T0336728

Handbook of Research on Organizational Transformations through Big Data Analytics

Madjid Tavana
La Salle University, USA

Kartikeya Puranam
La Salle University, USA

A volume in the Advances in Business Information
Systems and Analytics (ABISA) Book Series

An Imprint of IGI Global

Managing Director:	Lindsay Johnston
Managing Editor:	Austin DeMarco
Director of Intellectual Property & Contracts:	Jan Travers
Acquisitions Editor:	Kayla Wolfe
Production Editor:	Christina Henning
Development Editor:	Allison McGinniss
Typesetter:	Amanda Smith
Cover Design:	Jason Mull

Published in the United States of America by
Business Science Reference (an imprint of IGI Global)
701 E. Chocolate Avenue
Hershey PA, USA 17033
Tel: 717-533-8845
Fax: 717-533-8661
E-mail: cust@igi-global.com
Web site: http://www.igi-global.com

Library of Congress Cataloging-in-Publication Data

Handbook of research on organizational transformations through big data analytics / Madjid Tavana and Kartikeya Puranam, editors.

  pages cm

 Includes bibliographical references and index.

 Summary: "This book not only catalogues the existing platforms and technologies, it explores new trends within the field of big data analytics (BDA) by presenting new and existing research materials and insights on the various approaches to BDA"-- Provided by publisher.

  ISBN 978-1-4666-7272-7 (hardcover : alk. paper) -- ISBN 978-1-4666-7273-4 (ebook) -- ISBN 978-1-4666-7275-8 (print & perpetual access) 1. Data mining. 2. Big data. 3. Organizational change. I. Tavana, Madjid, 1957- editor. II. Puranam, Kartikeya, 1981-

  QA76.9.D343.H48 2015   2014036388
  006.3'12--dc23

This book is published in the IGI Global book series Advances in Business Information Systems and Analytics (ABISA) (ISSN: 2327-3275; eISSN: 2327-3283)

British Cataloguing in Publication Data
A Cataloguing in Publication record for this book is available from the British Library.

For electronic access to this publication, please contact: eresources@igi-global.com.

Advances in Business Information Systems and Analytics (ABISA) Book Series

Madjid Tavana
La Salle University, USA

ISSN: 2327-3275
EISSN: 2327-3283

Mission

The successful development and management of information systems and business analytics is crucial to the success of an organization. New technological developments and methods for data analysis have allowed organizations to not only improve their processes and allow for greater productivity, but have also provided businesses with a venue through which to cut costs, plan for the future, and maintain competitive advantage in the information age.

The **Advances in Business Information Systems and Analytics (ABISA) Book Series** aims to present diverse and timely research in the development, deployment, and management of business information systems and business analytics for continued organizational development and improved business value.

Coverage

- Geo-BIS
- Data Management
- Decision Support Systems
- Business Models
- Statistics
- Legal information systems
- Strategic Information Systems
- Algorithms
- Business Process Management
- Business Decision Making

IGI Global is currently accepting manuscripts for publication within this series. To submit a proposal for a volume in this series, please contact our Acquisition Editors at Acquisitions@igi-global.com or visit: http://www.igi-global.com/publish/.

Titles in this Series

For a list of additional titles in this series, please visit: www.igi-global.com

Business Technologies in Contemporary Organizations Adoption, Assimilation, and Institutionalization
Abrar Haider (University of South Australia, Australia)
Business Science Reference • copyright 2015 • 337pp • H/C (ISBN: 9781466666238) • US $205.00 (our price)

Business Transformation and Sustainability through Cloud System Implementation
Fawzy Soliman (The University of Technology, Australia)
Business Science Reference • copyright 2015 • 300pp • H/C (ISBN: 9781466664456) • US $200.00 (our price)

Effects of IT on Enterprise Architecture, Governance, and Growth
José Carlos Cavalcanti (Federal University of Pernambuco, Brazil)
Business Science Reference • copyright 2015 • 307pp • H/C (ISBN: 9781466664692) • US $195.00 (our price)

Technology, Innovation, and Enterprise Transformation
Manish Wadhwa (Salem State University, USA) and Alan Harper (South University, USA)
Business Science Reference • copyright 2015 • 378pp • H/C (ISBN: 9781466664739) • US $195.00 (our price)

Analytical Approaches to Strategic Decision-Making Interdisciplinary Considerations
Madjid Tavana (La Salle University, USA)
Business Science Reference • copyright 2014 • 417pp • H/C (ISBN: 9781466659582) • US $225.00 (our price)

Information Systems and Technology for Organizational Agility, Intelligence, and Resilience
Hakikur Rahman (University of Minho, Portugal) and Rui Dinis de Sousa (University of Minho, Portugal)
Business Science Reference • copyright 2014 • 355pp • H/C (ISBN: 9781466659704) • US $235.00 (our price)

ICT Management in Non-Profit Organizations
José Antonio Ariza-Montes (Loyola Andalucia University, Spain) and Ana María Lucia-Casademunt (Loyola Andalucia University, Spain)
Business Science Reference • copyright 2014 • 297pp • H/C (ISBN: 9781466659742) • US $215.00 (our price)

Security, Trust, and Regulatory Aspects of Cloud Computing in Business Environments
S. Srinivasan (Texas Southern University, USA)
Information Science Reference • copyright 2014 • 325pp • H/C (ISBN: 9781466657885) • US $195.00 (our price)

Remote Workforce Training Effective Technologies and Strategies
Shalin Hai-Jew (Kansas State University, USA)
Business Science Reference • copyright 2014 • 450pp • H/C (ISBN: 9781466651371) • US $265.00 (our price)

IGI GLOBAL
DISSEMINATOR OF KNOWLEDGE
www.igi-global.com

701 E. Chocolate Ave., Hershey, PA 17033
Order online at www.igi-global.com or call 717-533-8845 x100
To place a standing order for titles released in this series, contact: cust@igi-global.com
Mon-Fri 8:00 am - 5:00 pm (est) or fax 24 hours a day 717-533-8661

List of Contributors

Table of Contents

Detailed Table of Contents

Dennis T. Kennedy, La Salle University, USA
Dennis M. Crossen, La Salle University, USA
Kathryn A. Szabat, La Salle University, USA

Big Data Analytics has changed the way organizations make decisions, manage business processes, and create new products and services. Business analytics is the use of data, information technology, statistical analysis, and quantitative methods and models to support organizational decision making and problem solving. The main categories of business analytics are descriptive analytics, predictive analytics, and prescriptive analytics. Big Data is data that exceeds the processing capacity of conventional database systems and is typically defined by three dimensions known as the Three V's: Volume, Variety, and Velocity. Big Data brings big challenges. Big Data not only has influenced the analytics that are utilized but also has affected technologies and the people who use them. At the same time Big Data brings challenges, it presents opportunities. Those who embrace Big Data and effective Big Data Analytics as a business imperative can gain competitive advantage.

Sema A. Kalaian, Eastern Michigan University, USA
Rafa M. Kasim, Indiana Tech University, USA

Predictive analytics and modeling are analytical tools for knowledge discovery through examining and capturing the complex relationships and patterns among the variables in the existing data in efforts to predict the future organizational performances. Their uses become more common place due largely to collecting massive amount of data, which is referred to as "big data," and the increased need to transform large amounts of data into intelligent information (knowledge) such as trends, patterns, and relationships. The intelligent information can then be used to make smart and informed data-based decisions and predictions using various methods of predictive analytics. The main purpose of this chapter is to present a conceptual and practical overview of some of the basic and advanced analytical tools of predictive analytics. The chapter provides a detailed coverage of some of the predictive analytics tools such as Simple and Multiple-Regression, Polynomial Regression, Logistic Regression, Discriminant Analysis, and Multilevel Modeling.

In light of recent research that has begun to examine the link between textual "big data" and social phenomena such as stock price increases, this chapter takes a novel approach to treating news as big data by proposing the intelligent investment decision-making support model based on opinion mining. In an initial prototype experiment, the researchers first built a stock domain-specific sentiment dictionary via natural language processing of online news articles and calculated sentiment scores for the opinions extracted from those stories. In a separate main experiment, the researchers gathered 78,216 online news articles from two different media sources to not only make predictions of actual stock price increases but also to compare the predictive accuracy of articles from different media sources. The study found that opinions that are extracted from the news and treated with proper sentiment analysis can be effective in predicting changes in the stock market.

Distributed data mining and ensemble learning are two methods that aim to address the issue of data scaling, which is required to process the large amount of data collected these days. Distributed data mining looks at how data that is distributed can be effectively mined without having to collect the data at one central location. Ensemble learning techniques aim to create a meta-classifier by combining several classifiers created on the same data and improve their performance. In this chapter, the authors use concepts from both of these fields to create a modified and improved version of the standard stacking ensemble learning technique by using a Genetic Algorithm (GA) for creating the meta-classifier. They test the GA-based stacking algorithm on ten data sets from the UCI Data Repository and show the improvement in performance over the individual learning algorithms as well as over the standard stacking algorithm.

Inverse simulation involves finding the control inputs required to achieve a particular performance measure. The designer simulates the process numerically by varying the controllable input for generating desirable output. Clearly, this trial and error is not efficient and effective. This chapter proposes a "stochastic approximation" algorithm to estimate the necessary controllable input parameters within a desired accuracy given a target value for the performance function. The proposed algorithm is based on iterative Newton's method using a single-run simulation to minimize the expected loss function (i.e. risk function). The validity of the input parameter estimates are examined by applying it to some reliability and queuing systems with known analytical solutions.

This chapter examines the similarities and differences between big data and knowledge management. Big data has relatively little conceptual development, at least from a strategy and management perspective. Knowledge management has a lengthy literature and decades of practice but has always explicitly focused only on knowledge assets as opposed to precursors like data and information. Even so, there are considerable opportunities for cross-fertilization. Consequently, this chapter considers data from McKinsey Global Strategies on data holdings, by industry, and contrasts that with data on knowledge development, essentially the intangible assets found in the same industries. Using what we know about the variables influencing the application of intangible assets such as knowledge and intelligence, we can then better identify where successful employment of big data might take place. Further, we can identify specific variables with the potential to grant competitive advantage from the application of big data and business analytics.

Chapter 7

Many of the skills that define analytics are not new. Nonetheless, it has become a new source of competitive advantage for many corporations. Today's workforce, therefore, must be cognizant of its power and value to effectively perform their jobs. In this chapter, the authors differentiate the role of a business analyst by defining the appropriate skill level and breadth of knowledge required for them to be successful. Business analysts fill the gap between the experts (data scientists) and the day-to-day users. Finally, the section on Manufacturing Analytics provides real-world applications of Analytics for companies in a production setting. The ideas presented herein argue in favor of a dedicated program for business analysts.

Chapter 8

The terms big data, analytics, and business intelligence are often used in the media, with much attention on Fortune 500 enterprises. Small and medium-sized businesses (SMEs) also handle large amounts of data, and it is important to their decision making and planning. This chapter explores options for handling Big Data in SMEs. It presents a framework that considers not just the volume of data, but the variety of types of data, the velocity in which data is created and transmitted, the importance of data veracity, and its value in transforming small and medium-sized enterprises. SMEs need to work with big data, and doing so will impact their business models and require them transform themselves. Their transformation will be ongoing because all indicators show that the volume of data is rising and will continue to do so simply because of the trends related to customer interaction.

The authors present the experiences of a professor and a team of students who found that social media and predictive analytics go hand-in-hand when designing effective marketing campaigns (in this case, fundraising for a community of nonprofit organizations). The students of a medium-sized southwestern private university assisted a large southwestern city with the social media marketing efforts for the city's first Big Give fundraising. The organizers then told the students that the internal goal for the 24-hour event was $1.5 million USD. The campaign resulted in 21,361 gifts made for a grand total of $2,095,606.50 USD (approximately 40% greater than was forecasted). It was estimated by the organizers that the most significant contributing factor to the greater performance of the campaign was the social media efforts of the students. The average number of donations raised by the 467 organizations that participated was 45.52 for an overall average of $3,527.09 USD.

This chapter introduces the role of Business Analytics (BA) in Performance Management (PM), thus explaining the theoretical and practical concepts of BA, Performance Management Analytics (PMA), and organizational performance; the overview of performance measurement and PM; the application of Performance Management System (PMS) through BA; and the significance of BA in PMA. This chapter also explains the practical areas of BA and their advantages within the foundation of PM. BA can be used to validate causal relationships within traditional input, process, output, and outcome categories toward business success. Extending the domain of PM to PMA requires new business data analysis skills to gain organizational effectiveness. PMA fills the existing gap between PMS and effective PM adoption. Understanding the role of BA in PM will significantly enhance the organizational performance and achieve business goals in the global business environments.

Chapter 11

We are living at a time when change is the only constant in our lives. This is also true for organizations, which have to communicate these changes effectively to their employees. Internal communications are therefore increasingly garnering attention. In this regard, immense efforts should be made to create high levels of awareness and understanding about a new change project. Organizations use a variety of tools to communicate this information effectively. However, employee awareness and understanding can also vary on the choice of internal communications tools. This chapter presents the results of research carried out in Slovenia in 2012, where an experiment was conducted on 165 individuals. The individuals who took part in the experiment were exposed to information distributed through three different tools used in internal communications. Empirical data concerning the views of awareness and understanding of information according to the three internal communications tools are evaluated and presented.

Chapter 12

In Lih Ong, Universiti Tunku Abdul Rahman, Malaysia
Pei Hwa Siew, Universiti Tunku Abdul Rahman, Malaysia

Many organizations have recognized the importance of increasing commitment towards delivering long-term success of Business Intelligence (BI). However, effective BI strategies and governance to accommodate the rapid growth of data volumes are still scarce. Furthermore, there appears to be low usage rates of BI and analytics among business users. Consequently, many organizations are still positioned at either low or moderate levels in the BI maturity chart. In view of these issues, this chapter explores and develops a multi-dimensional BI maturity model that serves as a guideline to lift the BI capabilities of an organization for effectively planning, assessing, and managing BI initiatives. The focus of this research is to assess the current BI maturity level in Malaysian organizations and identify factors that affect the BI maturity. It also examines the effect of organization's demographic variables (i.e., types of industry, organizational size, and age of BI initiatives) on the BI maturity.

Chapter 13

Ekaterini Galanou, Qatar University, Qatar
Marios Katsioloudes, Qatar University, Qatar

This chapter presents an empirical study that examines the co-alignment between the Strategic Decision-Making Process (SDMP) and cultural contextual factors in developing a more completely specified model of innovation performance in a different setting from the Arab Middle East, namely Qatar. The key variables in this model consist of four strategic decision-making process dimensions (speed, degree of rationality, political behavior, and individual involvement), four culture attributes (locus of control, decision style, collectivistic orientation, and hierarchy), and innovation performance as an outcome variable in terms of process and product/service practice. The survey from 140 public and private organizations improves our understanding in three major issues: first, that SDM practices have a direct and more significant impact on process innovation performance than product/service innovation performance; second, that innovation performance is both process- and context-specific; and third, certain characteristics of the location support culture-specific awareness.

Chapter 14

Marius Octavian Olaru, University of Modena and Reggio Emilia, Italy
Maurizio Vincini, University of Modena and Reggio Emilia, Italy

Collaborative business making is emerging as a possible solution for the difficulties that Small and Medium Enterprises (SMEs) are having in recent difficult economic scenarios. In fact, collaboration, as opposed to competition, may provide a competitive advantage to companies and organizations that operate in a joint business structure. When dealing with multiple organizations, managers must have access to unified strategic information obtained from the information repositories of each individual organization; unfortunately, traditional Business Intelligence (BI) tools are not designed with the aim of collaboration so the task becomes difficult from a managerial, organizational, and technological point of view. To deal with this shortcoming, the authors provide an integration, mapping-based, methodology for heterogeneous Data Warehouses that aims at facilitating business stakeholders' access to unified strategic information. A complete formalization, based on graph theory and the RELEVANT clustering approach, is provided. Furthermore, the authors perform an experimental evaluation of the proposed method by applying it over two DW instances.

The approach of knowledge management, business intelligence, and customer relationship management was used as theoretical technologies in order to build an intelligence enterprise framework. Since the business intelligence process can create additional customer value through knowledge creation with the customer, business intelligence can provide users with reliable, accurate information and help them make decisions. Customer relationship management focuses on the integration of customer information and knowledge for finding and keeping customers to grow customer lifetime value. Therefore, integrating intelligence enterprise is needed in order to respond to the challenges the modern enterprise has to deal with and represents not only a new trend in IT but also a necessary step in the emerging knowledge-based economy. In intelligent enterprise operations, KM contains business models, processes, competence, implementation, performance assessment, and enterprise in information, organization, and e-commence processes.

The nature of SCM research is constantly evolving and must address a variety of concerns like poor service, large inventory levels, and friction among suppliers and manufacturers. Analytical databases and techniques in SCM are an important part of this research. Many researchers and practitioners have depended on secondary data, but given the dynamic nature of global competition, more recent and relevant data must be gathered. These efforts need to be geared to the development of properly managed supply chain relationships and corporate sustainability initiatives that ultimately promote broad-based sustainable development objectives for the good of people, plants, and profits (i.e., triple bottom-line).

Chapter 17

During the pre-purchase stage, consumers look for information in the external environment to verify marketers' claims, and by doing so, they are likely to encounter some reliable independent information such as consumer reports or technical reports. Using a Discrete Choice Experiment, this chapter shows that consumers use marketers' claims as reference points and record the independent information they encounter as either gain or loss. Moreover, consistent with Prospect Theory, losses loom larger than gains. However, the valuations of losses/gains do not differ for brands with different strengths.

Chapter 18

Reda Mohamed Hamou, Dr. Moulay Taher University of Saïda, Algeria
Abdelmalek Amine, Dr. Moulay Taher University of Saïda, Algeria

This chapter studies a boosting algorithm based, first, on Bayesian filters that work by establishing a correlation between the presence of certain elements in a message and the fact that they appear in general unsolicited messages (spam) or in legitimate email (ham) to calculate the probability that the message is spam and, second, on an unsupervised learning algorithm: in this case the K-means. A probabilistic technique is used to weight the terms of the matrix term-category, and K-means are used to filter the two classes (spam and ham). To determine the sensitive parameters that improve the classifications, the authors study the content of the messages by using a representation of messages by the n-gram words and characters independent of languages to later decide what representation ought to get a good classification. The work was validated by several validation measures based on recall and precision.

Chapter 19

Mariya Sodenkamp, University of Bamberg, Germany
Konstantin Hopf, University of Bamberg, Germany
Thorsten Staake, University of Bamberg, Germany & ETH Zurich, Switzerland

Smart electricity meters allow capturing consumption load profiles of residential buildings. Besides several other applications, the retrieved data renders it possible to reveal household characteristics including the number of persons per apartment, age of the dwelling, etc., which helps to develop targeted energy conservation services. The goal of this chapter is to develop further related methods of smart meter data analytics that infer such household characteristics using weekly load curves. The contribution of this chapter to the state of the art is threefold. The authors first quadruplicate the number of defined features that describe electricity load curves to preserve relevant structures for classification. Then, they suggest feature filtering techniques to reduce the dimension of the input to a set of a few significant ones. Finally, the authors redefine class labels for some properties. As a result, the classification accuracy is elevated up to 82%, while the runtime complexity is significantly reduced.

Chapter 20

Md. Hossain, North South University, Bangladesh
Rashedur M. Rahman, North South University, Bangladesh

This chapter offers a model for automated library material utilization that is based on knowledge discovery using association rules. Processing the circulation data of the library to extract the statistics and association utilization of the materials for departments is a great achievement that makes the analysis easier for calculating material utilization. Moreover, processing the circulation data of the library, two important dimensions, namely concentration and connection (Kao, Chang, & Lin, 2003), could be explored among departments and library members. This can make the analysis easier by calculating weights in those two important dimensions to make the decision about budget allocation. This chapter analyses the circulation data of North South University Library and suggests that efficient management and budget allocation can be achieved by using the above-mentioned metrics.

    N. Hemachandra, Indian Institute of Technology Bombay, India
    Puja Sahu, Indian Institute of Technology Bombay, India

Normally distributed data arises in various contexts and often one is interested in estimating its variance. The authors limit themselves in this chapter to the class of estimators that are (positive) multiples of sample variances. Two important qualities of estimators are bias and variance, which respectively capture the estimator's accuracy and precision. Apart from the two classical estimators for variance, they also consider the one that minimizes the Mean Square Error (MSE) and another that minimizes the maximum of the square of the bias and variance, the minmax estimator. This minmax estimator can be identified as a fixed point of a suitable function. For moderate to large sample sizes, the authors argue that all these estimators have the same order of MSE. However, they differ in the contribution of bias to their MSE. The authors also consider their Pareto efficiency in squared bias versus variance space. All the above estimators are non-dominated (i.e., they lie on the Pareto frontier).

    Salim Lahmiri, ESCA School of Management, Morocco & University of Quebec at Montreal,
      Canada

This chapter applies the Backpropagation Neural Network (BPNN) trained with different numerical algorithms and technical analysis indicators as inputs to forecast daily US/Canada, US/Euro, US/Japan, US/Korea, US/Swiss, and US/UK exchange rate future price. The training algorithms are the Fletcher-Reeves, Polak-Ribiére, Powell-Beale, quasi-Newton (Broyden-Fletcher-Goldfarb-Shanno, BFGS), and the Levenberg-Marquardt (LM). The standard Auto Regressive Moving Average (ARMA) process is adopted as a reference model for comparison. The performance of each BPNN and ARMA process is measured by computing the Mean Absolute Error (MAE), Mean Absolute Deviation (MAD), and Mean of Squared Errors (MSE). The simulation results reveal that the LM algorithm is the best performer and show strong evidence of the superiority of the BPNN over ARMA process. In sum, because of the simplicity and effectiveness of the approach, it could be implemented for real business application problems to predict US currency exchange rate future price.

    Sankar Kumar Roy, Vidyasagar University, India
    Deshabrata Roy Mahapatra, Vidyasagar University, India

In this chapter, the authors propose a new approach to analyze the Solid Transportation Problem (STP). This new approach considers the multi-choice programming into the cost coefficients of objective function and stochastic programming, which is incorporated in three constraints, namely sources, destinations, and capacities constraints, followed by Cauchy's distribution for solid transportation problem. The multi-choice programming and stochastic programming are combined into a solid transportation problem, and this new problem is called Multi-Choice Stochastic Solid Transportation Problem (MCSSTP). The solution concepts behind the MCSSTP are based on a new transformation technique that will select an appropriate choice from a set of multi-choice, which optimize the objective function. The stochastic constraints of STP converts into deterministic constraints by stochastic programming approach. Finally, the authors construct a non-linear programming problem for MCSSTP, and by solving it, they derive an optimal solution of the specified problem. A realistic example on STP is considered to illustrate the methodology.

Chapter 24
Abbas Keramati, University of Tehran, Iran
Niloofar Yousefi, University of Central Florida, USA
Amin Omidvar, Amirkabir University of Technology, Iran

Credit scoring has become a very important issue due to the recent growth of the credit industry. As the first objective, this chapter provides an academic database of literature between and proposes a classification scheme to classify the articles. The second objective of this chapter is to suggest the employing of the Optimally Weighted Fuzzy K-Nearest Neighbor (OWFKNN) algorithm for credit scoring. To show the performance of this method, two real world datasets from UCI database are used. In classification task, the empirical results demonstrate that the OWFKNN outperforms the conventional KNN and fuzzy KNN methods and also other methods. In the predictive accuracy of probability of default, the OWFKNN also show the best performance among the other methods. The results in this chapter suggest that the OWFKNN approach is mostly effective in estimating default probabilities and is a promising method to the fields of classification.

Preface

We are in the age of big data. Easy access to information and the successful usage of the information in the last decade has shown how important big data is to both large and small organizations. Big Data Analytics (BDA) is an overarching concept that incorporates a variety of software and analytical tools such as data mining, data warehousing, and data analytics. The ultimate use of BDA is to provide actionable information that can be used by decision makers at all levels to improve a company's bottom line. Everyone—from executive decision makers to managers who make day-to-day operational decisions—can use BDA, which democratizes the decision-making process and removes the need to rely solely on a decision maker's expertise in the area. The greatest challenge in implementing BDA applications is not simply about having the right technology and relevant expertise but also making sure that the data used is relevant and error-free.

This book provides the framework to exploit the synergies among traditionally diverse topics, such as the fields of data mining, quantitative methods, and decision support systems, in a more practical, application-driven format. It aims to provide tools to allow organizations to effectively use BDA platforms and technologies and make faster, smarter, data-driven, and real-time decisions. The following presents an introduction to each chapter.

CHAPTER 1

In the chapter titled "Business Analytics and Big Data: Driving Organizational Change," Crossen, Szabat, and Kennedy present a general overview of Big Data Analytics. They argue that even though data and data analytics allows managers to measure and therefore know much more about their businesses it does not eliminate the need for intuition and experience. It does change long-standing ideas about the value of experience, the nature of experience, and the practice of management.

CHAPTER 2

In the chapter titled "Predictive Analytics," Kalaian and Kasim present a conceptual and practical overview of some of the modeling tools and methods that can be used to perform predictive analytics. The conceptual overview provides analysts with the skills necessary to understand and conduct reliable and valid predictive analytics and interprets the reported conclusions based on using a specific predictive analytics technique. The predictive modeling methods that are covered in the chapter are (1) Simple Linear Regression, (2) Multiple Linear Regression, (3) Polynomial Regression, (4) Logistic Regression, (5) Discriminant Analysis, and (6) Multilevel Modeling.

CHAPTER 3

In the chapter titled "Using Big Data Opinion Mining to Predict Rises and Falls in the Stock Price Index," Kim, Jeong, and Jeong study opinion mining. Unstructured text data exist in diverse media content forms, ranging from blogs to social network service posts, but news articles have continually been of particular interest for their influence on different sectors of society. This study takes another step towards advancing the literature by proposing the intelligent investment decision-making support model based on opinion mining under which the continuous flow of massive news is regarded as unstructured text "big data," and both the automatic clipping and parsing of news and the tagging of vocabulary sentiment eventually allow for inferences to be made regarding the opinions on stock price fluctuations.

As a result of analyzing the underlying positive/negative sentiments of opinions contained in news articles, extracting the observed patterns, and using them to predict increases in stock prices, the study found that while it is important to consider contextual factors such as the media source from which the stories originate, opinions that are extracted from the news and treated with proper sentiment analysis can be effective in predicting movements in the stock market.

CHAPTER 4

In the chapter titled "A Modified Stacking Ensemble Machine Learning Algorithm Using Genetic Algorithms," Sikora and Al-Laymoun make an important contribution in making traditional machine learning algorithms more efficient and scalable in tackling big data and data mining problems. It takes a well-known and widely applied ensemble machine learning technique of stacking and modifies it using genetic algorithms for integrating the model learned by various machine-learning algorithms. The modified algorithm uses the concept of distributed data mining to decompose a large data set among different machine learning algorithms and uses a genetic algorithm to learn an optimal weighted vector for integrating the outcomes of these algorithms.

They test their algorithm on ten data sets from the UCI data-mining repository. Based on the results, they show statistically significant improvement in the performance of their algorithm over the standard stacking algorithm and over the best machine-learning algorithm on a majority of the data sets.

CHAPTER 5

In the chapter titled "Organizational Performance-Design Process: A Discrete-Events Simulation Approach," Hossein Arsham studies the concept of prescriptive simulation. The author's method is a single-run simulation approach to the design problem: "What should be the controllable input parameter value to achieve a desired output value?" He uses a "stochastic approximation" to estimate the necessary design parameters within a range of desired accuracy for a given target value of the performance measure. The main idea of the solution algorithm is based on stochastic Newton's method, together with recent single-run simulation development. The overall algorithm minimizes a loss function that measures the deviation from a target value. The validity of the presented algorithms is demonstrated by the application to a reliability and queuing system with a known analytical solution. The algorithms in this chapter are presented in English-like, step-by-step format to facilitate implementation under different computational environments. An immediate future extension is to develop an expert system that makes the algorithms more practically applicable for end-users.

CHAPTER 6

In the chapter titled "Data, Information, and Knowledge: Developing an Intangible Assets Strategy," Erickson and Rothberg investigate how the fields of knowledge management and intellectual capital have always distinguished between data, information, and knowledge. One of the basic concepts of the field is that knowledge goes beyond a mere collection of data or information, including know-how based on some degree of reflection. The related concept of intellectual capital deals with valuable organizational knowledge assets that, while not formal enough to rate a designation as intellectual property, deserve the attention of managers. Intellectual capital is valuable enough to be identified, managed, and protected. The authors explore the methods to better understand the idea of big data and how it relates to knowledge assets as well as provide a justification for bringing proven knowledge management strategies and tools to bear on big data and business analytics.

CHAPTER 7

In the chapter titled "Business Analytics for Business Analysts in Manufacturing," Wilder and Ozgur discuss how business analytics is taught in the curriculum. They define Data Scientist, Business Analyst, and Business User discussing the differences between them and emphasizing the business analyst. They provide examples and applications of analytics in manufacturing companies based on the work and consulting experience of the authors. They conclude the chapter with a note that emphasizes the duties of business analysts.

CHAPTER 8

In the chapter titled "Big Data Transforming Small and Medium Enterprises," Schaeffer and Olson provide a first look at the role Big Data can play in transforming Small and Medium-Sized Enterprises (SMEs). Small and medium-sized businesses are now realizing that the amount of data they handle is both large and important to their decision making and planning. The authors present a framework that adds "value" to the traditional four "Vs" of Big Data: Volume, Variety, Velocity, and Veracity.

CHAPTER 9

In the chapter "Nonprofit Fundraising Transformation through Analytics" by David George Vequist IV, the reader will learn from the experiences of a professor and a team of students who found that social media and predictive analytics go hand-in-hand when designing effective marketing campaigns (in this case, fundraising for a community of nonprofit organizations).

This chapter summarizes a micro-case study of how 28 students of a medium-sized southwestern private university assisted a large southwestern city with the social media marketing efforts for the city's first Big Give fundraising campaign (May 6th, 2014) which benefitted 467 non-profit organizations.

CHAPTER 10

In the chapter titled "The Role of Business Analytics in Performance Management," Kijpokin Kasemsap studies how performance management analytics can potentially increase the effectiveness of a performance management system. Organizations have been developing sophisticated performance management systems to support decision makers with relevant information. The performance management framework, different performance management indicators, and information and communication technology-based supporting tools presented in this research would be a valuable aid to help business organizations measure the performance of their corresponding operational processes.

CHAPTER 11

In the chapter titled "Evaluation of Information Awareness and Understanding through Different Internal Communication Tools," Sedej and Mumel study internal communication tools available to organizations. Their aim is to see which one can provide high levels of information awareness and understanding in times of introducing change, when employees cope with strong feelings such as anxiety, uncertainty, and even fear of the unknown. In the chapter, the authors considered three internal communication tools—written message, audio recording, and video clip—and conducted an experiment. The results reveal that different internal communication tools bring different levels of awareness and understanding of the change concerned.

CHAPTER 12

In the chapter titled "Empirical Investigation on the Evolution of BI Maturity in Malaysian Organizations," Ong and Siew investigate the state of BI in Malaysian organizations. The authors argue that organizations cannot determine which path of organizational strategy to follow for further improvement and continuous business growth in the future. This chapter explores and develops a multi-dimensional BI maturity model that can be used to guide organizations in their effort to move toward a higher maturity level in their BI initiatives. The focus of this research is to assess the current BI maturity level in Malaysian organizations and factors that affect the BI maturity.

This research provides contributions from both theoretical and practical perspectives. From theoretical perspective, this research contributes to the context understanding of BI maturity model as well as the key dimensions and associated factors deemed important by BI stakeholders. From a practical perspective, the BI maturity model serves as the fundamental framework for an organization to assess existing BI implementation and uncover the key weaknesses of BI in organizations.

CHAPTER 13

In the chapter titled "Cultural Integration with Strategic Decision-Making Process in Determining Innovation Performance: Evidence from an Arab Country Setting," Galanou and Katsioloudes investigate the interplay between cultural integration and strategic decision making. Qatar and its neighbors are all resource-poor apart from oil (and often gas), and thus, they find themselves competing tooth-to-tooth in their similar efforts at diversification and on the same grounds. It is only in the last few years that analysts have raised the specter of a single mineral or natural resource-dependant country becoming trapped by the realities of internal as well as external factors at the current juncture of globalization. Innovation by becoming a policy priority in these countries can support a sustained productivity growth through creating distinctiveness. The chapter contributes to the discussion of whether countries can confront their innovation challenges and embark on the high road to development.

CHAPTER 14

In the chapter titled "A Data Warehouse Integration Methodology in Support of Collaborating SMEs," Olar and Vincini address one of the main difficulties facing Small and Medium Enterprises that collaborate, namely the need to exchange and integrate strategic information concerning the organizations. In this context, the authors describe a complete, semi-automatic information integration methodology that allows companies to more easily integrate their Data Warehouses and Business Intelligence repositories, thus facilitating the collaboration effort of companies and enterprises. The integration methodology presented here is thoroughly described and is articulated in three main steps: semantic mappings generation, schema integration, and instance integration. Although it fits the classic approach of data integration methodologies, the innovative idea is to exploit schema knowledge to identify similar/identical dimensional attributes and to subsequently use the generated mappings to *consistently* integrate dimensional attributes. Remarkably, not only does this eliminate schema heterogeneity, but it also increases the dimensions of analysis that each DW has.

CHAPTER 15

In the chapter titled "Business Intelligence, Knowledge Management, and Customer Relationship Management Technological Support in Enterprise Competitive Competence," Ming-Chang Lee attempts to create an intelligence enterprise framework and discuss the implementation of this framework. E-business functions like Enterprise Resource Planning (ERP) and related systems, such as Supply Chain Management (SCM) and Customer Relationship Management (CRM), help in the incorporation of decision support tools and technologies. Effective Knowledge Management (KM) enhances products, improves operational efficiency, speeds up deployment, increases sales and profits, and creates customer satisfaction. Therefore, there is need for an integrated framework that links e-business, KM, CRM, and BI in order to respond to the challenges the modern enterprise has to deal with. The main contribution of this chapter is that it attempts to create an intelligence enterprise framework and discusses the implementation of this framework.

CHAPTER 16

In the chapter titled "Process Improvements in Supply Chain Operations: Multi-Firm Case Studies," Alan Smith discusses the need for successful Supply Chain Management (SCM) considerations, trends in SCM, and related databases and analytics, the collaborative nature of successful SCM, and case studies in SCM. A total of four companies are showcased in the Pittsburgh, PA, area, representing both service and manufacturing, highlighting their approaches to successful SCM practices, using technology, collaboration, and database management. Through the discussion of the various companies and managerial styles involved in this chapter, it explores the common theme in terms of the SCM and process improvements that these companies implemented: a focus on software-based solutions.

However, it is important to note that software and database applications alone will not solve a firm's supply chain issues. Only when coupled with well-designed processes, controls, training, and monitoring will a supply chain process improvement project yield truly successful results. The solutions discussed in the chapter focus on coordinated efforts to harness the potential of new technologies that promote increased information sharing and collaborative activities through mutual trust and properly managed supplier relationships.

CHAPTER 17

In the chapter titled "Consumer Information Integration at Pre-Purchase: A Discrete Choice Experiment," Dalman and Min use Prospect Theory as the theoretical underpinning to investigate how consumers combine the different information that varies in credibility (and uncertainty) they encounter at the purchase stage by conducting a Discrete Choice Experiment (DCE).

Findings from the DCE, using cell phone service providers as the category of investigation and dropped call rates as the main attribute on which marketers make numerical claims, suggest that consumers use marketers' claims as a reference point. Later, when they encounter credible third party information (i.e. an independent company that tests different service providers for dropped call rates), they compare the new information to this reference point and record it either as gain or loss.

This chapter not only contributes to the literature by answering a managerially important question, but it also makes a theoretical contribution by introducing an existing theory in a new relevant research venue. Moreover, this chapter uses DCE as a methodological tool, which is relatively easy for managers to consider.

CHAPTER 18

In the chapter titled "Using Data Mining Techniques and the Choice of Mode of Text Representation for Improving the Detection and Filtering of Spam," Hamou and Amine study spam-detecting techniques. Bayesian spam filtering is a powerful technique for dealing with unwanted email. It adapts to the patterns of mail and produces a false positive rate low enough to be acceptable. This technique has many advantages, as it adapts to its user, takes the entire message into account, is sensitive to the user, is multi-lingual and international, and particularly, avoids false positives, allowing it to classify legitimate messages as spam, and it is difficult to deceive. For the second technique, the choice fell on the k-means because it is based on unsupervised learning and the initialization problem does not arise since it is known and equal to two (spam and ham).

The contribution consists of the hybridization of both supervised and unsupervised techniques. The authors also show an interest in the representation of data by n-grams because they have a very good advantage because of their independence to the language used. Assessment measures were used to validate the work, and very satisfactory results that reflect the strategy implemented and confirm the choice of the policy hybridization used were obtained.

CHAPTER 19

In the chapter titled "Using Supervised Machine Learning to Explore Energy Consumption Data in Private Sector Housing," Sodenkamp, Hopf, and Staake study the problem of promoting energy efficiency using networked electricity meters that measure and communicate consumption information at a high resolution in time. These so-called smart meters offer, besides improvements to the utilities' billing processes, timely consumption feedback for residential customers, render dynamic tariff schemas possible, and provide input to home automation systems. Ultimately, smart meters should help households reduce their electricity consumption and motivate shifting loads to support the integration of renewable, fluctuating electricity sources. Recent studies show little response to incentives for load shifting, mostly due to the poor design of feedback campaigns and deficient data protection practices. The disappointing performance of smart metering is not a problem of the technology but resides in an insufficient information extraction from metering data.

The authors contribute to providing the missing link between smart meters and powerful energy efficiency measures. They develop and test supervised machine-learning techniques that automatically extract energy-relevant household characteristics from electricity load profiles with high accuracy.

CHAPTER 20

In the chapter titled "Application of Data Mining Techniques on Library Circulation Data for Library Material Acquisition and Budget Allocation," Hossain and Rahman offer two models for automated budget allocation using ID3 algorithm and association rules.

In the first model proposed in their research, the circulation data of library is processed to explore two important dimensions, namely concentration and connection among departments and library members. The value of concentration and connection is calculated from the number of records, the distribution of material categories used, and the relation between categories and subjects. The authors obtained the degree of concentration for a department by measuring information entropy using ID3 algorithm. In the second model, the circulation data of library is processed to extract the statistics and association utilization of the materials for a particular department that makes the analysis easier for calculating material utilization for the budget allocation. The authors obtained the degree of support for categories of a department by measuring the association in transactions using association rule algorithm and the confidence from the tuples of the transactions.

To demonstrate the effectiveness of their model, circulation data of eight years was collected from the automated library of North South University, the first and one of the leading private universities in Bangladesh. The authors believe the knowledge attained from this research to allocate the budget for the library will save a large amount of time and cost.

CHAPTER 21

In the chapter titled "Some Aspects of Estimators for Variance of Normally Distributed Data," Hemachandra and Sahu study how the inherent random error in normally distributed data is a cumulative of a variety of errors. As a result, one can approximate the distribution of this random error to be a normal random distribution with zero mean. To capture the behaviour of the data, it is important to estimate its variance. There are many criteria to find the "best" estimator of a parameter. Most of them make use of bias and variance of the estimator to measure its quality. The authors propose a minimax estimator, from the same class, that compares the bias and variance of the estimator as a multi-criteria problem. They compare this estimator to some of the estimators in the existing literature, such as the Uniformly Minimum Variance Unbiased Estimators (UMVUE), the optimal Mean Squared Error (MSE) estimator, and Maximum Likelihood Estimator (MLE).

For moderate to large ("Big Data") sample sizes, the estimators are almost similar on the scale of mean squared error. However, with this measure, it is difficult to determine the contribution of the components, the squared bias, and the variance towards the error incurred by the estimator. One framework to capture the relative nature of the squared bias and variance is to view their comparison as a multi-criteria optimization problem and identify the Pareto frontier on this space. The authors show that all of the above estimators are Pareto optimal since one cannot reduce one component without increasing the other.

CHAPTER 22

In the chapter titled "An Exploration of Backpropagation Numerical Algorithms in Modeling US Exchange Rates," Salim Lahmiri postulates that the difficulty of forecasting exchange rates arises from the inherent non-linearity and non-stationarity in exchange rate time series. The widely used ARMA model is a univariate process that is based on the linearity assumption about the data-generating process. This assumption is not satisfied for exchange rate data. Because of their general nonlinear function mapping capabilities and robustness to noisy data, artificial neural networks models have received increasing attention in exchange rate forecasting.

The motivation of this chapter is twofold. First, it aims to explore the effectiveness of different numerical techniques in the training of the BPNN, including conjugate gradients, quasi-Newton, and the Levenberg-Marquardt (LM) algorithm. The goal is to identify which algorithm allows achieving higher prediction accuracy of the future exchange rate. Second, it uses genetic algorithms in a way that objectively determines the optimum number of hidden layers and neurons.

CHAPTER 23

In the chapter titled "Solving Solid Transportation Problem with Multi-Choice Cost and Stochastic Supply and Demand," Roy and Mahapatra study the solid transportation problem. The Solid Transportation Problem (STP) is an important extension of the traditional Transportation Problem (TP) where other constraints besides source and destination constraints, such as product type constraints or transportation mode constraints, are dealt with.

This study proposes a novel method called Multi-Choice Stochastic Solid Transportation Problem (MCSSTP) to aid the DMs in selecting the appropriate choice of cost to a particular route from the multi-choice costs of several routes for transporting the goods from origins to destinations through the capacities. A real-life case of a reputed Betel leaves supplier company is presented.

CHAPTER 24

The chapter titled "Default Probability Prediction of Credit Applicants Using a New Fuzzy KNN Method with Optimal Weights," by Keramati, Yusefi, and Omidvar, has two major objectives. Their first objective is to provide a comprehensive academic review regarding credit scoring and propose a classification scheme to classify the articles. The second objective is to propose the Optimally Weighted Fuzzy K-Nearest Neighbor (OWFKNN) method for credit scoring and compare it with other algorithms.

The authors utilized Australian consumer credit data set and German credit scoring data from the UCI Repository of Machine Learning databases to figure out the accuracy of the credit scoring methods. They selected several common methods that have been recently used in credit scoring in order to compare OWFKNN with other methods in terms of classification accuracy.

Madjid Tavana
La Salle University, USA

Kartikeya Puranam
La Salle University, USA

Chapter 1

Business Analytics and Big Data:
Driving Organizational Change

Dennis T. Kennedy
La Salle University, USA

Dennis M. Crossen
La Salle University, USA

Kathryn A. Szabat
La Salle University, USA

ABSTRACT

Big Data Analytics has changed the way organizations make decisions, manage business processes, and create new products and services. Business analytics is the use of data, information technology, statistical analysis, and quantitative methods and models to support organizational decision making and problem solving. The main categories of business analytics are descriptive analytics, predictive analytics, and prescriptive analytics. Big Data is data that exceeds the processing capacity of conventional database systems and is typically defined by three dimensions known as the Three V's: Volume, Variety, and Velocity. Big Data brings big challenges. Big Data not only has influenced the analytics that are utilized but also has affected technologies and the people who use them. At the same time Big Data brings challenges, it presents opportunities. Those who embrace Big Data and effective Big Data Analytics as a business imperative can gain competitive advantage.

INTRODUCTION

Generations of technological innovations have evolved since the 1970's. Decision support systems (DSS) have emerged as one of the earliest frameworks intended to assist complex decision making through user-friendly interfaces, rudimentary database relationships, basic visualization capabilities, and pre-defined query proficiencies. A typical cycle of activities within a DSS network began with decision makers (Zeleny, 1987) defining a problem requiring a solution. After defining the problem and exploring possible alternatives, a decision model was developed that eventually would guide the decision makers toward implementation. This model-building phase of the process was an iterative approach to resolving organizational problems (Shim, 2002).

DOI: 10.4018/978-1-4666-7272-7.ch001

As a logical progression, supplementary support systems were being funded within the C-suite. Executive support systems were developed to obtain timely access to information for competitive advantage. These inter-networking infrastructures became possible because of distributed computing services, online analytical processing and business intelligence applications.

Today, it is the demand for the application of analytics to Big Data that is driving an expansion of information technology that will continue at an accelerating rate (Davenport, 2014). Big Data and analytics, now possible because of advances in technology, have changed the way organizations make decisions, manage business processes, and create new products and services.

Informed Decision Making

In any organization, it is essential that strategic decisions have executive level support. Exploring Big Data using analytical support systems has strategic, as well as tactical importance. This is not a modernistic view, rather one of historic precedence and contemporary necessity (Bughin, 2010; Ewusi-Mensah, 1997; Jugdev, 2005; Poon, 2001). Furthermore, Vandenbosch (1999) clearly established a relationship between how organizations can enable competitiveness and use methods and techniques for focusing attention, improving understanding, and scorekeeping. In recent years, numerous studies have validated the premise that business analytics informs decision making. Davenport, Harris and Morison (2010) show that business analytics produces smarter decisions. Business analytics has changed the way organizations make decisions. Organizations are making informed decisions because business analytics enables managers to decide on the basis of evidence rather than intuition alone. While business analytics does not eliminate the need for intuition and experience, it changes long standing ideas about the value of experience, the nature of experience and the practice of management (McAfee & Brynjolfsson, 2012).

Improved Business Processes

Many large organizations are burdened with an array of process modeling intended to improve the decision making hierarchy (Dijkman, 2011). If an organization has been in business for several decades, managing these processes is time-prohibitive and expensive because a team is required to manage and refine them. As organizations adopt business process management systems to automate key business processes, integration with business intelligence remains equally important. Making data from business processes available for business intelligence in near real-time allows organizations to proactively manage business processes through improved insight into performance. Business analytics not only changes the way organizations evaluate business processes but also how they manage business processes.

Empowering Products and Services

Nothing more effectively moves change in the business environment as does competition. Products and services evolve as competitive information is obtained and analyzed. Data has become widely available at historical discounts allowing organizations to manage their employees. Data also allows vendors the ability to adjust pricing based on archival and real-time sales. Similarly, considerations for complementary products and services are based on consumer behavior (Brown, 2011). These activities can take place only if data can be accessed and analyzed.

If a company makes things, moves things, consumes things, or works with customers, the company has increasing amounts of data about these activities (Davenport, 2013). Powerful data-gathering and analysis methods can provide an opportunity for developers of products and services. They can create more valuable products and services from the analysis of data.

The impact of business analytics and Big Data is measurable. The following sections describe: (a) what business analytics is, (b) the methods and techniques of business analytics and (c) the effect of Big Data on traditional analytics processes, tools, methods and techniques.

BUSINESS ANALYTICS: WHAT IS IT?

In today's business environment, few would argue against the need for business analytics. It provides facts and information that can be used to improve decision making, enhance business agility and, provide competitive edge.

Many academics and practitioners have defined *business analytics* or *analytics* in slightly different ways. Davenport and Harris (2007 p. 7) define *analytics* as "the extensive use of data, statistical and quantitative analysis, explanatory and predictive models, and fact-based management to drive decisions and actions." Lustig, Dietrich, Johnson, and Dziekan, (2010) at IBM proposed that business analytics include analytics and what Davenport and Harris (2007 p.7) define as business intelligence, "a set of technologies and processes that use data to understand and analyze business performance." At IBM, the term business analytics applies to:

1. **Software Products:** Including business intelligence and performance management, predictive analytics, mathematical optimization, enterprise information management, and enterprise content and collaboration;
2. **Analytic Solutions Areas:** Such as industry solutions, finance/risk/fraud analytics, customer analytics, human capital analytics, supply chain analytics;
3. **Consulting Services:** Outsourced business processes and configured hardware (Lustig et al. 2010).

These authors further refine business analytics into three categories: descriptive analytics, predictive analytics and prescriptive analytics. Davenport (2010) defined business analytics as the broad use of data and quantitative analysis for decision making within organizations. These definitions highlight four key aspects of business analytics: data, technology, statistical and quantitative analysis, and decision making support.

The Analytics Section of the Institute for Operations Research and Management Science (INFORMS) is focused on promoting the use of data-driven analytics and fact-based decision making in practice. The Section recognizes that analytics is seen as both

1. A complete business problem solving and decision making process, and
2. A broad set of analytical methodologies that enable the creation of business value.

Consequently, the Section promotes the integration of a wide range of analytical techniques and the end-to-end analytics process. INFORMS (2012 p. 1) defines analytics as "the scientific process of transforming data into insight for making better decisions."

A Science and an Art

In our view, business analytics is the use of data, information technology, statistical analysis, and quantitative methods and models to support organizational decision making and problem solving. The main categories of business analytics are:

1. **Descriptive Analytics:** The use of data to find out what happened in the past or is currently happening;
2. **Predictive Analytics:** The use of data to find out what could happen in the future; and
3. **Prescriptive Analytics:** The use of data to prescribe the best course of action for the future.

Business analytics will not provide decision makers with any business insight without models; that is, the statistical, quantitative, and machine learning algorithms that extract patterns and relationships from data and expresses them as mathematical equations (Eckerson, 2013). Business analytics, clearly, is a science.

However, business analytics is also an art. Selecting the right data, algorithms and variables, and the right techniques for a particular business problem is critical. Equally critical is clear communication of analytical results to end-users. Without an understanding of what the model discovered and how it can benefit the business, the decision maker would be reluctant to act on any insight gained. One of the best ways to tell a data story is to use a compelling visual. Organizations today are using a wide array of data visualization (dataviz) tools that help uncover valuable insight in easier and more user-friendly ways.

BUSINESS ANALYTICS: METHODS AND TECHNIQUES

This section provides an overview of key methods and techniques within each of the main categories of business analytics: descriptive, predictive and prescriptive.

Descriptive Analytics

Descriptive analytics is the use of data to reveal what happened in the past or is currently happening in the present. As presented in Figure 1, the methods and techniques within descriptive analytics can be classified by the purpose they serve.

Reporting and visual displays provide information about activities in a particular area of business. They answer questions such as: What happened? What is happening now? How many? How often? Where? Methods and techniques include both standard, predetermined report generation and ad hoc, end-user created report generation. Dashboards and scorecards are also included in this category. A dashboard is a visual display of the most important information needed to achieve objectives. A scorecard is a visualization of measures and their respective targets, with visual indicators showing how each measure is performing against its targets.

Analysis, Query and Drill Down provide descriptive summaries, retrieve specific information from a database, and move deeper into a chain of data, from higher-level information to more detailed, focused information. They answer questions such as: What exactly is the problem? Why is it happening? What does this all mean? The methods and techniques within this classification include data descriptive

Figure 1. Descriptive analytics

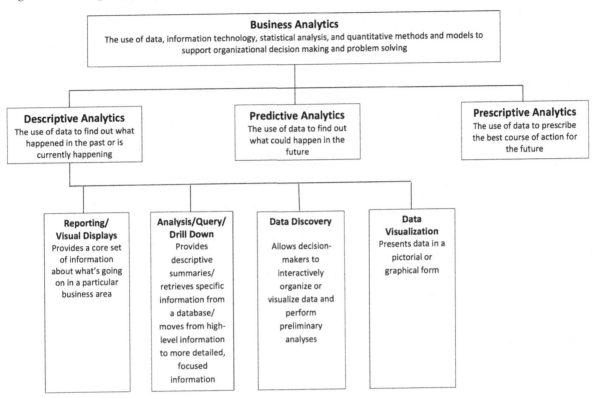

summaries provided by statistics (analysis), database manipulation capabilities provided by information systems technologies (query), and database navigation capabilities provided by information systems technologies (drill down).

Data Discovery allows decision makers to interactively organize or visualize data. Some of the previously mentioned methods and techniques can be considered traditional business intelligence. While data discovery can answer similar questions as traditional business intelligence, it is a departure from the traditional because it emphasizes interactive analytics rather than static reporting. Data discovery allows for easy navigation of data and quick interactive question-asking. These capabilities help the end-user gain new insights and ideas. Data discovery is recognized as critical to business data analysis because of the rise of Big Data. Methods and techniques in this category include statistics, text and sentiment analysis, graph analysis, path and pattern analytics, machine learning, visualization and complex data joins (Davenport, 2013).

Data Visualization capability is an important feature of data discovery because it visually represents patterns or relationships that are difficult to perceive in underlying data. Dataviz also facilitates communication of what the data represent, especially when skilled data analysts communicate to business decision makers. In this context, the picture is truly worth a thousand words.

There are a variety of conventional ways to visualize data: tables, histograms, pie charts, and bar graphs. Today, there are also very innovative, creative approaches to present data. When selecting a visualization for data, it is important to:

1. Understand the data to be visually represented, including its size and cardinality;
2. Determine what relationships or patterns are being communicated;
3. Know the audience; and
4. Use a visual that conveys the information in the most direct and simplest way (SAS, 2012).

Predictive Analytics

Predictive analytics is the use of data to discover what could happen in the future. The questions that can be answered with predictive analytics include: What will happen next? What trends will continue? As shown in Figure 2, predictive analytics encompasses a variety of methods and techniques from statistics and data mining and can be used for purposes of prediction, classification, clustering, and association.

Prediction assigns a value to a target based on a model. Techniques include regression, forecasting, regression trees, and neural networks. Classification assigns items in a collection to target categories or classes. Techniques include logistic regression, discriminant analysis, classification trees, K-nearest Neighborhood, Naïve Bayes, and neural networks. Clustering finds natural groupings in data. Cluster analysis falls within this category. Association finds items that co-occur and specifies the rules that govern their co-occurrence. Association rule discovery, also known as affinity analysis belongs to this category.

Figure 2. Predictive analytics

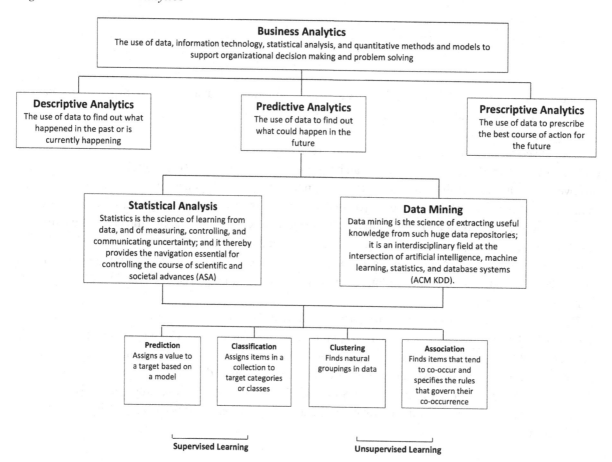

Within the field of data mining, techniques are described as supervised or unsupervised learning. In supervised learning, the variables under investigation can be split into two groups: explanatory variables and dependent variables, also called the target. The objective of the analysis is to specify a relationship between the explanatory variables and the dependent variables. In unsupervised learning, all variables are treated the same; there is no distinction between explanatory and dependent variables.

Prescriptive Analytics

Prescriptive analytics is the use of data to prescribe the best course of action for the future. The questions that can be answered with prescriptive analytics include: What if we try this? What is the best that can happen? As depicted in Figure 3, prescriptive analytics encompasses a variety of methods and techniques from management science including optimization and simulation.

Optimization provides means to achieve the best outcome. Optimizations are formulated by combining historical data, business rules, mathematical models, variables, constraints, and machine learning algorithms. Stochastic Optimization provides means to achieve the best outcome that address uncertainty in the data. Sophisticated models, scenarios, and Monte Carlo simulations are run with known and randomized variables to recommend next steps and display if/then analysis.

BUSINESS ANALYTICS: IMPACT OF BIG DATA

Data and data analytics allows managers to measure, and therefore, know much more about their businesses. They can then directly translate that knowledge into improved decision making, business process performance, and products and services. In recent years, businesses have experienced the emergence of Big Data.

Figure 3. Prescriptive analytics

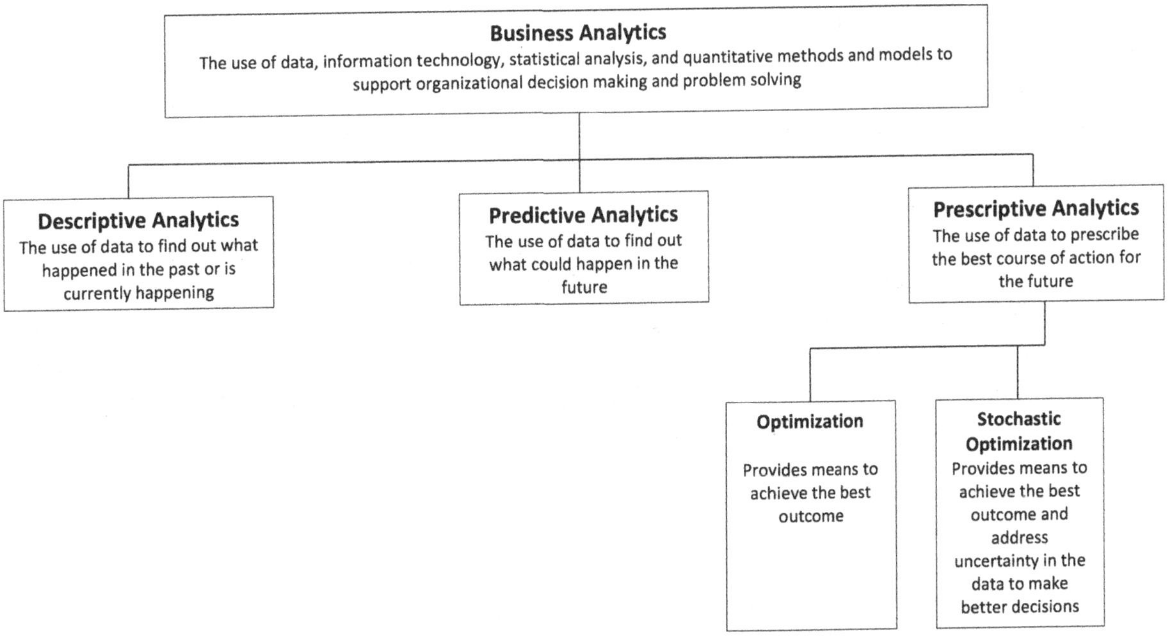

What Exactly is Big Data?

Big Data is data that exceeds the processing capacity of conventional database systems; the data is too big, moves too fast, or doesn't fit the structures of database architectures (inside-bigdata.com). Big Data is typically defined by three dimensions known as the Three V's: volume, variety, and velocity. Volume refers to the amount of data, typically in the magnitude of multiple terabytes or petabytes. Variety refers to the different types of structured and unstructured data, such as: transaction-level data, video, audio, and text. Velocity is the pace at which data flows from sources, such as: business processes, machines, networks, social media sites, and mobile devices. Now an additional V has surfaced, veracity. This fourth V refers to the biases, noise, and abnormality in data. Veracity is an indication of data integrity and trust in the data.

Big Data Means Big Challenges

Big Data brings with it big challenges. The technology, the analytic techniques, and the people, as well as the data, are all somewhat different from those employed in traditional business analytics. In recent years, tools to handle the volume, velocity, and variety of Big Data have improved. For example, new methods of working with Big Data, such as Hadoop and MapReduce, have evolved as alternatives to traditional data warehousing. However, these new technologies require a new IT skills set for integrating relevant internal and external sources of data, and this can present a challenge (McAfee, A., and Brynjolfsson, 2012). Not only does Big Data require advanced technologies, Big Data requires advanced analytics. In addition to the higher level traditional business analytics techniques, Big Data uses advanced techniques such as text analytics, machine learning, and natural language processing.

Together, these changes in technologies and techniques present managerial challenges that require organizational change. Organizations must manage change effectively to realize the full benefits of using Big Data. Leadership, talent, and company culture must adapt.

The intrinsic resistance to organizational change can be effectively mitigated with time and education. The dedication and diligence of actionable leadership can positively govern culture change within the organization. Leadership can also provide on-going support for malleable technology and adaptive talent acquisition, as well as for building a management team that is cognitively tactical in its decision making responsibilities. While critical, these management challenges can be overcome in organizations desiring to build integrated capabilities without the immediate need for large capital investments (McAfee, 2012). However, these organizational refinements must be recognized as preexisting conditions during the on-going transition period.

Furthermore, contemporary leaders must have the ability to respond to market issues that are both managerial and technical by nature (Tallon, 2008). This includes the ability to hire properly. Talent management and the acquisition of knowledgeable personnel are essential for dynamically adapting organizations. The strategy is to achieve competitive advantage with a maturing resource pool (Bartlett, 2013). The alternative strategy of acquiring talent and knowledge only by educating existing human capital is not a solution for either the short or the intermediate term.

Most importantly, unless managers have the ability to convert corporate goals, objectives, competencies, and resourcefulness into meaningful outcomes, organizations will fall short of the cyclical requirements essential for instilling creativity within talented people (Farley, 2005). Along with these challenges, organizational leaders must understand the nuances of technology, the value-added reasons for change, the constraints on human capital, and the impact that sequential implementation will have throughout the entire adaptive process (Hoving, 2007).

Big Data Analytics Means Big Opportunities

While the name may change in the future, Big Data is here to stay. According to Brynjolfsson and McAfee (2012), organizations in almost all industries can enhance their operations and strategic decision-making by implementing Big Data analytics programs:

Almost no sphere of business activity will remain untouched by this movement. We've seen Big Data used in supply chain management to understand why a carmaker's defect rates in the field suddenly increased, in customer service to continually scan and intervene in the health care practices of millions of people, in planning and forecasting to better anticipate sales on the basis of a data set of product characteristics (p.1).

Increasingly, organizations seeking competitive advantage need to enable, learn from, and use data. Those who embrace Big Data and effective data analytics as a business imperative can gain competitive advantage in the rapidly evolving digital economy (Johnson, 2012).

REFERENCES

Bartlett, C., & Ghoshal, S. (2013). Building competitive advantage through people. *Sloan Management Review*, *43*(2).

Brown, B., Chui, M., & Manyika, J. (2011). Are you ready for the era of 'big data'. *The McKinsey Quarterly*, *4*, 24–35.

Brynjolfsson, E., & McAfee, A. (2012). Big Data's Management Revolution. In The promise and challenge of big data. Harvard Business Review Insight Center Report.

Bughin, J., Chui, M., & Manyika, J. (2010). Clouds, big data, and smart assets: Ten tech-enabled business trends to watch. *The McKinsey Quarterly*, *56*(1), 75–86.

Davenport, T. (2010). *The New World of "Business Analytics*. International Institute for Analytics.

Davenport, T. (2013). *The Rise of Data Discovery*. Retrieved from http://www.asterdata.com/resources/assets/The_Rise_of_Data_Discovery.pdf

Davenport, T. (2014). *Big Data at Work: Dispelling the Myths, Uncovering the Opportunities*. Harvard Business Review Press.

Davenport, T., & Harris, J. (2007). *Competing on Analytics: The New Science of Winning*. Boston, MA: Harvard Business School Publishing Corporation.

Davenport, T., Harris, J., & Morison, R. (2010). Analytics at Work: Smarter Decisions, Better Results. Boston, MA: Harvard Business School Publishing Corporation. Retrieved from http://www.sas.com/resources/asset/IIA_NewWorldofBusinessAnalytics_March2010.pdf

Day, G. S. (1994). The capabilities of market-driven organizations. *Journal of Marketing*, 58(4), 37–54. doi:10.2307/1251915

Dijkman, R., Dumas, M., Van Dongen, B., Käärik, R., & Mendling, J. (2011). Similarity of business process models: Metrics and evaluation. *Information Systems*, 36(2), 498–516. doi:10.1016/j.is.2010.09.006

Eckerson, W. (2013). *Analytical Modeling is Both Science and Art*. Retrieved from http://searchbusinessanalytics.techtarget.com/opinion/Analytical-modeling-is-both-science-and-art

Ewusi-Mensah, K. (1997). Critical issues in abandoned information systems development projects. *Communications of the ACM*, 40(9), 74–80. doi:10.1145/260750.260775

Farley, C. (2005). HR's role in talent management and driving business results. *Employment Relations Today*, 32(1), 55–61. doi:10.1002/ert.20053

Hoving, R. (2007). Information technology leadership challenges - past, present, and future. *Information Systems Management*, 24(2), 147–153. doi:10.1080/10580530701221049

INFORMS Analytics. (n.d.). Retrieved from https://www.informs.org/Sites/Getting-Started-With-Analytics/What-Analytics-Is

Johnson, J. (2012). *Big Data + Big Analytics = Big Opportunity*. Financial Executive International.

Jugdev, K., & Müller, R. (2005). A retrospective look at our evolving understanding of project success. *Project Management Journal*, 36(4), 19–31.

Langley, A. (1999). Strategies for theorizing from process data. *Academy of Management Review*, 24(4), 691–710.

Lustig, I., Dietrich, B., Johnson, C., & Dziekan, C. (2010). *The Analytics Journey. Retrieved from analyticsmagazine.com*

McAfee, A., & Brynjolfsson, E. (2012). Big data: The management revolution. *Harvard Business Review*, 90(10), 60–68. PMID:23074865

Poon, P., & Wagner, C. (2001). Critical success factors revisited: Success and failure cases of information systems for senior executives. *Decision Support Systems*, 30(4), 393–418. doi:10.1016/S0167-9236(00)00069-5

SAS Business Intelligence Solutions. (2012). *Data Visualization Techniques: From Basics to Big Data with SAS® Visual Analytics*. Retrieved from http://www.sas.com/offices/NA/canada/downloads/IT-World2013/Data-Visualization-Techniques.pdf

Shim, J. P., Warkentin, M., Courtney, J. F., Power, D. J., Sharda, R., & Carlsson, C. (2002). Past, present, and future of decision support technology. *Decision Support Systems*, *33*(2), 111–126. doi:10.1016/S0167-9236(01)00139-7

Tallon, P. P. (2008). Inside the adaptive enterprise: An information technology capabilities perspective on business process agility. *Information Technology Management*, *9*(1), 21–36. doi:10.1007/s10799-007-0024-8

Vandenbosch, B. (1999). An empirical analysis of the association between the use of executive support systems and perceived organizational competitiveness. *Accounting, Organizations and Society*, *24*(1), 77–92. doi:10.1016/S0361-3682(97)00064-0

Wilson, H., Daniel, E., & McDonald, M. (2002). Factors for success in customer relationship management (CRM) systems. *Journal of Marketing Management, 18*(1-2), 193-219.

Zeleny, M. (1987). Management support systems: Towards integrated knowledge management. *Human Systems Management*, *7*(1), 59–70.

KEY TERMS AND DEFINITIONS

Big Data: Data that exceeds the processing capacity of conventional database systems.

Business Analytics: Use of data, information technology, statistical analysis, and quantitative methods and models to support organizational decision making and problem solving.

Descriptive Analytics: Use of data to find out what happened in the past or is currently happening.

Predictive Analytics: Use of data to find out what could happen in the future.

Prescriptive Analytics: Use of data to prescribe the best course of action for the future.

Variety: Refers to the different types of structured and unstructured data.

Velocity: The pace at which data flows from sources.

Veracity: Refers to the biases, noise, and abnormality in data.

Volume: Refers to the amount of data, typically in the magnitude of multiple terabytes or petabytes.

Chapter 2
Predictive Analytics

Sema A. Kalaian
Eastern Michigan University, USA

Rafa M. Kasim
Indiana Tech University, USA

ABSTRACT

Predictive analytics and modeling are analytical tools for knowledge discovery through examining and capturing the complex relationships and patterns among the variables in the existing data in efforts to predict the future organizational performances. Their uses become more common place due largely to collecting massive amount of data, which is referred to as "big data," and the increased need to transform large amounts of data into intelligent information (knowledge) such as trends, patterns, and relationships. The intelligent information can then be used to make smart and informed data-based decisions and predictions using various methods of predictive analytics. The main purpose of this chapter is to present a conceptual and practical overview of some of the basic and advanced analytical tools of predictive analytics. The chapter provides a detailed coverage of some of the predictive analytics tools such as Simple and Multiple-Regression, Polynomial Regression, Logistic Regression, Discriminant Analysis, and Multilevel Modeling.

INTRODUCTION

Predictive analytics, which is also referred to as predictive modeling techniques, are used in a variety of disciplines and fields of study such as business, management, engineering, marketing, technology, actuarial science, information systems, health informatics, and education. Predictive modeling methods are quantitative statistical techniques that are used most often to make future business predictions and decisions based on past historical data (Evans & Lindner, 2012). Kuhns and Johnson (2013) defines predictive modeling as "the process of developing a mathematical tool or model that generates an accurate prediction" (p. 2). Their uses become more common place due largely to

1. Collecting massive amount of data, which is referred to as "big data"; and
2. Increasingly complex nature of related predictive research and problems.

DOI: 10.4018/978-1-4666-7272-7.ch002

The main objective of predictive modeling is to predict an unknown value of a dependent (outcome) variable from known values of a set of exploratory independent (predictor) variables by analyzing and capturing the relationships between the dependent and independent variables in any research problem (Maisel & Cokins, 2014; Siegel 2014). The results and findings of these analyses are then used to make future predictions such as predicting specific future trends, risks, and behavior patterns. Consumer purchasing patterns, consumer loyalty, credit risks, credit limits, tax fraud, unemployment rates, and consumer attrition are examples of such predictions of future trends and consumer behavior patterns that the businesses and organizations often deal with.

Generally, predictive modeling is a complex data analytic process, of which predictive model building is only a part of the analytic process. The predictive analytics process includes:

1. Understanding the predictive research problem and the massive data to be analyzed.
2. Managing the data, preparing the data for analysis.
3. Analyzing the data and building the analytic models.
4. Evaluating the results and accuracy of the predictive modeling.
5. Deploying and tailoring the final models to directly addressing the original predictive research problem.

One of the most difficult tasks for predictive analysts, researchers and students conducting predictive modeling is identifying the most appropriate predictive analytic technique that can be utilized to answer a particular research oriented business question. In addition, the type and number of the dependent variables are two important primary factors to determine the appropriateness of the predictive modeling technique that can be used for a particular business problem. Provost and Fawcett (2013) stated that the success in today's data-driven businesses requires being able to think about how to correctly apply the principles, concepts, and techniques of predictive modeling to particular predictive business problems.

With the rise of using the internet and electronic devices (e.g., smart phones) to collect massive amount of data as well as technological advances in computer processing power and data storage capabilities, the demand for effective and sophisticated knowledge discovery and predictive modeling techniques has grown exponentially over the last decade. These knowledge discovery and predictive analytics techniques help business executives and policy makers make informed decisions to solve complex organizational and business problems. For example, the survival of businesses and organizations in a knowledge-and-data driven economy is derived from the ability to transform large quantities of data and information to knowledge (Maisel & Cokins, 2014; Siegel 2014). This knowledge can be used to make smart and informed data-based decisions and predictions using predictive analytics techniques. In fact, a decade ago, most such data was not collected or entirely overlooked as a key resource for business and organizational success because lack of knowledge and understanding of the value of such information (Hair, 2007).

Although Business Data Analytics (BDA) is commonly viewed from three major perspectives: descriptive, predictive, and prescriptive (Evans & Lindner, 2012), the focus of this chapter is only on predictive analytics. Therefore, the main purpose of this chapter is to present a conceptual and practical overview of some of the modeling tools and methods that can be used to perform predictive analytics. The conceptual and methodological overview provides analysts with the skills necessary to understand and conduct reliable and valid predictive analytics and interpret the reported conclusions based on the use of specific predictive analytic technique. The predictive modeling methods that are covered in the chapter are:

1.   Simple Linear Regression,
2.   Multiple Linear Regression,
3.   Polynomial Regression,
4.   Logistic Regression Analysis,
5.   Discriminant Analysis, and
6.   Multilevel Modeling.

The focus of each of the following six sections of the chapter are:

1.   Providing the definition and detailed description for each of the descriptive analytics techniques;
2.   Stating the assumptions for each of the methods;
3.   Testing the parameters of the coefficients for each of the predictive analytics techniques;
4.   Evaluating the overall fit of the predictive model to the data; and
5.   Providing the predictive models for the methods.

1. SIMPLE REGRESSION ANALYSIS

Simple regression analysis is a statistical method for analyzing and modeling the relationship between a continuous dependent variable and one continuous or categorical independent variable to build a predictive model for making future predictions.

The main goals of the simple linear regression analyses are to:

1.   Identify and explain the best model that represents the linear relationships between a quantitative dependent variable and one quantitative continuous or categorical independent variable, and
2.   Predict the value of the dependent variable given the specific values of the independent variable based on the best specified model.

In simple linear regression analysis, the linear relationship between a dependent variable and a known independent (predictor) for n individuals (cases) is represented by the following simple linear regression model:

$$Y_i = \alpha + B X_i + e_i \tag{1}$$

where, Y_i is the value of the dependent (outcome) variable for the ith individual in the population; α, is a constant that represents the intercept of the regression line (model) with the Y-axis. That is, it is the value of the outcome variable Y when the value of the independent variable (X) is equal to zero; B is the regression coefficient of the independent variable (X) in the regression model and it represents the slope of the regression line, which can be interpreted as the amount of change in the dependent (outcome) variable for one unit change in the independent (predictor) variable (X); X_i is the value of the individual i for the independent (predictor) variable; and e_i represents the amount by which the observed value of the dependent variable deviates from the predicted value for an individual i from the estimated simple regression model. If all error terms are randomly scattered around the regression line, their total sum will be 0.

A scatterplot of the actual data points of the independent and dependent variables is often called a bivariate scatterplot, is often used to graphically portray the linear relationship between the predictor variable (X) and the dependent variable (Y). A regression line that represents the best fit of the regression model is usually drawn through the scatterplot data points to portray the direction and the extent of the deviations of the actual values from their predictive ones.

Assumptions of Simple Linear Regression Analysis

Simple linear regression analysis is based on specific assumptions about the data that is used in regression analysis. Meeting these assumptions is necessary in order to achieve the best linear estimation of the parameters of the regression model. These assumptions are:

1. The error terms (e_i) are independent and identically normally distributed with mean equal to zero.
2. The relationship between the dependent and the independent variables is linear.
3. The errors of fitting the regression model are not correlated with the independent (predictor) variable.
4. The distribution of the errors of the regression model for each value of the independent variable (X) has an approximately normal distribution with constant variance across all values of the independent (predictor) variable X. This assumption is referred to as "homoscedasticity" or "equality of variances."

As a result of testing the assumptions, if the relationship between the dependent and the independent variables appears to be nonlinear (curvilinear) then a polynomial regression should be used to analyze the data instead of the linear regression. If there are sufficient number of cases and no violations of the assumptions evident, then it is safe to interpret the linear regression analysis results (Tabachnik and Fidell, 1996).

Testing the Coefficients of Simple Linear Regression

A t-statistic can be used to test whether or not the associated population parameter of the regression coefficient, B = 0. The t-statistic is computed by dividing the estimated B by the standard error of the estimated B. In simple linear regression, testing the regression coefficient B is equivalent to testing the significance of the simple regression model.

Predictions using Simple Linear Regression

Predictive regression models are used to

1. Predict the values of the dependent variable given known values of an independent (predictor) variable within the given range of the independent variable (X) values, and
2. Evaluate the accuracy in predicting (that is, evaluating the fitting of the regression line to the data) the unknown values of the dependent variable from known values of the independent variable.

The predicted value ($\hat{Y}$) of the dependent variable (Y) in simple linear regression is represented as follows:

$$\hat{Y}_i = a + b \, X_i \tag{2}$$

where, "a" is the estimated intercept of the population parameter, α. "b" is the estimated regression coefficient of the population's regression coefficient parameter, B, for the independent variable.

The accuracy of the predicted values of a particular Y value is found by subtracting the corresponding predicted value of the dependent variable, $\hat{Y}$, from the original value of the dependent variable, Y. This difference is called the error of prediction (Y_e) and represented as:

$$Y_e = Y - \hat{Y} \tag{3}$$

2. MULTIPLE LINEAR REGRESSION ANALYSIS

In multiple linear regression analysis, which is an extension of the simple linear regression, the linear relationship between a dependent variable and two or more known independent (predictor) variables ($X_1, X_2, ..., X_k$) in the population is represented by the following linear model:

$$Y_i = \alpha + B_1 X_{i1} + B_2 X_{i2} + ... + B_k X_{ik} + e_i \tag{4}$$

where, Y_i is the value of the dependent (outcome) variable for individual i; α is the intercept of the regression model, which is the value of the dependent variable Y when all predictors in the model have values equal to zero; $B_1, B_2, ..., B_k$ are the regression coefficients for the k independent variables X_{i1}, $X_{i2, ..., } X_{ik}$ respectively. Each of these coefficients represents the contribution of its associated predictor X on the dependent variable Y while holding other predictors in the model constants. Similar to the simple regression model, e_i represents the amount by which the observed value of the dependent variable deviates from the predicted value for an individual i from the estimated multiple regression model. If all the error terms are randomly scattered around the regression line, their total sum will be 0. This regression model is considered as a linear model because none of the independent (predictor) variables are exponential variables (e.g., raised to the power 2, 3, etc.).

The main goals of the multiple linear regression analyses where the researcher or analyst have two or more independent variables in the regression model are to:

1. Identify and explain the best model that captures and represents the linear relationships between a quantitative dependent variable and two or more quantitative and categorical independent variables, and
2. Predict the value of the dependent variable given the specific values of the multiple independent variables based on the best fitted model.

Assumptions of Multiple Linear Regression Analysis

Multiple linear regression analysis is based on specific assumptions about the data. Meeting these assumptions is necessary in order to achieve the best linear estimation of the parameters of the regression model. These assumptions are:

1. The dependent variable is normally distributed.
2. The relationship between the dependent variable and each of the multiple independent variables is linear.
3. The independent variables in the regression model are not correlated.
4. The errors are not correlated with each of the independent (predictor) variables.
5. The error terms (e_i) are independent and identically normally distributed with mean equal to zero and a constant variance. The later requirement of equal variances is referred to as "homoscedasticity" or "equality of variances" assumption.

Testing Beta Coefficients in Multiple Linear Regression

A t-test can be used to test whether or not the associated population parameter $B_i = 0$ given all the other independent (predictor) variables in the specified regression model. F-statistic tests whether or not all of the regression coefficients, B_i for all of the variables in the regression model are simultaneously equal to zero $(B_1 = B_2 = \ldots = 0)$.

Predictions using Multiple Linear Regression

As in simple linear regression, predictive regression models are used to

1. Predict the values of the dependent variable given known values of the independent (predictor) variables, and
2. Evaluate the degree of accuracy in prediction (that is, evaluating the fitting of the regression model to the data) of the unknown values of a dependent variable from multiple known independent variables (George & Mallery, 2010).

The predicted value $(\hat{Y})$ of the dependent variable (Y) in multiple linear regression is represented as follows:

$$\hat{Y}_i = a + b_1 X_{i1} + b_2 X_{i2} + \ldots\ldots + b_k X_{ik} \tag{5}$$

where, "a" is the estimated intercept of the population parameter, α; and $b_1, b_2, \ldots, b_k$ are the estimated regression coefficients of the regression coefficient parameters, $B_1, B_2, \ldots, B_k$ for the independent variables $X_{i1}, X_{i2}, \ldots, X_{ik}$ respectively.

As in simple regression, the accuracy of the predicted values of any Y value can be found by subtracting the predicted value of the dependent variable, $\hat{Y}$, from that particular original value of the dependent variable, Y. This difference is called the error of prediction (Y_e) and represented as:

$$Y_e = Y - \hat{Y} \tag{6}$$

Evaluating the Adequacy of the Fitted Regression Model

As part of the regression model building process, it is necessary to evaluate the goodness of fit of the model and test the statistical significance of the estimated parameters. Commonly used statistics to evaluate the fit of the model to the data are R^2 and F-test. A t-test is used to test each of the individual parameters of the model (the intercept and the regression coefficients).

R^2 Statistic

The coefficient of determination (R^2) is a descriptive measure of goodness-of-fit. It is a measure of the proportion of the total variance in the dependent variable (Y) that is accounted for and explained by the linear combination of the independent variables in the regression model. It represents the squared correlation between the actual values of the dependent variable (Y) and the predicted values of Y obtained from the regression equation. Its numeric value ranges from 0 to 1 and the closer R^2 statistic is to the value 1, the better the fit of the estimated regression line to the data.

3. POLYNOMIAL REGRESSION

Polynomial regression is used instead of the linear regression analysis when the relationship between the dependent and independent variable are not linear. For example, if the relationships between the dependent variable and the independent variable have curvilinear relationships (e.g., quadratic, cubic) then the linear regression model cannot be used. In this case the most appropriate predictive analytical tool will be using the polynomial regression methods. It is more appropriate because it provides a better model fit and more accurate estimates of the regression coefficients. The polynomial regression model for quadratic data is represented as:

$$Y_i = \alpha + B_1 X_{1i} + B_2 X_{1i}^2 + e_i \tag{7}$$

This regression model is not linear because it contains the nonlinear exponential variable, X_{1i}^2, which is simply the actual values of the independent variable, X_{1i} squared.

Predictions using Polynomial Regression

As in simple linear regression, predictive regression models are used to:

1. Predict the values of the dependent variable given known values of independent (predictor) variables, and
2. Evaluate the degree of accuracy in prediction (that is, evaluating the fitting of the regression line to the data) of the unknown value of the dependent variable from nonlinearly related independent variables.

The predicted value ($\hat{Y}$) of the dependent variable (Y) in the polynomial linear regression is represented as follows:

$$\hat{Y}_i = a + b_1 X_{i1} + b_2 X_{i1}^2 \tag{8}$$

where, "a" is the estimated intercept of the population regression parameter, α; and b_1 and b_2 are the estimated polynomial regression coefficients of the regression parameters, B_1 and B_2 for the nonlinearly related independent variables X_{i1} and X_{i1}^2 (X_{i1} squared) respectively.

4. LOGISTIC REGRESSION

Logistic regression is similar to regression analysis in that both techniques identify a set of continuous and/or categorical (nominal, discrete) independent variables that best predicts the dependent variable. The major difference between logistic regression and multiple regression is that the dependent variable in the logistic regression is a categorical variable while the dependent (outcome) in multiple regression is a quantitative continuous variable. Carlberg (2013) stated that logistic regression is the most valuable method in the predictive analytics toolbox.

Logistic regression is a predictive analytic method for predicting a membership of subjects into one of two or more groups or classifying a manufacturing product into categories such as whether a product is defective or not defective. When the dependent variable consists of only two groups, the logistic regression is referred to as binary or binomial logistic regression. When the dependent variable consists of three or more groups, the logistic regression is referred to as multinomial logistic regression (Mertler and Vannatta, 2005). Although logistic regression can be used for predicting memberships and classifications into two or more groups or categories, our focus in this chapter will be on dichotomous (binary) dependent variables with only two groups or categories. For example, in logistic regression application with a dependent (outcome) variable consisting of two categories, the categories might be values such as membership or non-membership in a group, buyers or not buyers of a product, on time bill payers or nonpayers. The two categories of the group membership (dependent variable) are usually coded as "0" and "1" with a code of "1" is assigned to "membership" or "success" cases and a code of "0" is assigned to "non-membership" or "failure" cases. This coding process helps to have more straightforward interpretations of the results of the logistic regression.

Logistic regression produces a regression equation that predicts the probability of whether an individual will fall into one category of group membership (e.g., "pays on time") or the other category (e.g., "doesn't pay on time"). If the dependent variable consists of only two categories, logistic regression estimates the odds outcome of the dependent variable given a set of quantitative and/or categorical independent variables. Unlike regression analysis, logistic regression does not directly model the values of the dependent variable. However, it does model the probability of the membership to a particular group or category.

Logistics regression analysis starts with calculating the *"Odds"* of the dependent variable, which is the ratio of the probability that an individual (case) is a member of a particular group or category, p(y) divided by the probability that an individual is not a member of the group or category [1- p(y)]. It is represented as follows:

Odds = p(y) / [1 − p(y)]   (9)

It is important to note that unlike the probability values, which range from 0 to 1, the values of the odds can theoretically range from 0 to infinity.

In order to establish a linear relationship between the odds and the independent variables in the logistic regression model, the odds need to be transformed to *logit* (log-odds) by taking the natural logarithm (*ln*) of odds. The logarithmic transformation creates a continuous dependent variable of the categorical dependent variable and it is represented as follows:

Logit p(y) = ln (Odds) = ln {p(y) / [1 − p(y)]}   (10)

As in simple linear regression, simple logistic regression has one binary dependent (outcome) variable and one continuous or categorical independent (predictor) variable. It is represented as follows:

ln {p(y) / [1 − p(y)]} = $\alpha + \beta X$ (11)

The logistic regression for multiple independent variables is represented as follows:

Logit p(y) = $\alpha + B_1 X_1 + B_2 X_2 + ... + B_k X_k$ (12)

where, α is the intercept; B_1, B_2, ... B_k are the logistic regression coefficients of the predictor variables X_1, X_2, ..., X_k respectively.

Interpreting the Logistic Regression Coefficients

In order to interpret the logistic regression coefficients, there is a need to calculate the difference in the odds. When the independent variable is a continuous variable, the difference (change) between the calculated odds when y=0 and y=1 is:

Odds D = $e^{\alpha} (e^{\beta} - 1)$ (13)

The value of $e^{\beta} - 1$ represents the difference (change) between the two Odds (y=0 and y=1) and is presented in Equation 13 as (Odds D) because e^{α} is constant. The numerical value of e is 2.178. This difference can be written as a percentage as follows:

(Odds D)% = $100 (e^{\beta} - 1)$ (14)

Therefore, when the independent variable X is continuous, the (Odds D)% can be interpreted as a one-unit change in the independent variable X, the odds will change by (Odds D)%. When the independent variable is a categorical variable, the change of the odds becomes the odds ratio. For example, X is a dichotomous variable with two values 0 and 1 (X=0 and X=1). In this case, the change is measured by the ratio of the two odds rather than the difference between the two odds. This odds-ratio is represented as e^{β} and interpreted as a one-unit change in the independent variable, X, the odds will change multiplicatively by e^{β}. An odds-ratio of 2.05 indicates that there is about a two-fold greater chance of occurrence of the event (e.g., group membership) given one unit increase in X.

Testing Beta Coefficients in Logistic Regression

In linear regression, the significance of an individual regression coefficient, which represents a unit change in the dependent variable for each unit change in the predictor, is assessed by t-test statistic. In logistic regression, the regression coefficients, which represent the change in the logit for each unit change in the predictor, are assessed by the Wald statistic. Wald statistic (W) is the ratio of the square of the logistic regression coefficient (β^2) to the square of the standard error of the coefficient (SE^2) and represented as follows:

$$W = \beta^2 / SE^2 \tag{15}$$

The Wald statistic has an approximate Chi-square distribution.

Cox-Snell R^2 and Nagelkerke R^2 Statistics

Cox-Snell R^2 and Nagelkerke R^2 Statistics are measures, which provide a logistic regression analogy to R^2 in simple- and-multiple linear regression. The Nagelkerke measure is a modification of the Cox-Snell measure to ensure that it varies from 0 to 1 (as does R^2 in simple- and-multiple linear regression).

5. DISCRIMINANT ANALYSIS

Discriminant Analysis, which is also known as discriminate function analysis, is a statistical technique that uses the information from a set of independent variables to predict the value of a discrete (categorical) dependent variable, which represents the mutually exclusive groups in the predictive model. Therefore, discriminant analysis is a useful analytic method for building a predictive model of group membership (dependent variable) based on observed characteristics (independent variables) for each individual case in the data. The main goal of the discriminant analysis is to identify a combination of independent variables (predictors) that provide the best discrimination between groups in efforts to accurately predict a membership in a particular group. In other words, the focus of the discriminant analysis is to best separate or discriminate a set of two or more groups using a set of predictors (Field, 2009). The discriminate functions are a linear combination (transformation) of the predictor variables, which are created such that the difference between group (e.g., member and non-member) means on the transformed variable are maximized (Field, 2009). For two categories, only one discriminate function is estimated; and for three categories, two discriminate functions are estimated. For two categories, the discriminate function is represented in the following form:

$$D_1 = b_1 X_1 + b_2 X_2 + \ldots\ldots + b_k X_k \tag{16}$$

where, $b_1, b_2, \ldots, b_k$ are the discriminate coefficients of the predictor variables $X_1, X_2, \ldots, X_k$ respectively. These discriminate functions are used to generate discriminate scores for individual cases and classify cases into the groups (in this case, two groups).

In sum, discriminant analysis starts by identifying and describing one or more discriminate functions (D) of a set of independent variables (predictors) that are generated from a sample of cases (individuals) for which group membership is known. Then, the discriminate function can be applied to another sample of new sample of cases with known values for the predictor variables, but unknown group membership (George & Mallery, 2010). This process of dividing the total cases into two samples is referred to as cross-validation.

Discriminant analysis differs from regression analysis because the dependent variable in discriminant analysis is discrete (categorical) rather than continuous, which is the case in regression analysis. Also, discriminant analysis is similar to logistic regression because it also explains and predicts a categorical dependent variable based on known continuous and categorical independent variables (predictors). But, logistic regression is preferable in applications where we have only two groups or categories and the assumption of normality of the independent variables is violated, which is a fundamental assumption of the discriminant analysis.

Assumptions of Discriminant Regression Analysis

As in any statistical methodology, discriminant analysis is based on specific and required assumptions about the data. Meeting these assumptions is a necessary condition in order to have the best discriminant functions that correctly predict group membership. These assumptions are:

1. The independent (predictor) variables are assumed to have multivariate normal distributions.
2. The individual cases (subjects) should be independent from each other.
3. The within-group variance-covariance matrix of the independent (predictor) variables should be equal across the multiple groups of the dependent variable.

6. MULTILEVEL MODELING

Businesses and organizations often collect massive amount of data, which most often has hierarchical (multilevel) structures. For example, employees nested within companies, patients within doctors, employees within managerial departments or organizational units, or investors within financial organizations are examples of such basic two-level nested structured data. Multilevel modeling (Hierarchical Linear Modeling) methods can be used to analyze and model different kinds of hierarchically structured data such as

1. Two-level structured data with a quantitative continuous dependent variable at the first level,
2. Three-level structured data with a quantitative continuous dependent variable at the first level, and
3. Two-level structured data with a dichotomous (binary) categorical dependent variable at the first level.

Although multilevel models can analyze and model hierarchically structured data with different kinds of dependent variables and two or more hierarchical levels, our focus in this chapter is on analyzing and modeling two-level structured data with continuous dependent (outcome) variables, where individuals are grouped (nested) within organizations.

Multilevel structured data presents analytical challenges that cannot be handled by the traditional regression analysis methods because we have regression model for each level of the multilevel data (Raudenbush & Bryk, 2002; Kalaian & Kasim, 2006; Kalaian, 2008). For example, for the two-level organizational data where we have employees nested within organizations, we have two regression models. One is level-1 regression model (employee-level) and the other is level-2 regression model (organization-level). In this basic two-level multilevel model, researchers are primarily interested in assessing the effects of both the individual employees' characteristics as well as the organizational characteristics (predictors) on the individual employee's dependent (outcome) variable. For instance, satisfaction, performance, production, and achievement are examples of such dependent variables.

In general, the multilevel modeling methods analyze and model all the levels (lower and higher levels) in the hierarchy by taking into consideration the interdependence of individuals nested within the higher level of hierarchy (e.g., organizations). For example, in a two-level analysis, the emphasis is on how to model the effect of explanatory variables (predictors) at macro-level on the relationships occurring at the micro-level. In other words, multilevel modeling describe and analyze the hierarchical relationships between variables at one level of analysis (micro-level) that are affected by variables at another higher level of the hierarchy (macro-level). Researchers and predictive analysts across all disciplines often incorrectly analyze and draw inferences regarding relationships in hierarchically structured data based on aggregating or disaggregating the data to be able to use the traditional predictive analytic methods such as regression analysis, logistic regression, polynomial regression (Raudenbush and Bryk, 2002; Kalaian and Kasim, 2006; Kalaian, 2008).

Level-1 (Micro-level) Model

Level-1 (micro-level) model specifies the relationships among independent explanatory variables (predictors), X_{ij}, and the outcome (dependent) variable, Y_{ij} (Raudenbush & Bryk, 2002; Hox, 2002; Kalaian & Kasim, 2006; Kalaian, 2008). Given that we have micro-level individuals of size n_j nested within j macro-level organizations, the Level-1 (micro-level) model is represented as:

$$Y_{ij} = B_{oj} + B_{1j} X_{ij} + r_{ij} \tag{17}$$

where, B_{0j} represents the intercept of the Level-1 model and B_{1j} represents the Level-1 regression coefficient capturing the relationship between the dependent (outcome) variable and the predictor variable X_{ij}. The term r_{ij} represents Level-1 random errors and are assumed to be distributed normally with mean zero and variance, σ^2.

Level-2 (Macro-level) Model

Level-2 model specifies the relationships among the level-2 characteristics as independent explanatory variables (predictors) and the level-1 regression estimates, such as the intercept and the slope(s). Thus, the intercept and slope estimates for each organization from the level-1 model then used as outcome variables in the level-2 models (Raudenbush & Bryk, 2002; Kalaian & Kasim, 2006; Kalaian, 2008). The Level-2 (macro-level) regression model, which is represented as:

$$B_{oi} = \gamma_{00} + \gamma_{01} W_j + U_{oj} \tag{18}$$

and,

$$B_{1j} = \gamma_{10} + \gamma_{11} W_j + U_{1j} \tag{19}$$

where $i = 1, 2, 3, ..., n_j$ individuals within organization j ($j = 1, 2, 3, ..., J$ macro-level organizations). W_j is a Level-2 (macro-level) predictor (e.g., organization size, organization type). γ_{00}, γ_{01}, γ_{10}, and γ_{11} are Level-2 fixed effects regression coefficients. U_{oj} and U_{1j} are the Level-2 random residual errors. In this case with an intercept and one predictor in the level-1 model, these two random residual errors are assumed to have a multivariate normal distribution with a zero mean vector and variance-covariance matrix with τ_{00}, τ_{01}, and τ_{11} components (Raudenbush & Bryk, 2002; Hox, 2002; Kalaian & Kasim, 2006; Kalaian, 2008).

Multilevel Models without Predictors

The no predictor model, which is much simpler than the full multilevel model (presented above), is a multilevel model with no explanatory variables included in the level-1 (micro-level). This no predictor model is referred to in the literature as unconditional model or null model.

Micro-Level (Level-1) Model with No Predictors

This no predictor micro-level model is represented as:

$$Y_{ij} = B_{oj} + r_{ij} \tag{20}$$

where, Y_{ij} is the outcome for individual employee i in organization j. B_{oj} is the mean of the outcome in organization j. r_{ij}, is the level-1 error. The variance of r_{ij} equals σ^2.

Macro-Level (Level-2) Model with No predictors

At the second level (macro-level), the intercept B_{oj} from level-1 is allowed to vary randomly across organizations. Thus, this model is represented as:

$$B_{oj} = \gamma_{00} + U_{oj} \tag{21}$$

where, γ_{00} is the overall grand mean of the outcome across all macro-level organizations. U_{oj} is the error term representing the deviation of each organization's mean outcome from the grand mean, γ_{00}. The variance of $U_{oj} = \tau_{00}$.

R² for Multilevel Modeling

As in traditional regression analysis, the amount of variance explained in the two-level multilevel modeling is represented by R^2. The variance estimates from the null (no predictors included in the multilevel model) and full multilevel models (predictors are included in the multilevel model) can be used to estimate R^2 for the Level-1 and Level-2 models (Hox, 2002; Raudenbush & Bryk, 2002; Kalaian & Kasim, 2006; Kalaian, 2008). R^2 for the Level-1 model represents the percentage of variance in the Level-1 outcome accounted for by the Level-1 predictor (s) and can be estimated as follows:

$$R^2_{\text{Level-1}} = (\sigma^2_{\text{No Predictor Model}} - \sigma^2_{\text{full Model}}) / \sigma^2_{\text{No predictor Model}} \tag{22}$$

Two R^2 are estimated for the Level-2 model, one is for the intercept and the other is for the regression slope. R^2 for the Level-2 intercept represents the percentage of the intercept variance accounted for by the Level-2 predictors and is estimated as follows:

$$R^2_{\text{Level-2 intercept}} = (\tau_{00\text{-No Predictor Model}} - \tau_{00\text{-full Model}}) / \tau_{00\text{-No Predictor Model}} \tag{23}$$

R^2 for the Level-2 (macro-level) slope represents the percentage of the slope variance accounted for by the Level-2 predictors and is estimated as follows:

$$R^2_{\text{Level-2 slope}} = (\tau_{11\text{-No Predictor Model}} - \tau_{11\text{-full Model}}) / \tau_{11\text{- No Predictor Model}} \tag{24}$$

Estimating and Testing of Multilevel Regression Coefficients

Three kinds of parameters are estimated when analyzing two-level hierarchically structured data. One is estimating the regression coefficients (γ) for the Level-2 model, which represent the fixed effects parameter estimates. Multilevel modeling provides t-statistic for testing the fixed effects parameter estimates. It tests the hypothesis that these estimates are significantly different from zero. The second is estimating the Level-1 regression coefficients, which represent the random coefficients and these coefficients vary across groups. Finally, the third is estimating the variance of the Level-1 residuals (variance of r_{ij}), which is σ^2 and the variance-covariance matrix of the Level-2 residuals (τ_{00} represents the variance of U_{0j}, τ_{11} represents the variance of U_{1j}, and τ_{01} represents the covariance of U_{0j} and U_{1j}). Multilevel modeling provides chi-square tests for the Level-2 residual variances (τ_{00} and τ_{11}) to test the hypothesis that these residual variances are significantly different from zero (Raudenbush & Bryk, 2002; Kalaian & Kasim, 2006).

Assumptions of the Multilevel Modeling

As in any statistical methodology, multilevel modeling (Hierarchical Linear Modeling, HLM for short) is based on several assumptions. Meeting these assumptions insures the validity of the HLM fixed and random effects' coefficients estimates, testing these coefficients, and the accuracy of the overall fit of the multilevel model to the hierarchically structured data (Raudenbush & Bryk, 2002; Kalaian & Kasim, 2006). The assumptions for the two levels of the hierarchical linear model are:

1. Level-1 (micro-level) predictors and residual errors are independent.
2. Level-1 (micro-level) residual errors are independent and normally distributed.
3. Level-2 (macro-level) random errors are independent and have a multivariate normal distribution.
4. Level- 2 (macro-level) residual errors and predictors are independent.
5. Level-1 (micro-level) and Level-2 (macro-level) residual errors are independent.

Predictions using Multilevel Modeling

Predictive multilevel modeling can be used to predict the values of the individual dependent variable given known values of independent (predictor) variables for the two levels of the multilevel model. The predicted value of the dependent variable (Y_{ij}) in multilevel modeling is represented as follows:

$$Y_{ij} = \gamma_{00} + \gamma_{01} W_j + \gamma_{10} X_{ij} + \gamma_{11} W_j X_{ij} + U_{oj} + U_1 X_{ij} + r_{ij} \qquad (25)$$

This equation is obtained by substituting the Level-2 models into the Level-1 model. As we can see that the random error in the predictive multilevel model has a complex form, which is a combination of the errors of the two levels and represented as $U_{oj} + U_{1j} X_{ij} + r_{ij}$.

Multilevel Software Packages

Because of the advancement of the statistical methods and the computer technologies, within the last three decades many specialized software packages have been developed to analyze hierarchically structured data. Software packages such as HLM6 (Raudenbush, Bryk, Cheong, & Congdon, 2004), SPSS, MLnWin, and SAS Proc Mixed, are examples of such commercial software.

FUTURE TRENDS

In the near future, we are expected to witness a renaissance in the use of the predictive analytics. It is expected that predictive analytics to be applied increasingly across a broad variety of fields of study and its applications to be global. It is also expected that its applications to revolutionize the ability of businesses and organizations to identify, understand, and predict future organizational outcomes such as trends, risks, and behavior patterns (Hair, 2007). In addition, it is expected that more advanced predictive analytics will be adopted, developed, and used to solve complex business problems using massive data sets. Further, it is expected that the demands for data analysts including predictive analysts will increase.

Furthermore, future and emerging trends will include a meaningful understanding of the hierarchical systems structured in large data sets. For example, organizational performances necessitate predictive analytical methods that can handle large-scale data (big data) with multiple levels of the hierarchical structures. Therefore, we believe that there is a solid theoretical and practical foundation for progress in predictive analytics toward the emergence of new analytical tools for big data with two or more levels and different types of variables.

As a consequences of these future demands, most universities across the nation and worldwide are developing new programs for undergraduate and graduate degrees in business data analytics (BDA) in which courses in predictive analytics are included in the program. We are also witnessing the phenomena of new textbooks have been published on this topic (Evans & Lindner, 2012; Maisel & Cokins, 2014; Siegel 2014).

CONCLUSION

Predictive analytics and modeling are advanced statistical techniques to assess and explain the relationships or patterns among variables in the existing (recent and past) data in efforts to predict the future performances, risks, trends, and behavior patterns. The uses and applications of predictive modeling are becoming more common due largely to collecting massive amount of data, which is referred to as "big data" and the increased need to transform large quantities of data into intelligent information such as trends, patterns, and relationships that can be used to make smart and informed data-based decisions and predictions.

Our main purpose in this chapter has been to present a conceptual and practical overview of some of the modeling tools and methods that can be used by analysts and researchers to accurately perform the predictive analytics for their data. The conceptual overview provides students, researchers, and analysts with the skills necessary to interpret the business and scientific reports that employed one or more of the various predictive analytic techniques.

Since predictive analytics and modeling cover a wide-range of analytical and modeling techniques, all the methods are impossible to be covered in a single chapter. Therefore, in this chapter, we chose to cover some of the important methods that are most commonly used by predictive analysts and researchers across a wide spectrum of fields of study. Various single-level predictive analytics such as simple and multiple linear regression analyses, polynomial regression, logistic regression, and discriminant analysis were covered. In addition, multiple-level predictive analytics such as multilevel modeling designed for analyzing hierarchically structured data were also covered.

REFERENCES

Carlberg, C. (2013). *Predictive Analytics: Microsoft Excel*. Pearson Education, Inc.

Evans, J. R., & Lindner, C. H. (2012). Business Analytics: The Next Frontier for Decision Sciences. *Decision Line*, *43*(2), 4–6.

Field, A. (2009). *Discovering Statistics Using SPSS* (3rd ed.). London: Sage Publications, Inc.

George, D., & Mallery, P. (2010). *SPSS for Windows Step by Step: A Simple Guide and Reference 18.0 Update* (11th ed.). Boston, MA: Pearson Education, Inc.

Hair, J. F. Jr. (2007). Knowledge creation in marketing: The role of predictive analytics. *European Business Review*, *19*(4), 303–315. doi:10.1108/09555340710760134

Hox, J. (2002). *Multilevel analysis: Techniques and applications*. Mahwah, NJ: Lawrence Erlbaum Associates.

Kalaian, S. A. (2008). Multilevel Modeling Methods for E-Collaboration Data. In N. Kock (Ed.), *Encyclopedia of E-Collaboration* (pp. 450–456). Hershey, PA: IGI Global.

Kalaian, S. A., & Kasim, R. M. (2006). Hierarchical Linear Modeling. In L. Salkind (Ed.), *Encyclopedia of Measurement and Statistics* (pp. 433–436). Thousand Oaks, CA: SAGE.

Kuhns, M., & Johnson, K. (2013). *Applied Predictive Modeling*. New York: Springer. doi:10.1007/978-1-4614-6849-3

Maisel, L. S., & Cokins, G. (2014). *Predictive Business Analytics: Forward Looking Capabilities to Improve Business Performance*. Hoboken, NJ: John Wiley & Sons, Inc.

Mertler, C. A., & Vannatta, R. A. (2005). *Advanced and Multivariate Statistical Methods* (3rd ed.). Glendale, CA: Pyrczak Publishing.

Provost, F., & Fawcett, T. (2013). *Data Science for Business*. Sebastopol, CA: O'Reilly Media, Inc.

Raudenbush, S. W., & Bryk, A. S. (2002). *Hierarchical Linear Models: Applications and Data Analysis Methods* (2nd ed.). Thousand Oaks, CA: Sage Publications, Inc.

Raudenbush, S. W., Bryk, A. S., Cheong, Y., & Congdon, R. T. (2004). *HLM 6: Hierarchical Linear and Nonlinear Modeling*. Chicago: Scientific Software International.

Siegel, E. (2014). *Predictive Analysis: The Power to Predict Who will Click, Buy, Lie, or Die*. Indianapolis, IN: John Wiley & Sons, Inc.

Tabachnick, B. G., & Fidell, L. S. (1996). *Using Multivariate Statistics* (3rd ed.). New York: Harper Collins.

KEY TERMS AND DEFINITIONS

Discriminate Analysis: Discriminant Analysis is a predictive analytic technique that uses the information from a set of independent variables to predict the value of a discrete (categorical) dependent variable, which represents the mutually exclusive groups in the predictive model.

Logistic Regression: Logistic regression is a predictive analytic method for describing and explaining the relationships between a categorical dependent variable and one or more continuous or categorical independent variables in the recent and past existing data in efforts to build predictive models for predicting a membership of individuals or products into two groups or categories.

Multilevel Modeling: Multilevel modeling are advanced analytical methods to describe, explain, and capture the hierarchical relationships between variables at one level (micro-level) of the existing data that are affected by variables at higher level of the hierarchy (macro-level) in efforts to predict future performances, risks, trends, and behaviors.

Multiple Linear Regression: Multiple linear regression analysis methods are analytic techniques for explaining, analyzing and modeling the linear relationships between a continuous dependent variable and two or more independent variables in the recent and past existing data in efforts to build predictive models for making future business performance and risk predictions.

Polynomial Regression: Polynomial regression is a predictive analytics method that is used instead of the linear regression analysis (simple or multiple linear regression analyses) for describing and explaining the nonlinear relationships between the dependent and independent variables in the recent and past existing data in efforts to predict future performances, risks, and behaviors.

Predictive Analytics: Predictive analytics and modeling are statistical and analytical tools that examine and capture the complex relationships and underlying patterns among variables in the existing data in efforts to predict the future organizational performances, risks, trends, and behavior patterns.

Simple Linear Regression: Simple linear regression analysis methods are analytic techniques for explaining, analyzing and modeling the linear relationships between a continuous dependent variable and an independent variable in the recent and past existing data in efforts to build predictive models for making future business performance and risk predictions.

Two-Level Multilevel Model: Refers to analytic methods for data with two levels where individuals (micro-level) are nested within organizational groups (macro-level) and there are independent variables (predictors) characterizing each of the two levels of the multilevel model.

Chapter 3
Using Big Data Opinion Mining to Predict Rises and Falls in the Stock Price Index

Yoosin Kim
University of Texas – Arlington, USA

Michelle Jeong
University of Pennsylvania, USA

Seung Ryul Jeong
Kookmin University, Korea

ABSTRACT

In light of recent research that has begun to examine the link between textual "big data" and social phenomena such as stock price increases, this chapter takes a novel approach to treating news as big data by proposing the intelligent investment decision-making support model based on opinion mining. In an initial prototype experiment, the researchers first built a stock domain-specific sentiment dictionary via natural language processing of online news articles and calculated sentiment scores for the opinions extracted from those stories. In a separate main experiment, the researchers gathered 78,216 online news articles from two different media sources to not only make predictions of actual stock price increases but also to compare the predictive accuracy of articles from different media sources. The study found that opinions that are extracted from the news and treated with proper sentiment analysis can be effective in predicting changes in the stock market.

1. INTRODUCTION

With the development of ICT, emergence of the Internet, and the expansion of the smartphone-led mobile environment, the digital revolution is accelerating. A huge amount of digital data is being created from both daily and corporate activities. In recent years, the collective form of such large volumes of digital data has taken on the label of 'big data' and much interest has begun to be taken in their utiliza-

DOI: 10.4018/978-1-4666-7272-7.ch003

tion (Madden, 2012; Manovich, 2011). Particularly compelling is the need to find and take advantage of the rapidly expanding supply of available unstructured text data, as such information can directly and indirectly reflect certain tendencies of their respective authors, including their opinions, emotions, interests, and preferences (Pang & Lee, 2008).

Unstructured text data exist in diverse content forms, ranging from news articles, blogs, and social network service (SNS) posts, to information found in Q&A forums and Voice of the Customer (VOC) feeds. Particularly of interest to this study is the data found in news articles. The news media produce and digitize a large quantity of news articles daily, distributing them worldwide. Such mass-produced news articles influence all sectors of society, but are especially believed to be closely correlated with stock price. For one, while changes in the stock market, due to their accompanying complexities, cannot be explained solely by changes in the market's fundamentals, one possible alternative explanation involves news. Even without any distinctive changes in the market fundamentals, the price can often fluctuate depending on the appearance of a particular news story. This may be due to the fact that news contains explanations of various real-world events, as well as predictions of future changes and directions in politics, society, and the economy. This close relationship between news and stock prices leads people to expect to learn of new investment opportunities and/or earn profits via news, and allows market participants to predict, albeit partially, the stock market fluctuations. It is thus feasible to imagine that with the proper analysis of news content, and the accurate distinction between favorable and adverse issues that arise in the stock market, stock price can be predicted, thereby creating economic profits (Fu, Lee, Sze, Chung, & Ng, 2008; Gillam et al., 2002; Mitchell & Mulherin, 1994; Mittermayer & Knolmayer, 2006; Schumaker & Chen, 2009; Sehgal & Song, 2009).

Although previous studies have indicated that news may influence stock prices (Fu et al., 2008; Mittermayer & Knolmayer, 2006), they mainly targeted news on particular events or individual corporate news, making it difficult to generalize these effects to the real world in which a myriad of news on different topics is produced and distributed daily. It is a challenge to identify not only which piece of news, among a continuous flow of a variety of news stories, is especially crucial in influencing stock prices, but how each news story brings about such effects. Moreover, a variety of news content, including daily market situations, future prospects, and evaluations of corporate performances, is written and disseminated in real time, and it is not easy to clearly determine whether such contents have actual causal impact on the market, and if so, whether those effects are positive or negative. After all, hard news attempts to cover both positive and negative aspects of the stock markets in an effort to keep the tone neutral, making it difficult to identify the underlying valence that may or may not be present (Kim, Kim, & Jeong, 2012).

Existing studies have attempted to analyze relatively simple news stories that cover particular events in conjunction with the stock prices responding to such news, as well as the link between stock price fluctuations and the presence of related news that could potentially have influenced such results. Given the slew of news that is being produced by diverse media platforms and sources, there has also been a recent increase in attention to the need for converting unstructured forms of massive amounts of data into meaningful information, but so far, only preliminary efforts have been made.

Thus, in order to overcome such limitations in the field, this study proposes the intelligent investment decision-making support model based on opinion mining, in which a continuous flow of massive news is regarded as unstructured text big data and leads to the automatic clipping and parsing of news and tagging of vocabulary sentiment, and consequently, inferences regarding the opinions on stock price fluctuations. The prototype experiment for sentiment polarity tagging developed and applied a subject-oriented sentiment dictionary specifically for the stock market domain, rather than a general purpose sentiment dictionary. Afterwards, the main experiment selected two somewhat different media sources, underwent machine learning, and tested predictive accuracy within three different experimental groups, thereby comparing the accuracy of stock price increase/decrease predictions across different media sources.

This is a new attempt to consider news as big data, to analyze the positive/negative meaning of news, to extract various patterns, and to utilize them in predicting stock prices. By proposing an intelligent investment decision-making support model designed to automatically gather, process, and analyze un-structured news texts from the Internet, this study fills a crucial gap in the current literature. In addition, in order to verify the model, both the prototype experiment for the development of the subject-oriented sentiment dictionary and the main experiment for predicting actual stock price index rise were carried out; in the process, this study introduced an experimental model that could be applied to similar areas.

2. RELATED WORKS

2.1 Opinion Mining

Opinion mining, as a sub-discipline within data mining and computational linguistics, is referred to as the computational techniques used to extract, classify, understand, and assess the opinions expressed in various online news sources, social media comments, and other user-generated content (Chen, & Zimbra, 2010). 'Sentiment analysis' is often used in opinion mining to identify sentiments, affect, subjectivity, and other emotional states in the online text (Boderndort & Kasier, 2010).

Works on opinion mining include showing the effectiveness of automatic mining of movie reviews and summarization of movies (Zhuang, Jing, & Zhu, 2006), proposing a technique that allows ranked product reviews to appear in lists that correspond to the intentions of the searcher (Yune, Kim, & Chang, 2010), and showing how market moods monitored from Twitter may be used to predict the flow of stock prices (Bollen, Mao, & Zeng, 2011). Similarly, much work has focused on predicting stock prices using news opinion mining (Mittermayer & Knolmayer, 2006; Schumaker & Chen, 2009; Ahn & Cho, 2010; Sehgal & Song, 2009; Paik et al., 2007).

In order to more accurately extract opinions and sentiments from a text, it is very important to build a lexicon of opinion mining. A properly developed lexicon will ensure that the opinion mining yields useful results (Boderndort & Kasier, 2010). Furthermore, sentiment word dictionaries are more effective when domain specific characteristics are taken into consideration (Yu, Kim, Kim, & Jeong, 2013).

Table 1 outlines the main differences among data mining, text mining, and opinion mining.

Table 1. Differences in opinion, text, and data mining

Opinion Mining	A series of processes used to identify sentiment, nuance, and the author's attitude shown in texts, to turn them into meaningful information, and to use it in decision making
Text Mining	A process used to extract and process useful information from texts, or even to evaluate the subjects of texts from text databases based on natural language processing technology
Data Mining	A series of processes used to explore and model patterns and relations between data hidden in large-volume data, to turn them into meaningful information applicable to work, and to apply the information in corporate decision making

2.2 Stock Prediction Using the News

Much work over the years has continued to prove that news is closely related to stock prices. In particular, with the recent explosive increase in the amount of unstructured text data from the internet, mobile channels, and SNS, there have been attempts to use such data to predict stock movements.

In one study, researchers used NewsCATS (News Categorization and Trading System; a stock prediction system consisting of three engines, i.e., news pre-treatment, categorization and trading), to analyze media news on specific companies, and experimented with a comparison between the flow of news and stock price fluctuations (Mittermayer & Knolmayer, 2006). Similarly, another study gathered, analyzed and extracted individual investors' opinions disclosed on the web, conducted sentiment analyses, and predicted the stock values of three companies via machine learning (Sehgal & Song, 2009). A third study developed a machine learning system called AZFinText (Arizona Financial Text System) to infer stock price predictive variables from the news, and showed higher returns than the market average through trading simulation (Schumaker & Chen, 2009).

Among a series of studies conducted in Korea, one study proposed the use of an automatic news classifier and showed that using pattern matching-based news classification was 69% accurate when predicting whether stock prices will rise, and 64% accurate when predicting whether they will fall (Paik et al., 2007). Similarly, another study extracted features from news texts to compare stock price variations, and experimented with a classifier to predict whether specific companies' stock prices would go up or down, using the Naïve Bayesian model (Ahn & Cho, 2010). Researchers in a third study suggested an intelligent investment model by text opinion mining to analyze the sentiments of 'news big data,' and used logistic regression analysis to show that predictions achieved an accuracy rate of 70.0% for increases in stock prices and 78.8% for decreases (Kim et al., 2012).

3. APPROACH

3.1 System Overview

Figure 1 shows the overall outline of the system used in this study. The first step was news gathering. We retrieved a scraping of online economic news from "Naver" (www.naver.com), the largest Korean search portal, and stored the data in a database. The next step consisted of natural language processing (NLP) in order to extract sentiment from unstructured news texts. We removed inappropriate characters such as punctuation, numbers, and html tags. The remaining words were used to build a sentiment dictionary. We then conducted 1) sentiment analysis and opinion mining using the sentiment word dictionary, and 2) supervised learning experiments aimed at predicting rises and falls in stock prices.

3.1.1 Gathering of News: Clipping

In order to build 'news big data', massive amounts of news data need to be automatically gathered and accumulated in real time. Therefore, this model used the clipping method, targeting Naver's securities sections featuring economic news from all domestic economic-related media.

Figure 1. System overview

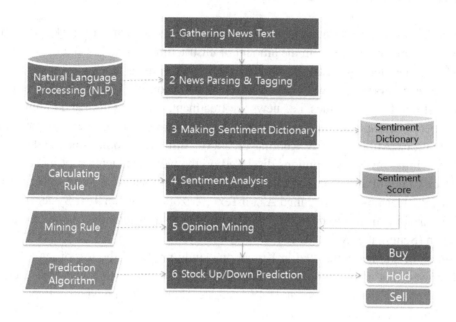

1.   Access the target site,
2.   Clip individual news content (i.e., texts),
3.   Classify only necessary content and store data, and
4.   Repeatedly clip news within the targeted time period.

3.1.2 News Parsing and Polarity Tagging

Clipped news texts were analyzed by the natural language processing morpheme analyzer module, where each vocabulary word was compared with the words listed in the sentiment dictionary, and was subsequently given a positive or negative sentiment polarity tagging. Such sentiment polarity-tagged words were converted into individual news-based opinions according to the opinion calculation rule.

In this parsing process, several pre-treatment stages were deemed necessary to remove noise that was unnecessary or uninterpretable, to ensure opinion mining was performed with only the items that could clearly offer news opinions.

In order to extract opinions, parsed news contents underwent tagging. As such, this study adopted the bag-of-words model by which to compare words parsed by the morpheme analyzer module with words in the sentiment dictionary, and to tag and score relevant words' polarity value. However, a subject-oriented sentiment dictionary was developed to comprise words that were mainly used and analyzed as meaningful in the context of stock markets, instead of general words. This was because if a vocabulary dictionary that reflects the specific domain characteristics is developed and used, it can boost the effect of analyzing big data by discovering opinion patterns from massive data.

3.1.3 Extraction of News Opinions

The next stage was to use sentiment-tagged words to evaluate the opinions of news. Using the aforementioned polarity-tagged vocabulary, as well as the frequency of vocabulary appearance in the news, we derived the news opinion index, which was subsequently converted into an opinion index of an entire day's worth of news.

Opinion vocabulary tagging can classify each word into positive (1) or negative (0), but stages beginning with news opinion extraction will have a quantification process, and each news opinion index will again be converted into a day's news opinion index. Through a comparison with stock price index direction, this enables training aimed at extracting optimal opinion critical values for classifying stock price increase/decrease, and accordingly, the prediction of stock price direction.

As mentioned above, in order to predict the stock price rise/fall according to each news opinion index, it is necessary to set the critical value aimed at distinguishing between positive/negative news. Instead of proposing a specific critical value as a discrimination criterion, this study experimented with the prediction accuracy change patterns and precision of stock price rise/fall according to changing critical values, thereby aiming to determine optimal critical values and classification conditions.

3.2 Data Collection

For this experiment, we used scraping technology to gather 78,216 economic news articles by media companies M and H from Naver, over a period of one year (2011).

The experiment divided the data into two sets of news articles: articles from the first seven months (January 1 - July 31, 2011) as a learning data set, and articles from the latter five months (August 1 - December 31, 2011) as a verification data set. Of all the articles in the data set, the number of news articles by media company M amounted to 44,305, while that of media company H amounted to 33,911.

3.3 Sentiment Analysis

Analyzing the sentiment of the news involves recognizing and defining the 'emotional state' expressed in the text. The sentiment word dictionary plays a crucial role in opinion mining to build linguistic resources, which classify sentiment polarity, quantify the breadth of sentiment, and discriminate between sentiments. In one specific study, a stock domain specific dictionary showed greater accuracy compared with general sentiment dictionaries in terms of its ability to predict price stock movements (Yu et al., 2013). Similarly, we extracted each sentiment word from the news using NLP, calculated the sentiment score, and mined the opinion. Figure 2 shows a flow diagram of the development process of a sentiment word dictionary aimed at predicting rises and falls in stock prices.

More specifically, two phases are required in order to develop a sentiment word dictionary. The first phase consists of deleting 'stop words/characters' (i.e., punctuation, numbers, English words, one-character words), extracting high performance words using term frequency, and removing duplicate words and proper nouns used as product names.

The next phase comprises forming an opinion of the news by calculating the probability of recurrence of certain sentiment words. The sentiment of a word is defined as the ratio of the resulting number of stock price increases or decreases to the total number of news containing the word; the calculation formula is expressed as follows:

Figure 2. Development of a sentiment dictionary

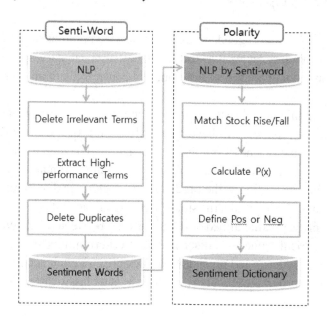

$$Word(i, j)$$

$$= \begin{cases} 1 \begin{pmatrix} Doc(j)\,including\ Word(i), \\ Doc(j)\,next\ day\ stock\ price\ rise \end{pmatrix} \\ 0\,(the\ rest) \end{cases}$$

$$Word(i).NumDocs$$
$$= the\ total\ number\ of\ news\ that$$
$$includes\ Word(i)$$

$$Word(i).SentiScore = \frac{\sum_{i=1}^{n} Word(i, j)}{Word(i).NumDocs}.$$

In the formula, the score for a sentiment word ranges from a maximum of 1 (i.e., fully positive sentiment) to a minimum of 0 (i.e., fully negative sentiment). The sentiment score of a news article is calculated based on the average sentiment score for all sentiment words contained in the news. Likewise, the sentiment score for a day is calculated by the average sentiment score of the total news of that day.

3.4 Stock Predictions

An opinion for prediction is decided to be positive or not at a certain critical value. Based on the sentiment score of that opinion, the stock price for the next trading day is predicted to rise, or, conversely, predicted to fall. Therefore, the setting of an appropriate critical value for predicting stock price fluctuation is crucial. Figure 3 shows a flow diagram of the learning experiment for predicting stock prices.

In addition, we compared the news offered by two different media sources, and measured the prediction accuracy of each media source using the selected critical values.

4. EXPERIMENTS AND RESULTS

4.1 Evaluation

The accuracy of opinion mining in new sentiment analysis, which is defined as the percentage of correctly predicted sentiments, can be evaluated using statistical measures such as recall, precision, and F1 score (Mittermayer & Knolmayer, 2006; Paik et al., 2007). The quality of the results is measured by comparing two standard performance measures, namely, recall and precision. In general, there is an inverse relationship between recall and precision. An ideal learning model would have both high recall and high precision. Sometimes, recall and precision are combined together into a single number called F1, which represents a harmonic mean of recall and precision:

Figure 3. Experimental model overview

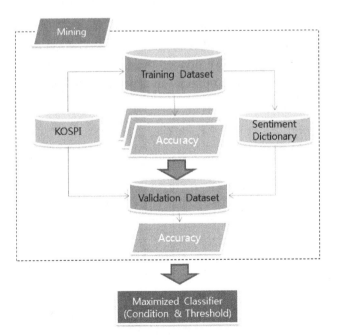

$$F1Score = \frac{2 \times Recall \times Precision}{Recall + Precision}$$

4.2 Analyzing Sentiment

In previous works, the use of a domain specific dictionary when analyzing news sentiment with a sentiment word dictionary was shown to have greater predictive accuracy than the use of a general dictionary (Yu et al., 2013). As a result, we developed a stock market-specific dictionary to evaluate the sentiment of the words appearing in the news. In order to develop a stock domain specific dictionary, we performed NLP on our full sample of 78,216 news articles. At the first parsing, we had over ten million words; after completing several pre-processing and selection procedures, we compiled a list of 700 sentiment words. We calculated a sentiment score for each of the selected words using the sentiment scoring formula described above. Table 2 lists a few examples of the sentiment words we used.

If the sentiment score of a word is closer to 1.0, it means that the word is more positive. Conversely, if a score is closer to 0.0, the word is considered more negative. As the results showed, rarely did any of the words display extremely negative or positive polarity; in fact, most words fell in the middle range, i.e., 0.3 ~ 0.7.

The sentiment scores of news (*NewsOpn*) were calculated using a sentiment scoring formula. The sentiment score of a day (*DayOpn*) was converted into stock price fluctuation prediction variables. We made attempts to determine the threshold (i.e., critical value) that would yield the highest predictive accuracy via repeated tests at various increments.

4.3 Predicting Increases/Decreases in Stock Price

The aim of the main experiment was to determine whether there is a correlation between news sentiment and the rise or fall of stock prices, and whether the results of prediction differ according to different media sources. For the main experiment, we divided the data set into three groups: media source M, media source H, and M+H combined. The opinions in news from media source M showed the highest

Table 2. Sample of sentiment words

Neg-Word	Score	Pos-Word	Score
double dip	0.167	pump-priming	0.700
freeze	0.246	confidence	0.692
defense	0.296	expand	0.677
slump	0.333	improve	0.647
compare	0.341	peak	0.625
basis	0.365	agree	0.612
require	0.365	leading stock	0.608
base rate	0.365	strong	0.565
fear	0.366	buy	0.563
range of drop	0.382	sudden rise	0.563

predictive accuracy, 65.2%, at the critical value of 0.22. In contrast, the opinions in news from media source H showed 60.3% predictive accuracy at the critical value of 0.19. The difference in accuracy between the two media sources was about 5%, which means that M's news, compared to H's news, could predict with greater accuracy any rises and falls in stock prices. Even in terms of the actual content of the news articles, media source H has a tendency of presenting macroeconomic infrastructure and post-incident evaluations, while media source M tends to present stock market situations, prospects and so forth in a relatively clearer tone

On the other hand, the opinions of news from both M+H combined showed 60.1% predictive accuracy at the critical value of 0.11. This may have been due to the fact that an analysis of combined news articles from two different media sources made the classification of opinions unclear, thereby lowering accuracy.

For verification, critical values drawn from the training data sets were applied to the test data sets, and the predictive accuracy of each group was tested. Media source M news' opinions, which showed the highest predictive accuracy in the training data set, also showed the highest accuracy in the test data set, with an accuracy rate of 54.8%. Media source H news' opinions showed an accuracy rate of 52.3%, a lower rate than that obtained by the training data set. The combined set of news from both M+H showed a very low level of accuracy at just 48.1%.

While the above results are focused on determining the threshold and predictive accuracy through the training and test data sets, the next thing that needs to be examined is how the prediction was performed to assess the quality of prediction. As mentioned in the Evaluation section, in order to assess the prediction quality, we calculated the F1 score. Generally, if the predictive accuracy is higher, the result is better; when the level of accuracy is identical, the higher the F1 score, the higher the degree of predictive power.

Table 3 shows each experimental group's predictive accuracy and F1 score based on the training data sets. The results showed that media source M news had the highest predictive accuracy (0.652) and F1 score (0.626), compared to the other experimental groups, meaning that overall, news from media source M has the best predictive probability.

We then tested the predictive accuracy and quality of the test data set, using the threshold from the training data set. The results are shown in Table 4. Media M's news still displayed the highest predictive power. Although its accuracy was 0.10 points lower compared to the accuracy displayed with the training data, it still resulted in a high predictive accuracy level of 0.550 and an F1 score of 0.630. In other words, it seems that the rises and falls in stock prices can be sufficiently predicted using news opinion mining.

Overall, the results of this experiment showed that although there are differences in the level of predictive accuracy and quality depending on media source, fluctuations in stock prices can be predicted using news opinions, and that proper sentiment analysis and an appropriate threshold, as learned through opinion mining, can be effectively used to predict changes in the actual stock market.

Table 3. Predictive quality using training data

Training Data	Max Critical Point	Accuracy ∝	F1 Score
M	0.22	0.652	0.626
H	0.19	0.603	0.526
M+H	0.11	0.594	0.736

Table 4. Predictive quality using test data

Training Data	Max Critical Point	Accuracy ∝	F1 Score
M	0.22	0.550	0.630
H	0.19	0.523	0.532
M+H	0.11	0.484	0.652

In summary, we showed that through a process of extracting opinions from clipped and classified news data, and determining an appropriate critical value and threshold, it is possible to predict the rises and falls in stock price. However, we should be aware that the differing characteristics of different media sources can sometimes render the results of opinion mining somewhat ambiguous and lower its predictive power.

5. CONCLUSION

Under the assumption that news and stock prices have a close correlation, this study sought to find patterns in the news that could be useful in predicting positive and negative fluctuations in stock prices. Existing studies show that the news influences stock prices, and a number of studies on stock price prediction have been made using actual news articles. However, we have made a novel attempt at compiling from a mass of unstructured news big data, a sentiment word dictionary specific to the stock domain, in order to analyze 'sentiment' and to mine opinions that would help predict stock price fluctuations.

As a result of building a stock domain specific dictionary via NLP of more than 78,000 news articles taken from two different media sources, calculating sentiment scores for news opinions, and conducting a stock prediction experiment, we found that while opinions extracted from the news could be useful in making solid predictions about stock market price movements, the accuracy of these predictions could vary depending on the media from which the news originated.

REFERENCES

Ahn, S., & Cho, S. B. (2010). Stock Prediction Using News Text Mining and Time Series Analysis. *KIISE 2010 Conference*, *37*, 364-369.

Boderndort, F., & Kasier, C. (2010). Mining Customer Opinions on the Internet A Case Study in the Automotive Industry. In *Proceedings of Third International Conference on Knowledge Discovery and Data Mining*, (pp. 24-27). Phuket, Thailand: Academic Press.

Bollen, J., Mao, H., & Zeng, X. (2011). Twitter mood predicts the stock market. *Journal of Computational Science*, *2*(1), 1–8. doi:10.1016/j.jocs.2010.12.007

Chen, H., & Zimbra, D. (2010). AI and Opinion mining. *IEEE Intelligent Systems*, *25*(3), 74–80. doi:10.1109/MIS.2010.75

Fu, T., Lee, K., Sze, D., Chung, F., & Ng, C. (2008). Discovering the Correlation between Stock Time Series and Financial News. In *Proceedings of IEEE/WIC/ACM International Conference on Web Intelligence and Intelligent Agent Technology*, (pp. 880-883). Sydney: IEEE. doi:10.1109/WIIAT.2008.228

Gillam, L., Ahmad, K., Ahmad, S., Casey, M., Cheng, D., Taskaya, T., et al. (2002). Economic News and Stock Market Correlation: A Study of the UK Market. In *Proceedings of Conference on Terminology and Knowledge Engineering*. Retrieved January 12, 2014, from http://www.cs.surrey.ac.uk/BIMA/People/M. Casey/downloads/Publications/2002_gillam_ahmad_ahmad_casey_cheng_taskaya_oliveira_manomaisu-pat_economic_news_and_stock_market_correlation.pdf

Kim, Y., Kim, N., & Jeong, S. R. (2012). Stock-index Invest Model Using News Big Data Opinion Mining. *Journal of Intelligent Information Systems*, *18*(2), 143–156.

Madden, S. (2012). From Databases to Big Data. *IEEE Internet Computing*, *16*(3), 4–6. doi:10.1109/MIC.2012.50

Manovich, L. (2011). Trending: The Promises and the Challenges of Big Social Data. In M. K. Gold (Ed.), *Debates in the Digital Humanities*. Minneapolis, MN: The University of Minnesota Press.

Mitchell, M. L., & Mulherin, J. H. (1994). The Impact of Public Information on the Stock Market. *The Journal of Finance*, *49*(3), 923–950. doi:10.1111/j.1540-6261.1994.tb00083.x

Mittermayer, M. A., & Knolmayer, G. F. (2006). NewsCATS: A News Categorization and Trading System. In *Proceedings of 6th International Conference in Data Mining*, (pp. 1002-1007). Hong Kong: Academic Press.

Paik, W., Kyoung, M. H., Min, K. S., Oh, H. R., Lim, C., & Shin, M. S. (2007). Multi-stage News Classification System for Predicting Stock Price Changes. *Journal of the Korea Society for Information Management*, *24*(2), 123–141. doi:10.3743/KOSIM.2007.24.2.123

Pang, B., & Lee, L. (2008). Opinion Mining and Sentiment Analysis. *Foundations and Trends in Information Retrieval*, *2*(1-2), 1–35. doi:10.1561/1500000011

Schumaker, R. P., & Chen, H. (2009). Textual Analysis of Stock Market Prediction Using Breaking Financial News: The AZFinText System. *ACM Transactions on Information Systems*, *27*(2), 12. doi:10.1145/1462198.1462204

Sehgal, V., & Song, C. (2009). SOPS: Stock Prediction using Web Sentiment. In *Proceedings of Seventh IEEE International Conference on Data Mining – Workshop*, (pp. 21-26). IEEE.

Yu, Y., Kim, Y., Kim, N., & Jeong, S. R. (2013). Predicting the Direction of the Stock Index by Using a Domain-Specific Sentiment Dictionary. *Journal of Intelligent Information Systems*, *19*(1), 92–110.

Yune, H., Kim, H., & Chang, J. Y. (2010). An Efficient Search Method of Product Review using Opinion Mining Techniques. *Journal of KIISE: Computing Practices and Letters*, *16*(2), 222–226.

Zhuang, L., Jing, F., & Zhu, X. (2006). Movie Review Mining and Summarization. In *Proceedings of 15th ACM International Conference on Information and Knowledge Management*, (pp. 43-50). New York, NY: ACM.

KEY TERMS AND DEFINITIONS

Opinion Mining: The computational techniques used to extract, classify, understand, and assess the opinions expressed in various online news sources, social media comments, and other user-generated content.

Parsing: Determining the parse tree (or syntactic structure) of a given sentence, based on grammatical analysis.

Polarity: The grammatical category associated with the distinction between affirmative and negative forms.

Precision: The fraction of retrieved instances that are relevant. High precision means that an algorithm returned substantially more relevant results than irrelevant.

Recall: The fraction of relevant instances that are retrieved. High recall means that an algorithm returned most of the relevant results.

Sentiment Analysis: Identifying sentiments, affect, subjectivity, and other emotional states in online text.

Sentiment: A complex combination of feelings and opinions as a basis for action or judgment.

Chapter 4
A Modified Stacking Ensemble Machine Learning Algorithm Using Genetic Algorithms

Riyaz Sikora
University of Texas – Arlington, USA

O'la Al-Laymoun
University of Texas – Arlington, USA

ABSTRACT

Distributed data mining and ensemble learning are two methods that aim to address the issue of data scaling, which is required to process the large amount of data collected these days. Distributed data mining looks at how data that is distributed can be effectively mined without having to collect the data at one central location. Ensemble learning techniques aim to create a meta-classifier by combining several classifiers created on the same data and improve their performance. In this chapter, the authors use concepts from both of these fields to create a modified and improved version of the standard stacking ensemble learning technique by using a Genetic Algorithm (GA) for creating the meta-classifier. They test the GA-based stacking algorithm on ten data sets from the UCI Data Repository and show the improvement in performance over the individual learning algorithms as well as over the standard stacking algorithm.

1. INTRODUCTION

According to some estimates we create 2.5 quintillion bytes of data every day, with 90% of the data in the world today being created in the last two years alone (IBM, 2012). This massive increase in the data being collected is a result of ubiquitous information gathering devices, such as sensors used to gather climate information, posts to social media sites, digital pictures and videos, purchase transaction records, and cell phone GPS signals to name a few. With the increased need for doing data mining and analyses on this big data, there is a need for scaling up and improving the performance of traditional data mining and learning algorithms. Two related fields of distributed data mining and ensemble learning aim to ad-

DOI: 10.4018/978-1-4666-7272-7.ch004

dress this scaling issue. Distributed data mining looks at how data that is distributed can be effectively mined without having to collect the data at one central location (Zeng et. al., 2012). Ensemble learning techniques aim to create a meta-classifier by combining several classifiers, typically by voting, created on the same data and improve their performance (Dzeroski & Zenko, 2004; Optiz & Maclin, 1999). Ensembles are usually used to overcome three types of problems associated with base learning algorithms: the statistical problem; the computational problem; and the representational problem (Dietterich, 2002). When the sample size of a data set is too small in comparison with the possible space of hypotheses, a learning algorithm might choose to output a hypothesis from a set of hypotheses having the same accuracy on the training data. The statistical problem arises in such cases if the chosen hypothesis cannot predict new data. The computational problem occurs when a learning algorithm gets stuck in a wrong local minimum instead of finding the best hypothesis within the hypotheses space. Finally, the representational problem happens when no hypothesis within the hypotheses space is a good approximation to the true function *f*. In general, ensembles have been found to be more accurate than any of their single component classifiers (Optiz & Maclin, 1999; Pal, 2007).

The extant literature on machine learning proposes many approaches regarding designing ensembles. One approach is to create an ensemble by manipulating the training data, the input features, or the output labels of the training data, or by injecting randomness into the learning algorithm (Dietterich, 2002). For example, Bagging learning ensembles, or bootstrap aggregating, introduced by Breiman (1996), generates multiple training datasets with the same sample size as the original dataset using random sampling with replacement. A learning algorithm is then applied on each of the bootstrap samples and the resulting classifiers are aggregated using a plurality vote when predicting a class and using averaging of the prediction of the different classifiers when predicting a numeric value. While Bagging can significantly improve the performance of unstable learning algorithms such as neural networks, it can be ineffective or even slightly deteriorate the performance of the stable ones such as k- nearest neighbor methods (Breiman, 1996).

An alternative approach is to create a generalized additive model which chooses the weighted sum of the component models that best fit the training data. For example, Boosting methods can be used to improve the accuracy of any "weak" learning algorithm by assigning higher weights for the misclassified instances. The same algorithm is then reapplied several times and weighted voting is used to combine the predictions of the resulting series of classifiers (Pal, 2007). Examples of Boosting methods include AdaBoost, AdaBoost.M1 and AdaBoost.M2 which were proposed by Freund and Schapire (1996). In a study conducted by Dietterich (2000) comparing the performance of the three ensemble methods Bagging, Randomizing and Boosting using C4.5 on 33 datasets with little or no noise, AdaBoost produced the best results. When classification noise was added to the data sets, Bagging provided superior performance to AdaBoost and Randomized C4.5 through increasing the diversity of the generated classifiers. Another approach is to apply different learning algorithms to a single dataset. Then the predictions of the different classifiers are combined and used by a meta-level-classifier to generate a final hypothesis. This technique is called "stacking" (Dzeroski & Zenko, 2004).

In this paper we use concepts from ensemble learning and distributed data mining to create a modified and improved version of the stacking learning technique by using a genetic algorithm (GA) for creating the meta-classifier. We use Weka-3, the suite of machine learning and data mining algorithms written in Java for all our experiments. We use concepts from distributed data mining to study different ways of distributing the data and use the concept of stacking ensemble learning to use different learning algorithms on each sub-set and create a meta-classifier using a genetic algorithm. We test the GA-based stacking algorithm on ten data sets from the UCI Data Repository and show the improvement in performance over the individual learning algorithms as well as over the standard stacking algorithm.

The rest of the paper is organized as follows. In the next section we describe the stacking ensemble learning approach. In Section 3, we describe our modified stacking algorithm using genetic algorithm. Section 4 describes the data sampling and decomposition technique we have used. In Section 5, we present the results and discussion. Finally, we conclude in Section 6.

2. STACKING ENSEMBLE LEARNING

In the standard stacking algorithm shown in Figure 1, n different subsets of the training data set are created by using stratified sampling with replacement in which the relative proportion of the different classes is maintained in all the subsets. Each subset of the training set used to determine the performance of the classifiers on the training set. A meta classifier in the form of relative weight for each classifier is created by assigning a weight to a classifier that is proportional to its performance.

Figure 1. Standard stacking ensemble learning

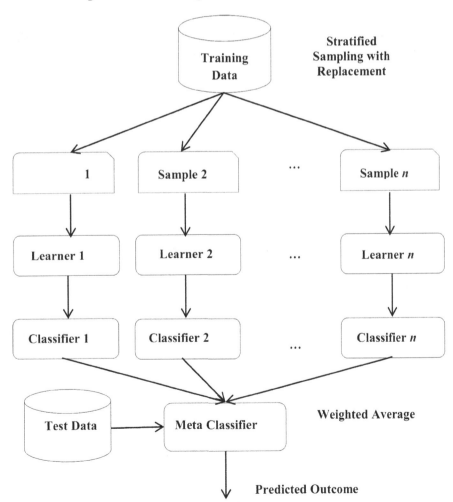

When evaluating an instance from the test set, every classification algorithm in Weka-3 gives a class distribution vector for that instance that gives the probability of that particular instance belonging to a given class. We can represent the class distribution vector over c classes for the jth classifier by a 1 x c vector as follows:

$$\Delta_j = [\delta_{1j} \quad \delta_{2j} \quad \cdots \quad \delta_{cj}] \quad 1 \leq j \leq n \tag{1}$$

where,

$$0 \leq \delta_{ij} \leq 1 \quad \forall \ 1 \leq i \leq c$$

$$\sum_i \delta_{ij} = 1$$

The class distribution vectors for the n classifiers can then be represented by an n x c matrix as follows:

$$\Delta = [\Delta_1, \Delta_2, \ldots, \Delta_n]^T \tag{2}$$

The meta-classifier creates a weight distribution vector that gives relative weight to different classifiers. The weight distribution vector over n classifiers is represented as follows:

$$\Theta = [\theta_1 \quad \theta_2 \quad \cdots \quad \theta_n] \tag{3}$$

where,

$$0 \leq \theta_j \leq 1$$

$$\sum_j \theta_j = 1$$

Given the class distribution matrix and the weight distribution vector, the meta-classifier evaluates each instance of the test set by using the following 1 x c class distribution vector:

$$\Delta' = \Theta \cdot \Delta = [\delta'_1, \delta'_2, \ldots, \delta'_c] \tag{4}$$

where,

$$\delta_i{}' = \sum_j \theta_i \delta_{ij}$$

As mentioned above, in the standard stacking algorithm the meta-classifier weight distribution vector Θ is created by assigning a weight to a classifier that is proportional to its performance. In the next section we discuss using a genetic algorithm to learn the weight distribution vector.

3. GENETIC ALGORITHM BASED STACKING ENSEMBLE LEARNING

Genetic Algorithms (GAs) (Goldberg, 1989) combine survival of the fittest among string structures with a structured yet randomized information exchange to form a search algorithm. GAs have been used in machine learning and data mining applications (Aci, Inam & Avci, 2010; Freitas, 2002; Agustin-Blas et. al.; Sikora & Piramuthu, 2005). GAs have also been used in optimizing other learning techniques, such as neural networks (Sexton, Sriram & Etheridge, 2003).

The stacking ensemble learning using genetic algorithm as the meta-learner is shown in Figure 2. The training data set is split into a training subset and a holdout subset. The training subset is further split into *n* subsets using stratified sampling with replacement, which are used by different learning algorithms to create *n* classifiers. The genetic algorithm is then used to learn a weight distribution vector that creates the meta classifier for predicting the test set instances.

In our case, the GA implements a weight distribution vector Θ as an individual member of the population. Each population member is therefore a vector of weights for each classifier, that all add up to 1.0. Based on some initial set of experiment runs we chose the following operators and parameter values for the GA. We used tournament selection of size 2 as the selection operator, a standard one-point crossover operator, and a mutation operator where one value from the vector of weights for an individual is randomly changed by a small amount. When an operator creates an invalid vector, i.e., whose weights do not add up to 1.0, we simply normalize the vector by dividing each weight value by the sum of all weights. We used a population size of 30 and the probabilities of crossover and mutation as 0.7 and 0.1 respectively. Note that the aim of our study was not to find the optimal parameter settings for the GA. In most cases the optimum settings would vary with data sets. Instead, our goal is to show the efficacy of this modified algorithm in general.

The GA begins by creating a random population of weight distribution vectors. The evaluation of each population member is done by evaluating the corresponding meta-classifier created by using its weight distribution vector on the holdout subset. The fitness of each member is then calculated to be the prediction accuracy of that meta-classifier on the holdout subset. Using the fitness of each population member, the GA then performs the tournament selection to select members for the next generation. It then applies the crossover and mutation operators to create a new generation of weight distribution vectors. The above process is repeated for 3000 generations, and the best weight distribution vector from its final population is selected to create the meta-classifier.

In the next section we give details about the data sampling and data decomposition techniques that were applied.

Figure 2. Stacking ensemble learning using genetic algorithm as meta learner

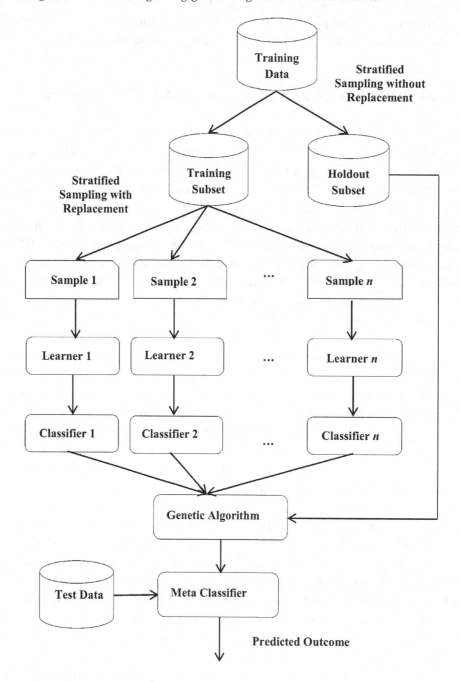

4. DATA SAMPLING AND DECOMPOSITION

The data sampling and decomposition shown in Figures 1 and 2 can be done either along instances or along attributes as depicted in Figure 3. In the instance-based decomposition, each sample receives only a subset of the total instances from the original data set. In the attribute-based decomposition, each sample receives a subset of the attributes from the original data set. We use two parameters to control

Figure 3. Instance-based and attribute-based decomposition

	a_1	a_2	a_3	...	a_n
X_1	x^1_1	x^1_2	x^1_3	...	x^1_n
X_2	x^2_1	x^2_2	x^2_3	...	x^2_n
X_3	x^3_1	x^3_2	x^3_3	...	x^3_n
...					
X_m	x^m_1	x^m_2	x^m_3	...	x^m_n

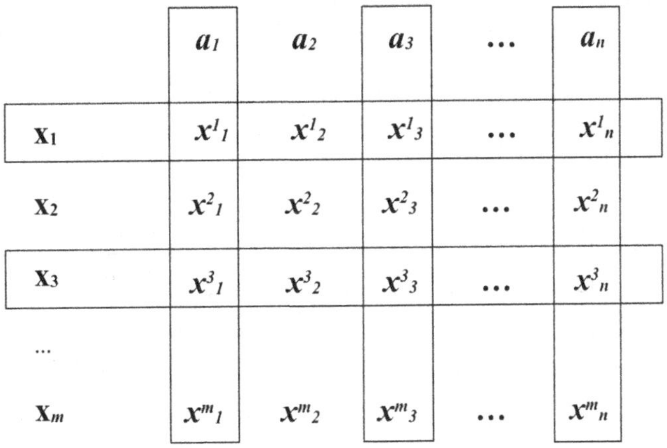

the type and amount of decomposition. For instance-based decomposition we use the parameter $0 < pEx \leq 1$ that gives the proportion of the examples/instances that are selected for each subset. For attribute-based decomposition we use the parameter $0 < pAtt \leq 1$ that gives the proportion of the attributes that are selected for each subset.

These two data decomposition techniques also have practical implications for distributed data mining. In many scenarios data is naturally distributed and it is infeasible or impractical or insecure to collect all the data at one site for data mining. In such cases, it is important to do local data mining at the individual sites and then integrate the results. In some cases, the number of attributes might be too large for a standard learning algorithm to handle. By showing the efficacy of the stacking method presented in this paper, we also provide an efficient mechanism of doing distributed data mining in such instances.

5. RESULTS AND DISCUSSION

The data sets used for the study were taken from the UCI Data Repository. Table 1 gives a summary of the ten data sets that were used for all the experiments. Both versions of the stacking algorithm were implemented in Java using the WEKA machine learning suite. The following five learning algorithms were used in both versions of the stacking algorithm: J48 (Quinlan, 1993), Naïve Bayes (John & Langley, 1995), Neural Networks (Kim & Han, 2000), IBk (Aha & Kibler, 1991), and OneR (Holte, 1993). In all experiments the data sets were split 80/20 into a training set and a holdout set as shown in Figure 2. In the first set of experiments, $pAtt = 1$ and $pEx = 0.5$ were used. In other words, only instance-based decomposition was used with each sample getting half of the instances from the training data set. Table 2 shows the performance results on the testing set of the two versions of the stacking algorithm along with those of the individual learning algorithms before they are used for creating the meta-classifier. Both versions of the stacking algorithm were run ten times with different random number seeds, and all the results are average of those ten runs. Results (p values) of the 1-sided paired t-test are also reported to show the significance of the improvement in performance of the standard stacking algorithm over the best learning algorithm, and the improvement in performance of the stacking algorithm using GA as the meta-learner. Significant values (at 0.01 level of significance) are highlighted in bold. Except for

Table 1. Information about the data set

Data Set	Attributes	Instances	Attribute Characteristics
Poker	11	25010	real
Letter Recognition	16	20000	integer
Chess	6	28056	categorical
Adult	14	48842	categorical, continuous
Nursery	8	12960	categorical, continuous
Shuttle	9	58000	integer
Mushroom	22	8124	categorical
Pen Digits	16	10992	categorical
Telescope	11	19020	categorical, integer
Block Classification	10	5473	integer, real

Table 2. Predictive performance results for pAtt = 1 and pEx = 0.5

Data Set	Individual Learners' Accuracy					Stacking			Stacking with GA		
	J48	Naïve Bayes	NN	IBk	OneR	Accuracy	Time (Sec)	p	Accuracy	Time (Sec)	p
Poker	50.96	50.14	50.29	50.50	50.27	51.25	1235.9	0.460234	52.17	1585.1	0.09515
Letter Recognition	81.12	72.52	75.14	79.45	66.97	90.80	1933.6	*6.83E-12*	94.15	2949.5	*5.98E-06*
Chess	52.33	43.00	45.83	46.52	42.19	57.03	2155.2	*0.000296*	62.75	6970.7	*3.2E-05*
Adult	55.15	54.96	53.98	54.25	52.67	55.37	30993.7	0.078302	55.83	35142.8	*0.010929*
Nursery	94.08	92.11	94.33	94.37	89.73	97.16	945.9	*6.91E-10*	99.52	487.2	*2.29E-06*
Shuttle	95.60	91.85	92.19	92.81	92.40	95.28	726.6	0.22935	99.91	1805.4	*0.019958*
Mushroom	99.95	97.28	98.18	98.63	98.59	99.99	12021.8	*0.007484*	99.96	5219.5	0.148333
Pen Digits	94.00	89.89	91.25	93.17	82.16	98.00	1172.6	*1.57E-10*	99.14	573.3	*2.63E-05*
Telescope	84.08	78.25	80.62	81.19	79.10	84.26	339.1	0.248141	85.86	256.8	*6.39E-08*
Block Classification	96.56	91.99	93.33	93.77	93.67	96.87	167.1	0.075069	96.89	86.9	0.458774

the Nursery data set, J48 was the best performing individual learning algorithm on all data sets. The standard stacking algorithm was able to improve the prediction accuracy on five of the ten data sets. The modified stacking algorithm with GA was however able to improve on the performance of the standard stacking algorithm on seven out of the ten sets. The best improvement in performance was on the Chess set, where the modified stacking algorithm was able to improve the prediction accuracy by more than 10% compared to the standard stacking algorithm. The training time is also reported for both versions of the stacking algorithm. On average the modified stacking algorithm takes more time than the standard stacking algorithm since it involves running the GA. Note that both the versions of the stacking algorithm were implemented as sequential algorithms. The training time can be considerably reduced by running the individual learning algorithms in parallel.

In the second set of experiments, *pAtt* = 0.5 and *pEx* = 0.5 were used. In other words, both instance-based and attribute-based decomposition were used with each sample getting on-average half of the instances containing only half of the attributes from the training data set. Table 3 shows the results for this set of experiments. As before, significant values (at 0.01 level of significance) are highlighted in bold. Note that the performance of all algorithms across the board was worse than in the first set of experiments since they were using only half of all the attributes. J48 was still the best individual algorithm in seven out of the ten sets. The standard stacking algorithm was able to improve the prediction accuracy on four of the ten data sets. The modified stacking algorithm with GA was able to improve on the performance of the standard stacking algorithm on six out of the ten sets. The best improvement in performance was again on the Chess set, where the modified stacking algorithm was able to improve the prediction accuracy by more than 69% compared to the standard stacking algorithm. The training time is also reported for both versions of the stacking algorithm. As before, the modified stacking algorithm takes more time than the standard stacking algorithm since it involves running the GA. The exceptions are the last four data sets for which the modified stacking algorithm is more efficient.

In both sets of experiments, the modified stacking algorithm was able to improve the performance of the standard stacking algorithm in majority of the data sets tested. This shows the potential of using a genetic algorithm to improve the performance of ensemble learning algorithms. Note that there was no attempt to tailor the ensemble learning algorithm for a given data set. One could possibly improve the performance of this modified stacking algorithm independently for each data set even further by fine tuning several parameters such as, the number and type of individual learning algorithms, the parameters of each of these individual algorithms, the value of *pAtt* and *pEx*, and the parameters of the genetic algorithm.

Table 3. Predictive performance results for pAtt = 0.5 and pEx = 0.5

Data Set	Individual Learners' Accuracy					Stacking			Stacking with GA		
	J48	Naïve Bayes	NN	IBk	OneR	Accuracy	Time (Sec)	*p*	Accuracy	Time (Sec)	*p*
Poker	50.21	50.03	49.93	49.95	49.89	50.05	516.8	0.06231	51.89	848.3	*0.005858*
Letter Recognition	59.68	48.77	51.66	57.53	49.33	79.60	1106.6	*4.26E-05*	84.45	2107.2	0.074477
Chess	26.82	25.03	27.04	27.21	26.27	23.99	1368.5	*1.49E-05*	40.65	2337.8	*6.03E-05*
Adult	53.73	53.44	53.39	53.29	52.73	54.30	9457.2	0.39323	55.82	14365	*0.007819*
Nursery	62.23	61.20	62.39	62.75	61.24	80.86	215	*0.003262*	84.52	375.5	0.263822
Shuttle	96.41	92.40	93.32	94.33	93.97	98.77	661.8	0.100216	95.26	964.3	0.233893
Mushroom	98.99	95.14	96.28	97.04	95.01	99.20	3032.4	0.426326	99.92	1933	0.098741
Pen Digits	83.93	78.50	80.87	84.18	74.62	93.28	539.7	*0.000319*	96.59	356.7	*0.002485*
Telescope	77.14	74.84	75.41	75.64	74.27	78.99	204.1	0.217304	82.44	174.6	*0.007871*
Block Classification	95.10	90.39	91.30	91.97	92.05	95.13	92.2	0.474408	95.93	54.8	*0.013562*

6. CONCLUSION

In this paper we presented a modified version of the standard stacking ensemble algorithm that uses a genetic algorithm to create an ensemble. We also tested two data decomposition techniques to distribute the data over the individual learning algorithms in the ensemble. We tested the GA-based stacking algorithm on ten data sets from the UCI Data Repository and showed the improvement in performance over the individual learning algorithms as well as over the standard stacking algorithm. We are currently also working on testing the robustness of the algorithm in the presence of noise.

REFERENCES

Aci, M., Inam, C., & Avci, M. (2010). A hybrid classification method of k nearest neighbors, Bayesian methods and genetic algorithm. *Expert Systems with Applications*, *37*(7), 5061–5067. doi:10.1016/j.eswa.2009.12.004

Agustin-Blas, L., Salcedo-Sanz, S., Jimenez-Fernandez, S., Carro-Calvo, L., Del-Ser, J., & Portilla-Figueras, J. (2012). A new grouping genetic algorithm for clustering problems. *Expert Systems with Applications*, *39*(10), 9695–9703. doi:10.1016/j.eswa.2012.02.149

Aha, D. W., Kibler, D., & Albert, M. K. (1991). Instance-based learning algorithms. *Machine Learning*, *6*(1), 37–66. doi:10.1007/BF00153759

Breiman, L. (1996). Bagging predictors. *Machine Learning*, *24*(2), 123–140. doi:10.1007/BF00058655

Dietterich, T. G. (2000). An experimental comparison of three methods for constructing ensembles of decision trees: Bagging, boosting, and randomization. *Machine Learning*, *40*(2), 139–157. doi:10.1023/A:1007607513941

Dietterichl, T. G. (2002). Ensemble learning. In The handbook of brain theory and neural networks, (pp. 405-408). Academic Press.

Džeroski, S., & Ženko, B. (2004). Is combining classifiers with stacking better than selecting the best one? *Machine Learning*, *54*(3), 255–273. doi:10.1023/B:MACH.0000015881.36452.6e

Freitas, A. A. (2002). *Data mining and knowledge discovery with evolutionary algorithms*. Springer. doi:10.1007/978-3-662-04923-5

Freund, Y., & Schapire, R. E. (1996, July). *Experiments with a new boosting algorithm* (Vol. 96). ICML.

Goldberg, D. E. (1990). *Genetic algorithms in search, optimization and machine learning*. Reading, MA: Addison-Wesley.

Holte, R. C. (1993). Very simple classification rules perform well on most commonly used datasets. *Machine Learning*, *11*(1), 63–90. doi:10.1023/A:1022631118932

IBM. (2012). *Bringing Big Data to the Enterprise*. Retrieved from http://www-01.ibm.com/software/data/bigdata/

John, G. H., & Langley, P. (1995, August). Estimating continuous distributions in Bayesian classifiers. In *Proceedings of the Eleventh Conference on Uncertainty in Artificial Intelligence* (pp. 338-345). Morgan Kaufmann Publishers Inc.

Kim, K. J., & Han, I. (2000). Genetic algorithms approach to feature discretization in artificial neural networks for the prediction of stock price index. *Expert Systems with Applications, 19*(2), 125–132. doi:10.1016/S0957-4174(00)00027-0

UCI Machine Learning Repository. (n.d.). *Center for Machine Learning and Intelligent Systems.* Retrieved from http://archive.ics.uci.edu/ml/

Opitz, D., & Maclin, R. (1999). Popular ensemble methods: An empirical study. *Journal of Artificial Intelligence Research, 11*, 169–198.

Pal, M. (2007). Ensemble learning with decision tree for remote sensing classification. *World Academy of Science. Engineering and Technology, 36*, 258–260.

Quinlan, J. R. (1993). *C4. 5: Programs for machine learning* (Vol. 1). Morgan Kaufmann.

Sexton, R. S., Sriram, R. S., & Etheridge, H. (2003). Improving decision effectiveness of artificial neural networks: A modified genetic algorithm approach. *Decision Sciences, 34*(3), 421–442. doi:10.1111/j.1540-5414.2003.02309.x

Sikora, R., & Piramuthu, S. (2005). Efficient genetic algorithm based data mining using feature selection with Hausdorff distance. *Information Technology Management, 6*(4), 315–331. doi:10.1007/s10799-005-3898-3

Weka-3: Data Mining with Open Source Machine Learning Software in Java. (n.d.). Retrieved from http://www.cs.waikato.ac.nz/ml/weka/

Zeng, L., Li, L., Duan, L., Lu, K., Shi, Z., & Wang, M. et al. (2012). Distributed data mining: A survey. *Information Technology Management, 13*(4), 403–409. doi:10.1007/s10799-012-0124-y

KEY TERMS AND DEFINITIONS

Classification: Classification is the problem of identifying to which of a set of categories a new observation belongs.

Distributed Data Mining: Applying data mining in a non-centralized way.

Ensemble Learning: The process of solving complex problems by intelligently generating and using multiple learning algorithms.

Genetic Algorithm: Heuristic procedure that mimics evolution through natural selection.

Machine Learning: Algorithms that learn and adapt when new data is added to it.

Meta-Classifier: A classifier, which is usually a proxy to the main classifier, used to provide additional data preprocessing.

Stacking: A type of ensemble learning.

Chapter 5
Organizational Performance-Design Process:
A Discrete-Events Simulation Approach

Hossein Arsham
University of Baltimore, USA

Shaya Sheikh
University of Baltimore, USA

ABSTRACT

Inverse simulation involves finding the control inputs required to achieve a particular performance measure. The designer simulates the process numerically by varying the controllable input for generating desirable output. Clearly, this trial and error is not efficient and effective. This chapter proposes a "stochastic approximation" algorithm to estimate the necessary controllable input parameters within a desired accuracy given a target value for the performance function. The proposed algorithm is based on iterative Newton's method using a single-run simulation to minimize the expected loss function (i.e. risk function). The validity of the input parameter estimates are examined by applying it to some reliability and queuing systems with known analytical solutions. (Keywords: Performance management by simulation; prescriptive analysis for parameter setting; decision support for product and service design; data analysis and design; inverse business performance measure.)

1. INTRODUCTION

Business models transform managerial inputs into useful information for managerial decisions of performance measures.

A Short Review of Business Decisions and Performance Measures

The following provides a brief review of literature on business decision-making, the linkage between decision-making and business performance evaluation. This review is focusing on three basic elements that are the forces and conditions surrounding decision-making, the scope and nature of business decision-making, and the impact of that decision-making on business performance.

DOI: 10.4018/978-1-4666-7272-7.ch005

Harnish (2012) looks at a dozen companies that made decisions that changed their businesses. The authors trace circumstances in which the decision happened and the results. Making Smart Decisions by Harvard Business Review on (2011) is a collection of ten articles and is not focused on any central theme. The book is instructional in nature and is aimed at helping business leaders to make bold decisions that challenge the status quo. It offers the best practices and ideas for smart decision-making. Davenport (2012) focuses on presenting the use of analytics in optimizing business performance and includes guide to analytics strategy, planning, organization, implementation and usage. It covers building better analytics, as well as gathering data. This is not an empirical study but an application of principles for working managers.

There are some books focusing on business performance measurement that connect to decision-making.

Neel (2007) is a textbook for MBA students and practitioners; it examines the leading ideas in business performance measures. It contains well-written chapters on measuring performance from different functional areas of business, theoretical foundations of performance, frameworks and methodologies, practical applications, specific measures and emerging issues and trends. Davenport (2012) provides a guide to business performance analytics strategy, implementation, and management. It utilizes large amounts of data and analytics to implement effective actions. It helps managers to understand what are the consequences of their actions by providing analytical techniques, practices and research for competitive advantage. This book is intended to improve performance on a case-by-case basis by focusing on the individual firm.

Hope & Player (2012) are concerned with improving organizational efficiency. The premise is to highlight and answer the question: "what is the practice and how effective is it? What is the performance potential of the practice? What needs to be done to maximize the potential of the practice?" The authors believe the tools the performance measures may be sound in theory; however, they are misused by most organizations. Tools are often used without asking what is the problem that needs to be solved.

Taticchied (2010) discusses measuring and managing the performance of a business. The book introduces new contexts and themes of application and presents emerging research areas, such as sustainability. This textbook is highly specialized with its focus on new performance measurement techniques that are aimed at students, academics, and practitioners.

What the immediately preceding compilation shows is that most books on measuring performance are recent.

Recognizing that many enterprises have been pursuing process innovation or improvement to attain their performance goals by aligning business process with enterprise performances. Hana *et al.* (2009) proposes a two-stage process analysis for process (re)design that combines the process-based performance-measurement framework and business process simulation. Target business processes that need improvement are identified and processed for a newly designed and then using simulation to predict the performance.

Bourne (2003) *et al.*, reviewed the different performance-measurement system-design processes published in the literature and created a framework for comparing alternative approaches. He reviewed journal articles on performance-measurement systems and concluded that, the performance-measurement literature is at the stage of identifying difficulties and pitfalls to be avoided based on experience and the performance-measurement literature lacks consideration of implementation.

Advancements in computing power, availability of PC-based modeling and simulation, new and efficient computational methodology, such as single-run gradient estimations Robertazzi (2000), are allowing leading-edge, simulation modeling to pursue investigations in systems analysis, design, and control processes that were previously beyond reach of the modelers and decision makers. Simulation models continue to be the primary method by which performance designers obtain information about complex stochastic systems, such as telecommunication networks, health service, corporate planning, financial modeling, production assembly lines, and flexible manufacturing systems. These systems are driven by the occurrence of discrete events; and complex interactions within these discrete events occur over time. For most discrete event systems (DES), no analytical methods are available; so DES must be studied via simulation. Descriptive simulation models are studied to understand their performance, while prescriptive simulation models are used to determine the best ways to improve their performance. In particular, one is often interested in how system performance depends on the system's design parameter v, which could be a vector. However, we are using a scalar parameter v for both static and dynamic system applications.

Design is an iterative decision-making process. For example, the aim of a product design is improving the competitiveness of a manufacturing enterprise by developing products that are easier, faster, and less expensive to make, while maintaining required standards of functionality, quality, and marketability, White Jr. (1998). Any system design approach must be balanced against competing objectives of cost, risk, lifecycle properties, and other criteria.

Murray-Smith (2013), uses parameter perturbations and response differencing to variation of parameters of a model in making engineering design decisions. It describes how parameter sensitivity analysis can be carried out for inverse simulations generated through approximate transfer function inversion methods and also through the use of feedback principles.

Osmundson (2000) uses a descriptive, object-oriented model to measure performance at certain discrete levels for the design factors. Frey et al (2007) applied non-simulation approaches to enhancing performance-measure accuracy, namely by applying theory of inventive problem solving, axiomatic design, and highly optimized tolerance. The central idea is that design decision-making under uncertain environments is perceptual rather than conceptual, Hutton & Klein (1999). The performance-measure analysis includes analysis and system verification and validation, Zhang and Ma (2005), and Marchant (2010).

While the above modes are mostly descriptive, de Weck & Jones (2006) developed a prescriptive non-simulation design model. Its basic idea is to implement an inverse design method that starts from a desired vector of performance requirements and works backwards to identify acceptable solutions in the design space. To achieve this, gradient-based is implemented as a multivariable search algorithm that manipulates the null set of the Jacobian matrix. For a non-gradient based optimization, see for example Huynh (2011) using orthogonal array experiment; see e.g., Hedayat *et al.* (1999), to solve a class of performance optimization problems encountered in systems design.

Handley *et al.* (1999) designed a comprehensive descriptive model-driven experimentation. The model is used to analyze the dynamic behavior of the model; an input scenario has been created that is used in the experimental setting to determine the desirable level of performance measure. Similarly Wang & Dagli (2011) proposed an executable system that analyzes the model through animation tools for validation purposes, and then for what-if analysis to find the system design parameters. These approaches are certainly time-consuming and costly way to determine design parameters.

Fortune editors do follow businesses closely, and they used that as a basis for highlighting a handful of business decisions that do appear to be tied to better performance, Ross & Lam (2011). Our purpose is to provide the link between decision-making and performance measurers. The kinds of business decisions that will be investigated are those related directly to performance measure. The decision-making process will be introduced in the context of performance measure, including how the controllable input variables of business decisions is related to the dependent variable of business performance.

This chapter proposes a direct approach to the design problem by using a "stochastic approximation" to estimate the necessary design parameters within a range of desired accuracy for a given target value of the performance function. The proposed solution algorithm is based on Newton's methods using a single-run simulation to minimize a loss function that measures the deviation from a target value.

The following section formalizes the design of a prescriptive modeling process.

Almost all stochastic systems performance evaluation can be formulated as an estimation of an expected value. Consider a system with continuous parameter $v \in V \subseteq R$, where V is an open interval. Let

$$J(v) = E_{Y|v}\left[Z(Y)\right] \tag{1}$$

be the steady-state, expected performance measure, where Y is a random vector with known probability density function (pdf), f(y;v) depends on v, and Z is the performance measure. For example, in a reliability system, J(v) might be the mean time to failure; Z is the lifetime of a system; Y is the lifetime of the components; and v might be the components' mean lifetimes. In general, v is the parameter of the underlying pdf.

In systems analysis, we resort to simulation when Z is either unknown or is too complicated to calculate analytically.

Before proceeding further, we distinguish between discrete event static systems (DESS) and discrete event dynamic systems (DEDS). Dynamic systems evolve over time; static systems do not evolve over time. Examples of dynamic systems are queueing systems; examples of static systems are reliability systems. Note that, while in DESS, Y is a multidimensional vector' in DEDS, Y represents a stochastic process.

Simulation is needed to estimate J(v) for most DESS and DEDS. The principal strength of simulation is its flexibility as a systems analysis tool for highly complex systems.

In discrete event systems, Monte Carlo simulation is usually needed to estimate J(v) for a given value $v = v_0$. By the law of large numbers

$$\hat{J}(V_0) = \frac{1}{n}\sum_{i=1}^{n} Z(y_i) \tag{2}$$

converges to the true value, where y_i, i = 1, 2, ..., n are independent, identically distributed random vector realizations of Y from f (y; v_0), and n is the number of independent replications. The numerical result based on (2) is only a point estimate for J(v) at $v = v_0$. The numerical result based on (2) is a solution to a system analysis: Given the underlying pdf with a particular parameter value v_0, estimate the output function J(v_0). The direct problem is widely used in stochastic system analysis. Now, we pose the system design problem: given a target output value of the system and a parameterized pdf family, find an input value for the parameter that generates such an output. The solution to the design problem has potential application in stochastic system analysis and design. Mathematical formulation of the design problem is as follows:

Given τ, find $v \in V \subseteq R$ subject to $J(v) = \tau$, where

$$J(v) = E_{Y|v}\left[Z(Y)\right] = \int Z(y)f(y;v)dy, \tag{3}$$

- $Z: R^m \to R$ is a system performance measure.
- $Y \in R^m$ is a random vector (or a truncated stochastic process) with pdf f (y; v).

The design problem is essentially backwards. The output is given, but the input must be determined. This is easiest to appreciate when a designer wants to match experimental data in order to obtain some basic parameters. The designer simulates the process numerically and obtains an approximation for that same output. The goal is to match the numerical and experimental results as closely as possible by varying the values of input parameters in the numerical simulation. Analyzing this, clearly, the output is there, and it is the input quantity that needs to be determined. The most obvious difficulty in solving the design problem is that one cannot simply calculate a straightforward solution and be done. Since varying the input must set the output, an iterative method of solution is implied. In the case when v is any controllable or uncontrollable parameter, the designer is interested in estimating $J(v)$ for a *small* change in $v = v_0$ to $v = v_0 + \delta v_0$. This is the so-called what-if problem that is a direct problem. However, when v is a controllable input, the decision maker may be interested in the goal-seeking problem; i.e., "What value of input parameter v will achieve a desired the output value J_0?" While the what-if problem has been extensively studied, the goal-seeking simulation problem is relatively new. Design interpolation based on regression models provides an indirect approach to solve the design problem. In this treatment, one simulates the system for many different values of $v = v_0$ and then one approximates the response surface function $J(v)$. Finally, the fitted function is used to interpolate to obtain in order the unknown parameter v. Since the shape of $J(v)$ function is unknown, this approach is tedious, time-consuming and costly. Moreover, in random environments, the fitted model might have unstable estimates for the coefficients. The only information available about $J(v)$ is general in nature; for example, continuity, differentiability, invertability, and so on.

The simulation models based on (2), although simpler than the real-world system, are still a very complex way of relating input (v) to output $J(v)$. Sometimes a simpler analytic model may be used as an auxiliary to the simulation model. This auxiliary model is often referred to as a local response surface model {known also as a metamodel, Friedman (1996)}. Local response surface models may have different goals: model simplification and interpretation, Clymer (1995); optimization, Arsham (1996, 1998a, 2008); Yakowitz et al (2000)' what-if analysis, Arsham (1989); and generalization to models of the same type. The following Taylor series can be used as an auxiliary model.

$$J(v) = J(v_0) + 'vJ'(v_0) + ('v)^2J''(v_0)/2 + \ldots, \tag{4}$$

where $\delta v = v - v_0$, and the primes denote derivatives. This local response surface model approximates J(v) for small δv. To estimate J(v) in the neighborhood of v_0 by a linear function, we need to estimate the nominal J(v) based on (2) and its first derivative. Traditionally, this derivative is estimated by crude Monte Carlo; i.e., finite difference which requires rerunning the simulation model. Methods that yield enhanced efficiency and accuracy in estimating, at little additional cost, are of great value.

There are few ways to obtain efficiently the derivatives of the output with respect to an input parameter, Arsham (2008). The most straightforward method is the Score Function (SF). The SF approach, Kleijnen & Rubinstein (1996), and Rubinstein & Shapiro (1998) is the major method for estimating the performance measure and its derivative, while observing only a single sample path from the underlying system. The basic idea of SF is that the derivative of the performance function, J'(v), is expressed as expectation with respect to the same distribution as the performance measure itself.

This chapter treats the design problem as a simulation (as opposed to regression) problem. By this approach, we are able to apply variance reduction techniques (VRT) used in the direct problem. Specifically, we embed a stochastic version of Newton's method in a recursive algorithm to solve the stochastic equation J(v) = J for v, given J at a nominal value v_0.

The explicit use of a linear local response surface model is the target parameter design: Given a desired value J = J(v), find the prerequisite input parameter v.

Most performance design methods essentially involve a framework for arriving at a target value for product, process, and service attributes, through a set of experiments that include Monte Carlo experiments. To solve the product design problem, we will restrict our model to the first order expansion. For a given J(v), the estimated δv using (4) is

$$\hat{\delta v} = \frac{\left[J(v) - J(\hat{v}_0) \right]}{J'(\hat{v}_0)}, \tag{5}$$

provided that the denominator in (5) does not vanish for any v_0 in interval V.

The remainder of this chapter is divided into eight sections. In the next section, we introduce the decision maker's modeling environment. It is followed by an outline on uses of single-run gradient estimation of the performance measure by Score Function method. This section includes an outline on the necessary tools for solving efficiently the parameter design-setting problem. Section 4 formally formulates the product parameters design target decision. Based on this formulation, a recursive solution algorithm for estimating the parameter design with desirable accuracy is presented. Sections 7 and 8 illustrate the proposed method for reliability and queuing systems, respectively. Finally, Section 9 provides some concluding remarks and ideas for further research and extensions.

2. DECISION-MAKER'S MODELING ENVIRONMENT

The modeling techniques are the way of representing the systems. The model must be well-tuned to the purpose it is intended. Since a model of a system is a re-presentation of the system that contains those elements that affect the objective of our decision, it is important to identify the most important elements and to categorize them. The desired output usually determines the controllable inputs. The input into a system can be classified either as controllable or uncontrollable. Time-horizons for the modeling review must be selected that are short enough so that the uncontrollable inputs (or probabilistic knowledge of them) will not change significantly. Even for short time-horizons, one might consider the time discounting factor for future periods, Arsham (1987). The output is often called performance measure (or indicator) for the system.

It is a fact that, in any organization, when an indicator to measure performance exists, then productivity improves. Moreover, when performance is measured and reported, the rate of improvement accelerates.

Clearly, when structures and systems are aligned, they facilitate empowerment. When they are not, they work against it. The following paragraphs explain the elements of a model and the sequence by which they must be understood by the designer.

1. **Performance Measure (or Indicator):** Measuring expected product performance is at the top of the designer's concerns. In a competitive market, the development of an effective performance measure (or indicator) is seen as increasingly important by many Performance management as a cyclical process. It starts with effective and efficient planning (e.g., the average waiting time of customers in a local bank, compared with other neighboring banks).
2. **Uncontrollable Inputs:** These come from the decision maker's environment.
   a. Uncontrollable inputs often create the problem and constrain the actions (e.g., arrival rate of customers to a bank, at certain time period of the day).
3. **Parameters of the Business:** Parameters are the constant elements that do not change during the time horizon of the decision review. These are the factors partially defining the decision problem (e.g., total number of customers, different services that the bank provides, etc.).
4. **Controllable Inputs:** The collection of all possible courses of action the decision maker
   a. (i.e., the designer) might take (Average service time determined by number of cashiers at different periods of time in a given day). These inputs are the parameter design with which we are concerned. Their values determine the performance of the product or service. The influential controllable input can be recognized by factor screening methods, Morrice, and Bardhan (1995).
5. **Interactions Involving These Components:** These are logical dependencies among all the above components, e.g., the process that a customer goes through between entering and leaving the bank.
6. **Action:** Action is the ultimate decision for the product design parameter that achieved a desirable performance measure. These parameter settings are determined after enough experiments are done with different sets of controllable inputs. This action is the strategy, i.e., purposeful decision that results in the desirable performance measure (e.g., what is the number of cashiers during certain time period of a day).
7. **Scope and Limitations:** For clarification of the scope and limitation of this chapter, the following provides descriptions of the other similar phrases to avoid any possible confusion.
8. **Reverse Engineering:** The process of discovering the technological principles of a device, object, or system through analysis of its structure, function, and operation. As an example of reverse engineering, recently an unmanned U.S. drone fell in the hands of a hostile foreign government. It is believed that, it was sent to some aero-engineering lab, where their engineers attempted to figure out its parts, its main functional structures, and their working mechanism.

9. **Feasibility Problem and Goal-Seeking Indicators:** In most business decision-making, the manager wishes to achieve a specific goal for the organization's overall objective, while satisfying the constraints of the model. The user does not particularly want to optimize. This type of problem is usually called a feasibility problem. In such situations, the decision-maker aims at satisfying or making incremental changes, rather than optimizing. This is so, because the human mind has a bounded rationality and hence cannot comprehend all alternatives. In the incremental approach to decision-making, the manager takes only small steps, or incremental moves, away from the existing system. This is usually accomplished by a "local search" to find a "good enough" solution. This problem is referred to as "satisficing problem", "feasibility problem", or the "goal-seeking" problem. Therefore, the aim is to achieve a global improvement to a level that is good enough, given current information and resources. One reason that a decision maker manager overestimates the importance of the optimal strategy is that organizations often use indicators as "proxies" for satisfying their immediate needs. Most managers pay attention to indicators, such as profit, cash flow, share price, etc., to indicate survival rather than as a goal for optimization. Another approach is to use "Goal Programming" models that deal precisely with problems of constraint satisfaction, without necessarily having a single objective. Basically, they look at measures of constraint violation and try to optimize them.

3. CONSTRUCTION OF POLYNOMIAL LOCAL RESPONSE SURFACE MODEL BY SINGLE-RUN SIMULATION

Simulation models, although simpler than real-world systems, are still very complex tools for relating input parameters (v) to performance measures J(v). Sometimes a simple analytical model may be used as an auxiliary to the simulation model. This auxiliary local response surface model is often referred to as a metamodel, Friedman (1996). In this treatment, we have to simulate the system for some different values of (v) and then use a "goodness-of-fit" regression. We fit a response surface to these data. Clearly, coupling the simulation model with the Score Function method enhances the efficiency of constructing a local response surface model. A local response surface model can also be constructed by using sensitivities in a Taylor expansion of J(v) in the neighborhood of $v = v_0$. The resulting local response surface model can be used for characterization (such as increasing/decreasing, and convexity/concavity) of the response surface.

Let

$$J(v) = E_{Y|v}\left[Z(Y)\right] = \int Z(y)f(y;v)dy,$$ (6)

where

- Z is a system performance measure,
- $Y \in R^m$ is a random vector (or a truncated stochastic process) with pdf f (y; v)

be the steady state performance measure, then

$$J'(v) = \int \left[Z(y)f(y;v) \right]' dy \tag{7}$$

where the prime (') denotes the derivative with respect to v. Note that, despite the fact that y depends on v, only the function Z.f is subject to differentiation with respect to v. From (7) it follows that

$$J'(v) = \int Z(y)f'(y;v)dy = E_{Y|v}\left[Z(Y).S \right] \tag{8}$$

where $S = f'(y;v) / f(y;v)$ is the Score Function, called Likelihood Ratio in latter papers, i.e., L'Ecuyer (1995). Differentiation is with respect to v. This is subject to that, $f'(y;v)$ exists, and $f(y;v)$ is positive for all $v \in V$, where V is an open interval, and the mild condition, L'Ecuyer (1995); that the differentiation and the integration operators are interchangeable, A necessary and sufficient condition for the interchangeability used above is that there must be no discontinuity in the distribution with position depending on the parameter v, Arsham (2008). Similarly, the second derivative is

$$J''(v) = \int \left[Z(Y)S'f(y;v) + Z(Y)Sf'(y;v) \right] dy \\ = E_{Y|v}\left[Z(Y).H \right] \tag{9}$$

where

$$H = S' + S^2. \tag{10}$$

In the multidimensional case, the gradient and Hessian of J(v) could be obtained in a straightforward manner by generalizing these results, Arsham *et al.* (1989). The estimator for the first and second derivatives based on (8) and (9) are given by:

$$\hat{J}'(v) = \sum_{i=1}^{n} Z(y_i)S(y_i;v)/n \tag{11}$$

$$\hat{J}''(v) = \sum_{i=1}^{n} Z(y_i)H(y_i;v)/n \tag{12}$$

where

$$S(y_i;v) = f'(y_i;v)/f(y_i;v) \tag{13}$$

and

$$H(y_i;v) = f''(y_i;v)/f(y_i;v). \tag{14}$$

Notice that both (11) and (12) estimators are evaluated at $v = v_0$, and y_i 's are the same n independent replications used in (2) for estimating the nominal performance $J(v_0)$; therefore they are quite efficient in terms of computation cost. Estimates obtained by using (11) and (12) are unbiased, consistent, and they converge to the true values in the sense of the mean squared error, Arsham *et al.* (1989). The estimated gradient can also be used in solving optimization problems by simulation, Arsham (2008). Other applications of sensitivity information include stability analysis Arsham (1998a).

The following subsection provides a descriptive presentation of other approaches to gradient estimations. For the full algorithmic implementations and their interrelationships, see Arsham (1998b) and references therein.

3.1 Other Derivative Estimation Techniques

In the design, analysis, and operation of Discrete Event Systems (DES), any information about the derivative $dJ(v)/dv$ is useful to managers, for example, in determining the rate of change, estimating sensitivity information, etc.

The following approaches avoid any numerical problems associated with the finite-differencing ratio as an approximation to the derivative; they are based on *a single simulation run*, and the methods have the potential for real-time applications.

3.1.1 Finite Difference Approximation

Kiefer and Wolfowitz (1952) proposed a finite difference approximation to the derivative. One version of the Kiefer-Wolfowitz (K-W) technique uses two-sided finite differences. The first fact to notice about the K-W estimate is that it requires 2N simulation runs, where N is the dimension of vector parameter v. If the decision maker is interested in gradient estimation with respect to each of the components of v, then 2N simulations must be run for each component of v. This is inefficient. The second fact is that it may have a very poor variance, and it may result in numerical calculation difficulties.

3.1.2 Simultaneous Perturbation Methods

The simultaneous perturbation stochastic approximation (SPSA) algorithm introduced by Spall (2000, 2003), has attracted considerable attention. There has recently been much interest in recursive optimization algorithms that rely on measurements of only the objective function to be optimized, not requiring direct measurements of the gradient of the objective function. Such algorithms have the advantage of not requiring detailed modeling information describing the relationship between the parameters to be optimized and the objective function. For example, many systems involving complex simulations or human beings are difficult to model, and could potentially benefit from such an optimization approach. The SPSA algorithm operates in the same framework as the above Kiefer-Wolfowitz methods, but SPSA has the strong advantage of requiring a much lower number of simulation runs to obtain the same quality of result. The essential feature of SPSA--which accounts for its power and relative ease of use in difficult multivariate optimization problems--is the underlying gradient approximation that requires only TWO objective function measurements, regardless of the dimension of the optimization problem. One variation of basic SPSA uses only ONE objective function measurement per iteration. The underlying theory for SPSA shows that the N-fold savings in simulation runs per iteration (per gradient approximation) translates directly into an N-fold savings in the number of simulations to achieve a given quality of solution to the optimization problem. In other words, the K-W method and SPSA method take the same number of iterations to converge to the answer, despite the N-fold savings in objective function measurements (e.g., simulation runs) per iteration in SPSA.

SPSA can be seriously limited by, for example, the stability constraints of the system; e.g., traffic intensity must remain positive but less than one for steady state sensitivity estimation, Arsham (2008a).

3.1.3 Perturbation Analysis

Perturbation analysis (PA), Cassandras (1993), Fu (2002), computes (roughly) what simulations would have produced, had v been changed by a "small" amount, without actually making this change. The intuitive idea behind PA is that a sample path constructed using v is frequently structurally very similar to the sample path using the perturbed v. There is a large amount of information that is the same for both of them. It is wasteful to throw this information away and to start the simulation from scratch with the perturbed v. In PA, moreover, we can let the change approach zero to obtain a derivative estimator without numerical problems. We are interested in the effect of a parameter change on the performance measure. However, we would like to realize this change by keeping the order of events exactly the same. The perturbations will be so small that only the duration, not the order, of the states will be affected. This effect should be observed in three successive stages:

Step 1: How does a change in the value of a parameter vary the sample duration related to that parameter?
Step 2: How does the change in the individual sample duration reflect itself as a change in a subsequent particular sample realization?
Step 3: Finally, what is the relationship between the variation of the sample realization and its expected value?

3.1.4 Harmonic Analysis

Another strategy for estimating the gradient simulation is based on the frequency domain method, which differs from the time domain experiments in that the input parameters are deterministically varied in sinusoidal patterns during the simulation run, as opposed to being kept fixed as in the time domain runs. The range of possible values for each input factor should be identified. Then, the values of each input factor, within its defined range, should be changed during a simulation run. In time series analysis, t is the time index. In simulation, however, t is not necessarily the simulation clock time. Rather, t is a variable of the model, which keeps track of certain statistics during each run. For example, to generate the inter-arrival times in a queueing simulation, t might be the variable that counts customer arrivals.

Frequency domain simulation experiments identify the significant terms of the polynomial that approximate the relationship between the simulation output and the inputs. Clearly, the number of simulation runs required to identify the important terms by this approach is much smaller than those of the other alternatives, and the difference becomes even more conspicuous as the number of parameters increases.

Figure 1 presents the main ideas and interrelationships among various gradient estimator techniques, Arsham (1998b).

Figure 1. Classification and unification of gradient estimation methods

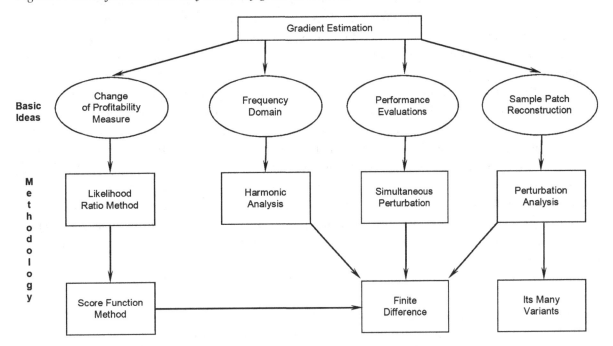

3.1.5 Some Additional Remarks on the Various Approaches

Using the Score Function (SF) method, the gradient can be estimated simultaneously, at any number of different parameter values, in a single-run simulation. The basic idea is that, the gradient of the performance measure function, $J'(v)$, is expressed as an expectation with respect to the same distribution as the performance measure function itself. Therefore, the sensitivity information can be obtained with little computational (not simulation) cost, while estimating the performance measure. It is well known that the crude form of the SF estimator suffers from the problem of linear growth in its variance as the simulation run increases. However, in the steady-state simulation, the variance can be controlled by run length. Furthermore, information about the variance may be incorporated into the simulation algorithm. A recent development has achieved improvement of the quality of SF estimates, Arsham (2008). Under regenerative conditions, the estimator can easily be modified to alleviate the problem of linear growth; yet the magnitude of the variance may be large for queueing systems with heavy traffic intensity. The heuristic idea is to treat each component of the system (e.g., each queue) separately, which synchronously assumes that individual components have "local" regenerative cycles. This approach is promising, since the estimator remains unbiased and efficient, while the global regenerative cycle is very long.

Now, we look at the general (non-regenerative) case. In this case, any simulation will give a biased estimator of the gradient, as simulations are necessarily finite. If n (the length of the simulation) is large enough, this bias is negligible. However, as noted earlier, the variance of the SF sensitivity estimator increases with increase in n; so, a crude SF estimator is not even approximately consistent. There are several ways to attack this problem. The variation of SF estimator is often high, when all past inputs contribute to the performance and the scores from all are included. When one uses batch means, keeping the length of the batch small reduces the variation.

A second way is to reduce the variance of the score to such an extent that we can use simulations long enough to effectively eliminate the bias. This is the most promising approach. Implementing the standard variance reduction techniques (VRT), such as importance sampling, the variance may be reduced further. Finally, we can simply use a large number of independent identically distributed replications of the simulation.

PA and SF (or LR) can be unified, Arsham (1998b). Further comparison of the PA and SF approaches reveals several interesting differences. Both approaches require an interchange of expectation and differentiation. However, the conditions for this interchange in PA depend heavily on the nature of the problem, and must be verified for each application, which is not the case in SF. Therefore, in general, it is easier to satisfy SF unbiased conditions. PA assumes that the order of events in the perturbed path is the same as the order in the nominal path, for a small enough change in v, allowing the computation of the sensitivity of the sample performance for a particular simulation. For example, if the performance measure is the mean number of customers in a busy period, the PA estimate of the gradient with respect to any parameter is zero! The number of customers per busy period will not change if the order of events does not change.

In terms of ease of implementation, PA estimators may require considerable analytical work on the part of algorithm developer, with some "customization" for each application, whereas SF has the advantage of remaining a general definable algorithm whenever it can be applied.

Perhaps the most important criterion for comparison lies in the question of accuracy of an estimator, typically measured through its variance. If an estimator is strongly consistent, its variance is gradually reduced over time and ultimately approaches zero. The speed with which this happens may be extremely important. Since in practice, decisions normally have to be made in a limited time, an estimator whose variance decreases fast is highly desirable. In general, when PA does provide unbiased estimators, the variance of these estimators is small. PA fully exploits the structure of DES and their state dynamics by extracting the needed information from the observed sample path, whereas SF requires no knowledge of the system other than the inputs and the outputs. Therefore when using SF methods, variance reduction is necessary. The question is, "can the variance be reduced enough to make the SF estimator useful in all situations to which it can be applied? The answer is certainly "yes." Using the standard variance reduction techniques can help, but the most dramatic variance reduction (VR) occurs using new methods of VR, such as conditioning, which is shown numerically to have a mean squared error that is essentially the same as that of PA.

Estimating system performance for several scenarios via simulation generally requires a separate simulation run for each scenario. In some very special cases, (to prevent confusion, in this paragraph we use random variable X instead of Y) such as the exponential density $f(x; v) = ve^{-vx}$, one could have obtained the perturbed estimate using Perturbation Analysis directly as follows. Clearly, one can generate random variate X by using the following inverse transformation:

$$X_i = \left(\frac{1}{v}\right) \text{Ln}\left(\frac{1}{U_i}\right)$$

where Ln is the natural logarithm and U_i is a random number distributed Uniformly [0,1], see e.g., Knuth (2011). In the case of perturbed v, the counterpart realization using the same U_i is

$$X_i = \left[\frac{1}{(v+'v)}\right] Ln\left(\frac{1}{U_i}\right).$$

Clearly, this single-run approach is limited, since the inverse transformation is not always available in closed form.

4. TARGET-SETTING PROBLEM IN DESIGN

Most system performance design, Clymer (1995), such as product, process, and service design, involve a framework for arriving at a target value for a set of experiments, which may include Monte Carlo experiments. A random quality loss function $L(Z_i)$ for a given system can be expanded in the neighborhood of the target value τ as follows:

$$L\left(Z_i\right) = L(\tau) + (Z_i - \tau)L'(\tau) + (Z_i - \tau)^2 L''(\tau)/2 + \dots \quad (15)$$

Since the optimal loss is zero at τ, Equation (15) reduces to the following quadratic approximation

$$L\left(Z_i\right) = K\ (Z_i - \tau)^2. \quad (16)$$

In (16), K is some constant that can be determined in terms of the customer's tolerance limit $(\tau - \delta v)$, which suggests that the product performs unsatisfactorily when Z_i slips below this limit. Given that the cost to customer is A dollars, then $K = A/\delta v^2$. Without loss of generality, for simplicity let K=1.

The goal of parameter design is to choose the setting of the design parameter v that minimizes the average loss (the risk function). The risk function $R(\tau)$ is the expected value of the loss function, which can be shown as:

$$R(\tau) = E\left\{L\left(Z_i\right)\right\} = (J - \tau)^2 + Var\left(Z_i\right), \quad (17)$$

This risk function measures the average loss due to a product performance that is proportional to the square of the deviation from the target value τ, as shown in Figure 2. A parabolic representation estimates the quality loss, expressed monetarily, that results when quality characteristics deviate from the target values.

The cost of this deviation increases quadratically as the characteristic moves farther from the target value. The acceptance range is between J(L) and J(U). Below the lower limit, the product is rejected; or, above the upper limit, the product must be reworked.

The parabolic curve shown in Figure 2 represents the Taguchi loss function. From the curve, you can interpret that the amount of loss is minimum for the target (or nominal) value; and, as you deviate from the target, the amount of loss increases, even if you are within the specified limits of the process.

The non-adjustable variational noise; i.e.;

Figure 2. Tolerance concept in target design

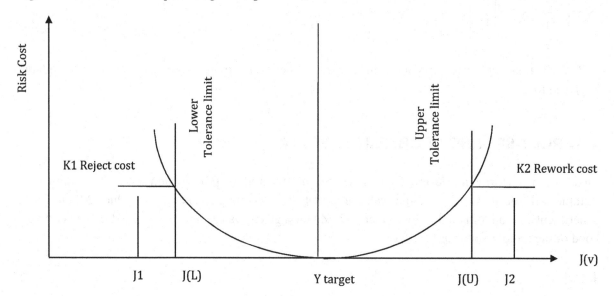

$$\mathrm{Var}\left(Z_i\middle|v\right)=\mathrm{Var}\left(Z_i\right),\tag{18}$$

is a measure of variation among products. However, the role of product design is to reduce the $(J - \tau)^2$ part of risk, which is our interest in this chapter. Note that all estimates involved in computing δv based on (5); i.e., in

$$\delta\hat{v}=\left[J\left(v\right)\text{-}J\left(\hat{v}_0\right)\right]/J'\left(\hat{v}_0\right)\tag{19}$$

are computed simultaneously from a single-run simulation of the nominal system ($v = v_0$). This was achieved by transforming all probability space to the nominal one. Note that, to estimate the derivative, we do not need to rerun the simulation. Estimating the derivatives adds only moderate computational cost to the base simulation.

5. ACCURACY OF THE ESTIMATE

In the design problem, the input parameter is random, while the output is fixed and given as a target value. Upon estimating the input parameter, we must provide a measure, such as a confidence interval, to reflect the precision of the estimate. To construct a confidence interval for δv using the estimator (19), let

$$A_i=J\left(v\right)\text{-}Z\left(y_i;\,v_0\right)\tag{20}$$

$$B_i = Z\left(yi;v_0\right)S\left(y_i;v_0\right) \tag{21}$$

and denote

$$A = \Sigma A_i/n, \text{ and } B = \Sigma B_i/n; \tag{22}$$

then

$$SS^2 = S_{11} - 2\hat{v}S_{12} + \left[\hat{v}\right]^2 S_{22} \tag{23}$$

where

$$S_{11} = \Sigma\left(A_i - A\right)^2/\left(n-1\right), \; S_{22} = \Sigma\left(B_i - B\right)^2/\left(n-1\right) \tag{24}$$

and

$$S_{12} = \Sigma\left(A_i - A\right)\left(B_i - B\right)/\left(n-1\right) \tag{25}$$

An exact $100\,(1-\alpha)\,\%$ confidence interval for δv is given by

$$P\left[n^{1/2} \frac{|\delta v\text{-}v|}{SS/B} \leq t_{n\text{-}1,1-\alpha/2}\right] \geq 1 - \alpha \tag{26}$$

where $t_{n\text{-}1,1-\alpha/2}$ is the $100\,(1-\alpha/2)$ percentile of Student's t distribution with $(n-1)$ degrees of freedom, see, e.g., Rubinstein & Shapiro (1998).

6. A RECURSIVE SOLUTION ALGORITHM

The solution to the design problem is a solution of the stochastic equation $J(v) = J$, which we assume lies in some bounded open interval V. The problem is to solve this stochastic equation by a suitable single-run simulation to ensure convergence as δv approaches zero. The following is a Robbins-Monro (1951) algorithm, see also Ruppert (1985), and Chen & Schmeiser (2001) for its modified versions, which is a root finding procedure for functions whose exact values are not known but are observed with noise. It involves placing experiment $j+1$ according to the outcome of experiment j immediately preceding it. That is,

$$\hat{v}_{j+1} = \hat{v}_j + d_j [\tau - J(v_j)]/J'(v_j) \tag{27}$$

where d_j is any sequence of positive numbers satisfying the following conditions:

$$\sum_{j=1}^{\infty} d_j = \infty \tag{28}$$

and

$$\sum_{j=1}^{\infty} d_j^2 < \infty . \tag{29}$$

The first condition is a necessary condition for the convergence δv to approach zero, while the second condition asymptotically dampens the effect of the simulation random errors Clark (1984) and Benveniste et al (1990). These conditions are satisfied, for example, by the harmonic sequence $d_j = 1/j$. With this choice, the rate of reduction of d_i is very high initially but may reduce to very small steps as we approach the root. Since simulation is partly statistical data generation, one performs simulation experimentation in order to generate "good" data. Instead, of classical $d_j = a / (a + j)$ with $a = 1$, we have performed some pilot-runs for integer values of $1 \leq a \leq 10$, and found that for $a = 9$ one gets considerable saving in number of iterations. Therefore, we have used the better choice $d_j = 9 / (9 + j)$ for the application presented in a latter section. However, as always, one must be careful in generalizing any results, since we have used specific applications. To estimate by simulation, the number of simulation runs (n) is critical. The confidence level of simulation output drawn from a set of simulation runs depends on the size of data set. The larger the number of runs, the higher is the associated confidence. However, more simulation runs also require more effort and resources for large systems. Thus, the main goal must be in finding the smallest number of simulation runs that will provide the desirable confidence. Since the needed statistics for the number of simulation runs was not available from an existing database, a pilot simulation run was used to determine the best $d_j = a / (a + j)$, $1 \leq a \leq 10$.

Usually, when modelers choose a DES approach, they often model the system as an open loop or nearly open loop system. Closing the loops should be an elemental task that a simulation modeler should take care of, even if the scope does not involve doing it. There must be awareness of system behavior, particularly if it is known that the system is under human decision-making processes/activities.

The parameter-setting algorithm is based on an iterative method using differentiation and a feedback structure. After simulation, the output $J(v)$ must be compared to the target value J_0. If the difference is acceptable, then the target is achieved by the current value and the iteration ends; otherwise, the iteration continues.

Since the adjustments are made in proportion to the recent value, we must be sure that the results remain finite. This requires that $J'(v)$ does not vanish for $v \in V$, where V is an open interval. To prevent excessive over-correction, we assume further that the solution lies in some finite interval V. Under some regularity condition such a continuity, this algorithm will converge in mean squared; moreover, it is an almost sure convergence. For some generalizations and studies concerning speed of convergence and acceleration techniques, see Dippon & Renz (1997). Finally, as in Newton's root-finding method Ruppert

(1985) and Clark (1984), it is impossible to assert that the method converges for just any initial $v = v_0$, even though J'(v) may satisfy the Lipschitz condition over V. The function f(x) satisfies the Lipschitz condition on [a, b] for finite real numbers a, and b, if for some real constant L, and for all x, y $\in$ [a, b],

$$\left|f(x)\text{-}f(y)\right| \leq L\left|x\text{-}y\right|$$

Intuitively, a Lipschitz continuous function is limited in how fast it can change: for every pair of points on the graph of this function, the absolute value of the slope of the line connecting them is no greater than a definite real number; this bound is called the function's "Lipschitz constant." For example $J(v) = v^{1/3}$ with an initial guess of $x = 1$. These numbers are growing (in absolute value) instead of converging. In fact, we have

$$v_n = \left(-1\right)^n 2^{n\text{-}1}$$

Hence the sequence fails to converge. However, it is clear that there is a root at $v = 0$. Notice that at $v = 0$, the derivative is undefined. Although it is Lipschitz continuous, however the derivative is unbounded at the origin, see also Pintér (2010).

Algorithm

- **Step 0:** Inputs
    - τ = Desired output
    - j = Iteration number
    - v_j = Controllable input parameter v
    - n = Sample size
    - U = Desired upper limit for absolute increment $u = v_{j+1} - v_j$
    - α = A desired significance level
- **Step 1:** Initialization
    - Set j=1
    - Set $v_j = v_0$
- **Step 2:** Estimations
    - $J(v_j)$ using (2)
    - $J'(v_j)$ using (9)
- **Step 3:** Computations
    - $$u = \frac{9\left[\tau\text{-}J\left(\hat{v}_j\right)\right]}{\left[\left(9+j\right) \ J'\left(\hat{v}_j\right)\right]}$$
    - If | u | < U
    - Construct 100(1- α)% confidence interval for v using (20)
    - Stop.

- Otherwise
  - Set $v_{j+1} = v_j + u$ and $j \rightarrow j+1$
- **Step 4:** Reset
  - Reset the seeds of random number generators to their initial values. Go to step 2.

Note that, by resetting the seeds to their initial values; we are using the Common Random Variate; see for example Rubinstein and Melamed (1998) for this and other variance reduction techniques.

7. DESIGN OF A RELIABILITY SUBSYSTEM

For most complex reliability systems, the performance measures, such as mean time to failure (MTTF), are not available in analytical form. We resort to Monte Carlo Simulation (MCS) to estimate MTTF function from a family of single-parameter density functions of the component's life with specific value for the parameter. The purpose of this section is to solve the design problem that deals with the calculation of the component's life parameters (such as MTTF) of a homogeneous subsystem, given a desired target MTTF for the system. A stochastic approximation algorithm is used to estimate the necessary controllable input parameter within a desired range of accuracy. The potential effectiveness is demonstrated by simulating a reliability system with a known analytical solution.

Consider a coherent reliability sub-system consists of four homogeneous elements; i.e., manufactured by an identical process, components having independent random lifetimes Y_1, Y_2, Y_3, and Y_4, which are distributed exponentially with rates $v = v_0 = 0.5$.

The first two and the last two elements are in series, while these two series, each with two components, are in parallel.

The system lifetime is $Z(Y_1, Y_2, Y_3, Y_4; v_0) = \max[\min(Y_3, Y_4), \min(Y_1, Y_2)]$. It is readily seen that the theoretical expected lifetime of this system is $J(v_0) = 3/(4 v_0)$, Barlow & Proschan (1998). Now we apply our results to compute a necessary value for v to obtain a particular value for $J(v)$, say $J(v) = 2$. For this reliability system, the underlying probability density function is:\

$$f(y;v) = v^4 \exp(-v\Sigma y_i), \quad i = 1, 2, 3, 4 . \tag{30}$$

The Score Function is

$$S(y) = f'(y; v)/f(y; v) = 4/v - \Sigma y_i, \quad i = 1, 2, 3, 4 , \tag{31}$$

$$H(y) = f''(y; v)/f(y; v)$$
$$= [v^2(\Sigma y_i)^2 - 8v(\Sigma y_i) + 12]/v^2, \quad i = 1, 2, 3, 4 \tag{32}$$

The estimated average lifetime and its derivative for the nominal system ($v = v_0 = 0.5$) based on (2) and (9) are

$$J\left(v_0\right) = \Sigma \ \max\left[\min\left(Y_{3,j}, Y_{4,j}\right), \ \min\left(Y_{1,j}, Y_{2,j}\right)\right]/n \tag{33}$$

and

$$\begin{aligned} &J'\left(v_0\right) \\ &= \Sigma \ \max\left[\min\left(Y_{3,j}, Y_{4,j}\right), \min\left(Y_{1,j}, Y_{2,j}\right)\right].S\left(Y_{i,j}\right)/n \end{aligned} \tag{34}$$

$$\begin{aligned} &J''\left(v_0\right) \\ &= \Sigma \ \max\left[\min\left(Y_{3,j}, Y_{4,j}\right), \min\left(Y_{1,j}, Y_{2,j}\right)\right].H\left(Y_{i,j}\right)/n \end{aligned} \tag{35}$$

respectively, where $Y_{i,j}$ is the jth observation for the ith component ($i = 1, 2, 3, 4$). We have performed a Monte Carlo experiment for this system by generating n = 10000 independent replications using SIM-SCRIPT II.5, CACI (1987), random number streams 1 through 4 to generate exponential variates Y_1, Y_2, Y_3, Y_4, respectively, on a PC. The estimated performance is J(0.5) = 1.5024, with a standard error of 0.0348. The first and second derivative estimates are -3.0933 and 12.1177 with standard errors of 0.1126 and 1.3321, respectively.

7.1 A Quadratic Metamodel

The response surface approximation in the neighborhood v = 0.5 is:

$$\begin{aligned} J\left(v\right) &= 1.5024 + \left(v - 0.5\right)\left(-3.0933\right) \\ &+ \left(v - 0.5\right)^2 \left(12.1177\right)/2 + ... \approx \end{aligned}$$

$$6.0589v^2 - 9.1522v + 4.5638 \tag{36}$$

A numerical comparison based on direct simulation and local response surface model (36) is given in Table 1. The relative error as presented is the difference between the metamodel and the analytical values. Notice that the largest error in Table 1 is 0.33% which could be reduced by either more accurate estimates of the derivatives or using a higher order Taylor expansion. A comparison of the errors indicates that the errors are smaller and more stable in the direction of increasing v. This behavior is partly due to the fact that lifetimes are exponentially distributed with variance 1/v. Therefore, increasing v causes less variance than the nominal system (with v = 0.50).

Table 1. A second order polynomial local response surface model and direct simulation

v	Analytic	Simulation	Metamodel	Abs.error(%)
0.40	1.8750	1.8780	1.8723	0.14
0.42	1.7857	1.7885	1.7887	0.17
0.44	1.7045	1.7072	1.7098	0.31
0.46	1.6304	1.6330	1.6359	0.33
0.48	1.5625	1.5650	1.5667	0.27
0.50	**1.5000**	**1.5024**	**1.5024**	**0.16**
0.52	1.4423	1.4446	1.4430	0.05
0.54	1.3889	1.3911	1.3884	0.04
0.56	1.3393	1.3414	1.3386	0.05
0.58	1.2931	1.2951	1.2937	0.05
0.60	1.2500	1.2520	1.2537	0.30

Now assume that the manufacturer wants to improve the average lifetime of the system to $J(v) = \tau = 2$. To achieve this goal, we have set $v_0 = 0.5$ and $U = 0.0001$ in the proposed algorithm. The numerical results are tabulated in Table 2.

The estimated input parameter to achieve the output $J(v) = \tau = 2$ is 0.375, on the fourth iteration. A 90% confidence interval based on this estimate using (20) is:

$$P[0.374 \leq v \leq 0.377] \geq 0.90 \tag{37}$$

Comparing the theoretical value $v_0 = 0.3750$, obtained from $J(v) = 3/(4v_0) = 2$, with our computational value suggests that the results based on the proposed algorithm are quite satisfactory. In fact, running this system with $v = 0.375$, and $n = 10000$, we obtained an estimated MTTF of $J(v) = 2.0000$. Hence the discrepancy in the estimated input parameter by this algorithm must be considered as a pure random error which can be reduced by increasing n. The metamodel (36) could also be applied to $J(v) = 2$ to estimate the desirable v. Solving the resulting quadratic metamodel equation, the relevant root is $v = 0.3725$. This result is an inferior estimate for v compared with the iterative method, although the accuracy of the latter comes with greater computational cost.

Table 2. Iterative decision parameter estimate for the reliability system

Iteration Number j	Fixed Input v_j	Estimated MTTF	Estimated Derivative	Change in v_j	New Input Parameter v_{j+1}
1	0.5000	1.5024	-2.9598	-0.1513	0.349
2	0.3487	2.1544	-6.0862	-0.0208	0.369
3	0.3694	2.0333	-5.4217	+0.0046	0.374
4	0.3740	2.0083	-5.2888	+0.0011	0.375

8. SERVICE SYSTEM DESIGN

This section presents implementation details and some statistical results on the efficiency of the proposed technique for a discrete event dynamic system. To evaluate the proposed single-run technique to solve the design problem, we have chosen to implement it on an M/G/1/∞ queuing system with a known analytical solution. Consider a single-server, first-come-first-served, Poisson input queue with arrival rate of 1 customer per unit of time. The server works according to a Gamma density

$$f\left(y;v\right)=y\ e^{-y/v}/v^2,\ v>0,\ y\geq 0. \tag{38}$$

The analytic solution for the expected steady-state waiting time as a performance measure, in this system is:

$$J\left(v\right)=\rho+(\rho^2+\sigma^2)/[2(1-\rho)] \tag{39}$$

which is obtained by using the Pollaczek-Khinchin formula, Gross (2009), where $\sigma^2 = \text{Var}(y) = 2v^2$ and ρ = traffic intensity =1/service rate = 2v. If we set the nominal value v = 0.25 for the nominal system, then $\sigma^2 = 0.125$ and $\rho = 0.5$ resulting in J(0.25) = 0.875.

To estimate J′ (v) for the nominal system, we will use the method of Batch Means. Other methods, such as Independent Replications or Regenerative Method could also be used.

Batch Means is a method of estimating the steady-state characteristic from a single-run simulation. The single run is partitioned into equal size batches large enough for estimates obtained from different batches to be approximately independent. In the method of Batch Means, it is important to ensure that the bias due to initial conditions is removed to achieve at least a covariance stationary waiting time process. An obvious remedy is to run the simulation for a period (say R customers) large enough to remove the effect of the initial bias. During this warm-up period, no attempt is made to record the output of the simulation. The results are thrown away. At the end of this warm-up period, the waiting times of customers are collected for analysis. The practical question is "How long should the warm-up period be?" Abate & Whitt (1987) provided a relatively simple and nice expression for the time required (t_p) for an M/M/1/∞ queue system (with traffic intensity ρ) starting at the origin (empty) to reach and remain within 100(1-p)% of the steady-state limit as follows:

$$t_p(\rho)=2C(\rho)\ \text{Ln}\{1/[\left(1-\text{p}\right)(1+2C(\rho))]\}/(1-\rho)^2 \tag{40}$$

where

$$C(\rho)=[2+\rho+(\rho^2+4\rho)^{1/2}]/4 \tag{41}$$

Some notions of $t_p(\rho)$ as a function of ρ and p, are given in Table 3.

Table 3. Time (t_p) required for an M/M/1 queue to reach and remain with 100(1-p)% limits of the steady-state value

Traffic Intensity	100p			
ρ	95.0	99.0	99.9	99.99
0.10	3.61	6.33	10.23	14.12
0.20	5.01	8.93	14.53	20.14
0.30	7.00	12.64	20.71	28.79
0.40	10.06	18.39	30.31	42.23
0.50	15.18	28.05	46.47	64.89
0.60	24.70	46.13	76.79	107.45
0.70	45.51	85.87	143.61	201.36
0.80	105.78	201.53	338.52	475.51
0.90	435.74	838.10	1413.7	1989.4

Although this result is developed for M/M/1/∞ queues, it has already been established that it can serve as an approximation for more general; i.e., GI/G/1/∞ queues, Whitt (1989). To compute the Score Function S, we need the density function of the steady-state process.

Clearly, for computational implementation, we need a truncated (say m-truncated) version of this process. The waiting time of customer t at steady state depends on values of the (m - 1) previous customers interarrival and service times. The dependency order m must be chosen so that the correlation between the waiting time of customer t and (t-m) is negligible. Notice that the order of dependency m is equivalent to the "Batch Size" widely discussed in simulation literature in connection with the method of Batch Means. We have chosen m = R large enough to ensure independency and not too large to create the singularity problem.

Let X_k and Y_k be the interarrival and service times of the kth customer at steady state, $k \geq R+1$. The underlying density function for the jth customer, $j \geq 2R+1$, in batch number i is:

$$f(v) = \sum_{k=j-m+1}^{j} f(y_k)f(x_k), \quad j=(i+1)R+1,(i+1)R+2,...,(i+2)R \tag{42}$$

where

$$f(x_k) = \exp(-x_k)$$

and

$$f(y_k) = \left[y_k \exp(-y_k/v)\right]/v^2 .$$

The expected waiting time for the nominal system is:

$$J(\hat{v}) = \sum_{i=1}^{n} \sum_{j=(i+1)R+1}^{(i+2)R} L_{i,j} / Rn \tag{43}$$

where $L_{i,j}$ is the waiting time of the jth customer in the ith batch. The Score Function S is:

$$S_{j,i} = -2m/v + \Sigma x_{j,k}/v^2 \tag{44}$$

For the nominal system ($v = v_0 = 2$), we have used $n = 500$ independent replications. In each run, we set $k = m = T = 100$. The estimated delay in the system and its derivative based on these simulation parameters are 1.007 and -0.951 with computed variance 0.001 and 0.012, respectively. Clearly, derivative estimators discussed in this chapter work much better for terminating models for which only a few number of observations are generated.

Consider the system described above. Assume we want to find a value for the controllable input parameter, service rate v, such that $J(v) = J = 0.8$. We have set $v_0 = 2$ and $U = 0.0001$ in the proposed algorithm. The simulation results are contained in Table 4. Our computations are performed on a PC using streams 1 and 2 of SIMSCRIPT II.5, CACI (1997) to generate the inter-arrival and service times, respectively.

The estimated input parameter to achieve the output $J(v) = 0.8$, is $v = 2.239$ with standard error 0.128. A 95% confidence interval for δv at the fifth iteration, based on the usual t-statistic is:

$$P[-0.016 \leq \delta v \leq 0.016] \geq 0.95 \tag{45}$$

A comparison of the analytical value $v = 2.25$, obtained from (39) with our estimated value suggests that the results based on the proposed algorithm are quite satisfactory. In fact, solving the direct problem using the same simulation parameters with $v_0 = 2.239$, the estimated expected waiting time turned out to be 0.800 with variance equal to 0.001. Hence the discrepancy in the estimated input parameter by this algorithm must be considered as a random error that can be reduced by increasing n.

Table 4. Estimated service rate to achieve a desirable steady state average delay in an M/G/1/∞ queue

Iteration Number	Fixed Input Parameter v_0	Estimated δv_0	Updated v_0
1	2	0.236	2.236
2	2.236	0.001	2.237
3	2.237	0.001	2.238
4	2.238	0.001	2.239
5	2.239	0.000	**2.239***

The method of Independent Replication has lower efficiency than the method of Batch Means for the steady-state perturbation analysis. In the Independent Replication method, the output data are collected over a period of length T in a simulation run over a period of length R + m + T; (T could be as small as 1). The ratio T/(R+m+T), which is the fraction of CPU time generating useful data, would be very small.

8.1 Determination of the Desirable Number of Simulation Runs

The two widely used methods for experimentation on simulation models are method of batch means, and independent replications. Intuitively, one may say the method of independent replication is superior in producing statistically a "good" estimate for the system's performance measure. In fact, not one method is superior in all cases, and it all depends on the traffic intensity ρ.

After deciding what method is more suitable to apply, the main question is determination of number of runs. That is, at the planning stage of a simulation, investigation of the question of number of simulation runs (n) is critical.

The confidence level of simulation output drawn from a set of simulation runs depends on the size of the data set. The larger the number of runs, the higher is the associated confidence. However, more simulation runs also require more effort and resources for large systems. Thus, the main goal must be to find the smallest number of simulation runs that will provide the desirable confidence.

8.2 Pilot Studies

When the needed statistics for the number of simulation runs calculation is not available from an existing database, a pilot simulation is needed.

For large pilot simulation runs (n), say over 30, the simplest number of runs determinate is:

$$[(Z_{\pm/2})^2 S^2]/\Delta_1^2 \tag{46}$$

where Δ_1 is the desirable absolute error, which is the half-length of the confidence interval with $100(1-\alpha)\%$ confidence interval and S^2 is the variance obtained from the pilot run.

One may use the following sample size determinate for a desirable relative error Δ_2 in %, which requires an estimate of the coefficient of variation (C.V. in %) from a pilot run with n over 30:

$$[(Z_{\pm/2})^2 (C.V.)^2]/\Delta_2^2 . \tag{47}$$

These sample size determinates could also be used for simulation output estimation of unimodal output populations, with discrete or continuous random variables, provided the pilot run size (n) is larger than (say) 30.

The aim of applying any one of the above number of runs determinates is to improve the pilot estimates at feasible costs. For both applications, we have set the sample size such that the relative precision does not exceed 10%. Again, the number of simulation run is determined by the desirable quality of simulation output, such as desirable coefficient of variation, while number of iterations depends upon desirable accuracy in estimating the parameter v.

9. CONCLUSION AND FUTURE RESEARCH

Conventional approaches to simulation involve finding the response of a system to a particular input or disturbance. Inverse simulation reverses this and attempts to find the control input required to achieve a particular response. The methodology is presented in the context of a reliability and queuing system application. Section 5 includes a presentation of a solution algorithm for the inverse simulation and issues of numerical stability and accuracy. The methodology includes an iterative method based on differentiation of the performance measure and use of feedback structures for generation of an inverse model, based on a stochastic version of Newton's method. Almost all discrete event systems simulation computation can be formulated as an estimation of an expected value of the system performance measure, which is a function of an input parameter of the underlying probability density function. In the ordinary system simulation, this input parameter must be known in advance to estimate the output of the system. From the designer's point of view, the input parameters can be classified as controllable and uncontrollable.

In this chapter, we considered the design problem: "What should be the controllable input parameter value to achieve a desired output value?"

As an alternative to other product design and development methods, the techniques introduced in this chapter should be welcomed by the systems designers; Ulrich & Eppinger (2011) discussed the pro and cons of the approach.

The approach used in this study was:

1.   To estimate the derivative of the output function with respect to the input parameter for the nominal system by a single-run, and on-line simulation;
2.   To use this estimated derivative in a Taylor's expansion of the output function in the neighborhood of the parameter; and finally,
3.   To use a recursive algorithm based on the Taylor's expansion to estimate the necessary controllable input parameter value within a desired accuracy.

Under some mild and reasonable conditions, the algorithm converges to the desired solution with probability 1. The efficiency of the proposed algorithm in terms of accuracy is tested using an M/G/1/∞ queueing service, as well as a reliability product design with satisfactory results. The approach has major implications for simulation modelers and practitioners in terms of time and cost savings. Simulation models are the replicas of the real systems, in general. While in this chapter, experiment was conducted on specific numerical examples; one might be able to make any other safe generalizations for other applications.

This chapter introduced the general concepts of inverse simulation. An effective solution algorithm for inverse simulation is presented from first principles. The impact of the proposed inverse simulation method in conveying real understanding about the discrete event properties of the systems is now made available. Inverse simulation method is also found to be of value for the validation and control of complex discrete event simulation models with numerical stability and desirable accuracy.

The proposed inverse simulation techniques can also be applied as a measuring tool and decision procedure for the validation of simulation models. In the course of future research:

1. We expect to introduce other efficient variance reduction techniques (VRT). The Common Random Variates as a VRT is already embedded in the algorithm. Notice that since

$$E[S]=E\ [Ln\ f\ ]'$$
$$=\int [Ln\ f\ ]'\ f\ dx=\int f\ 'dx=[\int f\ dx]'=0 \tag{48}$$

We can express the gradient in terms of covariance between Z and S

$$J'(v)=Cov[Z(Y),\ S]=E[Z\ S]-E[Z]E[S]. \tag{49}$$

and

$$J'(v)=E[Z(Y)S]+\alpha E[S] \tag{50}$$

where α could be the optimal linear control. Note also that (6) can be written as:

$$J'(v)=\int Z(y)f\ '(y;v)dy$$

$$=\int Z(y)[f\ '(y;v)/\ \varphi(y;v)]\varphi(y;v)dy \tag{51}$$

The best choice for φ is the one proportional to Z(y) f ' (y; v). This minimizes the variance of J'(v); however, this optimal φ depends on the performance function Z(y), which is not known in advance for most cases. One may use the empirical version of Z(y) f ' (y; v). We recommend a pilot run to study the effectiveness of these and other variance reduction techniques before implementing them.

2. We expect to extend our methodology to higher order Taylor's expansion. We believe that there is a tradeoff between number of iterations, sample size, and the order of Taylor's expansion. Clearly, estimating the second derivative requires a larger sample size n, but less iteration is required to achieve the same accuracy.
3. We also expect to extend our methodology to the design problems with two or more unknown parameters by considering two or more relevant outputs to ensure uniqueness. By this generalization, we could construct a linear system of stochastic equations to be solved simultaneously by multidimensional versions of the stochastic approximation proposed in Benveniste et al (1990) as well as the Newton method, Ruppert (1985) using the second order derivatives (e.g., Hessian).
4. The algorithms in this chapter are presented in English-like, step-by-step format to facilitate implementation in a variety of operating systems and computers, thus improving portability. However, there is a need to develop an expert system that makes the algorithms more practically applicable to simulation in performance system design.

ACKNOWLEDGMENT

We are most appreciative to the reviewers for their careful readings, useful comments and suggestions that are incorporated in the final version. The National Science Foundation Grant CCR-9505732 supports this work.

REFERENCES

Abate, J., & Whitt, W. (1987). Transient behavior of M/M/1 queue: Starting at origin. *Queueing Systems*, 2(1), 41–65. doi:10.1007/BF01182933

Arsham, H. (1987). A stochastic model of optimal advertising pulsing policy. *Computers & Operations Research*, 14(3), 231–239. doi:10.1016/0305-0548(87)90026-8

Arsham, H. (1996). Stochastic optimization of discrete event systems simulation. *Microelectronics and Reliability*, 36(10), 1357–1368. doi:10.1016/0026-2714(96)00044-3

Arsham, H. (1998a). Techniques for Monte Carlo optimizing. *Monte Carlo Methods and Applications*, 4(3), 181–230. doi:10.1515/mcma.1998.4.3.181

Arsham, H. (1998b). Algorithms for sensitivity information in discrete-event systems simulation. *Simulation Practice and Theory*, 6(1), 1–22. doi:10.1016/S0928-4869(97)00011-6

Arsham, H. (2008). *Gradient-based optimization techniques for discrete event systems simulation. In B. W. Wah (Ed.), Wiley Encyclopedia of Computer Science and Engineering* (Vol. 2, pp. 1–17). New York: Wiley.

Arsham, H., Feuerverger, A., McLeish, D., Kreimer, J., & Rubinstein, R. (1989). Sensitivity analysis and the 'what-if' problem in simulation analysis. *Mathematical and Computer Modelling*, 12(2), 193–219. doi:10.1016/0895-7177(89)90434-2

Barlow, R., & Proschan, F. (1998). *Statistical Theory of Reliability and Life Testing Probability Models.* New York: Holt Rinehart & Winston.

Benveniste, A., Metivier, M., & Priouret, P. (1990). *Adaptive Algorithms and Stochastic Approximations.* New York: Springer-Verlag. doi:10.1007/978-3-642-75894-2

Bourne, M., Neely, A. J., & Platts, K. (2003). Implementing performance measurement systems: A literature review. *The International Journal of Business Performance Management*, 5(1), 1–24. doi:10.1504/IJBPM.2003.002097

CACI PC Simscript II.5. (1987). Introduction and User's Manual. San Diego, CA: CACI.

Cassandras, C. (1993). *Discrete Event Systems: Modeling and Performance Analysis.* Irwin.

Chen, H., & Schmeiser, B. (2001). Stochastic root finding via retrospective approximation. *IIE Transactions*, 33(3), 259–275. doi:10.1080/07408170108936827

Clark, D. (1984). Necessary & sufficient conditions for the Robbins-Monro method. *Stochastic Processes and Their Applications, 17*(2), 359–367. doi:10.1016/0304-4149(84)90011-5

Clymer, J. (1995). System design & evaluation using discrete event simulation with AI. *European Journal of Operational Research, 84*(1), 213–225. doi:10.1016/0377-2217(94)00327-9

Davenport, T. (2012). *Enterprise Analytics: Optimize Performance. Process, and Decisions Through Big Data.* FT Press.

de Weck, O., & Jones, M. (2006). Isoperformance: Analysis and design of complex systems with desired outcomes. *Systems Engineering, 9*(1), 45–61. doi:10.1002/sys.20043

Dippon, J., & Renz, J. (1997). Weighted means in stochastic approximation of minima. *SIAM Journal on Control and Optimization, 35*(5), 1811–1827. doi:10.1137/S0363012995283789

Frey, D., Palladino, J., Sullivan, J., & Atherton, M. M. (2007). Part count and design of robust systems. *Systems Engineering, 10*(3), 203–221. doi:10.1002/sys.20071

Friedman, L. (1996). *The Simulation Metamodel.* Norwell, MA: Kluwer Academic Publishers. doi:10.1007/978-1-4613-1299-4

Fu, M. (2002). Optimization for simulation: Theory vs. practice. *INFORMS Journal on Computing, 14*(3), 192–227. doi:10.1287/ijoc.14.3.192.113

Glynn, P. (1990). Likelihood ratio derivative estimation for stochastic systems. *Communications of the ACM, 33*(10), 75–84. doi:10.1145/84537.84552

Gross, D. (2009). *Fundamentals of Queueing Theory.* New York: John Wiley and Sons.

Hana, H., Kanga, J., & Songb, M. (2009). Two-stage process analysis using the process-based performance measurement framework and business process simulation. *Expert Systems with Applications, 36*(3), 7080–7086. doi:10.1016/j.eswa.2008.08.035

Handley, H. A., Zaidi, Z. R., & Levis, A. H. (1999). *The use of simulation models in model driven experimentation.* George Mason University.

Harnish, V. (2012). *The Greatest Business Decisions of All Time.* New York: Time Home Entertainment.

Hedayat, A., Sloane, N., & Stufken, J. (1999). *Orthogonal Arrays: Theory and Applications.* New York, NY: Springer. doi:10.1007/978-1-4612-1478-6

Hope, J., & Player, S. (2012). *Beyond Performance Management: Why, When, and How to Use 40 Tools and Best Practices for Superior Business Performance.* Harvard Business Review Press.

Hutton, R., & Klein, G. (1999). Expert decision making. *Systems Engineering, 2*(1), 32–45. doi:10.1002/(SICI)1520-6858(1999)2:1<32::AID-SYS3>3.0.CO;2-P

Huynh, T. (2011). Orthogonal array experiment in systems engineering and architecting. *Systems Engineering, 14*(2), 208–222. doi:10.1002/sys.20172

Kiefer, J., & Wolfowitz, J. (1952). Stochastic estimation of the maximum of a regression function. *Annals of Mathematical Statistics, 23*(3), 462–466. doi:10.1214/aoms/1177729392

Kleijnen, J., & Rubinstein, R. (1996). Optimization and sensitivity analysis of computer simulation models by score function method. *European Journal of Operational Research, 88*(3), 413–427. doi:10.1016/0377-2217(95)00107-7

Knuth, D. (2011). *The Art of Computer Programming.* New York: Addison-Wesley Professional.

L'Ecuyer, P. (1995). Note: On the interchange of derivative and expectation for likelihood derivative estimation. *Management Science, 41*(4), 738–748. doi:10.1287/mnsc.41.4.738

Marchant, A. (2010). Obstacles to the flow of requirements verification. *Systems Engineering, 13*(1), 1–13.

Morrice, D., & Bardhan, I. (1995). A weighted least squares approach to computer simulation factor screening. *Operations Research, 43*(5), 792–806. doi:10.1287/opre.43.5.792

Murray-Smith, D. (2013). The application of parameter sensitivity analysis methods to inverse simulation models. *Mathematical and Computer Modelling of Dynamical Systems, 19*(1), 67–90. doi:10.1080/13873954.2012.696271

Neely, A. (2011). *Business Performance Measurement: Theory and Practice.* London: Cambridge University Press.

Osmundson, J. (2000). A systems engineering methodology for information systems. *Systems Engineering, 3*(2), 68–76. doi:10.1002/1520-6858(2000)3:2<68::AID-SYS2>3.0.CO;2-A

Pintér, J. (2010). *Global Optimization in Action: Continuous and Lipschitz Optimization: Algorithms. Implementations and Applications.* New York: Springer.

Review, H. B. (2011). *Making Smart Decisions.* Harvard Business Review Press.

Robbins, H., & Monro, S. (1951). A stochastic approximation method. *Annals of Mathematical Statistics, 22*(3), 400–407. doi:10.1214/aoms/1177729586

Robertazzi, Th. (2000). *Computer Networks & Systems: Queueing Theory and Performance Evaluation.* New York, NY: Springer. doi:10.1007/978-1-4612-1164-8

Ross, Ph. (1996). *Taguchi Techniques for Quality Engineering.* New York: McGraw Hill.

Ross, R., & Lam, G. (2011). *Building Business Solutions: Business Analysis with Business Rules.* New York: Business Rule Solutions Inc.

Rubinstein, R., & Shapiro. (1998). A. *Discrete Event Systems: Sensitivity Analysis and Stochastic Optimization by the Score Function Method.* Wiley.

Ruppert, D. A. (1985). Newton-Raphson version of the multivariate Robbins-Monro procedure. *Annals of Statistics, 13*(2), 236–245. doi:10.1214/aos/1176346589

Spall, J. (2000). Adaptive stochastic approximation by the simultaneous perturbation method. *IEEE Transactions on Automatic Control, 45*(10), 1839–1853. doi:10.1109/TAC.2000.880982

Spall, J. (2003). *Introduction to Stochastic Search and Optimization: Estimation, Simulation, and Control.* New York, NY: Wiley. doi:10.1002/0471722138

Taticchi, P. (2010). *Business Performance Measurement and Management: New Contexts, Themes and Challenges*. New York: Springer. doi:10.1007/978-3-642-04800-5

Ulrich, E., & Eppinger, S. (2011). Product Design and Development. McGraw-Hill/Irwin.

Wang, R., & Dagli, C. (2011). Executable system architecting using systems modeling language in conjunction with colored Petri nets in a model-driven systems development process. *Systems Engineering*, *14*(4), 383–409. doi:10.1002/sys.20184

White, K. Jr. (1998). Systems design engineering. *Systems Engineering*, *1*(4), 285–302. doi:10.1002/(SICI)1520-6858(1998)1:4<285::AID-SYS4>3.0.CO;2-E

Whitt, W. (1989). Planning queueing simulation. *Management Science*, *35*(11), 1341–1366. doi:10.1287/mnsc.35.11.1341

Yakowitz, S., L'Ecuyer, P., & Vazquez-Abad, F. (2000). Global stochastic optimization with low-dispersion point sets. *Operations Research*, *48*(6), 939–950. doi:10.1287/opre.48.6.939.12393

Zhang, H., & Ma, D. (2005). A Systems Engineering approach to Occupant Protection System design and optimization through modeling and simulation. *Systems Engineering*, *8*(1), 51–61. doi:10.1002/sys.20020

Chapter 6
Data, Information, and Knowledge:
Developing an Intangible Assets Strategy

G. Scott Erickson
Ithaca College, USA

Helen N. Rothberg
Marist College, USA

ABSTRACT

This chapter examines the similarities and differences between big data and knowledge management. Big data has relatively little conceptual development, at least from a strategy and management perspective. Knowledge management has a lengthy literature and decades of practice but has always explicitly focused only on knowledge assets as opposed to precursors like data and information. Even so, there are considerable opportunities for cross-fertilization. Consequently, this chapter considers data from McKinsey Global Strategies on data holdings, by industry, and contrasts that with data on knowledge development, essentially the intangible assets found in the same industries. Using what we know about the variables influencing the application of intangible assets such as knowledge and intelligence, we can then better identify where successful employment of big data might take place. Further, we can identify specific variables with the potential to grant competitive advantage from the application of big data and business analytics.

INTRODUCTION

The growth of interest in big data has prompted both enthusiasm and skepticism. The advent of huge databases and the cheap computing power allowing storage and analysis promises substantial opportunities, and so the enthusiasm. But the opportunities won't accrue by themselves, there needs to be a structure for analysis and action. Hence the skepticism. Data and insight need to be paired in order to reap the full potential of analytics.

DOI: 10.4018/978-1-4666-7272-7.ch006

In addressing this dichotomy, it can be useful to view big data as part of a range of intangible assets of the organization. Placing it squarely within existing theory, empirical results we have on big data and other intangible assets allows us to more carefully examine how it might be effectively employed by organizations. Further, these existing results can be discussed in the context of structures and tools that have successfully been applied to intangible assets, including knowledge management and competitive intelligence, bringing already identified success factors into the discussion. The result will include more specific guidance for organizations moving into big data, business analytics, and business intelligence.

BACKGROUND

The idea that intangible assets exist and may have something to contribute to the success of organizations is long-standing. Schumpeter's (1934) innovation work suggested that new ideas come from less tangible inputs of the firm. Nelson and Winter's (1982) evolutionary theory suggested that better management of such intangibles could lead to competitive advantage. This conceptualization fits nicely with the resource-based theory of the firm (Wernerfelt, 1984), and, thus, it was a short step to the conclusion that intangibles might be a key resource granting unique, sustainable advantage. And with some additional definitional development, intangibles became equated with organizational knowledge, and the knowledge-based theory of the firm was suggested (Teece, 1998; Grant, 1996). Knowledge workers (Drucker, 1991) were a key to organizational success and effective means of measuring and managing knowledge assets could be an explicit strategy for gaining such success.

The definitional step was not a large one, as a fairly lengthy literature also exists in the knowledge management (KM) field characterizing the nature of the assets. Indeed, Ackoff's (1989) DIKW (data, information, knowledge, wisdom) hierarchy permeates the field. Purposeful definitions distinguished data (observations) from information (data in context) and knowledge (information subjected to experience and reflection) (Zack, 1999). This is a key distinction as the value suggested by most KM work comes from the knowledge, the know-how built up over time that can then be used by the creator, shared with others, and/or captured by the organization. Data and information, while important precursors of knowledge, don't necessarily have any value in and of themselves in the traditional KM view. Some trends are now present that suggest an expanded interpretation of what intangibles are of value, which we'll discuss shortly.

Before that, let's capture some of the mainstream thinking about knowledge management and its companion discipline, intellectual capital. As noted, everything begins with an acceptance that intangible assets, particularly knowledge, have value. As such, organizations have an interest in measuring and managing such a valuable asset. One important aspect of such an approach is better understanding knowledge, starting with the distinction between tacit (personal, hard to express) and explicit (codifiable, easier to share, capable of becoming an organizational asset) knowledge (Polanyi, 1967; Nonaka & Takeuchi, 1995). The nature of the knowledge is important in dictating how it can be grown, as well as appropriate techniques for doing so. Nonaka & Takeuchi (1995) captured this dynamic in their SECI or "ba" framework, laying out the four potential transfers of knowledge (tacit to tacit, tacit to explicit, explicit to explicit, and explicit to tacit) and the nature of the growth these generate (socialization, externalization, combination, internalization).

Further, specific techniques are also associated with the knowledge types, so tacit transfers will usually involve more personal approaches (mentoring, communities of practice, storytelling) (Choi & Lee, 2003; Schulz & Jobe, 2001; Boisot, 1995) while explicit can employ information technology solutions (knowledge markets) (Matson, Patiath & Shavers, 2003; Thomas, Kellogg & Erickson, 2001; Brown & Duguid, 1991).

Choice of approach depends on other variables besides the nature of the knowledge. Other aspects of the knowledge matter, such as complexity or stickiness (McEvily & Chakravarthy, 2002; Zander & Kogut, 1995; Kogut & Zander, 1992). Organizational characteristics also play a role, factors such as absorptive capacity (Cohen & Levinthal, 1990), social capital (Nahapiet & Ghoshal, 1998), and resident social networks (Liebowitz, 2005). In short, there is valuable knowledge within organizations but how it is best utilized depends on a variety of circumstantial aspects revolving around the knowledge itself, information technology, systems, and human behavior.

The sister discipline of KM is intellectual capital, based on establishing metrics for these intangible knowledge assets. If one is to better manage knowledge, one needs to be able to identify and measure it. The field has evolved to a common representation of intellectual capital being composed of three parts: human capital, structural capital, and relational capital. This view came from practice (Edvinsson & Malone, 1997), academia (Bontis, 1999), and the mainstream business press (Stewart, 1997). Human capital generally refers to job-specific experience or know-how, structural capital has to do with persisting knowledge of the organization such as corporate culture or installed systems, while relational capital deals with knowledge about external relationships, including customers.

Another related discipline is competitive intelligence (CI), and that's the place we first start to get a wider view of what valuable intangible assets might be. KM and intellectual capital are all about knowledge assets, with data and information as only potential inputs, not valuable assets in and of themselves. With CI, not only are all forms of intangibles potential clues to competitor intentions and behavior, but analysts take any insights about competitors to the next level of actionable intelligence. As a consequence, there are similarities between KM and CI but also differences that serve to inform both disciplines (Erickson & Rothberg, 2012; Rothberg & Erickson, 2005). CI grew out of practice, much like KM (Prescott & Miller, 2001; Gilad & Herring, 1996; Fuld, 1994). As such, the field often focuses on sources of data, information and knowledge and techniques for obtaining such intangibles (Fleisher & Bensoussan, 2002; McGonagle & Vella, 2002). Analytical techniques are then used to process collected intangibles and develop deeper insights, intelligence, that can be acted upon in support of an organization's competitive strategy (Gilad, 2003; Wright, Picton & Callow, 2002; Raouch & Santi, 2001; Bernhardt, 2003). In a number of ways, the concept of intelligence, used in this context, has similarities to the wisdom component of Ackoff's original DIKW framework.

And we see that extended in other, newer representations of "intelligence". Andreou, Green & Stankosky (2007) constructed a framework rationalizing the standard intellectual capital typology with other intangibles of the organization (which may or may not fit in the standard typology, depending on one's preferences). Their categories included human capital, organizational capital, innovation and customer capital, market capital (incorporating competitive intelligence and enterprise intelligence), and decision effectiveness (strategic decision-making, akin to the actionable intelligence discussed earlier). The important thing to note is the clear connection between the established theory surrounding knowledge assets and the wider perspective of business intelligence, business analytics, and big data. The similarities in terminology, concepts, and purpose are all there.

BIG DATA

Indeed, the theory developing around big data does reference the KM literature as a forerunner of this new direction in employing organizational intangibles. (Bose, 2009; Jourdan, Rainer & Marshall, 2008). Increased amounts of data, cheaper storage, increased computing power, and other drivers have given firms the ability to better use all intangible assets, but particularly the data and information resources discussed earlier. Data from operations (enterprise systems, supply and distribution channels), transactions (customer relationship management), and communications (Google Analytics, social media) are easily and cost-effectively stored on a routine basis by firms (Vance, 2011a). This big data can then be mined and analyzed for useful insights, processes referred to as business intelligence, business analytics, marketing intelligence, marketing analytics, and so forth (Bussey, 2011; Vance, 2011b). Manyika, et. al. (2011) note concrete competitive advantages gained such as real-time experimentation, tighter segmentation, algorithm-driven and more objective decisions, and dispersed idea generation for innovation.

The conceptual basis of big data has characterized the "three V's" as the keys to evaluating an organization's capabilities: volume of data, velocity of input and output, and variety (Laney, 2001). The growth of these v's define the growth in big data and have allowed the new analysis techniques leading to new insights and more effective strategic and tactical decisions (Beyer & Laney, 2012). As a result, big data is rapidly growing in terms of metrics such as data storage (Liebowitz, 2013; Manyika, et. al., 2011) and as a new buzz word. But it's critical to keep in mind that a database itself is of only limited value without some means of processing and analyzing it. Databases and related systems can enhance decision-making, but they require the analytic/intelligence component, with some degree of human interaction, to live up to the promise of big data (Zhao, 2013).

This is where some combination of what we know about KM and big data could be helpful. As noted earlier, KM has often been overly focused on the more developed "knowledge" in organizations, to the detriment of data and information that the big data movement is showing to be of similar value. On the other hand, KM does rely on some analysis to identify valuable knowledge and has a deep literature (and practical application) in the human element of managing intangibles with the help of information technology (Matson, Patiath & Shavers, 2003; Thomas, Kellogg & Erickson, 2001).

The potential cross-fertilization is suggested in an oft-cited McKinsey Global Services (MGS) study already noted a couple of times in this chapter (Manyika, et. al., 2011). The report tracks data storage/usage by industry and firm, identifying the presence of big data holdings. But it also discusses "ease of capture", essentially related to an industry/firm's ability to take advantage of whatever big data it has. Further, ease of capture is divided into four indicators: talent, data-driven mindset, IT intensity, and data availability. The first two, as described, are immediately recognizable as parts of human capital, discussed frequently in KM and intellectual capital circles. The talent in the organization encompasses the skills and know-how of employees while a data-driven mindset relates to top management and what valuable knowledge they bring to the table. Talent could also describe the ability of an organization's people to deal with external relationships, and is so also relevant to relational capital. Similarly, IT intensity relates to structural capital in the standard intellectual capital universe. This is a less exact match, as structural capital typically includes matters like corporate culture and social capital or networks as well, but there is clear overlap. Data availability less obviously fits with the intellectual capital typology, but does relate to the intersection between data/information and the people who need to employ them. And, again, that is a core concern of KM systems as well.

From this vantage point, it's a short step to concluding that industries/firms already well-versed in KM might have some advantages in employing big data capabilities as well. Given the connection of the MGS indicators to KM/intellectual capital characteristics, one can easily extend the knowledge value found in those characteristics to enhanced ability to manage big data. We'll look specifically at that possibility by combining the data from the MGS big data study with a database we've built that assesses KM potential and achievement in various industries. From that vantage point, we should be able to draw some conclusions concerning which industries have the highest likelihood of benefiting from substantial data holdings.

BIG DATA AND KNOWLEDGE

The metrics of intellectual capital are a field of study unto themselves. Essentially the stock measurement of the more dynamic flow concept of knowledge management, intellectual capital assesses the level of knowledge assets at a particular point in time. Numerous techniques are available and have been used in one form or another. Sveiby (2010) lists over forty intellectual capital metrics, varying between those using financial measures or not and those using top-down (full firm) vs. bottom-up (within firm) approaches. The latter are much employed in the field and useful for case studies or comparisons across a small number of firms. Well-known techniques such as the Balanced Scorecard (Kaplan & Norton, 1992) and Skandia Navigator (Edvinsson & Malone, 1997) fall into this category. Such metrics allow assessment of overall organizational intellectual capital and have been applied in studies looking to determine the impact of such knowledge assets on financial returns (Tan, Plowman & Hancock, 2007; Chen, Chang & Hwang, 2005; Pulic, 2004; Firer & Williams, 2003). These tools can even be used to estimate the impact of individual parts of intellectual capital (human, structural, relational capital) on financial results (Lev & Radhakrishnan, 2003; Marr & Schiuma, 2001).

While useful, the internal data needed for such studies makes them impractical for comparing large numbers of firms. For such purposes (and ours) a more broad-based, if less detailed metric makes more sense. Here, we employ a version of Tobin's q (Tobin & Brainard, 1977). Tobin's q has been used as a measure of the intangible assets of the firm, taking the difference between market capitalization (value of the firm) and replacement value of assets (tangible assets). As replacement value can be difficult to estimate, a common variation is to use market cap and book value. We take that one step further and also employ market cap to asset value so as to eliminate the impact of debt on the analysis. Further we use a ratio of the values rather than the difference so as to minimize the impact of size differences between firms and allow direct comparisons.

We obtained our data by drawing the full population of firms listed on North American exchanges with annual revenue above $1 billion. Using the I/B/E/S database, we included the years 2005-2009. Firms were included when they met the sales threshold, not included when they did not or when they left the database because of merger or some other reason. As a result, over 2,000 firms are included with over 7,000 observations. Data were organized by SIC code with annual firm results averaged across industry. These results are paired with the MGS results showing big data by industry (Stored Data, US Industry) and by firm within these industries (Stored Data per Firm). Table 1 provides the data, including both Tobin's q variations.

Table 1. Big data and knowledge assets, by industry

Industry	Stored Data per Firm (terabytes)	Stored Data, US Industry (petabytes)	Industry (SIC)	Market Cap/ Book ($\mu = 2.68$)	Market Cap/ Assets ($\mu = 1.02$)
Security & Investment Services	3,866	429	Security Brokers (6211)	1.52	0.19
Banking	1,931	619	Commercial Banks (6020)	1.61	0.14
Communications & Media	1,792	715	Telecom, television (48)	2.29	0.72
Utilities	1,507	194	Electric, gas (49)	1.93	0.54
Government	1,312	848			
Discrete Manufacturing	967	966	Electronics, Equipment, Instruments (36, 37, 38)	2.94	1.33
Insurance	870	243	Insurance (63)	1.44	0.41
Process Manufacturing Resource Industries	831	694	Pharms, Chemicals, Plastics (28) Petroleum/Natural Gas (13),	2.99	1.39
	825	116	Lumber/Wood (24)	2.06, 1.66	1.04, 0.68
Transportation	801	227	Transportation (40-45)	2.21	0.61
Retail	697	364	Retail (53-59)	3.29	1.18
Wholesale	536	202	Wholesale (50-51)	2.18	0.94
Health Care Providers Education	370	434	Health Services (80)	2.65	0.85
Professional Service	319	269	Educational Services (82)	5.07	2.34
	278	411	Advertising (731)	2.82	1.00
Construction	231	51	Construction (16)	3.49	1.07
Consumer & Recreational Services	150	105	Amusement & Recreation (79)	2.71	0.91

DISCUSSION

What do these results tell us? Initially, there are a number of clear patterns in the overall data. The two metrics for intangibles/knowledge assets generally agree. The industries with intangible ratios above the average for the full database are the same according to both of these versions of Tobin's q, market cap/book and market cap/assets. Those below the average are also similar. There are differences in magnitude that illustrate the differences between the metrics. The financial industries at the top of the table, security and investment services and banking, are both much further below the global average when using the market cap/asset ratio. This is expected, as the difference in the denominator of the two ratios is total asset value vs. net asset value (assets less liabilities). As financial services industries tend to have high levels of financial assets (big denominator in the market cap/asset metric) which are balanced by similarly high levels of financial liabilities (dropping the denominator substantially in the market cap/book metric), the result shown here isn't surprising. Indeed, it shows how debt levels affect the choice of metric—they have a lot of assets but most are investments or borrowings from customers, and that shows up. In some studies, such differences matter. Here, the general agreement between the two methods suggests that we're on pretty safe ground using either.

The table also shows no apparent relationship between the big data measure (by firm) and the intangibles measure. The top industries in terms of available data (the financial industries, communications, utilities) are not the top industries in terms of creating valued intangible assets, what we have called knowledge (discrete and process manufacturing, retail, education). This could mean that the data aren't highly valued as an asset in and of themselves, that the analytics part of big data is required to generate the insights that aid in making strategic, tactical, and operational decisions. Relatedly, firms or industries with some track record in installing systems to better manage intangible assets (knowledge management), that have shown an ability to capitalize on intangibles by identifying, capturing, and leveraging them, are those adding value.

Both of these explanations fit with theory. Any basic explanation of big data includes not just the collection and storage of data but also the analytics or intelligence aspects that find insights within the mass of bytes. Just because firms possess a great deal of data doesn't mean they have the capability of doing much with it. The intangible asset metrics here suggest just that—the value of the intangibles isn't associated just with possessing big data, there must be something else.

And, as discussed earlier, the ability to take diverse intangible assets of all types: data, information, and knowledge and turn them into actionable intelligence is at the heart of our current thinking about managing intangibles, whether we call it knowledge management or look to some broader term. Indeed, the comparison of disciplines such as competitive intelligence, wherein all inputs can be of some use in strategy and planning, is a useful contrast to the narrower field of knowledge management with it focus on creating and sharing only knowledge assets. There's no good reason why data and information can't inform knowledge management practices and outcomes in the same manner. And, indeed, that appears to be the direction KM and related fields of intelligence are moving.

FUTURE TRENDS

For now, we can conclude a few things from these results. Initially, there are industries that are probably better prepared to take advantage of the big data trend. Again, those that have a track record in turning intangibles into value would likely be more ready to analyze and learn from basic data and information. While there will be sharable learnings that might allow other industries to catch up, decision-makers would probably be well-advised to consider whether their industry shows evidence of an ability to process data and information into higher-level intangible outputs. As illustrated in Table 1, these would include process and discrete manufacturing, retail, and education as a first pass. Following next would be industries such as oil and gas, construction, and professional services. While it might be common sense that the availability of data shouldn't be the first criterion for significant investment in big data, this analysis provides some further support for that idea and some guidance for decision-makers.

A second conclusion is that a great deal more research is needed on the characteristics of industries that generate such different conditions for applying big data or business analytics programs. We know something of the circumstances for investing in big-ticket KM, that variables such as knowledge characteristics (tacit/explicit, complex), type of knowledge (human, structural, or relational capital), industry conditions (life cycle stage, where on value chain knowledge is important), and other such things can matter (Erickson & Rothberg, 2012). But even these are far from conclusive and the entire field of intangibles needs more work as to where and when to put in the effort and money to effectively manage them. In this case, a first glance suggests that industries centered on transmission and distribution of funds, resources, goods, or people might generate a lot of data, but there isn't necessarily a lot of higher-level knowledge to be discerned from them. Those industries that do have some potential involve manufacturing operations, supply chains and distribution channels, and, perhaps, more consumer marketing. Whether these can be broken further down into aspects like tacit knowledge or human capital would be a good starting point for future research. But there certainly appears to be something of interest deeper within the data.

CONCLUSION

This paper combines published information on big data potential in a variety of industries with a dataset assessing knowledge management capabilities in similar industries. The latter specifically measures intangible asset values in resident firms but is a common proxy of KM levels. In doing so, we begin to bring together some of the diverse strains from the study of intangible assets. Clear similarities are apparent in the range of intangible assets studied in business, ranging from data to information to knowledge to wisdom/intelligence. It makes sense to us to try to blend what we know so as to better understand each topic and discipline.

In particular, we look to the extensive literature on knowledge management, intellectual capital, and competitive intelligence in order to better understand the prominent current trends in big data, business analytics, and business intelligence. KM, in particular, has shown interest in how intangible assets are grown from various inputs and includes studies of the human/information systems interface and interactions.

As a result of the big data statistics and related industry KM data, we can identify some industries which show more promise than others. Those with evidence of successful development of intangible assets include both product and process manufacturing, retail, and education. Others, even with high levels of big data, don't have nearly the track record of success. These industries may have more of a challenge in benefitting from the big data trend. For the future, we should look more deeply into why we see different results in different industries. Again, KM may provide some guidance, having identified relevant variables such as tacit/explicit knowledge, type of intellectual capital, industry conditions, and other related matters.

REFERENCES

Ackoff, R. (1989). From data to wisdom. *Journal of Applied Systems Analysis, 16*, 3–9.

Andreou, A. N., Green, A., & Stankosky, M. (2007). A framework of intangible valuation areas and antecedents. *Journal of Intellectual Capital, 8*(1), 52–75. doi:10.1108/14691930710715060

Bernhardt, D. (1993). *Perfectly legal competitive intelligence—How to get it, use it and profit from it.* London: Pitman Publishing.

Beyer, M. A., & Laney, D. (2012). *The importance of 'big data': A definition.* Retrieved from https://www.gartner.com/doc/2057415

Boisot, M. (1995). Is your firm a creative destroyer? Competitive learning and knowledge flows in the technological strategies of firms. *Research Policy, 24*(4), 489–506. doi:10.1016/S0048-7333(94)00779-9

Bontis, N. (1999). Managing organizational knowledge by diagnosing intellectual capital: Framing and advancing the state of the field. *International Journal of Technology Management, 18*(5-8), 433–462. doi:10.1504/IJTM.1999.002780

Bose, R. (2009). Advanced analytics: Opportunities and challenges. *Industrial Management & Data Systems, 109*(2), 155–172. doi:10.1108/02635570910930073

Brown, J. S., & Duguid, P. (1991). Organizational learning and communities-of-practice: Toward a unified view of working, learning, and innovation. *Organization Science, 2*(1), 40–57. doi:10.1287/orsc.2.1.40

Bussey, J. (2011, September 16). Seeking safety in clouds. *The Wall Street Journal*, p. B8.

Chen, M., Chang, S., & Hwang, Y. (2005). An empirical investigation of the relationship between intellectual capital and firms' market value and financial performance. *Journal of Intellectual Capital, 6*(2), 159–176. doi:10.1108/14691930510592771

Choi, B., & Lee, H. (2003). An empirical investigation of KM styles and their effect on corporate performance. *Information & Management, 40*(5), 403–417. doi:10.1016/S0378-7206(02)00060-5

Cohen, W. M., & Levinthal, D. A. (1990). Absorptive capacity: A new perspective on learning and innovation. *Administrative Science Quarterly, 35*(1), 128–152. doi:10.2307/2393553

Drucker, P. F. (1991). The new productivity challenge. *Harvard Business Review, 69*(6), 69–76. PMID:10114929

Edvinsson, L., & Malone, M. (1997). *Intellectual capital*. New York: Harper Business.

Erickson, G. S., & Rothberg, H. N. (2012). *Intelligence in action: Strategically managing knowledge assets*. London: Palgrave Macmillan. doi:10.1057/9781137035325

Firer, S., & Williams, M. (2003). Intellectual capital and traditional measures of corporate performance. *Journal of Intellectual Capital, 4*(3), 348–360. doi:10.1108/14691930310487806

Fleisher, C. S., & Bensoussan, B. (2002). *Strategic and competitive analysis: Methods and techniques for analysing business competition*. Upper Saddle River, NJ: Prentice Hall.

Fuld, L. M. (1994). *The new competitor intelligence: The complete resource for finding, analyzing, and using information about your competitors*. New York: John Wiley.

Gilad, B. (2003). *Early warning: Using competitive intelligence to anticipate market shifts, control risk, and create powerful strategies*. New York: ANACOM.

Gilad, B., & Herring, J. (Eds.). (1996). *The art and science of business intelligence*. Greenwich, CT: JAI Press.

Grant, R. M. (1996). Toward a knowledge-based theory of the firm. *Strategic Management Journal, 17*(Winter), 109–122. doi:10.1002/smj.4250171110

Jourdan, Z., Rainer, R. K., & Marshall, T. E. (2008). Business intelligence: An analysis of the literature. *Information Systems Management, 25*(2), 121–131. doi:10.1080/10580530801941512

Kaplan, R. S., & Norton, D. P. (1992). The balanced scorecard: Measures that drive performance. *Harvard Business Review, 70*(1), 71–79. PMID:10119714

Kogut, B., & Zander, U. (1992). Knowledge of the firm, combinative capabilities, and the replication of technology. *Organization Science, 3*(3), 383–397. doi:10.1287/orsc.3.3.383

Laney, D. (2001). *3D data management: Controlling data volume, velocity and variety.* Retrieved November 1, 2013 from http://blogs.gartner.com/doug-laney/files/2012/01/ad949-3D-Data-Management-Controlling-Data-Volume-Velocity-and-Variety.pdf

Lev, B., & Radhakrishnan, S. (2003). The measurement of firm-specific organizational capital. *NBER Working Paper #9581.*

Liebowitz, J. (2005). Linking social network analysis with the analytical hierarchy process for knowledge mapping in organizations. *Journal of Knowledge Management, 9*(1), 76–86. doi:10.1108/13673270510582974

Liebowitz, J. (Ed.). (2013). *Big data and business analytics.* Boca Raton, FL: CRC Press/Taylor & Francis. doi:10.1201/b14700

Manyika, J., Chui, M., Brown, B., Bughin, J., Dobbs, R., Roxburgh, C., & Hung Byers, A. (2011). *Big data: The next frontier for innovation, competition and productivity.* McKinsey Global Institute.

Marr, B., & Schiuma, G. (2001). Measuring and managing intellectual capital and knowledge assets in new economy organisations. In M. Bourne (Ed.), Handbook of performance measurement. London: Gee.

Matson, E., Patiath, P., & Shavers, T. (2003). Stimulating knowledge sharing: Strengthening your organizations' internal knowledge market. *Organizational Dynamics, 32*(3), 275–285. doi:10.1016/S0090-2616(03)00030-5

McEvily, S., & Chakravarthy, B. (2002). The persistence of knowledge-based advantage: An empirical test for product performance and technological knowledge. *Strategic Management Journal, 23*(4), 285–305. doi:10.1002/smj.223

McGonagle, J., & Vella, C. (2002). *Bottom line competitive intelligence.* Westport, CT: Quorum Books.

Nahapiet, J., & Ghoshal, S. (1998). Social capital, intellectual capital, and the organizational advantage. *Academy of Management Review, 23*(2), 242–266.

Nelson, R. R., & Winter, S. G. (1982). *An evolutionary theory of economic change.* Cambridge, MA: Harvard University Press.

Nonaka, I., & Takeuchi, H. (1995). *The knowledge-creating company: How japanese companies create the dynamics of innovation.* New York: Oxford University Press.

Polanyi, M. (1967). *The tacit dimension.* New York: Doubleday.

Prescott, J. E., & Miller, S. H. (2001). *Proven strategies in competitive intelligence: Lessons from the trenches.* New York: John Wiley and Sons.

Pulic, A. (2004). Intellectual capital—does it create or destroy value? *Measuring Business Excellence,* *8*(1), 62–68. doi:10.1108/13683040410524757

Raouch, D., & Santi, P. (2001). Competitive intelligence adds value: Five intelligence attitudes. *European Management Journal, 19*(5), 552–559. doi:10.1016/S0263-2373(01)00069-X

Rothberg, H. N., & Erickson, G. S. (2005). *From knowledge to intelligence: Creating competitive advantage in the next economy.* Woburn, MA: Elsevier Butterworth-Heinemann.

Schulz, M., & Jobe, L. A. (2001). Codification and tacitness as knowledge management strategies: An empirical exploration. *The Journal of High Technology Management Research, 12*(1), 139–165. doi:10.1016/S1047-8310(00)00043-2

Schumpeter, J. A. (1934). *The theory of economic development.* Cambridge, MA: Harvard University Press.

Stewart, T. A. (1997). *Intellectual capital: The new wealth of nations.* New York: Doubleday.

Sveiby, K.-E. (2010). *Methods for measuring intangible assets.* Retrieved from http://www.sveiby.com/articles/IntangibleMethods.htm

Tan, H. P., Plowman, D., & Hancock, P. (1997). Intellectual capital and the financial returns of companies. *Journal of Intellectual Capital, 9*(1), 76–95.

Teece, D. J. (1998). Capturing value from knowledge assets: The new economy, markets for know-how, and intangible assets. *California Management Review, 40*(3), 55–79. doi:10.2307/41165943

Thomas, J. C., Kellogg, W. A., & Erickson, T. (2001). The knowledge management puzzle: Human and social factors in knowledge management. *IBM Systems Journal, 40*(4), 863–884. doi:10.1147/sj.404.0863

Tobin, J., & Brainard, W. (1977). Asset markets and the cost of capital. In R. Nelson & B. Balassa (Eds.), *Economic progress, private values, and public policy: Essays in honor of William Fellner.* Amsterdam: North Holland.

Vance, A. (2011a, September 12). The data knows. *Bloomberg Businessweek,* 70-74.

Vance, A. (2011b, March 7). The power of the cloud. *Bloomberg Businessweek,* 52-59.

Wernerfelt, B. (1984). The resource-based view of the firm. *Strategic Management Journal, 5*(2), 171–180. doi:10.1002/smj.4250050207

Wright, S., Picton, D., & Callow, J. (2002). Competitive intelligence in UK firms, A typology. *Marketing Intelligence & Planning, 20*(6), 349–360. doi:10.1108/02634500210445400

Zack, M. H. (1999). Managing codified knowledge. *Sloan Management Review, 40*(4), 45–58.

Zander, U., & Kogut, B. (1995). Knowledge and the speed of transfer and imitation of organizational capabilities: An empirical test. *Organization Science, 6*(1), 76–92. doi:10.1287/orsc.6.1.76

Zhao, D. (2013). Frontiers of big data business analytics: Patterns and cases in online marketing. In J. Liebowitz (Ed.), *Big data and business analytics* (pp. 43–68). Boca Raton, FL: CRC Press/Taylor & Francis. doi:10.1201/b14700-4

KEY TERMS AND DEFINITIONS

Big Data: Large amounts of data generated and stored by an enterprise, often in the areas of operations, transactions, and/or communications.

Business Analytics/Intelligence: Analysis of big data for strategic, tactical, and/or operational insights.

Competitive Intelligence: Gathering and analyzing data, information, and knowledge relating to a competitor or related topic, resulting in actionable intelligence.

Data: Observations.

Information: Data in context.

Intellectual Capital: Knowledge assets of the organization, commonly thought to be made up of human capital (job-related knowledge), structural capital (persisting knowledge assets of the organization such as systems or culture), and relational capital (knowledge relating to external entities).

Intelligence: Actionable insights.

Knowledge Management: Methods to identify, organize, and leverage knowledge assets through further distribution and sharing.

Knowledge: Know-how or expertise.

Chapter 7
Business Analytics for Business Analysts in Manufacturing

Coleen Wilder
Valparaiso University, USA

Ceyhun Ozgur
Valparaiso University, USA

ABSTRACT

Many of the skills that define analytics are not new. Nonetheless, it has become a new source of competitive advantage for many corporations. Today's workforce, therefore, must be cognizant of its power and value to effectively perform their jobs. In this chapter, the authors differentiate the role of a business analyst by defining the appropriate skill level and breadth of knowledge required for them to be successful. Business analysts fill the gap between the experts (data scientists) and the day-to-day users. Finally, the section on Manufacturing Analytics provides real-world applications of Analytics for companies in a production setting. The ideas presented herein argue in favor of a dedicated program for business analysts.

INTRODUCTION

Business Analytics is something most people have heard about but fewer know or can agree on the definition. Some argue it is nothing new, simply another word for Business Intelligence. Others argue Business Intelligence and Business Analytics are two different disciplines, each with their own set of skills and software (Gnatovich, 2006). The purpose of this paper is not to debate these issues; the two terms will therefore be used interchangeably. The focus herein is to position Business Analytics, by any name, in the undergraduate curriculum in a manner that best serves students. This task will begin with a discussion on the value of analytics to today's businesses and will follow with suggestions on how to incorporate it into the curriculum. The expected challenges to implementing these ideas will be summarized in a separate section ending with ideas for future research.

DOI: 10.4018/978-1-4666-7272-7.ch007

BUSINESS VALUE

Business Intelligence/Business Analytics (BI/BA) is the process of gathering and transforming raw data into actionable insights yielding better decisions. Transforming data into insights is not a new discovery. Analysis of the 1854 Cholera Epidemic in London is one of many early examples. Edward Tufte describes at length in his book, Visual Explanations, how John Snow used data and graphics to convince local authorities that the source of the epidemic was a water pump on Broad Street. Later in 1958, an IBM Journal article is credited as the first documented reference of the term Business Intelligence; it did not become popular, however, until the 1980s with the advent of Decision Support Systems (Kalakota, 2011). So, why are many higher education institutions just now creating Analytics majors, minors, and institutes?

Throughout history, businesses have adopted innovative management programs in order to remain competitive. In the early 1800s it was standardized parts. In the late 1800s, it was the era of scientific management followed by mass production. In the 1980s, businesses found their competitive advantage in lean production initiatives (Heizer & Render, 2011). A recent Harvard Business Review article identifies analytics as the next source of competitive advantage for companies (Barton & Court, 2012).

Big Data has become an enabler for analytics. Big Data is the current phrase used to describe the changes in the accumulation of data over the past decade; the distinguishing factors of which are volume (2.5 exabytes per day), velocity (speed at which data is created), and variety (images, texts, videos, etc.) (McAfee & Brynijolfsson, 2012). Big Data has opened the flood gates for data analysis to achieve heights not possible in the recent past.

Business schools are responsible for preparing students to succeed in current and future business environments. According to a survey of CIOs, analytics and business intelligence was ranked as the number one technology priority; a position it has occupied in three of the last five years. Seventy percent of the CIOs rated mobile technologies as the most disruptive force with which they will be confronted in the next ten years, followed by big data and analytics each at fifty-five percent (Gartner Inc., 2013).

Analytics is a ubiquitous term in modern media. It is not difficult to find a story about a company using analytics to gain competitive advantage. Analytics is redefining companies. Overstock.com's CEO once referred to his company as "a business intelligence company" not an online retailer (Watson, 2013). Several best-selling data-driven books have also attracted attention with catchy titles such as Freakanomics: a Rogue Economist Explores the Hidden Side of Everything and Super Crunchers: Why Thinking-By-Numbers is the New Way to be Smart. Hollywood has contributed as well with a block-buster movie "Moneyball" in which baseball players are evaluated using analytics; the film was nominated for six-academy awards. Google has created an Analytics service to help businesses monitor the effectiveness of their websites. And, Google's Chief Economist, Hal Varian, said in a recent interview with James Manyika, "I keep saying the sexy job in the next ten years will be statisticians" (McKinsey & Co., 2009).

The value derived from analytics runs the gamut from cost savings to increased revenues. Nucleus Research found that analytics returns $10.66 for every dollar invested (Nucleus Research, 2011). Examples in marketing and managing customer relationships dominate the literature. Capital One, for example, used analytics to grow its customer base and increase the likelihood that customers will pay their bills. They conducted over 30,000 experiments a year using different incentives to find the best strategy (Davenport, 2006). Sears Holdings used data clusters to reduce the time it takes to generate new sales promotions from eight weeks to one week. The new promotions were even better than previous ones because they were more personalized and targeted to the individual consumer (McAfee & Brynijolfsson, 2012). Netflix, an early adopter of analytics, launched a million-dollar contest to anyone able to improve its movie recommendation performance by 10%; two of the top teams combined efforts to eventually win the prize with a 10.06% improvement (MacMillan, 2009).

Analytics opportunities are not exclusive to marketing departments. Talent analytics is one of several new terms used to describe the application of analytics to Human Resources. Companies are using analytics to help them improve everything from attracting new talent to making staffing decisions and evaluating performance (Davenport, Harris, & Shapiro, 2010). Location analytics is also gaining momentum. Companies are integrating geographic information systems (GIS) with other data sources to gain new insights about their business. Bankers are using location analytics to look at households and how they compare to their neighbors (Ferguson, 2012). Video analytics is yet another spin-off from the analytics family. AutoMotion Management, a North Carolina car wash chain, is using its video and analytics to both manage queues in real-time and to collect data for historical reporting (Zalud, 2013).

The skills needed to pursue the vast array of opportunities are almost as varied as the opportunities; the best place to begin perhaps is to look at the different levels of expertise that are required in an organization. Watson (2013) describes three skill levels corresponding to three different career paths as follows:

- **Data Scientist:** A data scientist's skill set must include "a solid foundation in math, statistics, probability, and computer science" with the ability to write code at the forefront (Davenport & Patil, 2012, p. 74).
- **Business Analyst:** Business analysts "simply need enough conceptual knowledge and quantitative skills to be able to frame and interpret analyses in an effective way," (Manyika, et al., 2011, p. 105).
- **Business Users:** Business users need to understand how data is stored, how to access it, and how to analyze it at a basic level.

McKinsey Global Institute estimates that by 2018 the talent shortage for those described as data scientists is estimated to be 140,000 to 190,000 and nearly 1.5 million for those described as business analysts (Manyika, et al., 2011).

ANALYTICS IN THE CURRICULUM

It is understood that business students are best served when they meet the expectations of industry; in other words, they have skills that are in demand. The first of the three skill levels, to be discussed, are those required of a data scientist. The title of data scientist was created by D.J. Patil and Jeff Hammerbacher in 2008; they were each working at LinkedIn and Facebook at the time (Davenport & Patil, 2012). Data scientists typically hold advanced degrees in a quantitative discipline. For this reason, companies typically use them to do the more challenging analyses and/or larger capital projects. These professionals know how to use advanced statistical methodologies and are adept at constructing complex models. Ideally, such a degree would be part of a dedicated institute such as North Carolina State's Institute for Advanced Analytics. Most schools do not have the resources to pursue this path and need to choose from an existing platform; as long as the program is housed in one of the STEM (Science, Technology, Engineering, and Mathematics) disciplines, it should possess the necessary rigor required for the role of a data scientist.

The next skill level, to be discussed, is for the role of a business user. Their analytical responsibilities are primarily centered on descriptive statistics. They tend to look backwards at what has already happened. They need to use a company's resources (data marts, warehouses) to access data and produce simple reports. Their primary knowledge base is in a business discipline that defines their work; for example, marketing, sales, or accounting. In addition to their core discipline, these professionals need courses in data management and basic statistics.

The final group and focus of this paper are business analysts. The McKinsey Global Institute referred to this group as "data-savvy managers." They are often in positions that allow them to identify and exploit opportunities. In order to fulfill their responsibilities, they need to have a solid foundation in business complemented by analytical studies. Academia needs to take an integrated approach to the curriculum of these professionals covering topics in data management, statistics, and communication, along with a business functional area such as marketing, finance and operations. This multi-discipline skill set is desirable in a data scientist as well; the difference between the two is in the weighting - data scientists' studies are weighted heavier on the quantitative side whereas business analysts are weighted more on the business side.

It is imperative that the quantitative skills are reinforced in the business functional areas with projects and case studies. It is also highly recommended that courses for data scientists are not combined with those for business analysts and business users. It is tempting to teach general concepts to reach a larger audience thereby lowering costs but research has shown this method to be ineffective (Moore, 2001). Business students need business examples to facilitate their learning; it is unrealistic, in most cases, to present a generalized exponential growth model for bacteria and expect students to transfer the application to continuous compounding of interest.

Business analysts do not need to be experts in the various analytical tools. As "data-savvy managers," they need to have confidence in the processes used by data scientists in order to identify opportunities and to fully exploit the results. Statistics departments are not usually structured to teach business functional content. Recruiters are often frustrated with where to find quantitative business students (Wixom, B. et.al 2011). An obvious choice to mitigate these frustrations is to position the quantitative courses (data management and statistics) within the business school. In a study of the top fifty U.S. undergraduate business schools, it was found that 68% of the schools taught the first statistics course in the business school and 81% did the same for the second course (Haskin & Krehbiel, 2011). Using these institutions as sources of "best practices," it makes sense to position the quantitate courses within business schools. Further support may be found by looking at the preferences of recruiters. When practitioners were asked from where they hired business intelligence skills, 449 replied business schools, 158 computer sciences, 111 mathematics, and 109 engineering (Wixom B., et al., 2011).

One of the authors worked in an operations research (OR) department for a large manufacturing company in a capacity which today would be called a data scientist. Personal stories follow to illustrate the importance of developing data-savvy managers.

- A valuable profitability model was developed using linear programming. Upper-level familiar with the methodology used to produce them. No manager is going to risk their career endorsing something they do not understand.

- A new chemical lab was in the planning stage of construction. The chemical testing machines were seven-figure expenditures. The team leader did not want to purchase more machines than absolutely necessary to deliver a given service level. The team leader had an analytical background and recognized the value of using data to drive decisions. He also realized the stakes involved and escalated the problem to the OR team to resolve.

The first example was not used by the company because the decision makers were not data-savvy managers; opportunities and profits were compromised. In the second example, the manager was data-savvy, and used the information to make an informed decision.

Analytics/Optimization Examples in Manufacturing

- Soap Manufacturing Company was having problems with their capacity limitations. We established priority classes and wrote an optimization program to optimize the schedule given the priority classes. The priority classes automatically updated themselves. You can see the specifics in Production Planning Journal year 1997 (Brown & Ozgur, 1997; Ozgur, 1998).
- In scheduling sequence-dependent set-ups for like items, we first used a cluster analysis method to group like items. In a cable assembly system, there were 93 cables produced on an automatic assembly line. We came-up with three groups/clusters of cables and once the cables are classified into 3 clusters of similar cables another program was used to sequence each cluster, once each cluster was scheduled another program was devised to combine the three clusters in an optimal way. Of course, each time subsets of items were selected, posing a different problem each time. (Ozgur & Bai, 2010; Ozgur & Brown, 1995).
- In a problem faced by an Aerospace parts manufacturing company, there were defective units produced. It was the responsibility of management to determine out of 150 units of a single part which items were defective. We established that using discriminant analysis method after using regression analysis method. This was a manufacturing company that produced parts and supplied an aerospace industry company. We repeated this procedure for 110 parts produced by the Aerospace parts manufacturing company. This was a consulting assignment.
- An appliance manufacturing company used SAS to help with quality control. Quality Control software was primarily used for predictive analysis of product defects. This was a consulting assignment.
- A Fastener Manufacturing Company was interested in the optimal torque settings of their fasteners. They didn't want the fasteners torque settings be too tight or too loose. The optimization program was designed to come up with optimal torque settings for their fasteners (Meek & Ozgur, 1991; Meek & Ozgur, 1989).
- A chemical components supplier to a steel manufacturing who supplies an automobile manufacturing company. The automobile manufacturing company passes back their quality standards back to steel manufacturing company who in turn passes back its standards back to chemical components manufacturing company. One of the authors was hired as a consultant for the chemical components company about improving their process capability. The company was using statistical software and trying to improve capability by increasing C_p and C_{pk} above 1.333.

CONCLUSION

The course of study for business analysts can no longer be as simple as a double major between business and mathematics; it requires its own plan of study. In their article (Wilder & Ozgur 2015) demonstrate an example of an undergraduate curriculum for Business Analytics. The role of a business analyst (data-savvy manager) does not require traditional mathematical skills that include the mechanical operations best performed by a computer. The traditional delivery of this type of education is for students to take quantitative courses from a mathematics or statistics department. The proposal herein is to move this responsibility to business schools. It is not the mathematics that is important for these business students; it is their problem solving abilities which requires knowledge of the business first. Adversaries will argue that it is dangerous for data-savvy managers to conduct simple data analyses without fully understanding the mathematics behind the underlying tools. Mistakes will be made as they are today. Good data-savvy managers will call on data scientists when the problems are complex or critical to the organization's success. A greater mistake is not to offer students an alternative analytics career path. Forcing students to take courses beyond their level of interest will satisfy no one.

Complacency is a comfortable choice but it must not be tolerated. Skill gaps between student graduates and market needs are noticeable. The information systems curricula of the top 50 business schools were examined to look at what schools were doing to help close this gap. In general, more managerial courses were being added to curriculums and more technical courses were being dropped (Benamati, Ozdemir, & Smith, 2010).

A cogent argument has been presented to position an undergraduate analytics program for business analysts within the school of business. The basis for such action is two-fold. First, the level of expertise for a business analyst is different than that for a data scientist. The focus of their quantitative studies should be on problem solving abilities, not mathematics. Since business analysts solve business problems it is business knowledge that will drive their resolution. Business knowledge is found in business schools. Second, a change in pedagogy is necessary. Data scientists need to know how and why mathematical models work. Business analysts need to recognize opportunities, frame problems, and interpret the results.

The ideas presented herein are innovative because they target an audience that has been neglected in the past – business analysts. Their hybrid education was traditionally delivered with a double major, not with a distinct program of its own. Execution necessitates that the program be delivered at the undergraduate level of a business school as a declared minor/major of student.

REFERENCES

Barton, D., & Court, D. (2012). Making Advanced Analytics Work For You. *Harvard Business Review*, *90*(10), 79–83. PMID:23074867

Benamati, J. H., Ozdemir, Z. D., & Smith, H. J. (2010). Aligning Undergraduate IS Curricula with Industry Needs. *Communications of the ACM*, *53*(3), 152–156. doi:10.1145/1666420.1666458

Brown, R., & Ozgur, C. (1997). Priority Class Scheduling: Production Scheduling for Multi-objective Environments. *Production Planning and Control*, *8*(2), 762–770. doi:10.1080/095372897234650

Chen, H., Chiang, R. H., & Storey, V. C. (2012). Business Intelligence and Analytics: From Big Data to Big Impact. *Management Information Systems Quarterly, 36*(4), 1165–1188.

Davenport, T. H. (2006). Competing on Analytics. *Harvard Business Review, 84*(1), 98–107. PMID:16447373

Davenport, T. H., Harris, J., & Shapiro, J. (2010). Competing on Talent Analytics. *Harvard Business Review, 88*(10), 52–58. PMID:20929194

Davenport, T. H., & Patil, D. (2012). Data Scientist: The Sexiest Job of the 21st Century. *Harvard Business Review, 90*(10), 70–76. PMID:23074866

Ferguson, R. B. (2012). Location Analytics: Bringing Geography Back. *MIT Sloan Management Review, 54*(2), 1–5.

Gartner Inc. (2013). *Press Release: Gartner Executive Program Survey of More Than 2,000 CIOs Shows Digital Technologies Are Top Priorities in 2013.* Available at http://www.gartner.com/newsroom/id/2304615

Gnatovich, R. (2006). *Business Intelligence Versus Business Analytics—What's the Difference?* Available at http://www.cio.com/article/18095/Business_Intelligence_Versus_Business_Analytics_What_s_the_Difference

Haskin, H. N., & Krehbiel, T. C. (2011). Business statistics at the top 50 US business programmes. *Teaching Statistics,* 92–98.

Heizer, J., & Render, B. (2011). *Operations Management* (10th ed.). Upper Saddle River, NJ: Prentice Hall.

Kalakota, R. (2011). *Gartner says – BI and Analytics a $12.2 Bln market.* Available at http://practicalanalytics.wordpress.com/2011/04/24/gartner-says-bi-and-analytics-a-10-5-bln-market/

MacMillan, D. (2009). *Netflix, AT&T are Real Winners of Netflix Prize.* Available at http://www.businessweek.com/the_thread/techbeat/archives/2009/09/netflix_att_are.html

Manyika, J., Chui, M., Brown, B., Bughin, J., Dobbs, R., Roxburgh, C., & Byers, A. H. (2011). *Big data: The next frontier for innovation, competition, and productivity.* Available at http://www.mckinsey.com/insights/business_technology/big_data_the_next_frontier_for_innovation

McAfee, A., & Brynijolfsson, E. (2012). Big Data: The Management Revolution. *Harvard Business Review, 90*(10), 61–68. PMID:23074865

McKinsey & Company. (2009). *Hal Varian on how the Web challenges managers.* Available at http://www.mckinsey.com/insights/innovation/hal_varian_on_how_the_web_challenges_managers

Meek, G., and Ozgur, C. (1989, August). Prevailing Locknut Torque Variations. *Journal of Fastener Technology International,* 58-60.

Meek, G., & Ozgur, C. (1991). Torque Variation Analysis. Indagationes Mathematicae, *41*(1), 1–16.

Moore, D. S. (2001). Undergraduate Programs and the Future of Academic Statistics. *The American Statistician, 55*(1), 1–6. doi:10.1198/000313001300339860

Nichols, W. (2013). Advertising Analytics 2.0. *Harvard Business Review*, *91*(3), 60–68. PMID:23593768

Nucleus Research. (2011). *Analytics Pays Back $10.66 for every dollar spend*. Available at http://nucleusresearch.com/research/search/

Ozgur, C. (1998). Capacity Constrained Resource Scheduling: A Decision Utility Approach. *International Journal of Operations and Quantitative Management*, *4*(3), 1–21.

Ozgur, C., & Bai, L. (2010, March/June). Hierarchical Composition Heuristic for Asymmetric Sequence Dependent Single Machine Scheduling Problems. *Operations Management Research*, *3*(1), 98–106. doi:10.1007/s12063-010-0031-5

Ozgur, C., & Brown, J. R. (1995). A Two-Stage Traveling Salesman Procedure for the Single Machine Sequence Dependent Scheduling Problem. *OMEGA, International Journal of Management Science*, *23*(2), 205–219. doi:10.1016/0305-0483(94)00057-H

Tufte, E. R. (2010). *Visual Explanations*. Cheshire, CT: Graphics Press LLC.

Watson, H. J. (2013). The Business Case for Analytics. *BizEd*, *12*(3), 49–54.

White, M. A., & Bruton, G. D. (2011). *The Management of Technology and Innovation*. Mason, OH: South-Western.

Wilder, C. R., & Ozgur, C. O. (2015). Business Analytics Curriculum for Undergraduate Majors. *INFORMS Transactions on Education,* 15(2), 1-8.

Wixom, B. (2011). *Survey Finds Disconnect Between BI Education, Industry Needs*. Available at http://www.itbusinessedge.com/cm/community/features/interviews/blog/survey-finds-disconnect-between-bi-education-industry-needs/?cs=47562

Wixom, B., Ariyachandra, T., Goul, M., Gray, P., Kulkarni, U., & Phillips-Wren, G. (2011). The Current State of Business Intelligence in Academia. *Communications of the Association for Information Systems*, *29*, 299–312.

Wixom, B. H., Ariyachandra, T., & Mooney, J. (2013). *BI Congress Communications*. Available at http://www2.commerce.virginia.edu/bic3/communications.asp

Zalud, B. (2013, February). Nine Shades of Analytics, Anything but Grey. *Security*, *50*(2), 36–50.

KEY TERMS AND DEFINITIONS

Analytics in Manufacturing: The use of statistical techniques to solve real world manufacturing problems.

Big Data: The current phrase used to describe the changes in the accumulation of data over the past decade; the distinguishing factors of which are volume (2.5 Exabyte's per day), velocity (speed at which data is created), and variety (images, texts, videos, etc.).

Business Analysts: A person needs enough conceptual knowledge and quantitative skills to be able to frame and interpret analyses of a business problem involving big data in an effective way.

Business Analytics: The use of statistics and other operations research techniques, such as simulation, decision trees and other operations research techniques.

Business Intelligence: The process of gathering and transforming raw data into actionable insights yielding better decisions.

Data Driven Companies: Companies that have real world problems involving big data and business analytics.

Data Scientist: The skill set must include "a solid foundation in math, statistics, probability, and computer science" with the ability to write code at the forefront.

Chapter 8
Big Data Transforming Small and Medium Enterprises

Donna M. Schaeffer
Marymount University, USA

Patrick C. Olson
National University, USA

ABSTRACT

The terms big data, analytics, and business intelligence are often used in the media, with much attention on Fortune 500 enterprises. Small and medium-sized businesses (SMEs) also handle large amounts of data, and it is important to their decision making and planning. This chapter explores options for handling Big Data in SMEs. It presents a framework that considers not just the volume of data, but the variety of types of data, the velocity in which data is created and transmitted, the importance of data veracity, and its value in transforming small and medium-sized enterprises. SMEs need to work with big data, and doing so will impact their business models and require them transform themselves. Their transformation will be ongoing because all indicators show that the volume of data is rising and will continue to do so simply because of the trends related to customer interaction.

DEFINITION AND ECONOMIC IMPACT OF SMALL AND MEDIUM ENTERPRISE

The definition of small and medium (SMEs) varies across countries. An enterprise is any entity engaged in an economic activity. SMEs play an important economic role in developed and developing countries. They provide jobs for many people and foster a spirit of entrepreneurship and innovation.

In the United States, firms that employ fewer than 500 employees are considered SMEs with farms and service-oriented firms further classified according to annual revenues (United States International Trade Commission, 2010). The vast majority of SMEs are firms with fewer than 20 employees. Although large corporations garner most media attention, there are some indications that small businesses are a major player in the United States' economy. Small businesses represent more than 99 percent of U.S. firms with employees and account for 49 percent of private sector employment (SBA, 2012). Freudenberg et al. (2012) indicated that small businesses account for 43% of sales and 51% of the Gross Domestic

DOI: 10.4018/978-1-4666-7272-7.ch008

Product in the United States. The Small Business Administration Office of Advocacy (United States Small Business Administration, 2012) estimates that, of the 18.5 million net new jobs created in the United States between 1993 and 2011, small businesses (less than 500 employees) accounted for 11.8 million, or 64 percent.

In the European Union, designation as an SME is based on the number of employees and the annual turnover or balance sheet. An SME may have up to 250 employees, and annual turnover of €50 m or a balance sheet of €43 m (European Commission, 2003). In the enlarged European Union of 25 countries, there are 23 million SMEs, and these provide jobs for 75 million people (European Commission, 2003). Many SMEs are quite small, for example, the average European enterprise employs less than10 people (European Commission, 2003).

In the Asia-Pacific region, SMEs are usually enterprises that employ no more than 250 employees, although there is no generally accepted definition. In China, Hong Kong, and Indonesia, the classification includes no more than 100 employees. Other countries in the Asia-Pacific region use a combination of employment and assets (Taiwan Ministry of Economics Affairs, 2006). SMEs comprise over 95 percent of the economy of the Asia – Pacific region.

On the African continent, the definition varies according to industry, but in general an SME has no more than 200 employees. In Egypt, the maximum number of employees an SME may have is 20, while in Morroco, the number is 200 (Gibson and van der Vaart, 2008). Various information sources put the percentage of SMEs from 80% to 99% of all firms (SMEAfrica.net, 2014; Fjose et al, 2010); and employ 60% of working population (SMEAfrica.net, 2014). Fjose et al (2010) estimates SMEs comprise more than 95 percent of all firms in Sub-Saharan Africa, and in South Africa, small and medium-sized enterprises make up 91% of businesses, provide employment to about 60% of the labor force and account for roughly 34% of that nation's Gross Domestic Product. Fjose, Grunfeld, and Green (2010) report that SMEs account for over one-third of the nation's employment in Malawi, Kenya, Zambia, and Ivory Coast.

A survey of global SMEs by Oxford Economics (2013) revealed that they are affected by increasing global competition. Global expansion is a priority for 34% of respondents. The same survey shows respondents expect the percentage of revenue generated outside of their home countries and the number of countries in which SMEs do business will grow sharply in the next three years. Successfully navigating these trends require a focus on business transformation. Two-thirds of the respondents are at some point in the transformation process—either planning, executing, or recently completed. Nearly two-thirds of SMEs say transformation is essential to staying ahead of the competition, and over half say technology developments are making their traditional ways of doing business obsolete.

Technology is a major element of transformation. Most surveys and reports indicate that investing in new technologies is a top strategic priority for SMEs. Business analytics are a key element of transformation, but current literature suggests SMEs struggle with data accuracy and quality.

THE INFORMATION TECHNOLOGY FOUNDATION FOR BIG DATA TRANSFORMING SMEs

Given the wide variety of industries and locations in which SMEs operate, as well as the differences in numbers of employees and amounts of revenue, it is understandable that the adoption of information technology (IT) in SMEs around the world varies. Several industry studies show SMEs account for as much as half of all IT spending globally.

A 2013 survey of 1,000 global IT professionals reports a 19% percent increase in SMEs' IT budgets in the first half of 2013 over previous years, and this is the largest increase since 2010 with hardware purchases, especially tablet devices, accounting for the bulk of IT spending (Spiceworks, 2013).

In Africa, the Middle East, and Turkey, SMEs account for 30% of IT spending, but the level of maturity of the technology is low and the infrastructure is weak (Topbas, 2012). In the Gujarat, India, SMEs have increased spending on IT by as much as 20% over 2012 because partnerships and clients require advanced ERP systems and other systems (Umarji, 2013). Globally, over half of the respondents in an Oxford Economics survey report increased collaborations with other firms via online business networks and platforms to drive innovation and growth.

In the United States, The National Small Business Association (2010) found that computers have a significant role in small business with 98% of respondents of a survey agreeing that it is important to keep up with technology. Many respondents reported having websites, purchasing supplies online, banking online, and using social media for business networking. Kim et al. (2013) studied the Web 2.0 practices of one hundred small and medium sized enterprises (SMEs) in the United States. The organizations consisted of those ranked one of the fifty best SMEs to work for in America, as well as fifty randomly selected enterprises. Most of the fifty best SMEs had adopted Web 2.0 in various degrees, but the other SMEs needed to increase their efforts to improve their performances, to connect with consumers and to remain competitive.

IDC (2012) reported spending on information technology by SMEs in the United States to be $53.0 billion in 2011 and expected that figure to exceed $138 billion in 2012. SMEs account for 10% of the investment in information technology worldwide (IDC, 2012). SMEs are spending increasing more of their budgets on cloud technology (Dyson, 2013). As a result, spending on security is increasing and is expected to pass $5.6 billion in 2015 (Eddy, 2012). A survey commissioned by Brother International Corporation (2013) also indicates just over half of small business owners in the United State surveyed (51%) viewed technology tool-related capital investments such as new software, mobile apps, and cloud computing services as a top priority for investment.

A survey (Kass, 2013) of 173 small business owners or managers in the United States demonstrated they are actively using five different devices including laptops, desktops, smartphones, and tablets. Some owners and managers reported regularly using as many as 12 different devices (Kass, 2013).

Staffing is a challenge. Nearly half of SMEs are actively seeking to acquire digital skills through hiring, training, or partnering with third-party providers (Oxford Economics, 2013). It is difficult for SMEs to find workers with the right skills and to afford competitive pay scales. This skills gap can be a roadblock to adopting cloud and analytics technologies.

The Dimensions of Big Data

"Big data" is high-volume, high-velocity and high-variety information assets that demand cost-effective, innovative forms of information processing for enhanced insight and decision making (Beyer & Laney, 2012). In addition to considerations about its volume, velocity, and variety, big data requires veracity.

Volume

High volume refers to data sets with sizes ranging from a few dozen terabytes to many petrabytes of data in a single data set. This volume of data is typically beyond the ability of commonly used software tools to capture, curate, and store data (Kuznetsky, 2010) as well as the ability to process the data within a tolerable elapsed time (Snijders, Matzat, & Reips, 2012). The volume also complicates the ability to share, transfer, and analyze the data (Vance, 2012).

While conducting a large project, data processing and storage needs could rise to the petabyte level. A petabyte is a term for an amount of computer storage; it is a unit of information equivalent to 1000 terabytes or 10^15 bytes. While terms like bit and gig have entered everyday vocabulary, authors try to explain a petabyte to the general public. A petabyte has been described as four times the amount of information in the United States Library of Congress or approximately 223,000 DVDs (McKenna, 2013), 20.0 million four-drawer filing cabinets filled with text (Mozy, 2009), or the memories of 800 human beings (Kurzweil, 2005). The amount of information generated is expected to grow fifty times over by 2020 (Nevitt, 2013). IBM (2012) has estimated 2.5 quintrilllion bytes of data are created daily. Frank Moss (2011) stated:

Computers, smart phones, GPS devices, embedded microprocessors, sensors — all connected by the mobile Internet — are forming a 'societal nervous system' that is generating a cloud of data about people that is growing at an exponential rate. Every time we perform a search, tweet, send an email, post a blog, comment on one, use a cell phone, shop online, update our profile on a social networking site, use a credit card, or even go to the gym, we leave behind a mountain of data, a digital footprint, that provides a treasure trove of information about our lifestyles, financial activities, health habits, social interactions, and much more.

One might wonder why an SME would "need" to engage such volumes of data. Implicit in the above statements is the idea that a successful business will "of necessity" need to interact with customers via social media. This is not simply a "text" interaction and definitely includes pictures and video. Thus the days of running an accounting system that uses a megabit of data have given way to pictures that use a megabit for each picture and videos that are 10+ megabits per instance. This will be true for all businesses in the future.

Velocity

Velocity refers to the speed of movement of the data. This is about both the customer and the business experience. In the case of the customer, the wait for data to get to them must be short. If the wait is very long, the customer leaves and there is no sale. On the business side a long wait, means delayed information for decision making and delayed information for serving customers. The problem of timing exacerbates the issue of speed. In some cases it is still possible to interact with customers via email. This would be an asynchronous experience and timing would not matter. However, the trend is for more synchronous interaction, especially in social media. The result is a need for more velocity.

Thus, the velocity aspect of big data required high speed connectivity and broad bandwidth. SMEs in large urban areas may have sufficient bandwidth to handle big data projects, but those in the more rural or underdeveloped areas may not have access to high-speed bandwidth. Drobo's (2012) study discovered 46 percent of small business owners in the United States don't have the bandwidth or sufficiently reliable networks for cloud storage. Rather, small business owners opt for a hybrid backup and storage solution of onsite and offsite.

In effect, SMEs are likely to be dependent on vendors to supply their storage service. The likely architecture for this is a line from the business to the Internet which lets them access services that third parties provide to their customers. While this might support SMEs even in remote areas, the solution increases risk.

Variety

Variety refers to both the types of things that data is collected about and the details about these items. For the first item it would be items like customers and accounts as examples. In the second area an illustration is found in these two ways of keeping information about customers. In one case the data collected is the customer number and the customer name. This would have less variety than collecting data about customer that includes some demographic data and the customer's preferences. This second example would have much more variety.

Big data is inherently high variety; but the data generated and used by small businesses may be more limited in scope. The limited variety of data inhibits the predictive capabilities and discovering the unexpected information that big data projects tout as beneficial. Mowbrey (2009) describes four different types of data that a small business might typically store in a cloud. The four types of data include information about customers, accounts such as payments, operating data, and activity data that tracks when and for which applications the business' account with the service provider is used.

The types of data noted by Mowbrey (2009) could each expand into large volumes of data as the variety of information kept about the item expands. Since SMEs have customers as well as items, the data types may be applied to customers as well. In fact, as a social media approach to customers and items is taken, both the variety and volume increases.

Veracity

Veracity refers to the ability of the small enterprise to rely on the correctness – or truthfulness – of the data. An example once again involves the customer. If the SME is a bookstore and the customer data shows that the customer has bought the last four books by a given author, it seems like common sense to try to market the author's newest book to that customer. However, if that customer bought the new book yesterday and this transaction is not recorded, the customer is erroneously contacted in the hopes of a sale. This could cause customers to view communications from the bookstore as a "nuisance," creating a reputation problem for this small bookstore.

In some cases it is possible for the very nature of big data to mitigate against this problem. For example, if the issue can be addressed by aggregate data (e.g. averages) the large size of the data set helps to provide aggregate data that is more useful. In the bookstore example, the amount of sales of the author's new book might in and of itself indicated that targeted "tweets" might not be needed!

Value

The last component of this framework is value. This is the idea that the big data effort is ultimately profitable for SMEs. For any business, increased sales and decreased costs provides this value. This can be done with big data in SMEs, but it likely done with vendors and the limited expertise found within the SME. Cloud services, and software as a service are solutions.

The System of Big Data

To effectively gather and use big data for decision making, a system is required to capture, curate, manage, and process the data. Systems, or large parts of systems, may already be in use in a small business. For example, a small business with a web presence can track online visitors to its site via a simple technology such as cookies or more sophisticated visitor analytic tools. SMEs can track who is visiting the site, where they are coming from, how long they stay, and which pages they browse. This information can be used in targeted marketing campaigns.

Data can be captured via point-of- sale (POS) terminals or other devices. POS terminals are the hardware used to manage the selling process with a salesperson-accessible interface in the location where a transaction takes place. During 2012, the number of POS terminals per 100,000 adults ranged from 0 to 4,890 (World Bank, 2012). GAO Research, Inc. (2012) estimates there are 10 million payment terminals in the United States, but there is no data about how many of these systems are in place in SMEs. With advances in Near-Field Communications (NFC) technologies, POS terminals are evolving into mobile payment systems. NFC is a set of standards that enable wireless communications between smartphones that are in very close proximity.

Cenicola (2013) identified several technologies that SMEs may have in place via which data can be captured – customer relationship management (CRM) systems, websites and visitor/lead analytic tools, email marketing tools, blogs, or electronic payments. Data could also be captured via web-based Voice of Internet Protocol (VoIP) telephone systems (Totka, 2013). In many cases, these technologies are provided to small businesses by other firms, such as Salesforce.com for CRM or Google for analytics, or tools like Constant Contact or Wordpress for specific applications.

The volume of data that is available due to POS, mobile payment systems, or other systems can be overwhelming to a small business owner. As mentioned earlier, data can quickly reach the petabyte level. Many SMEs opt to store their data using services in "the cloud." For example, Amazon Web Services provides the use of Amazon's computing infrastructure, including a power, storage, and e-commerce software. Other examples include Google Apps, a platform on which companies they can run and store their own applications and data in the cloud and Salesforce.com, a customer relationship management software.

Big Data, SMEs, and the Cloud

The use of the cloud for data storage among SMEs varies across the globe. The Brother Small Business Survey (2013) reports that 35% of respondents in the United States use the Cloud for data storage, but 42% are not using the cloud at all. Perhaps SMEs don't understand the concept - 46% of respondents understood "cloud" somewhat, while 27% responded that they didn't understand it well or at all. This is consistent with other findings. A survey of 239 SMEs in the United States found that 46% of respondents believe that public cloud storage is not a fit for their business (Drobo, 2012). This is not the case globally – a 2013 survey of 1,000 SMEs located throughout the world found that 61% of respondents already use cloud computing, with an additional 12% planning to invest in software as a service and cloud computing (Spiceworks, 2013).

Mowbrey (2009) points out that Service Level Agreements (SLAs) for cloud computing services do not always make it clear what rights the providers have to use the data they store. For many providers, the data is only monetarized when it is sold. Small business owners need to seek clarification. For example, the Amazon S3 storage service has "buckets" around the world, and users may choose which the region in which they want to store their data. Choice is factored by issues such as geographic proximity to handle latency issues, geographic remoteness for redundancy and disaster recovery purposes, legal and regulatory requirements, or costs.

The use of the cloud raises data veracity issues. A study conducted by Techaisle (2012) shows that it is important for SMEs to maintain ownership of data and that may not always be the case with cloud services. In some industries and countries, there are strong regulations about data; for example, the Attorney General in Minnesota filed suit with a health care provider over lax security of thousands of patients' digital health records (Lynn, 2013).

CONCLUSION

Considering the needs noted above, SMEs need to work with big data. The needs impact a variety of aspects of the SMEs up to and including their business models, which will require serious transformation. SMEs face an ongoing transformation because all indicators show that the volume of data is rising and will continue to do so simply because of the trends related to customer interaction. This leaves SMEs with the problem of how to participate in big data. The cloud is a good option. However, several sources indicate SMEs are reluctant to enter the cloud. This is likely related to issues of control, particularly ownership. Additionally, there is an access problem due to the difference in the way small and medium businesses access the Internet. Realistically, the difference isn't that surprising since many smaller companies still rely on consumer broadband and wireless services for access. Only one-third of SMEs have actually invested in networking infrastructure, as a recent IDC (2012) study estimated.

One of the important benefits of big data is the ability to discover relationships that were not previously known which is essential to the innovation which is required for transformation, but this benefit may be unavailable to SMEs. This is likely because while SMEs will certainly generate the volume of data that is associated with big data, they are unlikely to generate the variety of data usually associated with big data. Interestingly, a collection of SMEs would have that variety. However, accomplishing this would require the technology and the bandwidth to carry it.

Because access to bandwidth is a problem for more than one aspect of SME's involvement in big data, might this be a time to expand the opportunities provided by the Internet? The Internet2 Consortium recently upgraded its network backbone to a 100-Gigabit, Ethernet-enabled, 8.8-terabit-per-second optical network. Though usually used by education and government, allowing access to this network by the SME's would increase available bandwidth making innovation and transformation possible.

REFERENCES

Asia-Pacific Economic Cooperation. (2013). *SMEs in the APEC Region*. Retrieved from http://www.apec. org/Groups/SOM-Steering-Committee-on-Economic-and-Technical-Cooperation/Working-Groups/~/me dia/20ABF15DB43E498CA1F233DFF30CF88D.ashx

Beyer, M. A., & Laney, D. (2012). *The importance of 'big data': A definition*. Gartner Report, June version, ID G00235055.

Brother International Corporation. (2013, March 19). *Brother small business survey 2013*. Retrieved from http://www.brother-usa.com/PressReleases/brother%202013%20smb%20survey%20press%20 release%20%20final.pdf

Cenicola, M. (2013, April 29). Three steps to incorporate big data into your small business. *Forbes*. Retrieved from http://www.forbes.com/sites/theyec/2013/04/29/3-steps-to-incorporate-big-data-into-yoursmall-business/

Curry, E., Freitas, A., & O'Riain, S. (2010). The role of community-driven data curation for enterprises. In D. Wood (Ed.), *Linking enterprise data* (pp. 25–47). Boston, MA: Springer. doi:10.1007/978-1-4419-7665-9_2

Drobo Incorporated. (2012). *SMB IT 2012 Survey Results*. Retrieved from http://www.drobo.com/down-loads/docs/SR-0137-00_SMB-virt-survey-q3-q4-2012.pdf

Dyson, C. K. (2013, January 9). Can the cloud help small businesses? *Wall Street Journal*. Retrieved from http://online.wsj.com/article/SB10001424127887323706704578230641145851624.html

Eddy, N. (2012, May 30). *Small-business security spending to top $5.6B in 2015*. Retrieved from http://www.eweek.com/c/a/Security/Small-Business-Security-Spending-to-Top-56-Billion-in-2015-IDC875794/?kc=rss

European Commission. (2003). *The New SME Definition*. Retrieved from http://ec.europa.eu/enterprise/ policies/sme/files/sme_definition/sme_user_guide_en.pdf

Fjose, S., Grunfeld, L.A., & Green, C. (2010). *SMEs and Growth in Sub-Saharan Africa*. MENON-publication. Number 14/2010.

Freudenberg, B., Tran-Nam, B., Karlinsky, S., & Gupta, R. (2012). A comparative analysis of tax advisers' perception of small business tax law complexity: United States, Australia and New Zealand. *Australian Tax Forum, 27*(4), 677-718. Retrieved from http://ssrn.com/abstract=2190692

Gibson, T., & van der Vaart, H. J. (2008). *Defining SMEs: A Less Imperfect Way of Defining Small and Medium Enterprises in Developing Countries*. The Brookings Institute.

IDC. (2012, March). *U.S. small and medium-sized business 2012–2016 forecast: Sizing the SMB markets for PCs and peripherals, systems and storage, networking equipment, packaged software, and IT services*. IDC.

Kass, L. (2013, May 07). *Survey results reveal top five reasons small businesses are turning to cloud file management.* Retrieved from http://www.sugarsync.com/blog/2013/05/07/survey-results-reveal-top-fivereasons-small-business-are-turning-to-cloud-file-management/

Kim, H. D., Lee, I., & Lee, C. K. (2013). Building Web 2.0 enterprises: A study of small and medium enterprises in the United States. *International Small Business Journal, 31*(2), 156–174. doi:10.1177/0266242611409785

Kurzweil, R. (2005). *The singularity is near.* New York: Viking.

Kuznetsky, D. (2010). *What is big data?.* Academic Press.

Lynn, S. (2013, June 4). Small business cloud myths: Busted! *PC Magazine.* Retrieved from http://www.pcmag.com/article2/0,2817,2419823,00.asp

McKenna, B. (2013). What does a petabyte look like? *Computer Weekly.* Retrieved from http://www.computerweekly.com/feature/What-does-a-petabyte-look-like

Moss, F. (2011). *The sorcerers and their apprentices: How the digital magicians of the MIT media lab are creating the innovative technologies that will transform our lives.* New York: The Crown Publishing Group.

Mowbray, M. (2009). *The fog over the grimpen mire: Cloud computing and the law.* HP Laboratories: HPL-2009-99. Retrieved from http://www.hpl.hp.com/techreports/2009/HPL-2009-99.pdf

Mozy, Inc. (2009). *How much is a petabyte?* Retrieved from http://mozy.com/blog/misc/how-much-is-apetabyte/

National Small Business Association. (2010). *Small business technology survey.* Washington, DC: Author.

Nevitt, C. (2013, March 18). What is a petabyte? *Financial Times.* Retrieved from http://www.ft.com/cms/s/2/bc7350a6-8fe7-11e2-ae9e-00144feabdc0.html#axzz2WD55Twcz

Oxford Economics. (2013). *SMES: Equipped to compete.* Retrieved from http://cdn.news-sap.com/wp-content/blogs.dir/1/files/SAP-SME-analysis-presentation.pdf

GAO Research. (2012). Retrieved from http://www.gaoresearch.com/POS/pos.php

Schroeck, M., Shockley, R., Smart, J., Romero-Morales, D., & Tufano, P. (2012). *Analytics: The real world use of big data.* Somers, NY: IBM Corporation.

SMEAfrica. (2014). Retrieved from http://smeafrica.net

Snijders, C., Matzat, U., & Reips, U.-D. (2012). Big data: Big gaps of knowledge in the field of internet science. *International Journal of Internet Science, 1,* 1–5. Retrieved from http://www.ijis.net/ijis7_1/ijis7_1_editorial.pdf

Spiceworks. (2013). *Annual Report on Small and Midsize Business Technology Plans and Purchase Intent.* Retrieved from http://itreports.spiceworks.com/reports/spiceworks_voice_of_it_state_of_smb_2013_1h.pdf

Sugarsynch. (2013). Retrieved from http://www.sugarsync.com/blog/2013/05/07/survey-results-reveal-topfive-reasons-small-business-are-turning-to-cloud-file-management/

Taiwan Ministry of Economic Affairs. (2006). *White Paper on Small and Medium Enterprises in Taiwan*. Retrieved from http://www.moeasmea.gov.tw/eng/2006whitepaper/2006white.asp)

Topbas, G. (2013, 08 April). Empowering Qatar's SMEs using cloud technology. *The Edge: Qatar's Business Magazine*. Retrieved from http://www.theedge.me/empowering-qatars-entrepreneurs-and-smes-using-cloud-technology/

Totka, M. (2013, May 21). How a small business can use big data. *Small Business Operations*. Retrieved from http://smallbiztrends.com/2013/05/small-business-can-use-big-data.html

Umarji, V. (2013, May 27). Gujarat SMEs increase IT spending by 20%. *Business Standard*. Retrieved from http://www.business-standard.com/article/sme/gujarat-smes-increase-it-spending-by-20-113052700986_1.html

United States International Trade Commission. (2010). *Small and Medium-Sized Enterprises: Overview of Participation in U.S. Exports*. Retrieved from http://www.usitc.gov/publications/332/pub4125.pdf

United States Small Business Administration. (2012). Washington, DC: Author.

Vance, A. (2010, April 22). Start-up goes after big data with hadoop helper. *New York Times Blog*. Retrieved from http://bits.blogs.nytimes.com/2010/04/22/start-up-goes-after-big-data-with-hadoophelper/?dbk

World Bank. (2012). Retrieved from http://data.worldbank.org/indicator/FB.POS.TOTL.P5

KEY TERMS AND DEFINITIONS

Big Data: Data sets that are too large and complex to handle with traditional information technology tools.

Business Transformation: Big changes in organizational processes or technologies in response to changes in the market.

Cloud Computing: The use of remote servers hosted on the Internet to store and process data.

High Volume: Data sets with sizes ranging from a few dozen terabytes to many petrabytes of data in a single data set.

Information Technology: The hardware, software, and communications networks used by an enterprise.

Small and Medium Business Enterprises: The definition varies according to industry and country, typically employing less than 250 employees.

Variety: Different types of things that data is collected about and different details about these items.

Velocity: Speed of the network.

Veracity: Accurateness.

Chapter 9
Nonprofit Fundraising Transformation through Analytics

David George Vequist IV
University of the Incarnate Word (UIW), USA

ABSTRACT

The authors present the experiences of a professor and a team of students who found that social media and predictive analytics go hand-in-hand when designing effective marketing campaigns (in this case, fundraising for a community of nonprofit organizations). The students of a medium-sized southwestern private university assisted a large southwestern city with the social media marketing efforts for the city's first Big Give fundraising. The organizers then told the students that the internal goal for the 24-hour event was $1.5 million USD. The campaign resulted in 21,361 gifts made for a grand total of $2,095,606.50 USD (approximately 40% greater than was forecasted). It was estimated by the organizers that the most significant contributing factor to the greater performance of the campaign was the social media efforts of the students. The average number of donations raised by the 467 organizations that participated was 45.52 for an overall average of $3,527.09 USD.

INTRODUCTION

According to David Amerland in a 2014 article off of Social Media Today:

ROI is the dirty word in social media. The moment it's aired you get one of two responses: flashy numbers (clicks, visitor figures, reTweets, Likes and +1s) or mushy concepts (brand appeal, brand impact spread, influence rise or social media visibility). Both lead to discontent amongst clients and marketers who know what they are doing.

The reason we have such an approach lies in the way we have traditionally approached metrics in social media marketing. Surely there are better ways or surer methods (from: Social Media Analytics: From Return on Investment to Return on Involvement. June 14th, 2014).

DOI: 10.4018/978-1-4666-7272-7.ch009

In this chapter, the reader will get to learn from the experiences of a professor and a team of students who found that social media and predictive analytics go hand-in-hand when designing effective marketing campaigns (in this case, fundraising for a community of nonprofit organizations).

This case study started when a professor of a medium-sized southwestern private university was approached by the leadership of a non-profit community association (late in 2013) for a large southwestern city to assist with the social media marketing efforts for the city's first Big Give fundraising campaign. The Big Give is part of a national program called Give Local America whereby communities across the U.S.A. (run by the organizations Kimba & Network for Good, see here: http://www.givelocalamerica. org/#page-1) work together to help raise money for local nonprofits on one single day. In 2014, that 24-hour online giving day was on Tuesday, May 6th and $53,715,113.40 was raised from 306,099 gifts from all across the nation (Anonymous, 2014).

In this large southwestern city, this year (2014) was the first year for the various stakeholders of the city to participate in the annual day of giving and therefore multiple resources were utilized to help pull it together. As part of the efforts, the previously mentioned professor involved his BBA Capstone II students to run the social media efforts for the entire city and the 467 organizations (all nonprofits) that were involved. The Capstone II class is the second in a series of two Capstone classes required for all Bachelor of Business Administration (BBA) students at the university. The first Capstone class teaches the students how to conduct a theoretical case analysis of a publicly-traded organization and to ultimately suggest goals and strategies for this organization. In the second class, utilized by the city's stakeholders for the Big Give, the students are required to work with an outside client to help them with a pre-arranged consulting project (arranged prior to the semester by the professor teaching the class) and are graded on the quality of their final deliverables and a presentation made to the clients at the end of the class. At this university, all BBA students graduate only after having practiced using their skills and knowledge in a 'real world' situation with an actual consulting client.

The 28 students were introduced to the client, the executive director (ED) of the city's non-profit association organization and a contractor hired to help coordinate the overall fundraising campaign, on January 29th, 2014 and were instructed to get into five teams to work on developing and implementing strategies for the largest social media applications to help the city's stakeholders and the various non-profit organizations (467 by the cutoff date) to fund raise on May 6th, 2014. The students were then told by the organizers that the internal goal for the 24 hour event was $1.5 million USD. The five teams were self-selected to work with the following five social media channels:

1.   Facebook;
2.   YouTube;
3.   Twitter;
4.   Instagram; and
5.   LinkedIn.

The five social media platforms that were selected for the students to concentrate their efforts on were considered the largest and most active channels at the time and were jointly agreed upon by both the organizers, the professor and the students.

The students began working on the campaign on February 3rd, 2014 and continued until the campaign culminated on May 6th, 2014. They gave weekly updates to both the client and the professor who facilitated the projects. In addition, as the students began to implement some of the social media strategies based on the suggestions in the literature and the analytics they were collecting, they went through an editorial process which included a graduate student assistant, assigned by the university, who monitored the content for appropriateness (also audited by the client and the professor of the class). After the campaign was over, the students then presented their findings on May 8th, 2014 to the organizers, the Capstone professor, key stakeholders in the community, and faculty & administrators of the university. The students turned in printed (and electronic) deliverables and slide decks with their after-action reports and suggestions for future campaigns.

SOCIAL MEDIA ANALYTICS

Social media has become an increasingly important medium for non-profits to use for fund raising and to grow awareness in their communities of how they are helping those that they serve (Buckheit, n.d.). In fact, it is suggested by Goldberg in 2012 that "now, more than ever, organizations are using their online networks—and those that took advantage of the tools were better able to ramp up their fundraising efforts" (Goldberg, 2012). Online giving (which is most impacted by social media sources) in 2012 already accounted for over 8% of all monies received by non-profits in the U.S.A. (Kapin, 2012). Successful campaigns can be found throughout the literature (some examples- Goldberg, 2012; Hibbard, 2010; and Folsom, n.d.) and the one element that seems to contribute a great deal to their success is an emphasis on analytics as part of the campaign.

According to Gow predictive analytics are "a way of making decisions by taking the data of past performance, and using that data to expect future performance" (2014). The professor found that as the classroom consulting project evolved- the students became more and more aware that in order to have an impact on actual fundraising outcomes (total number of donations and dollars raised) that they had to focus on the analytics and actual successful strategies that have been supported in the literature (Folsom, n.d.). The students were able to move beyond just settling on trying to raise awareness to strategies that were more likely to be successful because there was empirical and quantitative evidence showing it has increased engagement and/or actual giving/buying behaviors (Buckheit, n.d.). And more importantly, they began to tie the social media content into a more integrated (and synergistic) strategy for the specific nonprofit entities and the overall Big Give campaign. As Gow (2014) concisely summarizes, "predictive marketing analytics are great for determining your social media strategy as it relates to content."

For purposes of this chapter, some of the best analytical work, by four of the social media channels:

1. Facebook;
2. YouTube;
3. Twitter; and
4. Instagram, as summarized by the students in their final deliverables can be found below:

Facebook

According to the student's research the following analytical trends were found for the Facebook social media channel (from Baer, n.d.):

- *Huge Uptick in Facebook's Influence on Purchase:* Last year, 68% of Americans using social networks said that none of those networks had an influence on their buying decisions. This year, just 36% said that there was no influence. Now, 47% say Facebook has the greatest impact on purchase behavior (compared to just 24% in 2011). Incidentally, Twitter ranks below "other" at 5%. If you want to drive purchase behaviors within social networks, Facebook is the one and only game to play, statistically speaking.
- *Facebook via Mobile Continues to be a Major Factor:* 54% of Facebook members have used the social network via a phone, and 33% use a phone as their primary way to access Facebook. This despite the fact that the Facebook mobile experience and mobile apps are mediocre, at best. Here's hoping the Instagram guys can jump start it. If so, watch for these numbers to soar.
- *Facebook is the Most Addicting of the Social Networks:* 23% of Facebook's users check their account five or more times EVERY DAY. The mean number of daily look-ins by Facebook users is 4. Are we really so interesting that we have to keep up with our friends' inanities every 90 minutes? Evidently, yes.

YouTube

According to the student's research the following analytical trends were found for the YouTube social media channel (excerpt from Jasinsky, Bravo, Olsen, Solano, & Rodriguez, 2014):

- *Social Media Guide:* (Developing a) social media guide (that...) is intended to show ("The Big Give") and their non-profits how to successfully create a YouTube campaign. Another thing they can do with this guide is use it to raise more funds throughout the year (See an example in Lab, 2013).
- *Google Grants:* We suggested that "The Big Give S.A." apply for Google Grants. If they are awarded a grant, they will be able to spend $10,000 a month through AdWords and other Google affiliates (Anonymous, 2014a). Listed in the guide are all of the rules and regulations for staying qualified with Google Grants.
- *YouTube for Non-Profits:* This strategy should be used to help promote videos for the non-profits in a way that they organizations can attract more views and donations to a specific cause. The main focus of YouTube for Non-profits is to help build an awareness of both the company and what they support (Anonymous, 2013).
- *Building Buzz Marketing:* If "The Big Give S.A." and the non-profits that are involved start to post videos a few weeks in advance, they will get people talking about the specific event. This type of marketing has been shown successful through campaigns such as "Kony 2012" and various Hollywood 'blockbusters' (Anonymous, 2014c and Kapin, 2012).

Twitter

According to the student's research the following analytical trends were found for the Twitter social media channel (excerpt from Lopez, Martinez, Rowell, Rodriguez, Speakmon, & Torres, 2014):

- ***Automated Tweet Prompt:*** *Automated tweet prompts allow social media users to share an online activity with their followers or friends. Nonprofits can use this tool to allow donors to share with their followers the fact that they just donated to their nonprofits. This could potentially bring new donors to any cause. Ben & Jerry's recently used automated tweet prompts to allow users to share posts with their followers. The company wanted to bring awareness to World Fair Trade Day. They used a microsite that allowed users to "donate" their unused character space on a Twitter post. The microsite would then fill the leftover space with a tweet promoting World Fair Trade Day. This required no effort from the user. According to MDG Advertising, 39% of people said that they would donate if they saw that a friend posted about a cause on social media, and 34% would repost the donation request (Goldberg, 2012).*

- ***Peer-to-Peer Fundraising:*** *Peer-to-peer fundraising allows for the creation of donor sites for individual fundraising pages (Fonseca, 2014). These can be set up for both firms that want to encourage employees to donate, as well as individual supporters wanting to raise money for a specific nonprofit. The links to these pages can be shared through e-mail or on any social media site, and it is meant to encourage friends and followers on these sites to donate to a cause their friend is passionate about.*
  - ○ *Amplify Austin implemented fundraiser pages in their second give day in 2014 and raised a total of $740,580 from this source (Anonymous, n.d.1).*
  - ○ *Comfort Zone Camp, a nonprofit that helps children cope with the loss of a loved one utilized peer-to-peer fundraising. 781 pages were created; the average page raised $498 each, which resulted in a total of $522,000 raised.*

- ***Promoted Accounts:*** *Promoted Accounts is a tool that can be used from Twitter specifically to gain followers. The Promoted Account targets users by geography, interest, and gender. Twitter gives users the option to set up a maximum budget they'd like to use on the campaign, and will only pay per follower gained. McDonald's Canada is good example of a success story when using promoted accounts. McDonald's Canada wanted to grow its followers by targeting users who used certain keywords or hashtags. McDonald's had a total budget of $15,000, which led them to gaining 9,500+ followers. They also received 14,200 profile views and received a 4% engagement rate. The online marketplace CustomMade connects buyers with makers of customizable products. The company wanted to attract and connect with users on Twitter who would be interested in custom products. They used Promoted Accounts to target users with similar interests. This resulted in a 111% increase in followers and a 3.30% average engagement rate for Promoted Tweets (Anonymous, n.d.2 and Ranadive, 2013).*

- ***Engage Top Tweeters:*** *It is important for (the Big Give) to utilize influential Twitter users in order for the event and cause to gain maximum reach in the community (Tressler, 2013). In order to understand the impact that social media influencers could potentially have on (the Big Give) campaign, it is important to utilize a past model: SXSW4Japan. Leigh Durst, a veteran in digital marketing, organized an event in Austin during SXSW in 2010 that was centered on helping Japan's earthquake victims. She initially worked with key social media influencers to spread the word on ways people could contribute, both off and online. Eventually, several major musicians recorded live-stream music sessions and created an album with proceeds going to the American Red Cross. Pepsi and Samsung also joined in on the cause. The results of using social media influencers to initially spread the word were $125,000 online donations in a short period of time.*

Instagram

According to the student's research the following analytical trends were found for the Instagram social media channel (excerpt from Chambers, Little, Lugo, Melendez, & Vasquez, 2014):

- ***Best Time of Day to Post:*** *According to a study done on TrackMaven (as reported by Lee, 2014), Fortune 500 companies tend to post photos on Instagram most frequently on Thursday. However, in terms of effectiveness, as measured by the number of total interactions per 1,000 followers, Thursdays were no better than any other day of the week for posting, the study found. Fortune 500 companies also tend to overwhelmingly post photos on Instagram during business hours, with posts spiking between 3-4 P.M. EST. However, posts during business hours are only 6% more effective than off hour posts.*
- ***Hashtag Effectiveness:*** *According to the same study conducted by TrackMaven (as reported by Lee, 2014), the number of hashtags used in a post also influences the number of interactions with that particular post. The study found that the "magic number" for hashtags is five. Posts with five hashtags had the highest effectiveness, based on an average of 21.21 interactions per 1,000 followers. Posts with greater than five hashtags started to decline in effectiveness, though they were still more popular than posts with 1-4 hashtags. The report was based on an analysis of the 123 active Instagram accounts of Fortune 500 companies. TrackMaven examined all of the posts by these companies since the launch of Instagram through September 17, 2013.*
- ***Infographics:*** *We will start with some facts of how information is processed by the brain. An entire half of our brain is dedicated to visual function. 65% of the population is visual learners. Visual images are processed 60,000 times faster in the brain than text is. Most people only remember about 20% of what they read. Stanford's Persuasive Technology Lab notes than 4.1% of people say a website's design is the number one criterion for discerning the credibility of the company. Images are processed simultaneously while text is processed sequentially. In just two years infographic search volumes have increased by over 800%. Publishers who use infographics experience growth in traffic at an average of 12% more than those who don't. Visual content drives engagement. In fact, just one month after the introduction of Facebook timeline for brands, visual content saw a 65% increase in engagement, according to a study performed by Simply Measured (Gardner, n.d.).*

- ***Get Followers Involved:*** *A great component of Instagram is the ability to make your followers feel as if they're getting a sneak peak in to your world. Thus, it would be wise to take advantage of this feeling of exclusivity by offering images of special promotions. Instagram can also be used as a way to run contests for followers, which can lead to increased engagement.*

FINDINGS

It was estimated by the organizers that the most significant contributing factor to the greater performance of the campaign than expected: 21,361 gifts made for a grand total of $2,095,606.50 USD raised (approximately 40% greater than was forecasted), was the social media efforts of the students. In fact, it was suggested that the social media analytical work and strategies developed were 'best practices' for non-profits worldwide. The average number of donation raised by the 467 organizations that participated was 45.52 for an overall average of $3,527.09 USD. The range for the number of donations went from a high of 579 (for a non-euthanasia campaign for animals) to a low of one (1) donation (12 different organizations) with a median of 25. Overall, the campaign helped all 467 nonprofit organizations raise at least one (1) donation of $25.00 USD (the minimum given) and with a maximum amount of $41,448.00 USD (given to a faith-based homeless serving ministry) and a median of $1,570.00 USD.

CONCLUSION

In conclusion, it is suggested by the organizers of the event that a strong focus on social media analytics helped the students to develop strategies which led to greater than expected performance in their Big Give fundraising performance. As suggested by Gow (2014) predictive analytics allow for better organizational decisions by utilizing data from past performance (both your own as well as others) and using it to improve future performance of social media campaigns. Stein (2014) reports that 59% of Americans say they donated to a charity after following them on a social network. She offers that this may be "even better than word-of-mouth marketing" and it means that "nonprofits are marketing themselves – and people are responding." Social media marketing allows nonprofits the opportunity to connect with people on a personal level by introducing them to their core mission. However, based on this micro-case study, the actual performance increases may be due to using the analytics (both the data and the meta-data) created by the social media marketing to improve decision making and increase customer fundraising behaviors. In addition, as the professor found, both using class-based client consulting projects and getting the students to focus on the secondary literature available about successful practices helped them move beyond just settling on trying to raise awareness to developing strategies that had empirical and quantitative evidence behind them showing they increased engagement and/or actual giving/buying behaviors.

REFERENCES

Amerland, D. (2014). Social Media Analytics: From Return on Investment to Return on Involvement. *Social Media Today*. Retrieved July 8th 2014 from: http://www.socialmediatoday.com/david-amerland/2510061/social-media-analytics-return-investment-return-involvement-video

Anonymous. (2013). YouTube for non profits 101. *GuideStar*. Retrieved July 6th 2014 from: http://www.guidestar.org/ViewCmsFile.aspx?ContentID=4631

Anonymous. (2014a). Give Local America. *Give Local America*. Retrieved July 8th 2014 from: http://www.givelocalamerica.org/#page-1

Anonymous. (2014b). Google for Nonprofits. *Google*. Retrieved July 6th 2014 from: http://www.google.com/nonprofits/join/

Anonymous. (2014c). Join the campaign to end extreme poverty. *One*. Retrieved July 6th 2014 from: http://www.one.org/us/about/

Anonymous. (n.d.a). The Greatest 24 Hours to Crank Up the Giving. *Amplify Austin*. Retrieved July 6th 2014 from: https://amplifyatx.ilivehereigivehere.org/content/whatsAmplify

Anonymous. (n.d.b). *Twitter for Business*. Retrieved July 6th 2014 from: https://business.twitter.com/products/promoted-tweets

Baer, J. (n.d.). 11 Shocking New Social Media Statistics in America. *Convince and Convert*. Retrieved July 6th 2014 from: http://www.convinceandconvert.com/social-mediaresearch/11-shocking-new-social-media-statistics-in-america/

Buckheit, C. (n.d.). 5 Savvy Nonprofits Using Eye-Catching Online Pledges to Advocate, Educate and Grow Email Lists. *Carol Buckheit RSS*. Retrieved July 8th 2014 from: http://www.carolbuckheit.org/2012/02/29/5-savvy-nonprofits-using-eye-catching-onlinepledges-to-advocate-educate-and-grow-email-lists/

Chambers, D., Little, M., Lugo, E., Melendez, F., & Vasquez, V. (2014). *Instagram*. Final Deliverable for Spring 2014 Semester BMGT 4381 (section 1) Course. Presented May 8th, 2014 (Unpublished).

Folsom, W. (n.d.). Little Giants, Big Money: Lessons in Social Media Fundraising From a Liberal Arts College. *Nonprofit Hub*. Retrieved July 8th 2014 from: http://www.nonprofithub.org/featured/little-giants-big-money-lessons-social-media-fundraising-liberal-arts-college/

Fonseca, D. (2014). *Peer-to-peer fundraising*. Retrieved July 6th 2014 from: http://info.firstgiving.com/blog/?Tag=peer-to-peer%20fundraising

Gardner, O. (n.d.). Why Do Infographics Make Great Marketing Tools? [Infographic] – Unbounce. *Unbounce Latest Posts RSS*. Retrieved July 6th 2014 from: http://unbounce.com/content-marketing/why-do-infographics-make-great-marketing-tools/

Goldberg, E. (2012). How Nonprofits Used Social Media To Increase Giving In 2012 (INFOGRAPHIC). *The Huffington Post*. Retrieved July 7th 2014 from: http://www.huffingtonpost.com/2012/12/18/nonprofits-social-media-2012_n_2325319.html

Gow, G. (2014). Why Are Predictive Marketing Analytics A Problem? *Crimson Marketing*. Retrieved July 6th 2014 from: http://crimsonmarketing.com/predictive-marketing-analytics-problem/

Hibbard, C. (2010). How One Man Used Social Media to Raise $91,000 for Charity. *Social Media Examiner RSS*. Retrieved July 7th 2014 from: http://www.socialmediaexaminer.com/howone-man-used-social-media-to-raise-91000-for-charity/

Jasinsky, D., Bravo, E., Olsen, A., Solano, J., & Rodriguez, K. (2014). *You Tube*. Final Deliverable for Spring 2014 Semester BMGT 4381 (section 1) Course. Presented May 8th, 2014 (Unpublished).

Kapin, A. (2012). *Infographic a peek inside donation trends and why we support charities*. Retrieved July 7th 2014 from: http://www.frogloop.com/care2blog/2012/3/23/infographic-2012-nonprofit-benchmarks. html

Lab, Y. N. (2013). YouTube playbook guide. *YouTube*. Retrieved July 6th 2014 from: http://static.google-usercontent.com/media/www.youtube.com/en/us/yt/advertise/medias/pdfs/playbook-for-good.pdf

Lee, J. (2014). Facebook Posts See More Engagement After Hours, Weekends [Study]. *ClickZ*. Retrieved July 7th 2014 from: http://www.clickz.com/clickz/news/2349587/facebook-posts-see-more-engagement-after-hours-weekends-study

Lopez, V., Martinez, C., Rowell, E., Rodriguez, A., Speakmon, A., & Torres, A. (2014). *Twitter*. Final Deliverable for Spring 2014 Semester BMGT 4381 (section 1) Course. Presented May 8th, 2014 (Unpublished).

Ranadive, A. (2013). Promoted Tweets drive offline sales for CPG brands. *Twitter Blogs*. Retrieved July 6th 2014 from: https://blog.twitter.com/2013/promoted-tweetsdrive-offline-sales-for-cpg-brands

Stein, K. (2014). 7 facts your CEO needs to know about the work you do on social media. *Dog-eared Social*. Retrieved July 8th 2014 from: http://www.kierastein.com/7-facts-your-ceo-needs-to-know-about-the-work-you-do-on-social-media/#sthash.lJew1cYc.dpuf

Tressler, S. (2013). *Ten of San Antonio's Top Tweeters*. Retrieved July 6th 2014 from: http://www.mysan-antonio.com/news/local/article/Ten-of-San-Antonio-s-top-tweeters-4755978.php

KEY TERMS AND DEFINITIONS

Analytics: Analytics is defined as the scientific process of transforming data into insight for making better decisions.

Case Study: A particular instance of something used or analyzed in order to illustrate a thesis or principle.

Fundraising: Fundraising is the process of collecting donations of money or other resources from people or organizations.

Nonprofit Organization: An organization that uses it profits internally and does not distribute it as dividends or profits to investors.

Predictive Analytics: Predictive analytics is the process of extracting patterns from past data in order to predict future outcomes and trends.

Social Media Analytics: Social media analytics is the process of information gathering on the Internet and analyzing the gathered data to make better decisions.

Social Media Marketing: Marketing strategy used to attract attention to product using social media channels like Facebook, Twitter and YouTube.

Chapter 10
The Role of Business Analytics in Performance Management

Kijpokin Kasemsap
Suan Sunandha Rajabhat University, Thailand

ABSTRACT

This chapter introduces the role of Business Analytics (BA) in Performance Management (PM), thus explaining the theoretical and practical concepts of BA, Performance Management Analytics (PMA), and organizational performance; the overview of performance measurement and PM; the application of Performance Management System (PMS) through BA; and the significance of BA in PMA. This chapter also explains the practical areas of BA and their advantages within the foundation of PM. BA can be used to validate causal relationships within traditional input, process, output, and outcome categories toward business success. Extending the domain of PM to PMA requires new business data analysis skills to gain organizational effectiveness. PMA fills the existing gap between PMS and effective PM adoption. Understanding the role of BA in PM will significantly enhance the organizational performance and achieve business goals in the global business environments.

INTRODUCTION

The driving force of BA is to create a win-win situation between business partners through creating valuable trust, strong commitment and improved organizational performance. To gain the business success, it is crucial to continuously monitor and evaluate the individual partners' performances within the business networks. It is quite challenging to know how BA should assess the organizational performance. These business competition requirements challenge PM to effectively support the decision making process. BA is an emerging field that can potentially extend the domain of PM to provide an improved understanding of business dynamics toward better decision making. Many organizations across the globe have been using BA as a competitive differentiator in their operations (Xavier, Srinivasan, & Thamizhvanan, 2011). Organizations have been developing more sophisticated PMS to support decision makers with relevant information. Increased business competition requires more rapid and sophisticated information and data analysis (Schlafke, Silvi, & Moller, 2013). A collaborative business aspires to reach competitiveness, world

DOI: 10.4018/978-1-4666-7272-7.ch010

excellence and business agility within the market segments (Ferreira, Shamsuzzoha, Toscano, & Cunha, 2012). The business networking paradigm implements common strategies and goals, upholds mutual trust, interoperable processes and infrastructures for business practices (Zacharia, Nix, & Lusch, 2009).

In order to manage performance effectively, top executives in organization need to be aware of information processing tendencies and practices within the organization in order to choose a suitable PMS (Sahoo & Jena, 2012). PM is a shared process of the day-to-day management of employees based on their agreement of objectives, knowledge, skills, and competence requirements (Sahoo & Jena, 2012). PM potentially makes the most significant contribution to organizational learning and helps to raise organizational efficiency and promote business growth (Adhikari, 2010). PMS is used to evaluate performance data and identify key success factors (KSFs) within an organization (Schlafke et al., 2013). PMS is commonly used to illustrate an organization's essential means (Garengo, Biazzo, & Bititci, 2005; Broadbent & Laughlin, 2009). PMA is about the data and analytical methods to understand relevant business dynamics, to effectively control key performance drivers, and to actively increase organizational performance (Schlafke et al., 2013). PMA can be a potential success factor of the use of PMS. Conventional PMS focuses on controlling strategy execution, while it is less interested in understanding business dynamics for strategy formulation and decision making (Schlafke et al., 2013). PMA provides a possible explanation for the missing link between highly sophisticated PMS and their effective business implementation. The relationship between the distribution of such PMA systems and organizational success is inconclusive (Micheli & Manzoni, 2010). This chapter introduces the role of BA in PM, thus explaining the theoretical and practical concepts of BA, PMA, and organizational performance; the overview of performance measurement and PM; the application of PMS through BA; and the significance of BA in PMA.

Background

Advanced data analysis, scenario planning, and predictive capabilities are the functions to cope with the complexity, uncertainty, and volatility (Schlafke et al., 2013). These are supported by a continuously grown amount of data which are available for organizations. Organizations have started to focus on analytical approaches to deal with data. PMA can increase the effectiveness of PMS. PMA supports the selective capturing, control, and communication of tangible and/or intangible elements in a causality-based coupling of inputs, processes, outputs, and outcomes. Different BA methods can be used to identify and verify the mentioned causal couplings within PM. These BA-related methods can be qualitative but they can also be adopted with a more analytical level of design. The analytical approach can discover new or hidden business dynamics at a strategic level. Demand forecasting, price setting, customer value prediction, marketing effectiveness evaluation, and supply chain management (SCM) intelligence are the examples of BA. Analytical approaches that support PM are always based on information systems. PMA evolves when different areas of expertise merge are combined with analytical methods.

ROLE OF BUSINESS ANALYTICS IN PERFORMANCE MANAGEMENT

This section introduces the concepts of BA, PMA, and organizational performance; the overview of performance measurement and PM; the application of PMS through BA; and the significance of BA in PMA.

Concept of Business Analytics

The term "business analytics" refers to the extensive use of data, statistical and quantitative analysis, explanatory and predictive models and fact-based management to drive decisions and actions (Davenport & Harris, 2007). Referring to an appendix, "analytics is the field of data analysis. Analytics often involves studying past historical data to research potential trends, to analyze the effects of certain decisions or events, or to evaluate the performance of a given tool or scenario. The goal of analytics is to improve the business by gaining knowledge which can be used to make improvements or changes." BA includes the application of mathematical, statistical, and econometric methods to test and verify proposed causal relationships. BA can work on multiple sources from ''drill-down'' accounting data (i.e., revenue and cost breakdowns) to more sophisticated sources for understanding and exploring performance drivers' dynamics, and can contribute to the success of strategic planning in organization (Klatt, Schlafke, & Moller, 2011). BA should be the first rather than the last step in the decision-making process (Davenport, Harris, & Morison, 2010). In order to effectively use the BA, certain requirements need to be fulfilled first. Effective BA underlies many aspects (i.e., data availability, information technology (IT) infrastructure, and business data analysis skills). An analytical management system's potential is strong in an organization that has an advanced IT infrastructure such as an enterprise resource planning (ERP) system, data warehouse, data mining system, or customer relationship management (CRM) (Schlafke et al., 2013). Referring to an appendix, "business analytics is a process of determining and understanding the effectiveness of various organizational operations. Business analytics can be either focused on internal or external processes. Different specializations exist, encompassing most major aspects of business, including risk analysis, market analysis, and supply chain analysis." If BA is supposed to work properly in both PM and strategic planning, it requires a comprehensive amount of specific data (Klatt et al., 2011).

Many organizations collect much data on their performance in various business areas. This is related to a misunderstanding when organizations assume they can only manage what they are actually able to measure. Measuring performance is not a performance driver that is useful for gaining competitive advantage. The key concern should be to find a way to understand performance data and transform them into usable information that can effectively support management and strategic planning (Mouritsen, 2004). This problem of finding causal structures in performance data is addressed through applying BA, which can improve strategic planning and management efficiency by signaling opportunities and threats, changes in markets and competitors' behavior, internal processes, as well as customer or supply chain profitability drivers. BA helps organizations identify KSFs by uncovering the causal relationships, thus allowing organizations to visualize what effectively drives financial performance now and what will drive it in the future (Klatt et al., 2011).

Concept of Performance Management Analytics

PMA can be used in all functional management areas such as research and development (R&D), human resources, and marketing (Schlafke et al., 2013). PMA uses multiple sources ranging from "drill down" accounting data (i.e., revenue and cost breakdowns) to more sophisticated mathematical, statistical, and econometric methods that can provide insights into the dynamics of performance drivers (Schlafke et al., 2013). A more analytical PM systematically uses BA to identify, use, and prove the quantitative relationships between the inputs, processes, outputs, and outcomes (Schlafke et al., 2013). PM exclusively deals with the deployment of PMA and delivers crucial information to drive decisions and actions within PM (Davenport & Harris, 2007). The role of analytical PM is to effectively support the understanding, exploration, and exploitation of business dynamics and opportunities (Schlafke et al., 2013). However, the gathering of the required data for the effective use of BA can be a problem for an organization (Schlafke et al., 2013).

Some performance drivers are difficult to measure, especially intangible values. Therefore, organizations that generate their business values with intangible values might not have as much data as others and are not in a position to start using BA. BA uses the past data which can be very misleading because such data are not always a good predictor of current and future performance. There are two different maturity levels, namely applications that focus on the identification and use of cause-and-effect relations for performance optimization on a logical level (management accounting applications); and techniques that combine logical reasoning with more complex and sophisticated mathematical, statistical, or econometric models (analytical methods). Effective PMA occurs among the IT-based applications, management accounting applications, and the analytical methods. When used together, data and analysis tools have the potential to provide useful support for decision making. Decisions based on the use of analytical tools are normally better than those made without (Klatt et al., 2011). Therefore, their obvious competitive advantage and their increasing importance within PM make PMA a critical subject for further empirical research.

Concept of Organizational Performance

The success and sustainability of an organization depends on performance of the organization and how their objectives are carried out to its effect (Sahoo & Jena, 2012). Organizations are trying to manage performance of each employee, team and process to ensure that the goals are met in an efficient and effective manner consistently (Sahoo & Jena, 2012). Organizational performance is commonly used as a dependent variable for business research and is considered to be one of the most important constructs in the field of management (Pagell & Gobeli, 2009; Richard, Devinney, Yip, & Johnson, 2009). Measuring and analyzing organizational performance has an important role in turning goals into reality, which in today's competitive environment is paramount to the success and survival of an organization (Popova & Sharpanskykh, 2010). Referring to an appendix, "organizational performance is an analysis of a company's performance as compared to goals and objectives. Within corporate organizations, there are three primary outcomes analyzed: financial performance, market performance and shareholder value performance." Ricardo and Wade (2001) explained that achieving organizational goals and objectives is known as organizational performance. Ricardo and Wade (2001) suggested that organizational success shows high return on equity; and this organizational success become possible regarding the establishment of PMS in organization.

According to Richard et al. (2009), organizational performance encompasses three specific areas of organizational outcomes: (a) financial performance (i.e., profits, return on assets, and return on investment); (b) product market performance (i.e., sales and market share); and (c) shareholder return (i.e., total shareholder return and economic value added). Organizational performance can be measured as an overall outcome of the strategy implemented by the organization for a product or an industry (Neely, 2007). Organizational performance refers to the degree of achievement of the mission at work place that builds up the employees' job (Cascio, 2006). Different researchers have different thoughts about organizational performance. Organizational performance is a continuous process to controversial issue among organizational researchers. Organizational performance does not only mean to define problem but it is also for solution of problem in business (Hefferman & Flood, 2000). Daft (2000) stated that organizational performance is the capability to effectively and efficiently accomplish its goals through using organizational resources.

Competitive advantage and organizational performance results are a consequence of firm-specific resources and capabilities that are costly for competitors to imitate (Rumelt, 1987; Barney, 1991). In the knowledge-based view, analysis of capabilities has incorporated human, social and organizational resources next to economic and technical resources (Theriou & Chatzoglou, 2008). Organizations that possess stocks of organizational knowledge characterized as uncommon or idiosyncratic, stand a good chance of generating and sustaining high returns (Raft & Lord, 2002). Banerjee and Kane (1996) stated that for the measurement of organizational performance, there is a need for integration of financial and non-financial measures. Kaplan and Minton (1994) stated that financial performance measures are important although other performance indicators such as product innovation, product leadership, employee morale, and customer satisfaction can be much better performance indicators for future profitability and organizational performance. Regarding operational performance, the most common measures are unit cost, quality, delivery, flexibility, and speed of new product introduction (Ahmad & Schroeder, 2003).

OVERVIEW OF PERFORMANCE MEASUREMENT AND PERFORMANCE MANAGEMENT

PM is an essential management function to achieve competitive advantage through a process that leads to a number of organizational outcomes. Referring to an appendix, "business performance management is a business management approach which looks at the business as a whole instead of on a division level. Business performance management entails reviewing the overall business performance and determining how the business can better reach its goals. This requires the alignment of strategic and operational objectives and the business' set of activities in order to manage performance." Few researches provide the evidence that regular use of PM system results in the improved outcomes (Hoque & James, 2000; Ahn, 2001). PM is related to a number of things regarding specification of qualitative and quantitative requirements of given tasks and responsibilities, caring behavior at work, preparing people to work hard and making them smarter, increase in job involvement, raising individual and team commitment and engagement, increasing job satisfaction and ensuring quality and quantity of products or services that all lead to a satisfactory level of employees' performance and competitiveness ensuring the growth of an organization in an industry (Adhikari, 2010). To manage and measure the performance of individuals, it is essential to consider behavior, process and outcomes. Performance may be quantitative, qualitative or both. Quantitative performance is related to the use of organizational resources such as budget, number of outputs produced or number of assignments undertaken in a given time. The qualitative performance is measured against operational quality such as accuracy and error. Organizational performance depends on different organizational factors such as personality, leadership, team, and system (Armstrong & Baron, 1998).

Neely, Gregory, and Platts (1995) stated that PM includes three interrelated elements: individual measures that quantify the efficiency and effectiveness of actions; a set of measures that combine to assess the organizational performance as a whole; and a supporting infrastructure that enables data to be acquired, collated, sorted, analyzed, interpreted and disseminated. Referring to an appendix, "performance management is an assessment of an employee, process, equipment or other factor to gauge progress toward predetermined goals." The set of performance measures used to identify the performance are focused on providing a balanced scope of the current business. The performance measurement should reflect global business outcomes in terms of financial and non-financial performance measures, internal and external measures, and efficiency and effectiveness measures (Kaplan & Norton, 1992). PM through financial performance measures has long been used to assess the performance of individual partners in the business networks (Ferreira et al., 2012). Collaborative performance measures enable the decision making that strategically manages the collaborative enterprise itself. The implementation of an information and communication technology (ICT)-based tool supports the fulfilling of the objective to conduct the necessary performance measurement activities within the business networks. The performance measurement and PM need the deployment of an integrated ICT tool across organizational boundaries to enhance information exchange among the business partners in the business networks.

Referring to an appendix, "performance measure is a quantifiable indicator used to assess how well an organization or business is achieving its desired objectives." The ICT tool provides equity, flexibility, reliability, responsiveness and information sharing, which are the prime requirements for an effective and efficient performance measurement precondition. ICT-based infrastructure should reduce the complexity of specifying and obtaining information related to the performance measures in the business networks. The PM framework, different PM indicators and ICT-based supporting tool would be a valuable aid to measure the performance of operational processes. Referring to an appendix, "operational performance management is the alignment of the various business units within a company in order to ensure that the units are helping the company achieve a centralized set of goals. This is done by reviewing and optimizing the operations of the business units."

Regarding collaborative business, the performances are usually measured and evaluated through the collection of data in terms of key performance indicator (KPI), KSF, and key performance factor (KPF) across the organizational borders (Ferreira et al., 2012). KSF can be termed the factor that is identified as the driver of stakeholders' strategy and their success. KSF is the most important success factor for the key stakeholders (La Forme, Genoulaz, & Campagne, 2007). The term KSF is also named key strategic factor (Kenny, 2005). Another performance measurement factor is KPF, which can be defined as the factor that drives the success factor and organizational performance. KPF requires a cause-and-effect analysis, and is considered as an enabler for an organization's successful business operation. As KPF has higher impact on other factors, it requires priority in improvement and monitoring. KPI is a performance measurement factor used by different stakeholders in the business community (Ferreira et al., 2012). KPI is a variable that measures a performance factor quantitatively. KPI is considered as the selected factor that represents the overall organizational performance (Ferreira, Silva, Strauhs, & Soares, 2011). The number of KPIs for assessing an organizational performance depends on the available data structure or the complexity of the performance measurement process.

Organizations require a sustainable PM system to improve organizational effectiveness (Sahoo & Jena, 2012). Before implementing the process of performance measurement, managers and top executives need to follow a specific PM framework where each step of performance measurement is consecutively performed (Ferreira et al., 2012). Before implementation, three factors related to PMS have to be considered (i.e., incentives, costs, and strategic feedback system) as shown in the following (Sahoo & Jena, 2012):

1. **Incentives:** Performance measures can generate inappropriate behavior because of the procedure linked to formal or informal incentive structures. The incentives linked to a certain performance can create pressure to focus on the easily solved problems while ignoring more challenging problems (Bruttel, 2005).
2. **Costs:** The costs associated with performance measurement are often immediate while the benefits of it are realized after a long period of time or sometimes are even uncertain.
3. **Strategic Feedback System:** When the feedback from the PMS is only concentrated on short-term results than on strategy implementation and success, the success of the feedback system becomes doubtful.

A successful PMS ensures that work performed by employees accomplishes the goals and mission of the organization (Sahoo & Jena, 2012). Three PMSs utilized by the manufacturing industries include balanced scorecard (BSC), benchmarking, and terminal operated production program (TOPP) as shown in the following (Sahoo & Jena, 2012):

1. **BSC:** BSC, first developed by Kaplan and Norton (1996), is a tool that tracks the execution of an organizational vision. Referring to an appendix, "BSC is a management practice that attempts to complement drivers of past performance with the drivers of future performance in an organization." BSC is a management system that focuses the efforts of people, throughout the organization, toward achieving strategic objectives (Sharma & Djiaw, 2011). BSC is extensively used for both strategic and operational purposes in business (Sahoo & Jena, 2012). BSC is a measurement framework which has integrated the non-financial performance measures to traditional financial systems which gives the executives a balanced wholesome outlook on organizational performance. Most of the high performing organizations emphasize on business innovation and growth perspectives of BSC (Silk, 1998; Olson & Slater, 2002). Anderson and Lanen (1999) stated that information on customer expectations, customer satisfaction, competitor's performance, internal information, on-time delivery, unit product cost, and product quality are significant for strategy formulation through BSC procedure. There is an increase in use of non-financial performance measures such as on-time delivery, customer satisfaction, and productivity (Joshi, 2001).
2. **Benchmarking:** Benchmarking is one of the most continuous improvement tools for transferring knowledge and innovation into organization, which determines a positive impact on competitiveness of the business and work processes, as well as represents best practices which establishes performance goals. Referring to an appendix, "benchmarking is a measurement of the quality of the organizational policies, products, strategies, and their comparison with standard measurements or similar measurements of its peers." Performance benchmarking as a tool for continuous improvement is more prominently adopted among the developed countries than the developing countries (Jarrar & Zairi, 2001; Yusuff, 2004; Maire, Bronet, & Pillet, 2005). For example, the performance benchmarking in Indian manufacturing sector is a relatively new concept though it has been adopted worldwide as an instrument of continuous improvement. Benchmarking was initially developed by Xerox as a continuous and systematic process of evaluating organizations recognized as industry leaders so as to understand the best practices and establish rational performance goals for itself (Sahoo & Jena, 2012). However, it must be acknowledged that benchmarking initiative does not automatically provide the solutions in organization. The organization needs to find the right performance measures for comparison so as to analyze the performance gap and to realize some innovative solutions (Carpinetti & Melo, 2002; Rohlfer, 2004; Berrach & Cliville, 2007).

3.   **TOPP:** TOPP is a new performance measurement system which was developed by SINTEF (1992), in Norway in partnership with the Norwegian Institute of Technology, the Norwegian Federation of Engineering Industries, and 56 participating enterprises. TOPP is a type of questionnaire that determines the organizational performance in the areas of manufacturing. This questionnaire consists of three parts of which; one part obtains information regarding the organization as a whole, second part determines how the enterprise operates, and finally the third part focusing on 20 specific areas within the enterprise that may need improvement such as marketing, design, technological planning, product development, financial management, and human resource management. TOPP is related to three performance measurement dimensions (i.e., effectiveness: optimal application to satisfy customers' needs; efficiency: suitable utilization of enterprise and economic resources; and ability to change: capability to strategically handle organizational changes) (Sahoo & Jena, 2012).

The target indicators are measured to identify the acceptable level. If the values are not acceptable to the managerial team, they are improved and followed by taking corrective actions. The accepted values are compared with the target values and checked out for differences if there are any. If differences exist between the measured values and the target values, the indicators are revised and the cycle restarts. The measured values are stored for future record if there are no differences between the actual values and target values. In this generic step, managers can keep track of their operational processes in a more professional way. The target-setting performance indicators may be valuable to managers in producing the best performance within the organization. Managers who rely on valid and reliable performance measures may use them in process development and take corrective actions in case of poor performance. Each organization is set up with a specific mission and vision based on its performance indicators.

Before proceeding with any performance measurement activities, the most essential part is to collect the required data (Ferreira et al., 2012). During the data collection period, it is important to define the target value, measurement period, owner of the data, measurement formula, unit of the data and starting time of the collected data. Reviewing the performance measures is essential in order to define the success of any organization. This review result displays the current situation of an organization and reflects its organizational performance within a definite period of time. Periodic performance evaluation guides the organization or a business network to target future performance values. In each reviewing process, the performance values are collected within a pre-specified time, which has a start date and end date. The performances are made transparent with each other within the business network and they provide necessary suggestions or guidelines for future improvements if there are any activities or processes which are underperforming among the collaborative business partners (Ferreira et al., 2012).

Performance factors should provide a concise overview of the collaboration's performance. The performance measures for such networked businesses must be treated with more intensity. PM process encourages organization to update or improve their performance (Trkman, 2010; Le Dain, Calvi, & Cheriti, 2011; Lima, Guerrini, & Carpinetti, 2011). In a collaborative business, PM depends on the performance of the individual partners' knowledge and capabilities (Evans, Roth, & Sturm, 2004; Chiesa, Frattini, Lazzarotti, & Manzini, 2009; Yin, Qin, & Holland, 2011). The nature of PM has been most extensively and effectively investigated as the process of quantifying the efficiency and effectiveness of action. It is obvious from such a definition that performance requires a number of measures to assess and needs an infrastructure to measure and manage (Elbashir, Collier, & Davern, 2008; Glykas, 2011). An implicit concern in the literature on performance measurement is that it includes the development of strategies in order to improve organizational performance based on insights provided by the performance measures (Ittner, Larcker, & Randall, 2003; Li, Huang, & Tsai, 2009).

To measure and manage the performance in the business networks, it is necessary to implement some kind of methodology that can contribute to supporting successful collaboration (Busi & Bititci, 2006). PM models are based on a specific performance concept to build a PM framework that can focus on specific purposes and support the decision makers (Ferreira et al., 2012). PM framework describes the interrelationships of various performance indicators with their corresponding stakeholders. The stakeholders can be the business community, virtual organization, broker, partner, and customer (Ferreira et al., 2012). In any kind of PM framework for business collaboration, the first and most essential feature is to identify the strategy and vision of the business network, which is followed by the execution and output analysis. The second level of the PM framework is execution and monitoring, where the collaborative performance measures are determined for monitoring purposes. At this level, various performance measures are optimized in term of business process execution and business network management vision.

During performance optimization, the reporting is done related to business needs and functionalities. The progress of the performance measures is reviewed to enable the value-added feedback process. In the execution process, corporate and partnership priorities within the business networks are monitored for the purpose of comparing the actual and target values of the performance indices. The final level of the PM framework is to analyze the performance levels or outcomes from the coordinated business networks. In this stage, the key value drivers and metrics of business are evaluated in order to assess the operational excellence in the business networks. Various performance indicators are checked out to compare the target values and the output results. This process is done for the purpose of measuring the balance between the customer expectation and satisfaction level. At this level of the PM framework, the value-added measurements are stored to facilitate the necessary learning process and benchmarking for the purpose of producing operational excellence within the business networks. The complete life cycle of PM framework is related to the performance indices regarding the collected feedback (Ferreira et al., 2012).

Application of Performance Management System through Business Analytics

The need for an efficient and effective PMS has increased over the last decade (de Waal & Counet, 2009). It has been shown that the use of PMS improves the performance and overall quality of an organization (Lawson, Stratton, & Hatch, 2003; de Waal & Coevert, 2007). PMS is needed which is able to pursue all maintenance efforts made by the organization which is synchronized to organizational strategy (Sahoo & Jena, 2012). PMS is used on a daily basis for controlling and managing the organization (deWaal, 2003). The successful implementation of PMS depends on accommodating the human element in management control (Holloway, Lewis, & Mallory, 1995). PMS is a good starting point for a systematic discussion of the potential links to BA (Schlafke et al., 2013). PMA can be seen as a refinement of PMS. The different streams of research provide definitions of the PM characteristics that constitute the PMS (Bourne, Neely, Mills, & Platts, 2003; Berry, Coad, Harris, Otley, & Stringer, 2009; Broadbent & Laughlin, 2009). Strategic PM focuses on the link between organizational strategy and performance measurement systems (Kloot & Martin, 2000; Chenhall, 2005; Kaplan & Norton, 2008). The strategic PMS links the organizational strategy to performance measures, operations, human resources, performance evaluations, IT, customer and supplier networks, and value chain in organization (Chenhall, 2005). The combination of performance-driven behavior and regular use of the PMS leads to the improved results (deWaal, 2003; Bauer, Tanner, & Neely, 2004). Effective utilization of PM system is critical to enhance organizational performance and achieve a competitive position in the global marketplace (Neill & Rose, 2006; Kovacic, 2007; Franceschini, Galetto, Maisano, & Mastrogiacomo, 2010).

The changing business environment engenders difficult challenges in designing and implementing effective PMS in organization for the management. PMS needs to be integrated with the organizational strategies to enable high degree of business success. In addition, several organizational initiatives can be developed in an organization to enhance the employees' performance through PMS perspectives (i.e., top management, involvement and participation, review process, feedback system, and compensation) as shown in the following (Sahoo & Jena, 2012):

1. **Top Management:** There should be clear agreement and commitment among the top management on strategy, goals, measures, and performance targets to be implemented within the organization.
2. **Involvement and Participation:** The involvement of all organizational employees toward achieving the established performance parameters is crucial. Involvement of managers and employees in developing and implementing PMS enhances trust and ownership of the performance measures. Clearly defined measures of performance would enable the managers to select an adequate PMS for their organization.
3. **Review Process:** The managers in organization should be focused on continuous review of the PMS in order to determine whether the actions plans to fill the gaps between performance measures and goals are being achieved or not. The focus of PMS should be on continuous improvement and learning rather than on control.
4. **Feedback System:** A prompt and formal feedback system must be enabled for successful performance measurement. Efficient communication and feedback system would detect any loopholes within the system and would aid the managers in organization to correct it.
5. **Compensation:** A well-defined compensation plan must be introduced for the employees in order to avoid any conflict in organization.

From an organizational perspective, Simons (1995) stated that PMS plays an important role in an organization. PMS must be designed in an instrumental and functional way, and must be communicated to the different user groups (Tucker, Thorne, & Gurd, 2009). Ferreira and Otley (2009) explained a comprehensive PSM framework that outlines the possible key aspects of the PM process (Berry et al., 2009; Ferreira & Otley, 2009; O'Grady, Rouse, & Gunn, 2010). It is essential to test if the combination of structural and behavioral aspects in practice influences the success of implementing and using PMS and organizational performance (de Waal & Counet, 2009). According to Ferreira and Otley (2009), PMS should identify and communicate the vision and mission of an organization, and show how the attention of managers and employees can be focused on that vision and mission; identify the KSFs and illustrate how they can be brought to the attention of managers and employees; illustrate the organizational structure and reveal how this structure affects a design and use of PMS; highlight the organizational strategies and show which PM processes and activities are required for their implementation; illustrate the key performance measures; identify the appropriate performance targets for the key performance measures and show how they should be chosen; identify the already existing performance evaluation processes; set the rewards for target achievement; and illustrate the information flows that can support the PM processes and activities.

Organizations need to ensure that the right data are available, and the quality of data is good before they try to find procedures in order to transform the data into information that can effectively support the management and control of performance, and thereby implement the proposed features of PMS (Ittner & Larcker, 2003; Mouritsen, 2004; Taticchi, Tonelli, & Cagnazzo, 2010). BA helps build such a business connection and effectively provide the business decision makers with additional information. PM framework should capture, elaborate on, and analyze the existing information, while recognizing the important means and ends within an organization (Neely, Adams, & Kennerley, 2002; Garengo et al., 2005; Broadbent & Laughlin, 2009). PM framework should control and manage the achievement of organizational outcomes. In addition, PM framework should show how organizational performance is measured, and display the links between the different performance measurement systems and the tools (Sousa, Carpinetti, Groesbeck, & Van Aken, 2005; Andersen, Henriksen, & Aarseth, 2006). PM identifies the KSFs within an organization. Feedback and feedforward loops from various levels of the organization and the impact of the external environment should be considered in the PM framework (Bititci, Carrie, & McDevitt, 1997).

Significance of Business Analytics in Performance Management Analytics

Many organizations collect a great deal of data on their performance in different business areas (Schlafke et al., 2013). Businesses do not obtain a competitive advantage by measuring their performance. In a competitive market, organizations need to understand business dynamics, value creation, possible opportunities, and potential threats to create competitive advantage (Schlafke et al., 2013). In dynamic business environment along with the increasing heterogeneity in the marketplace, manufacturing organizations, especially small and medium-sized enterprises (SMEs), are challenged for the adaptation of rapid market changes. This rapid change of market exerts extra pressure on the manufacturing organizations to concentrate on their core competencies and search for competitive advantages and innovations (Ferreira et al., 2012).

To sustain such a competitive business environment, organizations have to cooperate with each other with the objective of meeting customers' needs effectively and efficiently (Chituc & Azevedo, 2005). The business cooperation provides the flexibility and mobility for business enterprises to be successful in largely saturated markets (Camarinha-Matos, Afsarmanesh, & Ollus, 2005). The challenge of collaborative business is to identify the factors that affect the evolution of the performance measurement system used by different business partners in organizations (Ferreira et al., 2012). With more demanding customers and highly competitive markets, the need for greater responsiveness among business partners is crucial. Organizations in the business networks are required to implement new performance measures to reflect new business priorities regarding the current market need (Kennerley & Neely, 2003; Popova & Sharpanskykh, 2010; Ferreira et al., 2011). In a collaborative enterprise, customers and suppliers get access to performance information beyond their own organizations and offer access to performance information to the other business partners in organizations within the collaborative business networks (Holmberg, 2000; Ireland & Bruce, 2000; Busi & Bititci, 2006).

BA aims to support managers in understanding and structuring the business dynamics, including the disclosure of the assumed business interactions, for example, between the business and economic shifts (Schlafke et al., 2013). BA creates multiple advantages for managers in organization (Schlafke et al., 2013). BA can be used to test the impact of PM strategy. PMA provides the evidence of potential competitive business dynamics in organization (Schlafke et al., 2013). The increasing relevance of PMA is due to the fast-growing hypercompetitive effect (D'Aveni, 1994). PMA is related to the changes in internal processes, customers, and supply-chain drivers of organizational profitability. PMA creates a basis for the effective application of PMS (Schlafke et al., 2013). PMA delivers crucial information by capturing, combining, and analyzing multiple sources of data (i.e., operational, financial, internal, external, qualitative, and quantitative data). PMA is essential for fact-based decision making within PMS (Schlafke et al., 2013). PMA can be a tool to create a competitive advantage within hypercompetitive environment (Davenport et al., 2010).

Based on proven assumptions and key environmental impact factors, PMA enables the testing of the strategic strength. The desired performance results can be traced back to strategic business development, or whether random changes can provide valuable insights into the future strategic orientation. Analytics can create a basis for improving decisions over time. If managers in organization use logic and explicit supporting data to make a decision, the decision-making process can be followed and made. In addition, analytics can be used to objectify decisions by allowing a more formal reporting in the decision-making process. This competitive advantage does not seem to be fully exploited, since many organizations do not even make use of strategic process reporting. An investment in PMA in order to analyze critical interfaces or operations can contribute to accelerating the execution of tasks and reduce the risk of time-consuming mistakes by identifying previous causes of errors.

The operational efficiency is improved by cutting costs caused by spending unnecessary time on poorly managed tasks (Schlafke et al., 2013). Analytics can help managers learn from business changes in the modern business world. The application of PMA can improve the understanding of markets' and customers' behavior. Using a longer timeframe can reveal critical reactions to these targets due to external changes, legislative amendments, or social trends, which can be used to expect future changes. Although these competitive advantages are undeniable, the design and the use of an analytical PMS require a comprehension of the business model in organization, as well as its performance factors, key success processes, information, data sources, and the formulation of the algorithms that convert data, transactions, and events into management actions. According to PMA, organizations doing pioneering work effectively create a competitive advantage toward business success (Davenport et al., 2010). Despite all the competitive advantages through using BA, the majority of organization does not use BA because of the skills and experiences. The challenges that prevent them from doing so are various. Some managers might not have the skills needed to implement and understand BA. Other managers rely on their experience and have not faced a situation that has convinced them that they should do otherwise to improve the organizational performance.

CONCLUSION

This chapter introduced the role of BA in PM, thus explaining the theoretical and practical concepts of BA, PMA, and organizational performance; the overview of performance measurement and PM; the application of PMS through BA; and the significance of BA in PMA. This chapter also explained the practical areas of BA and their advantages within the foundation of PM. BA can be used to validate causal relationships within traditional input, process, output, and outcome categories. BA can deliver facts about the effects of relationships among different business indicators. Existing data on KPI can be brought into the organization's bigger picture. Using this competitive advantage in business is a complex challenge for implementing PM in organization. The suitable match between the organization and PMS is essential for business success. The function of PMS has a significant positive impact on employees' performance when it is successfully implemented in organization.

This chapter also explained certain issues on implementation of PMS in the manufacturing organizations such as costs, lack of strategic feedback system, and incentive schemes which undermine the efficiency of PMS in organization. Improvisation of PM through BA is an ongoing process, and the organization needs to strive to attain optimal level of business value and to enhance the business potential. Therefore, the process of measuring and managing the manufacturing PMS needs frequent reviewing and monitoring to combat an increasingly globalized business environment. In order to create a basis for the effective PMA application, extending the domain of PM to PMA requires new business data analysis skills toward better organizational effectiveness. PMA fills the existing gap between PMS and the effective PM adoption. Research should focus on the "what, why, how and when" of PMA within PMS (Busco, Quattrone, & Riccaboni, 2007). In addition, an answer is required to the question whether BA can deliver a positive impact on information quality and decision-making effectiveness. On an instrumental level, the combinations and couplings between analytical methods and PM tools should be implemented and utilized in organization. PM education would have to be redesigned and integrated into BA topics. Furthermore, business decision makers require new IT and business analysis skills. Understanding the role of BA in PM will significantly enhance the organizational performance and achieve business goals in the global business environments. Future research directions should broaden the understanding of other BA contexts and should examine the causal model among BA variables in the knowledge-based organizations. In addition, future research should emphasize analytical tools, the relevance of analytical PM, and the organizational integration of utilizing BA in organization.

REFERENCES

Adhikari, D. R. (2010). Human resource development (HRD) for performance management The case of Nepalese organizations. *International Journal of Productivity and Performance Management, 59*(4), 306–324. doi:10.1108/17410401011038883

Ahmad, S., & Schroeder, R. G. (2003). The impact of human resource management practices on operational performance: Recognizing country and industry differences. *Journal of Operations Management, 21*(1), 19–43. doi:10.1016/S0272-6963(02)00056-6

Ahn, H. (2001). Applying the balance scorecard concept: An experience report. *Long Range Planning, 34*(4), 441–461. doi:10.1016/S0024-6301(01)00057-7

Andersen, B., Henriksen, B., & Aarseth, W. (2006). Holistic performance management: An integrated framework. *International Journal of Productivity and Performance Management, 55*(1), 67–78. doi:10.1108/17410400610635507

Anderson, S. W., & Lanen, W. N. (1999). Economic transition, strategy, and the evolution of management accounting practices: The case of India. *Accounting, Organizations and Society, 24*(5-6), 379–412. doi:10.1016/S0361-3682(97)00060-3

Armstrong, M., & Baron, A. (1998). *Performance management handbook*. London, UK: IPM.

Banerjee, J., & Kane, W. (1996). Informing the accountant. *Management Accounting, 74*(9), 30–32.

Barney, J. B. (1991). Firm resources and sustained competitive advantage. *Journal of Management, 17*(1), 99–120. doi:10.1177/014920639101700108

Bauer, J., Tanner, S. J., & Neely, A. (2004). Benchmarking performance measurement: A consortium benchmarking study. In A. Neely, M. Kennerly, & A. Waters (Eds.), *Performance measurement and management: Public and private* (pp. 1021–1028). Cranfield, UK: Centre for Business Performance.

Berrach, L., & Cliville, V. (2007). Towards an aggregation performance measurement system model in a supply chain context. *Computers in Industry, 58*(7), 709–719. doi:10.1016/j.compind.2007.05.012

Berry, A. J., Coad, A. F., Harris, E. P., Otley, D. T., & Stringer, C. (2009). Emerging themes in management control: A review of recent literature. *The British Accounting Review, 41*(1), 2–20. doi:10.1016/j.bar.2008.09.001

Bititci, U. S., Carrie, A. S., & McDevitt, L. (1997). Integrated performance measurement systems: A development guide. *International Journal of Operations & Production Management, 17*(5), 522–534. doi:10.1108/01443579710167230

Bourne, M., Neely, A., Mills, J., & Platts, K. (2003). Implementing performance measurement systems: A literature review. *International Journal of Business Performance Management, 5*(1), 1–24. doi:10.1504/IJBPM.2003.002097

Broadbent, J., & Laughlin, R. (2009). Performance management systems: A conceptual model. *Management Accounting Research, 20*(4), 283–295. doi:10.1016/j.mar.2009.07.004

Bruttel, O. (2005). Are employment zones successful? Evidence from the first four years. *Local Economy, 20*(4), 389–403. doi:10.1080/00207230500286533

Busco, C., Quattrone, P., & Riccaboni, A. (2007). Management accounting issues in interpreting its nature and change. *Management Accounting Research, 18*(2), 125–149. doi:10.1016/j.mar.2007.04.003

Busi, M. M., & Bititci, U. S. (2006). Collaborative performance management: Present gaps and future research. *International Journal of Productivity and Performance Management, 55*(1), 7–25. doi:10.1108/17410400610635471

Camarinha-Matos, L. M., Afsarmanesh, H., & Ollus, M. (2005). Ecolead: A holistic approach to creation and management of dynamic virtual organizations. In L. M. Camarinha-Matos, H. Afsarmanesh, & A. Ortiz (Eds.), *Collaborative networks and their breeding environments* (pp. 3–16). New York, NY: Springer-Verlag. doi:10.1007/0-387-29360-4_1

Carpinetti, L. C. R., & Melo, A. M. D. (2002). What to benchmark? A systematic approach and cases. *Benchmarking: An International Journal, 9*(3), 244–255. doi:10.1108/14635770210429009

Cascio, W. F. (2006). *Managing human resources: Productivity, quality of life, profits*. Burr Ridge, IL: McGraw-Hill/Irwin.

Chenhall, R. (2005). Integrative strategic performance measurement systems, strategic alignment of manufacturing, learning and strategic outcomes: An exploratory study. *Accounting, Organizations and Society, 30*(5), 395–422. doi:10.1016/j.aos.2004.08.001

Chiesa, V., Frattini, F., Lazzarotti, V., & Manzini, R. (2009). Performance measurement of research and development activities. *European Journal of Innovation Management, 12*(1), 25–61. doi:10.1108/14601060910928166

Chituc, C. M., & Azevedo, A. L. (2005). Multi-perspective challenges on collaborative networks business environment. In L. M. Camarinha-Matos, H. Afsarmanesh, & A. Ortiz (Eds.), *Collaborative networks and their breeding environments* (pp. 25–32). New York, NY: Springer-Verlag. doi:10.1007/0-387-29360-4_3

D'Aveni, R. (1994). *Hypercompetition.* New York, NY: Free Press.

Daft, R. L. (2000). *Organization theory and design.* Cincinnati, OH: South-Western College.

Davenport, T., & Harris, J. G. (2007). *Competing on analytics.* Boston, MA: Harvard Business School Press.

Davenport, T. H., Harris, J. G., & Morison, R. (2010). *Analytics at work: Smarter decisions, better results.* Boston, MA: Harvard Business School Press.

de Waal, A. A. (2003). Behavioural factors important for the successful implementation and use of performance management systems. *Management Decision, 41*(8), 688–697. doi:10.1108/00251740310496206

de Waal, A. A., & Coevert, V. (2007). The effect of performance management on the organizational results of a bank. *International Journal of Productivity and Performance Management, 56*(5-6), 397–416. doi:10.1108/17410400710757114

de Waal, A. A., & Counet, H. (2009). Lessons learned from performance management systems implementations. *International Journal of Productivity and Performance Management, 58*(4), 367–390. doi:10.1108/17410400910951026

Elbashir, M. Z., Collier, P. A., & Davern, M. J. (2008). Measuring the effects of business intelligence systems: The relationship between business process and organizational performance. *International Journal of Accounting Information Systems, 9*(3), 135–153. doi:10.1016/j.accinf.2008.03.001

Evans, S., Roth, N., & Sturm, F. (2004). Performance measurement and added value of networks. In L. M. Camarinha-Matos & H. Afsarmanesh (Eds.), *Collaborative networked organizations: A research agenda for emerging business models* (pp. 147–152). New York, NY: Springer-Verlag. doi:10.1007/1-4020-7833-1_18

Ferreira, A., & Otley, D. (2009). The design and use of performance management systems: An extended framework for analysis. *Management Accounting Research, 20*(4), 263–282. doi:10.1016/j.mar.2009.07.003

Ferreira, P. S., Shamsuzzoha, A. H. M., Toscano, C., & Cunha, P. (2012). Framework for performance measurement and management in a collaborative business environment. *International Journal of Productivity and Performance Management, 61*(6), 672–690. doi:10.1108/17410401211249210

Ferreira, R. P., Silva, J. N., Strauhs, F. R., & Soares, A. L. (2011). Performance management in collaborative networks: A methodological proposal. *Journal of Universal Computer Science, 17*(10), 1412–1429.

Franceschini, F., Galetto, M., Maisano, D., & Mastrogiacomo, L. (2010). Clustering of European countries based on ISO 9000 certification diffusion. *International Journal of Quality & Reliability Management, 27*(5), 558–575. doi:10.1108/02656711011043535

Garengo, P., Biazzo, S., & Bititci, U. S. (2005). Performance measurement systems in SMEs: A review for a research agenda. *International Journal of Management Reviews, 7*(1), 25–47. doi:10.1111/j.1468-2370.2005.00105.x

Glykas, M. M. (2011). Effort based performance measurement in business process management. *Knowledge and Process Management, 18*(1), 10–33. doi:10.1002/kpm.364

Heffernan, M. M., & Flood, P. C. (2000). An exploration of the relationship between managerial competencies organizational, characteristic and performance in an Irish organization. *Journal of European Industrial Training, 24*(2), 128–136. doi:10.1108/03090590010321098

Holloway, J., Lewis, J., & Mallory, G. (1995). *Performance measurement and evaluation.* London, UK: Sage.

Holmberg, S. (2000). A system perspective on supply chain measurement. *International Journal of Physical Distribution & Logistics, 30*(10), 847–868. doi:10.1108/09600030010351246

Hoque, Z., & James, W. (2000). Linking balanced scorecard measures to size and market factors: Impact on organizational performance. *Journal of Management Accounting Research, 12*(1), 1–18. doi:10.2308/jmar.2000.12.1.1

Ireland, R., & Bruce, R. (2000). CPFR: Only the beginning of collaboration. *Supply Chain Management Review, 4*(4), 80–89.

Ittner, C. D., & Larcker, D. F. (2003). Coming up short on nonfinancial performance measures. *Harvard Business Review, 81*(11), 88–98. PMID:14619154

Ittner, C. D., Larcker, D. F., & Randall, T. (2003). Performance implications of strategic performance measurement in financial service firms. *Accounting, Organizations and Society, 28*(7-8), 715–741. doi:10.1016/S0361-3682(03)00033-3

Jarrar, Y. F., & Zairi, M. (2001). Future trends in benchmarking for competitive advantage: A global survey. *Total Quality Management, 12*(7-8), 906–912. doi:10.1080/09544120100000014

Joshi, P. L. (2001). The international diffusion of new management accounting practices: The case of India. *Journal of International Accounting, Auditing & Taxation, 10*(1), 85–109. doi:10.1016/S1061-9518(01)00037-4

Kaplan, R. S., & Norton, D. P. (1992). The balanced scorecard – measures that drive performance. *Harvard Business Review, 70*(1), 71–79. PMID:10119714

Kaplan, R. S., & Norton, D. P. (1996). *The balanced scorecard: Translating strategy into action.* Boston, MA: Harvard Business School Press.

Kaplan, R. S., & Norton, D. P. (2004). *Strategy maps: Converting intangible assets into tangible outcomes.* Boston, MA: Harvard Business School Press.

Kaplan, R. S., & Norton, D. P. (2008). Mastering the management system. *Harvard Business Review*, *86*(1), 63–77. PMID:18271319

Kaplan, S. N., & Minton, B. A. (1994). Outside activity in Japanese companies: Determinants and managerial implications. *Journal of Financial Economics*, *36*(2), 225–258. doi:10.1016/0304-405X(94)90025-6

Kennerley, M., & Neely, A. (2003). Measuring performance in a changing business environment. *International Journal of Operations & Production Management*, *23*(2), 213–229. doi:10.1108/01443570310458465

Kenny, G. (2005). *Strategic planning and performance management: Develop and measure a winning strategy.* London, UK: Butterworth-Heinemann/Elsevier.

Klatt, T., Schlafke, M., & Moller, K. (2011). Integrating business analytics into strategic planning for better performance. *The Journal of Business Strategy*, *32*(6), 30–39. doi:10.1108/02756661111180113

Kloot, L., & Martin, J. (2000). Strategic performance management: A balanced approach to performance management issues in local government. *Management Accounting Research*, *11*(2), 231–251. doi:10.1006/mare.2000.0130

Kovacic, A. (2007). Benchmarking the Slovenian competitiveness by system of indicators. *Benchmarking: An International Journal*, *14*(5), 553–574. doi:10.1108/14635770710819254

La Forme, L., Genoulaz, F. A. G., & Campagne, J. P. (2007). A framework to analyze collaborative performance. *Computers in Industry*, *58*(7), 687–697. doi:10.1016/j.compind.2007.05.007

Lawson, R., Stratton, W., & Hatch, T. (2003). The benefits of a scorecard system. *CMA Management*, *77*(4), 24–26.

Le Dain, M. A., Calvi, R., & Cheriti, S. (2011). Measuring supplier performance in collaborative design: Proposition of a framework. *R & D Management*, *41*(1), 61–79. doi:10.1111/j.1467-9310.2010.00630.x

Li, Y. H., Huang, J. W., & Tsai, M. T. (2009). Entrepreneurial orientation and firm performance: The role of knowledge creation process. *Industrial Marketing Management*, *38*(4), 440–449. doi:10.1016/j.indmarman.2008.02.004

Lima, R. H. P., Guerrini, F. M., & Carpinetti, L. C. R. (2011). Performance measurement in collaborative networks: A proposal of performance indicators for the manufacturing industry. *International Journal of Business Excellence*, *4*(1), 61–79. doi:10.1504/IJBEX.2011.037249

Maire, J., Bronet, V., & Pillet, M. (2005). A typology of best practice for a benchmarking process. *Benchmarking: An International Journal*, *12*(1), 45–60. doi:10.1108/14635770510582907

Micheli, P., & Manzoni, J. F. (2010). Strategic performance measurement: Benefits, limitations and paradoxes. *Long Range Planning*, *43*(4), 465–476. doi:10.1016/j.lrp.2009.12.004

Mouritsen, J. (2004). Measuring and intervening: How do we theorize intellectual capital management? *Journal of Intellectual Capital*, *5*(2), 257–267. doi:10.1108/14691930410533687

Neely, A. D. (2007). *Business performance measurement: Unifying theory and integrating practice.* Cambridge, UK: Cambridge University Press. doi:10.1017/CBO9780511488481

Neely, A. D., Adams, C., & Kennerley, M. (2002). *The performance prism: The scorecard for measuring and managing stakeholder relationship.* London, UK: Financial Times Prentice Hall.

Neely, A. D., Gregory, M. J., & Platts, K. W. (1995). Performance measurement system design: A literature review and research agenda. *International Journal of Operations & Production Management, 15*(4), 80–116. doi:10.1108/01443579510083622

Neill, S., & Rose, G. M. (2006). The effect of strategic complexity on marketing strategy and organizational performance. *Journal of Business Research, 59*(1), 1–10. doi:10.1016/j.jbusres.2004.12.001

O'Grady, W., Rouse, P., & Gunn, C. (2010). Synthesizing management control frameworks. *Measuring Business Excellence, 14*(1), 96–108. doi:10.1108/13683041011027481

Olson, E. M., & Slater, S. F. (2002). The balanced scorecard, competitive strategy, and performance. *Business Horizons, 45*(3), 11–16. doi:10.1016/S0007-6813(02)00198-2

Otley, D. T. (1999). Performance management: A framework for management control systems research. *Management Accounting Research, 10*(4), 363–382. doi:10.1006/mare.1999.0115

Pagell, M., & Gobeli, D. (2009). How plant managers' experiences and attitudes toward sustainability relate to operational performance. *Production and Operations Management, 18*(3), 278–299. doi:10.1111/j.1937-5956.2009.01050.x

Popova, V., & Sharpanskykh, A. (2010). Modeling organizational performance indicators. *Information Systems, 35*(4), 505–527. doi:10.1016/j.is.2009.12.001

Raft, A., & Lord, M. (2002). Acquiring new technologies and capabilities: A grounded model of acquisition implementation. *Organization Science, 13*(4), 420–441. doi:10.1287/orsc.13.4.420.2952

Ricardo, R., & Wade, D. (2001). *Corporate performance management: How to build a better organization through measurement driven strategies alignment.* Oxford, UK: Butterworth-Heinemann.

Richard, P. J., Devinney, T. M., Yip, G. S., & Johnson, G. (2009). Measuring organizational performance: Towards methodological best practice. *Journal of Management, 35*(3), 718–804. doi:10.1177/0149206308330560

Rohlfer, S. (2004). Benchmarking concepts in the UK and Germany: A shared understanding among key players? *Benchmarking: An International Journal, 11*(5), 521–539. doi:10.1108/14635770410557735

Rumelt, R. P. (1987). *The competitive challenge.* Cambridge, MA: Ballinger.

Sahoo, C. K., & Jena, S. (2012). Organizational performance management system: Exploring the manufacturing sectors. *Industrial and Commercial Training, 44*(5), 296–302. doi:10.1108/00197851211245059

Schlafke, M., Silvi, R., & Moller, K. (2013). A framework for business analytics in performance management. *International Journal of Productivity and Performance Management, 62*(1), 110–122. doi:10.1108/17410401311285327

Sharma, R. S., & Djiaw, V. (2011). Realising the strategic impact of business intelligence tools. *VINE: The Journal of Information and Knowledge Management Systems, 41*(2), 113–131. doi:10.1108/03055721111134772

Silk, S. (1998). Automating the balanced scorecard. *Management Accounting, 79*(11), 38–44.

Simons, R. (1995). *Levers of control, how managers use innovative control systems to drive strategic renewal.* Boston, MA: Harvard Business Review Press.

SINTEF. (1992). *TOPP: A productivity program for manufacturing industry.* Trondheim, Norway: NTNF/NTH.

Sousa, G. W. L., Carpinetti, L. C. R., Groesbeck, R. L., & Van Aken, E. (2005). Conceptual design of performance measurement and management systems using a structured engineering approach. *International Journal of Productivity and Performance Management, 54*(5-6), 385–399. doi:10.1108/17410400510604548

Taticchi, P., Tonelli, F., & Cagnazzo, L. (2010). Performance measurement and management: A literature review and a research agenda. *Measuring Business Excellence, 14*(1), 4–18. doi:10.1108/13683041011027418

Theriou, G. N., & Chatzoglou, P. D. (2008). Enhancing performance through best HRM practices, organizational learning and knowledge management - A conceptual framework. *European Business Review, 20*(3), 185–207. doi:10.1108/09555340810871400

Trkman, P. (2010). The critical success factors of business process management. *International Journal of Information Management, 30*(2), 125–134. doi:10.1016/j.ijinfomgt.2009.07.003

Tucker, B., Thorne, H., & Gurd, B. (2009). Management control systems and strategy: What's been happening. *Journal of Accounting Literature, 28*(1), 123–163.

Xavier, M. J., Srinivasan, A., & Thamizhvanan, A. (2011). Use of analytics in Indian enterprises: An exploratory study. *Journal of Indian Business Research, 3*(3), 168–179. doi:10.1108/17554191111157038

Yin, Y., Qin, S., & Holland, R. (2011). Development of a design performance measurement matrix for improving collaborative design during a design process. *International Journal of Productivity and Performance Management, 60*(2), 152–184. doi:10.1108/17410401111101485

Yusuff, R. M. (2004). Manufacturing best practices of the electric and electronics firms in Malaysia. *Benchmarking: An International Journal, 11*(4), 361–369. doi:10.1108/14635770410546764

Zacharia, Z. G., Nix, N. W., & Lusch, R. F. (2009). An analysis of supply chain collaborations and their effect on performance outcomes. *Journal of Business Logistics, 30*(2), 101–123. doi:10.1002/j.2158-1592.2009.tb00114.x

KEY TERMS AND DEFINITIONS

Analytics: The field of data analysis. Analytics often involves studying past historical data to research potential trends, to analyze the effects of certain decisions or events, or to evaluate the performance of a given tool or scenario. The goal of analytics is to improve the business by gaining knowledge which can be used to make improvements or changes.

Balanced Scorecard (BSC): Management practice that attempts to complement drivers of past performance with the drivers of future performance in an organization.

Benchmarking: A measurement of the quality of the organizational policies, products, strategies, and their comparison with standard measurements or similar measurements of its peers

Business Analytics: Process of determining and understanding the effectiveness of various organizational operations. Business analytics can be either focused on internal or external processes. Different specializations exist, encompassing most major aspects of business, including risk analysis, market analysis, and supply chain analysis.

Business Performance Management: A business management approach which looks at the business as a whole instead of on a division level. Business performance management entails reviewing the overall business performance and determining how the business can better reach its goals. This requires the alignment of strategic and operational objectives and the business' set of activities in order to manage performance.

Operational Performance Management: The alignment of the various business units within a company in order to ensure that the units are helping the company achieve a centralized set of goals. This is done by reviewing and optimizing the operations of the business units.

Organizational Performance: An analysis of a company's performance as compared to goals and objectives. Within corporate organizations, there are three primary outcomes analyzed: financial performance, market performance and shareholder value performance.

Performance Management: An assessment of an employee, process, equipment, or other factor to gauge progress toward predetermined goals.

Performance Measure: A quantifiable indicator used to assess how well an organization or business is achieving its desired objectives.

Chapter 11
Evaluation of Information Awareness and Understanding through Different Internal Communication Tools

Tanja Sedej
Research and Research, LLC, Slovenia

Damijan Mumel
University of Maribor, Slovenia

ABSTRACT

We are living at a time when change is the only constant in our lives. This is also true for organizations, which have to communicate these changes effectively to their employees. Internal communications are therefore increasingly garnering attention. In this regard, immense efforts should be made to create high levels of awareness and understanding about a new change project. Organizations use a variety of tools to communicate this information effectively. However, employee awareness and understanding can also vary on the choice of internal communications tools. This chapter presents the results of research carried out in Slovenia in 2012, where an experiment was conducted on 165 individuals. The individuals who took part in the experiment were exposed to information distributed through three different tools used in internal communications. Empirical data concerning the views of awareness and understanding of information according to the three internal communications tools are evaluated and presented.

1. INTRODUCTION

More than ever before the need for efficient and effective internal communications is becoming a key benchmark for organizational success all over the world. Organizations face heightened local and global competition, rapid technological development and increasingly demanding customers every day (Sankar, 2010; Teixeira et al., 2012). Truong (2005, p. 56) believes that the ability of organizations to compete and survive in a global environment will depend on their ability to be flexible and to adapt to changing

DOI: 10.4018/978-1-4666-7272-7.ch011

market needs, while Khalil and Mady (2005, p. 39) describes the international economic environment which has experienced drastic changes in last decades as fierce cost wars, slow market growth, decline of productivity and decreasing protectionism. Kini and Basaviah (2013, p. 98) explains that organizations are constantly striving to refine and optimize processes, improve efficiencies and reduce costs. Consequently, they are eagerly looking for solutions as to how to successfully cope and manage these changes, which are occurring with ever growing intensity and frequency in today's dynamic business environment.

The most successful organizations develop and implement internal communication programs that focus on the needs of their employees and the ability of organizations to cope with the changes. Argenti (2007, p. 139) also believes that organizations with effective communication strategy are usually more successful. Today, as change is the only constant in the lives of organizations, rapid development can also be seen in the area of internal communications. New technology is seeping into every aspect of everyday life and internal communications in organizations are no exception.

The crucial role of internal communications–especially during times of introducing change–has not only been noted in academic circles but also in the practice of managers and experts because only well-informed, motivated and committed employees can contribute to a positive realization of the vision and business objectives of any organization. Croft in Cochrane (2005, p. 18) stress that internal communication activities are a priority factor during implementation of change. It is essential to understand that change of behaviour is long-term goal that cannot be achieved overnight.

However, to communicate in an organization successfully, internal communications need to raise high levels of awareness and understanding of the change that is being implemented. But there is also another aspect that has been widely neglected: the right selection of internal communication tools can lead either to great success or total failure. Nonetheless, compared to other research fields, little has been done so far. However, existing research has identified that internal communications that facilitate information awareness and understanding are critical factors for success (Theaker, 2004; Sande, 2009; Merrell, 2012).

One of the main tasks of internal communication professionals is therefore to really understand the potential of internal communication tools in such a way that encourages employees to contribute eagerly to achieving business goals. This research verifies and advances existing literature by including broader knowledge on the potential of internal communication tools at times when change is being introduced. The central goal is to ascertain what kind of impact careful selection of internal communication tools has on levels of awareness and understanding of change by its employees, and which internal communication tools work better in times of change from the three carefully chosen tools.

Above all, the research results on awareness and understanding of information conducted with different tools appears to be indispensable, because in times of rapid change and new technologies an in-depth view and due consideration is certainly required.

2. THEORETICAL BACKGROUND

2.1 The Essential Role of Internal Communications

As mentioned above, there is often a deeply held belief that the function of internal communications is extremely important in an organization. However, in order to confirm this statement, it is first necessary to clarify what we really mean when we talk about internal communications.

The role and scope of internal communications is in fact anything but clearly defined, and a wide range of expressions that indicate internal communications introduce additional confusion into an understanding of the discipline. Kitchen and Daly (2002) even call for a re-definition and intensive discussion on the field of internal communications.

The term "internal communications" is preferred by many academics (Orsini, 2000; Henderson & McAdam, 2003; Dolphin, 2005; Kalla, 2005; Nisar, 2006; Mumel, 2008; McDougall, 2012). However, academic professionals often use other terms such as internal communication (Smidts et al., 2005, Buckingham, 2008; Grimshaw & Barry, 2008; Linke & Zerfass, 2011), communication with employees (Argenti, 1996; Barrett, 2002; Jo & Shim, 2005; O'Neil, 2008), communications with employees (Stein, 2006), employee relations (Grunig & Hunt, 1984; Kalleberg & Rognes, 2000), organizational communication (Kreps, 1990; Luss & Nyce, 2004; Lammers & Barbour, 2006; Cheney & Ashcraft, 2007) organizational communications (Motiwalla & Aiken, 1993), etc.

Nevertheless, the high potential for the rapid development–and very broad nature and scope–of internal communications has led to a number of different definitions, and therefore the inconsistent, even occasional misuse, of the term in practice. Based on the literature review, it can be concluded that numerous and varied definitions of internal communications exist. In view of the facts presented above, the existing definitions of internal communications were selected. Argenti (2007, p. 37) points out that internal communication in the 21st century is more than just simply a method or publication. This is also confirmed by Nisar (2006, 1), who believes that the scope of internal communication can be very broad, ranging from keeping employees informed on a regular basis about how to achieve the business strategy to disseminating information about recent changes, while Orsini (2000, p. 31) justifies this broad area by stating that internal communication can take the written, spoken and virtual forms that occur among individuals and groups.

In essence, internal communications mean the collection, design and transmission of information to employees and monitoring their interpretation in a way that would lead to achieving personal and organizational goals. Kreps (1990, p. 11) concurs and explains that organizational communication is a process in which employees obtain relevant information about the organization and the changes that occur in it, while Justinek and Sedej (2011, p. 230) point out that internal communications must be flexible enough to adapt smoothly to business needs. In the definition and exploration of internal communications, Dolphin (2005, p. 172) relies on the connection with the function of corporate communication, while van Riel (1995, p. 13) defines and describes internal communication as an element of organizational communication. Since the turn of the century, many experts including Argenti (2007) emphasize that the critical importance of internal communications lies in creating a healthy corporate culture, the potential to promote and implement organizational change.

Furthermore, employees today work in a turbulent, ever changing and dynamic environment and this is also the main reason why internal communications are becoming not only more important, but also a more complex, extensive and urgent professional area that needs to be carefully planned and managed. Among others Wenrich and Ahmad (2009, p. 56) stress that communication represent critical issue to combat inevitable resistance to change.

Internal communication is therefore a complex and essential process with which employees get to know, among other things, the business strategy and coordinate the daily tasks that are essential to the functioning of the organization. Kitchen (1997, p. 80) points out that employees can be effective and efficient in their work only if they are well informed and fully understand the objectives of the organization, their place in its hierarchy and their contribution to fulfilling the objectives of the organization. According to Mumel (2008, p. 162), a well-set internal communication system does not focus only on the fluid flow of information and daily working tasks, but also on clarifying the real meaning (purpose) of these tasks. Turner (2003, 8) further explains that communications are becoming increasingly difficult due to the diversified and pluralistic nature of contemporary society organizations and the different modes of organizational function. Consequently, there is no longer a one-size-fits-all communication model that would be successful.

Nevertheless, internal communications are one of the most important businesses challenges, especially in periods when an organization faces major changes. It represents an activity that is carried out constantly, but still too often without careful consideration. Its importance is summed up well by Kitchen (1997, p. 80), who points out that internal communication is a systematic method of communication between employees in an organization. Its main purpose is to build and maintain a healthy and positive relationship among employees, which has a positive impact on the organizational outcome. Therefore, internal communications are too important to be left to unplanned and even random activities. They must be carefully and systematically planned, organized and monitored, and transformed when necessary.

As the world of internal communication rapidly evolves, management is becoming increasingly aware of the importance of the function. More importantly, managers understand the contribution to the greater engagement of employees. Despite the fact that ever more attention is devoted to internal communications, Smidts et al. (2001) believe that internal communication is still a neglected management instrument.

Overall, as established internal communications are not only a way of informing employees, but rather creating and cultivating employee relationships, which are based on trust and cooperation, this leads to highly motivated and committed employees and, as a result, to improved business results.

2.2 Internal Communications during Change Processes

The success of a change process depends on many equally important background factors. One of them is certainly the planning and implementation of internal communications. It can sometimes be difficult to separate the change and internal communications from each other. In practice, these two fields are very closely intertwined in order to deliver a positive outcome to the organization.

Therefore, it is important that management sees employees as having the crucial influence on company performance. This tight link is also explained by Lewis (1999, p. 44), who notes that the communication process and the introduction of organizational changes are inextricably linked. Within this context, Holtz (2004, pp. 165-166) believes that internal communication is of paramount importance, particularly in times of change, while Richardson and Denton (1996, p. 203) add that it represents a difficult task to manage. Nevertheless, Kreps (1996) points out that internal communications enable the company to implement change successfully at an individual as well as organizational level.

Numerous attempts to introduce changes in organizations end in failure and often the failure is a result of reckless internal communications and the resulting lack of acceptance of change by employees. Companies tend to communicate positive messages, but managers often prefer to remain silent when negative changes occur. Nevertheless, communication is a way to avoid uncertainty because employees may resist change if it is carried out inappropriately (Young & Post, 1993, pp. 32-33). Wojtecki and Peters (2000, p. 1) confirm the importance of internal communications, and indicate that the constant changes in today's reality in the workplace cause significant psychological pressure in the workforce, who are understandably concerned about their survival and quality of life. People who work under stress can lose up to 80 percent of their ability to process information appropriately.

In times of stress, the majority of employees have no desire to investigate and search for answers to the many questions they have interest in or concerns about. A rapid and fluid flow of information becomes a crucial and critical area in organizations where changes are faced. The worst choice for a manager to do is to limit communication or remain in the background. Unfortunately, this still happens far too often. It is necessary to realize that silence is a response that encourages speculation that could be prevented or at least mitigated by open communication. Although the great importance of communication in organizations during times of change is widely accepted, there are still many specific areas that have been insufficiently explained.

2.3 Raising Awareness and Understanding through Internal Communication Tools

Despite the great importance of internal communications during times of change, thus far it has been carried out in only a small number of studies that have examined internal communication tools used in a time of change in organizations. Thus, Wojtecki and Peters (2000) investigated the internal communication tools in times of change in a situation where concerns are high and confidence is low. They offer insight into the main reasons why employees require more communication that is not based on tools that require the use of technology at these times. Orsini (2000), among others, discovered that internal communications represent a significant challenge for organizations, especially in times of uncertainty and change. In the organization studied, management tactics such as personal letters, newsletters and monthly communications transmitted to all employees were helpful, but not enough. The feedback received was that it was necessary to do more.

In general, the results of the research carried out on internal communication tools during times of change often point to the importance of sound selection (Young & Post, 1993; Richardson & Denton, 1996; Goodman & Truss, 2004; Merrell, 2012), but we can conclude that this complex area has still been only partly investigated.

Nevertheless, internal communication tools must be chosen carefully, especially during times of change. Chen et al. (2009, p. 32) stresses that information systems must be flexible to satisfy user requirements, particularly in changing environments, while Merrell (2012, p. 20) points out that effective change management must be based on an understanding of the unique needs of the organization and its employees, and consequently applying relevant knowledge to choose the most appropriate tools to cope with change successfully.

The optimal selection of internal communication tools is related to their ability to effectively transfer information to target groups and provide awareness and understanding of change and encourage the employee commitment. Austin and Currie (2003, p. 236) believe that managers should use a variety of the tools available and find innovative ways to establish strong ties with employees, and to provide information as soon as it is known. In this context Smythe (1996, p. 42) points out that the key issue is in choosing the right communication tools to creatively relay stories about new procedures, processes and products, and to embed them into the context of a corporate vision that encourages and motivates employees.

The number of new possibilities to communicate in organization has been rapidly increasing in last two decades (Lengel & Daft, 1998; Lydon, 2005; Richardson & Denton, 1996). There is no doubt that new technologies have been having a great impact on employees: in the main, not by supplanting traditional internal communication tools but instead by creating new ways to interact and build relationships among employees. In this context Arnold and Sohrabi et al. (2012, p. 14) adds that in today's increasingly technological environment organizations need to be kept up to date with novelties in their related field, while Arnold and Sutton (2007, p. 1) also adds that information technology has made information presentation and dissemination much more affordable.

2.4 Achievement of Internal Communication Objectives

The internal communication tools for communicating organizational change can also differ in line with the objectives set. This mirrors Theaker's (2004, p. 180) thoughts as he states that only when the objectives have been set it is possible to choose the appropriate communication methods (tools).

Various authors identify and define the different objectives of internal communications. Sande (2009, p. 29) considers that communication is divided into four levels of receiver outcome. These are: awareness, understanding, commitment and ownership. In order to achieve these different levels, there are four levels of sender activity. These are to inform, interact, engage and enable. Smythe (1996, p. 42) believes that there are two key communication objectives in change management. The first is for employees to achieve an understanding of what will change in the organization and why, and the other is to generate a process where employees can contribute to designing and implementing change with its knowledge.

Based on a review of articles as well as the technical and scientific literature available, we determined three communication objectives which are critical in the selection of internal communication tools: awareness, understanding and commitment.

The first step in achieving the internal communications objectives for introducing change is to create a high level of awareness that it is necessary to introduce such changes. The second step is to make employees understand the changes and, if necessary, the third step follows, which is to generate commitment for their implementation, often with the involvement of employees in the process. It is therefore important to carefully plan and use the optimal combination of internal communication tools in accordance with the objectives set.

When establishing the first objective–awareness–it takes a lot less time, effort and energy to achieve understanding or commitment. Informing employees, which is especially crucial in achieving awareness, is based primarily on the simple transmission of information. Achieving high levels of understanding is usually a more complex task, since it is often necessary to establish a dialogue. Employee commitment, which is particularly vital when organizations implement complex change, represents the biggest challenge. It is therefore necessary to establish a high level of interaction and strong relationships between employees.

In times of change, the aim of each organization should be to achieve the greatest possible degree of awareness and understanding, as well as the commitment of employees regarding the implementation of the change. Many organizations still only follow the first objective presented–merely to achieve awareness by providing information, which is disseminated vertically from senior management down the line with the expectation that employees will uncritically accept the information and incorporate it into the daily activities. It is often only when employee frustration and reduced productivity occurs that a broader range of activities is devoted to internal communications.

3. RESEARCH

3.1 Methods

In order to effectively implement their goals, vision and mission organizations have at their disposal a wide range of internal communications tools to choose from. The challenge does not lie in the use of all possible and available internal communications tools, but in the selection of those, which will facilitate the most effective communication in accordance with the organizational culture. The main hypothesis states that different internal communication tools used during times of change give different result on awareness and understanding of information.

The conducted research reveals that different internal communication tools bring different levels of awareness and understanding of the change concerned. In other words, not all messages are received in a planned way once they have reached employees. This is also the main reason why organizations should give much more thought to the appropriate selection of internal communication tools.

Based on an extensive review of the theoretical framework–the existing literature, articles and research–we have planned and conducted an experiment, in which the main focus was to achieve high levels of change awareness and understanding through a variety of internal communication tools.

First, theoretical information was gathered about how successful internal communications, change management, internal communication tools and setting goals are defined and interrelated. Existing research and analytical reasoning on change process and internal communications were used to construct and design a research framework.

The framework was then tested empirically with the experiment in October 2012 on 165 post-graduate students at the Faculty of Economics and Business. We planned the experiment so that the selected participants were a relatively homogenous group, as they were between 21 and 24 years old and all studying towards obtaining the same level of education in the field of business.

A total of 165 individuals participated in the research experiment, of whom 35 percent received information via a written message, 30 percent in the form of an audio recording and 35 percent by a video clip. The experiment was conducted in the framework of regular activities held in the lecture rooms of the faculty, equipped with all the necessary technical equipment. The experiment was not announced in advance.

3.2 Design of the Experiment

The experiment was very carefully planned in such a way that all the participants took part under the same conditions, with the exception of the changing independent variables. We identified and selected internal communication tools as the independent variables, and determined that awareness and understanding of the information, which was provided to the randomly selected groups, would be the dependent variable (Figure 1). First group received the information via written message, the second group via audio recording and the third group via video clip.

The main planned stages of the experiment were precisely and consciously implemented (Figure 2). We determined three main phases of experiment: transmission of information, verifying information awareness, and understanding and determination of learning types. For this purpose we created and formed a message that was provided to all the individuals via three internal communication tools. After serious consideration, we decided to select a relatively challenging topic on organizational change. The content referred to the change of a two-tier to one-tier corporate governance system.

Figure 1. The design of the experiment

	Group 1	Group 2	Group 3
Independent variable	Written message	Audio recording	Video clip
Dependent variable	Level of information awareness and understanding		

Figure 2. The main phases of the conducted experiment

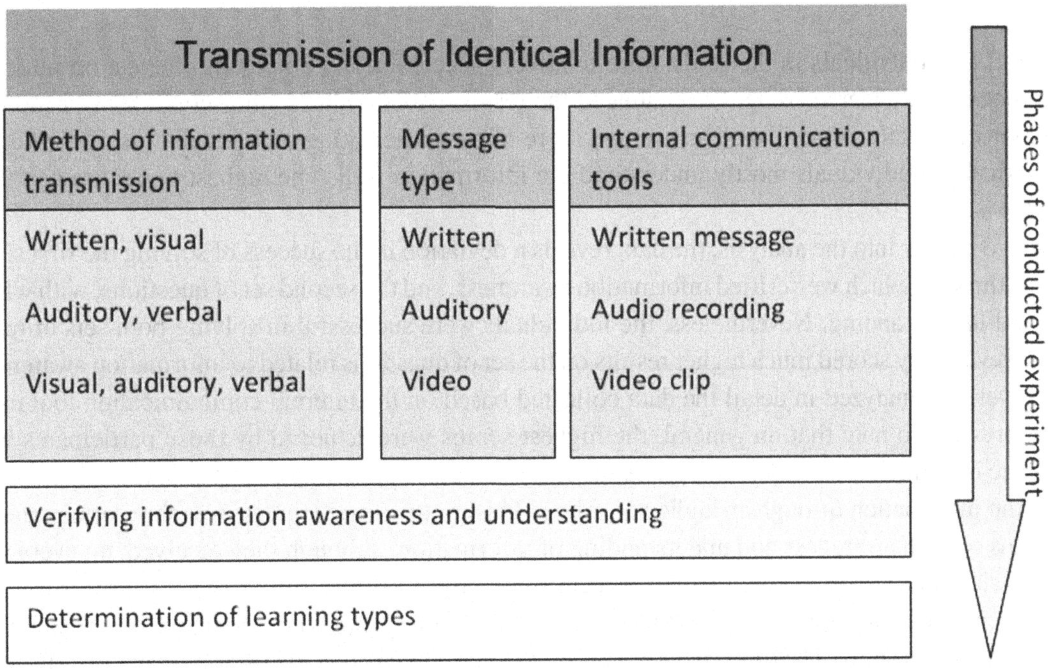

Transmission of Identical Information			
Method of information transmission	**Message type**	**Internal communication tools**	
Written, visual	Written	Written message	
Auditory, verbal	Auditory	Audio recording	
Visual, auditory, verbal	Video	Video clip	
Verifying information awareness and understanding			
Determination of learning types			

Phases of conducted experiment

153

The awareness and understanding of the information sent was verified on the basis of a carefully formed test, which was also identical for all the individuals participating. The test was composed of questions on two different themes. The order of the two sets of questions was mixed. The first set of test questions related to awareness of the information. The main purpose was to check if the individuals were familiar with the information. The second set of test questions related to understanding the information. With this set of questions we examined whether individuals really understood the information presented. In other words, the information was not submitted directly, but was transformed in such a way to encourage the participants to process and rethink the information they had received, and thereby consider the correct answer to the question.

The next step of the research was the second questionnaire on the determination of learning types. With this questionnaire we classified participants as one the three learning types, since we consider that they are closely related to the verification of success of information awareness and understanding, and the introduction of changes in the organization. The three main learning types are visual, auditory and kinesthetic (Brooks, 1996; Greene, 1993; O'Connor & Seymour, 1996). In short, the visual type perceives the world especially in the form of pictures and images, the auditory type is mostly responsive to sounds and voices, and the kinesthetic type is particularly sensitive to things that are associated with a specific sense.

The results of experiment were evaluated and the theoretical assumptions were challenged empirically. The sample in this study shows how crucial the right tool selection is for successful internal communications.

3.3 Results

3.3.1 Information Awareness and Understanding

On average, the individuals in the study were relatively successful in completing the test on information awareness and understanding. We evaluated the results of individuals who scored 50% or more of the questions correctly as positive. The average score of all participating individuals was 59%. We can conclude that the individuals mostly understood the information well. The highest test score was 94% and the lowest was 19%.

As we go deeper into the analysis, the data reveals a deviation in the success of solving the first set of questions, through which we verified information awareness, and the second set of questions, with which we verified understanding. Nevertheless, the individuals were successful in solving both sets of questions. However, they scored much higher results on the set of questions related to information awareness.

Moreover, we analyzed in detail the data collected based on the internal communication tool used. It was interesting to note that, in general, the highest scores were achieved by those participants who received the information via video clip, while the lowest results were achieved by those participants who received the information through an audio recording. This group of participants was the worst performing in terms of both awareness and understanding of information, although they received, on average, a positive evaluation (a score higher than 50 percent).

The order of the participants' performance is almost the same, even when we take a closer look only on information awareness. The most successful were the participants that received information via video clip and written message (Figure 3). The third and last place belongs to those participants to whom the information was transmitted via an audio recording.

Figure 3. Box-plot participant performance on the awareness of information sent via three internal communication tools

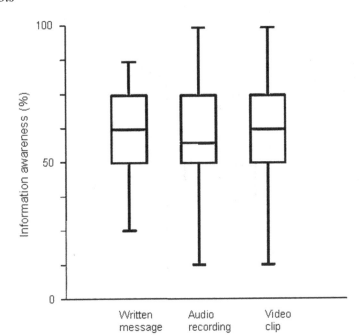

Furthermore, when we analyzed data on the understanding of information (Figure 4). Far in the foreground in terms of performance are those participants who received information via video clip. In second and third place, with an average positive evaluation, are those participants who received information in writing and via audio recording.

Far worse results were achieved by those participants to whom information was transmitted via voice recording. They passed the test on information awareness, but were on average unsuccessful in the test where we verified the understanding of information.

We can clearly establish that the most appropriate internal communication tool for achieving high results in terms of both information awareness and understanding is via video clip. With regard to achieving information awareness, a good substitute for a video clip is also a written message, whereas when it comes to achieving understanding of the information, the results show that an audio recording or a written message are not the preferred modes.

3.3.2 Information Awareness and Understanding Considering Learning Types

The second part of the experiment included the "Learning types" test, with which we verified the learning types (visual, auditory and kinesthetic) that participated in research. The data collected was used for an in-depth analysis. As expected, the research shows the dominance of those with a predominantly visual type with a 51% share, followed by auditory and last by kinesthetic type.

Figure 4. Box-plot participant performance on the understanding of information sent via three internal communication tools

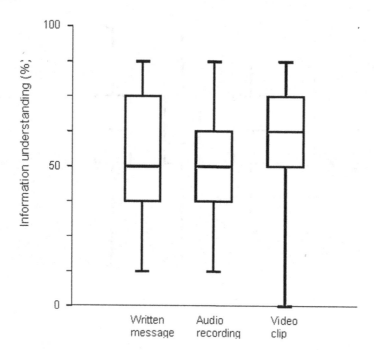

As we go deeper in the analysis, it is interesting to note that the conducted experiment reveals that the most successful participants in completing the whole test were those with a predominantly auditory and visual type. In third place came those participants with a predominantly kinesthetic type.

Interestingly, participants with a predominantly kinesthetic type did not achieve a score of 50 per cent, which means that they were, on average, negatively assessed in completing the test. While the other two groups with a predominantly auditory and visual type were both relatively successful, they both attained a total score of approximately 61 percent.

The performance of participants on information awareness was the highest by those dominated by visual and auditory type (Figure 5). Indeed, far worse results were achieved by participants with a predominantly kinesthetic type.

Furthermore, the participants' performance in understanding information also depended on the learning types (Figure 6). Analysis reveals that the first place was taken by participants with the dominant visual type, other two places with the auditory type and the kinesthetic type.

3.3.3 Information Awareness and Understanding Considering Learning Types and Three Internal Communication Tools

Finally, our focus was on the link between the participants' performance on awareness and understanding of the information, taking into accounts both learning types and different internal communication tools.

Figure 5. Box-plot participant performance on information awareness considering learning types

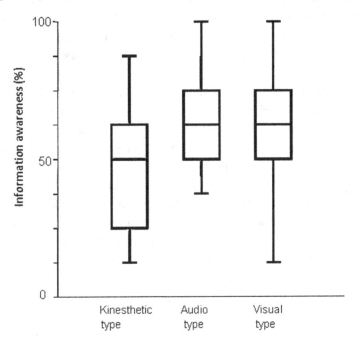

Figure 6. Box-plot participant performance on information understanding considering learning types

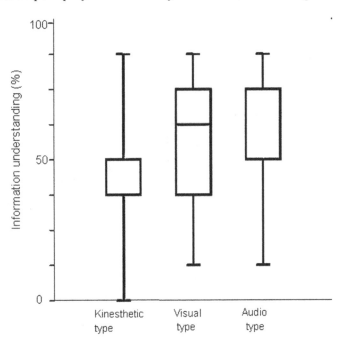

Individuals with a predominantly auditory type, on average, were the most successful in completing the test when they had received information via written message and voice recording, while the individuals with a predominantly visual type were most successful when the information was transmitted via video clip. Individuals with a predominantly kinesthetic type achieved the highest scores, when they received the information via written message.

Firstly, a review of the performance of individuals on the awareness and understanding of information transmitted via written message considering the learning type is presented in Figure 7. Individuals who have received information via written communication and were also ranked with predominantly auditory types were the most successful in terms of information awareness, while in terms of understanding also individuals with a predominantly auditory type were ranked first. The third place once again in terms of information awareness or understanding taken by individuals with kinesthetic type dominance.

The next stage is a more detailed review on the performance of individuals on the awareness and understanding of information transmitted by a voice clip considering learning types (Figure 8). As expected, the most successful individuals on awareness and understanding of information analysed individually were those with a predominantly auditory type, followed by representatives of visual types, and then by kinesthetic types.

Lastly, a more detailed insight into the performance of individuals on awareness and understanding of the information via the video clip, considering the learning types is provided (Figure 9).

Individuals with a predominantly visual type achieved the highest scores not only in overall results, but also on awareness and understanding of information individually. They were closely followed by representatives of the auditory type, and then representatives of the kinesthetic type.

Figure 7. Box-plot participant performance on information awareness and understanding sent via written message considering learning types
Note: A: auditory type, K: kinesthetic type, V: visual type.

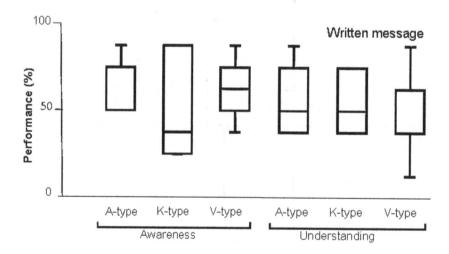

Figure 8. Box-plot participant performance on information awareness and understanding sent via voice clip considering learning types
Note: A: auditory type, K: kinesthetic type, V: visual type.

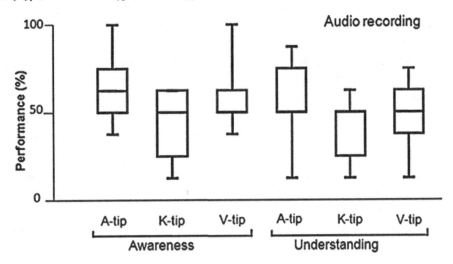

Figure 9. Box-plot participant performance on information awareness and understanding sent via video clip considering learning types
Note: A: auditory type, K: kinesthetic type, V: visual type.

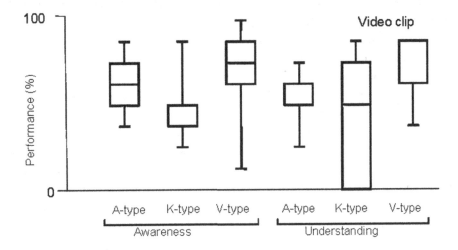

4. DISCUSSION

The high levels of information awareness and understanding represent two of the key factors of success in realizing organizational changes. As a result, if organizations wish to achieve both objectives at the same time–awareness and understanding of the information about the changes–they need to consider internal communication tools more accurately and systematically.

Before deciding on which internal communication tool to select, managers need to clarify which goals they will follow. In order to be successful at achieving awareness and understanding of organizational change by its employees, more resources, time and energy are needed than if only goal awareness requires realization. If achieving awareness is enough, less attention is needed. If extensive understanding is required, more complex consideration is necessary.

As we have established, a video clip was the most appropriate tool to achieve the awareness and understanding of information when compared to a written message and audio recording. The highest achieved results were therefore noted for information provided in visual–auditory–verbal mode. Second place was taken by written communication. The third and last place belongs to audio recording–the mode through which participants achieved the lowest results in overall results as on awareness and understanding separately.

In order to achieve the highest level of information awareness, the results showed that the best way is video clip, but that a good substitute for this was also a written message. In order to achieve the highest levels of understanding of information, the best method was also video clip, with second place still belonging to the written message. Nevertheless, it is also clear that the results are much worse regarding the understanding of information transmitted by written message compared to the results for information awareness, but still much better than the transmission of information using an audio recording.

Regardless of the medium used, the most successful individuals on test were in general those with the auditory type dominance. Moreover, we cannot overlook the fact that they were only slightly more effective than the visual types, who were also very successful in the overall result of the awareness and understanding of information. The research also shows that individuals with a predominantly kinesthetic type were the least successful in completing the questionnaire.

Only when we analyzed the results on information awareness and understanding separately were we able to see the whole picture. In order to achieve the highest level of information awareness, regardless of the mode of transmission, the most successful individuals were interestingly those with a predominantly auditory and visual type, while in achieving information understanding the most successful individuals were those with a predominantly visual type.

The lowest overall scores on questionnaire, irrespective of the medium–both in terms of information awareness and understanding–were achieved by individuals with kinesthetic type dominance. We can conclude beyond doubt that the internal communication tools selected were unsuitable for this type of individual. Although these selected tools are commonly used in business, especially written messages and video clips, it would be more accurate to consider how to integrate other internal communications tools that also facilitate all the other senses in order to also ensure effective communication with kinesthetic types.

Individuals with a predominantly auditory type generally achieved the highest scores on questionnaire when they received the information by a written message (visual–written) or an audio recording (auditory–verbal).

Individuals with a predominantly visual type were generally the most successful on solving questionnaire of information awareness and understanding when they received information by a video clip (visual - auditory–verbal). Photos, images and presentations are an important element of communication with visual types. Consequently, the best mode of information transmission in order to be successfully adopted by visual types is the one that contains the visual - auditory - verbal mode.

Individuals with a predominantly kinesthetic type were, on average, the most effective when they received information via written message. In order to achieve improved results, it is important to include the other senses. The results of the experiment evidently show that information transmitted with the three internal communication tools selected was poorly accepted by kinesthetic types.

5. CONCLUSION

Today's employees are constantly faced with information overload and the huge impact of ever-changing technology, which should also take its rightful place in internal communications. This means that internal communications need to become a more deliberate and accountable function, similar to all the other functions in the organization.

Consequently, the central question of the research conducted was as follows: Does an awareness and understanding of information about change vary if different internal communication tools are used? As demonstrated by the research results, we can confirm the hypothesis as it can be concluded that different tools are appropriate for different goals (awareness and understanding). Therefore, internal communication must not neglect consideration of the internal communication goals that drive the overall goals of the organization.

As for the research, the various strengths and weaknesses of internal communication tools were apparently revealed. The results hint at further opportunities and risks if the selection of internal communication tools does not form part of overall internal communication considerations. As is evident, the three tools that were verified in the experiment show different abilities to generate awareness and understanding of information.

In conclusion, the research contributes to a better understanding of the issue in a practical sense and also represents a progress in theory, since so many traditional and modern potential internal communication tools are available for communicating effectively in the workplace.

Nonetheless, the findings cannot be used without limitation. Only three of many possible internal communication tools were selected and evaluated in the research. The selection of different tools could be extended and altered in further research undertaken. Furthermore, this research included only individuals located in one country. Consequently, it would be interesting to see if the research results differ between countries and cultures.

ACKNOWLEDGMENT

The authors would like to thank the anonymous reviewers and the editor for their insightful comments and suggestions.

REFERENCES

Argenti, P. A. (1996). Corporate communication as a discipline–Toward a Definition. *Management Communication Quarterly, 10*(1), 73–97. doi:10.1177/0893318996010001005

Argenti, P. A. (2007). *Corporate communication*. New York: McGraw-Hill.

Arnold, V., & Sutton, S. G. (2007). The Impact of Enterprise Systems on Business and Audit Practice and the Implications for University Accounting Education. *International Journal of Enterprise Information Systems, 3*(4), 1–21. doi:10.4018/jeis.2007100101

Austin, J., & Currie, B. (2003). Changing organisations for a knowledge economy: The theory and practice of change management. *Journal of Facilities Management, 3*(2), 229–243. doi:10.1108/14725960410808221

Barrett, D. J. (2002). Change communication: Using strategic employee communication to facilitate major change. *Corporate Communications, 7*(4), 219–231. doi:10.1108/13563280210449804

Brooks, M. (1996). *Zbližanje in ujemanje*. Kranj: Ganeš.

Buckingham, I. (2008). Communicating in a recession: Employee must engage with the brand during tough times. *Strategic Communication Management, 12*(3), 7.

Chen, R. S., Sun, C. M., Helms, M. M., & Jih, W. J. (2009). Factors Influencing Information System Flexibility: An Interpretive Flexibility Perspective. *International Journal of Enterprise Information Systems, 5*(1), 32–43. doi:10.4018/jcis.2009010103

Cheney, G., & Ashcraft, K. L. (2007). Considering "The Professional" in Communication Studies: Implications for Theory and Research Within and Beyond the Boundaries of Organizational Communication. *Communication Theory, 17*(2), 146–175. doi:10.1111/j.1468-2885.2007.00290.x

Croft, L., & Cochrane, N. (2005). Communicating change effectively. *Management Services, 49*(1), 18.

Dolphin, R. R. (2005). Internal Communications: Today's Strategic Imperative. *Journal of Marketing Communications, 11*(3), 171–190. doi:10.1080/1352726042000315414

Greene, R. H. (1993). *Nov način komunikacije: Praktični nasveti za boljše poslovno in družinsko sporazumevanje*. Ljubljana: Alpha Center.

Grimshaw, J., & Barry, M. (2008). How mature is your internal communication: Empowering the function to demonstrate its strategic value to the organization. *Strategic Communication Management, 12*(3), 28–29.

Grunig, J. E., & Hunt, T. (1984). *Managing Public Relations*. New York: Harcourt Brace Jovanovich College Publishers.

Henderson, J., & McAdam, R. (2003). Adopting a learning-based approach to improve internal communications: A large utility experience. *International Journal of Quality & Reliability Management, 20*(6/7), 774–794. doi:10.1108/02656710310491212

Holtz, S. (2004). *Corporate conversations: a guide to crafting effective and appropriate internal communications*. New York: AMACOM.

Jo, S., & Shim, S. W. (2005). Paradigm shift of employee communication: The effect of management communication on trusting relationships. *Public Relations Review*, *31*(5), 277–280. doi:10.1016/j.pubrev.2005.02.012

Justinek, G., & Sedej, T. (2011). Knowledge sharing as a part of internal communication within internationalized companies. In *Knowledge as business opportunity: Proceedings of the Management, Knowledge and Learning International Conference 2011*. Celje: International School for Social and Business Studies.

Kalla, H. (2005). Integrated internal communications: A multidisciplinary perspective. *Corporate communication. International Journal (Toronto, Ont.)*, *10*(4), 302–314.

Kalleberg, A. L., & Rognes, J. (2000). Employment Relations in Norway: Some Dimensions and Correlates. *Journal of Organizational Behavior*, *21*(3), 315–335. doi:10.1002/(SICI)1099-1379(200005)21:3<315::AID-JOB23>3.0.CO;2-1

Khalil, O. E. M., & Mady, T. (2005). IT Adoption and Industry Type: Some Evidence from Kuwaiti Manufacturing Companies. *International Journal of Enterprise Information Systems*, *1*(4), 39–55. doi:10.4018/jeis.2005100103

Kini, R. B., & Basaviah, S. (2013). Critical Success Factors in the Implementation of Enterprise Resource Planning Systems in Small and Midsize Businesses: Microsoft Navision Implementation. *International Journal of Enterprise Information Systems*, *9*(1), 97–117. doi:10.4018/jeis.2013010106

Kitchen, J. P. (1997). *Public relationship: Principles and Practice*. London: International Thomson Business Press.

Kitchen, J. P., & Daly, F. (2002). Internal communication during the change management. *Corporate communications. International Journal (Toronto, Ont.)*, *7*(1), 46–53.

Kreps, G. L. (1990). *Organizational Communication: Theory and Practice* (2nd ed.). New York: Longman.

Lammers, J. C., & Barbour, J. B. (2006). An Institutional Theory of Organizational Communication. *Communication Theory*, *16*(3), 356–377. doi:10.1111/j.1468-2885.2006.00274.x

Lengel, R., & Daft, R. L. (1988). The selection of communication media as an executive skill. *The Academy of Management Executive*, *11*(3), 225–232. doi:10.5465/AME.1988.4277259

Lewis, L. K. (1999). Disseminating information and soliciting input during planned organizational change: Implementers' targets, sources and channels for communicating. *Management Communication Quarterly*, *13*(1), 43–75. doi:10.1177/0893318999131002

Linke, A., & Zerfass, A. (2011). Internal communication and innovation culture: Developing a change framework. *Journal of Communication Management*, *15*(4), 332–348. doi:10.1108/13632541111183361

Luss, R., & Nyce, S. A. (2004). *Connecting Organizational Communication to Financial Performance: The Methodology Behind the 2003/2004 Communication ROI Study*. Retrieved April 30, 2007, from http://www.watsonwyatt.com/research/reports.asp

Lydon, S. (2006). *Common Sense in a Changing world: Ipsos MORI Employee Relationship Management*. Retrieved may 15, 2011, from http://www.ipsos-mori.com/_assets/erm/common-sense-in-a-changing-world.pdf

McDougall, M. (2012). Prioritizing internal communications. *Canadian HR Reporter*, 25(14), 22.

Merrell, P. (2012). Effective Change Management: The Simple Truth. *Management Services*, 56(2), 20–23.

Motiwalla, L., & Aiken, M. (1993). An organizational communications perspective on knowledge-based mail systems. *Information & Management*, 25(5), 265–272. doi:10.1016/0378-7206(93)90075-5

Mumel, D. (2008). *Komuniciranje v poslovnem okolju*. Maribor: De Vesta.

Nisar, T. (2006). *Organising electronic-based channels of internal communications*. Southampton, UK: University of Southampton, Information and Management.

O'Connor J., & Seymour, J. (1996). *Spretnosti sporazumevanja in vplivanja*. Žalec: Sledi.

O'Neil, J. (2008). Measuring the Impact of Employee Communication on Employee Comprehension and Action: A Case Study of a Major International Firm. *The Public Relations Journal*, 2(2), 1–17.

Orsini, B. (2000). Improving internal communications. *Internal Auditor*, 57(6), 28–33.

Richardson, P., & Denton, K. (1996). Communicating change. *Human Resource Management*, 35(2), 203–216. doi:10.1002/(SICI)1099-050X(199622)35:2<203::AID-HRM4>3.0.CO;2-1

Riel van, C. (2005). Principles of Corporate Communication. Harlow, MA: Prentice-Hall.

Sande, T. (2009). Taking charge of change with confidence. *Strategic Communication Management*, 13(1), 28–31.

Sankar, C. S. (2010). Factors that improve ERP implementation strategies in an organization. *International Journal of Enterprise Information Systems*, 6(2), 15–34. doi:10.4018/jeis.2010040102

Smidts, A., Pruyn, A. T. H., & Van Riel, C. B. M. (2001). The impact of employee communication and perceived external prestige on organizational identification. *Academy of Management Journal*, 44(5), 1051–1062. doi:10.2307/3069448

Smythe, J. (1996). The changing role of internal communication in tomorrow's company. *Managing Service Quality*, 6(2), 41–44. doi:10.1108/09604529610109756

Stein, A. (2006). Employee communications and community: An exploratory study. *Journal of Public Relations Research*, 18(3), 249–264. doi:10.1207/s1532754xjprr1803_3

Teixeira, P., Brandão, P. L., & Rocha, A. (2012). Promoting Success in the Introduction of Health Information Systems. *International Journal of Enterprise Information Systems*, 8(1), 17–27. doi:10.4018/jeis.2012010102

Theaker, A. (2004). *Priročnik za odnose z javnostmi*. Ljubljana: GV Založba.

Truong, D. (2005). Methodologies for Evaluating Investment in Electronic Data Interchange. *International Journal of Enterprise Information Systems*, 1(3), 56–68. doi:10.4018/jeis.2005070104

Turner, P. (2003). *Organisational communication: The role of HR professional*. London: CIPD.

Wenrich, K. I., & Ahmad, N. (2009). Lessons Learned During a Decade of ERP Experience: A Case Study. *International Journal of Enterprise Information Systems*, 5(1), 55–75. doi:10.4018/jeis.2009010105

Wojtecki, J. G., & Peters R. G. (2000). Communicating organizational change: information technology meets the carbon-based employee unit. *The 2000 Annual, 2,* 1-16.

Young, M., & Post, J. E. (1993). Managing to communicate, communicating to manage: How leading companies communicate with employees. *Organizational Dynamics, 22*(1), 31–43. doi:10.1016/0090-2616(93)90080-K

KEY TERMS AND DEFINITIONS

Change Management: Change management is a process, approach or method that increases the likelihood that employees will successfully manage through a change process.

Information Awareness: Achieving awareness is based primarily on informing employees through simple forms of information transmission within organizations.

Information Understanding: Achieving information understanding is usually a complex task, since it is often necessary to establish a dialogue among employees within organizations.

Internal Communication Objectives: Setting internal communication objectives provides a clear focus, how to communicate with employees for achieving overall organizational results.

Internal Communication Tools: Through internal communication tools with informing, creating dialogue, and relationships among employees communication objectives can be achieved.

Internal Communications: Internal communications represent a function responsible for effective communications among employees within organizations.

Organisational Change: Organization change is an organizational transition from its current state to a desired future state.

Organizational Information Transmission: Organizational information transmission is an act or process of transmitting information within organizations.

Chapter 12
Empirical Investigation on the Evolution of BI Maturity in Malaysian Organizations

In Lih Ong
Universiti Tunku Abdul Rahman, Malaysia

Pei Hwa Siew
Universiti Tunku Abdul Rahman, Malaysia

ABSTRACT

Many organizations have recognized the importance of increasing commitment towards delivering long-term success of Business Intelligence (BI). However, effective BI strategies and governance to accommodate the rapid growth of data volumes are still scarce. Furthermore, there appears to be low usage rates of BI and analytics among business users. Consequently, many organizations are still positioned at either low or moderate levels in the BI maturity chart. In view of these issues, this chapter explores and develops a multi-dimensional BI maturity model that serves as a guideline to lift the BI capabilities of an organization for effectively planning, assessing, and managing BI initiatives. The focus of this research is to assess the current BI maturity level in Malaysian organizations and identify factors that affect the BI maturity. It also examines the effect of organization's demographic variables (i.e., types of industry, organizational size, and age of BI initiatives) on the BI maturity.

INTRODUCTION

In today's rapidly changing business environment, maintaining a competitive advantage and moving toward a higher level of maturity are recognized as essential for an organization to maximize business value from business intelligence (BI) investments. However, such movement is constrained by the availability of resources in their organizations. A survey of 392 BI professionals conducted in 2008 reported that only 28 percent of respondents described their BI implementation as being in advanced stages (TDWI, 2008). According to another 2010 survey of 308 individuals (involving executives, management, and users), many organizations are still at the lower levels of a maturity chart in their use of BI due to poor usage of advanced BI capabilities (Wailgum, 2010).

DOI: 10.4018/978-1-4666-7272-7.ch012

Despite an increased interest in BI, it is surprising that little empirical study has actually been conducted on BI maturity assessment through the extensive studies on BI maturity, especially in Malaysian context. The review of extant literature also shows that there is a lack of academic research in providing systematic guidelines for this evolutionary transformation path. Thus, this research gives emphasis to the development and examination of a BI maturity model with the goal of eventually using the model to guide organizations in their effort to move toward a higher maturity level in their BI initiatives. It synthesizes different viewpoints of BI into a comprehensive model that takes into account critical dimensions, commonly mentioned in the literature. It also aims to study the effect of demographic variables (in terms of types of industry, organizational size, and age of BI initiatives) on BI maturity in an organization.

BUSINESS INTELLIGENCE

From a historical standpoint, the underlying concept of BI is not new one. It has existed over the last 50 years in the area of information systems (IS). According to Wixom et al. (2011), the origins of BI can be traced back to the early 1970s when decision support systems (DSS) were first introduced. Over the years, numerous applications such as executive information systems (EIS), online analytical processing (OLAP), data mining, predictive analytics, and dashboards have emerged and added to the domain of decision support applications (Watson and Wixom, 2007).

The term "business intelligence" was first used by Hans Peter Luhn in 1958 in an IBM journal article. However, BI became widely recognized in the 1990s only after it was used by Howard Dresner, a research analyst of Gartner Group in 1989 (Shollo and Kautz, 2010). According to Power (2002), Howard Dresner explained BI as "a set of concepts and methods to improve business decision making by using fact-based support systems" (p. 128).

Even though there has been a growing interest in BI area, there is no commonly accepted definition of BI. The literature shows that the definition of BI has evolved from a one-dimensional view to a multi-dimensional view (Vitt et al., 2010). Drawing upon extant literature, it was found that the scope and definition of BI have been extended to include the idea that it is product, not just a process. As noted in the study of Jourdan et al. (2008), BI is viewed as both a process and a product. Petrini and Pozzebon (2009) provided a similar distinction of perspectives to BI in terms of technical and managerial perspectives. Shariat and Hightower (2007) characterized BI as a composition of process, technology, and product. Based on the definitions from various sources, four main focus of BI were identified for this research, namely organizational management, process, technology, and outcome as summarized in Table 1.

PROPOSED BI MATURITY MODEL

The review of the extant literature on BI maturity models reveals that capability maturity model (CMM) and TDWI's BI maturity model are considered as the most suitable reference model for BI implementation. It is evident that CMM was being widely accepted and used to shape various maturity studies in IS research (Sen et al., 2006; Russell et al., 2010). TDWI's BI maturity model can be applied to organizations in different industries and it outlines the path that majority of organizations undertake when evolving their BI infrastructure. However, CMM does not take into account the issues in determining the success of BI systems implementation among their quality goals.

Table 1. Four main focus areas of BI

BI Focus	Description
Organizational management	The focus of BI is related to how an organization is structured to support the business processes and ensure long term success of BI implementation, such as having clear vision statement, strong support from management and obtaining sponsorship to secure the necessary funding.
Process	BI can be viewed as a process which integrates, analyzes and transforms data collected from internal and external sources into information so that users at all levels are able to support decision making process and take actions.
Technology	BI can be described as the usage of architectures, tools, applications, and technologies in facilitating various BI processes such as collecting, storing, analysing, and providing access to data to enable users make effective decisions in support of organizational perspective.
Outcome	BI is considered as the product or result of performing BI-related processes such as analyzing business data (e.g., information, knowledge, insights) which are useful to organizations for their business activities and decision making.

In view of this, a BI maturity model is proposed to address BI issues and provide a systematic method for organizations to achieve improvement based on the concept of CMM and TDWI's BI maturity model. This so-called MOBI (Malaysian Organizations' Business Intelligence) maturity model was built on a five-point scale (i.e. Initial, Repeatable, Defined, Managed, and Optimizing) which corresponds to the five maturity levels of BI. This model addressed some of the weaknesses of existing BI maturity models (e.g. Sen et al., 2006; Davenport and Harris, 2007; Sacu and Spruit, 2010) such as the lack of empirical data for validation and focus on one or two specific areas.

As can be perceived through Figure 1, the MOBI maturity model incorporates all the components that are critical to test different aspects of an organization's BI capabilities but are missing from all the BI maturity models reviewed in this research. By combining these components, it will show the overall BI maturity level of an organization. All the BI related components were then grouped into four dimensions: organizational management, process, technology, and outcome.

RESEARCH METHODOLOGY

This research focuses on the development and evaluation of a multi-dimensional BI maturity model encompassing relevant dimensions and associated components for assessing the BI maturity level in Malaysian organizations. The structured questionnaire survey approach was used to evaluate the proposed BI maturity model and validate the research objectives. The survey questionnaire contains two sections: Section A and B. Section A of the questionnaire sought information about the background data of participants and organizations. In Section B, an item was constructed for each component within the four dimensions (i.e., organizational management- 11 items, process- 5 items, technology- 6 items, and outcome- 3 items), with the total of 25 items. A five-point scale which corresponds to the five levels of maturity was used where scale 1 indicates the lowest level (i.e., Initial) and scale 5 indicates the highest level (i.e., Optimizing). The respondents were instructed to give a rating to each of the components within the four dimensions shown in Table 2, based on their understanding and perspectives.

A preliminary investigation was conducted to validate the content and reliability of the survey instrument before the empirical study was undertaken. The adoption of content validation approach in this

Figure 1. MOBI maturity model

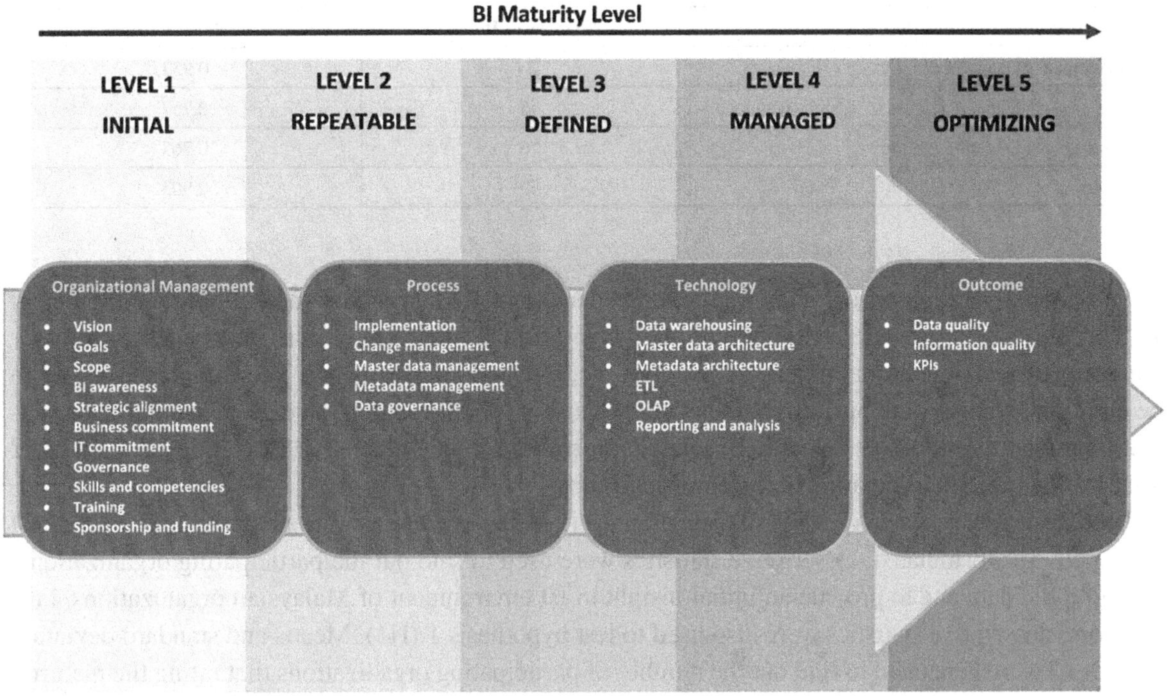

Table 2. Four dimensions with the subcomponents in each dimension

Dimension	Components
Organizational management	Vision, Goals, Scope, BI Awareness, Strategic Alignment, Business Commitment, IT Commitment, Governance, Skills and Competencies, Training, Sponsorship and Funding
Process	Implementation, Change Management, Master Data Management, Metadata Management, Data Governance
Technology	Data Warehousing, Master Data Architecture, Metadata Architecture, ETL, OLAP, Reporting and Analysis
Outcome	Data Quality, Information Quality, KPIs

research ensures that the instrument is comprehensive enough to measure the concepts being studied. Five experts in the BI area were engaged to assess logical consistencies and validate conciseness of each question in the questionnaire. The comments collected from these experts led to several minor modifications of the wording, length, and item sequence in the questionnaire to reflect their feedback.

Meantime, a reliability test was carried out using Cronbach's alpha, which measures the internal consistency of the survey questionnaire, which consists of 25 items measuring the components built into each dimension. The questionnaire has demonstrated a high level of internal reliability among items in which the Cronbach's alpha values coefficient of the four dimensions ranging from 0.757 to 0.937 as shown in Table 3. Since the Cronbach's alpha values for all the four dimensions exceeded the minimum acceptance level of 0.70 as recommended by Hair et al. (2010), it can be inferred that the questionnaire was well constructed and reliable.

Table 3. Cronbach's alpha of the survey instrument

Dimension	Number of Items	Cronbach's Alpha
Organizational management	11	0.937
Process	5	0.757
Technology	6	0.765
Outcome	3	0.903

Subsequently, the empirical study was conducted in selected Malaysian organizations that implement BI. The questionnaires were distributed through email or hand-delivered to the members of top senior management and operational managers from BI- or IT-related departments. The samples involved in the empirical studies were purposively selected because it is believed that the experience of the participants is imperative to obtain valuable BI related information in the selected organizations. A total of 52 organizations were participating in the empirical study.

Both descriptive and inferential statistical analysis methods were used to analyse the data and test the hypotheses formulated. Descriptive statistics were used to find out the participating organizations' demographic data and to provide an initial insight to BI environment of Malaysian organizations. Furthermore, descriptive statistics were also used to test hypothesis 1 (H1). Means and standard deviation (Std. Dev.) were generated to find out the number of participating organizations that rating the maturity level for each component that built into the four dimensions of BI such as organizational management, process, technology and outcome. Then, an average of the rating scores in each dimension was used to determine the current BI maturity level in Malaysian organizations. Besides, inferential statistics such as independent-samples t-test and one-way ANOVA test were used to test hypotheses 2 (H2), 3 (H3), and 4 (H4). Independent-samples t-test and one-way ANOVA (analysis of variance) test were also used to test the effect of demographic variables on BI maturity.

RESULTS OF DATA ANALYSIS

This section briefly describes and discusses our results. It includes data regarding BI maturity level in Malaysian organizations and results of hypothesis tests. The respondents were asked about their opinions on the factors that would likely affect BI maturity level of their organizations. Figure 2 shows that most of the respondents (88 percent) believed that data quality will affect their organizations' BI maturity level. This was followed by business commitment (75 percent), skills and competencies (71 percent), IT commitment (56 percent), technologies and tools (54 percent), and training (52 percent).

Additionally, 48 percent of respondents indicated that vision, strategy, and goals will also influence BI maturity. Meanwhile, 33 percent of respondents considered change management process as one of the factors and 23 percent of respondents stated sponsorship and funding is also another factor that affects BI maturity. There were 12 percent of respondents added a few other factors such as data governance, organization culture, expertise availability, data integration, data ownership, information quality, user adaptability, and data usage to support business.

Figure 2. Factors that would likely affect BI maturity level in the participating organizations

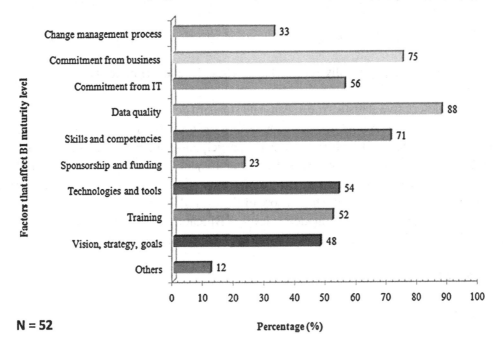

The findings show that the participating organizations' BI maturity tends to be influenced through the combination of various key factors. These influencing factors were denoted as some components and then mapped into four dimensions to compose BI maturity model as illustrated in Figure 1.

Table 4 reveals an overview of average mean scores that 52 participating organizations attained for each dimension. Overall, technology and outcome dimensions had achieved the highest BI maturity with average mean score of 3.25 respectively. Whereas, the process dimension had attained the lowest BI maturity with average mean score of 3.00.

The findings suggest that the participating organizations have put much emphasis on their BI tools and architectures, as well as BI quality in terms of data, information, and KPIs. Furthermore, it seemed that the participating organizations did not provide a strong platform for governance and training at various levels to support BI workflows and business processes. These findings highlight that there was not only one dimension that affects the level of BI maturity in an organization. Rather, several dimensions usually come together to contribute to BI maturity level.

Table 4. Average mean scores of each dimension that built into MOBI maturity model

Dimension	Mean	Std. Dev.
Organizational management	3.13	0.75
Process	3.00	0.66
Technology	3.25	0.67
Outcome	3.25	0.67
Overall BI Maturity	**3.16**	**0.57**

The Results of H1 Testing

The following hypothesis was tested:

H1: Malaysian organizations generally achieved a moderate level of BI maturity.

To test H1, the descriptive statistics (i.e. means and standard deviation) seem to be the most appropriate method for analysis. The average response for each of the dimensions is around the midpoint (3) of the five-point scale (see Table 4). This means that the participating organizations show a moderate level of maturity for the four dimensions to assess the BI maturity in their organizations. Then, the overall BI maturity score was calculated based on the average mean scores attained for the four dimensions. As can be seen in Table 4, the average mean score of the overall BI maturity is 3.16. This reflects that the Malaysian organizations are still at moderate level of BI maturity and have not fully obtained all the potential benefits from their BI investments. Therefore, H1 has been substantiated.

The Results of H2 Testing

The following hypothesis was tested:

H2: The type of industry has significant effect on the BI maturity.

An independent-samples t-test was used to test H2 to examine whether the service and non-service industries have significant effects on the BI maturity. The p value was found to be significant ($t = 2.051$, $p = 0.046$) (see Tables 5 and 6). The data provide enough evidence to reject the null hypothesis ($p < 0.05$). Therefore, there was strong evidence to support H2 that the types of industry had significant effects on the BI maturity.

The results of the comparative analysis of each component that built into the four dimensions (i.e., organizational management, process, technology, and outcome) to measure the BI maturity based on types of industry (i.e. service and non-services industries) are further discussed in the following subsections. Past studies (e.g., Olbrich et al., 2012; Raber et al., 2013) claimed that the environment of an organization could affect the evolution of BI maturity. The study of Shanks et al. (2012) also highlighted that service industries are very information-intensive, requiring more scrutinizing and reporting functionalities to address explorative and routine problems than non-service industries.

Table 5. Descriptive statistics for BI maturity level and types of industry

BI Maturity Level			
Types of Industry	**N**	**Mean**	**Std. Dev.**
Service	32	3.28	0.57
Non-service	20	2.96	0.53

Table 6. T-test results for BI maturity level and types of industry

BI Maturity Level	Levene's Test for Equality of Variance		T-Test for Equality of Means		
	F	Sig.	t	df	Sig. (2-Tailed)
Equal variances assumed	0.349	0.555	2.051	50	0.046*
Equal variances not assumed			2.085	42.603	0.043

* $p < 0.05$.

Organizational Management Dimension by Types of Industry

Table 7 shows the comparison between service and non-service organizations based on the 11 components of the organizational management dimension. As depicted in Table 7, the results show that the organizational management from service industries achieved higher mean score for all components than the non-service industries. BI is often associated with service industries, especially financial and healthcare industries. Specifically, service organizations focus on the information flow and interaction between people (e.g., customers) to deliver quality service. Thus, service organizations are more likely to have a stronger organizational focus especially on sponsorship and funding component with mean score of 3.72, followed by vision, goals, and IT commitment components with mean score of 3.56 respectively.

Furthermore, since service organizations are labour- and knowledge-intensive, the skills and competencies of service employees are higher than non-service organizations. In term of training component, both industries have a similar maturity level (i.e., level 2), which could be affected by the business and IT strategies formulated in their organizations.

On the other hand, non-service organizations scored lower maturity level (i.e., level 2) for strategic alignment, governance, and business commitment components compared to service organizations. This could be probably due to non-service organizations focus largely on internal operations instead of service processes and view BI as an IT-driven initiative.

Table 7. Descriptive analysis for organizational management dimension and types of industry

Component	Types of Industry			
	Service		Non-Service	
	Mean	Std. Dev.	Mean	Std. Dev.
Vision	3.56	0.88	3.10	0.79
Goals	3.56	0.84	3.15	0.81
Scope	3.09	1.00	3.05	1.05
BI awareness	3.31	0.90	3.05	1.00
Strategic alignment	3.09	1.17	2.75	0.91
Skill and competencies	3.22	0.75	2.85	0.59
Business commitment	3.28	1.02	2.70	0.73
IT commitment	3.56	1.11	3.00	0.86
Governance	3.00	1.16	2.55	0.89
Training	2.63	0.79	2.50	0.69
Sponsorship and funding	3.72	1.40	3.15	1.63

Process Dimension by Types of Industry

Table 8 depicts the comparison between service and non-service organizations based on the five components of the process dimension. The results reveal that organizations from the service industries achieved higher mean score for almost all components than the organizations from non-service industries, except for master data management component.

In particular, non-service organizations have recorded a lower maturity level (i.e., level 2) for implementation and data governance components. This may be related to the low degree of business commitment for coordination, product diversification, and highly complex supply chains making the non-service organizations (e.g., manufacturing and retail industries) difficult to evolve to a higher level.

In term of change management component, service organizations scored slightly higher although both industries have a lower maturity level (i.e., level 2). This implies that service organizations are putting more efforts in handling changes since the business processes in service environment are normally cross-organizational boundaries. Additionally, both industries have a similar maturity level (i.e., level 3) for metadata management component. This signifies that the organizations have not centrally documented policies and standards regarding the creation and maintenance of metadata, which contributes to the moderate level of metadata management.

For master data management component, service organizations fall within level 2 (mean = 2.91) although it is very close to non-service organizations which are situated at level 3 (mean = 3.10). This indicates that master data management is higher importance to non-service organizations. Possible reason could be due to the larger need in the maintenance and optimization of the substantial data volumes about products and raw materials in non-service organizations, especially for manufacturing and semiconductors industries. In contrast, service organizations deal with services and other intangible goods that cannot be depicted easily as concrete data, compared to physical goods.

Technology Dimension by Types of Industry

Table 9 reveals the comparison between service and non-service organizations based on the six components of the technology dimension. From Table 9, the results show that organizations from service industries achieved higher mean score for all the components than the organizations from non-service industries, except master data architecture component. Specifically, service organizations scored at level

Table 8. Descriptive analysis for process dimension and types of industry

Component	Types of Industry			
	Service		Non-Service	
	Mean	Std. Dev.	Mean	Std. Dev.
Implementation	3.22	1.04	2.75	0.55
Change management	2.94	1.11	2.50	0.76
Master data management	2.91	1.06	3.10	0.91
Metadata management	3.03	1.23	3.00	1.21
Data governance	3.44	1.08	2.85	0.81

Table 9. Descriptive analysis for technology dimension and types of industry

Component	Types of Industry			
	Service		Non-Service	
	Mean	Std. Dev.	Mean	Std. Dev.
Data warehousing	3.53	0.80	3.35	0.75
Master data architecture	2.97	1.23	3.05	0.89
Metadata architecture	2.91	1.15	2.75	0.72
ETL	3.91	0.73	3.10	0.85
OLAP	3.53	0.92	3.10	0.97
Reporting and analysis	3.28	1.02	3.20	0.83

3 with mean score of 3.05 while non-service scored at level 2 with mean score of 2.97. This difference could be explained by the unique requirements and complexity of decision making on non-service environment which places an emphasis on the master data quality in facilitating the exchange of information between applications.

Of the four components (i.e., data warehousing, ETL, OLAP, and reporting and analysis), both industries attained a similar maturity level (i.e., level 3). In terms of ETL and OLAP components, the mean scores of service industries are fairly higher than non-service industries. This result could be due to service organizations place greater demand for more advanced functionalities to support customer-related activities in real time basis.

Besides, there is only a slight difference in mean score between service (mean = 3.53) and non-services (mean = 3.35) industries for data warehousing component. This could be due to some service organizations are moving towards real time data warehousing with the implementation of BI services in business transaction workflow. As a result, this puts service industries higher on data warehousing component than non-services industries. With regard to reporting and analysis component, the mean scores for both service and non-service industries are about the same (3.28 and 3.20 respectively). Apart from that, both industries were positioned in the same maturity level (i.e., level 2) for metadata architecture component with mean score of 2.91 and 2.75 respectively. This highlights that there is a lack of business support and commitment within non-service environment.

Outcome Dimension by Types of Industry

Table 10 shows the comparison between service and non-service organizations based on the three components of the outcome dimension. The results show that organizations from service industries achieved higher mean scores for all components compared to the organizations from non-service industries. With regard to data quality and information quality components, both industries fall within same maturity level (i.e., level 3). Unlike data within non-service environment that can only be used for single products, data and information within service environment can be produced and consumed by end users simultaneously. This explains why service industries place more efforts on improving quality of data and information.

In term of KPIs component, service organizations scored higher maturity level (i.e., level 3) with mean score of 3.50 than non-service organization with mean score of 2.90. This could be attributed to the higher degree of integration and improvement in cross-functional service processes that are customer-

Table 10. Descriptive analysis for outcome dimension and types of industry

Component	Types of Industry			
	Service		Non-Service	
	Mean	Std. Dev.	Mean	Std. Dev.
Data quality	3.22	0.71	3.00	0.65
Information quality	3.47	0.80	3.15	0.75
KPIs	3.50	0.72	2.90	1.02

oriented. For instance, service organizations in banking industries focus more on KPIs such as service time and waiting time. Unlike non-service industries, it appears that their KPIs are still function-oriented such as product quality and inventory balances.

The Results of H3 Testing

The following hypothesis was tested:

H3: The organizational size has a significant effect on the BI maturity.

The One-Way ANOVA test was used to test H3 to analyze whether or not the organizational size has a significant effect on BI maturity. The p value was large ($p = 0.740$) indicating that the null hypothesis could not be rejected ($p > 0.05$) (see Tables 11 and 12). Hence, there was not enough evidence to support H3. This indicates that the organizational size had no significant effect on BI maturity.

Table 11. Descriptive statistics for BI maturity level and organizational size

BI Maturity Level			
Organizational Size	N	Mean	Std. Dev.
Small (1 – 1000)	16	3.16	0.48
Medium (1001 – 5000)	19	3.23	0.57
Large (> 5000)	17	3.08	0.66

Table 12. ANOVA results for BI maturity level and organizational size

ANOVA Table		Sum of Squares	df	Mean Square	F	Sig.
BIMat * OrgSize	Between Groups	0.201	2	0.100	0.303	0.740
	Within Groups	16.242	49	0.331		

The research findings differ from previous studies (e.g., Elbashir et al., 2008; Raber et al., 2013; Ramamurthy et al., 2008) which indicated that organizational size has an impact on BI initiative. In general, the larger the organization, the more mature the organization is. However, the results show that the mean score of three size groups are relatively close to each other (see Table 12). This reflects that even though small- and medium-sized organizations do not involve in big scale of operations as large-sized organization, they leverage same advantages from the best practice processes and technology improvements that were developed specifically for larger organizations. As a result, small- and medium-sized organizations are able to gain equivalent benefits and have a higher BI maturity level similar to larger organizations.

Nonetheless, the result was supported by the study of Levy and Powell (2004) which stated that "small- and medium-sized enterprises (SMEs) have as much need for BI as large firms" (p. 24). The study of Guarda et al. (2013) also reported that most of today's SMEs experience similar BI challenges as large organizations. Hence, the size of an organization does not matter especially in the advancement of technology aspect.

Furthermore, the comparative analysis of each component that built into the four dimensions (i.e., organizational management, process, technology, and outcome) to measure the BI maturity based on organizational size (i.e. small-, medium- and large-sized organizations) was conducted which revealed more findings.

Organizational Management Dimension by Organizational Size

Table 13 depicts the comparison of each component in the organizational management dimension based on organizational size. With regard to business commitment component, medium-sized organization scored slightly lower maturity score (mean = 2.95) compared to small- (mean = 3.12) and large-sized (mean = 3.13) organizations (see Table 12). This implies that medium-sized organizations are shifting towards business-driven BI initiatives. In term of governance component, small-sized organizations

Table 13. Descriptive analysis for organizational management dimension and organizational size

Component	Organizational Size					
	Small		Medium		Large	
	Mean	Std. Dev.	Mean	Std. Dev.	Mean	Std. Dev.
Vision	3.31	1.01	3.37	0.90	3.47	0.72
Goals	3.31	1.20	3.47	0.61	3.41	0.71
Scope	3.06	1.12	3.11	0.99	3.06	0.97
BI awareness	3.31	1.08	3.16	0.90	3.18	0.88
Strategic alignment	2.94	1.24	2.84	1.17	3.12	0.86
Skill and competencies	3.13	0.62	3.11	0.66	3.00	0.87
Business commitment	3.13	1.09	2.95	0.97	3.12	0.86
IT commitment	3.69	1.20	3.37	0.96	3.00	0.94
Governance	3.00	1.10	2.95	0.97	2.53	1.18
Training	2.56	0.63	2.68	0.89	2.47	0.72
Sponsorship and funding	3.06	1.61	4.05	1.27	3.29	1.53

scored slightly higher maturity score (mean = 3.00) than medium- (mean = 2.95) and large-sized (mean = 2.53) organizations. This implies that they still lack of necessary authority on BI-related decisions.

Apart from that, medium-sized organizations scored higher maturity score (mean = 4.05) than small- (mean = 3.06) and medium-sized (mean = 3.29) organizations for the sponsorship and funding component. This was probably due to medium-sized organizations recognizing the importance of obtaining high level of sponsorship and funding to increase end user adoption and greater access to resources. Meantime, this was an evident that medium-sized organizations scored higher mean score for the scope component (mean = 3.11) than small- and large-sized organizations with the mean score of 3.06 respectively.

Process Dimension by Organizational Size

Table 14 illustrates the comparison of each component in process dimension based on organizational size. The results showed that three groups of organizations have a similar maturity level for change management (i.e., level 2) and data governance (i.e., level 3) components.

With regard to implementation component, the results reveal that large-sized organizations scored higher mean score (mean = 3.12), followed by medium- (mean = 3.05) and small-sized (mean = 2.94) organizations. One of the possible reasons for this result is the implementation strategy chosen by the organizations. Specifically, large- and medium-sized organizations tend to use phased approach. Although many small-sized organizations favoured phased approach but there is a few of organizations applied big-bang approach.

In term of master data management and metadata management components, small- and medium-sized organizations have slightly higher mean scores than large-sized organizations. This could be due to bigger organizations have a larger amount of master data and metadata as well as more complex business processes to be handled.

Technology Dimension by Organizational Size

Table 15 reveals the comparison of each component in the technology dimension based on organizational size. Out of six components in technology dimension, the results show that three groups of organizations have a similar maturity level for five components. Except for master data architecture component, medium-sized organizations have a higher maturity level (i.e., level 3) than small- and large-sized organizations (i.e., level 2). This could be related to the low degree of cross-functional collaboration and absence of enterprise-level architectural planning.

Table 14. Descriptive analysis for process dimension and organizational size

Component	Organizational Size					
	Small		Medium		Large	
	Mean	Std. Dev.	Mean	Std. Dev.	Mean	Std. Dev.
Implementation	2.94	0.85	3.05	0.78	3.12	1.11
Change management	2.75	1.13	2.79	0.79	2.76	1.15
Master data management	3.13	0.96	2.95	1.13	2.88	0.93
Metadata management	3.06	1.00	3.11	1.33	2.88	1.32
Data governance	3.13	0.96	3.47	0.84	3.00	1.23

Table 15. Descriptive analysis for technology dimension and organizational size

Component	Organizational Size					
	Small		Medium		Large	
	Mean	Std. Dev.	Mean	Std. Dev.	Mean	Std. Dev.
Data warehousing	3.25	0.86	3.58	0.77	3.53	0.72
Master data architecture	2.88	0.72	3.21	1.36	2.88	1.11
Metadata architecture	2.75	0.93	2.84	1.02	2.94	1.09
ETL	3.63	0.81	3.63	1.01	3.53	0.80
OLAP	3.00	1.10	3.63	0.90	3.41	0.80
Reporting and analysis	3.25	0.68	3.32	1.00	3.18	1.13

With regard to data warehousing component, small-sized organizations have a mean score of 3.25 that is close to medium- and large-sized organizations with mean scores above 3.50. This highlights that even small-sized organizations are now using data warehouses to meet rapidly growing business demands and maintain a competitive advantage over their competitors.

There is a gradient in maturity of metadata architecture component among the three groups of organizations (i.e., small-sized with mean score of 2.75, medium-sized with mean score of 2.84, and large-sized with mean score of 2.94). This indicates that the organizations primarily focused on technical and operational metadata without recognizing the significance of business metadata.

In term of ETL component, large-sized organizations have a slightly lower mean score of 3.53 compared to small- and medium-sized organizations with similar mean score of 3.63. This reflects the widespread adoption of standard ETL tools for managing data validation and migration.

Apart from that, small-sized organizations have a lower mean score of 3.00 for the OLAP component than medium- and large-sized organizations with mean scores above 3.40. This difference indicates that larger organizations show a greater interest implementation of integrated OLAP to automate cube maintenance tasks.

As for the reporting and analysis component, small- and medium-sized organizations achieved a slightly higher mean score of 3.25 and 3.32 respectively, compared to large-sized organizations with mean score of 3.18. This highlights many small- and medium-sized organizations are now evolving towards advanced reporting and analysis capabilities.

Outcome Dimension by Organizational Size

Table 16 illustrates the comparison of each component in the outcome dimension based on organizational size. The results show that three groups of organizations have a similar maturity level (i.e., level 3) for all the components.

With regard to data quality and information quality components, large-sized organizations scored lower mean scores compared to small- and medium-sized organizations. This could be attributed to the lack of standardization and integration strategies to handle large amounts of data and information across applications and databases.

Table 16. Descriptive analysis for outcome dimension and organizational size

Component	Organizational Size					
	Small		Medium		Large	
	Mean	Std. Dev.	Mean	Std. Dev.	Mean	Std. Dev.
Data quality	3.19	0.66	3.21	0.71	3.00	0.71
Information quality	3.56	0.73	3.42	0.77	3.06	0.83
KPIs	3.44	0.63	3.21	1.13	3.18	0.81

Furthermore, there is a gradient in maturity of KPIs component among the three groups of organizations (i.e., large-sized with mean score of 3.18, followed by medium-sized with mean score of 3.21, and small-sized with mean score of 3.44). Possible reason could be that smaller organizations with narrow business focus have lesser KPIs, whereas larger organizations have multiple departments making it difficult to share and integrate diversified KPIs which in turn leading to lower maturity.

The Results of H4 Testing

The following hypothesis was tested:

H4: The age of BI initiatives has a significant effect on the BI maturity.

The One-Way ANOVA test was also used to test H4 to examine whether or not the different ages of BI initiative have significant effects on BI maturity. From the following statistics and ANOVA results (see Tables 17 and 18), the p value was rather large ($p = 0.155$) indicating that the null hypothesis could not be rejected ($p > 0.05$). Thus, there was not enough evidence to support H4. It can be concluded that the age of BI initiatives did not have any significant effects on the BI maturity.

The results are in contrast with Eckerson's study (2007a) which reported that the BI initiatives that have existed for longer period of time indicates a high level of maturity. This might due to organizations that are new to BI could excel at their BI evolution due to the deployment of new technologies and adaptability to changes. The study of Williams and Williams (2007) stated that age difference is not a factor in determining BI maturity, rather it depends on the ability of an organization to align, leverage, and deliver BI.

Table 17. Descriptive statistics for BI maturity level and age of BI initiatives

BI Maturity Level			
Age of BI Initiatives	N	Mean	Std. Dev.
Less than 5 years	14	2.91	0.69
5 – 6 years	18	3.24	0.47
More than 6 years	20	3.26	0.52

Table 18. ANOVA results for BI maturity level and age of BI initiatives

ANOVA Table		Sum of Squares	df	Mean Square	F	Sig.
BIMat * AgeBI	Between Groups	1.206	2	0.603	1.940	0.155
	Within Groups	15.236	49	0.311		

In addition, the comparative analysis of each component that built into the four dimensions (i.e., organizational management, process, technology, and outcome) to measure the BI maturity based on the age of BI initiatives was conducted which revealed more findings. The age of BI initiatives consists of three groups.

Organizational Management Dimension by Age of BI Initiatives

Table 19 reveals the comparison of each component in the organizational management dimension based on age of BI initiatives. The results show that all the three age groups have similar maturity level (i.e., level 3) for vision, goals, business commitment, IT commitment, and sponsorship and funding components.

Of the three age groups, BI initiatives that have existed for less than 5 years received lower maturity level (i.e., level 2) in term of scope, BI awareness, and skill and competencies components. This is particularly true since some of the organizations are still in the early stages of BI implementation.

With regard to strategic alignment component, BI initiatives that have existed for less than 5 years and 5 to 6 years received lower maturity level (i.e., level 2) than the remaining age groups (i.e., level 3). On top of that, all three age groups have similar maturity level (i.e., level 2) for governance and training components.

Table 19. Descriptive analysis for organizational management dimension and age of BI initiatives

Component	Age of BI Initiatives					
	Less than 5 Years		5 – 6 Years		More than 6 Years	
	Mean	Std. Dev.	Mean	Std. Dev.	Mean	Std. Dev.
Vision	3.07	1.07	3.56	0.78	3.45	0.76
Goals	3.07	0.92	3.39	0.85	3.65	0.75
Scope	2.71	1.20	3.22	0.81	3.20	1.01
BI awareness	2.86	0.95	3.33	1.03	3.35	0.81
Strategic alignment	2.71	1.27	2.89	1.08	3.20	0.95
Skill and competencies	2.86	0.86	3.33	0.59	3.00	0.65
Business commitment	3.00	1.11	3.11	1.08	3.05	0.76
IT commitment	3.21	1.25	3.56	0.92	3.25	1.02
Governance	2.64	0.93	2.94	0.87	2.85	1.35
Training	2.36	0.84	2.83	0.79	2.50	0.61
Sponsorship and funding	3.43	1.70	3.44	1.50	3.60	1.43

Process Dimension by Age of BI Initiatives

Table 20 shows the comparison of each component in the process dimension based on age of BI initiatives. With regard to implementation component, BI initiatives that have existed for less than 5 years received highest mean score (mean = 3.21) than other two age groups. This implies that some organizations have accelerated their starting point of BI implementation resulting in higher maturity score.

In term of change management component, all three age groups have similar maturity level (i.e., level 2) for change management component. However, BI initiatives that have existed for less than 5 years received lowest mean score (mean = 2.43) which probably due to insufficient funding and resources for change management. As organizations grow, there is a need for a fully centralized master data management system to manage large and complex master data. This was evident that BI initiatives that have existed for 5 to 6 years and more than 6 years scored higher maturity level (i.e., level 3) for master data management component than those have existed for less than 5 years.

In term of metadata management component, it is surprising that BI initiatives that have existed for 5 to 6 years recorded a higher maturity level (i.e., level 3) than the rest of the age groups (i.e., level 2). This implies that there is limited awareness about the importance of maintenance, publication or sharing of metadata within some organizations resulting in a lower maturity level. Lastly, all the three age groups have similar maturity level (i.e., level 3) for data governance component.

Technology Dimension by Age of BI Initiatives

Table 21 shows the comparison of each component in the technology dimension based on age of BI initiatives. Overall, BI initiatives that have existed for less than 5 years received lowest mean scores for all the components, followed by BI initiatives that have existed for 5 to 6 years and more than 6 years. The results show that all three age groups have similar maturity level (i.e., level 3) for data warehousing, ETL, and OLAP components. With regard to master data architecture component, BI initiatives that have existed for less than 5 years achieved lower maturity level (i.e., level 2) than the remaining two age groups. This could be due to the lack of management support and insufficient funding.

However, BI initiatives that have existed for 5 to 6 years achieved higher maturity level (i.e., level 3) for metadata architecture component compared to the remaining two age groups. Possible reason could be that there is a lack of understanding of the importance of business metadata.

Table 20. Descriptive analysis for process dimension and age of BI initiatives

Component	Age of BI Initiatives					
	Less than 5 Years		5 – 6 Years		More than 6 Years	
	Mean	Std. Dev.	Mean	Std. Dev.	Mean	Std. Dev.
Implementation	3.21	1.19	2.94	0.64	3.00	0.92
Change management	2.43	1.02	2.94	1.00	2.85	0.99
Master data management	2.71	0.91	3.00	0.91	3.15	1.14
Metadata management	2.79	1.25	3.44	0.92	2.80	1.36
Data governance	3.29	1.14	3.11	0.96	3.25	1.02

Table 21. Descriptive analysis for technology dimension and age of BI initiatives

Component	Age of BI Initiatives					
	Less than 5 Years		5 – 6 Years		More than 6 Years	
	Mean	Std. Dev.	Mean	Std. Dev.	Mean	Std. Dev.
Data warehousing	3.07	0.83	3.39	0.78	3.80	0.62
Master data architecture	2.79	1.25	3.06	1.06	3.10	1.07
Metadata architecture	2.57	1.16	3.11	0.83	2.80	1.01
ETL	3.43	1.09	3.67	0.84	3.65	0.75
OLAP	3.00	1.24	3.33	0.84	3.65	0.75
Reporting and analysis	2.79	0.98	3.33	0.77	3.50	1.00

On top of that, BI initiatives that have existed for less than 5 years scored lower maturity level (i.e., level 2) for reporting and analysis component than the remaining two age groups. This could be attributed to the cost, complexity, and learning curve of sophisticated BI tools.

Outcome Dimension by Age of BI Initiatives

Table 22 depicts the comparison of each component in the outcome dimension based on age of BI initiatives. The results show that there is a gradient in maturity of data quality and information quality components among the three age groups of organizations. In particular, BI initiatives that have existed for less than 5 years received lower maturity level (i.e., level 2) compared to BI initiatives that have existed for 5 to 6 years and more than 6 years with higher maturity level (i.e., level 3). This is particularly true that smaller organizations often have inadequate funding and resources to manage data and information quality.

With regard to KPIs component, all three age groups of organizations have a similar maturity level (i.e., level 3). In particular, BI initiatives that have existed for 5 to 6 years scored higher mean score of 3.39 than the remaining two age groups. This indicates that the efforts to improve organizational performance with the development of integrated KPIs.

The overall results of all the four tested hypotheses and the decision of acceptance or rejection for each hypothesis are summarized in Table 23.

Table 22. Descriptive analysis for outcome dimension and age of BI initiatives

Component	Age of BI Initiatives					
	Less than 5 Years		5 – 6 Years		More than 6 Years	
	Mean	Std. Dev.	Mean	Std. Dev.	Mean	Std. Dev.
Data quality	2.79	0.80	3.22	0.55	3.30	0.66
Information quality	2.79	0.89	3.39	0.61	3.70	0.66
KPIs	3.14	1.03	3.39	0.70	3.25	0.97

Table 23. Summary of hypotheses testing and the decisions

Hypothesis	Decision
H1: Malaysian organizations generally achieved a moderate level of BI maturity.	H1 has been substantiated. The findings indicated that Malaysian organizations generally achieved a moderate level of the maturity. The average mean score of the overall BI maturity for the four dimensions is 3.16.
H2: The types of industry have significant effects on the BI maturity.	H2 has been substantiated. The findings indicated that the types of industry had significant effects on the BI maturity.
H3: The organizational size has a significant effect on the BI maturity.	Fail to support H3. The findings indicated that the organizational size had no significant effect on the BI maturity.
H4: The age of BI initiatives has a significant effect on the BI maturity.	Fail to support H4. The findings indicated that the age of BI initiatives had no significant effect on the BI maturity.

FUTURE TRENDS

Following the introduction to big data, BI still plays a vital role in facilitating decision making and competitive advantage. Specifically, mobile and cloud technologies will continue to lead the BI trend to give businesses the access to massive amount of data on demand.

While this research has developed and attested the efficacy of a BI maturity model, the results presented have to be interpreted with some limitations in mind. First, the sample sizes are not representative of all Malaysian organizations. Therefore, further in-depth studies are needed to establish the comprehensiveness and validity of this maturity model and consistent results.

Another limitation of this research is the cross-sectional nature of the data collected due to the limited resources and time. Although this BI maturity model is supported by empirical data, theoretical assumptions, and previous research findings, further research can extend existing work by conducting longitudinal and experimental studies to examine the changes of BI maturity of an organization over time. Such studies are useful and can serve as benchmarks to organizations that plan to improve BI.

CONCLUSION

This research develops a multi-dimensional BI maturity model and studies the effects of demographic variables such as types of industries, organizational size, and age of BI initiatives on the maturity. Four main dimensions (i.e. organizational management, process, technology, and outcome) along with the associated components in each dimension had been identified through the review of extant academic and practitioner literatures.

The survey results showed that Malaysian organizations are at level 2 (i.e., Repeatable) to level 4 (i.e., Managed) of BI maturity. This reflects that the Malaysian organizations are still at moderate level of BI maturity and have not fully obtained all the potential benefits from their BI investments. The findings also revealed that the technology and outcome dimensions have higher effects on the BI maturity in an organization. These results suggest that organizations need to coordinate their improvement activities across four dimensions so that they can reap full benefits of BI and attain desired level of BI maturity. Aside from that, the results obtained from the hypotheses testing showed that among the three demographic variables (i.e. types of industry, organizational size and age of BI initiatives), only the types of industry had significant effects on the BI maturity.

The development and validation of a multi-dimensional BI maturity model in this research could make a significance contribution to the body of knowledge in the area of management of BI initiative. Specifically, this maturity model overcomes the limitations of existing BI maturity models that mainly focus on one or two specific areas. Besides, this research could add to the contextual understanding of BI maturity and the key dimensions deemed important for the success of BI implementation. Such an understanding can help the organizations to analyze their BI from various perspectives.

Although some studies of BI maturity have been made in other countries, there are no previous studies exist that investigate the maturity issues of BI in Malaysia. So, it is believed that the research findings could be used as guideline for organizations in Malaysia and other countries to better identify their current BI state and start balancing all the aspects and take actions towards achieving the desired maturity level, thereby enabling continuous business growth in the future.

REFERENCES

Davenport, T. H., & Harris, J. G. (2007). *Competing on analytics: The new science of winning*. Boston, MA: Harvard Business School Press.

Dayal, U., Castellanos, M., Simitsis, A., & Wilkinson, K. (2009). Data integration flows for business intelligence. In *Proceedings of the 12th International Conference on Extending Database Technology: Advances in Database Technology* (pp. 1-11). New York: ACM. doi:10.1145/1516360.1516362

Eckerson, W. W. (2007a). *2007 TDWI BI benchmark report*. Retrieved December 24, 2013, from http://tdwi.org/~/media/86FE9B6DA255431C84E20570BBFFF3EB.pdf

Eckerson, W. W. (2007b). *Beyond the basics: Accelerating BI maturity*. Retrieved March 8, 2013, from http://download.101com.com/pub/tdwi/Files/SAP_monograph_0407.pdf

Elbashir, M. Z., Collier, P. A., & Davern, M. J. (2008). Measuring the effects of business intelligence systems: The relationship between business process and organizational performance. *International Journal of Accounting Information Systems*, *9*(3), 135–153. doi:10.1016/j.accinf.2008.03.001

Guarda, T., Santos, M., Pinto, F., Augusto, M., & Silva, C. (2013). Business intelligence as a competitive advantage for SMEs. *International Journal of Trade, Economics and Finance*, *4*(4), 187–190.

Hair, J. F., & Anderson, R. E. (2010). *Multivariate data analysis*. Upper Saddle River, NJ: Prentice Hall.

Jourdan, Z., Rainer, R. K., & Marshall, T. E. (2008). Business intelligence: An analysis of the literature. *Information Systems Management*, *25*(2), 121–131. doi:10.1080/10580530801941512

Levy, M., & Powell, P. (2004). *Strategies for growth in SMEs: The role of information and information systems*. Oxford, UK: Butterworth-Heinemann.

Olbrich, S., Poppelbuß, J., & Niehaves, B. (2012). Critical contextual success factors for business intelligence: A Delphi study on their relevance, variability, and controllability. In *Proceedings of the 45th Hawaii International Conference on System Science* (pp. 4148-4157). Washington, DC: IEEE Computer Society. doi:10.1109/HICSS.2012.187

Paulk, M. C., Curtis, B., Chrissis, M. B., & Weber, C. V. (1993). Capability maturity model. *IEEE Software*, *10*(4), 18–27. doi:10.1109/52.219617

Petrini, M., & Pozzebon, M. (2009). Managing sustainability with the support of business intelligence: Integrating socio-environmental indicators and organisational context. *The Journal of Strategic Information Systems*, *18*(4), 178–191. doi:10.1016/j.jsis.2009.06.001

Power, D. J. (2002). *Decision support systems: Concepts and resources for managers*. Westport, CT: Greenwood Publishing Group.

Raber, D., Wortmann, F., & Winter, R. (2013). Situational business intelligence maturity models: An exploratory analysis. In *Proceedings of the 46th Hawaii International Conference on System Sciences* (pp. 4219-4228). Wailea, HI: IEEE Computer Society. doi:10.1109/HICSS.2013.483

Ramamurthy, K., Sen, A., & Sinha, A. P. (2008). An empirical investigation of the key determinants of data warehouse adoption. *Decision Support Systems*, *44*(4), 817–841. doi:10.1016/j.dss.2007.10.006

Russell, S., Haddad, M., Bruni, M., & Granger, M. (2010). Organic evolution and the capability maturity of business intelligence. In *Proceedings of the 16th Americas Conference on Information Systems* (pp. 4271-4280). Lima, Peru: AMCIS.

Sacu, C., & Spruit, M. (2010). BIDM: The business intelligence development model. In *Proceedings of the 12th International Conference on Enterprise Information Systems* (pp. 288-293). Lisboa, Portugal: SciTePress.

Sen, A., Sinha, A. P., & Ramamurthy, K. (2006). Data warehousing process maturity: An exploratory study of factors influencing user perceptions. *IEEE Transactions on Engineering Management*, *53*(3), 440–455. doi:10.1109/TEM.2006.877460

Shanks, G., Bekmamedova, N., Adam, F., & Daly, M. (2012). Embedding business intelligence systems within organisations. In A. Respicio & F. Burstein (Eds.), *Fusing Decision Support Systems into the Fabric of the Context* (pp. 113–124). Amsterdam, The Netherlands: IOS Press.

Shariat, M., & Hightower, R. Jr. (2007). Conceptualizing business intelligence architecture. *Marketing Management Journal*, *17*(2), 40–46.

Shollo, A., & Kautz, K. (2010). Towards an understanding of business intelligence. In *Proceedings of the 21st Australasian Conference on Information Systems* (pp. 1-10). Brisbane, Australia: ACIS.

Tapia, R. S., Daneva, M., & van Eck, P. (2007). Validating adequacy and suitability of business-IT alignment criteria in an inter-enterprise maturity model. In *Proceedings of the 11th IEEE International Enterprise Distributed Object Computing Conference* (pp. 202-213). Washington, DC: IEEE Computer Society. doi:10.1109/EDOC.2007.19

TDWI. (2008). *TDWI BI benchmark report: Organizational and performance metrics for BI teams.* Retrieved December 19, 2013, from http://mfhammond.com/yahoo_site_admin/assets/docs/TDWI-BIBenchmarkReport.242122912.pdf

Vitt, E., Luckevich, M., & Misner, S. (2010). *Business intelligence: Making better decisions faster.* Redmond, WA: Microsoft Press.

Wailgum, T. (2010). *Biggest barriers to business analytics adoption: People.* Retrieved November 12, 2013, from http://www.cio.com.au/article/367783/biggest_barriers_business_analytics_adoption_people/

Watson, H. J., & Wixom, B. H. (2007). Enterprise agility and mature BI capabilities. *Business Intelligence Journal, 12*(3), 4–6.

Williams, S., & Williams, N. (2007). *The profit impact of business intelligence.* San Fracisco, CA: Morgan Kaufmann.

Wixom, B., Watson, H., & Werner, T. (2011). Developing an enterprise business intelligence capability: The Norfolk Southern journey. *MIS Quarterly Executive, 10*(2), 61–71.

KEY TERMS AND DEFINITIONS

Analytics: Davenport et al. (2007) describe analytics as "the extensive use of data, statistical and quantitative analysis, explanatory and predictive models, and fact-based management to drive decisions and actions" (p. 7).

Business Intelligence: Business intelligence (BI) refers to "a collection of data warehousing, data mining, analytics, reporting and visualization technologies, tools, and practices to collect, integrate, cleanse, and mine enterprise information for decision making" (Dayal et al., 2009, p. 1).

Capability Maturity Model: Capability maturity model (CMM), a well-known software process improvement model, was developed by Watts S. Humphrey and his team members from Software Engineering Institute (SEI) of Carnegie Mellon University in 1986 (Paulk et al., 1993). CMM is structured into five maturity levels: initial, repeatable, defined, managed, and optimizing.

Data Warehouse: The function of data warehouse (DW) is to "collect and store integrated sets of historical data from multiple operational systems and feeds them to one or more data marts" (Williams and Williams, 2007, p. 201).

ETL: Williams and Williams (2007) defines extract, transformation, and loading (ETL) as a "process that extracts data from source systems, potentially changes it (transformation process), and loads it into target data stores in the BI/DW environment" (p. 201).

Maturity Model: Tapia et al. (2007) defines maturity model as "a framework that describes, for a specific area of interest, a number of levels of sophistication at which activities in this area can be carried out" (p. 203).

OLAP: Online analytical processing (OLAP) tools "allow the user to query, browse, and summarize information in an efficient, interactive, and dynamic way" (Shariat and Hightower, 2007, p. 41).

Chapter 13

Cultural Integration with Strategic Decision-Making Process in Determining Innovation Performance:
Evidence from an Arab Country Setting

Ekaterini Galanou
Qatar University, Qatar

Marios Katsioloudes
Qatar University, Qatar

ABSTRACT

This chapter presents an empirical study that examines the co-alignment between the Strategic Decision-Making Process (SDMP) and cultural contextual factors in developing a more completely specified model of innovation performance in a different setting from the Arab Middle East, namely Qatar. The key variables in this model consist of four strategic decision-making process dimensions (speed, degree of rationality, political behavior, and individual involvement), four culture attributes (locus of control, decision style, collectivistic orientation, and hierarchy), and innovation performance as an outcome variable in terms of process and product/service practice. The survey from 140 public and private organizations improves our understanding in three major issues: first, that SDM practices have a direct and more significant impact on process innovation performance than product/service innovation performance; second, that innovation performance is both process- and context-specific; and third, certain characteristics of the location support culture-specific awareness.

INTRODUCTION

As international interactions increase in frequency and importance, there is an enduring need to know how managers make decisions in different parts of the world, despite the recognized existence of different decision-making approaches (Nutt, 1984; Brouthers et al., 2000; Dean and Sharfman, 1993;, Dean et al., 1993) . This knowledge is critical since a distinctive prevailing decision style reflects differences

DOI: 10.4018/978-1-4666-7272-7.ch013

in cultural values and the relative needs for achievement, affiliation, power and information (Abbas Ali 1989; M. Martinsons & R. Davison, 2007). Particularities of cultures give birth to respective management practices and decisions, personal motivation, and the ways in which information is interpreted (e.g. Laurent, 1983; Hickson and Pugh, 2001; Whitley,2000; Hofstede, 2001; Hayat Kabasakal, e.t.c, 2012; House et al. 2004; Trompenaars 1998). Despite the fact that the influence of societal (or national) values on how decisions are made, research literature is lacking for determining the effect of cultural factors on the Arab strategic decision making process (J. Hammoud,2011 ; A. Ali, 1995; A.J. Ali, 1995; Mellahi, 2003;Mellahi et al, 2010; Riddle et al, 2007; S. Elbanna & J. Child, 2007). Therefore, this bundle of evidence is significant because of the increasing interest of Western nations concerning the growing affluence of Arab countries, especially that of the Gulf States as a critical part of the world economy. Despite the profound interest in the theme, the influence of Arab business culture remains unclear (J. Hammoud, 2011; A. Ali, 1995; Mellahi, 2003;Mellahi & Budhwar, 2010). But, Arabs have not been static in the face of globalization and other changes that have challenged their world (Baraket, 1993; Hill et al., 1998).

This study aims at contributing to the body of knowledge regarding the role of culture in the SD making process in terms of determining performance. It extends traditional cultural studies to explore the within-nation cultural specificities of a particular country and enhance the development of cross-cultural theories and methodology. This procedure builds upon the significance of the executives' cultural values in shaping SDs, by exploring a number of specific national characteristics of the top level managers (e.g. locus of control, decision style, collectivistic orientation, hierarchy) as well as a number of dimensions characterizing the process of making SDs (e.g. degree of rationality, speed, political behavior, individual involvement).

Since Gulf countries are being transformed to a huge potential market and a critical part of the world economy, western companies are attracted in positioning themselves in the region. This paper brings up some useful observations to integrate knowledge of strategic management from a cross-cultural perspective by contrasting western and Arab viewpoints on the investigated issues of hypotheses. To the extent that a society's cultural values impact managerial decision making practices and organizational performance, this research adds to that understanding and introduces new findings when certain cultural value orientations are applied to other different cultural domains. Such knowledge of cultural differences is anticipated to advance mutual understanding and lead to a successful partnership with companies and organizations in an Arab culture.

It is fact that there is a need for a cultural insight before deciding if management concepts are able to be transferred to the Arab countries and how these concepts can be applied using the most effective way. This will cater to the practicing managers' needs to be better prepared for the challenges of being global managers. Furthermore, monumental changes are taking place in the gulf countries and that would enable them to gain a lot of attention for studying this region and its corporations (Zahra, 2011).

In view of these suggestions the State of Qatar is of particular importance taking into account its culture and extensive outlook on change and development. In recent years, Qatar has emerged as one of the better known and more highly regarded Gulf States, in part because of its immense natural gas reserves (the third largest in the world) but also, and more importantly, because of recent strategy of branding initiatives. These strategies seem to have been deliberately designed to put the State on the international map (Peterson, J E, 2006). Additionally, Qatar encompasses the constraints and challenges of small states. In addition, it is representative of the recently established, oil- producing Arab economies, with Bedouin culture such as those of Saudi Arabia, Kuwait, Oman, and the U.A.E (Elbana, 2012). As one of the Gulf's petroleum-driven, traditionally inclined, micro-states, it will be valuable to report the way and the extent that managers in Qatar have positive attitudes toward management knowledge and organizational innovation. The subject takes essential value of interest assuming that Qatar as a small state will always be a small one, but it's responsiveness to innovation management practice would be the means in order to take the lead in the global competition. The critical point for this study is to provide some insight into how will the unique and vibrant cultures of the Gulf region react and respond to an increasing level of interaction with Western business counterparts.

THEORETICAL BACKGROUND

The formulated research model used is presented in Figure 1. It is a simple linear model of the relationship between the independent and dependent variables. The model therefore is descriptive in nature and assumes the influence of management characteristics in terms of cultural idiosyncrasies, on the strategic decision-making process that results in an impact on the innovation performance. The cultural factors, and SDM process practices and innovation performance constructs are discussed in the next subsections. Figure 1 summarizes the hypotheses within the conceptual framework of this study that will be developed below. A (+) sign indicates a positive influence and a (-) sign indicates a negative relationship between the two variables.

Arab Cultural Factors

Owing to the issue that organizations are culture bound and managers are not separable from their indigenous cultures (Gannon, 1994; Hickson and Pugh, 2002) scholars contend that the Arab society has its unique social and cultural environment. Kavoossi, (2000) and Weir (1993) emphasized the single characteristics of the Arab culture and commented that the driving forces of the study of Arab management are

Figure 1. Research conceptual model

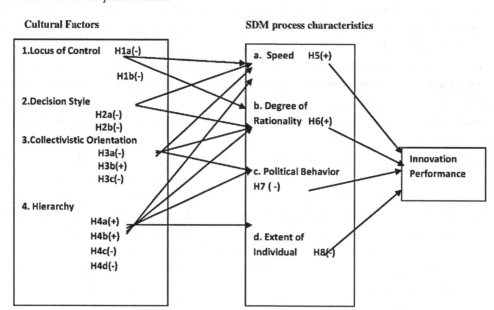

the Islamic, social, and political life of these countries. Studies that set dimensional frameworks for the study of culture include those by Hofstede (2001, 2004), Schwartz (1999), Trompenaars and Hampden-Turner (1997), and the GLOBE study (House et al., 2004). The view that manager's cultural indicators have considerable influence on decision processes has been supported by a number of researchers, such as Avinash Malshe, 2012; Jamil Hammoud 2011, I. Forstenlechner & K. Mellahi,2011. The works of Abbas J. Ali, 2010, D. Weir & K. Hutchings, 2005 and Hofstede, 2001 as well as others have shown how organizational strategies, structures, etc. can be influenced by the cultural indicators of leaders (e.g. patriarchal and collectivism, power distance, uncertainty avoidance index, mutual consultation, tolerance of ambiguity and dedication, fatalism & religious legitimacy). In a top executive survey comparing and contrasting American and Egyptian management styles, J. Parnell & T. Hatem (1999,) reported that cultural characteristics (e.g. long term focus, high tolerance for ambiguity, high leadership ambition, social alienation) is deeply embedded in management behavior. Finally, transformational leadership theory also supports the notion that a leader's personality characteristics (risk taking, innovation, social adroitness) are predictors for major changes in organizational innovation (Conger and Kanungo, 1987; Howell and Higgins, 1990).On the contrary, Shuhong Wang and Xiang Yi (2012), adopt different cultural dimensions/characteristics. A meaningful categorization, based on their study of the relevant literature, resulted in understanding how a pair of important individual cultural value orientations (allocentrism and idiocentrism) affects organizational behavior and performance in Chinese companies. This does not negate the significance of other aspects but more theoretical and empirical research is needed. Taras' team of researchers (Vas Taras, Julie Rowney, Piers Steel) have produced a very comprehensive and illuminating set of insights in the area. In 2009, after having concluded an extensive research of 121 instruments for measuring culture, they provided a historical overview and analyzed how culture has been operationalized over the last half a century. Their analysis identified twenty-six most popular facets of culture which could be grouped, with a few exceptions, into four major blocks related to Hofstede's dimensions of Individualism–Collectivism, Masculinity–Femininity, Uncertainty Avoidance, and Time Orientation. Building on the previous empirical advances and existing theory, this paper stipulates that a great portion of these cultural partners can be clustered under four sets of knowledge: the locus of control, decision style approach, collectivistic orientation, and hierarchy.

SDM Process Characteristics

Due to the fact that the SD making process has many dimensions, most existing strategy-making process models do not totally capture its complexity and variety (Hart and Banbury, 1994). To do this, the SD making process has to be investigated from several sights. Eisenhardt and Zbaracki (1992) suggest that researchers who want to realize this attempt should develop a broader agenda for investigating SDs in organisations so that to create a more realistic view of the SD making process. Several scholars have in fact integrated different opinions on the decision making process in their researches of it (e.g. Dean and Sharfman, 1996; Eisenhardt, 1989; Elbanna and Child, 2007; Hart and Banbury, 1994; Papadakis, 1998).In reviewing and consolidating the literature, this study emerges four dimensions of SDM practices namely degree of rationality and speed (as representatives of the synoptic formalism model) and both political behavior and the extent of individual Involvement (as representatives of the political incrementalism model). These four variables have been pillars of SDM process in the seminal study of Rajagopalan et al., (1993). Moreover, the specified characteristics have been interested in an empirical investigation by many other researchers in the field of the SD making process (Dean and Sharfman, 1993; Hough and White, 2003; Dean et al., 1993; Baum and Wally, 2003; Cray et al., 1988; Hickson et al., 1986). Although the dimensions included in this research capture the major common aspects of SDM practices, they cannot be considered as complete. Other factors identified in the literature such as ritual, leisure, conformity, humanistic, trust, harmony, face-to-face interaction, interpersonal relationship (Branine, 2002; Chr. Robertson et. al 2001; Metcalfe, 2007; Mellahi, 2006 ; Weir, 2000; Whiteoak et al., 2006) are not included in this research. Although the excluded factors are of great interest, they are not encompassed due to "the length of the survey, and the concerns regarding the parsimony of measurement instruments" (Li et al., 2006).

Innovation Effectiveness

Innovation is recognized to play a central role in creating value and sustaining competitive advantage to the organizations (Rowley, Baregheh, ot Sambrook, 2011). So, abandoning the emphasis on lowering costs and rigid organizational structures, they direct their attention instead to value-creation for the customer, to innovation and to flexibility, to becoming the first user of new ideas, new process, new products, etc. (Grant, 1998; Prastacos et al., 2002; Teece et al. 1997). Furthermore, previous research has shown a positive link between innovation performance and firm performance (Alegre, Lapiedra, & Chiva, 2006). As Bolwijn and Kumpe (1990) argued, the competitive environment today requires organizations to pursue more complex dimensions of performance, most notably quality and innovation. As developing countries (particularly Arab countries) become crucial partners in global competition, they are diligently examining the means and drivers of growing their local and national economies. Within this context, innovation is broadly considered to be the very first natural means for their departure to achieve this desired growth. Although, innovation consists of successful exploitation of new ideas it stands to be the least explored one, which is partially due to the newness of this field (Vrgovic, Glassman, Walton, & Vidicki, 2012). Apart from the earlier discussion, what can be further stressed here is that innovation performance is a significant concern for developing and particularly Arab countries in which macro-economic decisions of governance are thought to be more important than the other environmental factors for firms in strategic decision making process. In addition, Arab managers tend to think that they have limited control over the external environment, so they may direct their efforts towards controlling the immediate, internal environment (Papadakis et al., 1998; Zehir C. & M. Oszahin, 2008) and tailor their SDMP accordingly. The role of construct measuring practices of innovation performance has been a major element in the literature of organizational innovation. The study therefore prioritizes the aspect for measuring product and process innovation on the basis of several criteria which are captured and comprehended in previous empirical studies of innovation, such as Avlonitis et al., 1994, Deshpande et al., 1993, Miller and Friesen, 1982, and Subramanian and Nilakanta,1996. These criteria are the number of innovations, the speed of innovation, the level of innovativeness (novelty or newness of the technological aspect), and being the 'first' in the market.

HYPOTHESIS DEVELOPMENT

The Relationships between Cultural Factors and the SDMP

Building on the need for a broader contextualizing perception in the linkage among societal-level measures and business environment (Early ;2006,p.928), a schedule with 8 item hypotheses is developed that addresses concerns in capturing the manifestation of four national culture value dimensions in managerial SDM context and their cumulative impact on organizational performance in terms of innovation.

Locus of Control Will Reflect Both the Speed and Ratio of Rationality of the SDMP

As one of the most commonly used individual characteristics in human behavior, locus of control was found to be related to the expected organizational performance (Boon et al., 2000; Halikias and Panayotopoulou, 2003). Locus of control perception refers to the extent to which individuals believe that they can control events affecting them (Rotter, 1954; Rossier et al., 2005). Researchers explained that managers with internal locus of control believe that the consequences of their behavior stem from their own efforts, while external managers believe that events are beyond their control (Rotter, 1954; Twenge et al., 2004; Oliver et al., 2006). Research has shown that Arab management practices are characterized by emphasis on uncertainty avoidance and maintenance of in-group harmony (Hofstede, 1980, 1991; Ouchi, 1980) compelling managers to moderate any documented open conflicts (Dawes & Massey, 2005). As such, they like to go by the rulebook to reduce risks and uncertainty while they engage in less rational decision making. As an inclination to relieve the anxiety of making important decisions, and to psychologically reduce the feeling of uncertainty, Arab managers orientate themselves on social norms like 'Wasta' (connections), "Inshallah' (God-willing). But, these "caste system" actions cause obstacles to the rationality of decision making, such as managers' distraction from the normal SDM process, paucity of pertinent, reliable and timely information (Abdul Wahad,1979;Omar,1984). At the same time they are not tolerant of employees' spontaneous actions or deviation from the formal rules using more aggressive export behaviour (Bjerke & Abdulrahim, 1993; Muna, 1980). These practices in the Arab managerial behavior may be further supported by the fact that, the religion and inherited cultural norms and traditions makes a shape of cultural identification, providing a socialization control in order to achieve growth and transition. It has been argued that they exert more power within the organisation, which again is expected to reduce problem-solving dissension (Ali, 1990, 1998; Dadfar, 1993; Weir, 1998, 2001; Budhwar and Mellahi, 2006). This kind of control depends apparently on more time to accomplish targets. Following this line of reasoning, Arab managers establish a relationship first, then build connections, and only actually come to the heart of the intended business at a later meeting. This process is very time consuming, yet once an agreement has been established verbally, it is considered an absolute contract that will certainly lead to the termination of a business relationship when managers don't honor their obligations (Weir, 1998). The previous discussion suggests the following two hypotheses:

Hypothesis 1a: Perceived control by Arab managers is expected to be negatively correlated with the speed of strategic decision making.

Hypothesis 1b: Arab managers are expected to be negatively related to degree of rationality in strategic decision making, depending on their cultural mold to avoid uncertainty.

Arab Managers' Decision Making Approach Will Impact Both Decision 'Speed' and 'Degree of Rationality'

Arabic business society follows centralized decision-making practices (Baker & AbouIsmail, 1993) with top management exerting strong control and minimizing any deviations. Firm leaders not only conceptualize various strategic initiatives but also adopt a very hands-on approach by keeping a close watch over how their strategies are implemented on a day-to-day basis (Bhuian, 1998; Harris & Moran, 1987). In approaching the specific issue of managerial behavior in the Arab world, Hickson and Pugh (1995) respecting the distinctive sociocultural Arabian system, emphasized on the influence of four unique factors: foreign rule, the Western quest for oil, Bedouin/tribal traditions, and Islam. The magnitude of influence of each factor impedes management thought in the region adopting strict codes of top-down authoritative structure, often referred to as a 'Bedo-aucracy' or 'Sheikocracy' managerial style. Such is likely the matter of "order" (a critical phenomenon to organizational practice) that is preserved more by autocratic decision making than by establishing and following rules and regulations (Hofstede, 1980). Additionally, researchers understanding the perception of polychromic time culture, (Hall & Hall, 1990; Schneider & Barsoux, 2003; Trompenaars and Hampden-Turner, 2007) explained that Arab managers work on different tasks at once, are elastic, and don't get annoyed by interruption. Walker, (2003) pointed in his review that Arabs are inclined to do multiple tasks and several assignments at the same time. Hence, the concept of time for them is fluid and flexible but beyond a certain point there is danger to be managed precisely. It merely adds value to the hypothesis that Arab managers belonging in a highly-context culture, supposed to be connected in management practices with a holistic aspect (Adler, 2002). Nevertheless, Arab management thought has been portrayed as fragmented and directionless (Ali, 1990, 1995). Enlisting them may reduce the speed and effectiveness of the decision making.

Hypothesis 2a-2b: Reliance on an Arabian indigenous centralized decision style will be rated ineffective with

1. The speed of the SDM process, and
2. The degree of rationality.

Collectivistic Orientation Affects Speed, the Degree of Rationality, and Political Behavior

Considering the impact of various cultural characteristics composing the strategic profile of Arab managers, becomes distinctive to postulate the relationship between group orientation and speed, degree of rationality, political behavior. Ali, 1996; Al-Hegelan and Palmer, 1985; Sabri, 2004, approaching the issue of managerial practice in the Arab world, have demonstrated that managers are reluctant to delegate authority; avoid responsibility and risk-taking; prefer stable a lifestyle over rewarding but challenging work; and give priority to friendships and personal considerations over organizational goals and performance. With respect to temporal focus of human activity, Dedaussis states that Arabs' relationships tend to be hierarchical and collectivist (2004). Accordingly, Deresky (1994) and Mohamed et al (2008) point out that Arab culture may also be characterized highly by terms of context, verbal interaction and nonverbal communication where one needs to read between the lines and interpret covert clues. In essence, it is customary for Arabs to use terms and phrases that have double meanings, descend from the very general to the specific, avoid going directly to the point. Instead they prefer to loop around; they begin with social talk, discuss business for a while, loop round to general issues, and then go back to business. The above highlighted social characteristics translate into implicit and indirect expression of Hofestede's thoughts, and key information for a strongly collectivist Arab behavior (2008).Notably, studies of management in Arab countries (Weir, 2000; Assad, 2002) have found that too much centralization, overbearing bureaucracy, poor communication, lack of management skills and unrealistic performance issues such as the importance of personal factors over the needs of the organization exist. Also, nepotism, personal connections, favoritism significantly influence Arab managers decisions (Al-Hussaini, 1985; Barakat, 1983; Harastani, El-Sayed and Palmer, 1985). Critically from the above discussion there is a clear reflection of highly collectivistic, face-saving and status-consciousness values (Gregg, 2005) to the use of decision making. Eisenhardt's (1989) and C.Zehir and M. Ozsahin's (2007) findings related to the linkage between involvement and strategic decision-making speed, exemplified that extensive participation accelerates the pace of decision making (Eisenhardt, 1989, p. 561). Accordingly, the following hypotheses should be seen as tentative:

Hypothesis 3a-3c: Arab managers' collectivist value orientation with inclination towards the "task behavior" is expected to be

1. Negatively correlated with the speed of decision making,
2. Positively correlated with the degree of rationality,
3. Negatively related to political behavior.

Social Elite (Hierarchy) Has a Relationship with All the SDM Process Characteristics

In a cross-culture comparison of organizational culture between the Arab World and Japan, Dedaussis argues that Arabs' relationship to others tends to be hierarchical and collectivist (2004). This is revealed by respect for seniority and authority as determined by age, family, and sex and preference for hierarchical communication and bureaucratic organizations characterized by systems and structures that binds the individual to the group. There is a high tendency for managers to lean towards prestigious positions, being very title oriented. Ali and Sabri (2001) and Sabri (2007) observed that managerial style in organizations is characterized by high power and role cultures. Relatedly, firms follow centralized decision-making practices (Baker & AbouIsmail, 1993) with top management exerting strong control and minimizing any recognizing status hierarchy deviations (Baker & AbouIsmail, 1993). Hammoud J., 2011, sketching the profile of arab organizational culture criticizes "the leader turns into an individual possessing dictatorial power and authority reinforced by followers' unquestioning loyalty and trust". This mode of centralization is based on a basic managerial subscription to the assumptions of theory X in management science. In other terms, followers or workers are lazy, do not want responsibility, motivated my money and must be tightly controlled using threats and methods of punishment". These considerations lead to:

Hypothesis 4a: Arab top management team is expected to be positively correlated with the speed of the strategic decision making process.

The Intervention of Top Management Team Distracts Managers from the Normal Rational Process

The prevailing research suggests that organizational practices are political in nature, since decision makers play politics because they believe that they will be affected by the decision outcomes (Eisenhardt and Bourgeois, 1988). For this reason, they attempt to satisfy their personal needs by influencing the decision process. P. B. Smith et al. 2007 discussing the characterization of Arab leadership that has been provided by the GLOBE researchers (House et al., 2004), mention that effective managers from the Arab cluster were found to score significantly lower than those from elsewhere on charismatic, team-oriented or participative qualities. Interestingly, effective Arab managers were reported to score significantly higher on 'self-protective' traits, namely self-centeredness, status-consciousness, conflict induction and reliance on procedure. Considering this range of behaviors as a whole, there are reasons to accept that Arab top managers' strategic decisions are mostly limited to themselves and rely on less rational-comprehensive approach to decision making leading to rather misleading conclusions. In this regard, because of hierarchy, managers are considered as a source of guidance and decisions for the lower management team resulting an intervening role to most of the situations the degree of rationality. On the other hand, the top level managers may more easily be able to resolve conflict and refine harmony using superior position, which may be more effective in resolving responses. In view of the above, the below nominal hypotheses are entered:

Hypothesis 4b-d: Arab top management team is expected to be

1. Positively correlated with political behavior,
2. Negatively related to individual involvement, and
3. Negatively related to the degree of rationality.

The Relationship between the SDM Process and Innovation Performance

There is a significant body of empirical research examining the relationship between strategic decision-making speed and firm performance (Eisenhardt's, 1989; Judge and Miller,1991; Wally and Baum, 1994; Baum and Wally,2003). Despite this, little considerable empirical support has been directed towards the investigation among strategic decision-making speed and innovation performance (C. Zehir & Ozsahin, 2008; Vrgovic, et al., 2012; Fortuin, F T J. M., & (Onno) Omta, S. W. F 2009). Therefore, the particular research theme is attracting much attention, since firms move in an competitive area of increasingly global markets and shortened product life cycles (Judge and Miller, 1991, p. 449).The view that fast decision-making as a source of competitive advantage in volatile environments has been supported by a number of researchers, such as Stevenson & Gumpert, 1985; Jones, 1993, Ancona et al., 2001; Kepner-Tregoe, 2001; Judge and Miller 1991. In a similar vein, Grant (1998) and Teece et al. (1997) pointed out some important aspects of organization's survival and growth in a technologically sophisticated and highly competitive environment highlighting that firms need to be innovative and flexible, to be the first user of new ideas, new process, new products, etc. Baum and Wally, (2003, p. 1109) in studying SDM processes, went so far as to contend that "Fast decision speeds is expected to be improve competitive performance across environments because fast strategic decisions result in:

1. Early adoption of successful new products or improved business models that provide competitive advantages,
2. Early adoption of efficiency-gaining process technologies even in established industries, and/or
3. Preemptive organization combinations that enable economies of scale and knowledge synergies."

Furthermore, researchers (e.g. Meyer and Goes, 1988 ; Howell and Higgins 1990, Marshall and Vredenburg 1992; Kim et al., 1993; Phan P.H. 2000) concentrated on the effect of top management team characteristics in the emergence of innovation champions in organizations since they studied the beneficial type of organizational factors (strategies, and structures) as predictors and drivers of innovation approach. Due to the inconclusiveness of the available research and the literature discussed earlier from an Arab perspective, the following hypothesis is suggested:

Hypothesis 5: The faster the strategic decision making, the better the innovation performance.

Approaching innovation performance as a multidimensional phenomenon and a function of many variables (Subramanian, Nilakanta, 1996, Vigoda-Gadot et al., 2005 ; Dundon, 2005 ; Scriahina N., 2011; Fortuin & (Onno) Omta, 2009), strategic decision making speed and comprehensiveness have been recognized in the broader set of innovation performance criteria (Forbes,2000). The influential work of Miller & Toulouse, 1986; Miller & Droge, 1986 and Mark's perspective (1997) emphasize the role of decision makers stressing that strategic choices are, the hardest part of managing an organization today, for many reasons. The difficulty arises since the most preferred alternatives are unfeasible (Nutt, 1998). This composes the thought that once the top management team choose an alternative, they are getting to a process in which the problem is well defined, various alternatives are established, adequate information are gathered, alternatives are appraised and the best possible alternative is selected. That point can often be a long, complex, and challenging course of action requiring formal strategic planning, analytic rational decision making, and systems for measurement, control and co-ordination (Miller et all, 1998). A number of studies adopt rationality/comprehensiveness dimension (Dean and Sharfman, 1993; Fredrickson, 1984; Hough and White, 2003) in approaching strategic process and most research find empirical support for a positive relationship between performance and the rational processes of decision making (Papadakis et al. 1998; Jones et al., 1992). Providing strong empirical support Elbanna, 2006 showed that high performance leads to decisions that are more rational and less intuitive. Settling this line of reasoning, it is expected that managers tend to be more conservative and exert a more formal planning process in their decision making in order to reduce risk, especially in the case that the impact of the decision to be made is likely to be great. Closer to our argument, other research on Arab organizations (Ali, 1996; Al-Hegelan and Palmer, 1985; Sabri,2004) have noted that Arab managers are reluctant to delegate authority; and avoid responsibility and risk-taking. Additionally, Hofstede (2010) emphasized on a particular observed situation in Arab societies due to the combination of the two dimensions of power distance and uncertainty avoidance, resulting leaders have ultimate power and authority, and the rules, laws and regulations developed by those in power reinforce their own leadership and control. In other words, good performers are much likely to exhibit rationality in their strategic decision-making process.

Hypothesis 6: There is a positive relationship between the extent of rationality in the decision-making process of Arab managers and innovation performance.

As argued by Dean and Sharfman (1996), individual's "decision set" of interests, power bases and positions inside the organizations bring political tactics into decision-making process, exerting a harmful effect on the degree of political behavior and conflict. Thus, the majority of serious scholarly works on the subject resulted with evidence the significant negative relationship between performance and political behavior resting on the assumption that political decision process is not consistent with organizational goals, is unlikely to produce complete and accurate information and is not oriented to environmental constraints (Dean J. & Sharfman M.,1996;Vigoda-Gadot & Cohen,2004; Said Elbanna,2008). In others words, decision makers engaging in political tactics make less effective decisions than those who do not. Therefore, several authors, using another critical way, have suggested that politics may be beneficial in a rapidly changing environment as an important mechanism for organizational adaptation (Eisenhardt et al. 1997), may be useful for bargaining reducing uncertainty and increasing acceptance (Nutt, 1998) or may be facilitator in alleviating the path for the implementation of a strategic decision (Mintzberg,1998). Considering the Arab culture that highlights on maintaining harmony within a group, and establishing stability through a hierarchical and pyramidal class structure there is low likelihood of increasing political behavior and conflict. Based on the above analysis the following hypothesis is formed:

Hypothesis 7: Innovation performance is negatively related to Arab managers' political behavior in strategic decision-making.

Meanwhile, some researchers have viewed management involvement through autonomy and participation as the means for reducing inhibiting organizational barriers, facilitating creativity and supporting opportunistic business development (Spoull & Kiesler,1986;Huber, 1990;Cullupe et.all., 1992). However, Wally and Baum (1994,pp. 932-956) have stated that when in the organizations, the potential for process-slowing conflict is low (the result of a limited participation), strategic decision-makers can probably move through the intelligence and design activity phases more quickly than they would otherwise. They can also probably choose more quickly because they have little need to consult and build consensus. There is, however, the Arabic view, which reports that in the micro level of the Arab business organization, leadership style of Arab managers is often characterized as one of theory X style of management closely consistent with a highly dictatorial or authoritative mode (Hammoud J.,2011), . The previous discussion suggests the following hypothesis:

Hypothesis 8: The greater the participation/involvement of the SDM process in Arab management the lower the innovation performance.

While most of the published research, on different aspects of management, in Arab countries remains 'subjective, case study based, normative, and conceptual' (Elbaba, 2012; Hickson and Pugh, 2003;Zahra, 2011: 13), this study lends support on the research hypotheses basically based on relevant literature from the Arab exploration context according to Khalifa's (2001), Al-Buraey's (1990), Ahmad's (2006); Beekun's (2006); Ali's (2005),different perspectives .

RESEARCH METHODOLOGY

Sample and Data Collection: Sampling Profiles

To address the research hypotheses, a survey instrument was developed. Although the items and questions in the proposed questionnaire were adopted from existing studies, to improve the validity of the questionnaire, eliminate ambiguous or biased items, a small scale pilot study was pre-tested before the final questionnaire was sent out for full scale study. The results of this analysis indicated that variables in the study had acceptable reliability with Cronbach's alpha ranging from 0.7079 to 0.8542. Since English is the second official language in the State of Qatar, and the percentage of English-speaking business people is also very high, it was ensured that the wording and format of the questions were clear, precise, and did not confuse the reader. Measurement instrument for this exploratory study was used a self-administered questionnaire that was distributed to a randomly selected sample of 600 executive members of the Qatar Chamber (QC) via e- mail. Directing the interest to carry out a full scale study to provide a generalized picture of the Qatar economy, attention was focused on companies that were identified in the literature as recognizing to traditionally strong or rapid growth business sectors (private & public). These include: oil & gas well drilling, construction, manufacturing, services, insurance and real estate, wholesale, retail trade, and 'others' (hospitals, air transportation, agriculture, communication, and non-classifiable establishments). Building on Arbuckle' s scholarly work (2003) who specified a minimum number of cases required to ensure adequate power and validity for a particular form of multivariate analysis, this research used a 'proportional sampling ' procedure for the 7 economic sectors. The sample qualifying procedure was justified by the fact that overall, 140 respondents returned the questionnaire, yielding a relative restricted but acceptable total 23,3 per cent response rate. According to Baruch and Holtom's analysis (2008), " it is clear that studies conducted at the structural level seeking responses from organizational representatives or top executives are likely to experience a lower response rate". Additionally, it has been recognized that no theoretical evidence exists that suggests a significant nonresponse bias influence on culturally generated data (i.e., Shane et al., 1995; Miller et al., 1998). In order to minimize self-report bias in the data, we have informed the respondents that their names and the organizations' name are not needed for the survey. Conducting an exploratory research by the key-informant technique (Eyler, et al., 1999), the sample frame of potential respondents consisted of executive managers and vice presidents of the respective organizations. In other words, due to the fact that strategic decisions are an outcome that come from people who create them (Amason, 1996), the information for this analysis was acquired by using managers who are under the responsibility to make decisions delinquently of the position they have in the organization (e.g. Hickson et al., 1986).Personal characteristics of responding managers indicate that 100 per cent of the respondents are males; 43,4 per cent are above the age of 40; around 50 per cent hold a higher educational degree, 55 per cent have a long working experience in the organization (10 years or more); The organizational contingencies of the sample show that 62,4 per cent hold the position of CEO, president, and managing director who are nominated for making strategic decisions ; and the highest number of managers (36,7 per cent) were specialized in the "other" sector (construction, communication, oil, travel/tourism). In terms of organizational size, based on the number of employees, 86% of the respondents represent firms with 500 employees or less, with around 55% of them representing firms with less than 200 employees.

Research Instrument

The instrument developed in this study consists of three major parts with equal three types of variables. The first part comprises four constructs measuring cultural factors (locus of control, decision style, collectivistic orientation, hierarchy) while the second part includes other four constructs measuring characteristics of strategic decision making process (speed, degree of rationality, political behavior, extent of individual). The last part captures two constructs measuring different types of performance: product innovation performance and process innovation performance. The section on cultural factors had 44 items containing 15 items on Locus of Control, 16 items on Decision style, 7 items on Collectivistic Orientation, and 6 items on Hierarchy. Consistent with the designs of others (C. Miller & et. al., 1998; J. Fredrickson & T. Mitchell, 1984; K. Eisenhart & L. Bourgeois, 1988), the current survey quantitatively assessed managers' cultural reflections in their attitude characteristics relevant to decision making process, using a seven- point numerical scale rating of agreement. Based on Rotter (1966) and Dağ adaptation (1991), participants were asked to respond to fifteen statements to measure the degree of locus of control. Drawing on a modified version of one used by Muna (1980) and Al-Malik (1989) this study assesses the decision style of strategic decision making by using a scale included a description of five alternatives: autocratic, pseudo-consultative, consultative, participative, and delegatory. Managers were asked to indicate the one style that best described their behavior. The measure has been successfully used in national and cross-national studies including the Arab setting (D. Boussif,2010; A. Ali; 1992). Moreover, the present study pursued to employ the decision style variable using the five dimensions of style of the same 15-item measurement that was administrated by both Albaum and Herche's (1999) and Gerald A. et all's work (2008). To collect managers' work values of group orientation, the respective part of the cultural attitudes inventory instrument developed by Dorfman and Howell (1988) was used. Hierarchy was measured with 6 seven-point scales employing a disagreement/agreement format. They were drawn from the Cultural Attitudes Inventory Instrument, developed by Dorfman and Howell (1988). The section on SDMP characteristics consisted of 18 items (were allocated on speed, degree of rationality, political behavior, and extent of individual), based upon suggested typologies from earlier studies. To measure the degree of rationality, it was used by Dean and Sharfman's (1996) instrument, consisting of four seven-point Likert-type scales with options ranging from 1= not at all to 7=completely successful/extensively. The response format reflects an active attitude towards decision making and information gathering, inquiry, scrutiny. Following Baum and Wally, (2003), three decision scenarios were explored to measure decision speed:

1. An acquisition decision,
2. A new product introduction decision, and
3. A technology adoption decision.

A composite variable of six 7-point Likert type scales was used to capture the political behavior variable (Bacharach and Lawler, 1980; Dean and Sharfman 1996; Eisenhardt and Bourgeois 1988; Papadakis et al. 1998). To measure "the extent of individual" variable, the five-item scale of Torben J. Andersen (2001) was used. Although there are various typologies of comprehensively capturing the aspects of innovation performance, most studies have built the measuring construct primarily on product and process innovation (Prajogo and Sohal, 2001; Chen and Tsou, 2007; Gobeli and Brown, 1994; Yamin et al., 1997;Avlonitis et al., 1994; Deshpande et al.,1993; Miller and Friesen,1982). Consistent with the above mentioned researchers this study conceptualizes the section of innovation performance into the two categories of process innovation and product/service innovation (Tidd J, 1997; Zhuang L, 1999). As far as the measurement approach is concerned, the data was used in order to evaluate the innovative motives of the company against the industry competition. This method presented by Kraft (1990), and was used to minimize, a bias from subjective answers. Since nine questions were conducted to measure process innovation, and product/service innovation, responses to the questions were based on a seven-point Likert scale, ranging from much worse in industry to much better in industry.

Statistical Analysis of Measurement Model

Data analysis for this study involved two major steps: the data reduction process and the structural relationship analysis (Hair et al., 1995). The structural relationship analysis is effective when testing models that are path analytic with mediating variables, and include latent constructs that are being measured with multiple items (Luna-Arocas and Camps, 2008). It is assessed the overall model fit following Bollen's (1989) recommendation to examine multiple indices, since it is possible for a model to be adequate on one fit index but inadequate on many others. Exploratory factor analysis (EFA) with varimax rotation was performed on cultural factors, decision making practices and innovation performance in order to extract the dimensions underlying each construct. Table 1 shows the results of the EFA.

The reliability of the measurements in the survey was tested using Cronbach's alpha (a). The reliability coefficients (a) of each of the variables were as follows: locus of control (0,86), decision style(0,82), collectivistic orientation (0,78), hierarchy (0,80), speed(0,83), degree of rationality(0,79), political be-

Table 1. EFA, CFA, and reliability

Constructs	Final (No. of Items)	GFI	Cronbach's Alpha	S.D.	Means
Locus of control (locon)	4	0.958	0.8650	0.817	3.767
Decision Style(decst)	5	0.970	0.8142	0.802	3.592
Collectivistic orientation(color)	4	0.998	0.7953	0.902	3.918
Hierarchy(hier)	5	0.973	0.7851	0.706	3.613
Speed(sped)	3	0.953	0.7933	0.923	3.633
Degree of rationality (degrat)	4	0.983	0. 8332	0.698	3.367
Political behavior (polbeh)	6	0.978	0.9222	0.714	3.533
Extent of Individual (idin)	4	0.974	0.8907	0.878	3.434
Product innovation (inprod)	4	0.980	0.8674	0.709	3.609
Process innovation (inproc)	4	0.976	0.8580	0.884	3.542

havior(0,92), the extent of individual(0,84), product innovation (0,88), process innovation(0,87). The result shows that the Cronbach's alpha measures for the ten constructs surpass the threshold point of 0.7 suggested by Nunnally (1978).In order to examine the construct validity of each scale, confirmatory factor analysis (CFA) was employed. Based on the model used in this study, there are 43 items focusing on the ten dimensions of conceptual model. Table 2 shows that the goodness-of-fit index (GFI) and comparative fit index (CFI) exceeded the 0.9 criterion suggested by Kelloway (1981) which indicates that there is unidimensionality in the factors (Hart, 1994; Katos, 2010). The value of root mean square error of approximation (RMSEA) is less than 0.8 representing the required good approximation for an acceptable model. Since LISREL (see Joreskog and Sorbom, 2004) could estimate all parameters incorporated in the model, we can conclude that the model is well specified with: RMSEA=0,041, GFI=0,949, p-value= 0,063, CFI=0,981 (Li et al., 2006). The best competing model is presented in Table 2.

The differences of the variables incorporated in this study based on the number of team members who participated in decision making were tested. The importance of examining this difference is because the subsequent relationship analyses were conducted using the whole sample irrespective to this situational variable. The number of team members has appeared with great frequency in the literature navigation in strategic management and in arab strategic management as well that may influence strategic decision-making (Baum J. R. and Wally St., 2003; West & Anderson, 1996; Capon, Farley, and Hulbert, 1987; Fredrickson and Iaquinto, 1989). The responses were classified into three categories: 2-3 members in the management team that are directly involved in decision making process, 4-5 members in management team, and 1 person who makes decision for the company. One-way ANOVA test was used to test the mean differences of the ten variables used in this study with respect to these three categories. The result, as presented in Table 3, indicates significant gaps between the third group of respondents (i.e. 4-5 team members) and the first group (1 person) relating to several variables of the study. These gaps reflect variation of perceptions on decision making process between the number of people engaged in decision making in an organization.

RESULTS

Table 4 depicts bivariate Pearson's correlations between the mean variables of cultural factors, decision making practices and innovation performance, displaying that all correlations are positive and relatively strong. The four cultural factors have strong correlations amongst themselves. The correlations within cultural variables (ACF) are also relatively stronger than those between cultural variables and strategic

Table 2. Statistical structural indices of SEM model

Statistics	Structural Model
x^2/dF	1.33
p-value	0.063
GFI	0.949
AGFI	0.868
CFI	0.981
NFI	0.902
RMSEA	0.041

Table 3. ANOVA test for the composite variables based on the number of members in management team

Variables	1 Person(a) (N=75)	2-3 Mem(b) (N=32)	4-5 Mem(c) (N= 34)	Mean Difference
Locus of control (locon)	3.44	3.64	4.12	1-3**;2-3**
Decision Style(decst)	3.42	3.58	3.68	–
Collectivistic orientation(color)	3.75	3.96	4.11	1-3**
Hierarchy(hier)	3.44	3.66	3.75	–
Speed(sped)	3.22	3.55	3.69	1-3**
Degree of rationality (degrat)	3.49	3.60	3.75	–
Political behavior (polbeh)	2.85	2.95	2.99	1-3**
Extent of individual(idin)	4.13	4.24	4.36	–
Product innovation (inprod)	3.37	3.41	3.48	1-3**
Process innovation (inproc)	3.40	3.75	3.59	–

*Significant at $p < 0.05$;** significant at $p < 0.01$

a= 1 person for making decisions

b =2-3 members in management team

c = 4-5members in management team.

Table 4. Bivariate correlation among variables

	V1	V2	V3	V4	V5	V6	V7	V8	V9	V10
Locus of control (locon)	1.00									
Decision Style(decst)	0.662**	1.00								
Collectiv.orientat. (color)	0.533**	0.550**	1.00							
Hierarchy(hier)	0.555**	0.633**	0.560**	1.00						
Speed(sped)	0.733**	0.603**	0.512**	0.633**	1.00					
Degree of rationality (degrat)	0.601**	0.518**	0.643**	0.677**	0.672**	1.00				
Political behavior (polbeh)	0.513**	0.403**	0.392**	0.412**	0.511**	0.428**	1.00			
Extent of individual (idin)	0.388**	0.355**	0.275**	0.312**	0.276**	0.301**	0.566**	1.00		
Product innovation (inprod)	0.432**	0.433**	0.468**	0.352**	0.423**	0.334**	0.444**	0.251**	1.00	
Process innovation (inproc)	0.366**	0.258**	0.397**	0.412**	0.346**	0.422**	0.532**	0.466**	0.343**	1.00

decision making process variables (SDMP), indicating that these two constructs are distinct to each other. Both CF and SDMP variables show a strong and positive correlation with the two performance measures.

Nevertheless, correlation coefficients are used as first step indicators with respect to the support or not of the stated hypotheses, whilst the complete investigation of the hypotheses is undertaken using SEM, where the general rule for SEM is fulfilled (Bollen, 1993). The estimated path diagram for the proposed organizational innovativeness determination framework is presented in Figure 2. The boxes

Figure 2. Estimation results of the hypothesized framework

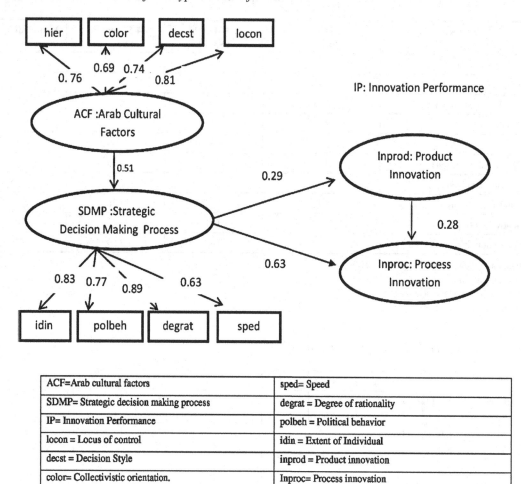

ACF=Arab cultural factors	sped= Speed
SDMP= Strategic decision making process	degrat = Degree of rationality
IP= Innovation Performance	polbeh = Political behavior
locon = Locus of control	idin = Extent of Individual
decst = Decision Style	inprod = Product innovation
color= Collectivistic orientation.	Inproc= Process innovation
hier =Hierarchy	

represent exogenous or endogenous observed variables and the circles represent the related latent variables. The light arrows indicate the observed variables that constitute the related latent variables and the bold arrows indicate the structural relationships between the corresponding variables. The numbers that are assigned to each arrow show the estimated standardized coefficients.

As presented in Figure 2, the results show that:

- Arab cultural factors have a direct and strong positive effect on strategic decision making process (0.51) supporting thus H1, H2, H3, and H4.
- Strategic decision making process has direct positive effect on innovation performance (0.63 for process innovation performance and 0.29 for product innovation performance), supporting thus H5, H6, H7 and H8. In addition the findings display that strategic decision making process fully mediate the relationship between Arab cultural factors and innovation performance.

Analytically, from the estimated results it is seen that the tested hypotheses were supported giving the following specific indications:

- The positive strength of correlation (0.51 at p<0.01) between ACF and SDMP is not satisfied highly to validate an exact multi-collinearity that could direct an imposing relationship between them (Tabachnick BG, Fidell LS.,2001). Therefore, it can be confirmed by the preliminary findings of the coefficient correlation that their distinct impact to each other. Additionally, the findings of the study specify the presence of mediating impact of SDMP between ACF and innovation performance.
- The ACF construct is robust, based on four experimental variables which are strongly loaded to the latent variable with rather equal values with error correlations being established between locus of control (locontr), decision style (destyl), collectivistic orientation (colorien), and hierarchy (hier). This technique is consistent with Anderson JC & Gerbing DW, 1988 recommendations, given the fact the researcher recognized to the items measuring the construct a logical and theoretical justification.
- In the same vein, there is no specific problem with the SDMP construct. Although the loading factor of ExtofId seems to be lower than the others, still keeps an acceptable level of range (above 0.5). In this connection, H1a-b, H2a-b, H3a-c, H4a-d, hypotheses are supported.
- As shown in the path analysis in Figure 2, SDMP variables increase (positive relationships) the two innovation performance variables. Therefore, responding to research hypotheses H5, H6, H7 and H8, the results expose the positive impact of SDMP on the two different types of innovation performance.

DISCUSSION OF RESULTS

According to Scriabina (2011), a crucial subject for managers is not whether they bear in mind that innovation is an art, but rather it is a process for organizational success based on their managerial actions. The thrust of this paper has been to examine this dimension in a rich country such as the State of Qatar as well as to determine whether the characteristics of the process of making SDs is deeply embedded in culture. In this regard Yang, Liu, Cao, and Li (2012) in their study concerning the influence of companies' external factors consider that government and social culture are two important environmental factors in determining innovation strategies and companies deal with different market and competition situations which also needs to be taken into consideration. The subject is fundamental to both theorists and practitioners, especially in fast growing countries such as the Qatar, for the assumption that performance derives from managerial actions to build relationships and have frequent interactions and communications between cultures, religions and civilizations in order to be able to work together and to lead effectively in the global competition. Following the study's findings, as hypothesized in H1, (internal) locus of control appears to reveal the negatively relationship on the degree of rationality and the speed during the making of the SD. This is in line with Lau and Woodman, (1995), who argue that internally oriented managers are less keen to take risks, and tending towards uncertainty avoidance. However, uncertainty avoidance is usually dealt with by gathering more information which then lengthens the SDM process (Schneider, 1989). The negative relationship between comprehensiveness/rationality and locus of control is consistent with past researches (Abdul Wahad,1979 ; Omar,1984) which points out that social norms and rituals arise the feeling of uncertainty and prevent the rationality of decision making. Second, as hypothesized in H2, the Qatari (Arabian) indigenous centralized decision style affects negatively the speed of the SDM process and the degree of rationality, indicating the results of other researches (Hall & Hall, 1990; Schneider & Barsoux, 2003; Trompenaars & Hampden-Turner, 2007; Adler 2002).Third, as hypothesized in H3, the collectivistic cultural orientation affects negatively the speed of decision making, and political behavior but positively the degree of rationality. Fourth, the study shows that hierarchy controls positively on the speed of decision making and political behavior, but negatively the degree of rationality and individual involvement in decision making process . This supports the previous suggestion from P. B. Smith et. al. 2007. Our research findings related to the positive linkage between strategic decision speed and innovation performance (H5) are in line with Zehir C.& Ozsahin M.'s work (2008), who indicate that the faster strategic decision making accelerates innovation performance. Thus, few more interesting findings have produced in terms of the integration between nation's cultural context and SDs process in determining innovation performance. On the one hand, the compatibility of cultural features with characteristics of decision making process is in line with findings reported in some studies (Ali,1998,1993; Al Faleh, 1987; Al Rasheed,2001) suggesting that organizations can observe their cultural diffusion in the face of globalization and other changes that have challenged their world (Baraket, 1993; Hill et al., 1998) and align it with other resources to build their competence and capabilities, including innovation. Overall, the study gained evidence to support its hypotheses indicating that Arab cultural drivers and forces influence organizational performance positively, particularly to the perception of innovation performance. However, Arab culture, much like other aspects of Arab society, has entered into a period of transition and the results of which remain premature (Jamil Hammoud,2011). From a practical point of view, Arab managers and mainly Qatari managers broaden their perspectives in serving customer needs through innovation by considering a proactive 'technology-push' approach than the reactive 'market-pull' approach that is more emphasized in the new product/service innovation context. Observing the particular findings it can be observed the differentiation in descending order, as follow: product innovation (0,27) and process innovation (0,64). However, the positive relationship between them (0,28) is aligned with Prajogo 's results (2005) which can be understood in a sense that the strategy for pursuing product innovation or broadening product variety often leads to adoption of process innovation. In particular, it is important for organizations to understand the cyclic role of product and process innovation in producing competitive advantage in the context of product life cycle (Tushman M, Nadler D. 1986). This is in line with the findings of Salim and Sulaiman (2011) and Fisher, (2001) where they note that innovation becomes a competitive advantage when it is based on in-depth understanding of customer needs, competitors' actions, and technological development. The aforementioned results confirm the hypotheses H6 and H7 that rationality and speed of decision making process influence innovation performance positively. Arab managers appear to comprehend that process innovation as a strategic goal can produce competitive advantage, for example, in terms of delivery, responsiveness, flexibility, or cost. Hence, the results of the study can be interpreted as nation-specific. One rational explanation is the fact that the research was conducted in Qatar dynamic business settings, one of the Gulf's petroleum-driven, traditionally inclined, micro-states, with relatively new companies since the country itself is a new rich state, reporting a competitive role in the global marketplace. Like most manufacturing-oriented countries, Qatar is moving towards creating a knowledge-based economy that is focused on innovation, using recent practices in its organizations.

Lastly, the results show that the low participation in strategic decision making influences innovation performance positively (H8). This support many authors arguments that the Arab managers are highly individualistic (e.g., Baali and Wardi, 1981; Elbanna et al., 2011; Zahra, 2011) but it contradicts to the strong theoretical suggestion that broad-based participation by management in the strategic planning and decision process enhances organizational outcomes (Hrebiniak and Joyce, 1984; Lines, 2004). Thus, Qatar's oil wealth and production have long been part of its branded image, and more recently, the country is confirmed by news articles that has the third largest natural gas reserves in the world. This in the lights of those findings leads to the single belief that centralized power in the process of accomplishing strategic goals, in the process of formalizing strategic goals and in the process of strategic decision making provides necessary flexibility and enhances innovation in the fast-moving environment to the state.

LIMITATIONS AND FUTURE STUDIES

Our survey was conducted in Qatar, a Gulf dynamic developing small country in which macro-economic decisions of governance are thought to be very important enhancing other environmental factors for firms in strategic decision making (market competitiveness, technological sophistication), while other surveys on strategic decision-making have been conducted in western countries. Thus, cultural differences to the specific State may have played a part in the results. Moreover, Qatari managers have the tendency to minimize control against the external environment. With this behavior, they can have the opportunity to direct their efforts towards controlling the immediate, internal environment of their companies (Papadakis et al., 1998, p. 134) and consequently conform to their strategic decision-making process. These results may be differentiated if the survey is extended to different sector organizations or to smaller firms. The survey should be extended so that results can be generalized. As a final note, it is important to comment on the clear existing gap in the literature in this region of the world. This suggests that it would be interesting to conduct a cross-country comparative study into other countries of the Gulf region, which may use other cultural and/or decision making process contexts as well as other methodologies to validate study findings, or explore additional facets of this interface.

ACKNOWLEDGMENT

The authors would like to thank the anonymous reviewers and the editor for their insightful comments and suggestions.

REFERENCES

Abdul Muhmin, A. (2005). Instrumental and interpersonal determinants of relationship satisfaction and commitment in industrial markets. *Journal of Business Research*, 58(5), 619–628. doi:10.1016/j.jbusres.2003.08.004

Abdul Wahab, A. (1979). *Decision-Making in Saudi Arabia*. Riyadh: Institute of Public Administration.

Adler, N. J. (2002).International Dimensions of Organizational Behaviour (4ed). Cincinnati, Ohio: South-Western.

Ahmad, K. (2006). *Management from the Islamic Perspective*. Kuala Lumpur: International Islamic University Malaysia.

Al-Buraey, M. A. (1990). *Management and Administration in Islam*. Saudi Arabia: Al-Dharan.

Al Faleh, M. (1987). Cultural Influences on Arab Management Development: A Case Study of Jordan. *Journal of Management Development, 6*(3), 19–34. doi:10.1108/eb051643

Al-Hegelan, H., & Palmer, M. (1985). Bureaucracy and development in Saudi Arabia. *The Middle East Journal, 39*(Winter), 48–59.

Al-Malik, S. (1989). *Strategic Decision Makers: A Study of Business and Government Executives in Saudi Arabia*. (Unpublished doctoral dissertation). Georgia State University.

Al Rasheed, A. (2001). Features of Traditional Arab Management and Organization in Jordan Business Environment. *Journal of Transnational Management Development, 6*(1-2), 27–53. doi:10.1300/J130v06n01_02

Albaum, G., & Herche, J. (1999). Management style comparisons among five European nations. *Journal of Global Marketing, 12*(4), 5–27. doi:10.1300/J042v12n04_02

Albaum, G., Herche, J., Yu, J., Evangelista, F., Murphy, B., & Poon, P. (2008). Differences in Marketing Managers' Decision Making Styles Within the Asia-Pacific Region. *Journal of Global Marketing, 21*(1), 63–78. doi:10.1300/J042v21n01_06

Alegre, J., Lapiedra, R., & Chiva, R. (2006). A measurement scale for product innovation performance. *European Journal of Innovation Management, 5*(4), 333–346. doi:10.1108/14601060610707812

Ali, J. A. (1989). Decision Style and Work Satisfaction of Arab Gulf Executives: A Cross-National Study. *International Studies of Management & Organization, 19*, 22–37.

Ali, J. A. (1990). Management theory in a transitional society: The Arab's experience. *International Studies of Management & Organization, 20*, 7–35.

Ali, J. A. (1993). Decision Making Style, Individualism and Attitudes Toward Risk of Arab Executives. *International Studies of Management & Organization,* (Fall): 23, 53–74.

Ali, J. A. (1995). Cultural discontinuity and Arab management thought. *International Studies of Management & Organization, 25*, 7–30.

Ali, J. A. (1995a). Cultural discontinuity in Arab management thought. *International Studies of Management & Organization, 25*, 7–30.

Ali, J. A. (1995b). Preface: Management in a sheiko-capitalist system. *International Studies of Management & Organization, 25*, 3–6.

Ali, J. A. (1998). The typology of the Arab individual: Implications for management and business organizations. *The International Journal of Sociology and Social Policy, 18*(11/12), 1–19. doi:10.1108/01443339810788551

Ali, J. A. (2005). *Islamic Perspectives on Management and Organization*. Cheltenham, UK: Edward Elgar Publishing.

Ali, J. A. (2010). Islamic challenges to HR in modern organizations. *Personnel Review*, *39*(6), 692–711. doi:10.1108/00483481011075567

Ali, J. A., & Sabri, H. (2001). Organizational culture and job satisfaction in Jordan. *Journal of Transnational Management Development*, *6*(1-2), 105–118. doi:10.1300/J130v06n01_06

Ali, J. A., & Schaupp, L. D. (1992). Value Systems as Predictors of Managerial Decision Styles of Arab Executives. *International Journal of Manpower*, *13*(3), 19–26. doi:10.1108/01437729210010274

Amason, A. C. (1996). Distinguishing the effects of functional and dysfunctional conflict on strategic decision making: Resolving a paradox for top management teams. *Academy of Management Journal*, *39*(1), 123–148. doi:10.2307/256633

Ancona, D. G., Okhuysen, G. A., & Perlow, L. A. (2001). Taking time to integrate temporal research. *Academy of Management Review*, *26*, 512–529.

Anderson, J. C., & Gerbing, D. W. (1988). Structural equation modeling in practice: A review and recommended two-step approach. *Psychological Bulletin*, *103*(3), 411–423. doi:10.1037/0033-2909.103.3.411

Arbuckle, J. L. (2003). *AMOS 5.0 update to the AMOS user's guide*. Chicago: SPSS.

Arendt, S., & Brettel, M. (2010). Understanding the influence of corporate social responsibility on corporate identity: Image, and Firm Performance. *Management Decision*, *48*(10), 1469–1492. doi:10.1108/00251741011090289

Avlonitis, G. J., Kouremenos, A., & Tzokas, N. (1994). Assessing the innovativeness of organizations and its antecedents: Project innovstrat. *European Journal of Marketing*, *28*(11), 5–28. doi:10.1108/03090569410075812

Baali, F., & Wardi, A. (1981). *Ibn Khaldun and Islamic Thought Style*. Boston, MA: Haland G K.

Baker, M., & AbouIsmail, F. (1993). Organizational buying behavior in the Gulf. *International Marketing Review*, *10*(6), 42–60. doi:10.1108/02651339310051614

Barakat, H. (1983). *Contemporary Arab Society: An Exploratory Sociological Study*. Beirut, Lebanon: Arab Unity Studies Center. (In Arabic)

Barakat, H. (1993). *The Arab World: Society, Culture and the State*. Berkeley, CA: University of California Press.

Baruch, Y., & Holtom, B. C. (2008). Survey response rate levels and trends in organizational research. *Human Relations*, *61*(8), 1139–1160. doi:10.1177/0018726708094863

Baruch, Y., & Ramalho, N. (2006). Communalities and distinctions in the measurement of organizational performance and effectiveness across for-profit and nonprofit sectors. *Nonprofit and Voluntary Sector Quarterly*, *35*(1), 39–65. doi:10.1177/0899764005282468

Baum, J. R., & Wally, S. (2003). Strategic decision speed and firm performance. *Strategic Management Journal, 24*(11), 1107–1129. doi:10.1002/smj.343

Beekun, R. E. (2006). *Strategic Planning and Implementation for Islamic Organizations*. Herndon, VA: The International Institute of Islamic Thought.

Bhuian, S. (1998). An empirical examination of market orientation in Saudi Arabian manufacturing companies. *Journal of Business Research, 43*(1), 13–25. doi:10.1016/S0148-2963(97)00130-6

Bjerke, B., & Abdulrahim, A. (1993). Culture's consequences: Management in Saudi Arabia. *Leadership and Organization Development Journal, 14*(2), 30–35. doi:10.1108/01437739310032700

Bollen, K. A. (1989). *Structural Equations with Latent Variables*. New York, NY: Wiley. doi:10.1002/9781118619179

Bollen, K. A., & Long, J. S. (1993). *Testing structural equation modeling*. Newbury Park, CA: Sage.

Bolwijn, P. T., & Kumpe, T. (1990). Manufacturing in the 1990s—productivity, flexibility, and innovation. *Long Range Planning, 23*(4), 44–57. doi:10.1016/0024-6301(90)90151-S

Boussif, D. (2010). Decision-Making Styles of Arab Executives: Insights from Tunisia. *Communications of the IBIMA, 2010* (2010), article ID 66660955. Retrieved February 12, 2013, http://www.ibimapublishing.com/journals/CIBIMA/cibima.html

Branine, M. (2002). Algeria's employment policies and practice: An overview. *International Journal of Employment Studies, 10*, 133–152.

Branine, M., & Pollard, D. (2010). Human resource management with Islamic management principles: A dialectic for a reverse diffusion in management. *Personnel Review, 39*(6), 712–727. doi:10.1108/00483481011075576

Brouthers, K. D., Brouthers, L. E., & Werner, S. (2000). Influences on strategic decision-making in the Dutch financial services industry. *Journal of Management, 26*(5), 863–883. doi:10.1177/014920630002600506

Budhwar, P., & Mellahi, K. (2006). Introduction: Managing human resources in the Middle East. In P. Budhwar & K. Mellahi (Eds.), *Managing Human Resources in the Middle* (pp. 1–19). London: Routledge.

Budhwar, P., & Mellahi, K. (2006). Human resource management in the Middle East: emerging HRM models and future challenges for research and policy. In Managing Human Resources in the Middle East (pp. 291-301). London: Routledge.

Budhwar, P., & Mellahi, K. (2007). Introduction: Human resources management in the Middle East. *International Journal of Human Resource Management, 18*(1), 2–10. doi:10.1080/09585190601068227

Capon, N., Farley, J. U., & Hulbert, J. M. (1987). *Corporate Strategic Planning*. New York, NY: Columbia University Press.

Carr, C. (1997). Strategic investment decisions and short-termism: Germany versus Britain. In V. Papadakis & P. Barwise (Eds.), *Strategic Decisions* (pp. 107–125). Boston, MA: Kluwer Academic Publishers. doi:10.1007/978-1-4615-6195-8_8

Chen, J., & Tsou, H. (2007). Information technology adoption for service innovation practices and competitive advantage: The case of financial firms. *Information Research, 12*, 1368–1613.

Child, J., & Tsai, T. (2005). The dynamic between firms' environmental strategies and institutional constraints in emerging economies: Evidence from China and Taiwan. *Journal of Management Studies, 42*(1), 95–125. doi:10.1111/j.1467-6486.2005.00490.x

Cosier, R., Schwenk, C. R., & Dalton, D. (1992). Managerial decision making in Japan, the U.S., and Hong Kong. *The International Journal of Conflict Management, 3*(2), 151–160. doi:10.1108/eb022710

Cray, D., Mallory, G. R., Butler, R. J., Hickson, D. J., & Wilson, D. C. (1988). Sporadic, fluid and constricted processes: Three types of strategic decision making in organizations. *Journal of Management Studies, 25*(1), 13–39. doi:10.1111/j.1467-6486.1988.tb00020.x

Dadfar, H. (1993). In search of Arab management, Direction and identity. In *Proceedings of the Arab Management Conference*. Bradford Management Centre, University of Bradford

Dağ, İ. (1991). Rotter'in iç-dış kontrol odağı ölçeğinin üniversite öğrencileri için güvenirliği ve eçerliği. *Psikoloji Dergisi, 7*, 10–16.

Dawes, P. L., & Massey, G. R. (2005). Antecedents of conflict in marketing's cross-functional relationship with sales. *European Journal of Marketing, 39*(11/12), 1327–1344. doi:10.1108/03090560510623280

Dean, J. W., & Sharfman, M. P. (1993). Procedural rationality in the strategic decision-making process. *Journal of Management Studies, 30*(4), 587–610. doi:10.1111/j.1467-6486.1993.tb00317.x

Dean, J. W., & Sharfman, M. P. (1996). Does decision process matter? A study of strategic decision making effectiveness. *Academy of Management Journal, 39*(2), 368–396. doi:10.2307/256784

Dean, J. W., Sharfman, M. P., & Ford, C. A. (1993). The relationship of procedural rationality and political behaviour in strategic decision-making. *Decision Sciences, 24*(6), 1069–1083. doi:10.1111/j.1540-5915.1993.tb00504.x

Dedoussis, E. (2004). A Cross-Cultural Comparison of Organizational Culture: Evidence from Universities in the Arab World and Japan. *Cross Cultural Management, 11*(1), 15–34. doi:10.1108/13527600410797729

Deresky, H. (1994). *International Management: Managing Across Borders and Cultures*. New York, NY: Harper Collins College Publ.

Deshpande, R., Farley, J. U., & Webster, F. E. Jr. (1993). Corporate culture customer orientation and innovativeness in Japanese firms: A quadrat analysis. *Journal of Marketing, 57*(1), 23–27. doi:10.2307/1252055

Dorfman, P. W., & Howell, J. P. (1988). Dimensions of national culture and effective leadership patterns: Hofstede revisited. In R. N. Farmer & E. G. McGoun (Eds.), *Advances in International Comparative Management (pp. 127-50)*. New York, NY: JAI.

Dundon, E. (2005). Innovation triangle. *Leadership Excellence, 22*, 16.

Dwairy, M., Achoui, M., Abouserie, R., Farah, A., Sakhleh, A., Fayad, M., & Khan, H. (2006). Parenting Styles in Arab Societies: A First Cross-regional Research Study. *Journal of Cross-Cultural Psychology, 37*(3), 230–247. doi:10.1177/0022022106286922

Earley, P. C. (2006). Leading cultural research in the future: A matter of paradigms and taste. *Journal of International Business Studies*, *37*(6), 922–931. doi:10.1057/palgrave.jibs.8400236

Eisenhardt, K. M. (1989). Making fast strategic decisions in high-velocity environments. *Academy of Management Journal*, *32*(3), 543–576. doi:10.2307/256434

Eisenhardt, K. M. (1997). Strategic decisions and all that jazz. *Business Strategy Review*, *8*(3), 1–3. doi:10.1111/1467-8616.00031

Eisenhardt, K. M., & Bourgeois, L. J. I. (1988). Politics of strategic decision making in high-velocity environments: Toward a midrange theory. *Academy of Management Journal*, *31*(4), 737–770. doi:10.2307/256337

Elbana, S. (2012). Slack, Planning and Organizational Performance: Evidence from the Arab Middle East. *European Management Review*, *9*(2), 99–115. doi:10.1111/j.1740-4762.2012.01028.x

Elbana, S., & Child, J. (2007). Influences on Strategic Decision effectiveness: Development and test of an integrative model. *Strategic Management Journal*, *28*(4), 431–453. doi:10.1002/smj.597

Elbanna, S. (2006). Strategic decision making: Process perspectives. *International Journal of Management Reviews*, *8*(1), 1–20. doi:10.1111/j.1468-2370.2006.00118.x

Elbanna, S. (2008). Planning and participation as determinants of strategic planning effectiveness: Evidence from the Arabic context. *Management Decision*, *46*(5), 779–796. doi:10.1108/00251740810873761

Elbanna, S., Ali, A. J., & Dayan, M. (2011). Conflict in strategic decision making: Do the setting and environment matter? *The International Journal of Conflict Management*, *22*(3), 278–299. doi:10.1108/10444061111152973

Eyler, A. A., Mayer, J., Rafii, R., Housemann, R., & Brownson, R. C. (1999). Key informant surveys as a tool to implement and evaluate physical activity interventions in the community. *Health Education Research*, *14*(2), 289–298. doi:10.1093/her/14.2.289 PMID:10387507

Fisher, M. (2001). Innovation, knowledge creation and systems of innovation. *The Annals of Regional Science*, *35*(2), 199–216. doi:10.1007/s001680000034

Forbes, D. P. (2000). *The strategic implications of managerial cognition and firm decision processes: evidence from a new venture context*. (Unpublished PhD thesis). New York University, New York, NY.

Forstenlechner, I., & Mellahi, K. (2011). Gaining legitimacy through hiring local workforce at a premium: The case of MNEs in the United Arab Emirates. *Journal of World Business*, *46*(4), 455–461. doi:10.1016/j.jwb.2010.10.006

Fortuin, F. T. J. M., & Omta, S. W. F. (2009). Innovation drivers and harriers in food processing. *British Food Journal*, *111*(8), 839–851. doi:10.1108/00070700910980955

Fredrickson, J. W. (1984). The comprehensiveness of strategic decision processes: Extension, observations, future directions. *Academy of Management Journal*, *27*(3), 445–466. doi:10.2307/256039

Fredrickson, J. W., & Laquinto, A. L. (1989). Inertia and creeping rationality in strategic decisions. *Academy of Management Journal*, *32*(3), 516–542. doi:10.2307/256433

Fredrickson, J. W., & Terence, R. M. (1984). Strategic Decision Processes: Comprehensiveness and Performance in an Industry with an Unstable Environment. *Academy of Management Journal, 27*(2), 399–423. doi:10.2307/255932

Friman, M., Garling, T., Millett, B., Mattsson, J., & Johnston, R. (2002). An analysis of international business-to-business relationships based on the commitment-trust theory. *Industrial Marketing Management, 31*(5), 403–409. doi:10.1016/S0019-8501(01)00154-7

Gallupe, R. B., Dennis, R. A., Cooper, A. W., Vallacich, S. G., Bastianutti, M. L., & Nunamaker, G. F. (1992). Electronic brainstorming and group size. *Academy of Management Journal, 35*(2), 350–369. doi:10.2307/256377

Gannon, M. (1994). *Understanding Global Cultures: Metaphorical Journeys Through 17 Countries.* Thousand Oaks, CA: Sage Publications.

Gobeli, D. H., & Brown, W. B. (1994). Technological innovation strategies. *Engineering Management Journal, 6*, 17–24.

Grant, R. M. (1998). Contemporary Strategy Analysis: Concepts, Techniques, Applications (3rd Ed.). Oxford, UK: Blackwell Publishing.

Gregg, G. S. (2005). *The Middle East: A Cultural Psychology.* Oxford, UK: Oxford University Press.

Haddad, R. (2003). Taking the Veil: Reem Haddad on Why Lebanese Women Are Covering Up. *New Internationalist, 360*, 3–12.

Hair, F., Anderson, R., Tatham, R., & Black, W. (1995). *Multivariate Data Analysis with Readings* (4th ed.). London, UK: Prentice-Hall.

Halikias, J., & Panayotopoulou, L. (2003). Chief executive personality and export involvement. *Management Decision, 41*(4), 340–349. doi:10.1108/00251740310468072

Hammoud, J. (2011). Consultative Authority Decision Making: On the Development and Characterization of Arab Corporate Culture. *International Journal of Business and Social Science, 2*, 141–148.

Harastani, H., & Al-Turki, M. (1985). *Patients Queuing in Out-Patient Clinics in Riyadh's Public Hospitals.* Riyadh, Saudi Arabia: Institute of Public Administration. (In Arabic)

Harris, P., & Moran, R. (1987). *Managing cultural differences* (2nd ed.). Houston, TX: Gulf Publishing Co.

Hart, P. M. (1994). Teacher quality of work life: Integrating work experiences, psychological distress and morale. *Journal of Occupational and Organizational Psychology, 67*(2), 109–132. doi:10.1111/j.2044-8325.1994.tb00555.x

Head, T. C., & Sorenson, P. F. (1993). Cultural values and organizational development: A seven-country study. *Leadership and Organization Development Journal, 14*(2), 3–7. doi:10.1108/01437739310032656

Hickson, D. J., & Pugh, D. S. (1995). *Management worldwide.* London, UK: Penguin Books.

Hickson, D. J., & Pugh, D. S. (2001). *Management worldwide: Distinctive styles Amid globalization* (2nd ed.). London, UK: Penguin Books.

Hill, C., Loch, K., Straub, D. W., & El-Sheshai, K. (1998). A Qualitative Assessment of Arab Culture and Information Technology Transfer. *Journal of Global Information Management, 6*(3), 29–38. doi:10.4018/jgim.1998070103

Hofstede, G. (1980). *Culture consequences: International differences in work-related values*. Beverly Hills, CA: Sage Publications.

Hofstede, G. (1991). *Cultures and organizations: software of the mind*. New York, NY: McGraw-Hill.

Hofstede, G. (2001). *Culture's Consequences: Comparing Values, Behaviors, Institutions and Organizations Across Nations* (2nd ed.). Thousand Oaks, CA: Sage Publications.

Hofstede, G. (2007). Asian management in the 21st century. *Asia Pacific Journal of Management, 24*(4), 411–420. doi:10.1007/s10490-007-9049-0

Hofstede, G. (2008). Dimensionalizing Cultures: The Hofstede Model in Context. *Online Readings in Psychology and Culture*. Retrieved February 10/2013 from Http://www.ac.wwu.edu/~culture/hofstede.htm

Hofstede, G. (2010). The Hofstede model: Applications to global branding and advertising strategy and research. *International Journal of Advertising, 29*(1), 85–110. doi:10.2501/S026504870920104X

Hofstede, G., & Hofstede, G. J. (2004). *Cultures and Organizations: Software for the Mind. Intercultural Cooperation and Its Importance for Survival* (2nd ed.). New York, NY: McGraw-Hill.

Hofstede, G., Hofstede, G. J., & Minkov, M. (2010). *Cultures and organizations: Software of the mind: Intercultural cooperation and its importance for survival* (3rd ed.). Cambridge, MA: McGraw Hill.

Hoskisson, R. E., Hitt, M. A., Johnson, R. A., & Grossman, W. (2002). Conflicting voices: The effects of institutional ownership heterogeneity and internal governance on corporate innovation strategies. *Academy of Management Journal, 45*(4), 697–716. doi:10.2307/3069305

Hough, J. R., & White, M. A. (2003). Environmental dynamism and strategic decision-making rationality: An examination at the decision level. *Strategic Management Journal, 24*(5), 481–489. doi:10.1002/smj.303

House, R. J., Hanges, P. J., Javidan, M., Dorfman, P. W., & Gupta, V. (2004). *Leadership, Culture, and Organizations: The GLOBE Study of 62 Societies*. Thousand Oaks, CA: Sage.

Howell, J. M., & Higgins, C. A. (1990). Champions of technological innovation. *Administrative Science Quarterly, 35*(2), 317–341. doi:10.2307/2393393

Huber, G. P. (1990). A theory of the effects of an advanced information technologies on organization designs intelligence and decision making. *Academy of Management Review, 15*, 47–71.

Iqbal, A. (2011). Creativity and innovation in Saudi Arahia: An overview. *Innovation: Management. Policy & Practice, 13*(3), 391–406. doi:10.5172/impp.2011.13.3.376

Jones, L. W. (1993). *High Speed, Management: Time-Based Strategies for Managers and Organizations*. San Francisco, CA: Jossey-Bass.

Jones, R. E., Jacobs, L. W., & Spijker, W. V. (1992). Strategic decision processes in international firms. *Management International Review, 32*, 219–237.

Joreskog, K. G., & Sorbom, D. (2004). *LISREL 8.7 for Windows, (computer software)*. Lincolnwood, IL: Scientific Software International INC.

Judge, W. Q., & Miller, A. (1991). Antecedents and outcomes of decision speed in different environmental contexts. *Academy of Management Journal, 34*(2), 449–463. doi:10.2307/256451 PMID:10111313

Kabasakal, H., Dastmalchian, A., Karacay, G., & Bayraktar, S. (2012). Leadership and culture in the MENA region: An analysis of the GLOBE project. *Journal of World Business, 47*(4), 519–529. doi:10.1016/j.jwb.2012.01.005

Katos, A. V. (2010). The influence of information and communication technologies on enabling trade: A cross-country investigation. *Journal of Information Technology Impact, 10,* 15–24.

Kavoossi, M. (2000). *The Globalization of Business and the Middle East: Opportunities and Constraints.* Westport, CT: Quorum Books.

Kelloway, E. K. (1998). *Using LISREL for structural equation modelling: a researcher's guide.* Newbury Park, CA: SAGE Publications.

Kepner-Tregoe, G. (2001). Hurry up and decide. *Business Week, 3732,* 16.

Khalifa, A. S. (2001). *Towards and Islamic Foundation of Strategic Business Management.* Kuala Lumpur, Malaysia: International Islamic University Malaysia.

Khaliq, A. (2009). Leadership and work motivation from the cross cultural perspective. *International Journal of Commerce and Management, 19*(1), 72–84. doi:10.1108/10569210910939681

Khatri, N., & Alvin, H. N. (2000). The role of intuition in strategic decision making. *Human Relations, 53*(1), 57–86. doi:10.1177/0018726700531004

Kim, Y., Song, K., & Lee, J. (1993). Determinants of technological innovation in the small firms of Korea. *R & D Management, 23*(3), 215–226. doi:10.1111/j.1467-9310.1993.tb00824.x

Kozan, M. K. (1993). Cultural and industrialization level influences on leadership attitudes for Turkish managers. *International Studies of Management & Organization, 23,* 7–17.

Kraft, K. (1990). Are product- and process-innovations independent of each other? *Applied Economics, 22*(8), 1029–1038. doi:10.1080/00036849000000132

Lau, C. M., & Woodman, R. W. (1995). Understanding organizational change: A schematic perspective. *Academy of Management Journal, 38*(2), 537–554. doi:10.2307/256692

Laurent, A. (1983). The Cultural Diversity of Western Conceptions of Management. *International Studies of Management & Organization, 13,* 75–96.

Lewin, A. Y., & Stephens, C. U. (1994). CEO attributes as determinants of organization design: An integrated model. *Organization Studies, 15*(2), 183–212. doi:10.1177/017084069401500202

Li, S., Ragu-Nathan, B., Ragu-Nathan, T., & Subba Rao, S. (2006). The impact of supply chain management practices on competitive advantage and organizational performance. *Omega, 34*(2), 107–124. doi:10.1016/j.omega.2004.08.002

Luna-Arocas, R., & Camps, J. (2008). A model of high performance work practices and turnover intentions. *Personnel Review*, *37*(1), 26–46. doi:10.1108/00483480810839950

Malshe, A., Al-Khatib, J., Al-Habib, M., & Ezzi, S. (2012). Exploration of sales-marketing interface nuances in Saudi Arabia. *Journal of Business Research*, *65*(8), 1119–1125. doi:10.1016/j.jbusres.2011.08.006

Mark, S. (1997). Delaying decisions stifles: Industrial management decision-making progress. *Management Decision*, *45*, 1622–1635.

Marshall, J. J., & Vredenburg, H. (1992). An empirical study of factors influencing innovation implementation in industrial sales organizations. *Journal of the Academy of Marketing Science*, *20*(3), 205–215. doi:10.1007/BF02723407

Martinsons, G. M., & Robert, D. M. (2007). Strategic decision making and support systems: Comparing American, Japanese and Chinese management. *Decision Support Systems*, *43*(1), 284–300. doi:10.1016/j.dss.2006.10.005

Melewar, T. C., Turnbull, S., & Balabanis, G. (2000). International advertising strategies of multinational enterprises in the Middle East. *International Journal of Advertising*, *19*, 529–547.

Mellahi, K. (2003). National culture and management practices: The case of GCCs. In M. Tayeb (Ed.), *International management: Theory and practices*. London, UK: Prentice-Hall.

Mellahi, K. (2006). Human resource management in Saudi Arabia. In P. Budhwar & K. Mellahi (Eds.), *Managing Human Resources in the Middle East*. London, UK: Routledge.

Mellahi, K., & Al-Hinai, S. (2000). Local workers in Gulf co-operation countries: Assets or liabilities? *Middle Eastern Studies*, *36*(3), 177–190. doi:10.1080/00263200008701323

Mellahi, K., & Budhwar, P. (2010). Introduction: Islam and human resource management. *Personnel Review*, *39*(6), 685–691. doi:10.1108/00483481011075558

Metcalfe, B. D. (2007). Gender and human resource management in the Middle East. *International Journal of Human Resource Management*, *18*(1), 54–74. doi:10.1080/09585190601068292

Meyer, A. D., & Goes, J. B. (1988). Organizational assimilation of innovations: A multilevel contextual analysis. *Academy of Management Journal*, *31*(4), 897–923. doi:10.2307/256344

Miller, C. C., Burke, M. L., & Glich, H. M. (1998). Cognitive Diversity among Upper-Echelon Executives: Implications for strategic decision processes. *Strategic Management Journal*, *19*(1), 39–58. doi:10.1002/(SICI)1097-0266(199801)19:1<39::AID-SMJ932>3.0.CO;2-A

Miller, D., & Droge, C. (1986). Psychological and traditional determinants of structure. *Administrative Science Quarterly*, *31*(4), 539–560. doi:10.2307/2392963

Miller, D., & Friesen, P. H. (1982). Innovation in conservative and entrepreneurial firms: Two models of strategic momentum. *Strategic Management Journal*, *3*(1), 1–25. doi:10.1002/smj.4250030102

Minkov, M. L., & Hofstede, G. (2011). The evolution of Hofstede's doctrine. *Cross Cultural Management: An International Journal*, *18*(1), 10–20. doi:10.1108/13527601111104269

Mintzberg, H. (1985). The organization as a political arena. *Journal of Management Studies*, *22*(2), 133–154. doi:10.1111/j.1467-6486.1985.tb00069.x

Mintzberg, H. (1998). *Strategy Safari: a Guided Tour Through the Wilds of Strategic Management*. London, UK: Prentice-Hall.

Mohamed, M. S., O'Sullivan, K. J., & Ribiere, V. (2008). A Paradigm Shift in the Arab Region Knowledge Evolution. *Journal of Knowledge Management*, *12*(5), 107–220. doi:10.1108/13673270810902975

Muna, F. (1980). *The Arab Executive*. New York, NY: St. Martin's Press.

Nunnally, J. (1978). *Psychometric theory*. New York, NY: McGraw-Hill.

Nutt, P. C. (1984). Types of organizational decision processes. *Administrative Science Quarterly*, *29*(3), 414–450. doi:10.2307/2393033 PMID:10268867

Nutt, P. C. (1998). Evaluating alternatives to make strategic choices. *Omega*, *26*(3), 333–354. doi:10.1016/S0305-0483(97)00068-6

Oliver, J. E., Jose, P. E., & Brough, P. (2006). Confirmatory Factor Analysis of the Work Locus of Control Scale. *Educational and Psychological Measurement*, *66*(5), 835–851. doi:10.1177/0013164405285544

Omar, A. (1984). *The Role of Training in Saudi Arabian Public Agencies*. Riyadh, Saudi Arabia: Institute of Public Administration.

Ouchi, W. G. (1980). Markets, bureaucracies, and clans. *Administrative Science Quarterly*, *25*(1), 129–141. doi:10.2307/2392231

Papadakis, V. M. (1998). Strategic investment decision processes and organizational performance: An empirical examination. *British Journal of Management*, *9*(2), 115–132. doi:10.1111/1467-8551.00078

Papadakis, V. M., Lioukas, S., & Chambers, D. (1998). Strategic decision-making processes: The role of management and context. *Strategic Management Journal*, *19*(2), 115–147. doi:10.1002/(SICI)1097-0266(199802)19:2<115::AID-SMJ941>3.0.CO;2-5

Parnell, A. J., & Hatem, T. (1999). Cultural Antecedents of Behavioural Differences between American and Egyptian managers. *Journal of Management Studies*, *36*(3), 399–418. doi:10.1111/1467-6486.00142

Peterson, J. E. (2006). Qatar and the World: Branding for a Micro-State. *The Middle East Journal*, *60*, 732–748.

Pettigrew, A. M. (1987). Strategy formulation as a political process. *International Studies of Management & Organization*, *7*, 78–87.

Phan, P. H. (2000). *Taking Back the Boardroom*. Singapore: McGraw-Hill.

Prajogo, I. D., & Amrik, S. S. (2006). The integration of TQM and technology/R&D management in determining quality and innovation performance. *Omega*, *34*(3), 296–312. doi:10.1016/j.omega.2004.11.004

Prastacos, G., Soderquist, K., Spanos, Y., & Wassenhove, L. V. (2002). An integrated framework for managing change in the new competitive landscape. *European Management Journal*, *20*(1), 55–71. doi:10.1016/S0263-2373(01)00114-1

Rajagopalan, N., Rasheed, M. A., & Datta, D. (1993). Diversification and performance: Critical review and future directions. *Journal of Management, 19*, 349–384. doi:10.1177/014920639301900207

Razzouk, N., & Al-Khatib, J. (1993). The nature of television advertising in Saudi Arabia: Content analysis and marketing implications. *Journal of International Consumer Marketing, 6*(2), 65–90. doi:10.1300/J046v06n02_06

Rettab, B., Ben Brik, A., & Mellahi, K. (2009). Study of management perceptions of the impact of corporate social responsibility on organisational performance in emerging economies: The case of Dubai. *Journal of Business Ethics, 89*(3), 371–390. doi:10.1007/s10551-008-0005-9

Rice, G. (1999). Islamic ethics and the implications for business. *Journal of Business Ethics, 18*(4), 345–358. doi:10.1023/A:1005711414306

Riddle, L., Ralston, D. A., Mellahi, K., Butt, A. N., & Dalgic, T. (2007). *Middle East managerial values: Evidence from five countries*. Philadelphia, PA: Academy of Management Meeting.

Robertson, J. C., Al–Khatib, A. J., Al–Habib, D. M., & Lanoue, D. (2001). Beliefs about Work in the Middle East and the Convergence Versus Divergence of Values. *Journal of World Business, 36*(3), 223–244. doi:10.1016/S1090-9516(01)00053-0

Rossier, J., Dahourou, D., & Mccrae, R. R. (2005). Structural and Mean-Level Analyses of the Five-Factor Model and Locus of Control: Further Evidence From Africa. *Journal of Cross-Cultural Psychology, 36*(2), 227–246. doi:10.1177/0022022104272903

Rotter, J. B. (1954). *Social Learning and Clinical Psychology*. New York, NY: Prentice-Hall. doi:10.1037/10788-000

Rotter, J. B. (1966). Generalized expectancies for internal versus external control of reinforcement. *Psychological Monographs, 80*(1), 1–28. doi:10.1037/h0092976 PMID:5340840

Rowley, J., Baregheh, A., & Samhrook, S. (2011). Towards an innovation-type mapping tool. *Management Decision, 49*(1), 73–86. doi:10.1108/00251741111094446

Sabri, H. (2004). Socio-cultural values and organizational culture. In K. Becker (Ed.), *Islam and Business*. New Brunswick, NJ: Haworth Press.

Sabri, H. (2007). Jordanian managers' leadership styles in comparison with the International Air Transport Association (IATA) and prospects for knowledge management in Jordan. *International Journal of Commerce and Management, 17*(1/2), 56–72. doi:10.1108/10569210710774758

Salim, I. M., & Sulaiman, M. (2011). Impact of organizational innovation on firm performance: Evidence from Malaysian-hased ICT companies. *Business and Management Review, 1*, 10–16.

Sawyerr, O. O., Ebrahimi, B. P., & Luk, V. W. M. (2003). Environment, executive information search activities, and firm performance: A comparative study of Hong Kong and Nigerian decision-makers. *International Journal of Cross Cultural Management, 3*(1), 67–92. doi:10.1177/1470595803003001851

Schneider, S. C. (1989). Strategy formulation: The impact of national cultural. *Organization Studies, 10*(2), 149–168. doi:10.1177/017084068901000202

Schneider, S. C., & Barsoux, J. L. (2003). Managing across cultures. (2ed.) Harlow, England: Prentice Hall.

Schneider, S. C., & Meyer, D. A. (1991). Interpreting and responding to strategic issues: The impact of national culture. *Strategic Management Journal, 12*(4), 307–320. doi:10.1002/smj.4250120406

Schwartz, S. H. (1999). A theory of cultural values and some implications for work. *Applied Psychology, 48*(1), 23–47. doi:10.1111/j.1464-0597.1999.tb00047.x

Scriabina, N. (2011). Organize how you innovate. *Quality Progress, 44,* 16–22.

Shane, S., Venkataraman, S., & MacMillan, I. (1995). Cultural differences in innovation championing strategies. *Journal of Management, 21*(5), 931–952. doi:10.1177/014920639502100507

Shrivastava, P., & Grant, J. H. (1985). Empirically derived models of strategic decision-making process. *Strategic Management Journal, 6*(2), 97–113. doi:10.1002/smj.4250060202

Smith, B. P., Achoui, M., & Harb, C. (2007). Unity and Diversity in Arab Managerial Styles. *International Journal of Cross Cultural Management, 7*(3), 275–289. doi:10.1177/1470595807083374

Spoull, L., & Kiesler, S. (1986). Reducing social context cues: Electronic mail in organizational communication. *Management Science, 32*(11), 1492–1512. doi:10.1287/mnsc.32.11.1492

Stevenson, H., & Gumpert, D. (1985). The heart of entrepreneurship. *Harvard Business Review, 63,* 85–94.

Subramanian, A., & Nilakanta, S. (1996). Organizational innovativeness: Exploring the relationship between organizational determinants of innovation, types of innovations, and measures of organizational performance. *Omega, 24*(6), 631–647. doi:10.1016/S0305-0483(96)00031-X

Tabachnick, B. G., & Fidell, L. S. (2001). *Using multivariate statistics* (4th ed.). Nedham Heights, MA: Allyn & Bacon.

Taras, V., Rowney, J., & Steel, P. (2009). Half a century of measuring culture: Review of approaches, challenges, and limitations based on the analysis of 121 instruments for quantifying culture. *Journal of International Management, 15*(4), 357–373. doi:10.1016/j.intman.2008.08.005

Teece, D., Pisano, G., & Shuen, A. (1997). Dynamic capabilities and strategic management. *Strategic Management Journal, 18*(7), 509–533. doi:10.1002/(SICI)1097-0266(199708)18:7<509::AID-SMJ882>3.0.CO;2-Z

Tidd, J., Bessant, J., & Pavitt, K. (1997). *Managing innovation: integrating technological, market, and organizational change.* Chichester, UK: Wiley.

Torben, J. A. (2001). Information technology, strategic decision approaches and organizational performance in different industrial settings. *The Journal of Strategic Information Systems, 10*(2), 101–119. doi:10.1016/S0963-8687(01)00043-9

Triandis, H. C., & Suh, E. M. (2002). Cultural influences on personality. *Annual Review of Psychology, 53*(1), 133–160. doi:10.1146/annurev.psych.53.100901.135200 PMID:11752482

Trompenaars, F., & Hampden-Turner, C. (1997). *Riding the Waves of Culture: Understanding Cultural Diversity in Business* (2nd ed.). London, UK: McGraw-Hill.

Tuma, E. H. (1988). Institutionalized Obstacles to Development: The Case of Egypt. *World Development, 16*(10), 1185–1198. doi:10.1016/0305-750X(88)90085-X

Tushman, M., & Nadler, D. (1986). Organizing for innovation. *California Management Review, 28*(3), 74–92. doi:10.2307/41165203

Twenge, M. J., Zhang, L., & Im, C. (2004). It's Beyond My Control: A Cross-Temporal Meta-Analysis of Increasing Externality in Locus of Control,1960-2002. *Personality and Social Psychology Review, 8*(3), 308–319. doi:10.1207/s15327957pspr0803_5 PMID:15454351

Vigoda-Gadot, E., & Cohen, A. (2004). *Citizenship and Management in Public Administration: Integrating Behavioral Theory and Managerial Thinking.* Cheltenham, UK: Edward Elgar.

Vigoda-Gadot, E., Shoham, A., Ruvio, A., & Schwabsky, N. (2005). *Innovation in the Public Sector.* Oslo, Norway: The University of Haifa & NIFU STEP.

Vogel, E. F. (1979). *Japan as Number One. Lessons for America.* Cambridge, MA: Harvard University Press. doi:10.4159/harvard.9780674366299

Vrgovic, P., Glassman, B., Walton, A., & Vidicki, P. (2012). Open innovation for SMEs in developing countries - an intermediated communication network model for collaboration beyond obstacles. *Innovation: Management. Policy & Practice, 14*(3), 290–303. doi:10.5172/impp.2012.14.3.290

Walker, D. M., Walker, T., & Schmitz, J. (2003). *Doing Business Internationally: The Guide to cross-Cultural Success* (2nd ed.). New York, NY: McGraw-Hill.

Wally, S., & Baum, J. R. (1994). Personal and structural determinants of the pace of strategic decision-making. *Academy of Management Journal, 37*(4), 932–956. doi:10.2307/256605

Wan, W. P., & Hoskisson, R. E. (2003). Home country environments, corporate diversification strategies, and firm performance. *Academy of Management Journal, 45*(1), 27–45. doi:10.2307/30040674

Wang, S., & Yi, X. (2012). Organizational justice and work withdrawal in Chinese companies: The moderating effects of allocentrism and idiocentrism. *International Journal of Cross Cultural Management, 12*(2), 211–228. doi:10.1177/1470595812439871

Weir, D. (1993). Management in the Arab world. In *Proceedings of the First Arab Management Conference.* University of Bradford Management Centre.

Weir, D. (1998). The fourth paradigm. In A. Al Shamali & J. Denton (Eds.), *Management in the Middle East.* Kuwait: Gulf Management Centre.

Weir, D. (2000).Management in the Arab middle east. In Managing in Emerging Countries. London, UK: Thomson Learning.

Weir, D. (2000). Management in the Arab Middle East. In M. Tayeb (Ed.), *International Business: Theories, Policies and Practices.* London, UK: Prentice Hall.

Weir, D. (2000). Management in the Arab World: A Fourth Paradigm? In A. Al-Shamali & J. Denton (Eds.), *Arab Business: The Globalisation Imperative.* Kuwait: Arab Research Center.

Weir, D., & Hutchings, K. (2005). Cultural embeddedness and contextual constraints: Knowledge sharing in Chinese and Arab cultures. *Knowledge and Process Management, 12*(2), 89–98. doi:10.1002/kpm.222

West, M., & Anderson, N. (1996). Innovation in top management teams. *The Journal of Applied Psychology, 81*(6), 680–693. doi:10.1037/0021-9010.81.6.680

Whiteoak, J. W., Crawford, N. G., & Mapstone, R. H. (2006). Impact of gender and generational differences in work values and attitudes in an Arab culture. *Thunderbird International Business Review, 48*(1), 77–91. doi:10.1002/tie.20086

Whitley, R. (2000). *Divergent Capitalisms. The Social Structuring and Change of Business Systems.* Oxford, UK: Oxford University Press.

Wright, M., Filatotchev, I., Hoskisson, R. E., & Peng, M. W. (2005). Strategy Research in Emerging Economies: Challenging the Conventional Wisdom. *Journal of Management Studies, 42*(1), 1–33. doi:10.1111/j.1467-6486.2005.00487.x

Yamin, S., Mavondo, F., Gunasekaran, A., & Sarros, J. A. (1997). Study of competitive strategy, organizational innovation and organizational performance among Australian manufacturing companies. *International Journal of Production Economics, 52*(1-2), 161–172. doi:10.1016/S0925-5273(96)00104-1

Yang, J., Liu, H., Gao, S., & Li, Y. (2012). Technological innovation of firms in China: Past, present, and future. *Asia Pacific Journal of Management, 29*(3), 819–840. doi:10.1007/s10490-010-9243-3

Zahra, S. (2011). Doing research in the (new) Middle East: Sailing with the wind. *The Academy of Management Perspectives, 25*(4), 6–21. doi:10.5465/amp.2011.0128

Zehir, C., & Ozsahin, M. (2008). A field research on the relationship between strategic decision-making speed and innovation performance in the case of Turkish large-scale firms. *Management Decision, 46*(5), 709–724. doi:10.1108/00251740810873473

Zhuang, L., Williamson, D., & Carter, M. (1999). Innovate or liquidate—are all organisations convinced? A two-phased study into the innovation process. *Management Decision, 37*(1), 57–71. doi:10.1108/00251749910252030

Zineldin, M. (2002). Globalisation, strategic co-operation and economic integration among Islamic/Arab countries. *Management Research News, 25*(4), 35–61. doi:10.1108/01409170210783188

Zuboff, S. (1988). *In the Age of the Small Machine.* New York, NY: Basic Books.

Chapter 14
A Data Warehouse Integration Methodology in Support of Collaborating SMEs

Marius Octavian Olaru
University of Modena and Reggio Emilia, Italy

Maurizio Vincini
University of Modena and Reggio Emilia, Italy

ABSTRACT

Collaborative business making is emerging as a possible solution for the difficulties that Small and Medium Enterprises (SMEs) are having in recent difficult economic scenarios. In fact, collaboration, as opposed to competition, may provide a competitive advantage to companies and organizations that operate in a joint business structure. When dealing with multiple organizations, managers must have access to unified strategic information obtained from the information repositories of each individual organization; unfortunately, traditional Business Intelligence (BI) tools are not designed with the aim of collaboration so the task becomes difficult from a managerial, organizational, and technological point of view. To deal with this shortcoming, the authors provide an integration, mapping-based, methodology for heterogeneous Data Warehouses that aims at facilitating business stakeholders' access to unified strategic information. A complete formalization, based on graph theory and the RELEVANT clustering approach, is provided. Furthermore, the authors perform an experimental evaluation of the proposed method by applying it over two DW instances.

1. INTRODUCTION

The Data Warehousing is the main Business Intelligence instrument for the analysis of large amounts of operational data. It permits the extraction of relevant information for decision-making processes usually inside one single organizations. In fact, Inmon defines it as a "subject-oriented, integrated, time-variant and non-volatile collection of data in support of management's decision making process" (Inmon, 1992).

DOI: 10.4018/978-1-4666-7272-7.ch014

Traditionally, one single Data Mart (a building block of the DW) is focused on a particular aspect or subject area (thus, subject-oriented) and is confined to a single department, and the union of all the company's Data Mart form the enterprise Data Warehouse.

DW integration is the process of combining strategic information from two or more heterogeneous Data Marts or Data Warehouses with the aim of providing users a unified view over the entire available information. The problem, although more and more frequent, has received little attention so far. There is in fact a series of scenarios where managers need to combine data and information from one or more Data Warehouses in order to obtain a unique overview of different areas of one single enterprise or a network of collaborating enterprises.

For example, in large organizations, different departments usually develop their separate, heterogeneous Data Mart without any knowledge about other departments. It is thus difficult for managers to have a coherent overview of the entire organization and to be able to take strategic decisions concerning all departments. Unfortunately, in such cases, the necessity of integration arises after the Data Warehouse has been built, and presents several difficulties due to the inherent heterogeneity of the data and to the different perspective with which different groups manage and represent the same data and information. The issue may be avoided when the integration goal is clearly defined *a priori* of the development phase. For example, Kimball proposes a design methodology, the Data Warehouse Bus Architecture for creating and maintaining common analysis dimensions for all DM of the group, eliminating thus schema and instance inconsistencies. The bus architecture creates "conformed dimensions", as either identical or strict mathematical subsets of the most granular and detailed dimensions (Kimball & Ross, 2002). This way, facts can be analyzed through a simple union of the different Data Marts.

Unfortunately, most of the times developers and analysts lack the vision of creating a cross-organization Data Warehouse from the beginning, or create the individual Data Marts without any intent for integration.

This is also the case when companies collaborate, form alliances, or one company acquires another company. On top of the business structure, managers need to access a series of strategic indicators that describe all the companies involved in the collaborative effort.

One single company's data is usually managed by a complex set of specialized tools, each with a specific task. Accessing all of it is a difficult objective, *per se*, because of to the distinct models that are used to represent each specific dataset. That is why accessing data from more than one company is not scalable, as the difficulty of managing the heterogeneity increases exponentially.

The goal of integrating data and structured information is rising also with the increasing adoption of specialized tools by Small and Medium Enterprises (SMEs), which initially used IT only as a support for the operational process. Subsequently, SMEs acknowledged the importance of IT in the strategic behavior of any firm seeking greater competitiveness (Blili & Raymond, 1993). SMEs provide an interesting setting as they are knowledge generators, but are poor at knowledge exploitation (Levy, Loebbecke & Powel, 2001). This means that they rarely capitalize on the data they produce and are not able to transform data and information into knowledge. Cooperation offers SMEs the possibility to access a larger array of resources and knowledge on which to capitalize for developing a deeper business vision and for obtaining competitive advantage.

A rather new perspective in business networks is CO-Opetition (Branderburger & Nalebuff, 1996), the simultaneous cooperation and competition between organizations. Although contradictory as concept, co-opetition allows companies to collaborate, exchange experience, knowledge and resources, and in the same time compete for strategic advantage. Of course, the ratio between competition and cooperation determines the behavior of the participants, and how much they are willing to share. Without any further analysis of the concept from a business point of view, we point out that the success of such a business network also depends on a proper IT infrastructure that allows knowledge sharing.

The driving forces behind integration tools adoption in SMEs may be seen both as a cause and as an effect of the economic process driving companies.

First of all, globalization of communication technology is facilitating the formation of SME networks. These inter-organizational networks, which are strategic partnerships or alliances among SME stakeholders, introduce a new organizational form into assumptions (Acs & Yeung, 1999). In fact, the ability of business to communicate at various levels of organizations has been in some cases a major drawback for organizations that wanted to form alliances, business networks or other kinds of collaboration and/ or interaction. The type of interaction among organizations implies a weaker or tighter coupling of the operational, managerial and strategic business process, which in exchange determines the type and amount of data and information that the IT infrastructure needs to handle. The advent of internet and modern enterprise networks, and specialized data management tools provided a great opportunity collaboration.

Secondly, even when IT is not an incentive for collaboration by itself, it is still required for allowing the business network creation. In this case, the adoption of modern IT tools is not a cause, but an effect of collaboration.

In any case, IT and information integration proves fundamental both for facilitating and allowing business collaboration.

The role of this paper is to present a DW integration methodology that facilitates the automatic exchange of strategic information between collaborating enterprises.

The advantages of an automatic methodology are numerous, and may be presented by comparing traditional data integration inside one DW with a higher-level approach.

1.1 High End Data Warehouse Integration

A Data Warehouse integrates and reconciles a different number of heterogeneous data sources (Figure 1) that reside across the entire company. The data sources may vary from flat files, spreadsheets, semi-structured data (like XML) to Database Management Systems (DBMSs) and web data (Calvanese et al., 2001).

Even after identifying the correct data sources to integrate for building the DW, the actual integration task itself requires managing a series of schema and instance level conflicts. In fact, the different data sources may contain the same information, but structured differently (e.g., different classes/entities/tables, etc.); even if the schema is very similar or identical, the instance values may differ (e.g., different names for the same real-life concept, different date format, abbreviations, etc.). Data coming from the data sources undergoes a series of changes and transformations before being loaded in the final Data Warehouse, through a series of operations called Extract-Transform-Load (ETL). This approach, however, is laborious, time consuming and mostly manual. It thus implies high costs for the companies (Vassiliadis, 2009).

Figure 1. Classical DW architecture

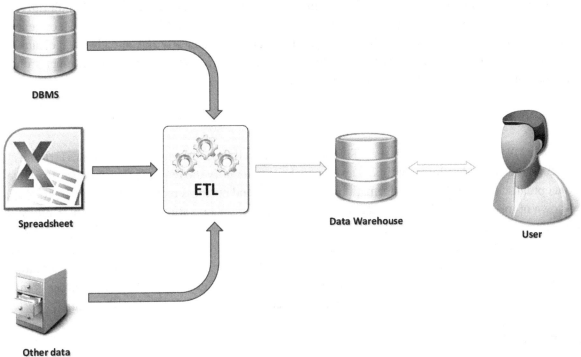

The DW creation and load procedure produces valuable information that among other characteristics should be available with the smallest delay and should be of elevated quality. When integrating information obtained from multiple DWs, one simple solution deriving from classical Data Warehousing would be to use extensive ETL procedures to combine all the data sources used to populate each and one of the individual DWs, into a unique data repository, usually called data staging area (Golfarelli & Rizzi, 2009), and on top of that build a new DW. This approach is a low-end DW integration.

We envision instead a more direct integration methodology where it is possible to combine the high-level information already available in the final DWs in a seamlessly way, allowing the end-users to benefit from a number of advantages, that are summarized as follows.

Data Quality

The integration of more than one data source into one unique, reconciled repository is a laborious task. Achieving it inside one single company, where the data sources, even if different, are somewhat similar could prove to be extremely difficult. Nonetheless, integrating multiple, heterogeneous operational data sources from more than one company means having to deal with an elevated number of schema and instance inconsistencies. In fact, developers may find themselves in cases where, due to schema and/or instance incompatibility, have to develop DWs based on partial, incomplete or even misleading information. We want to point out that this situation is useless or risky in applied cases, as the level of quality required inside DWs is extremely elevated. Managers, in fact, need to be able to make decision based on complete and extremely accurate information; otherwise, they may risk damaging the decision making process itself (Ballou & Tayi, 1999).

It is clear how having to cope with the integration of a potential high number of data sources makes the entire process prone to errors. Nevertheless, integrating the already available high-end, multidimensional information may reduce the complexity of the whole process, greatly reducing the risk of generating importation errors. Moreover, the information contained in each DW has already been cleansed and transformed in order to be easily interrogated, so the process needn't start from the raw operational data, but from the information available in the final DWs.

Time Consumption

During the DW building procedure, the ETL phase is the most time-consuming, in some cases arriving at 60-70% of the entire development time. Developers have to identify the required data sources, to create a conceptual schema of the final information that managers and business require (by using a bottom-up, top-down or mixed approach), and then to correctly map the initial operational data to the final information schema implementing at the same time intermediary processing steps by using ETL procedures. Although this phase may be in some way automated (for example, by using a more advanced ETL, like a semantic ETL (Bergamaschi, Guerra, Orsini, Sartori & Vincini, 2011)), the possibility of integrating the already available multi-dimensional information and skipping great part of the ETL process may reduce considerably the development time and effort required for the DW building procedure.

Business Network Flexibility

When using a traditional approach to integrating multiple, heterogeneous DWs, independently of the chosen architecture, the structure itself is static. Imagine, for example, the case in which a set of companies decide to collaborate, and after having identified the required data to integrate among their information repositories, the ETL sequences are developed for the actual integration. As pointed out, the process itself is time consuming and prone to errors. If at the end of the integration process, one or more companies decide to leave or to enter the business network, part or the entire integration process must be reengineered from the beginning, analyzing the compatibility of the new data schemas with the already available one, and reconciling both the schema and the instances of the given data sources. Again, having the possibility to integrate the already available multidimensional information allows a more rapid change in the structure of the business network, permitting organizations to enter or leave the network and thus increasing the dynamicity of the network.

Data Latency and Replication

One of the major drawbacks of today's Data Warehousing is the latency of the information gathered in the final DW. In fact, the ETL process is time-consuming not only when implemented, but also when it is executed, due to the extensive transformations that data usually has to undergo. When using a classical approach to DW integration (i.e., by means of ETL procedures), the process must be executed twice, for loading the local DW (that is usually maintained) and for refreshing the final global DW. In this situation, there is also the issue of the data replicated both in the local DW and in the final DW.

In addition, another important issue is that the time required for the refresh procedure of the DW increases exponentially with the amount of data, mainly due to the massive join queries executed for the retrieval of the correct data.

1.2 Motivating Example

Suppose the schemas in Figures 2 and 3 represent two example Data Warehouses of different organizations or Data Marts of two different divisions inside one large organization. Supposing they have been developed and implemented independently, integrating them is a difficult task. Specifically, developers must face two types of problems: schema and instance inconsistencies.

First, the conceptual schemas are different. Although belonging to different companies/groups and built for different purposes, the DWs present similar dimensions: the time hierarchy, the geographical and the class hierarchy. However, schema inconsistencies can be observed in all three dimensions, but the presence of inconsistencies does not necessarily mean that the dimensions are incompatible. In fact, they share the same type of information that is structured differently.

In Figure 2, for example, a month is aggregated in bimesters and quadrimesters and finally in years (or alternatively in semesters and years), while in the second DW a month is only aggregated in semesters and years. In this case, the first Data Warehouse has additional information with respect to the second Data Warehouse. This particular schema inconsistency induces the two different user groups to have a different perspective over the available information, although they may have access to the same information.

Figure 2. Example DW1

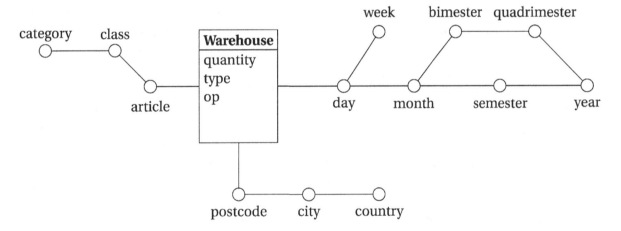

Figure 3. Example DW2

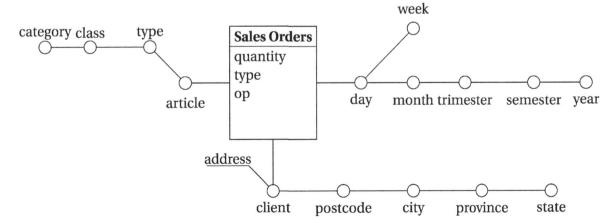

Apart from a possible different vision over the same information, this particular case highlights a possible integration issue. For example, a user of DW1 accessing both DWs might be interested in writing the following query: Q1: "select the types of articles that have been sold at least 100 times, having stock quantity less than 150, grouped by quadrimester and city". The Data Warehouse DW1 is easily accessible for obtaining stock information (as the time dimensions contain the two required aggregation levels); however, DW2 cannot provide this kind of information, as facts are not aggregated by bimester. This means that Q1 obtains no answer from the two DWs.

Query compatibility presents a serious difficulty when accessing heterogeneous data sources. In such cases, incompatibilities may be solved in two ways:

1. **Integrate Information Only from Compatible Sources:** This setting is complicated when integrating a large number of data sources as the user loses overview of what information is integrated;
2. **Discard Incompatible Queries:** In this case, the number of valid queries is drastically reduced by the data sources compatibility.

Compared to the previous example, real DWs have a much larger number of dimensions with more aggregation levels. That is why the possibility of encountering schema inconsistencies is much higher. Furthermore, different schemas may also induce different kinds of inconsistencies. For example, a concept may be represented as a dimensional attribute in one DW or a measure in the other DWs. Many of the types of inconsistencies are identical to the ones defined for databases (see (Sheth & Larson, 1990) and (Lenzerini, 2002) for a discussion and examples). Furthermore, in SMEs networks (like co-opetition) developers usually face the need to integrate a larger number of data sources, which further decreases the number of compatible queries.

The second possible inconsistency is the instance level inconsistency, which means representing the same information according to the same conceptual schema, but using different attribute values. Different working groups may represent the same information differently. For example, different groups may represent months using the full name (e.g., January, February, etc.) or bay abbreviation (e.g., Jan., Feb., etc.) or by a sequential number (e.g., 1, 2, 3,…). In this case, the information is the same; a direct value-equality approach would not be able to discover that an object refers to the same real-world concept.

Between two distinct, heterogeneous DWs there may be both types of inconsistencies, and information integration tools must be able to correctly discover and handle them.

This necessity is twofold: first, relevant information must be identified for integration purposes (what to integrate); however, identical concepts must be discovered to allow data reconciliation (how to integrate).

1.3 Paper Contribution

The purpose of this paper is to promote the concept of collaborating business process by providing an actual integration methodology as a support for collaborating organizations. In this context, we propose a three-step information integration methodology for a heterogeneous Data Warehouse environment aimed at providing collaborating companies a support in their business efforts.

2. RELATED WORK

Data Warehouse integration can be seen as a case of Data Integration, which has been an important research topic during the last decades. DW integration is a context-based DI solution where developers may exploit the available knowledge of the information to integrate. In fact, the information inside a DW is structured alongside multidimensional structures, in star-like schemas (e.g., the Dimensional Fact Model (Golfarelli, Maio & Rizzi, 1998)).

To the knowledge of the authors, there have been few attempts to formalize and solve the DW integration problem. Among them, (Kimbal & Ross, 2002) define the concept of conformed dimensions as dimensions that have consistent keys, consistent column names (i.e., dimensional attributes names), consistent attribute definitions and consistent attribute values. This is, of course, a design methodology and not a solution for a DW integration problem.

A more systematic solution is offered in (Torlone, 2008), where the author defines the dimension algebra (DA), as a set of operations (selection, projection and aggregation) that can be executed on any given dimensions. Moreover, a definition of a matching among dimensions is provided, and three properties that a matching may have: coherence, soundness and consistency. A matching that is coherent, sound and consistent is considered a perfect matching. Furthermore, the author provides a definition for compatible dimensions, with the aid of DA expressions. This approach is relevant for defining a solution from a theoretical perspective; however, the author doesn't provide a method to compute the solution for actual integrated purposes, as this is outside the scope of the paper.

In (Banek, Vrdoljak, Tjoa & Skocir, 2008), the authors provide a semantics-based methodology for the automated integration of heterogeneous DW schemas, based on earlier work in data integration (Bergamaschi, Sartori, Guerra, & Orsini, 2007; Madhavan, Bernstein, & Rahm, 2001). The methodology may be regarded as an alternative to the first step in our methodology, although we believe that a systematic approach, like the one we propose, may yield better results.

In the current paper, we use a subset of the semantic mappings defined in (Golfarelli, Mandreoli, Penzo, Rizzi & Turricchia, 2010), in particular we used the semantic mappings for dimensional attributes: equi-level, roll-up, drill-down and related.

3. DATA WAREHOUSE INTEGRATION

Creating multi-enterprise software components or delivering methods to integrate the already operational ones can provide a strong incentive for collaborating businesses. Such a goal, however, requires identifying and tackling a series of technological shortcomings; in particular the entire process must follow these steps:

1. Analyze the business strategy and identify the software tools that need to cooperate;
2. Analyze each individual tool and their internal and external model for storing/representing data, information and knowledge;
3. Develop interfaces that allow the exchange of the information among various tools/models;

Data Warehouse integration can be seen as a subcase of classical data integration (DI), where developers usually make use of mappings to express semantic similarities among similar attributes/concepts (Bergamaschi, Castano, De Capitani De Vimercati, Montanari & Vincini, 1998; Beneventano, Bergamaschi, Guerra & Vincini, 2001). The mappings are reused by query rewriting techniques to execute a global query over the local data sources and to integrate and reconcile data coming from different, compatible data sources. The experience accumulated in the two decades of DI research can also be used in DW integration, where similar mapping-based techniques may be used.

In this context, we propose a three step DW dimension integration methodology that is able to:

1. Identify similar dimensional attributes and generate semantic mappings;
2. Integrate and extend compatible dimension hierarchies;
3. Populate the imported dimension attributes with relevant information;

3.1 Generate Semantic Mappings

In this section, we present an instance level (Rahm, 2001) technique to automatically generate semantic mappings among different DW dimensional attributes. We rely on cardinality based properties, in particular on a graph-like structure that can be extracted to represent the different dimensional hierarchies of the two DWs, called cardinality-ratio (Bergamaschi, Olaru, Sorrentino, Vincini, 2012).

Consider, for example, that the time dimension on the first DW (Figure 2) contains all the days and months from January 1st 2001 to December 31st 2012 (12 complete years), the time dimension of the second DW (Figure 3) contains all the days from January 1st 2008 to December 31st 2013 (16 complete years), and that there is an inconsistency among the instances of the schemas, such that an intersection of the attribute values of the schemas is null. Although apparently the schema and the instances are different, they represent the same real-world concept, and some properties deriving from the general knowledge of that concept is maintained. For example, in both dimensions, a month is an aggregation of 30-31 days (i.e., the ratio among the number of distinct values of the attribute month and the number of distinct values of the attribute day), also a semester is an aggregation of 6 different months in both dimensions. This common information may be used to generate semantic mappings among similar dimension hierarchies.

In particular, we consider the dimension hierarchies as directed labeled graphs, where the label of each graph is the cardinality ratio among different dimension hierarchies (Figures 4 & 5). A connectivity matrix (Figure 7) is associated to each graph, each element of the matrix is greater than if there is a path among the two nodes.

The value of each element is the cardinality ratio among the two dimensional attributes that the nodes represent. Such cardinality ratio is computed as the multiplication of the labels of the arcs the path is composed of. In the example above, the lines of the connectivity matrix are assigned to the nodes day, week, month, bimester, quadrimester, semester and year respectively. Thus, the element , as a bimester is composed on average of two months. Similarly, the matrix is assigned to the second graph, and the lines correspond to the nodes day, week, month, trimester, semester, and year respectively.

Figure 4. Graph 1

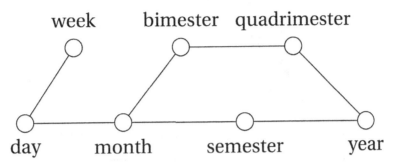

Figure 5. Graph 2

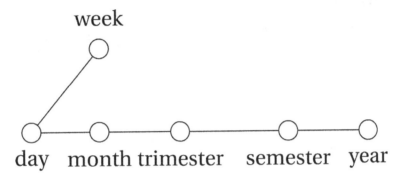

We then use Algorithm 1 to compute a common subgraph that is used to generate the semantic mappings. The algorithm, given an error , computes a maximum rank common square sub-matrix, whose element has a relative error of no more than from the average of the same elements in the initial matrices. The new matrix describes a subgraph, that approximates the two initial graphs with respect to the cardinality ratios by no more than a relative error of (Figure 6).

In the example above, similar names were used for the dimensional attributes/nodes, so that it is easier to visualize the kind of semantic correspondences that are maintained between the two initial graphs and the common subgraph. In real life cases, however, the attribute names are usually different, abbreviated, or are just labels with no particular meaning. In such cases, it is difficult to identify similar/identical dimensional attributes.

The node day of the common subgraph is obtained from the node day of the first graph and from the node day of the second graph. This means that the two initial nodes are the same. Similarly, the corresponding nodes week, month, semester and year are the same. Starting from these nodes, it is possible to generate semantic mappings between all the other dimensional attributes.

As mapping predicates, we used those defined in (Golfarelli, Mandreoli, Penzo, Rizzi & Turricchia, 2012), in particular the equi-level, drill-down, roll-up and related semantic predicates.

To generate semantic mappings, we use the following inference rules:

Let A, B be nodes of the first graph, and X, Y be nodes of the second graph, such that B is an aggregation of A and Y an aggregation of X.

Figure 6. Common subgraph

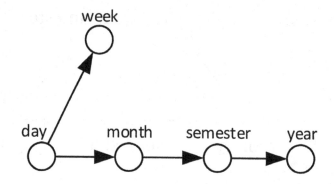

Figure 7. Connectivity matrices

$$M_1 = \begin{pmatrix} 1 & 6{,}99 & 30{,}43 & 60{,}86 & 121{,}72 & 182{,}58 & 365{,}16 \\ 0 & 1 & 0 & 0 & 0 & 0 & 0 \\ 0 & 0 & 1 & 2 & 4 & 6 & 12 \\ 0 & 0 & 0 & 1 & 2 & 0 & 6 \\ 0 & 0 & 0 & 0 & 1 & 0 & 3 \\ 0 & 0 & 0 & 0 & 0 & 1 & 2 \\ 0 & 0 & 0 & 0 & 0 & 0 & 1 \end{pmatrix} \qquad M_2 = \begin{pmatrix} 1 & 6{,}89 & 30{,}43 & 91{,}29 & 182{,}58 & 365{,}16 \\ 0 & 1 & 0 & 0 & 0 & 0 \\ 0 & 0 & 1 & 3 & 6 & 12 \\ 0 & 0 & 0 & 1 & 2 & 4 \\ 0 & 0 & 0 & 0 & 1 & 2 \\ 0 & 0 & 0 & 0 & 0 & 1 \end{pmatrix}$$

Algorithm 1. Cardinality ratio computation

```
C= {empty matrix}
    for every square sub-matrix  M₁ of the first matrix do
        for every square sub-matrix  M₂ of the second matrix do
```

$$\textbf{if} \quad \text{for every } i,j : m_{ij}, m_{ij} \in \left[\left(1-\epsilon\right)\frac{\left|a_{ij}-m_{ij}\right|}{2}, \left(1+\epsilon\right)\frac{\left|a_{ij}-m_{ij}\right|}{2} \right] \quad \textbf{then}$$

$$\textbf{if } \ rank\left(S_A\right) > rank\left(C\right) \ \textbf{then}$$

```
                C=new matrix of rank   rank(S_A)
                for every c_ij do
```

$$c_{ij} = \frac{\left|a_{ij}-m_{ij}\right|}{2}$$

```
                end for
            end if
        end if
    end for
  end for
return C
```

Rule 1: If A and X correspond to the same node in the subgraph, then A {equi-level} B.
Rule 2: If from Rule 1, B {equi-level} X, then A {drill-down} X and X {roll-up} A (Figure 8).
Rule 3: If from Rule 1, A {equi-level} X, then B {roll-up} X and X {drill-down} B (Figure 9).
Rule 4: If from Rule 1, B {equi-level} X, then A {roll-up} Y and Y {drill-down} A (Figure 10).
Rule 5: Add a {related} predicate for each other pair of nodes.

3.2 Experimental Evaluation

In order to validate our approach, we applied the matching technique to a scenario of three independent Data Warehouses. In particular, we analyzed the *sales* of three different companies, an automation technology company, a food producer and a fashion designer company. The reason for choosing such different companies is to further proof the underlying idea of the mapping step, which is that people

Figure 8. Rule 2

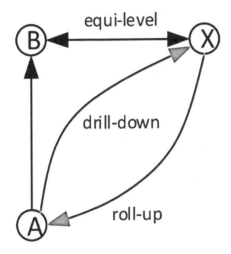

Figure 9. Rule 3

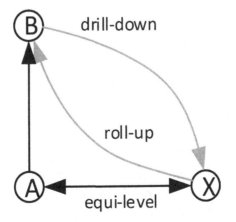

Figure 10. Rule 4

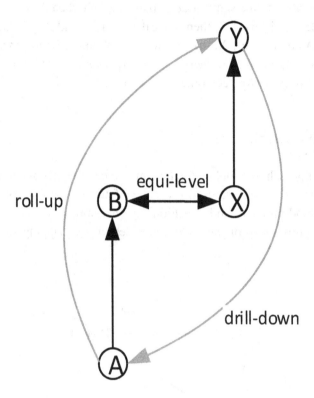

tend to categorize similar concepts in roughly the same way. In this case, the companies sell different types of products and services; however, the mapping methodology is still able to discover identical attributes in the different DWs.

For the testing purposes, the three DWs are generically called DW1, DW2 and DW3. They contain almost 250.000 purchase orders combined, all related to approximately 9.000 customers. The matching methodology was applied to common dimensions of the DWs in order to verify its efficiency.

The simplest test was time dimension that have an almost identical structure. Our expectation was that the common dimensional attributes matched with a low error ε because time hierarchies have a fixed structure over all DWs. Assuming the DW instances contain complete years, a month will contain 30-31 days, a trimester will be composed of three months, a year is formed of twelve months and four trimesters, etc.

Figure 11 shows the total number of instance values for each dimensional attribute in the selected DWs (blue numbers) and the cardinality-ratio between every two connected dimensional levels (red numbers). The common sub-dimension is shown in the Figure 12, and represents the two initial dimensions by an error of $\varepsilon = 4\%$.

The second test regarded the postcode hierarchies. Figure 13 contains the address dimensions of two of the DWs, and the related cardinalities.

Unlike the time hierarchy, the probability of having the same structure is lower. However, some similarities are maintained. A common sub-dimension was computed from the two original dimensions with an error $\varepsilon = 7,4\%$. Furthermore, we analyzed the instance values of the time and address (postcode) dimensions. Interestingly, while in the first case the values were 75% the same, in the second case the

Figure 11. Time dimensions

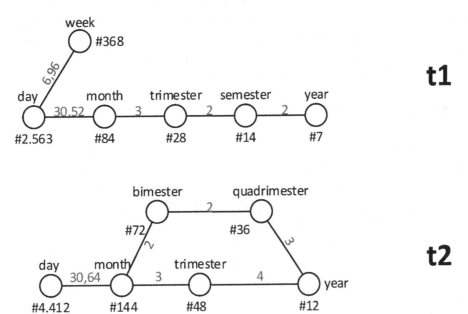

Figure 12. Time sub-dimension

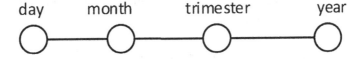

Figure 13. Postocode dimensions

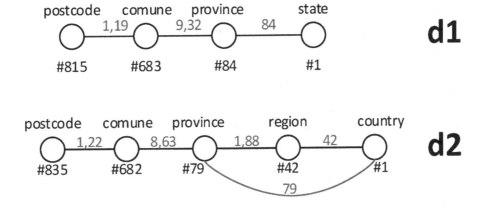

instance values overlapped only in 16% of the cases. This means that a *value*-matching approach would consider the first dimensions highly similar (75%) while the second dimensions would be considered with a low similarity value, although the dimensions are conceptually almost identical. This consideration further proves that value-matching approaches would not be reliable for completely independent, heterogeneous DWs.

The final test regarded the article dimension hierarchy. As expected, the sets of values of the dimensional attributes are completely disjoint because the companies sell different products/services. However, the mapping methodology is still able to compute a common subgraph with an error of $\varepsilon = 12\%$, and subsequently to correctly identify and map identical dimensional attributes.

Table 1 synthesizes the results of the validation process.

3.3 Schema Level Integration

The semantic mappings can be exploited to write and execute, where possible, queries over the two instances. The expressiveness of the queries is, however, limited to their compatibility, which means that some queries are simply impossible to execute on both instances, due to their schema level inconsistency; for example, the fact measures are not aggregable by bimester in the second instance of the given example, as the required information is not available.

A DW integration methodology must be general enough to be efficient in a variety of integration architectures, either involving two or more DWs. Some integration architectures, like the Peer-to-Peer DW (Golfarelli, Mandreoli, Penzo, Rizzi, & Turricchia, 2012) hypothesizes a network composed of a potentially large number of peers, each having its independent DW. In such scenario, the possibility of rewriting queries on all the peers is drastically reduced by the compatibility of the schemas. Some workarounds may include the possibility to deny the queries that are incompatible with all the nodes or to execute each query only on compatible nodes. This kind of approaches, however, may create confusion rather than provide a solution for the problem, as for some cases the end user may receive a unified answer obtained from all the nodes of the network, a part of the network, or may obtain data belonging only to the local node.

A possible solution may be to uniform similar dimensions, by importing, where possible, remote compatible dimension levels. For example, the time dimension in the first schema contains the bimester-quadrimester alternative path that is not available in the second schema, meaning that the users of the first schema have augmented analysis and interpretation possibilities compared to the users of the second schema. If, however, there is sufficient knowledge about the two schemas, the dimensional attributes may be imported in the remote schema, uniforming the users' capabilities to jointly interrogate the information repositories, in the same way. The schema knowledge in this case may be the mappings discovered in the first step of the presented methodology, that provide indication of how the dimensional attributes fit in the other schemas. This way, the missing attributes may be seamlessly integrated in the remote schema, by also generating the correct semantic relationships relatively to the other dimensional attributes available in the schema. For example, in the schemas in Figures 2 and 3, the province dimensional attribute was available only in the second schema, but can be also imported in the other schema (see Figure 14). From the first step, the mapping S2.*province {roll-up}* S1.*city* was derived from Rule 2 (blue line), so the *province* attribute is inserted in the schema S2 as an aggregation of *city*. Also, S1.*country {roll-up}* S2.*province*, so country is an aggregation or province in S1.

Table 1. Evaluation results

Article		Postcode		Day	
overlapping	ε	overlapping	ε	overlapping	ε
0 %	12 %	16 %	7,4 %	75 %	4 %

Figure 14. Example of the importation rule

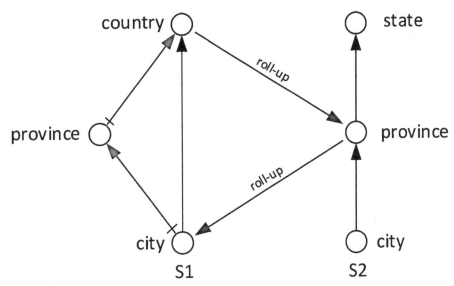

The reason the attribute was inserted as optional is that there may be the case that some cities in the instance of the first schema don't have a region, or none is deductible from the instance of the second schema. The concept will be explained in the next value importation section.

3.4 Importing Values with RELEVANT

One important step in the DW integration procedure is the integration and reconciliation of common information. This implies that:

1.   The newly imported attributes have to be populated with consistent values, and
2.   The possible inconsistencies among attribute values must be resolved.

For this purpose, we propose an extension of RELEVANT (RELEvant VAlues geNeraTor) (Bergamaschi, Sartori, Guerra & Orsini, 2007) that is specially conceived for the integration of multidimensional information.

RELEVANT performs clustering of attribute values and, for each cluster, identifies one relevant value, that is representative for the whole cluster. By applying the RELEVANT techniques to the values of the dimensional attributes, we obtain clusters of related dimension. The relevant value provided by each cluster is then used for populating the missing values of the newly imported dimensional attributes. In this way, RELEVANT is able to provide approximate values to the new dimension attributes.

Clusters of related elements are computed by using some similarity measures. In this extension of RELEVANT, clusters are created by means of two similarity measures:

1.   **Syntactic Similarity:** Compares the alphabets used for describing the attribute values;
2.   **Containment:** Measures the closeness of attributes belonging to different dimension.

In particular, the containment is based on the {roll-up}, {drill-down}, and {equi-level} mappings holding among the sources. Some further semantic measures based on lexical similarity and external ontologies can be exploited for dimensions belonging to specific domains, but this is outside the scope of the paper.

Example

Consider the attribute importation in the earlier example. For a more realistic example, consider that the newly inserted attribute must be populated using integrated information obtained from other three distinct information sources (Table 2) that contain related values.

The way we applied *RELEVANT* is similar to functional dependency reasoning, but rather than checking if a certain functional dependency holds, we enforce the one given by the roll-up relation, not on each individual values but rather on cluster of similar values. In other words, we impose that if two cities belong to the same cluster, then they must belong to the same cluster of region values. For example, the values "Torino" and "Turin" are in the same cluster, so the values of the region value must also belong in the same region. In the last instance (red values) there is no region specified, so the city "Turin" is assigned the representative value for the corresponding region cluster (Figure 15). Similarly, the city "Bologna" (red section in the table) is placed in the region "Emilia Romagna", which is the relevant value of its cluster.

Conflicts Resolution

One of the advantages of applying *RELEVANT* is the possibility to resolve instance level inconsistencies. In fact, having multiple information sources allows analysts to discriminate between allowed or incorrect attribute values in the given instances. For example, the regions of the city "Sicilia" must be in the same cluster, which is not the case in the example in Table 2. *RELEVANT* is able to detect that the region values do not belong in the same cluster, so the last one is discarded (Figure 16). In such cases, the ability to discriminate among correct or wrong information is given by the number of values in the

Table 2. Example of values

City	Region	City	Region
Roma	Lazio	Florence	Tuscany
Firenze	Toscana	Bologna	Emilia Romagna
Ferrara	Em.Romagna	Rome	Lazio
Milano	Lombardia	Turin	Piedmont
Palermo	Sicilia	Palermo	Piedmont
Palermo	Sicilia	Rome	null
Milano	Lombardia	Torino	null
Pisa	Toscana	Bologna	null
Rimini	E. Romagna	Palermo	null
Palermo	Sicilia	Firenze	null

Figure 15. Example clusters

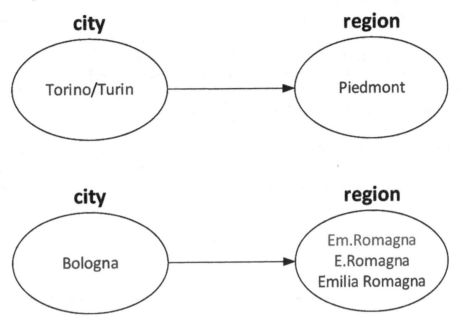

cluster. In this case, there are three values, two of which are correct, so a simple majority approach may be applied. In other cases, however, there may not be sufficient available information to be able to choose the right value. In any case, given the quality requirements in a DW we suggest human supervision in such scenarios.

4. CONCLUSION

As the economical context is evolving, DW integration will become an even more demanding challenge and managers and developers will seek new and innovative ways to obtain relevant information from different sources. Latency is already an issue in today's Data Warehousing, as the amount of data in a warehouse builds up incrementally; that is why combining information from multiple information repositories not only increases the development and execution time, but also increases the latency of data almost exponentially. Managers nowadays and in the future will require near real-time information, so the solution proposed in this paper may seem an obvious solution to some of the problems that they have to face nowadays.

Figure 16. Example of discarded values

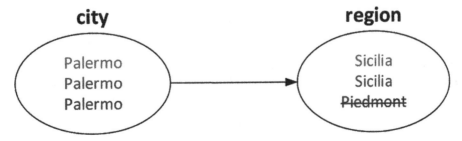

The work presented in this paper brought us to two general conclusions.

First of all, when dealing with collaborative business making, a clear distinction must be made between the dynamics of the business process and the integration methodology that is adopted. The business process dictates the sequence and type of interactions among parties, and the type of information and knowledge to be exchanged; meanwhile the methodology defines the technical background that the exchange process is operating in. The current paper defines a three step integration methodology that should be general enough to fit in any kind of collaborative business structure.

The second conclusion is that, although works fine when dealing with a limited number of sources, the current methodology shows its great potential when tackling a scenario with numerous organizations each having its own DW. In fact, introducing an automated methodology has the potential of drastically reducing the required development and execution of the integration phase, providing near real-time strategic information for managers.

REFERENCES

Acs, Z. J., & Yeung, B. (1999). *Small and Medium-Sized Enterprises in the Global Economy.* University of Michigan Press.

Ballou, D. P., & Tayi, G. K. (1999). Enhancing data quality in data warehouse environments. *Communications of the ACM, 42*(1), 73–78. doi:10.1145/291469.291471

Banek, M., Vrdoljak, B., Tjoa, A. M., & Skocir, Z. (2008). Automated Integration of Heterogeneous Data Warehouse Schemas. *International Journal of Data Warehousing and Mining, 4*(4), 1–21. doi:10.4018/jdwm.2008100101

Beneventano, D., Bergamaschi, S., Guerra, F., & Vincini, M. (2001). The Momis approach to Information Integration. In *Proceedings of the International Conference on Enterprise Information Systems (ICEIS 2001).* ICEIS.

Bergamaschi, S., Castano, S., De Capitani De Vimercati, S., Montanari, S., & Vincini, M. (1998). An Intelligent Approach to Information Integration. In *Proceedings of The 1st Conference on Formal Ontology in Information Systems (FOIS '98).* FOIS.

Bergamaschi, S., Guerra, F., Orsini, M., Sartori, C., & Vincini, M. (2011). A semantic approach to ETL technologies. *Journal of Data and Knowledge Engineering, 70*(8), 717–731. doi:10.1016/j.datak.2011.03.003

Bergamaschi, S., Olaru, M. O., Sorrentino, S., & Vincini, M. (2012). Dimension matching in Peer-to-Peer Data Warehousing. In *Proceedings of the International Conference on Decision Support Systems (DSS 2012).* DSS.

Bergamaschi, S., Sartori, C., Guerra, F., & Orsini, M. (2007). Extracting Relevant Attribute Values for Improved Search. *IEEE Internet Computing, 11*(5), 26–35. doi:10.1109/MIC.2007.105

Blili, S., & Raymond, L. (1993). Information Technology: Threats and Opportunities for Small and Medium-Sized Enterprises. *International Journal of Information Management, 13*(6), 439–448. doi:10.1016/0268-4012(93)90060-H

Branderburger, A., & Nalebuff, B. (1996). *Co-Opetition*. New York: Doubleday.

Calvanese, D., Castano, S., Guerra, F., Lembo, D., Melchiori, M., & Terracina, G. et al. (2001). Towards a Comprehensive Methodological Framework for Integration. In *Proceedings of the 8th International Workshop on Knowledge Representation meets Databases (KRDB 2001)*. KRDB.

Golfarelli, M., Maio, D., & Rizzi, S. (1998). The Dimensional Fact Model: A Conceptual Model for Data Warehouses. *International Journal of Cooperative Information Systems, 7*(2-3).

Golfarelli, M., Mandreoli, F., Penzo, W., Rizzi, S., & Turricchia, E. (2010). Towards OLAP query reformulation in Peer-to-Peer Data Warehousing. In *Proceedings of the International Workshop on Data Warehousing and OLAP (DOLAP 2010)*. DOLAP. doi:10.1145/1871940.1871950

Golfarelli, M., Mandreoli, F., Penzo, W., Rizzi, S., & Turricchia, E. (2012). OLAP Query Reformulation in Peer-to-Peer Data Warehousing. *Information Systems, 37*(5), 393–411. doi:10.1016/j.is.2011.06.003

Golfarelli, M., & Rizzi, S. (2009). *Data Warehouse Design: Modern Principles and Methodologies*. McGraw Hill.

Inmon, H. (1992). *Building the Data Warehouse*. New York: John Wiley & Sons, Inc.

Kimbal, R., & Ross, M. (2002). *The Data Warehouse Toolkit: The Complete Guide to Dimensional Modeling*. New York: John Wiley & Sons, Inc.

Lenzerini, M. (2002). Data Integration: A Theoretical Perspective. In *Proceedings of the Symposium on Principles of Database Systems (PODS 2002)*. PODS.

Levy, M., Loebbecke, C., & Powel, P. (2001). SMEs, CO-Opetition and Knowledge Sharing: The IS Role. In *Proceedings of the 9th European Conference on Information Systems*. Academic Press.

Madhavan, J., Bernstein, P. A., & Rahm, E. (2001). Generic Schema Matching With Cupid. In *Proceedings of the International Conference on Very Large Data Bases (VLDB 2001)*. VLDB.

Sheth, A., & Larson, J. (1990). Federated database systems for managing distributed, heterogeneous, and autonomous databases. *ACM Computing Surveys, 22*(3), 183–236. doi:10.1145/96602.96604

Torlone, R. (2008). Two Approaches to The Integration of Heterogeneous Data Warehouses. *Distributed and Parallel Databases, 23*(1), 69–97. doi:10.1007/s10619-007-7022-z

Vassiliadis, P. (2009). A Survey of Extract–Transform–Load Technology. *International Journal of Data Warehousing and Mining, 5*(3), 1–27. doi:10.4018/jdwm.2009070101

KEY TERMS AND DEFINITIONS

Business Intelligence: A set of tools, techniques, and methodologies for managing and analysing large quantities of operational data for obtaining aggregated, highly relevant strategic information.

Clustering: The process of identifying values that are similar by one or more criteria.

CO-Opetition: Business structure among participants that cooperate and compete simultaneously.

Data Integration: Methodologies used for solving heterogeneities between two or more different data sources and for presenting the final user an unique homogeneous view over all data sources.

Data Warehousing: Widely used IT architecture for storing large banks of information that can be accessed for analytical purposes.

Dimension Matching: The process of identifying similar elements in two different and heterogeneous Data Warehouse dimensions.

Small and Medium Enterprises (SMEs): Organizations of no more than 250 employees and a turnover lower than 50 million euros.

Chapter 15

Business Intelligence, Knowledge Management, and Customer Relationship Management Technological Support in Enterprise Competitive Competence

Ming-Chang Lee
National Kaohsiung University of Applied Science, Taiwan

ABSTRACT

The approach of knowledge management, business intelligence, and customer relationship management was used as theoretical technologies in order to build an intelligence enterprise framework. Since the business intelligence process can create additional customer value through knowledge creation with the customer, business intelligence can provide users with reliable, accurate information and help them make decisions. Customer relationship management focuses on the integration of customer information and knowledge for finding and keeping customers to grow customer lifetime value. Therefore, integrating intelligence enterprise is needed in order to respond to the challenges the modern enterprise has to deal with and represents not only a new trend in IT but also a necessary step in the emerging knowledge-based economy. In intelligent enterprise operations, KM contains business models, processes, competence, implementation, performance assessment, and enterprise in information, organization, and e-commence processes.

INTRODUCTION

How to create a sustainable competitive advantage have been the core issues of the enterprise management. Enterprise must adjust rapidly their policies and strategies in order to respond to sophistication of competition, customers and suppliers, globalization of business, international competition (Albescu, Pugna, & Paraschiv, 2008). Enterprise address these challenges have been developed in two different approaches: structured data management (BI) and unstructured content management (KM and CRM).

DOI: 10.4018/978-1-4666-7272-7.ch015

KM plays an important role in selecting the right information at the right time from several pertinent resources (Perko & Bobek, 2007) while converting it to useful insightful acumen so that an organization can get maximum benefits from it. Effective knowledge management helps the processing industry to accumulate core knowledge, build corporate intelligence and obtain a competitive edge. The aims of CRM at leverage investments in customer relations are to strengthen the competitive position and maximize returns. KM and CRM have been the focus of attention in organizations and academic contexts. KM and CRM both strive to obtain the constant benefits of competition through the optimization of the organizational resource in order to support commerce leading to competitive advantage (Gebert, Geib & Kolbe, 2003). Focusing on customer processes requires knowledge of considerable extent. Customer-focused companies provide three types knowledge, knowledge that customers demand, process the knowledge that customers pass to the company and processes knowledge about customer (Bueran, Schierholz, Kolbe, & Brenner, 2004). This means that knowledge support allows for performance enhancement in customer oriented business process.

CRM focuses on the integration of customer information, knowledge for finding and keeping customer to grow customer lifetime value. CRM requires continuant input of their information into the organization through CRM and the organization makes the information meaningful through KM. Therefore, the organization needs complete integration between KM and CRM to become successful in competitive market (Attafar, Sadidi, Attafar, & Shahin, 2013).

BI systems connected with CRM system and Enterprise Resource Planning (ERP) will provide an enterprise with a competitive advantage (Liautaud & Hammons, 2002). Systems of BI standard combine data from the environment e.g. statistics, financial and investment portals and miscellaneous dataset. BI provides adequate and reliable up-to-date information on different aspects of enterprise activities (Olszak & Ziemba, 2003). BI systems refer to decision making, information analysis and knowledge management, and human-computer interaction. Therefore, BI also often associated with systems such as Management Information Systems (MIS), Decision Support Systems (DSS), Executive Information Systems (EIS), management support systems and business / corporate performance management (O'Brien & Marakas, 2007).

The aim of this paper is to propose an integrated intelligence enterprise model for KM process, BI optimization and CRM process. This research begins with a presentation of the research model about the relationship between KM and BI, CRM between BI optimization and CRM between KM. Then under the conceptual model, we build the enterprise competence framework, intelligence enterprise process in order to enhance organizational competition advantage. Integrated framework illustrates how the three technologies can complement each other to improve organizational performance. A research conceptual framework denotes as Figure 1.

This chapter will proceed as follows: section 2 will discuss the background of the research; section 3 will use CRM process, KM process, and BI process to build intelligence enterprise framework; section 4 will discuss the enterprise business model, process, competence, implementation, assessment performance and enterprise in information, organization, and e-commence process; Section 5 is the conclusion.

Figure 1. Research conceptual framework

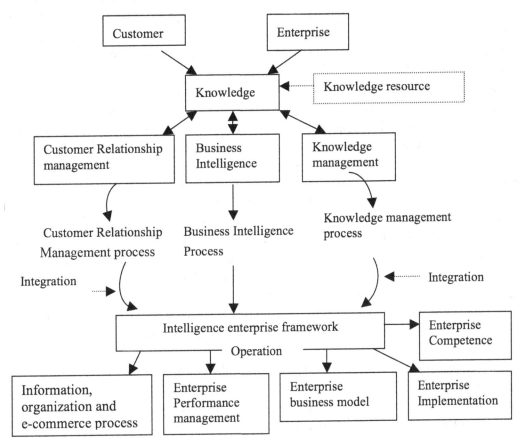

1. LITERATURE REVIEW

CRM has an important role to help organizations to keep their customers and to make them loyal. CRM role is more important in customer retention and in customer analysis (Jayashree & Shojace, 2011). The acquisition of customer knowledge, especially the potential knowledge is far more important than acquiring customer loyalty. Hence, the aim of CRM should be extended from customer loyalty to obtaining and exploring customer knowledge and making customer a value-added collaborator (Guangming, 2007). Due the lack of data integration, customers will need at each contact with the company to give back their data, which can cause their dissatisfaction and certain leaving. For this reason, this can be achieved be building customer data warehouse. Without functional integration of data warehouse as the foundation, there is on successful relationship with customers or acquiring new knowledge in the form of business intelligence, which means providing quality information (Habul, Piav-Velic & Kremic, 2012). A progressive CRM is enabled by BI applications and solutions which becomes the foundation of a successful customer intimacy strategy (Habul, Piav-Velic & Kremic, 2012).

KM makes an organization act as possible to secure its viability and to otherwise realize the best value of its knowledge assets (Karl, 1997). Common reasons to implement KM are to enable and foster organizational learning, to improve an organizational performance by link experts to each other, to apply best practices to future problems and opportunities, and to produce long-term competitive advantage (Gebert, Geib & Kolbe, 2003).

Some researchers explained the relation of KM with CRM. Managing customer knowledge has been the most important aspect of KM in many organizations, and KM capabilities have been found to be crucial factors in successful CRM-implementations (Croteus & Peter, 2003). A number of researchers have recently paid attention to the potential synergies of integration ideas from CRM and KM in both consumer and business markets (Bose & Sugumaran, 2003; Gebert, Geib & Kolbe, 2003; Massey, Montoya-Weiss & Holcom, 2001; Rowley, 2002; Rowley, 2004; Winer, 2001).

Some researchers explained the relation of KM with BI. Shehzad & Kham (2013) suggested that integrating KM with BI process enhanced organizational learning. Campbell (2006) proposed a framework to transform KM into BI. An insight into KM and BI integration reveals that BI transforms data into knowledge and information (Weidong, Weihui & Kunlomg, 2010). KM helps share knowledge to create new knowledge and provides BI with an understanding of business perspectives as well as estimation and outcome analysis. Campbell (2006) examines the results of KM processes on the overall BI and organizational performance by looking at the dynamics of innovation and the interconnected processes of knowledge which are needed to influence one's cerebral assets. Some researchers discussed KM and its components of BI and integration BI and KM (You, 2010; Cambell, 2006; Alwis, & Hartmann, 2008). Cheng & Peng (2011) analyze BI and KM, and explain their pros and cons followed by proposing a framework named the KMBI framework that integrates KM and BI. The integration KM and BI have features and the integration of both can maximize organizational efficiency and provide the best services to customer (Hanahadeh, Aiajlouni & Nawafleh, 2012).

Attafar, Sadidi, Attafar, & Shahin (2013) discuss the role of customer knowledge management in improving organization-customer relationship. This research identifies the integration barriers of CRM and KM in organizations in order to make clear the possibility of achieving CKM. The enterprise should fully explore and utilize customers' information to implement CKM and combine it with corporate knowledge (Guangming, 2007). The formation of customer knowledge competence is affected by four factors including customer information process, marketing-IT interface, senior management involvement as well as employee evaluation and reward system (Li & Calantone, 1998). Gebert, Geib, & Kolbe, (2003) emphasized empowering to customers and regarding customers as partners and acquiring customer knowledge through direct interaction with customers that is extension of CRM and KM. CKM seek opportunities for partnering with their customers as equal cop-creators of organizational value (Guangming, 2007).

Under the relation of KM with BI and the relation of CRM with BI in the above researches study, and the following reasons that the enterprise need to integrate CRM, KM and BI.

1. Integrating CRM, KM and BI in new strategy not only to store the competitor information but also to interpret the results and communicate them to decision factors provides real technological support for strategic management.
2. KM is the process which helps organizations to identify, select, organize, disseminate, and transfer knowledge and skills that are part of history of the organization and generally are unstructured (Manning, 2009).

3. CRM is an implementation of comprehensive solution that by integrating people, process and technology make a perfect communication among all activities of customers to enhance relationship of organizations and their customers (Handen, 2000).

4. KM strategies are more likely to be successfully implementation if an optimization based approach is adopted that implicitly shows the interactions between knowledge management initiatives and a set of optimization. Carrillo, Kamara & Anumba (2000) suggested that knowledge management could be integrated into key optimization indicators, and other optimization measurement approaches. Business intelligence process can create additional customer value through knowledge creation with customers (Kodama, 2005).

5. BI can quickly provide users with reliable, accurate information and help them make decisions of widely varying complexity. BI is the ultimate purpose of KM and a way of delivery of the right information in the right format, at the right hand and the right time (Murfitt, 2001). The most prominent advantage of BI in CRM is the rooting in personalization. Personalization of relations between company and customer help company to better understand and respond to the needs of each customer.

6. BI system plays a vital role in effective decision making in order to improving the business performance and opportunities by understanding the organization's environment through the systematic process of information (Venkatadri, Hanumat & Manjunath, 2010).

2. BUILDING INTELLIGENCE ENTERPRISE FRAMEWORK

2.1 Knowledge Management Process

Knowledge management is to manage and optimize knowledge chains to improve the strength of the overall business processes. Figure 2 is denoted as knowledge management chain process. This process uses to analyze most important knowledge management processes in corporation. This process uses for analyzing from knowledge creation to its application, a quantum of knowledge progresses through four primary stages: creation, diffusion, transfer, and application of knowledge (Alavi & Leidner, 2001).

2.2 Customer Relationship Management Process

Marketing, sales, and service are primary business functions (Poter & Milar, 1985). CRM is defined as an interactive process which leads to a balance between organization investments and satisfying customer's needs in order to maximize the profit (Hashemi & Hajiheydari, 2011). CRM business process

Figure 2. Knowledge management chain process

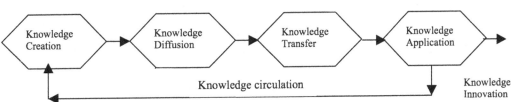

involves the processing of customer knowledge to pursue the goals of relationship marketing. There are four views and perspective for the CRM processes: Customer-facing level CRM processes (Moutot & Bascoul, 2008; Ragins & Greco, 2003), Customer-oriented CRM processes (Reinartz, Krafft & Hoyer, 2004), Cross-functional CRM processes (Geib, Reichold, Kolbe & Brenner, 2005) and CRM-Macro-level Processes (Payne & Frow, 2006). A quantum of CRM progresses through four primary stages: Strategic CRM, operational CEM and Analytical CRM. Figure 3 is CRM process.

CRM Process includes five processes: strategy development process, value creation process, multi-channel integration process, performance process, and information management process.

1. **Strategy Development Process:** The organizational business strategy detects that how it should be development and evolves over time, then it could instigate with a review of the organizational vision, and the industry and competitive environment (Geib, Reichold, Kolbe & Brenner, 2005; Plakoyiannaki & Saren, 2006). The organizational customer strategy entails the identification of the existing and potential customer base and recognition of the most appropriate form of customer segmentation (Plakoyiannaki & Saren, 2006).

2. **Value Creation Process:** In this process, programs for extracting and delivering value are developed based on the outputs of the strategy development process (Geib, Reichold, Kolbe & Brenner, 2005; Plakoyiannaki & Saren, 2006). The elements of process are:
    a. The value the customer receives,
    b. The value the organizational receive,
    c. Maximization the lifetime value of desired customer segments by the successful management of the value exchange of the co production processes (Plakoyiannaki & Saren, 2006).

The customer value process is an independent process to indicate for turning the organization's understanding toward producing product and delivering services that deliver value, and for incorporating the customer in the design and production of new products or services (Payne & Frow, 2005).

Figure 3. CRM process
Source: Rababah et al. (2011).

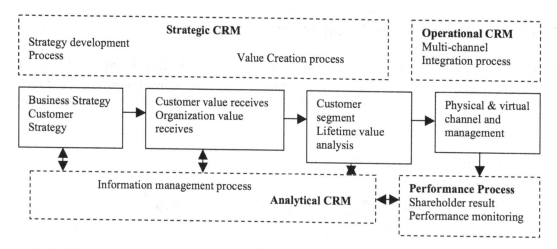

3. **Multi-Channel Integration Process:** The focus of this process is on:
    a. Deciding what channels to be used (e.g. sales force, outlets, direct marketing, e-commerce, and m-commerce),
    b. Ensuring highly positive interaction through the channel, and
    c. Creating a single unified view of the customer at the interaction through more than on channel (Plakoyiannaki & Saren, 2006).

In this process, create the value-adding activities with customer based on the outputs from the strategy process and development process and the value creation process (Plakoyiannaki & Saren, 2006).

4. **Performance Assessment Process:** The performance assessment process in which the assuring of achieving an organizational strategic aims in terms of CRM satisfactory standard is covered and the basis for establish future improvement (Plakoyiannaki & Saren, 2006). Payne & Frow (2005) uses the performance assessment process and the continuous monitoring of CRM activities over the time in order to capture customer feedback regarding CRM practice in the firm and to assure that both the organizational and the customer goals are achieved.
5. **Information Management Process:** Plakoyiannaki & Saren (2006) studied that the information management process provides a means of sharing relevant customer and other information throughout the enterprise and replicating the mind of the customer.

2. 3 Intelligence Enterprise Process

BI framework consists of four layers; each layer is dedicated to execute one major task of the system. Each upper layer interacts with the lower layer through Web services. The core functionalities of Data source layer are to provide primary data services from various heterogeneous data resources to Data cleansing layer, data will undergo the cleansing process for maintaining the data accuracy and integrity; this process would help to improve the information correctness. The business provides the core functionality to the Application layer. The Application layer presents user interface to the user by establishing the connection to provide various services like querying, analyzing and mining the data to the user in an interactive and visualized model (Venkatadri, Hanumat & Manjunath,. 2010). Figure 4 is BI process.

2.4 Enterprise Competence Framework

Market Knowledge competence is define as the processes that generate and integrate market knowledge (Li & Calsntone, 1998). Li & Calsntone (1998) suggested that market knowledge competence in new product development is composed three organizational processes:

Figure 4. BI process

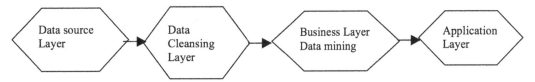

1.   Customer knowledge process,
2.   Competitor knowledge process, and
3.   Marking research and R&D interface.

This research conceptualizes enterprise's processes, which, together, generate and integrate business intelligence with the organization:

1.   Customer information process,
2.   Marking: IT (information technology interface),
3.   Management innovation,
4.   Employee reward,
5.   Organization performance, and
6.   BI systems (in Figure 5).

Customer Information processes refer to the set of behavioral activities that generate customer knowledge pertaining to customers' current and potential need for products and services (Li & Calantone, 1998). Marking – IT interface refers to the process by which marketing and information technology functions communicate and cooperate with each other. Management Innovation refers to the processes by which top management signals its support for generation and integration of customer knowledge within the firm (Campbell, 2003). The employee evaluation and reward system refer to the process by which employee behavior is aligned to the firm's goals of generating and integrating knowledge into the firm's marketing strategies. BI system may be analyzed from different perspectives. Decision makers and organizations should predominantly associate BI with organizational implementation of specific philosophy and methodology that would refer to work with information and knowledge, open communication, knowledge sharing along with the holistic and analytic approach to business process in organization (Olszak & Ziemba, 2007).

This model supports data analysis and decision making in different areas of organization performance. It includes:

Figure 5. BI systems
Source: Extended from Campbell (2003).

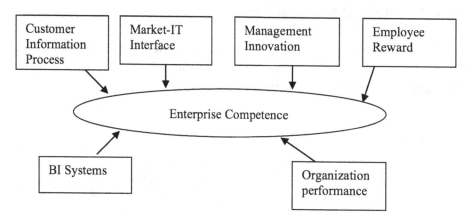

1. **Financial Analysis:** Involves reviewing of costs and revenues, calculation and comparative analysis of corporate income statements, analysis of corporate balance sheet and profitability, analysis financial markets, and sophisticated controlling.

2. **Marketing Analysis:** Involves analysis of sales receipts, sale profitability, profit margins, meeting sales targets, time of orders, actions undertaken by competitors, stock exchange quotations.

3. **Customer Analyses:** Concern time of maintaining contacts with customers, customer profitability, modeling customers' behavior and reactions, customer satisfaction, etc.

4. **Product Management Analyses:** Makes it possible to identify production bottlenecks and delayed orders, thus enabling organizations to examine product dynamics and to compare production results obtained by department or plants, etc.

5. **Logistic Analyses:** Enables to identify partners of supply chain quickly (Olszak & Ziemba, 2003; Olszak & Ziemba, 2007).

3. INTELLIGENCE ENTERPRISE OPERATION

3.1 Customer Knowledge (CK)

Customer knowledge is a kind of knowledge (also data or information which can be analyzed, interpreted and eventually converted to knowledge) in the areas of customer relationship, which has direct on indirect effect on our organizational performance (Zanjani, Rouzbehani & Dabbagh, 2008). As a consequence, managers must decide when to take a particular of CK seriously and when to discount it or look for more confirmation (Davenport, Harris & Kohli, 2001). Researchers identified three flows of information in customer business intelligence knowledge management (Paquette, 2006):

-   **Knowledge for Customer:** Satisfies customer's requirements for knowledge about products, the market and other relevant items.
-   **Knowledge about Customer:** Captures customers' background, motivation, expectation and preference for products or services.
-   **Knowledge from Customer:** Understands customers' needs pattern and/or consumption experience of products and/or services (Su, Chen & Sha, 2006).

3.2 Intelligence Enterprise Process

The integration of BI technologies and CRM systems provides the path to customer's loyalty. BI procession of full information about all transactions and customer's experience, companies can increase the delivered value. BI helps creation of real and complete image that will ensure the customer faster, better and easier decision making. Complementary use of CRM systems and BI provides a holistic approach to customers, which include improvements in company in satisfying its customers. Two technologies have been central in improving the quantitative and qualitative value of the knowledge available to decision makers: BI and KM. BI has applied the functionality, scalability, and reliability of database management systems to build large data warehouses, and to utilize data mining techniques to extract business advantage from the vast amount of available enterprise data. Figure 6 is denoted as intelligence enterprise process.

Figure 6. Intelligence enterprise process

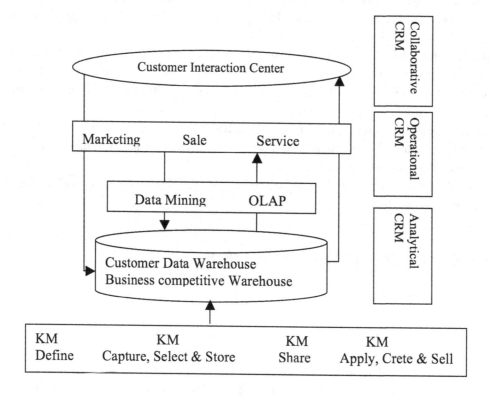

Sunasses & Sewry (2002) proposed that a knowledge life cycle of six steps:

1.   Select,
2.   Store,
3.   Share,
4.   Apply,
5.   Create, and
6.   Sell.

The select function is to select among the captured knowledge that which is appropriate. The store function is to properly codify and store the selected knowledge. The share function is to disseminate and transfer knowledge. The apply function is to use, integrated and reuse knowledge to carry out tasks and solve problems. The create function is to create new knowledge and to uncover the existing knowledge. The sell function is to use the knowledge to provide new products and services in order to consolidate customers and market and to create competitive advantages.

The CRM solution is based on: (Habul, Piav-Velic & Kremic, 2012).

- **Operational CRM:** Daily communication with clients. It provides support for font office business processes, such as sales, marketing, and service departments within the company.
- **Analytical CRM:** The collection, storage extraction, proceeding, reporting, and interpreting customer data.
- **Collaborative CRM:** All company's interaction with external entities, such as its customers, suppliers, and partners.

3.3 Intelligence Enterprise Model

The adopted model also examines how organizations can improve efficiency through enhanced organizational learning. The model consists of four layers: Operational Layer, BI and KM Layer, CRM layer and Output Layer (see Figure 7).

1. **The Operational Layer:** Operational systems are used to process daily transactions within an organization. Sometimes, such systems are referred as transaction processing systems, operational databases or online transaction processing systems. Operational systems can be mixture of manual and automated systems such as production, Inventory control, Sale, and Marketing, etc. The data available in this layer is fed to the BI and KM layer for further process.
2. **The BI and KM Layer:** This layer is an important layer for sorting, filtering, advanced search and query generation is all done within it. In this layer, we used the data warehouse, data mining, reports and graph components of the BI model. Input is generated by the operational layer and that input is passed to a data warehouse where data is processed according to the underlying input. Data is passed to the KM component to the model in this shape of reports and graphs to get the user feedback. The end result of this layer is provided as an output to the user in the form of summary reports and analytical graphs.

Figure 7. Layers of the intelligence enterprise model
Source: Extended from Shehzad and Khan (2013).

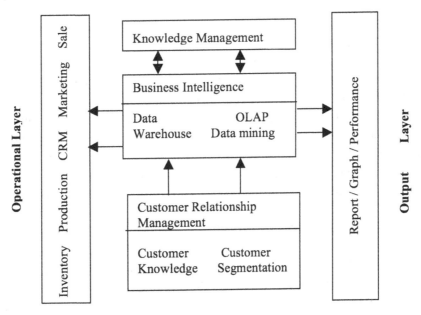

3. **The CRM Layer:** CRM layer can get more advantages from high technology corporations, financial services and telecommunication industries. CRM developed new strategies that accommodated work between understandings, sharing information and goes to increased customer satisfaction. Financial services can track the level of customer satisfaction, changing habits on buying and make a feedback to the organizations.

4. **The Output Layer:** This layer further filters the reports as per the user requirement, policy support and organizational templates.

There are four stages to operate the intelligence enterprise model.

Stage 1: Company provides information for the customers using tools available in the e-commerce process. Customers become familiar with the products and services of the company.

Stage 2: It helps the company to achieve initial knowledge from customer through the website. This information used for further analysis of appropriate information about potential customers' needs, wants and expectations.

Stage 3: Data extraction from previous steps would be categorized and from datasets. With the help of data mining techniques and applications, customer data could be analyze in order to provide information for improving business performance.

Stage 4: After market segmentation and choosing in right target market, knowledge extracted from previous stages would be applied in offering right products and services to the right customers.

3.4 Intelligence Enterprise Operation in Information, Organization, and E-Commerce Process

The Intelligence enterprise operation in information, organization and e-commerce process to types of knowledge was shown in Table 1.

3.5 Intelligence Enterprise Performance Management

The intelligence enterprise idea provides for an integrated analysis and evaluation of an enterprise by means of utilization of financial and non-financial indicators. The concept of the Balanced Scorecard (BSC) is one of the suggestions to be applied in enterprise. BSC is based on the assumption the ability to reach objectives that have been set by an enterprise should be discussed in the four basic dimensions (Kaplan & Norton, 1996). (1) Financial: required financial standing of an enterprise to release its mission, (2) Customer: the way an enterprise is perceived by customers to realize its mission, (3) Internal processes: which businesses are the most important to realize its mission, (4) Development and growth: which competencies and what kind of knowledge are indispensable to realize the mission. The BSC method highlights intellectual resources management as an important and integrating factor in the realization of organizational strategy. We summarize the intelligence enterprise performance management in Table 2.

3.6 Intelligence Enterprise Competence

Enterprise competence in knowledge about customers, knowledge for customer, tacit knowledge conversion, and knowledge from customers are shown in Table 3.

Table 1. Intelligence enterprise operation in information, organization, and e-commerce process

Categories of CK	Knowledge about Customers	Knowledge for Customers	Tacit Knowledge Conversion	Knowledge from Customers
In information	Information retrieval	Information Transfer	Information storage / distribution	Information application
	Competencies of acquiring and using customer knowledge	Competencies of acquiring, sharing and using customer knowledge	Competencies of providing data business competitive warehouse	Competencies of providing actual product preferences. Supplying payment and address information.
In customer	Product features/benefits/ identification	Customers' needs categorization	Market segmentation implementation	Extracting the needs pattern in each segment
In organization	Involves basic data exchange from the retailer to the customer, such as browsing, gathering information, and making product and price comparisons.	Involves the customer providing some personal information, by describing product automatic information exchange, such as data mining.	Involves the enterprise providing some data mining tools to drive their business forward.	Involves provision of private and monetary information, such as actual purchase preference, in order to complete the purchase of product or service
In e-commerce	Providing effective information and products and services using tools such as: e-catalogue and intelligent agents.	Gating basic information about customers and their need through cookies, forms, web bugs, transaction log, spy wares and click stream	Manipulate customer data sources applying data mining techniques, in order to extract useful knowledge about customers segments, potential market and needs in each segment	Applying extract knowledge from market to design product and services and revising market strategies.

Source: Extended from (Hashemi & Hajjheydari, 2011).

Table 2. Intelligence enterprise performance management

Dimension	Assessment Performance Indicators
Financial dimension	1. Analyzing profitability of products and services 2. Analysis of actual costs and financial flows 3. Analyzing profitability of products and services 4. Analyzing operational efficiency of a organization 5. Inform about the realization of an enterprise's strategy 6. Providing analyses of deviations from the realization of plans
Marketing dimension	1. Customer satisfaction 2. Loyalty of customer 3. Customer orientation 4. One-to-one market
Internal processes	1. Optimization of setting time 2. Shorter delivery time 3. Lower cost 4. Reduction of much efforts related knowledge acquisition 5. Rapid adoption of experience to a particular problem 6. Decrease in effort necessary to retain knowledge
Development and growth	1. Motivation of employee 2. Effectiveness of team 3. Training of staff 4. Improvement in information on customers

Table 3. Intelligence enterprise competence

Categories of Customer Knowledge	Knowledge about Customers	Knowledge for Customers	Tacit Knowledge Conversion	Knowledge from Customers
Enterprise Competence	Information retrieval	Information Transfer	Information storage / distribution	Information application
	Competencies of acquiring and using customer knowledge	Competencies of acquiring, sharing and using customer knowledge	Competencies of providing data business competitive warehouse	Competencies of providing actual product preferences. Supplying payment and address information.

3.7 Implementing in Intelligence Enterprise

The enterprise address these challenges have been developed in two different approaches: structured data management (BI) and unstructured content management (KM and CRM).

Technological aspects of the integrated systems primarily involve methods of knowledge creation, source of knowledge and information technology tools. The tasks of knowledge management are knowledge transparency, knowledge dissemination, knowledge development, and knowledge efficiency. Knowledge in order to be utilized effectively in the process of decision-making should be stored and created according to already testes research methods. Solutions based on artificial intelligence including fuzzy logic, intelligent agents, genetic algorithm, and case base reasoning etc.

The most important motives that support implementation of BI system in enterprise may include the following: (Liautaud & Hammond, 2002; Rasmussen, Goldy & Solli, 2002)

1. Transitioning from instinct and intuition decision making to objectivism that is based on the analysis of facts, indexes, balanced score cards, managerial cockpits, etc.
2. Forecasting enterprise development along with customer's and suppliers' behavior.
3. Match operational activities with realization of strategic objectives.
4. Rapid detecting of information that deviates from commonly accepted standards and procedures and that suggests some possibilities that new threats will emerge.
5. Shortening time that is necessary to analyze information, and decreasing a number of participants who are involve in analyzing and processing of information.
6. Unifying information transfers in order to make them more transparent and unifying roles of individuals who participate in decision making processes.

CRM applications can use more advantages of technology; CRM application provider can use technology to gathering data, producing knowledge to predicting the behavior of customer and patterns of trade. Central foundation to CRM applications are Data warehouses, Enterprise Resource Planning (ERP) system. The most important motives that support implementation of CRM system in enterprise may include the following: (Jayashree & Shojace, 2011)

1. Data warehousing transforms customers' related data into customer intelligence for finding the customers' behavior.

2. ERP serves as a strong base while CRM tries to connect front and back office applications to maintain the customer relationship and making loyal customers. ERP systems integrate all functional areas of the business with suppliers and customers (Chen & Popovich, 2003).

3. There are two main of them of data analysis techniques in CRM: (a) OLAP: Online Analytical Processing collects a group of data from databases that are related with each other in one or more dimensions, like location. (b) Data mining can extract information from a customers' data. Data mining helps CRM to find the behavior of customers and patterns of buying, finding market segmentation and finding potential customers. Therefore, organizations can predict customers' needs and increase customers' satisfaction.

4. The budget of organization should be considered during making CRM application; more expensive application can be used only in very large organizations so different types of applications are needed for different budgets.

5. Sellers use a lot of information that are related to their work and this information makes selling process easier. Information like historical sales and revenue reports, trade show and promotional event schedules are very important.

6. CRM collects and maintains all valuable information about the customers so the organizations can know about their customers for predicting their future behavior and producing other valuable knowledge for marketing more profit.

7. By gathering and storing customer data, and then using business intelligence to making information and making knowledge, by use of knowledge management system, CRM can improve its knowledge about clients.

8. By using new communication technologies in CRM organization can improve interaction between them and customers.

4. CONCLUSION

In this study, it proposes a framework for customer relationship management, business intelligence, and knowledge management process to provide basic information for potential customer, achieve information from customer and analyze gathered data to provide better services. This could lead to increased customer satisfaction, reduced marketing costs and more effective marketing and lower costs customer acquisition and retention. Through the process of CRM, BI, and KM, it has an intelligence enterprise framework. The operations of intelligence enterprise are model, process, and competence. The model consists of four layers: the operational Layer, the BI and KM layer, the CRM layer and the output layer in order to enhance organizational competition advantage. In this paper, it discusses the enterprise performance management and the implementing in enterprise. In order to achieve the full potential of the integration model application, further research should focus on the e-business strategy.

REFERENCES

Alavi, M., & Leidner, D. E. (2001). Review: Knowledge management and knowledge management system: conceptual foundations and research issue. *MIS Quarterly Journal, 25*(1), 107–136. doi:10.2307/3250961

Albescu, F., Pugna, I., & Paraschiv, D. (2008). Business Intelligence & Knowledge management – Technological support for strategic management in the knowledge based economy. *Revisit Information Economics, 4*(48), 5–12.

Alwis, R., & Hartmann, E. (2008). The use of tacit knowledge within innovative companies: Knowledge management in innovation enterprise. *Journal of Knowledge Management, 12*(1), 133–147. doi:10.1108/13673270810852449

Attafar, A., Sadidi, M., Attafar, H., & Shahin, A. (2013). The Role of Customer Knowledge (CKM) in Proving Organization Customer Relationship. *Middle-East Journal of Science Research, 13*(6), 829–835.

Bose, R., & Sugumaran, V. (2003). Application of knowledge management technology in customer relationship management. *Knowledge and Process Management, 10*(1), 3–17. doi:10.1002/kpm.163

Bueren, A., Schierholz, R., Kolbe, L., & Brenner, W. (2004), Customer knowledge management - improving performance of customer relationship management with knowledge management. In *Proceedings of the 37th Hawaii International Conference on System Sciences.* IEEE. doi:10.1109/HICSS.2004.1265416

Campbell, A. J. (2003). Creating customer knowledge competence: Managing customer relationship management programs strategically. *Industrial Marketing Management, 32*(5), 375–383. doi:10.1016/S0019-8501(03)00011-7

Campbell, A. J. (2006). The role of organizational knowledge management strategies in the quest for business intelligence. In *Proceedings of IEE International Conference on Engineering Management,* (pp. 231-236). IEE.

Carrillo, P. M., Kamara, J. M., & Anumba, C. J. (2000), Integration of knowledge management within construction business processes. In *Proceeding of the UK National Conference on Objects and Integration for Architecture, Engineering and Construction,* (pp. 95-105). Academic Press.

Chen, I. J., & Popovich, K. (2003). Understanding customer relationship management (CRM), people, process and technology. *Business Process Management Journal, 9*(5), 672–688. doi:10.1108/14637150310496758

Cheng, L., & Peng, P. (2011), Integration knowledge management and Business. In *Proceedings of 2011 Fourth International Conference on Business Intelligence and Financial Engineering (BIFE),* (pp. 307-310). BIFE. doi:10.1109/BIFE.2011.172

Croteus, A. M., & Peter, L. (2003). Critical success factors of CRM technological initiatives. *Canadian Journal of Administrative Sciences, 20*(1), 21–34. doi:10.1111/j.1936-4490.2003.tb00303.x

Davenport, T., Harris, J., & Kohli, A. (2001, Winter). How do they know their customer so well?. *MIT Sloan Management, Review,* 1-13.

Gebert, H., Geib, H., Kolbe, L., & Brenner, W. (2003). Knowledge-enabled customer relationship management: Integrating customer relationship management and knowledge management concepts. *Journal of Knowledge Management, 7*(5), 107–123. doi:10.1108/13673270310505421

Geib, M., Reichold, A., Kolbe, L., & Brenner, W. (2005). Architecture for customer relationship management approaches in Financial service. In *Proceedings of the 38th Annual Hawaii International Conference on System Sciences* (HICSS '05), (pp. 240.1-240.10). IEEE.

Guangming, Z. (2007). CRM- based customer knowledge management. In *Proceeding of International Conference on Enterprise and Management Innovation*, (pp. 417-421). Academic Press.

Habul, A., Piav-Velic, A., & Kremic, E. (2012). *Customer Relationship Management and Business. In Advances in Customer Relationship Management* (pp. 1–30). InTech.

Hanandeh, R., Aiajlouni, M. I. & Nawafleh, S. A. (2012). The impact of knowledge management system on business intelligence optimization. In *Proceeding of Business Intelligence and Knowledge Economy,* (pp. 1119-1125). Academic Press.

Handen, L. (2000). *Customer relationship management: A strategic imperative in the world of e-business.* New York: Join Wiley & Sons.

Hashemi, N., & Hajiheydari, N. (2011), Customer knowledge management framework in E-commerce. In *Proceedings of 2011 International Conference on E-business, Management and Economics.* IACSIT Press.

Jayashree, S., & Shojace, S. (2011). A critical analysis customer relationship management from strategic perspective. In *Proceedings of 2010 International Conference on E-business Management and Economics.* IACSIT Press.

Kaplan, R. S., & Norton, D. P. (1996). Using the balanced scorecard as a strategic management system. *Harvard Business Review, 74*(1), 75–85.

Karl, W. (1997). Knowledge management: An Introduction and Perspective. *Journal of Knowledge Management, 1*(1), 6–14. doi:10.1108/13673279710800682

Kodama, M. (2005). Customer value creation through knowledge creation with customers: Case studies of IT and multimedia business in Japan. *International Journal of Innovation and Learning, 2*(4), 357–385. doi:10.1504/IJIL.2005.006661

Li, T., & Calantone, R. J. (1998). The impact of market knowledge competence on new product advantage: Conceptualization and empirical examination. *Journal of Marketing, 62*(4), 13–29. doi:10.2307/1252284

Liautaud, R., & Hammond, M. (2002). *E-business intelligence: Turning information into knowledge into profit.* New York: McGraw-Hill.

Manning, N. P. D. (2009). Knowledge management. *Development Journal, 5*(2), 31–34.

Massey, A., Montoya-Weiss, M. M., & Holcom, K. (2001). Re-engineering the customer relationship: Leveraging knowledge assets at IBM. *Decision Support Systems, 32*(2), 155–170. doi:10.1016/S0167-9236(01)00108-7

Moutot, J. M., & Bascoul, G. (2008). Effects of sales force automation use on sale force activities and customer relationship management processes. *Journal of Personal Selling and Sales, 28*(2), 167–184. doi:10.2753/PSS0885-3134280205

Murfitt, S. (2001). *Using Business Intelligence*. Retrieved 14 August 2013, from http://www.digitrends/net/scripts

O'Brien, J. A., & Marakas, G. M. (2007). *Introduction to information Systems*. New York: McGraw-Hill.

Olszak, C. M., & Ziemba, E. (2003, June). Business intelligence as a key to management of an enterprise. *Proceeding of Information Science,* 855-863.

Olszak, C. M., & Ziemba, E. (2007). Approach to building and implementing business intelligence systems. *Interdisciplinary Journal of Information, Knowledge and Management, 2,* 135–148.

Paquette, S. (2006). *Customer knowledge management. In Encyclopedia of knowledge management.* Idea Group Inc.

Payne, A., & Frow, P. (2005). A strategic framework for customer relationship management. *Journal of Marketing Management, 69*(4), 167–176. doi:10.1509/jmkg.2005.69.4.167

Payne, A., & Frow, P. (2006). Customer relationship management: From strategy to implementation. *Journal of Marketing Management, 22*(1-2), 135–168. doi:10.1362/026725706776022272

Perko, L., & Bobek, S. (2007). An agent model in BI knowledge intensive environment. In *Proceedings of International Conference on Information Technology Interfaces.* Academic Press. doi:10.1109/ITI.2007.4283821

Plakoyiannaki, E., & Saren, M. (2006). Time and the customer relationship management process: Conceptual and methodological insights. *Journal of Business and Industrial Marketing, 2*(4), 218–230. doi:10.1108/08858620610672588

Poter, M. E., & Milar, V. E. (1985). How Information Gives you Competitive advantage. *Harvard Business Review, 4,* 149–160.

Rababah, K. Mohd, H. & Ibrahim, H. (2011). Customer Relationship Management (CRM) process from Theory to Practice: The pre-implementation Plan of CRM System. *International Journal of e-Education, e-Business, e-Management, e-Learning, 1*(1), 22-27.

Ragins, E. J., & Greco, A. J. (2003). Customer Relationship Management and E-Business: More than a Software Solution. *Review of Business, 24*(1), 25–30.

Rasmussen, N., Goldy, P. S., & Solli, P. Q. (2002). *Financial business intelligence, trends, technology, software selection, and implementation.* John Wiley & Sons.

Reinartz, W., Krafft, M., & Hoyer, W. D. (2004). The customer relationship management process: Its measurement and impact on performance. *JMR, Journal of Marketing Research, 41*(3), 293–305. doi:10.1509/jmkr.41.3.293.35991

Rowley, J. (2002). Reflections on customer knowledge management in e-business. *Qualitative market Research: An Internal Journal, 4,* 268–280.

Rowley, J. (2004). Relationship Marketing and Knowledge Management: Partnering Paradigms? *Industrial Management & Data Systems, 104*(2), 149–157. doi:10.1108/02635570410522125

Shehzad, R., & Khan, M. N. A. (2013). Integrating knowledge management with business intelligence process for enhance organizational learning. *International Journal of Software Engineering and its Applications, 7*(2), 83-92.

Su, C. T., Chen, Y. H., & Sha, D. A. (2006). Linking innovative product development with customer knowledge: A data-mining approach. *Technovation, 26*(7), 784–795. doi:10.1016/j.technovation.2005.05.005

Sunasses, N., & Sewry, D. A. (2002). A theoretical framework for knowledge management implementation. In *Proceeding of 2002 Annual Research Conference of the South African Institute of Computer Scientists and Information Technologies on Enablement through Technology (SAICSIT)*. Port Elizabeth, South Africa: SAICSIT.

Venkatadri, M., Hanumat, G. S., & Manjunath, G. (2010). A novel business intelligence system framework. *Universal Journal of Computer Science and Engineering Technology, 1*(2), 112–116.

Weidong, Z., Weihui, D., & Kunlomg, K. (2010). The relationship of business intelligence and knowledge. In *Proceedings of the 2nd IEE International Conference on Informational Management and Engineering (ICIE)*, (pp. 26-29). IEE.

Winer, E. (2001). A framework for customer relationship management. *California Management Review, 43*(4), 6–14. doi:10.2307/41166102

You, H. (2010). A knowledge Management Approach for real-time business intelligence. In *Proceedings of the 2nd IEE International Workshop on Intelligent Systems and Application (ISA)*. IEE.

Zanjani, M. S., Rouzbehani, R., & Dabbagh, H. (2008). proposes a conceptual model of customer knowledge Management: A study of CKM tools in British Dotcoms. *International Journal of Humanities and Social Science, 3*(5), 363–367.

KEY TERMS AND DEFINITIONS

Business Intelligence (BI): Activities that not only collect and process data, but also make possible analysis that results in useful-intelligent-solutions to business problems.

Customer Relationship Management (CRM): A customer service approach that focuses on building long-term and sustainable customer relationships that add value both for the customer and the selling company.

Data Warehouse (DW): A single, service-based data repository that allow centralized, security, and control over data.

Decision Support System (DSS): DSS are target systems that combine analytical models with operational data and supportive interactive queries and analysis for middle managers who face semi-structured decision situations hence DSS support the semi-structured and unstructured problem analysis.

E-Commerce (EC): EC is a broader term that encompasses electronically buying, selling, service customers, and interacting with business partner and intermediaries over the Internet.

Enterprise Competitive Competence: Core competences are the capabilities that are critical to an organization's achievement of competitive advantage.

Enterprise Resource Planning (ERP): ERP is business management software. It is usually a suite of integrated applications. A company can use to collect, store, manage and interpret data from many business activities.

Information Technology (IT): IT is the application of computers, networking, software programming, and other equipment and processes to store, process, retrieve, transmit, and protect information.

Knowledge Management (KM): The process of capturing or creating knowledge, storing it, updating it constantly, interpreting it, and using it whenever necessary.

Online Analytical Processing (OLAP): End user analytical activities, such as DSS modeling using spreadsheets and graphics that are done online.

Chapter 16
Process Improvements in Supply Chain Operations:
Multi-Firm Case Studies

Alan D. Smith
Robert Morris University, USA

ABSTRACT

The nature of SCM research is constantly evolving and must address a variety of concerns like poor service, large inventory levels, and friction among suppliers and manufacturers. Analytical databases and techniques in SCM are an important part of this research. Many researchers and practitioners have depended on secondary data, but given the dynamic nature of global competition, more recent and relevant data must be gathered. These efforts need to be geared to the development of properly managed supply chain relationships and corporate sustainability initiatives that ultimately promote broad-based sustainable development objectives for the good of people, plants, and profits (i.e., triple bottom-line).

1. INTRODUCTION

1.1 Successful SCM Considerations

Understanding that supply chain success depends on supplier performance can make supplier relationships, or their lack of, having a huge impact on revenue, inventory, and profitability. There have been a multitude of positive and negative links between suppliers that can directly or indirectly impact the overall operational success of companies, especially in terms of cost, quality, flexibility, and delivery metrics (Ketikidis, Hayes, Lazuras, Gunasekaran, & Koh, 2013; Mateen & More, 2013). ; Park & Min, (2013). Firms and their supply chains must control suppliers, and not let suppliers control their business, through increased levels of mutual benefit and respect. This is the issue where the efforts of lean operatrions to reduce the waste of inventory and time begins (Basu & Nair, 2012; Brito & Botter, 2012). It is critical to align performance with demand planning. Otherwise, too much of the demand planning horizon is frozen by unnecessarily long-lead times and too much variability in performance. The authors, van Weele and

DOI: 10.4018/978-1-4666-7272-7.ch016

Copyright © 2015, IGI Global. Copying or distributing in print or electronic forms without written permission of IGI Global is prohibited.

van Raaij (2014) made a plea to the academic community for Purchasing and Supply Management (PSM) to engage in greater efforts to adhere to a more rigorous approach to research. They distinguished supply chain management (SCM) as a different entity than PSM, as SCM has moved away from simply a focus on the flow of goods to examining more closely the relationships between different players along the supply chain in an attempt to control more than just inventory management-related concerns. Through the creation of value for a specific customer market, emphasis is placed on proceeding as efficiently as possible (as opposed to effectively). This task may be accomplished through strategic management, of which certain aspects will be examined in the present case study, but van Weele and van Raaij suggested that research into this subject may hold no value unless the findings are executed. As profits became a result of customer satisfaction, firms began to focus on excelling at their core competencies and outsourcing other aspects of their business and shifting to a more supplier-dependent climate. It was suggested that competitiveness was not entirely internal, but relies on external relationships with suppliers, as well. Still, the literature contained a lack of studies that display any new finding on how to leverage this internal knowledge within a firm. One of the purposed of this chapter is to address this apparent lack of multiple industrial studies on internal leverage of SCM-related information.

If management recognizes that SCM processes require integration throughout the organization and beyond with suppliers and customers, problems that may have been historically significant are caught and dealt with prior to them becoming a current issue or problem. Otherwise, gaps in the supply chain are created that can significantly hinder results. Using collaboration with key supply chain participants to provide additional focus and resources to the total supply chain is vital. Assessing the entire supply chain is critical for identifying critical areas, including suppliers, logistics-service providers, ports, and other potential risks that could disrupt a company's supply chain. Essentially, SCM is not only concerned with the management of the flow of goods and services within and without a firm, but maintaining the relationships among all stakeholders that support the supply chain. Goods and service involved in this flow traditionally include fresh raw materials, inventory, and finished products. Raw materials need to be transported using fast and efficient means to make the production process successful. The availability of raw materials and the fast nature of the production process dictates that raw materials need to be constantly available in large quantity and in good condition. Therefore, proper storage of raw materials comes in handy and consequently, this would necessitate adequate storage capacities.

SCM has traditionally concerned with the internal planning, design, execution and control of activities connected to the supply chain (Casadesus & de Castro, 2005; Miguel & Brito, (2011). These activities are usually intended to fulfill certain objectives, but management is always pressured to strategically leverage the supply chain to create net value. This means that firms have to put forth extra effort to enhance their productivity at all levels. Management has to ensure that their overhead expenses do not balloon beyond reasonable levels, which initially would limit profitability. Therefore, the difference that is realized between expenditure on production and revenues from sales constitutes the net value. Effective SCM should strive to ensure the creation of the largest possible net value, yet maintain positive customer and supplier relationships (Smith, 2011, 2012). Logistics also play a fundamental role in the outworking of activities pioneered by an organization. These concerns with the overall oversight of activities, plans, and procedures in which a firm participates can be overwhelming at times and their complex interactions should not be downplayed. In many instances, achieving a sensible form of logistics proves elusive and unrelenting. Consequently, logistics always require to be leveraged against any discrepancy related to harmful gossip of strangers. The leverage of logistics has the potential to determine the general direction that the firm would be willing to take in its SCM activities. Hence, SCM is directly involved with the leveraging of logistics, not just for one firm on a local scale, but also on a worldwide scale as reflected in large customer and vendor databases.

Proper management of the supply chain would also ensure the building of a competitive system of infrastructure. Basically, infrastructure is concerned with streamlining the exchange of information and the flow of products from the point of manufacture to the point of consumption such as the marketplace. Firms with a streamlined system of infrastructure have an upper hand in terms of realizing their potential in the supply chain. The quality of the SCM-related activities has a direct bearing on the quality of infrastructure (Bulcsu, 2011; Carvalho, Cruz-Machado, & Tavares, 2012; Hamidi, Farahmand, Sajjadi, & Nygard, 2012; Pettersson & Segerstedt, 2011). Few firms are able to operate entirely within their own industries. Majority of firms have to work within the limits and allowances stipulated by the industries within which they operate. The prevalence of many firms within the same industry creates a significant competitive environment. Nevertheless, each firm within the industry has an opportunity to create its own niche within the market; hopefully within a sustainability framework. Different firms adopt varying systems of infrastructure depending on their relative strengths and weaknesses. Therefore, proper supply-chain strategic initiatives should be capable of producing an efficient and competitive system of infrastructure (Kumar, Shankar, & Yadav, 2011; Mathirajan, Manoj, & Ramachandran, 2011; More & Babu, 2012; Paksoy & Cavlak, 2011).

1.2 Purpose of Chapter

The focus of this paper will be to explore the importance of interactions between SCM and social capital and review how major global companies further enhance its capability to approach this important operations management topic. In addition to the topics of SCM discussed thus far, e-procurement is also an important area to consider in the operations management process. This topic is discussed in more detail in an upcoming section. The operations management concept that is showcased in the present study specifically deals with the management of the buying and re-engineering a firm's supply chain, especially the managerial effects of operational and social capital on the buyer-supplier relationship. Since SCM is very important due to the numerous decisions regarding the supply chain can influence other decisions made by operations managers. As firms try to increase competitiveness through cost or customization, quality, cost reductions, and a product's speed to market, more emphasis is placed on the supply chain. Effective SCM looks to form partnerships with suppliers, in pursuing the firm's strategy to satisfy the end customer.

The available literature on SCM is extensive, as previously demonstrated, especially with respect to the value of collaborative buyer–supplier relationships; and recently a number of researchers have studied how value is created by building social capital among participating stakeholders for firms participating in such ventures. Most of these studies have been very supportive of social capital and collaborative supplier relationships, suggesting that social capital allows the firms to access and leverage resources resulting from their relationship. Management in many cases are able to reduce the likelihood of conflicts and promote cooperative behavior, as a result of their association's shared vision and trust. To this point, many SCM-related studies and literature have focused on the positive side of social capital. This chapter specifically deals with managing the social capital inherent in supply chains, even in recently acquired supply chains. In order to properly deal with such uncertainties in the supply chain, it is extremely important to create access to comprehensive databases and associated analytics to mediate such threats to lean operations.

2. SCM AND ANALYTICAL DATABASES

2.1 SCM Trends

In order to choose the right suppliers, management must be able to evaluate the tangible and intangible attributes associated with the many SCM decisions (Baxter & Hirschhauser, 2004; Biswas & Sarker, 2008; Browning & Heath, 2009; Cavaleri, 2008; Chan & Kumar, 2009). There are a number of research studies about supplier selection that concentrate on the evaluation of the supplier choice instead of researching the process of evaluating. Many operational managers focus more on cost and delivery performance measures than properly selecting partners in their global supply chains. Wu, Lin, and Kung (2013) suggested that this lack of focus on supply chain partnering its dynamics are due, in part, to multi-faceted processes and the many conflicting attributes to be considered. They suggested that using Fuzzy Multiple-Attribute Decision-Making (FMADM), a big-data analytical SCM tool, when making a supplier selection for a supply chain, may be the best approach. The importance of the supplier candidates can be compared using a linguistic value with a fuzzy number. This value and number help evaluate the importance of the chosen attributes, sub-attributes as well as the suppliers themselves. The decision making goes through a 12-step calculation to help rank the order of all alternatives.

Management must strive to be both sustainable and socially responsible in dealing with the operational effectiveness of their supply chains by reducing carbon footprint of their energy-dependent systems such as distribution, logistical, and warehousing functions in the ever changing market conditions, especially in the current global economic downturns. Projecting social responsibility is an important part the business culture today and part of an overall competitive strategy (Porter, 1996, 2008; Porter & Kramer, 2006; Rowe & Schlacter, 1978; Smith, 2007). Concurrently management needs to appropriately deal with stakeholder pressure and how such pressure a company's' willingness to practice sustainable supply chain management (SSCM) in order to create scales of corporate sustainability performance (CSP). According to a sustainability report produced by the United Nations Global Compact ("Supply Chain Sustainability: A Practical Guide for Continuous Improvement," 2010), a major driving force for implementing SSCM is to aid efforts to identify the highest priority supply chain issues for companies. This aid may be accomplished via appropriately evaluating their risks and opportunities and, ultimately, to build the internal support to move forward. Stakeholder pressure may be defined as the extent to which the focal organization is held accountable for its actions and decisions regarding product design, sourcing, production, or distribution to stakeholders (Wolf, 2014). The company uses a database Sustainalytics that has a multitude of companies that it has collected data on and in a stepwise process creates a CSP index.

Sustainalytics database, which has a multitude of companies that it has collected data on and in a stepwise process creates a CSP index, measures stakeholder pressure on issues ranging from product-related concerns to those of employee treatment. Sustainalytics' analysts identify concerns and assess an organization's reputation among stakeholders, according to these concerns. This information is used to propose an evaluation reflecting the social and environmental issues most relevant to stakeholders of an organization.

To assess stakeholder pressure on SCM issues, Wolf (2014) completed a comprehensive study to access this pressure, with the control variables set in this study were organization size, risk, and industry. The study proposed three competing models of the potential relationship between stakeholder pressure, SSCM, and CSP. With these goals to investigate, Wolf tried to decide which of the three models best fit information on the subset organizations from different industries? The findings revealed that the model, in which stakeholder pressure drives SSCM and SSCM in turn impacts CSP, does not fit the data best. Rather, a direct-effects model best represents the underlying data structure. The direct-effects model shows that SSCM is positively related to the perception of an organization as a sustainable one; suggesting that organizations benefit from proactive adoption of SSCM strategies. Reputation for an organization as ''good citizen'' increases by promoting environmental and social sustainability in their supply chains and improves legitimacy and access to key resources. This reputation has been captured in a measure of CSP, which is positively and significantly related to different types of SSCM strategies, practices, and policies. Interestingly, though, the findings indicate that stakeholder pressure does not moderate the SSCM-CSP relationship. This was somewhat surprising, as one would expect the effects of SSCM on CSP to diminish under conditions of high-stakeholder pressure. In essence, without being aware of a company's impact throughout all facets of business, one cannot fully assess their worth to the global marketplace.

2.2 Collaborative Nature of Successful SCM

Other researchers (Miguel & Brito, 2011; Paksoy & Cavlak, 2011; Pettersson & Segerstedt, 2011) have suggested that SCM, by its definition, applies to the collaborative relationships of members of different ranks of the supply chain and refers to common and agreed practices performed jointly by two or more organizations. When adopting the SCM, companies have to carry out a constant set of best-business management practices. The large-scale databases of customers and vendors involved in effective SCM typically involve the functions of information sharing, long-term relationship building, risk and reward sharing, cooperation, and process integration. Information sharing maps directly to knowledge exchange (Miguel & Brito, 2011). Long-term relationships can help reduce transaction costs through the development of trust and reputation. Strategic relationships can result in the exchange of knowledge and assure investment in specific assets. Cooperation and process integration can lead to the development of both specific assets and complementary resources. Databases and their management require significant amount of testing for accuracy among samples and SCM modules in order to ensure that there is a positive link to SCM on operational performance. All data collected and the decisions based on such results should make use of competitive priorities interlinked with operational performance.

Miguel & Brito (2011) suggested from their analytical findings that SCM impacted positively the operational performance as a whole and all the competitive priorities; hence, providing support for the cumulative capabilities perspective. There was ample evidence for an operational competence construct mediating the relationship between SCM and operational performance. From a resource-based view, the findings can be thought as an enlightening resource that summarizes the impacts of several operational initiatives. From a managerial perspective, these findings could reinforce the importance of pursuing a competitive advantage leading to excellent performance in all competitive priority dimensions simultaneously. Perhaps a significant part of success in manufacturing firms and companies, is the visibility through the entire supply chain. If there is visibility, information sharing, cooperation, process integration, and long-term relationships should all contribute to this SCM success. All of these factors allow for more of a smooth production process. Any significant delays or discrepancies among the various members in the chain can be very detrimental to the success of the company. These suppliers and manufactures have to work together so that all the members can see a positive effect on costs, quality, flexibility, and delivery.

Chamber, Kouvelis, & Wang (2006) reviewed a significant number of SCM articles between 1992-2006 in order to review, highlight, and summarize significant contributions to the field. The original intent was intended to analyze for suggestions for furthering SCM, as well as how to expand research in a conceptual overview of SCM dynamics from 1992-2006. It was obvious that SCM continues to be dominant issue in operations management, "that the ultimate core competency of an organization is SC (supply chain) design" (p. 451). Many of the major themes in SCM research were the traditional areas of supply chain dynamics, the Bullwhip Effect (BWE), supply chain capacity and sourcing decisions, SCM applications and practices, supply chain planning and scheduling, and approaches to teaching SCM. As the authors noted the strengths and weaknesses or shortcomings of SCM practices, highlighting some important concerns, of which they identified if a SCM practice allows for a disruption in production, long-term stock price performance, and equity risk. They found that the average abnormal stock return of firms that experienced disruptions was –40%. In essence, there are some "glaring inefficiencies" that still remain in many industries regarding inventory and logistics that SCM professionals need to actively address.

Other researchers have suggested that there is much work to be done linking operational and financial performance in SCM (Park & Min, 2013; Rajapakshe, Dawande, & Sriskandarajah, 2013; Rajeev, Rajagopal, & Mercado, 2013; Smith & Synowka, 2014). Typically, the operations manager situations usually involve dynamic concerns with multiple parties, yet much research has primarily been completed on single-agent problems (Chamber, et al., 2006). There must be certain successful operations management skills for the SCM professionals that involve functional, technical, leadership skills, coupled with a relative high level of global experience. Hence, effective SCM can provide sustainable advantages and barriers to entry, beyond the traditional scope SCM provides of efficiency and passing lower margins on to customers. Effective management of supply chain operations is critical to the success of any organization. Regardless of the type of business, supply chain processes can have a major impact on the organization's ability to deliver products and/or services to its customers. All successful companies must determine how to effectively partner with suppliers and design efficient processes to promote efforts to improve innovation, expedite product/service design, and reduce costs.

3. METHODOLOGY

3.1 Case Studies of Competitive SCM Practices

This study focuses on the complementarity of SCM metrics and lean management approaches within an analytical database environment. Supply chain metrics, in general, allow organizations to create a standard framework to assess its supply chain performance, including internal and external links in the chain. Downstream performance metrics have not been examined much in current literature, rather than on upstream supply chain performance (Chamber, et al., 2006). Upstream supply chain activities for manufacturers would typically include the suppliers and raw material manufacturers. Key participants in downstream supply chain performance are manufacturers, transporters, distributors, wholesalers, retailers, and end customers, which will be briefly discussed in the various case studies. Supply chain metrics can help members communicate and work together to improve the supply chain rather than each member working in isolation. The use of internal performance metrics can help in the elimination on non-value added items, allow for smoother product flows and more efficient use of time. The use of external performance metrics can increase communication among member firms and allow for the creation of increased end customer value through integrated supply chain activities.

The manufacturing companies are more similar than dissimilar in nature and scope, especially in terms of its clientele. Management at each firm faces unique challenges in utilizing its process strategies to continuously improve its operations in a highly competitive manufacturing environment. Commonly established case study procedures associated with SCM and manufacturing initiatives and improvements were followed in the present study (Nonthaleerak & Hendry, 2008; Smith, Smith, & Baker, 2011).

A combination of personal interviews of upper-to-middle management, as well as comments from convenient samples of employees were used to gather perceptions of the various firms' perceived metric-based SCM and supportive strategic initiatives that support their efforts for profitability, reasons for change and choice of solutions in SCM practices. In essence, much of the information, not just personal experiences, were obtained either directly from management or from the firms' websites, or a combination of both sources.

3.2 Sample Description

Organizations in different sectors can have vastly different challenges to overcome and solutions that work well for one company may have no applicability in another. To illustrate this fact, this chapter focuses on four separate companies in widely varying industries. In particular, a focused analysis is performed on process improvements made within the supply chain of each company. Pittsburgh, PA and its metropolitan area were chosen for its highly educated business environment (one of the major global headquarters in the U.S.), a stable workforce environment (one of the lowest unemployment rates of any major metropolitan domestic region) (Fleishe, 2014). The goal of this study is to illustrate the similarities and differences among the many challenges faced by supply chain managers in different industries and to highlight examples of how each company has addressed those challenges. It is important to remember that supply chain managers in all the companies are heavy dependent on creating and maintaining large-scale databases on their customers and vendors. Please note that the last section, specific adoptions in response to global competitive conditions, may not be as complete for all companies as access to particular data and general comments during the interview process in some cases were quite confidential and, hence, somewhat restricted.

4. COMPANY CASE STUDIES

4.1 McKesson Automation

4.1.1 Company Description and Background

Located in Cranberry Township, PA, McKesson Automation, a division on McKesson Corporation, is a manufacturer of robotic and other automated hardware systems geared towards the management, dispensing, packaging, and administration of medications in hospitals and other healthcare facilities. The particular area of supply chain process improvement focus is primarily JIT inventory management using electronic Kanban software.

4.1.2 History

McKesson Automation was originally founded by Sean McDonald in 1989 under the name Automated Healthcare. The initial product offered by the company was a massive enclosed robot responsible for filling the prescriptions of hospital patients. The first such unit was installed at Saint Clair hospital in 1992 and quickly rose to prominence as a forerunner in hospital pharmacy automation. Following six years of rapid growth, the company was acquired by McKesson Corporation in 1996. Since that time, the products offered by this division have grown to include medication dispensing cabinets, anesthesia carts, vertical lift modules for storing medications and other inventory items, along with oral solid medication dispensing and packaging machines among many others.

Currently, McKesson Automation's manufacturing division manages a 93,000 square foot facility in which they stock over 6100 purchased items in inventory which are sourced from 411 different vendors. The current on-hand inventory has a value of US$7.3M. The supply-chain team is responsible for managing vendor relations, parts ordering, receiving and restocking each of these items; a task that had grown increasingly challenging until five years ago.

4.1.3 Reasons for Change in SCM and Process Practices

In 2003, the materials management team made the decision to move to a Kanban-based system for inventory management, a classic technique in the implementation of JIT strategies. Over the course of the next several years, this major process change was slowly implemented for the vast majority of purchased items. This JIT approach was highly successful in helping to reduce inventory levels, streamlining the replenishment process and enabling greater flexibility to changes in demand. As the years progressed, the team was faced with a number of new challenges. In particular, as new products were brought to market, the growing number of inventory items led to a large number of Kanban cards being managed. The large volume of cards resulted in a greater volume of lost cards which eventually led to stock-outs. In addition, the continuous increase in the number of stocked items required a proportional amount of additional labor to manage. McKesson eventually reached a critical point at which it was unable to add any additional Kanban cards to the system and still improve efficiency levels.

In 2007, the team made the decision to investigate ways to further automate the Kanban system so as to reduce the amount of manual repetitive steps in the process. In addition, they wanted to provide real-time visibility to the status of inventory items throughout the entire manufacturing process to both internal users as well as to external suppliers. A number of different software packages were considered containing features that had been designed with these goals in mind.

4.1.4 Choice of Solution

The team conducted a brief competition among three separate vendors of electronic Kanban software solutions and eventually chose a package developed by Ultriva, Inc. This solution was chosen for a number of reasons. First, it offered a web-based interface that allowed for access by both internal manufacturing employees as well as external suppliers. The second key feature was a framework for developing ERP integrations which would remove the need to perform redundant data entry. One of the most compelling feature of the application, however, was its proprietary algorithms that allow it to analyze inventory usage and automatically adjust the Kanban loop size to minimize inventory levels while still preventing stock-outs.

The system manages the entire inventory cycle for any purchased item that is Kanban controlled. The Kanban cycle starts when a worker on the shop floor pulls material from inventory, a process which includes scanning the barcoded Kanban label. The system automatically relieves the material from inventory in the ERP system and simultaneously creates a blanket order release and notifies the appropriate supplier that more parts are needed. The supplier uses the system to accept the release, print a new Kanban label which they affix to the package, and process the shipment transaction. When the goods reach the dock, the receiving team scans the Kanban card which automatically performs a blanket order receipt in the ERP system. Goods are then placed into inventory, thereby completing the cycle. After several cycles, the application is able to analyze usage data and predict the optimal loop size. Loop size settings can be automatically or manually adjusted.

4.1.5 Adoption Process Details

After selection of the software, the team spent the next three months on system implementation as well as designing and developing the ERP integration layer. Integration points include supplier and item master records as well as blanket order release and receipt transactions. Following numerous training sessions with internal employees and external suppliers, rollout of the solution and accompanying process changes began in September 2007. New Kanban labels were printed and attached to all existing on-hand inventory. An initial batch of 15 suppliers was brought onto the platform during the launch and the remaining 15 suppliers were gradually brought in throughout the remainder of the year.

Initially, there were significant concerns regarding the willingness of suppliers to comply with and adhere to the new process McKesson was requiring of them. However, the vast majority of suppliers were highly affable to the new conditions of doing business. Although a small number of suppliers were unable or unwilling to comply, these vendors were quickly replaced by other suppliers.

Internal adoption of the new tools and processes was quick and seamless. Manufacturing personnel were accustomed to Kanban processes so the transition to a software-based Kanban solution was not a significant change. The only significant issues that occurred were related to transactions for consignment inventory items and those which were required to pass through inspection prior to being received. These issues were quickly addresses through minor changes to the integration procedures along with minor adjustments to material handling processes.

4.1.6 Results

Since its initial deployment, purchased inventory items have grown from 5033 parts to 6162 parts and the number of suppliers using the system has grown from 30 to 66. While the production level has remained relatively constant over that timeframe, the average raw inventory costs have been reduced from US$10.4M to US$7.3M; a reduction of 29.6%. Use of the software has also accelerated receiving time, reducing it from 12 minutes to 7 minutes per package. This allowed for the elimination of one position within the receiving department providing US$46K per year in savings. In addition, the reduction in time needed to communicate with suppliers has allowed the materials management team to cut the number of full time positions from 7 to 6 resulting in additional labor savings of US$87K per year.

Additional soft savings have been realized as well including a reduction in stock-outs, increased inventory turns, a 99% on-time delivery rating, the elimination of lost Kanban cards, increased inventory accuracy and near instantaneous communication between the plant and the supplier when inventory is consumed.

Overall, the manufacturing team estimates that implementation of this system has resulted in a bottom line cost savings of over US$16M over the past 5 years. This includes labor savings along with the savings achieved through raw inventory cost reductions over the 5 year period. The initial cost to implement the system was US$350K and ongoing maintenance has incurred an additional cost of US$50k per year. Over the 5-year period since implementation, the system has demonstrated an incredible 2586% return on investment (J. Norwood, personal communication, October 1, 2012).

McKesson Automation was founded on process automation. It is only natural for the organization to continue to find ways to automate internal processes as well. The process automation achieved through the electronic Kanban application has been tremendously beneficial to the organization and will continue to allow them to grow and expand their supply chain operations for many years to come. Future expansion of the electronic Kanban system will target shop floor operations and inventory movement from work center to work center.

4.2 Community Care, Inc. (CCI)

4.2.1 Company Description and Background

With offices in Pittsburgh, Greensburg, and Washington, Community Care, Inc. is a small regional privately held firm founded in 1986 that currently specializes in home health services (Community Care, Inc., 2012). Home health services refer to the delivery of skilled nursing care in the home arena (i.e., wound care, delivery of medicine, to name a few).

4.2.2 History

CCI initially entered the potentially the burgeoning homecare market of Southwestern Pennsylvania in the late 1980s. Homecare services are different than the home health services defined above. Homecare refers to the delivery of unskilled care to patients in a home setting (i.e., meal preparation, bathing). Currently CCI offers both home health and homecare-related services to its clients. At the time at the company entered into this area, homecare involved little in the way of government regulation, and most of the clientele paid for their services out of pocket. This meant that billing, documentation, credentialing of field staff, and a vast variety of other services were relatively simple tasks. Therefore, the day-to-day operation of the company could easily be performed by the two owners and a few office staff who dealt with clerical duties and some scheduling of services. This arrangement was in place for much of the first 10 years the business existed.

Since CCI is a service-related company the definition of its supply chain is somewhat different than a traditional manufacturing company. To keep things relatively simple and in context with the process improvement, CCI implemented, the supply chain will be defined as follows:

1. The procurement of raw materials that CCI performs can be equated to the function of recruitment and hiring of qualified field staff.
2. The intermediate goods that CCI transforms into the final product consist of their inventory of properly trained and credentialed field staff.
3. The distribution system is the scheduling mechanism that CCI has in place to properly staff all of its clients with the proper field staff.
4. The services of homecare and/or home health are the final finished products that CCI provides to its clientele (this includes the care and documentation of the care provided).

Although there are certainly other more detailed portions to CCI's overall supply chain, the above definition focuses on the main function of the business (delivery of home health and homecare services) and how they relate to the supply chain process improvement described in the following paragraphs.

4.2.3 Reasons for Change in SCM and Process Practices

During the first decade of CCI's existence, as described above, the nature of the services being provided by CCI and the overall number of clients, allowed for a reasonably small staff to run the daily operations of the company and provide quality care to their clients. In addition to the small number of office staff, the business was very much a "pen and paper" operation. Scheduling of clients was manually logged in a paper binder, phone numbers were kept in Rolodexes, patient records were stored in hard files, and even paychecks were hand written. Again, the size, scope and demands of the company allowed this arrangement to thrive for about a decade.

As with any reasonably successful and growing company, changes would have to take place operationally within CCI to allow the firm to remain successful and competitive in the growing Homecare/ Health sector. In addition to increased competition, during the late 1990's more government regulation and requirements crept into the Homecare portion of CCI's business. More stringent documentation of consumer care and more thorough screening, credentialing and training of field staff were required during this time as well.

Other factors associated that are rapidly changing homecare line of business, the company also wished to expand into the area of home health in the early 2000's. The operational requirements of providing home health services are much greater than those of Homecare. The administration of skilled care requires a field staff that is better trained and has clinical credentialing and experience far greater than that of an unskilled field staff. Patient documentation is far more complex in home health as compared to homecare-related delivery systems.

It was clear that in order to stay competitive in homecare and expand into the home health arena, significant changes would need to happen operationally to CCI and that the change would have a direct impact on the supply chain as defined above. That change was to design and implement a proprietary database that could manage the increasing demands of the supply chain of a growing and ever more regulated business. If the company were to survive and thrive in the coming decade the pen and paper would need to be traded for a database and computer network.

4.2.4 Choice of Solution

Changing a corporate culture from pen and paper to a computerized one is not a quick task and it was not in CCI's case. Over a three year period a computer network was designed and fully implemented. But more importantly, a centralized database with functionality specific to CCI's line of business was created internally. This database would change the supply chain as described earlier, with process improvements at each step of the chain. For example, the function of recruitment and hiring of field staff was greatly enhanced by having a centralized record of current, former and in-process employees. The former manual system relied on paper records and often the owners' memories. Now a recruiter could track things like termination reasons of former employees in a searchable electronic fashion to prevent re-hiring of ex-employees with poor past performance. Next, the function of managing CCI's inventory of properly trained and credentialed field staff could be managed quickly and accurately, something that was nearly impossible to do under the old manual system.

4.2.5 Adoption Process Details

Office employees are now informed by the computer system of expiring or missing employee credentialing instead of relying on the employee to remember to periodically check on these things. As a result, the problem of employees working without proper credentialing has been all but eliminated. Next, the supply chain function of distribution of services was vastly enhanced by the proprietary database. Just a few office staff can now efficiently and accurately manage the scheduling of hundreds of field staff to hundreds of patients. This task would be impossible to handle manually with so few office staff. This is probably the biggest process improvement and cost savings that CCI's centralized computer system has resulted in. Finally, the actual delivery of care has been greatly improved. Nursing staff is able to track patient progress through the database and create clinical forms automatically that were once manual processes. In addition, the system also stores patient documentation digitally. This enhances the archiving and retrieval of patient information again improving the function of delivery of services.

4.2.6 Results

The proof of positive results is that CCI is still a competitive and thriving business in the homecare and home health markets in Southwestern PA. Although the adoption process was not an overnight success, the corporate culture has done a 180-degree turn to embracing technology in the day to day operations of the business. Process improvements to CCI's supply chain are now often results of adjustments made to their proprietary database. This makes CCI more responsive to changes in their market. In order to keep a competitive advantage, healthcare companies (like any service company) must implement a sound information technology strategy to survive (Archer, Bajaj, & Zhang, 2008).

4.3 Knichel Logistics

4.3.1 Company Description and Background

Located in Gibsonia, PA, Knichel Logistics is a fully staffed, federally licensed third party logistics provider offering shipping, warehousing, transloading and other special services for its clients.

4.3.2 History

Knichel Logistics was founded in 1974 by William Knichel. He began by working in the railroad transportation industry. Since the company's inception, Knichel has earned a reputation in the transportation industry as a reliable and valuable logistics provider and has focused on superior customer service. During an interview with the current COO of Knichel Logistics, David Mudd, a number of details were uncovered about their part of the supply chain and what process improvements have been made (personal communication, October 19, 2012).

Currently, Knichel Logistics is strictly a third-party logistics provider servicing intermodal (train), over the road (truck) and LTL (less than full truckload) one-way moves. Mudd refers to their company as a transactional third-party logistics company, which means that they make their money off of single moves. A customer would use Knichel to give them the best possible mode of transportation at the best rate and fastest shipping time. For example, a customer in Cleveland, OH needs 20 pallets of a shipment of rice totaling 18,000 pounds moved to Los Angeles, CA by a certain date and they want to know the most cost effective way of getting it there. The customers generally want to know if it is cheaper to ship via intermodal or over the road routes and when they can expect their shipment to arrive. Knichel does not have any fortune 500 customers and they have no plans on procuring them. Knichel aims at keeping their customer base smaller so they can give each customer superior service and keep them loyal to Knichel. In addition, Mudd felt that Fortune 500 companies require significant attention for generally a 5% profit, since they are volume buyers and it is not in Knichel's strategy to try to obtain these customers. Knichel attracts small to mid-size customers that require more customer service and attention and are willing to pay a little bit more for Knichel to handle their shipment and show great interest in each transaction. They are able to give such great service (at a premium) because they keep 20-30% more staff than competitors in their industry. Knichel's strategy is to over communicate every single shipment and make sure there are no mistakes made. Customers that they deal with very much prefer frequent status updates on their shipments.

4.3.3 Reasons for Change in SCM and Process Practices

As Knichel grew, it became apparent that the company wanted to focus on continuous process improvement within their small piece of the big supply chain picture. They did not have the most technologically advanced computer software in the industry and wanted to make improvements in this area first, along with always improving total transaction time for customers.

Next, the organization wanted to address the nationwide shortage of commercial truck drivers due to CSA 2010. CSA, or Compliance, Safety, and Accountability, was a law made active in 2010 by the Department of Transportation in an effort to reduce crashes involving commercial trucks. The CSA foundation is attempting to identify behaviors that are statistically linked to increased incidences of crashes. CSA consists of seven Behavioral Analysis Safety Improvement Categories (BASICS), which consists of approximately 600 possible violations that are scored based on severity of the violations and are ranked in a percentile against other members of the group (https://roadsideresume.com/csa.html). David stated that this legislation affects Knichel because they rely on commercial truck rates to be fairly consistent. When this law was first made active, he felt that it made a nationwide shortage even worse and that drivers were being cited for things that they were never cited for in the past. For example, in the past, if a truck had a burned out tail light, the truck driver would be stopped for it and the company he or she was driving for may have been issued a citation for it. With CSA 2010, all drivers are being scored and cited for everything that happens with the trucks that they are driving, causing a large number of drivers to be deemed ineligible to be operating a commercial truck. This is causing a shortage, which vastly increases rates of commercial truck shipments.

Finally, Knichel needed to change the way that they handle LTL (i.e., less than full truck load) shipments. Costs have been rising in the commercial truck industry, and LTL shipments have become more and more cost prohibitive. Knichel needed a new strategy to address these concerns.

4.3.4 Choice of Solution

In response to the reasons needed for change, Knichel addressed them individually as they arose. First, Knichel wanted to upgrade its computer software in order to optimize the total transaction time. The total transaction time was all of the costs involved from the time the customer places an order until the time the order is delivered and payment received. He mentioned that in today's climate, you make more money when you can optimize total transaction time, including overhead expenses and labor. Their new upgrades are optimizing the way that they generate rates. Their rate analysts can input all of the customer needs and generate a myriad of shipping options that will best meet the needs of the consumer. It is increasing customer service and helping to keep everything consistent with rate analysts.

4.3.5 Adoption Process Details

In response to the recent commercial truck driver shortage, Knichel has a competitive advantage over competitors because they have a contract to use intermodal routes whereas some competitors do not. Management is working on a new strategy called truck conversion, which essentially is utilizing the rate analysts to convert some shipments that traditionally would have gone over the road route and converting it to an intermodal route. The company can take advantage of this situation, since much of their contracts to use intermodal route as well as utilizing the new operations strategy of the railway systems. Over a decade ago, intermodal route meant coast-to-coast shipments. However, intermodal can include over a 300-mile shipment and making the rate as comparable as they can to over the road rates.

Finally, to address the LTL costs rising and number of contracts falling, management decided that they were going to implement a trap and freight method. Basically, this method is essentially a process improvement in which they consolidate shipments starting in similar locations and ending in similar locations. David said an example would be if a shipment is going to take half a truck and is leaving Pittsburgh and another shipment taking half a truck is leaving from Cleveland and both are going to end up in Los Angeles, they will be perfect candidates for the new trap and freight method. The customers would now be charged ¾ of a truck versus a full truck, which saved money, but is making Knichel even more money than before. They are generating higher customer service because they are creating more value for their customers at the same time Knichel is getting a 50% profit bonus on each of these "trap and freight" shipments. If each customer is being charged ¾ of a truck, they are making more profits than before and are not expending much more resources to make this possible.

4.3.6 Results

In conclusion, Knichel Logistics and their COO David Mudd are always looking to new and innovative process improvements. When Knichel makes process improvements, it creates value for the customers in the form of saving money and increasing customer service as well as making Knichel more money and growth in a very competitive industry.

4.4 VEKA, Inc.

4.4.1 Company Description and Background

Another company that is working towards making supply chain improvements is VEKA, Inc. Current economic and internal changes have led to the necessity for a supply chain improvement. Competition is fierce in the housing market and VEKA needs to be an attractive supplier to current and potential customers in order to maintain or increase market share. The supply chain improvement that VEKA discovered to be beneficial is Electronic Data Interchange (EDI).

4.4.2 History

VEKA is a German-based, privately held multi-national corporation that has 25 extrusion facilities in 20 countries and has a headquarters in Fombell, PA. In North America, VEKA, Inc. serves as the headquarters to all the North American VEKA companies. The North American companies include VEKA South, Inc. in Texas, VEKA West, Inc. in Nevada, and VEKA Canada, Inc. in Alberta. VEKA is an extrusion facility which creates a vast array of polyvinyl chloride (PVC) products, such as window frames, door, fencing, decking, and railing profiles. For these products, many different replacement materials exist, but unlike those other materials, PVC will never need to be stained and will not chip, crack, peel or rot.

4.4.3 Reasons for Change in SCM and Process Practices

In 2007, the U.S. saw an economic crash of the housing market, which led to foreclosures and bankruptcies. As part of the global recession, a freeze resulted in the market since banks did not want risk lending out an uncollectible mortgage. Because consumers cannot obtain mortgage loans, most people cannot afford houses leading to a decrease in business for companies in the housing market, such as VEKA. Companies in the housing market have needed to make significant changes in order to maintain competitiveness during today's recession.

The apparent changes in the economy and its competitive restriction in the global marketplace hve caused many changes at VEKA. Because of the economic crash costs needed to be cut in order for VEKA to stay in business, but, unfortunately, VEKA initially cut labor costs, assets were sold, and no process improvements were made. In 2010, VEKA assigned a new Chief Executive Officer. CEO Joe Peilert's primary objective has been to work on cutting costs and improve the overall performance of VEKA North America. In addition, he has been trying to improve processes for the customer's benefit, so that the customer's jobs, as they are relative to VEKA, are easier and less time-consuming. These improvements are being made so that VEKA is a more attractive supplier in comparison to the competition, which is important when trying to make a profit in the housing market during today's difficult economy.

4.4.4 Choice of Solution

Recently VEKA has been courting the second largest window and door manufacturer in the U.S., which is a multimillion dollar industry. This company prides itself on its continuous improvements method and JIT manufacturing processes to meet customer needs and reduce costs. In order to get this company to sign a contract, VEKA would need to invest in Electronic Data Interchange (EDI), since the potential customer's large volume and process requires EDI. EDI is the structured transmission of data between organizations by electronic means, which is used to transfer electronic documents or business data from one computer system to another computer system without human intervention.

4.4.5 Adoption Process Details

Currently, the implementation of EDI is still in the beginning stages and will take time to become fully implemented. The first steps that are being taken are researching the information on EDI and software, in order for a smooth transition. VEKA already has an employee in Information Systems (IS), Rick Harmon, who has previous work experience using EDI and will take the lead in the implementation (personal communication, October 19, 2012). The company will be adding an EDI administrator, which include SAP FI/CO Consultant, SAP BI Consultant, and IBM Lotus Domino Administrator. Harmon is explaining the basics of EDI to member in the supply chain who will be directly affected by the implementation, so that employees will understand a more about EDI and understand how this will impact their duties. One worry that many have when they hear that certain aspects of their job will become automated is that VEKA will not need them and they will be eventually replaced. The advantages VEKA should allow employees to experience from the implementation should typically lead to more business and no reductions in staff will be necessary.

Initially for the VEKA implementation of EDI, only five documents will be used. Those documents are the Functional Acknowledgement (997), the Purchase Order (850), the Invoice (810), the Advance Ship Notice (856), and the Payment Order/Remittance Advice (820). The Functional Acknowledgement (997) is sent in response to any EDI document that is received. If VEKA receives a document, VEKA's computer system will send a 997, and if the customer sends a document, VEKA will receive a 997 from the customer's computer system. The 997 does not insure the validity of the business data contained in the document.

Next the Purchase Order (850) is an EDI purchase order that contains the same information that a paper purchase order would contain. EDI purchase orders are normally generated automatically from the customer's system as a result of a process such as the Material Requirements Planning (MRP) process. The implementation at VEKA will include both blanket and individual purchase orders. These EDI purchase orders are generated in a customer system, converted into a special format and will then be transmitted to VEKA's system. VEKA's system will convert the purchase order into a sales order systematically. At this point a Functional Acknowledgement will be sent to the customer system as receipt of the Purchase Order. Prior to this being implemented, the process now is that the customer faxes, emails, or calls in the purchase order, whereby the Customer Call Center (CCC or Order Entry) will manually key in the sales order into VEKA's system, then have a fellow employee double check for entry errors. The EDI process completely eliminates any human interaction or manual order entry, freeing up a tremendous amount of time so that CCC can spend that time helping customers over the phone and developing a strong vendor-customer relationship.

Another document is the Advance Ship Notice (856), which is generally an electronic Bill of Lading. The advantage to VEKA's customer is that the customer will receive the Advance Ship Notice prior to the truck arriving at their dock, so they can prepare for the incoming delivery. Accuracy is critical for this document to be useful, so any current problems with VEKA's warehouse and shipping process will need to be fixed prior to implementation and employees thoroughly trained. In addition, the use of this document can speed up payment once a consistent level of accuracy is proven by VEKA, since Mr. Harmon has seen that customers will typically start paying from this document if they are historically accurate.

One more EDI document VEKA will be using is the Invoice (810), which contains the same information as a paper invoice. The EDI invoice will be generated automatically when the shipment is sent to the customer. Similar to the Advance Ship Notice, EDI Invoices reduce time to receive payment because invoices are received by the customer the same day. The current process at VEKA is that the shipment is completed and sent then the invoice generates overnight and is printed the next morning. Next an employee looks through the invoices and then takes them to the front desk to be put in envelopes and mailed. All those steps and labor time will be eliminated if EDI is used.

Finally, the last EDI document to be used will be the Payment Order/Remittance Advice (820), which will work the same as a paper remittance advice received for cash application in Accounts Receivable. An 820 is usually accompanied by an Electronic Funds Transfer which is the term used in EDI for (ACH) electronic payments. This will also reduce time to receive payment, since there will be no wait time involved with waiting to receive payment through the mail. Overall these EDI documents and the processes involved will drastically eliminate wasted time.

4.4.6 Results

After implementation, VEKA will realize several advantages to its business. One immediate advantage would be the signing of a contract with a multimillion dollar window and door manufacturer. In addition, VEKA already has current customers in line to use EDI, which will lead to maintaining current customers and potentially increase sales on those customers. Due to the streamlined process, VEKA will also realize quicker and increased sales and inventory turns. Mr. Harmon has stated the time is crucial in the EDI process and is one reason companies implement EDI, because time is money. Because of this, inventory and sales turns increase because there is no wait time on the processing and transit of the electronic documents. This will lead to meeting lead times since the entire process will be quicker and lead to a decreased chance of stock outs. If a customer is not able to get material within the lead time, that could be a lost sale or additional costs for VEKA, because if the lead time cannot be met, VEKA promises to pay the freight costs. Another advantage is that VEKA will save money on the electronic documents by saving on labor time that would originally be used to manually enter those documents. This will also lead to more accurate documents due to less manual processing, causing fewer problems for the customer and for VEKA. Furthermore, VEKA will have to improve current processes in order to effectively implement EDI leading to improvements throughout the company. If something is not done right the first time, there is no opportunity for VEKA employees to backtrack to fix the mistake before documents get to the customer, since the documents are sent immediately. The employees involved will need to ensure that these processes are handled accurately.

Though EDI has not yet been implemented at VEKA, the improvements in the supply chain process can already be visualized. In order to effectively implement these new processes, a hefty amount of money will need to be spent on the software and thorough training of VEKA employees will need to be coordinated to ensure a smooth transition. The initial investment and work involved in the implementation will be minor in comparison to the vast amount of benefits. More importantly, VEKA customers will also benefit from this change causing VEKA to be a more attractive supplier than other PVC competitors.

5. CONCLUSION AND IMPLICATIONS

5.1 General Managerial Implications

Looking at the SCM-based and social capital challenges faced by each of the four organizations studied in this chapter should allow readers to understand that despite the differences in industry, there are many similarities in the high-level goals held by each company. An exploration of the different strategies and tactical approaches taken by each company helps to provide a glimpse into the vast realm of possible solutions that are being pursued to help improve efficiency, lower cost, boost innovation, and ultimately, enhance the organization's ability to compete in the marketplace.

One common theme that each of the improvements these companies implemented was a focus on software-based solutions, especially in terms of large data analytics. It is clear that with the global economy rebounding, SCM will be adopting 21st century software, database management, and its associated analytics for cost cutting, optimization, speed of deployment, agility and real-time process information and automation initiatives (Shacklett, 2010). However, it is important to note that software and database applications alone will not solve a firm's supply chain issues. Only when coupled with well-designed processes, controls, training, and monitoring will a supply chain process improvement project yield truly successful results (Snell, 2007). The main objective for every single firm is concerned with the realization of profits. All firms are involved in the production of goods and services. These goods and services are usually aimed at fulfilling certain needs within the consumer groups. Firms always have to weigh the availability of a niche within the market to guarantee the continuity of sales. Therefore, every firm needs to ensure that they incur the least amount of expenses in the provision of goods and services. Production costs are intertwined with other costs pertaining to storage, distribution, and marketing of goods and services. A proper economic analysis needs to be conducted by the organization to ascertain the level of demand within the market. This would lay the groundwork for the adoption of an appropriate marketing strategy.

A corporation has to acknowledge the inherent variations in its levels of supply and demand, which will make it possible for the firm to maximize its profitability. The size and quality of the market will determine the level of demand that is exerted on the goods produced within a country. An excess of demand will benefit manufacturers since they will be able to sell their products at higher prices. A reduced level of demand would have the converse effect. In this instance, the goods produced by a firm would not attract enough buyers in the market setting. Consequently, the profits would be reduced. On-the-other hand, if a firm supplies an abundant quantity of goods, the excessive supply would result in a glut of goods in the market. This would reduce the revenues realized by firms since excess products will have to be sold at throwaway prices in an attempt to cut losses. A reduced level of supply would create excessive demand in the market. Therefore, a firm needs to know the optimum level of demand and supply which they should maintain in an effort to maximize on the profits realized from business activities.

5.2 Dealing with Uncertainties

When many technologies and innovations are rushed into manufacturing a product/service, the designers have less time to properly prototype, simulate, identify, and remediation of the problems associated with converting design specifications into manufacturing processes. However, this uncertainty in what may be uncovered in the production process may serve as to level the playing field and allow creativity to new problems as they occur, instead of depending on older and more traditional methods of dealing with manufacturing inconsistencies. As noted by Michalski, Yurov, and Montes (2014), in developing a deep understanding of the relationship between SCM innovation, trust and symmetry, can significantly improve efficiencies of the SCM process. Basically, asymmetry may be defined as a lack of balance among relationship factors like joint decision-making process, information sharing, and multi-organizational relationships. Asymmetry directly affects business factors, such as knowledge, information, power, organizational structure, costs and benefits. The level of shared knowledge influences the ability of defining a collaborative agreement between the organizations. Therefore, access to comprehensive databases and associated analytics are essential to deal with uncertainty in the supply chain, coupled with an acknowledgement of a firm's social capital within supply chains. This basic thesis was reflected in the present case study of Pittsburgh-based manufacturing and service firms. As evident in any intensively competitive business environment, asymmetric operating conditions may have a direct influence on both trust and IT innovation, which greatly affects collaboration in the supply chain. Such influence will undoubtedly affect the performance of related inter-organizational agreements. In general, managers typically ignore the adverse effect of asymmetry on the influence of trust and innovation on the sustainability of SCM partnership agreements.

ACKNOWLEDGMENT

The author wishes to thank the reviewers for their input into the final chapter. Peer reviewing and editing are commonly tedious and thankless tasks.

REFERENCES

Archer, N., Bajaj, H., & Zhang, H. (2008). Supply management for home healthcare services. *Information Systems and Operational Research*, 46(2), 137–145. doi:10.3138/infor.46.2.137

Basu, P., & Nair, S. K. (2012). Supply chain finance enabled early pay: Unlocking trapped value in B2B logistics. *International Journal of Logistics Systems and Management*, 12(3), 334–353. doi:10.1504/IJLSM.2012.047605

Baxter, L. F., & Hirschhauser, C. (2004). Reification and representation in the implementation of quality improvement programmes. *International Journal of Operations & Production Management*, 24(2), 207–224. doi:10.1108/01443570410514894

Biswas, P., & Sarker, B. R. (2008). Optimal batch quantity models for a lean production system with in-cycle rework and scrap. *International Journal of Production Research*, 46(23), 6585–6610. doi:10.1080/00207540802230330

Brito, T. B., & Botter, R. C. (2012). Feasibility analysis of a global logistics hub in Panama. *International Journal of Logistics Systems and Management*, 12(3), 247–266. doi:10.1504/IJLSM.2012.047601

Browning, T. R., & Heath, R. D. (2009). Reconceptualizing the effects of lean on production costs with evidence from the F-22 program. *Journal of Operations Management, 27*(1), 23–35. doi:10.1016/j.jom.2008.03.009

Bulcsu, S. (2011). The process of liberalising the rail freight transport markets in the EU: The case of Hungary. *International Journal of Logistics Systems and Management, 9*(1), 89–107. doi:10.1504/IJLSM.2011.040061

Carvalho, H., Cruz-Machado, V., & Tavares, J. G. (2012). A mapping framework for assessing supply chain resilience. *International Journal of Logistics Systems and Management, 12*(3), 354–373. doi:10.1504/IJLSM.2012.047606

Casadesus, M., & de Castro, R. (2005). How improving quality improves supply chain management: Empirical study. *The TQM Magazine, 17*(4), 345–357. doi:10.1108/09544780510603189

Cavaleri, S. A. (2008). Are learning organizations pragmatic? *The Learning Organization, 15*(6), 474–481. doi:10.1108/09696470810907383

Chamber, C., Kouvelis, P., & Wang, H. (2006). Supply chain management research and production and operations management: Review, trends, and opportunities. *Production and Operations Management, 15*(3), 449–469.

Chan, F. T. S., & Kumar, V. (2009). Performance optimization of a legality inspired supply chain model: A CFGTSA algorithm based approach. *International Journal of Production Research, 47*(3), 777–791. doi:10.1080/00207540600844068

Fleishe, C. (2014). *Pittsburgh unemployment rate drops to 5.5 percent in May.* Retrieved July 2, 2014 from http://triblive.com/business/headlines/6373154-74/jobs-rate-reported#ixzz36KiyyJTa

Hafeez, K., Keoy, K. H. A., Zairi, M., Hanneman, R., & Koh, S. C. L. (2010). E-supply chain operational and behavioral perspectives: An empirical study of Malaysian SMEs. *International Journal of Production Research, 48*(2), 526–546. doi:10.1080/00207540903175079

Hamidi, M., Farahmand, K., Sajjadi, S. R., & Nygard, K. E. (2012). A hybrid GRASP-tabu search metaheuristic for a four-layer location-routing problem. *International Journal of Logistics Systems and Management, 12*(3), 267–287. doi:10.1504/IJLSM.2012.047602

Ketikidis, P. H., Hayes, O. P., Lazuras, L., Gunasekaran, A., & Koh, S. C. L. (2013). Environmental practices and performance and their relationships among Kosovo construction companies: A framework for analysis in transition economies. *International Journal of Services and Operations Management, 15*(1), 115–130. doi:10.1504/IJSOM.2013.050565

Kumar, P., Shankar, R., & Yadav, S. S. (2011). Global supplier selection and order allocation using FQFD and MOLP. *International Journal of Logistics Systems and Management, 9*(1), 43–68. doi:10.1504/IJLSM.2011.040059

Mateen, A., & More, D. (2013). Applying TOC thinking process tools in managing challenges of supply chain finance: A case study. *International Journal of Services and Operations Management, 15*(4), 389–410. doi:10.1504/IJSOM.2013.054882

Mathirajan, M., Manoj, K., & Ramachandran, V. (2011). A design of distribution network and development of efficient distribution policy. *International Journal of Logistics Systems and Supply Management*, *9*(1), 108–137. doi:10.1504/IJLSM.2011.040062

Michalski, M., & Yurov, K.M. & Montes, Botella, J. L. (2014). Trust and IT innovation in asymmetric environments of the supply chain management process. *Journal of Computer Information Systems*, *54*(3), 10–24.

Miguel, P. L., & Brito, L. A. L. (2011). Supply chain management measurement and its influence on operational performance. *Journal of Operations and Supply Chain Management*, *4*(2), 56–69.

More, D., & Babu, A. S. (2012). Benchmarking supply chain flexibility using data envelopment analysis. *International Journal of Logistics Systems and Management*, *12*(3), 288–317. doi:10.1504/IJLSM.2012.047603

Nonthaleerak, P., & Hendry, L. (2008). Exploring the six sigma phenomenon using multiple case study evidence. *International Journal of Operations & Production Management*, *28*(2), 279–303. doi:10.1108/01443570810856198

Paksoy, T., & Cavlak, E. B. (2011). Development and optimisation of a new linear programming model for production/distribution network of an edible vegetable oils manufacturer. *International Journal of Logistics Systems and Management*, *9*(1), 1–21. doi:10.1504/IJLSM.2011.040057

Park, B.-N., & Min, H. (2013). Global supply chain barriers of foreign subsidiaries: The case of Korean expatriate manufacturers in China. *International Journal of Services and Operations Management*, *15*(1), 67–78. doi:10.1504/IJSOM.2013.050562

Pettersson, A. I., & Segerstedt, A. (2011). Performance measurements in supply chains within Swedish industry. *International Journal of Logistics Systems and Management*, *9*(1), 69–88. doi:10.1504/IJLSM.2011.040060

Porter, M. E. (1996). What is strategy? *Harvard Business Review*, *74*(6), 61–78. PMID:10158474

Porter, M. E. (2008). Why America needs an economic strategy. *Business Week*, *4107*, 39-42. Retrieved September 15, 2014 from http://reddog.rmu.edu:2060/pqdweb?did=1589842131&sid=1&Fmt=2&clientId=2138&RQT=309&VName=PQD

Porter, M. E., & Kramer, M. R. (2006). Strategy and society: The link between competitive advantage and corporate social responsibility. *Harvard Business Review*, *84*(12), 78–92. PMID:17183795

Rajapakshe, T., Dawande, M., & Sriskandarajah, C. (2013). On the trade-off between remanufacturing and recycling. *International Journal of Services and Operations Management*, *15*(1), 1–53. doi:10.1504/IJSOM.2013.050560

Rajeev, V. (2013). Impact of service co-creation on performance of firms: The mediating role of market oriented strategies. *International Journal of Services and Operations Management*, *15*(4), 449–466. doi:10.1504/IJSOM.2013.054885

Rowe, K., & Schlacter, J. (1978). Integrating social responsibility into the corporate structure. *Public Relations Quarterly*, *23*(3), 7–12.

Shacklett, M. (2010). Supply chain software: The big spend. *World Trade, 100*, 16-18, 20, 22.

Smith, A. A., Smith, A. D., & Baker, D. J. (2011). Inventory management shrinkage and employee anti-theft approaches. *International Journal of Electronic Finance, 5*(3), 209–234. doi:10.1504/IJEF.2011.041337

Smith, A. D. (2011). Corporate social responsibility implementation: Comparison of large not-for-profit and for-profit companies. *International Journal of Accounting and Information Management, 19*(3), 231–246. doi:10.1108/18347641111169241

Smith, A. D. (2012). Gender perceptions of management's green supply chain development among the professional workforce. *International Journal of Procurement Management, 5*(1), 55–86. doi:10.1504/IJPM.2012.044154

Smith, A. D., & Synowka, D. P. (2014). Lean operations and SCM practices in manufacturing firms: Multi-firm case studies in HRM and visual-based metrics. *International Journal of Procurement Management, 7*(2), 183–200. doi:10.1504/IJPM.2014.059554

Snell, P. (2007). Focus on supply chain to retain edge. *Supply Management, 12*(8), 8.

Supply Chain Sustainability: A Practical Guide for Continuous Improvement. (2010). *United Nations Global Compact Report.* Retrieved September 15, 2014 from http://www.bsr.org/reports/BSR_UNGC_SupplyChainReport.pdf

van Weele, A., & van Raaij, E. (2014). The future of purchasing and supply management research: About relevance and rigor. *Journal of Supply Chain Management, 50*(1), 56–72. doi:10.1111/jscm.12042

Wolf, J. (2014). The relationship between sustainable supply chain management, stakeholder pressure and corporate sustainability performance. *Journal of Business Ethics, 119*(3), 317–328. doi:10.1007/s10551-012-1603-0

Wu, W.-Y., Lin, C.-T., & Kung, J.-Y. (2013). Supplier Selection in Supply Chain Management by Using Fuzzy Multiple-Attribute Decision-Making Method. *Journal of Intelligent & Fuzzy Systems, 24*(1), 175–183.

KEY TERMS AND DEFINITIONS

Corporate Sustainability Performance (CSP): CSP can be computed from large datasets in many ways and can be used as an index to measure movement for an enterprise into more sustainable strategic initiatives. One example is the Sustainalytics database, which has a multitude of companies that it has collected data on and in a stepwise process creates a CSP index, which measures stakeholder pressure on issues ranging from product-related concerns to those of employee treatment. Sustainalytics' analysts identify concerns and assess an organization's reputation among stakeholders, according to these concerns. This information is used to propose an evaluation reflecting the social and environmental issues most relevant to stakeholders of an organization.

Fuzzy Multiple-Attribute Decision-Making (FMADM): FMADM is a useful analytical SCM tool that can serve as an aid to management when making a supplier selection for a supply chain using an optimization algorithm. The approach is based on prioritizing and assigning the importance of the supplier candidates then comparing them using a linguistic value with a fuzzy number. These values and resulting numbers can help evaluate the importance of the chosen attributes, sub-attributes as well as the suppliers themselves. The decision-making goes through a 12-step calculation to help rank the order of all alternatives.

Inventory Management Problems: There are a number inventory management that occurs that are not due to shrinkage. Most of these problems tar based on inaccuracies that are based on poor management and record-keeping activities. Typically too much inventory can erode working capital and profits. It is important that management spends attention to supply projections, using past demand are a basis to improve upon and adjusting for identifying and quantifying less obvious patterns.

Lean Operations: The term lean operations common refer to a family of terms that are typically associated with quality assurance, JIT, reduced waste, process-focused operations that are very efficient and cost sensitive. Lean operations can refer to processes that are found in both service and manufacturing environments. Basically, lean operations are best business practices that minimize time of task, inventories on hand, supplies, and work-related instructions and steps in order to create desirable products and/or services that satisfy or exceed customer's expectations and producers' profitability goals. The basic philosophies of lean are grounded in the need to reduce human involvement in very standardized processes that result in reduced opportunities for waste to occur. It is assumed that analytical datasets are used to monitor processes and gather as complete and accurate information from the point-of sale to design-for-manufacturing and ultimate delivery to consumers without significant flaws and waste. The tools associated with lean operations includes six-sigma business practices to ensure adherence to stated goals to provide ensured companies become efficient in all value-added processes. Lean has become almost interchangeable waste reduction, value-added, and sustainability as management tries to identity opportunities to reduce waste, energy consumption, and variations from original design specifications in order to increase efficiency and profitability via changing practices.

Supply Chain Management/Performance: In basic terms, supply chain is the system of organizations, people, activities, information and resources involved in moving a product or service from supplier to customer. The configuration and management of supply chain operations is a key way companies obtain and maintain a competitive advantage. The typical manufacturing supply chain begins with raw material suppliers, or inputs. The next link in the chain is the manufacturing, or transformation step; followed the distribution, or localization step. Finally, the finished product or service is purchased by customers as outputs. Service and Manufacturing managers need to know the impact of supply on their organization's purchasing and logistics processes. However, supply chain performance and its metrics are difficult to develop and actually measure.

Sustainable Supply Chain Management (SSCM): SSCM may be perceived as the proper management of related environmental, social, and economic impacts in constructing and maintaining effective and efficient global supply chains. SSCM encourages governance practices at all levels of lifecycles of goods and services that reduce waste, ensure long-term maintainability and economic value of environmental and social well-being of all stakeholders' interest in the creation and delivery of products and services. Although it is a very difficult task to bring into the decision process of the rights and needs of all interested stakeholders in the marketplace, it is to the long-term benefit of the properly managed supply chain relationships and corporate sustainability initiatives that ultimately promote broad-based sustainable development objectives for the good of people, plant, and profits (i.e., triple bottom-line).

Chapter 17
Consumer Information Integration at Pre-Purchase:
A Discrete Choice Experiment

M. Deniz Dalman
Dogruluk International Transportation Co., Turkey & Ozdogruluk Custom Clearance Co., Turkey

Junhong Min
Michigan Technological University, USA

ABSTRACT

During the pre-purchase stage, consumers look for information in the external environment to verify marketers' claims, and by doing so, they are likely to encounter some reliable independent information such as consumer reports or technical reports. Using a Discrete Choice Experiment, this chapter shows that consumers use marketers' claims as reference points and record the independent information they encounter as either gain or loss. Moreover, consistent with Prospect Theory, losses loom larger than gains. However, the valuations of losses/gains do not differ for brands with different strengths.

INTRODUCTION

Consider a consumer choosing between two cell phone service providers. These two providers will make specific claims about their different attributes (e.g. less dropped call rates, coverage area etc.) through their advertising. Consumers then generally will look for information in the external environment to verify those claims and by doing so; they are likely to encounter credible independent information regarding these claims -such as consumer reports or technical reports. In this research, we investigate:

1. How consumers integrate and evaluate these different types of information before making a purchase decision, and
2. If this process is different for Well-Known vs. Less Known Brands.

DOI: 10.4018/978-1-4666-7272-7.ch017

Specifically, we argue that in situations where brands make claims on some experiential attributes, consumers use companies' claims as reference points. Later, when consumers find out about the independent third party information, they compare the new information to their reference level and record it as either gain or loss with losses having greater impact than gains on choice. However, the effect of gains vs. losses does not differ among brands with different strengths.

The objective of this chapter is twofold. Managerially, it investigates how consumers integrate different information they encounter at purchase stage. Methodologically, it offers a relatively new method for this context, i.e. a choice experiment.

BACKGROUND

Brands use attribute claims as signals of their quality (Kopalle and Lehmann, 2006), and consumers want to verify these claims before they make a purchase decision as consumers generally possess disbelief towards these claims (Obermiller and Spangenberg, 1998). In order to verify these claims, consumers engage in external search (e.g. through consumer reports, word of mouth, technical reports etc.). Attributes whose claims can be verified before purchase are called search attributes (e.g. size or color of the phone) and whose claims cannot be verified before the consumption are called experience attributes (e.g. coverage area or signal strength of the phone) (Jain, Buchanan, and Maheswaran, 2000; Nelson, 1970). Therefore, for experience attributes, consumers face with uncertainty even after external search. When faced with uncertainty, consumers evaluate the potential gains and losses of their choices and this evaluation is based on a reference point (Kahneman and Tversky, 1979). Since consumers use claims to set their expectations regarding the product performance (e.g. Goering, 1985; Kopalle and Lehmann, 1995), we argue that the claims serve as reference points when consumers make decisions. When consumers encounter highly credible independent information during external search, they will not only use claims to set expectations but also use them along with independent information they find as a shortcut to evaluate potential gains and losses of the alternatives. This will occur, as the third party information will have less uncertainty than company claims. Specifically, we argue that consumers will use product claims as reference points and then they will compare them with the high credible independent sources' information. If the independent source points out more than what brand claims, consumers will record this as a gain and if the independent source points out less than what brand claims, consumers will record this as a loss and both gains and losses will affect their buying likelihood. Moreover, consistent with the prospect theory (Kahneman and Tversky, 1979), we argue that the absolute value of losses will be more than the same size gains. Finally, consistent with prior research, we show the advantage of high equity brands over low equity brands in terms of buying likelihood but the evaluation of gains vs. losses for brands with different strengths does not differ.

This chapter contributes to the literature on Information Integration by offering a new context for investigation, as this research is first as to explain the phenomena from the advertising claims vs. third party information (TPI) perspective to our knowledge and it is the one of the few studies to incorporate the Prospect Theory into the pre-purchase stage of decision-making. Methodologically, this research is also one of the few studies that investigate the issue using a Discrete Choice Experiment.

This chapter has important Managerial Implications as well. First of all, marketers need to ensure their products live up to their claims as consumers rely on third party sources and losses loom larger than the gains. If consumers use marketers' claims as reference points and then compare them to the third party information to record as either gains or losses, marketers have different options depending on their and competitors' situation in the marketplace. For example, a marketer whose brand performs less than what it promised on lab tests can either change the reference point or challenge the authenticity of the third party source to create some ambiguity for the consumers.

The rest of the chapter is organized as follows. Next, we present our conceptual background leading to our hypotheses followed by a discrete choice experiment we conducted. We then discuss the implications of our research and conclude with the limitations of our research and offer some future research directions.

MAIN FOCUS OF THE CHAPTER

Companies often make specific claims on product attributes to signal their quality to consumers in the market (Kopalle and Lehmann, 2006) such as 3-hour battery life for laptops or MP3 players or 100 pages per minute for printers etc. However, for most of these attributes, consumers have to use and experience the product to be able to verify these claims. Products whose attributes can be objectively evaluated prior to purchase are called search products, whereas products whose attributes can be evaluated only after using the product are called experience products (Franke, Huhmann, and Mothersbaugh, 2004; Jain, Buchanan, and Maheswaran, 2000; Nelson, 1970). As a result, for experience products, consumers will face an uncertainty at the pre-purchase stage whether the product will perform as it promises (Ford, Smith, and Swasy, 1990). In addition to this inherent product variability, consumers do not believe company paid communication (Obermiller and Spangenberg, 1998), which increases the uncertainty for the consumers at pre-purchase stage further.

When faced with this uncertainty about claims at pre-purchase stage, consumers engage in external search to verify marketers' claims and look into different sources for this purpose such as Salespeople, Independent Consultants, Magazines, Consumer Reports, Technical Reports, and Friends and Family (Chen and Xie, 2005; Jarvis, 1998; Beales, 1981). At this stage consumers have some enduring beliefs about information sources learned through experience and socialization (Jarvis, 1998) and non-marketer related sources such as Third Party Reviews (TPRs) become important sources where consumers seek insight (Jiang, Jones, and Javie, 2008). These TPRs mainly serve consumers for coping with uncertainty they have in their decision-making (Akdeniz, Calantone, and Voorhees, 2013).

While external search is generally limited even for high involvement products (Beales et al 1981), Internet has reduced the search cost for consumers (Chen and Xie, 2005) and made TPRs widely available in public (Chen, Liu, and Chang, 2012). For example, Riler (1999) [cited in Chen and Xie, 2005] reports that 44% of online consumers indicated they consulted review websites before making a purchase. TPRs usually provide product info based on lab testing or expert evaluation (Chen and Xie, 2005) and consumers often rely on TPRs to provide them with accurate product quality information (Aiken and Boush, 2006; Klein and Ford, 2003).

The main reason consumers rely on TPRs is that consumers find them credible. Eisen (2004) defines credibility as "a person's perception of the truth of a piece of information" and it is related to source's ability and motivation to provide the truthful information (Kelman and Hovland, 1953). Therefore, in our opening example about cell phone providers above, when consumers face with marketers' claims about some important experiential attributes (e.g. dropped call rates), they are likely to look for information in the external environment to reduce their uncertainty and find some credible TPRs. Considering the reduced search costs due to technology and internet as we mentioned above, consumers will likely to find TPRs related to the specific claims marketers have.

The next step for consumers then is how to integrate these two pieces of information in their decision-making. Most cognitive theories of decision-making are interested in understanding how consumers assess values of different options based on their goals (Mellers et. al. 1997). In the scenario above, consumers' choice situation can be explained via Prospect Theory, considering the uncertainty for experience attributes and the distrust in marketers. Prospect Theory deals with risky choice situations where consumers cannot be sure of the outcomes (Kahneman and Tversky, 1979) and Prospect Theory is the formal theory of loss aversion (Abdellaoui, Bleichrodt, and Paraschiv, 2007). In choice situations like above where people are not sure of the outcomes, they interpret the outcomes as gains and losses relative to a reference point and are more sensitive to losses than gains (Abdellaoui, Bleichrodt, and Paraschiv, 2007).

Companies use product claims to influence consumer expectations about their products' quality (Goering, 1985). These expectations then lead to a) purchase decision and b) consumer (dis) satisfaction through the comparison of them against the actual performance (Kopalle and Lehman, 2006). Therefore, company claims are used as reference points that consumers hold the companies responsible for. However, company claims do not always convey the actual product quality (Jacoby and Szybillo 1995) and consumers generally have distrust in them (Obermiller and Spangenberg, 1998). For experience products, consumers can only verify these claims fully once they use the product due to this uncertainty. We argue that at the purchase stage consumers use company claims as reference points and when they face a credible information source (e.g TPR) that has less uncertainty than the claims, they compare the newly found (credible) information against the reference point. Consistent with the Prospect Theory, we also argue that if the findings of TPR is above the company claim, it will be recorded as gain and if the findings of TPR is below the company claim, it will be recorded as a loss. Formally:

H1a: At purchase stage, when consumers find a credible TPR that exceeds the company claims, it will be recorded as gain.

H1b: At purchase stage, when consumers find a credible TPR that is below the company claims, it will be recorded as loss.

As mentioned previously, one of the basic tenets of Prospect Theory is that gains and losses are treated differently with same sized losses loom larger than same sized gains (Kahneman and Tversky, 1979). Therefore:

H2: At purchase stage, after comparing the TPR information to the company claims, the absolute value of losses will be higher than the gains for consumers.

When consumers face uncertainty at purchase stage, TPR are not the only source to reduce the uncertainty. Even in the lack of such information, consumers use different external cues to reduce the uncertainty and the brand name is one of the most commonly used extrinsic information cues for consumers (Dodds, Monroe, and Grewal, 1991; Jacoby, Szybillo, and Busato-Schach, 1977). Strong, well-known brands (WKB) with strong brand equity have several advantages in the marketplace, which include (among others) higher brand preference (Feinberg et. al. 1992), and reduced consumer uncertainty (Mitchell and McGoldrick 1996; Erdem, Zhao and Valenzuela 2004; Gurhan-Canli and Batra 2004). Therefore, regardless of TPR information, we argue that strong, well-known brands will have choice advantage over less known brands (LKB) due to their lower uncertainty. Formally:

H3: Well known brands will have advantage over less known brands at purchase stage regardless of credible TPR information.

While we argue the advantage of well-known brands over less known brands regardless of TPR information, we do not hypothesize that advantage will lead to the differential evaluation of gains vs. losses for brands with different strengths.

In order to test our Hypotheses, we ran a Discrete Choice Experiment discussed in the next section.

STUDY

In order to shed light to these managerially important questions, a Discrete Choice Experiment (DCE) is conducted. We chose DCE as the research method, as it is a very suitable method for our research questions. DCE can 1) compare different models' goodness of fit, and 2) estimate the valuations of brands at the attribute level, based on deviations from a reference point.

Pretest

We chose cell phone providers as product category and dropped call rates as experience attributes. Considering the technical nature of the attribute and thus measurability, this allowed us to manipulate a high credibility source, which was an independent research company that tests different providers' dropped call rates. Our WKB was Verizon and our LKB was Telstra -a fictitious brand. Our theoretical model requires our stimuli to meet certain criteria. Namely, dropped call rates need to be important for consumers to consider when making a choice between cell phone providers and it should also have a considerable degree of uncertainty. Moreover, independent research company that tests different providers' dropped call rates need to be considered as a credible information source during purchase stage. And finally, Verizon and Telstra have to be seen as well-known and less known brands respectively. In order to test these, we conducted 2 pretests.

Our first pretest was designed to test our assumptions about the dropped call rates and the brands in the cell phone service provider category. 84 Undergraduate students participated in the pretest in exchange for extra credit. We first asked participants of their familiarity with both brands (Verizon and Telstra) on a 9-point scale (1: Unfamiliar, 9: Familiar). A paired sample t-test indicated that participants were more familiar with Verizon than Telstra ($M_{Verizon} = 8.15$ vs. $M_{Telstra} = 1.35$, $t = 33.24$ $p = .00$). We then asked the importance of dropped call rates in choosing one service provider over another on a 9-point scale

(1: Not at all important, 9: Very important). A one-sample t-test against the midpoint of 5 indicated that participants thought dropped call rates were an important factor in their choice (M = 5.76, t = 3.5 p = .001). As for uncertainty of the attribute, we asked the question separately for Verizon and Telstra which read as 'I am not sure of the level of dropped call rates I would get when using Verizon (Telstra)". The question was again on a 9-point scale (1: Strongly Disagree, 9: Strongly Agree). A one-sample t-test against the midpoint of 5 indicated that participants saw some degree of uncertainty for both brands but the uncertainty was much less for the well-known brand compared to the less known brand consistent with the branding literature ($M_{Verizon}$ = 4.11, t = -1.43 p = .002; $M_{Telstra}$ = 8.43, t = 30.48 p = .00).

Our second pretest with the participation of 29 undergraduate students was solely to measure the credibility of the independent research company specifically in our research setting. Therefore, we have shown participants similar scenario we would use in the DCE without mentioning specific brands (The scenario can be seen in Appendix A). In this scenario, we told participants how the independent research company finds out the actual dropped call rates (The research company has researchers in different cities that make calls, and record the number of dropped calls). We then asked participants rate the credibility of the independent research company on a 6-item scale adapted from McCroskey and Teven (1999). The items were on a 7-point bipolar scale (Inexpert/Expert, Untrustworthy/Trustworthy, Dishonest/Honest, Unethical/Ethical, Incompetent/Competent, Doesn't have my interests at heart / Has my interests at heart). The cronbach's alpha for the scale was .87. A one-sample t-test against the midpoint of 4 indicated that participants find the independent research company's findings credible under this scenario (M = 4.67, t = 3.09 p = .004).

Based on these two pretests, we decided to use Verizon, Telstra as our brands and dropped call rates for cell phones as our attributes in the DCE.

Discrete Choice Experiment

We ran the DCE with the participation of 114 undergraduate students (different students from the ones participated in the pretests but from the same sample pool). We manipulated the brands, claimed dropped call rates, and price all at two levels, and research company findings at 4 levels which lead to a $2^4 * 4^1$ design. In order to increase the believability, we have chosen all the levels corresponding the relative equity of the brands in the market. This meant that Verizon claims 4% and 6% dropped call rates and Telstra claims 6% and 8%. Moreover, the price levels for Verizon was $50 and $60, while they were $40 and $50 for Telstra. The research company findings were either at par with the claimed levels or +-2 below and above the claimed levels for dropped call rates (The levels we chose are shown in Table 1). Using the Addelman and Kempthorne Catalog, we chose the main effect only plan with 12 treatments. Therefore, participants were given 12 scenarios, where in each they were shown brand names, claimed dropped call rates, independent company's findings, and price. For each scenario, participants indicated their choice of brand by putting an X on the boxes given (participants also had an option of choosing neither of them). The choice scenario can be seen in Appendix B and a sample treatment is shown in Table 2.

Table 1. Stimuli for choice experiment

Verizon Claim	Telstra Claim	Verizon Price	Telstra Price	Research Company Findings
4%	6%	$50	$40	2%
6%	8%	$60	$50	4%
				6%
				8%
				10%

Table 2. Sample treatment in the study

Scenario 1			
	Verizon	Telstra	Neither of Them
Percentage of Dropped Calls	6%	8%	
Research Company's Finding	6%	10%	
Price	$50	$40	
Mark Your Choice			

RESULTS

We then analyzed the data using Limdep to test our Hypotheses. Our hypotheses 1a and 1b relies on our theoretical argument that TPR (independent research company findings in our case) will be evaluated against the brand claims and will be recorded as either gains or losses. In order to test this, we compared the goodness of fit of different alternative models using Limdep. Our Base Model was with alternative specific (for WKB and LKB) constants only. Our Model 1 was where participants use TPR and company claims independently. Our Model 2 was our main interest to test our hypotheses. In this model, we defined the TPR as gains and losses (where participants use claimed levels as reference point and compare the research company's findings to this reference and record them as either gain or loss) along with alternative specific parameters for WKB and LKB and company claims. All models also included price. Different models we tested can be seen in Table 3.

Table 3. Model specifications

Base Model	U(Verizon) = av U(Telstra) = at U(None) = 0
Model 1	U(Verizon) = av + a*claim + b*tpr + c*price U(Telstra) = at + a*claim + b*tpr + c*price U(None) = 0
Model 2	U(Verizon) = av + a*gain + b*loss + c*claim + d*price U(Telstra) = at + a*gain + b*loss + c*claim + d*price U(None) = 0

tpr: Third Party Review (Research Company Findings).

The Model 2 was significant and it improved the fit of the previous models significantly compared to Model 1. Therefore, we could show that consumers indeed recorded numbers as gains and losses rather than separately. This confirmed our Hypotheses 1a and 1b. Moreover, the brand effect could be seen on the alternative specific constants where WKB had an advantage over LKB as expected. The price coefficient was negative, as one would expect, indicating lower utility for increased price. The goodness of fits of different models and parameter estimates for Model 3 are reported in Tables 4 and 5 respectively.

These numbers were further verified with the fact that Verizon was chosen 70% of the time over Telstra. Therefore our Hypothesis 3 was confirmed.

The coefficient in the utility function of Model 2 for gains was ~.16 and for losses it was ~.69 indicating a strong loss aversion consistent with prospect theory. Therefore, our Hypothesis 2 was confirmed. We later tested a third model in which we used alternative specific parameters for gains and losses for WKB and LKB along with alternative specific parameters for WKB and LKB. However, the model was not significant. Therefore, it indicated no differential brand effects for gains and losses consistent with our expectations.

CONCLUSION

Developments in communication technology and the availability of information on the web led consumers to have access almost any information they want. While this brings many opportunities for companies (e.g. wider market reach), it also brings challenges, as managers need to be aware of and control related to their sectors and brands. For example, independent third party information about different products is widely available and consumers value this information more than they value the information coming from the marketers. However, little is known about how consumers integrated different sources of information. Therefore, managers need to understand how consumers integrate this information.

Table 4. Goodness of fits

Model	Log Likelihood Function
Base Model	-1002.611
Model 1	-834.9251*
Model 2	-825.7249**

*Significant improvement compared to Base Model
**Significant improvement compared to Model 1.

Table 5. Parameter estimates for Model 2

Variable	Coefficient	Standard Error	b/St.Er.	P[|Z|>z]
AV	10.76564373	.67468138	15.957	.0000
AT	8.805492065	.62374520	14.117	.0000
Gain	.1568979360	.72830043E-01	2.154	.0312
Loss	.6893320748	.72405324E-01	9.520	.0000
Claim	-.2608312567	.54938114E-01	-4.748	.0000
Price	-.1120948639	.10145707E-01	-11.049	.0000

E+nn or E-nn means multiply by 10 to + or -nn power.

This research has shown that brand claims not only serve reference points for expectations but also they are used as reference points to evaluate potential gains and losses for customers in availability of independent TPRs. Our research has both theoretical and practical implications. As theoretical implications, our findings from this study confirms our expectations that when brands make numerical claims on experience attributes, consumers use claims as reference points, and then compares them with the information from a credible source and record them as either gains or losses. To our knowledge, this is the first research that incorporates prospect theory into pre-purchase stage of decision-making. As for managerial implications, our research shows that managers need to look for different sources information before setting their claims as losses loom larger than gains.

FUTURE RESEARCH DIRECTIONS

The study we present is not without its limitations. First, we used student participants and their knowledge and attitude toward the category could be different than from general population. For example, younger generations are more technology savvy and they probably possess more knowledge of the cell phone category and brands within this category. Moreover, they are more likely to encounter a TPR because they use the Internet more than the general population. Therefore, future research should investigate the issue using a more representative sample. Moreover, future research should include more personality variables to see if the non-existence of the brand effect in this study holds for different groups (e.g. more knowledgeable consumers vs. less knowledgeable consumers).

DCE is relatively easy to conduct and can offer managers great insight about consumers' revealed preferences. Future research should test the applicability of DCE on different domains and also by adding different attributes and levels of those attributes.

REFERENCES

Abdellaoui, M., Bleichrodt, H., & Paraschiv, C. (2007). Loss aversion under prospect theory: A parameter-free measurement. *Management Science*, *53*(10), 1659–1674. doi:10.1287/mnsc.1070.0711

Aiken, K. D., & Boush, D. M. (2006). Trustmarks, objective-source ratings, and implied investments in advertising: Investigating online trust and the context-specific nature of internet signals. *Journal of the Academy of Marketing Science*, *34*(3), 308–323. doi:10.1177/0092070304271004

Akdeniz, B., Calantone, R. J., & Voorhees, C. M. (2013). Effectiveness of Marketing Cues on Consumer Perceptions of Quality: The Moderating Roles of Brand Reputation and Third-Party Information. *Psychology and Marketing*, *30*(1), 76–89. doi:10.1002/mar.20590

Beales, H., Mazis, M. B., Salop, S. C., & Staelin, R. (1981). Consumer search and public policy. *The Journal of Consumer Research*, *8*(1), 11–22. doi:10.1086/208836

Chen, Y., Liu, Y., & Zhang, J. (2012). When do third-party product reviews affect firm value and what can firms do? The case of media critics and professional movie reviews. *Journal of Marketing*, *76*(2), 116–134. doi:10.1509/jm.09.0034

Chen, Y., & Xie, J. (2005). Third-party product review and firm marketing strategy. *Marketing Science, 24*(2), 218–240. doi:10.1287/mksc.1040.0089

Dodds, W. B., Monroe, K. B., & Grewal, D. (1991). Effects of price, brand, and store information on buyers' product evaluations. *JMR, Journal of Marketing Research, 28*(3), 307–319. doi:10.2307/3172866

Eisend, M. (2004). Is it still worth to be credible? A meta-analysis of temporal patterns of source credibility effects in marketing. *Advances in Consumer Research. Association for Consumer Research (U. S.), 31*(1), 352–357.

Erdem, T., Zhao, Y., & Valenzuela, A. (2004). Performance of store brands: A cross-country analysis of consumer store-brand preferences, perceptions, and risk. *JMR, Journal of Marketing Research, 41*(1), 86–100. doi:10.1509/jmkr.41.1.86.25087

Feinberg, F. M., Kahn, B. E., & McAlister, L. (1992). Market share response when consumers seek variety. *JMR, Journal of Marketing Research, 29*(2), 227–237. doi:10.2307/3172572

Ford, G. T., Smith, D. B., & Swasy, J. L. (1990). Consumer skepticism of advertising claims: Testing hypotheses from economics of information. *The Journal of Consumer Research, 16*(4), 433–441. doi:10.1086/209228

Franke, G. R., Huhmann, B. A., & Mothersbaugh, D. L. (2004). Information content and consumer readership of print ads: A comparison of search and experience products. *Journal of the Academy of Marketing Science, 32*(1), 20–31. doi:10.1177/0092070303257856

Goering, P. A. (1985). Effects of product trial on consumer expectations, demand, and prices. *The Journal of Consumer Research, 12*(1), 74–82. doi:10.1086/209036

Gürhan-Canli, Z., & Batra, R. (2004). When corporate image affects product evaluations: The moderating role of perceived risk. *JMR, Journal of Marketing Research, 41*(2), 197–205. doi:10.1509/jmkr.41.2.197.28667

Jacoby, J., & Szybillo, G. J. (1995). Consumer research in FTC versus Kraft (1991): A case of heads we win, tails you lose? *Journal of Public Policy & Marketing*, 1–14.

Jacoby, J., Szybillo, G. J., & Busato-Schach, J. (1977). Information acquisition behavior in brand choice situations. *The Journal of Consumer Research, 3*(4), 209–216. doi:10.1086/208669

Jarvis, C. B. (1998). An exploratory investigation of consumers' evaluations of external information sources in prepurchase search. *Advances in Consumer Research. Association for Consumer Research (U. S.), 25*(1), 446–452.

Jiang, P., Jones, D. B., & Javie, S. (2008). How third-party certification programs relate to consumer trust in online transactions: An exploratory study. *Psychology and Marketing, 25*(9), 839–858. doi:10.1002/mar.20243

Kahneman, D., & Tversky, A. (1979). Prospect theory: An analysis of decision under risk. *Econometrica, 47*(2), 263–291. doi:10.2307/1914185

Kelman, H. C., & Hovland, C. I. (1953). Reinstatement" of the communicator in delayed measurement of opinion change. *Journal of Abnormal and Social Psychology, 48*(3), 327–335. doi:10.1037/h0061861 PMID:13061165

Klein, L. R., & Ford, G. T. (2003). Consumer search for information in the digital age: An empirical study of prepurchase search for automobiles. *Journal of Interactive Marketing, 17*(3), 29–49. doi:10.1002/dir.10058

Kopalle, P. K., & Lehmann, D. R. (1995). The effects of advertised and observed quality on expectations about new product quality. *JMR, Journal of Marketing Research, 32*(3), 280–290. doi:10.2307/3151981

Kopalle, P. K., & Lehmann, D. R. (2006). Setting quality expectations when entering a market: What should the promise be? *Marketing Science, 25*(1), 8–24. doi:10.1287/mksc.1050.0122

McCroskey, J. C., & Teven, J. J. (1999). Goodwill: A reexamination of the construct and its measurement. *Communication Monographs, 66*(1), 90–103. doi:10.1080/03637759909376464

Mellers, B. A., Schwartz, A., Ho, K., & Ritov, I. (1997). Decision affect theory: Emotional reactions to the outcomes of risky options. *Psychological Science, 8*(6), 423–429. doi:10.1111/j.1467-9280.1997.tb00455.x

Mitchell, V. W., & McGoldrick, P. J. (1996). Consumer's risk-reduction strategies: A review and synthesis. *International Review of Retail, Distribution and Consumer Research, 6*(1), 1–33. doi:10.1080/09593969600000001

Nelson, P. (1970). Information and consumer behavior. *Journal of Political Economy, 78*(2), 311–329. doi:10.1086/259630

Obermiller, C., & Spangenberg, E. R. (1998). Development of a scale to measure consumer skepticism toward advertising. *Journal of Consumer Psychology, 7*(2), 159–186. doi:10.1207/s15327663jcp0702_03

Piller, C. (1999). Everyone is a critic in cyberspace. *Los Angeles Times, 3*(12), A1.

Pratap Jain, S., Buchanan, B., & Maheswaran, D. (2000). Comparative versus noncomparative advertising: The moderating impact of prepurchase attribute verifiability. *Journal of Consumer Psychology, 9*(4), 201–211. doi:10.1207/S15327663JCP0904_2

ADDITIONAL READING

Anderson, N. H. (1981). *Information integration theory*. Acad. Press.

Ben-Akiva, M., Bradley, M., Morikawa, T., Benjamin, J., Novak, T., Oppewal, H., & Rao, V. (1994). Combining revealed and stated preferences data. *Marketing Letters, 5*(4), 335–349. doi:10.1007/BF00999209

Ben-Akiva, M., & Lerman, S. R. (1979). Disaggregate travel and mobility choice models and measures of accessibility. *Behavioural travel modelling*, 654-679.

Ben-Akiva, M. E., & Lerman, S. R. (1985). *Discrete choice analysis: theory and application to travel demand* (Vol. 9). MIT press.

Camerer, C. F. (2004). Prospect theory in the wild: Evidence from the field. Colin F. Camerer, George Loewenstein, and Matthew. Rabin, eds., Advances in Behavioral Economics, 148-161.

Keller, K. L., & Lehmann, D. R. (2006). Brands and branding: Research findings and future priorities. *Marketing Science*, 25(6), 740–759. doi:10.1287/mksc.1050.0153

List, J. A. (2004). Neoclassical theory versus prospect theory: Evidence from the marketplace. *Econometrica*, 72(2), 615–625. doi:10.1111/j.1468-0262.2004.00502.x

McFadden, D. (2000). Disaggregate behavioral travel demand's RUM side. *Travel Behaviour Research*, 17-63.

Moorthy, S., Ratchford, B. T., & Talukdar, D. (1997). Consumer information search revisited: Theory and empirical analysis. *The Journal of Consumer Research*, 23(4), 263–277. doi:10.1086/209482

Shocker, A. D., Ben-Akiva, M., Boccara, B., & Nedungadi, P. (1991). Consideration set influences on consumer decision-making and choice: Issues, models, and suggestions. *Marketing Letters*, 2(3), 181–197. doi:10.1007/BF02404071

Swait, J., & Louviere, J. (1993). The role of the scale parameter in the estimation and comparison of multinomial logit models. *JMR, Journal of Marketing Research*, 30(3), 305–314. doi:10.2307/3172883

Train, K. E. (2009). *Discrete choice methods with simulation*. Cambridge university press. doi:10.1017/CBO9780511805271

Tversky, A., & Kahneman, D. (1992). Advances in prospect theory: Cumulative representation of uncertainty. *Journal of Risk and Uncertainty*, 5(4), 297–323. doi:10.1007/BF00122574

KEY TERMS AND DEFINITIONS

Choice Experiment: An experiment designed to understand consumers' revealed preferences for different alternatives.

Dropped-Call: A phone conversation not completed due to technical problems.

Information Integration: How consumers combine different information from different sources cognitively.

Information Search: Consumers' look for information in the environment (i.e. consumer reports, testimonials, technical reports) to verify marketer's claims at the purchase stage.

Limdep: An econometric and statistical software package.

Pre-Purchase: A stage in consumer behavior where consumers compare and evaluate alternatives before acquiring the product.

Prospect Theory: A behavioral theory that investigates consumers' decision making for situations involving risk.

Third Party Information: Information that is not stemmed from marketer.

APPENDIX A

Not all cell phone calls are completed successfully. This is due to either the handsets not being able to pick up weak signals or the cell towers being too far resulting in weak signal.

According to industry statistics, the average dropped call rate is about 6%. However, this varies across cell phone firms depending on the number of the firm's cell towers.

Suppose you had to choose a cell phone service provider and dropped call rate is an important attribute for you.

The firms in the market are providing different handset technology that result in different dropped call rates. However, an independent third party Research Company has actually checked the claims of these firms. They found that actual dropped call rate sometimes matches the claim and sometimes is different from the claim (either better or worse). The research company has researchers in different cities that make calls, and record the number of dropped calls.

APPENDIX B

Not all cell phone calls are completed successfully. This is due to either the handsets not being able to pick up weak signals or the cell towers being too far resulting in weak signal.

According to industry statistics, the average dropped call rate is about 6%. However this varies across cell phone firms depending on the type of cell phone you may be using and number of the firm's cell towers.

Suppose you had to choose a cell phone service between two providers – *Verizon (Well-Known Company) or Telstra (Less Known Company)*. Verizon is the largest cell phone service provider with the best network and customer service. Telstra is a new provider which will use other providers' cell towers. It is a small company but growing quickly.

The firms are providing different handset technology that result in different dropped call rates. Of course, the prices of these phones also vary. However, independent third party Research Company has actually checked the claims of these firms and dropped call rates vary from company to company and the technology of the cell phone. They have researchers in different cities who make calls, and record the number of dropped calls. *However your calling locations will influence the actual dropped call rate that you experience.*

Given below are twelve scenarios of the two firms offering cell phone service at different prices (The prices shown are the monthly prices for the 1000 minutes plan). We also tell you *what the claimed dropped call rate is,* and *what dropped call rate the research company finds.* Please consider each scenario independently.

In each scenario, please indicate which cell phone service you would choose by putting an X in the box. If you would choose neither, then indicate that choice in the last column.

Chapter 18

Using Data Mining Techniques and the Choice of Mode of Text Representation for Improving the Detection and Filtering of Spam

Reda Mohamed Hamou
Dr. Moulay Taher University of Saïda, Algeria

Abdelmalek Amine
Dr. Moulay Taher University of Saïda, Algeria

ABSTRACT

This chapter studies a boosting algorithm based, first, on Bayesian filters that work by establishing a correlation between the presence of certain elements in a message and the fact that they appear in general unsolicited messages (spam) or in legitimate email (ham) to calculate the probability that the message is spam and, second, on an unsupervised learning algorithm: in this case the K-means. A probabilistic technique is used to weight the terms of the matrix term-category, and K-means are used to filter the two classes (spam and ham). To determine the sensitive parameters that improve the classifications, the authors study the content of the messages by using a representation of messages by the n-gram words and characters independent of languages to later decide what representation ought to get a good classification. The work was validated by several validation measures based on recall and precision.

INTRODUCTION

Unsolicited email, or spam, is a wound of electronic communication currently can represent up to 95% of the volume of mail processed on some servers. This is an ethical and economic issue of role that effectively fight against this scourge. Although the decision "spam / non-spam" is most often easy to take for a human. A message in circulation prevents address manually sorting the acceptable mail and

DOI: 10.4018/978-1-4666-7272-7.ch018

other. Spam is a global phenomenon and massive. According to the CNIL (The Commission Nationale de L'Informatique and Freedoms), spam is defined as follows: "The" spamming "or" spam "is to send massive and sometimes repeated, unsolicited emails, to individuals with whom the sender has never had contact, he has captured the email address erratically. "It was not until the late 90s that the problem of detection and spam filtering by content, drew attention to three areas of research that were not directly affected by e-mail: the information retrieval, data mining and machine learning.

Detection and spam filtering is a binary classification problem in which the email is classified as either Ham or spam. This area has experienced a wide range of methods for the classification among its techniques; the use of Bayes' theorem is the most famous. Bayesian filters work by establishing a correlation between the presence of certain elements (usually words) in a message and the fact that they usually appear in messages (spam) or in legitimate email (ham) to calculate the probability that the message is spam. Bayesian filtering spam is a powerful technique for the treatment of unwanted email. It adapts to the habits of mail each other and produces a false positive rate low enough to be acceptable.

This problematic leads us to do a study as to the representation of data (message corpus) to try to identify sensitive parameters that can improve the results of classification and categorization around detections and spam filtering. We know very well that supervised learning techniques yield the best results, it is for this reason that we have tried to inject a clustering algorithm (k-means) to try to minimize the intervention of expert.

STATE OF THE ART

Among the anti-spam techniques exist in the literature include those based on machine learning and those not based on machine learning.

The Techniques Not Based on Machine Learning

Heuristics, or rules-based, the analysis uses regular expression rules to detect phrases or characteristics that are common in spam, and the amount and severity of identified features will propose the appropriate classification of the message. The history and the popularity of this technology has largely been driven by its simplicity, speed and accuracy. In addition, it is better than many advanced technologies of filtering and detection in the sense that it does not require a learning period. Techniques based on signatures generate a unique hash value (signature) for each message recognized spam. Filters signature compare the hash value of all incoming mail against those stored (the hash values previously identified to classify spam e-mail). This kind of technology makes it statistically unlikely that a legitimate email to have the same hash of a spam message. This allows filters signatures to achieve a very low level of false positives. The blacklist is a technique that is simple common among almost all filtration products. Also known as block lists, blacklists filter e-mails from a specific sender. White lists, or lists of authorization, perform the opposite function, to correctly classify an email automatically from a specific sender. Currently, there is a spam filtering technology based on traffic analysis provides a characterization of spam traffic patterns where a number of attributes per email are able to identify the characteristics that separate spam traffic from non-spam traffic.

The Techniques Based on Machine Learning

Filtering techniques based on machine learning can be further categorized into, comprehensive solutions and complementary solutions. Complementary solutions are designed to work as part of a larger filtering system, providing support to primary filter (whether or not based on a machine learning approach). The solutions aim to build a comprehensive knowledge base that classifies independently all incoming messages.

Bayesian filtering spam (of the mathematician Thomas Bayes) is a system based on a large amount of spam and legitimate e-mails to determine whether an email is legitimate or not. To function properly, the corpus of spam (spam) and ham (legitimate email) should ideally contain several thousand "specimens." The support vector machine (SVM) is generated by the mapping of the data forming a non-linear characteristic of a space of higher dimension, where a hyperplane is formed that maximizes the margin between the sets. The hyperplane is then used as a nonlinear decision boundary when exposed to real data. Drucker & al applied this technique to spam filtering, testing it against the other three classification algorithms text: Ripper, Rocchio and building decision trees. Both trees stimulating and SVM provided a performance "acceptable". Neural networks are generally optimized by methods of learning probabilistic, in particular Bayesian. They are placed one hand in the family of statistical applications, that they enrich with one set of paradigms allowing to create fast classifications (Kohonen networks in particular), and on the other the family of artificial intelligence methods that they provide a perceptual mechanism independent of designer's own ideas and providing input information to formal logical reasoning.

Chhabra & al present a classifier based anti-spam on a Markov random field (MRF) model. This approach allows the spam classifier to consider the importance of the neighborhood relationship between words in an email message. Dependency between the words of natural language can be incorporated into the classification process, which is generally ignored by Bayesian classifiers. Characteristics of incoming e-mails are decomposed into feature vectors and are weighted super-increasing.

There are other anti-spam methods such as envelope filtering, filtering content, filtering by keywords or addresses, regular expression filtering, virus scanning and attachments, filtering server sender's Real-time Black hole List (RBL), SPF (Sender Policy Framework), integrity SMTP priority MX records, the gray list, and heuristic filtering or RPD Recurrent Pattern Detection. The following figure shows the classification of different approaches to spam filtering.

REPRESENTATION OF DATA

The natural language text cannot be directly interpreted by a classifier or by classification algorithms from which the need for a mathematical representation of the text in such a way that it can perform analytical processing thereon, retaining maximum semantics. The mathematical representation generally used is the use of a vector space representation space as target. The main feature of the vector representation is that each language is associated with a specific dimension in the vector space. Two texts using the same textual segments are therefore projected onto identical vectors.

Several approaches for the representation of texts exist in the literature, among which are the representation of sentences bag of words which constitutes the simplest and most used; representation bag phrases, lexical roots and of course the n-grams representation which is independent representation of natural language.

Figure 1. Classification of different approaches to spam filtering

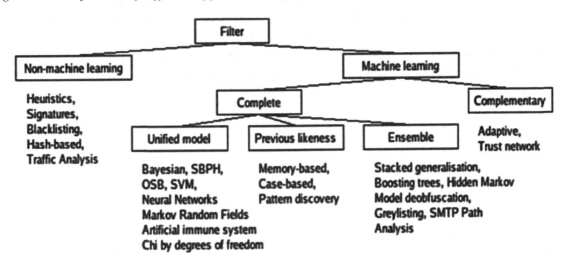

In general, the n-gram character is defined as a sequence of n consecutive characters and n-gram word as a sequence of n words. The principle of the n-gram character for a string of k characters surrounded by white, we generate (k +1) n-grams. An example of cutting the word "porte" in 2-gram is the following: "_porte_" _p, po, or, rt, te e_.

Once we extract all n-grams of a document we define the list of n-grams sorted in descending order of their frequency of occurrence. These methods are independent of language and neither the segmentation into linguistic units or pretreatments are needed. After the step of representing the n-grams, indexing documents is required. Once the components of the vectors chosen to represent a text, we must decide how to encode each coordinate of the vector. Given the occurrence of a term tk in document dj, each component of a vector is coded f (tk dj) where the function f must be determined.

A very simple function is the Boolean function defined by:

$$F = \begin{cases} 1 \ \text{if the term } t_k \text{ appears in document } d_j \\ 0 \ \text{if not} \end{cases}$$

This function is rarely used statistical methods because this coding removes information that can be useful: the appearance of the same word several times in a text can be an important decision. The most used function is the coding tf.idf.

This encoding uses a function of occurrence multiplied by a function which involves the inverse of the number of different documents in which a term appears. Function TFIDF (Salton et al., 1988), defined as follows: (Dziczkowski et al., 2008).

$$tfidf\left(t_k, d_j\right) = \#\left(t_k, d_j\right) . \log \frac{\left|T_k\right|}{\# T_k\left(t_k\right)}$$

where #(tk, dj) denotes the number of times tk occurs in dj, and # (tk) denotes the frequency of term tk in document corpus—i.e. the number of documents in which tk occurs, $|\text{Tr}|$ number of documents in the corpus. This function shows that the more often a term appears in a document, it is more representative, more the number of documents containing a term are important, this term is less discriminatory.

TF×IDF coding does not fix the length of texts, to this end, the coding TFC is similar to TF×IDF, but it sets the length of texts by cosine normalization, not to encourage longer.

$$TFC\left(t_k, d\right) = \frac{TFxIDF\left(t_k, d\right)}{\sqrt{\sum_k^{|r|}(TFxIDF\left(t_k, d\right))^2}}$$

At the end of this phase we obtain our document vector where each component indicates the weight of the term tk in the document.

We experienced in our study 2, 3, 4, and 5 grams characters, and 1 gram words.

In all areas of computing in which you want to automatically analyze a set of data, it is necessary to have an operator can accurately assess the similarities or dissimilarities that exist within the data. On this basis, it becomes possible to order the elements of the set, prioritize or to extract invariants.

To describe this operator in our area which is supervised and unsupervised classification of text document we use the term "similarity". This similarity is expressed by several types of vector distances (Hamou et al., 2010, 2012, 2013).

THE PROPOSED APPROACH

In our experiments, we used a corpus of data already categorized that we will detail in the next section, we will speak of the learning base. The Bayesian network that we construct will allow us to calculate the probability of a new message being spam.

After representation of textual documents corpus of spam, by various techniques of n-grams that are character n-grams and word n-grams, we construct the matrix term document for each type of representation, which represent the presence or absence of the document in terms coded as 1 and 0 respectively. We can find terms that appear in both spam and ham in and it is for this reason that we use the naive Bayes probabilistic model to calculate the new weighting of terms in the document-term matrix that we call the matrix category term. By the same model we do categorization (supervised learning) constructing the matrix document category using similarity distances. The points obtained are represented in a two-dimensional landmark (2D) which are displayed in Figures 2 and 3. Subsequently, we perform a clustering algorithm (k-means) (Figures 4 and 5) to obtain two new classes that we evaluate by measures based on recall and precision in this case the entropy and F-measure to know the percentage of documents correctly classified and unclassified ones. For each technical representation of texts, we note the best results for classification that at the end we can make a decision on what type of representation chosen for the detection and spam filtering. Before analyzing the results, we explain the methodology treatments.

Figure 2. Graphical representation of data by 1-gram word after weighting of Naïve Bayes

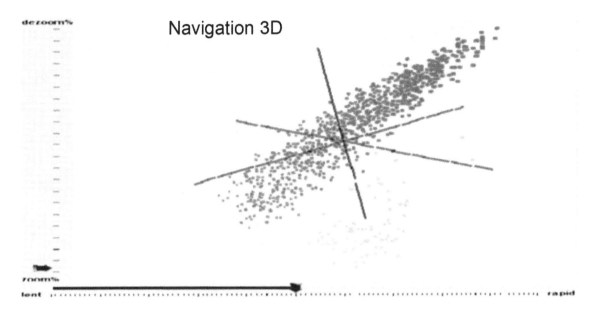

Figure 3. Graphical representation of data by the 4-gram characters after weighting Naïve Bayes

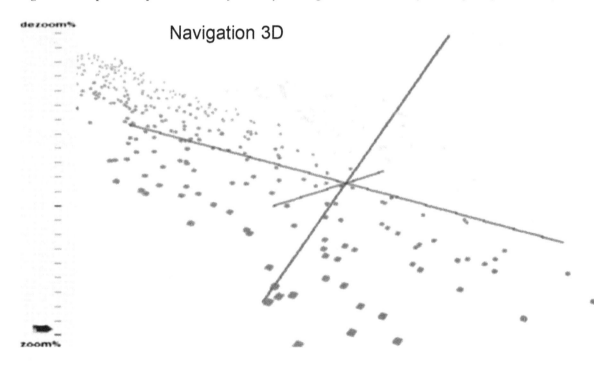

Figure 4. Graphical representation of data by 1-gram word after clustering by k-means

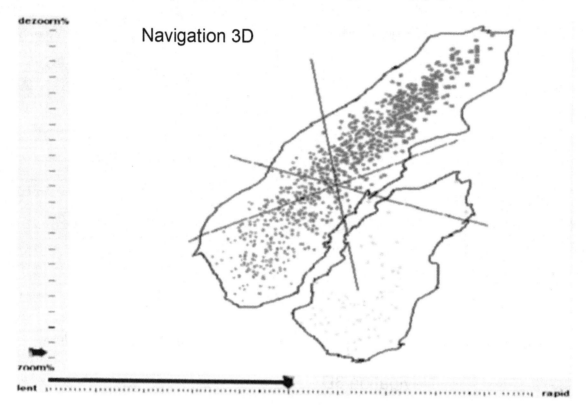

Figure 5. Graphical representation of data by the 4-gram characters after clustering by k-means

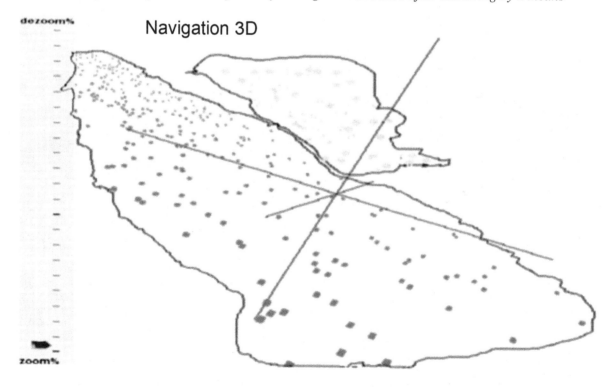

THE DETECTION AND BAYESIAN FILTERING OF SPAM

Bayesian filtering spam (of mathematician Thomas Bayes) is a system based on a large amount of spam and legitimate e-mails to determine whether an email is legitimate or not.

Some words have probabilities of appear in spam and legitimate mail. For example, most people frequently will encounter the word "Viagra" in their spam, but they rarely will encounter their legitimate emails. The filter does not know in advance the probabilities, which is why it takes a long time learning to evaluate them (Sahami et al., 1998).

Learning is the responsibility of the user, who must manually indicate whether a message is spam or not. For every word of every message "learned", the filter adjusts the probabilities of encountering this word in spam or legitimate mail and stores them in its database. For example, Bayesian filters are likely to have a high probability of spam for the word "Viagra", but a very low probability for words encountered in legitimate emails, such as names of friends and relatives of the user. After learning, the probabilities of words (also called likelihood functions) are used to calculate the probability that a message (all these words) is spam. Each word of the message, or at least every word "interesting" message contributes to the likelihood that the message is spam. This contribution is calculated using Bayes' theorem. Once the calculation for the entire message is finished, we compare its probability of being spam to an arbitrary value (eg 95%) to mark or unmark a message as spam.

Mathematical Foundations

The Bayesian spam filters based on Bayes' theorem. Bayes' theorem is used repeatedly in the context of spam:

- A first time to calculate the probability that the message is spam, since a given word appears in this message;
- A second time, to calculate the probability that the message is spam, considering all his words, or a significant subset of the words.
- Sometimes, to treat rare words.

Calculate the probability that a message containing a given word is a spam:

Suppose the suspicious message contains the word "Word". In 2009 most of the people accustomed to receive e-mail know that it is likely that the message is spam. The spam detection software ignores these facts; however, all he can do is calculating probabilities.

The formula for determining this probability is derived from Bayes' theorem, it is, in its most general form, to:

$$P\left(S \setminus M\right) = \frac{P\left(\frac{M}{S}\right).P\left(S\right)}{P\left(\frac{M}{S}\right).P\left(S\right) + P\left(\frac{M}{H}\right).P\left(H\right)}$$

where,

- P (S / M) is the probability that the message M is spam, knowing that the word "Word" is included.
- P (S) is the absolute probability that any message is spam.
- P (M / S) is the probability that the "Word" appears in spam messages.
- P (H) is the absolute probability that any message is not spam (ie, the "ham").
- P (M / H) is the probability that the "Word" appears in messages ham.

Spamicity

Recent statistics show that the current probability that any message being spam is at least 80%: ie: P (S) = 0.8 and P (H) = 0.2.

Most software Bayesian spam detection believe that there is no a priori reason that a received message is spam instead of ham, and consider the two cases as having equal probabilities of 50%, ie: P (S) = P (H) = 0.5.

Filters that make this assumption are called "non-biased", which means they do not have prejudices about incoming mail. This assumption simplifies the general formula:

$$P\left(S \setminus M\right) = \frac{P\left(M \setminus S\right)}{P\left(M \setminus S\right) + P\left(M \setminus H\right)}$$

This quantity is called spamicity the word "Word" and can be calculated. The number P (M\S) that appears in this formula is approximated by the frequency of messages containing "Word" among the messages identified as spam during the learning phase. Similarly, P (M\H) is approximated by the frequency of messages containing "Word" among the messages identified as the ham during the learning phase.

Of course, determine whether a message is spam or not relying solely on the presence of the word "Word" can lead to error, which is why the anti-spam software tries to consider several words and combine spamicités for determine the probability of assembly to be spam.

Clustering by K-Means

Clustering by K-means (MacQueen, 1967) is a commonly used technique to automatically partition a data set into k groups. It does this by selecting k initial cluster centers, and then iteratively refines them as follows:

```
Initialize centers μ₁, · · · μκ
```
- Repeat
- Assigning each point to its nearest cluster

$$C\ell \leftarrow xi \quad tel\,que\,\ell = arg \min_{k} \mathrm{d}\left(xi, \tfrac{1}{4}k\right)$$

- Recalculate the center µk of each cluster

$$\mu k = \frac{1}{Nk} \sum_{i \in Ck} xi$$

Where N_k is the number of data in the cluster C_k

- While $\left\| \Delta\mu \right\| > \varepsilon$

Complexity: O (KnI) for I: iterations

A visual result after clustering by k-means is illustrated in Figures 4 and 5.

It should be noted that 3D navigation software has been designed to represent the data and the different classifications performed in our study. The points in red represent ham and green points represent the spam.

RESULTS AND EXPERIMENTS

Data Used

The SMS Spam Corpus v.0.1 (hereafter the corpus) is a set of SMS tagged messages that have been collected for SMS Spam research. It contains two collections of SMS messages in English of 1084 and 1319 messages, tagged according being legitimate (ham) or spam.

This corpus has been collected from free or free for research sources at the Web:

- A list of 202 legitimate messages, probably collected by Jon Stevenson, according to the HTML code of the Webpage. Only the text of the messages is available. We will call this corpus the Jon Stevenson Corpus (JSC). It is available at: http://www.demo.inty.net/Units/SMS/corpus.htm.
- A subset of the NUS SMS Corpus (NSC), which is a corpus of about 10,000 legitimate messages collected for research at the Department of Computer Science at the National University of Singapore. The messages largely originate from Singaporeans and mostly from students attending the University. These messages were collected from volunteers who were made aware that their contributions were going to be made publicly available. The NUS SMS Corpus is avalaible at: http://www.comp.nus.edu.sg/~rpnlpir/downloads/corpora/smsCorpus/.
- A collection of between 82 and 322 SMS spam messages extracted manually from the Grumbletext Web site. This is a UK forum in which cell phone users make public claims about SMS spam messages, most of them without reporting the very spam message received. The identification of the text of spam messages in the claims is a very hard and time-consuming task, and it involved carefully scanning hundreds of web pages. The Grumbletext Web site is: http://www.grumbletext.co.uk/.

RESULTS AND DISCUSSION

To carry out our experiments, we opted by the following methodology:

1. Representation of documents in the corpus by:
   a. The 1-gram words.
   b. The 1-gram characters.
   c. The 2-gram characters.
   d. The 3-gram characters.
   e. The 4-gram characters.
   f. The 5-gram characters.
2. For each representation defined above, we performed experiments with and without cleaning the documents in the corpus.
3. Calculate the matrix document-term.
4. Compute the matrix-term category by probabilistic weightings.
5. Make a categorization (supervised learning) by the model-Naïve Bayes.
6. Data Visualization in a 3D coordinate system.
7. From the data thus found, we run a clustering algorithm (unsupervised learning) based on k-means to identify two classes of documents in this case the new ham and spam and therefore determine the confusion matrix or more precisely contingency table.
8. Evaluation of results measures based on recall and precision (F-measure and Entropy).

The corpus used contains 1084 documents divided into 82 spams and 1002 ham.

Referring to Tables 1 and 2, we will explain the results based on the contingency tables of the best results of the model in this case the 4-gram representations characters and 1-gram words with cleaning data, and 3-gram representation characters without data cleansing.

Table 1. Results of learning Naïve Bayes with data cleaning

Representation	# Term	# Spam	# Ham	Learning Time (s)	F_Measure	Entropy	Confusion Matrix	
							Spam	Ham
1-Gram Char	27	253	831	5	0, 8284	0,1522	72	181
							10	821
2-Grams Char	555	131	953	11	0,9433	0.0554	76	55
							6	947
3-Grams Char	3907	82	1000	17	0.9888	0.0111	77	7
							5	995
4-Grams Char	**12074**	**74**	**1010**	**62**	**0.9929**	**0.0067**	**74**	**0**
							8	**1002**
5-Grams Char	23516	56	1028	89	0.9798	0.0163	56	0
							26	1002
1-Gram Word	**2270**	**71**	**1013**	**16**	**0.9905**	**0.0088**	**71**	**0**
							11	**1002**

Table 2. Results of learning Naïve Bayes without data cleaning

Representation	# Term	# Spam	# Ham	Learning Time (s)	F_Measure	Entropy	Confusion Matrix	
							Spam	Ham
1-Gram Char	98	94	990	7	0.9851	0,0148	80	14
							2	988
2-Grams Char	2005	86	998	13	0.9944	0.0056	81	5
							1	997
3-Grams Char	9175	79	1005	53	0.9972	0.0028	79	0
							3	1002
4-Grams Char	20951	68	1016	83	0.9881	0.0107	68	0
							14	1002
5-Grams Char	33233	51	1033	96	0.9767	0.0176	51	0
							31	1002
1-Gram Word	4224	62	1022	34	0.9837	0.0139	62	0
							20	1002

Contingency table (or table of co-occurrence) is a tool often used when it is desired to study the relationship between two variables that take discrete values (or categories). In our case, the variables are in the columns, actual (also known as "Gold Standard") and in the lines, the result of the filter. The sum of each column gives the actual number of elements in each class and of each line gives the number of elements seen by the classifier in each class. Table 3 shows the form of the contingency table.

Tables 4, 5 and 6 show the contingency matrix representations that have given the best results with the evaluation criteria that we have outlined.

We present some evaluation metrics that we used in our experiments to validate our results.

ERROR RATE BY CLASS

(False positives and false negatives): it is the fraction of the number of objects in a category erroneously classified in another class.

$$FPR = \frac{FP}{VN + FP}$$

Table 3. Form of the contingency table

	True Spam	True Ham
Ranking Spam	VP	FP
Ranking Ham	FN	VN

VN: True negatives: Hams seen by the filter as hams or hams correctly classified.

FN: False negative: Spam seen as hams or spams not correctly classified.

VP: True positives: Spam seen as spam or spam correctly classified.

FP: False positive: Hams seen as spams or hams not correctly classified.

Table 4. Contingency table for 4-grams characters with cleaning

	True Spam	True Ham
Ranking Spam	74	0
Ranking Ham	8	1002

Table 5. Contingency table for 1-gram word with cleaning

	True Spam	True Ham
Ranking Spam	71	0
Ranking Ham	11	1002

Table 6. Contingency table for 3-grams characters without cleaning

	True Spam	True Ham
Ranking Spam	79	0
Ranking Ham	3	1002

$$FNR = \frac{FN}{VP + FN}$$

Based on Tables 4 and 5, which relate the results by doing the cleaning data before doing learning, and the above formulas, we calculate the error rate per class (spam and ham).

1. **4-Grams Characters with Cleaning:** FPR = 0; FNR = 8/82 = 0.0975.
2. **1-Gram Words with Cleaning:** FPR = 0; FNR = 11/82 = 0.134.
3. **3-Gram Characters without Cleaning:** FPR = 0; FNR = 3/82 = 0.0365.

Based on these evaluation results and the error rate for each class, we note that 3-grams Characters have the better performance than other types of representations and data cleansing reduces the performance of results.

RATE OF GOOD RANKING

(True positives and true negatives or sensitivity and specificity).

$$VPR = \frac{VP}{VP + FN} = 1 - FNR$$

$$VNR = \frac{VN}{VN + FP} = 1 - FPR$$

1. **4-Grams Characters with Cleaning:** VPR = 74/82 = 0.9025; VNR = 1002/1002 = 1.
2. **1-Gram Words with Cleaning:** VPR = 71/82 = 0.865; VNR = 1002/1002 = 1.
3. **3-Gram Characters without Cleaning:** VPR = 79/82 = 0.963; VNR = 1002/1002 = 1.

We see that the representation of data by 3-gram characters without data cleansing gives very good results given the very high sensitivity (VPR= 0.963) and a specificity equal to 1 (VNR).

PRECISION AND RECALL

The precision indicates the proportion of spam messages among detected as spam, while the recall is the ratio between the number of detected spam rightly and the total number of spams.

$$Precision = \frac{VP}{VP + FP}$$

$$Recall = \frac{VP}{VP + FN} = VPR$$

1. **4-Grams Characters with Cleaning:** Precision = 1; Recall = 74/82 = 0.9025.
2. **1-Gram Words with Cleaning:** Precision = 1; Recall = 71/82 = 0.865.
3. **3-Gram Characters without Cleaning:** Precision = 1; Recall = 79/82 = 0.963.

Both criteria have their origin in retrieval applications and are sometimes found in the assessment results spam filters.

It should be noted that the f-measure and entropy are defined as follows:

$$F\_measure = \frac{2 x Precision x Racall}{Precision + Racall}$$

$$Entropy = -precision \, x \, Ln\left(precision\right)$$

Hence,

1. **4-Grams Characters with Cleaning:** f-measure = 0.9929; Entropy ≈ 0.
2. **1-Gram Words with Cleaning:** f-measure = 0.9905; Entropy ≈ 0.
3. **3-Gram Characters without Cleaning:** f-measure = 0.9972; Entropy ≈ 0.

As regards the assessment by the F-measure and the entropy, we note very good results with almost zero entropy (close to zero) and F-measure close to 1.

ACCURACY

This is the total error rate, the two classes combined.

$$Accuracy = \frac{\left(VP + VN\right)}{\left(VP + FN + VN + FP\right)}$$

1. **4-Gram Characters with Cleaning:** Accuracy = 1076/1084 = 0.993.
2. **1-Gram Words with Cleaning:** Accuracy = 1073/1084 = 0.990.
3. **3-Gram Characters without Cleaning:** Accuracy = 1081/1084 = 0.997.

All evaluation results are summarized in Tables 7 and 8.

The following graphs provide an illustration on the sensitivity of the mode of representation on the quality of the result of our classifier.

Figure 6 shows that the 3-gram character provides better results compared to other forms of data representation since all documents ham were correctly classified because the classification error rate of ham is zero and is the case as for 4 and 5 grams characters, and 1 gram words, but the difference is that one of the modes of representation mentioned, i.e. the 3-gram characters, have the lowest rate of spam classification (3.66%).

We can clearly see that Figures 8 and 9 show that the best results are achieved for 3-gram characters, and especially without data cleaning because they have a high f-measure and low entropy.

Table 7. Evaluation results for different modes of representation without data cleaning

	Error Rate Class		Rate of Rank Well		Precision	Recall	Accuracy
	Spam	Ham	Spam	Ham			
1-Grams Char	2,44%	1,40%	97,56%	98,60%	85,11%	97,56%	98,52%
2-Grams Char	1,22%	0,50%	98,78%	99,50%	94,19%	98,78%	99,45%
3-Grams Char	3,66%	0,00%	96,34%	100,00%	100,00%	96,34%	99,72%
4-Grams Char	17,07%	0,00%	82,93%	100,00%	100,00%	82,93%	98,71%
5-Grams Char	37,80%	0,00%	62,20%	100,00%	100,00%	62,20%	97,14%
1-Gram Word	24,39%	0,00%	75,61%	100,00%	100,00%	75,61%	98,15%

Table 8. Evaluation results for different modes of representation with data cleaning

	Error Rate Class		Rate of Rank Well		Precision	Recall	Accuracy
	Spam	Ham	Spam	Ham			
1-Grams Char	18,06%	12,20%	87,80%	81,94%	28,46%	87,80%	82,38%
2-Grams Char	5,49%	7,32%	92,68%	94,51%	58,02%	92,68%	94,37%
3-Grams Char	0,70%	6,10%	93,90%	99,30%	91,67%	93,90%	98,89%
4-Grams Char	0,00%	9,76%	90,24%	100,00%	100,00%	90,24%	99,26%
5-Grams Char	0,00%	31,71%	68,29%	100,00%	100,00%	68,29%	97,60%
1-Gram Word	0,00%	13,41%	86,59%	100,00%	100,00%	86,59%	98,99%

Figure 6. Error rate per class for representation without cleaning

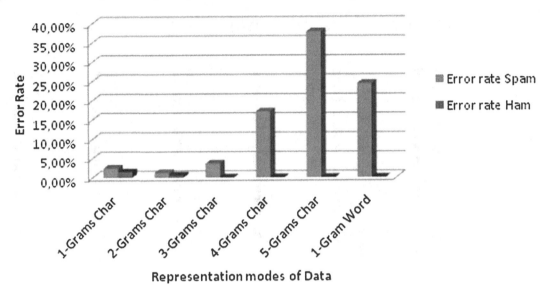

Figure 7. Rate of rank well for representation without cleaning

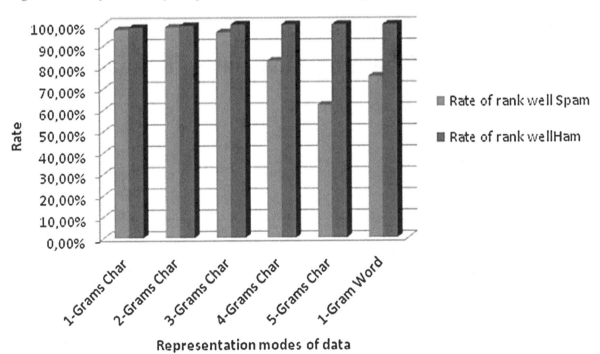

Figure 8. Results of learning by hybrid algorithm (f-measure)

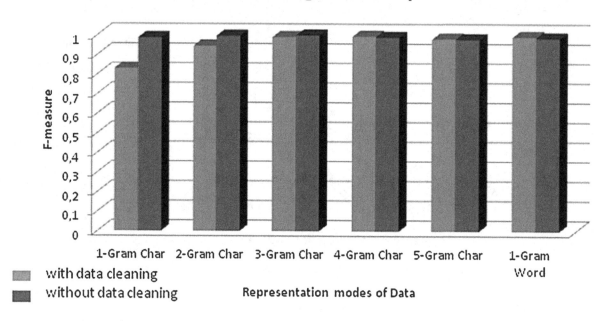

Figure 9. Results of learning by hybrid algorithm (Entropy)

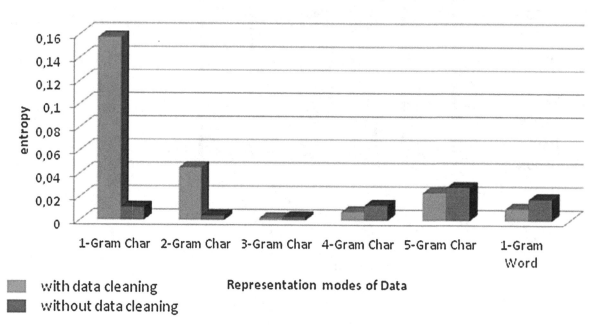

CONCLUSION

In this paper, we are interested in modes of representation of textual data in this case, the n-gram characters and words because its modes, which operate independently of languages, lexical roots are automatically captured and they are tolerant to the misspellings. The advantages of n-grams have led us to use them because a spam is text document written in any language and can contain text full of mistakes and written by anyone.

The results obtained have proved that the 3-gram characters are most likely to be used for this kind of problems that is detection and spam filtering without the cleaning step is to remove data terms (words tools) and 4-gram characters were the best with the data cleaning step.

Another index emerged as significant is the use of the data cleaning step because the best results were obtained without data cleansing, this is interpreted by the fact that the elimination of terms in this stage could harm the quality of classification because a term may have eliminated its importance to the calculation of the probability that the document is or is not spam.

In the future, we plan to experimenting unsupervised learning techniques because supervised learning techniques are very expensive.

ACKNOWLEDGMENT

The authors would like to thank the anonymous reviewers and the editor for their insightful comments and suggestions.

REFERENCES

Benevenuto, F., Rodrigues, T., Almeida, V., Almeida, J., Zhang, C., & Ross, K. (2008, April). Identifying video spammers in online social networks. In *Proceedings of the 4th International Workshop on Adversarial Information Retrieval on the Web* (pp. 45-52). ACM. doi:10.1145/1451983.1451996

Byun, B., Lee, C., Webb, S., Irani, D., & Pu, C. (2009, July). An anti-spam filter combination framework for text-and-image emails through incremental learning. In *Proceedings of the the Sixth Conference on Email and Anti–Spam (CEAS 2009)*. CEAS.

Chevalier, J. F., & Gramme, P. (2008). RANK for spam detection ECML-Discovery Challenge. In *Proceedings of ECML PKDD Discovery Challenge*. PKDD.

Cohn, D. A., Ghahramani, Z., & Jordan, M. I. (1996). Active learning with statistical models. *arXiv preprint cs/9603104*.

da Cruz, J. M. M. (2009, December 4). *Méthodologie d'évaluation des filtres anti-spam. Journées Réseaux*.

Deerwester, S. C., Dumais, S. T., Landauer, T. K., Furnas, G. W., & Harshman, R. A. (1990). Indexing by latent semantic analysis. *JASIS, 41*(6), 391–407. doi:10.1002/(SICI)1097-4571(199009)41:6<391::AID-ASI1>3.0.CO;2-9

Dziczkowski, G., & Wegrzyn-Wolska, K. (2008, December). An autonomous system designed for automatic detection and rating of film reviews. In *Proceedings of the 2008 IEEE/WIC/ACM International Conference on Web Intelligence and Intelligent Agent Technology* (vol. 1, pp. 847-850). IEEE Computer Society. doi:10.1109/WIIAT.2008.262

Gyöngyi, Z., Garcia-Molina, H., & Pedersen, J. (2004, August). Combating web spam with trustrank. In *Proceedings of the Thirtieth International Conference on Very Large Data Bases* (vol. 30, pp. 576-587). VLDB Endowment.

Hamou, R. M., Amine, A., & Boudia, A. (2013). A New Meta-Heuristic Based on Social Bees for Detection and Filtering of Spam. *International Journal of Applied Metaheuristic Computing, 4*(3), 15–33. doi:10.4018/ijamc.2013070102

Hamou, R. M., Amine, A., & Lokbani, A. C. (2012). The Social Spiders in the Clustering of Texts: Towards an Aspect of Visual Classification. *International Journal of Artificial Life Research, 3*(3), 1–14. doi:10.4018/jalr.2012070101

Hamou, R. M., Amine, A., & Lokbani, A. C. (2013). Study of Sensitive Parameters of PSO: Application to Clustering of Texts. *International Journal of Applied Evolutionary Computation, 4*(2), 41–55. doi:10.4018/jaec.2013040104

Hamou, R. M., Amine, A., & Rahmani, M. (2012). Visualisation and clustering by 3D cellular automata: Application to unstructured data. *International Journal of Data Mining and Emerging Technologies, 2*(1), 15-25.

Hamou, R. M., Amine, A., Rahmouni, A., Lokbani, A. C., & Simonet, M. (2013). Modeling of Inclusion by Genetic Algorithms: Application to the Beta-Cyclodextrin and Triphenylphosphine. *International Journal of Chemoinformatics and Chemical Engineering, 3*(1), 19–36. doi:10.4018/ijcce.2013010103

Hamou, R. M., Lehireche, A., Lokbani, A. C., & Rahmani, M. (2010). Representation of textual documents by the approach wordnet and n-grams for the unsupervised classification (clustering) with 2D cellular automata: A comparative study. *Computer and Information Science, 3*(3), 240–255.

Hamou, R. M., Lehireche, A., Lokbani, A. C., & Rahmani, M. (2010, October). Text clustering by 2D cellular automata based on the n-grams. In *Proceedings of Cryptography and Network Security, Data Mining and Knowledge Discovery, E-Commerce & Its Applications and Embedded Systems (CDEE),* (pp. 271-277). IEEE.

Heymann, P., Koutrika, G., & Garcia-Molina, H. (2007). Fighting spam on social web sites: A survey of approaches and future challenges. *IEEE Internet Computing, 11*(6), 36–45. doi:10.1109/MIC.2007.125

Hotho, A., Jäschke, R., Schmitz, C., & Stumme, G. (2006). *Information retrieval in folksonomies: Search and ranking.* Springer Berlin Heidelberg.

Kanich, C., Kreibich, C., Levchenko, K., Enright, B., Voelker, G. M., Paxson, V., & Savage, S. (2008, October). Spamalytics: An empirical analysis of spam marketing conversion. In *Proceedings of the 15th ACM Conference on Computer and Communications Security* (pp. 3-14). ACM. doi:10.1145/1455770.1455774

Kleinberg, J. M. (1999). Authoritative sources in a hyperlinked environment. *Journal of the ACM, 46*(5), 604–632. doi:10.1145/324133.324140

Longe, O. B. (2011). On the use of Imagebased Spam Mails as Carriers for Covert Data Transmission. Computer & Information Systems Journal, 15(1).

Sahami, M., Dumais, S., Heckerman, D., & Horvitz, E. (1998, July). A Bayesian approach to filtering junk e-mail. In *Learning for text categorization: Papers from the 1998 workshop* (*Vol. 62*, pp. 98-105). Academic Press.

Salton, G., & Buckley, C. (1988). Term-weighting approaches in automatic text retrieval. *Information Processing & Management, 24*(5), 513–523. doi:10.1016/0306-4573(88)90021-0

Saporta, G. (2011). *Probabilités, analyse des données et statistique*. Editions Technip.

Yerazunis, W. S. (2004, January). The spam-filtering accuracy plateau at 99.9% accuracy and how to get past it. In *Proceedings of the 2004 MIT Spam Conference*. MIT.

Chapter 19
Using Supervised Machine Learning to Explore Energy Consumption Data in Private Sector Housing

Mariya Sodenkamp
University of Bamberg, Germany

Konstantin Hopf
University of Bamberg, Germany

Thorsten Staake
University of Bamberg, Germany & ETH Zurich, Switzerland

ABSTRACT

Smart electricity meters allow capturing consumption load profiles of residential buildings. Besides several other applications, the retrieved data renders it possible to reveal household characteristics including the number of persons per apartment, age of the dwelling, etc., which helps to develop targeted energy conservation services. The goal of this chapter is to develop further related methods of smart meter data analytics that infer such household characteristics using weekly load curves. The contribution of this chapter to the state of the art is threefold. The authors first quadruplicate the number of defined features that describe electricity load curves to preserve relevant structures for classification. Then, they suggest feature filtering techniques to reduce the dimension of the input to a set of a few significant ones. Finally, the authors redefine class labels for some properties. As a result, the classification accuracy is elevated up to 82%, while the runtime complexity is significantly reduced.

DOI: 10.4018/978-1-4666-7272-7.ch019

1. INTRODUCTION

Smart grid technology is one of the main pillars of next-generation sustainable energy management. Detailed information about energy consumption is useful to both energy users and utilities. Energy providers can better forecast demand, improve meter-to-cash-processes, and manage supply, while customers get better control over their own electricity usage, costs, and caused carbon footprint. In the last decade, governments across Europe placed high hopes on smart metering as an indispensable means to improve energy efficiency in the residential sector.

Smart meters typically record energy consumption in 15- to 30- minute intervals, and the information is sent back to the energy supplier. The gained information then can be used to support grid optimization processes and to derive targeted interventions toward customers. Combined with direct consumer feedback, smart metering has been promised to increase energy efficiency by 5-15%, though the current field studies show savings of around 3% (Degen et al., 2013).

Given the lower-than-expected saving effects, European countries are moving from the euphoria regarding its potential. The reasons are high upfront costs, customers' privacy concerns, and, most importantly, lack of analytical implications from the data for policy and efficiency measures development. Meanwhile, utilization of the information from fine-grained consumption profiles is in its infancy. With current expectations running high – still burdened with a risk of disappointment – developing new analytical approaches of data processing, interpretation, and utilization remains one of the major challenges.

This work is aimed at filling the gap between raw smart metering consumption data and the information required for developing energy policy toward dwellings. We improve previous algorithms for household classification with predicting energy efficiency relevant characteristics (such as type of heating, size/age of house, number of inhabitants/children, etc.) from the consumption traces. In essence, we rely upon the pioneering work of Beckel et al. (Beckel et al., 2013) who showed that household properties can be inferred from fine-grained consumption data using supervised machine learning with accuracy above 60%. In short, we focus on three following aspects to improve the classification accuracy and to reduce runtime complexity of the Beckel et al.'s algorithm:

1. Extending the feature set,
2. Applying feature filtering methods, and
3. Refining property definitions.

For training and test of the proposed model, we relied upon the dataset acquired from the Irish Commission for Energy Regulation (CER) (Irish Social Science Data Archive, 2014). It contains 30-minute smart electricity meter and survey data from about 4200 private households collected during a 76-week period of 2009 and 2010 in Ireland. We analyzed one noise-free week (21-27.09.2009) without public holidays and with average weather conditions. The results show that the classification accuracy of the upgraded algorithm can be significantly improved (up to 82%), while reducing the computational complexity.

This chapter is organized as follows: Section 2 gives an overview of the related work. Section 3 describes our classification system. It is followed by a more detailed description of the underlying dataset, along with the proposed feature/property definition and feature selection methods in Section 4. Finally, Section 5 presents the attained results and main conclusions of this work.

2. STATE OF THE ART

Most of the existing research on defining household characteristics using power consumption data involves unsupervised machine learning techniques (e.g., Self-Organizing Maps, and k-Means clustering) (Verdu et al., 2006; de Silva et al., 2011; Chicco et al., 2006; Räsänen et al., 2008; Figueiredo et al., 2005; Sánchez et al., 2009). The underlying idea here is to identify households with repeatable/similar load traces. However, these approaches do not allow for deriving household properties explicitly, instead, human interpretation of the obtained patterns is needed. Another pitfall of these works is that they either rely upon small datasets (only 6 to 625 energy customers), including private households, companies and public service consumers (de Silva et al., 2011; Chicco et al., 2006; et al., 2005; Sánchez et al., 2009) or analyze annual data (Räsänen et al., 2008). As a result, these findings have theoretical nature; they have not found application in practical settings so far.

Recently, Beckel et al. (2013) showed that supervised machine learning can be used for inferring household properties – like their floor area or the number of persons living in them - from electricity consumption curves. They relied on the data from 3,488 private households, collected at a 30-minute granularity and for a period of more than 1.5 years. Their approach is based on extraction of 22 empirically defined features, application of four standard classifiers, and inference of 12 household properties. However, error rate higher than 35% hamper the adoption of this system by utility companies. Therefore, looking for ways to improve the accuracy is a major thrust of current research on household classification.

Definition of features is crucial to the success of any classifier. The essential task of time series dimensionality reduction is to find a mapping of initial high-dimensional data into the desired low-dimensional representation. Fine grained metering data (with measurement intervals less than 1 Hz) was initially used in nonintrusive load monitoring (NILM) (Zeifman & Roth, 2011; Hart, 1992) to trace the consumption of home appliances. For the purpose of household clustering and classification, data recorded with a much coarser granularity (typically one measurement every 15, 30, or 60 minutes) is sufficient. Applications based on such data are of particular interest to energy providers as this is the type of data that was collected during most of the smart meter trials so far (Beckel et al., 2013). However, in order to make such high-volume time series operationable, they have to be transformed into a handful of more representative characteristics. Some basic features (e.g., daily consumption, impact of certain daytimes, relation consumption mean/max) were suggested in (Chicco et al., 2006; Figueiredo et al., 2005; Sánchez et al., 2009). Beckel et al. (2012) presented a taxonomy of 22 features divided in four groups: consumption figures, ratios, temporal figures, and statistics. Indeed, further extension of this feature set may enable more precise prediction.

On the other hand, to efficiently manage large feature sets, it may be necessary to select those features that contribute, in the simplest sense, to classification accuracy and efficiency. The problem of feature selection is frequently solved using statistical methods (Ramsey & Schafer, 2002), where wrapper and filtering are two main approaches. Wrapper methods utilize the classifier on each feature selection step (Guyon et al., 2003) to calculate and optimize performance measures. Although the wrapper approach may obtain better performances, it is very resource intensive. In our work we rely on feature filtering methods that are independent on the classifier used. They select features according to their goodness of fit for the prediction task. Correlation coefficient is one of most commonly used filtering metrics (Hall, 1999), but it gives only a quantification of the coherence in the feature set and does not measure the expressiveness of one feature for a specific property. This task can be achieved by applying statistical tests, as suggested by Biesiada & Duch (2005). For a review of other feature filtering methods, the interested reader is referred to Saeys et al. (2007).

Improvement of the prior class distributions and thus classification accuracy may be arrived at by refining initial training set of class labels. Räsänen et al. (2008) and Sánchez et al. (2009) suggest some basic properties for segmentation of energy consumers. Beckel et al. (2013) conducted interviews with energy utilities to find important household characteristics for an energy-efficiency consulting task and used these results to formulate 12 properties for their classification system. Our work improves on Beckel et al's study in three ways:

1. **Extension of the Feature Set:** We expand the set of features from 22 to 88 and evaluate their impact on the classification performance.
2. **Application of Feature Filtering Methods:** Besides the commonly used correlation coefficient, we implement the KS-test and Pearson's eta-squared (Richardson, 2011) and evaluate their impact on the classification performance. Furthermore, we show that feature filtering produce at least the same classification performance as wrapper methods.
3. **Refining the Properties:** The underlying dataset offers a broader property definition and a more detailed distinction among households. We check whether an alternative class distribution affects the results.

3. SYSTEM DESIGN

Figure 1 illustrates the components of our classification system and their interaction.

Data Preparation

As an input, the system accepts SMD and customer survey data for the classification task. For dimensionality reduction features were extracted from the raw SMD and property values were determined from the survey data. Missing values in the dataset were handled different for the SMD and the survey data. We excluded all households with missing values in raw SMD, leaving us with about 3000 records. The records, for which the calculation of features was impossible, were also excluded. If one property value cannot be determined from the survey data the household is ignored in the classification only for this property, but not for the others.

Classification

For classification we use the k-Nearest Neighbor (kNN) and the Support Vector Machine (SVM) methods, as they were described in (Beckel et al., 2013). For SVM the default configuration (Meyer et al., 2014) was not changed, but for kNN we increased k to 20 for more robust classification results.

Evaluation

To evaluate the system robustness and the result quality we separate the entire dataset into training data and test data at a typical 2:1 ratio, as mentioned in (Han et al, 2011). The training data is used for feature selection and for the classifier training. After the classification step the right class labels from the test data (so called "ground truth") are compared with the labels assigned by the classifier, and the performance measures are calculated to evaluate the classification quality.

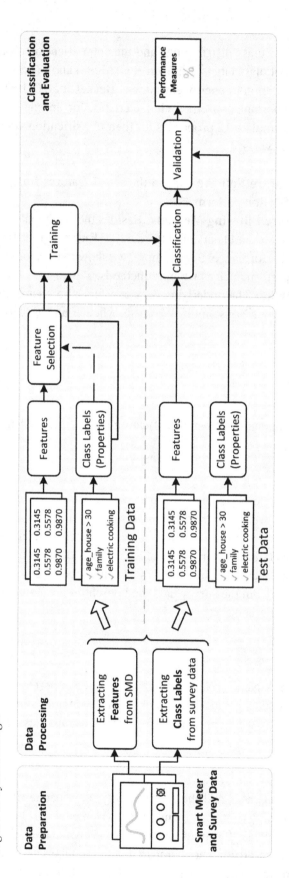

Figure 1. System design

4. DATA PROCESSING

The main scope of our work is the improvement of the data processing in the classification system with the goal to improve the classification performance. For recap, we differentiate between features (characteristics of the load profile) and properties (characteristics of the household producing the load profile).

Feature Definition

From the SMD of one week we extract 88 features where 22 features definitions are adopted from (Beckel et al., 2012). We add more features that consider the relations between the consumption on weekdays and on the weekend, parameters of seasonal and trend decomposition, estimations of the base load and some statistical features. A sample and the category tree of all implemented features are visualized in Figure 2.

Altogether the features include statistical aspects (like the variance, the auto-correlation and other statistical numbers), temporal aspects (like consumption levels, peaks, important moments, temporal deviations, values of time series analysis), consumption figures (like mean consumption in different times of the day and in different days) and finally different ratios (daytime-ratios and ratios between different days).

After the feature extraction, the values are normalized. This is performed separately on the training data and on the test data. In (Beckel et al, 2013) the normalization step is performed over the whole dataset, which might leads to inflated results, because the training data is not independent form the test data.

Feature Filtering

Using a huge amount of variables in a classification task involves the risk to over-train the classifier. Due to expansion of the feature set the importance of selecting the most meaningful features for each property is a key success factor of the whole classification system.

In contrast to wrapper methods used in (Beckel et al, 2013) we implement feature filtering methods. The main characteristic of them is that the FS takes place before the classifier training. The classification is performed only once on the selected features. This saves computational costs compared to the wrapper methods.

Correlation Based Feature Selection (CBFS)

In our first approach of feature filtering we applied the product-moment correlation coefficient to the whole feature set. This correlation coefficient is a measure for linear correlation between two statistical variables X and Y, which has a codomain of [-1;+1] where -1 denotes a negative and +1 denotes a positive correlation; if the coefficient takes the value 0 there is no correlation between the two variables.

$$-1 \leq r_{XY} = \frac{\sigma^2_{XY}}{\sigma_X \sigma_Y} \leq +1 \tag{1}$$

Thereby σ^2_{XY} denotes the covariance between X and Y and σ_X is the standard deviation of X.

Figure 2. Feature categories with examples of features

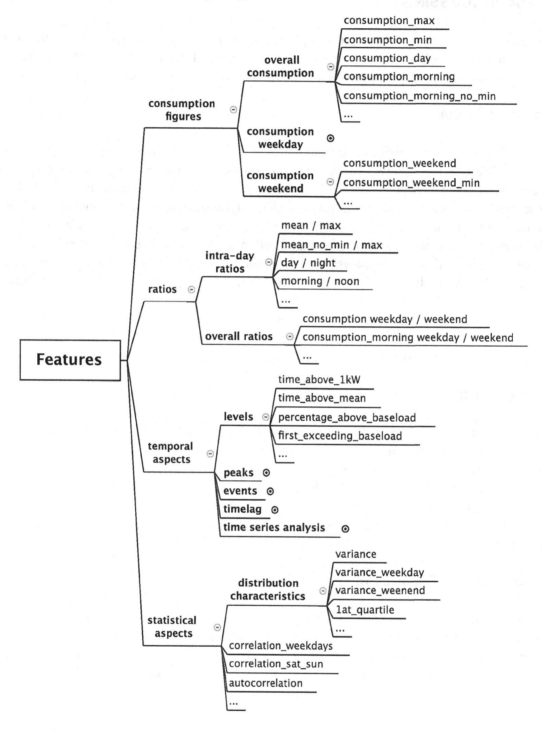

The FS algorithm calculates the row or column mean over the absolute values of the correlation-matrix and selects all features which have a mean correlation lower than a specific value that can be configured. During an empirical analysis we estimated a correlation-level of lower than *0.4* as appropriate.

KS-Test Based Feature Selection (KSBFS)

The second FS method utilizes a statistical test to find features, which have significantly different distributions for different classes of one property. The test statistic is therefore an effect-size measure for the features. The statistic for all feature values according the hypotheses:

H_0: The distribution in the two classes is equal.
H_1: The distribution is not equal.

We choose the Kolmogorov-Smirnov (KS) Test, because it is nonparametric and can compare empirical distributions of two samples. Furthermore the test can also be used with small samples.algorithm takes one property, e.g. single, which has two classes: Single and Not Single and calculates the test

η^2 Based Feature Selection (EBFS)

Another indicator for the expressiveness of a feature for a specific property is the η^2 correlation coefficient, which calculates the correlation between one quantitative variable X (interval or ratio scale) and one qualitative variable A (nominal or ordinal scale). The coefficient is defined as follows:

- i : Index of the class in A (i=1,…,k)
- $x_{i\mu}$: Value at the index μ (μ=1,…, n_i)
- $\bar{x}$: Average over all values of X
- σ_X^2 : Overall variance of X, can be divided into the spread in the classes + the spread between the classes.

The variance can then be calculated by Equation (2).

$$\sigma_X^2 = \frac{1}{n} \sum_{i=1}^{k} \sum_{\mu=1}^{n_i} \left(x_{i\mu} - \bar{x} \right)^2 \tag{2}$$

We calculate η^2 by Equation (3).

$$0 \leq \eta^2 = \frac{\frac{1}{n} \sum_{l=1}^{k} \left(\bar{x}_l - \bar{x} \right)^2 n_i}{\sigma_X^2} \leq 1 \tag{3}$$

The implantation of this measure in FS is analogously to the CBFS method and we configured the algorithm that all features with $\eta^2 \geq 0,003$ were selected. This number was also a result of our empirical analysis.

Combined Feature Selection (CombFS)

Lastly the idea is obvious to combine two of the presented methods to get a further improvement in the classification performance. Our algorithm here can be described as follows:

1. Find the most expressive feature using the KS test statistic and add it to the feature set.
2. Add all features to the feature set that have a low (product-moment) correlation to the first selected feature.

Property Definition

According to the fact that the CER survey data has more details as used in (Beckel et al, 2013; Beckel et al, 2012) we suggest two additional property sets: the first property set contains only bivalent definitions and the second set contains properties that have more than two characteristics (multivalent definition). The alternative definitions are given in Table 1. In some cases we added no new class labels but change the class borders deliberately to check whether different definitions influence the classification performance.

5. RESULTS

This section shows our improvements in the three goals of our research work, mentioned in Section 2.

For the evaluation of our system we use accuracy as performance measure for the classification system. It is calculated as follows:

$$accuracy = \frac{correct\,cases}{all\,cases} \tag{4}$$

Table 1. Three options of property definitions

Property	Reference Definition (Beckel et al., 2013)	Bivalent Definition	Multivalent Definition
#devices	Low (≤ 8) Medium (≤ 11) High (>11)	Few (≤ 23) Many (>23)	Low (≤ 21) Medium (≤ 25) High (>30)
employment	Employed Not Employed		Employed Unemployed Freelancer
age_house	Old (>30) New (≤ 30)	Old (>10) New (≤ 10)	<5, <10, <30, <75, >75
cooking	Electrical Not Electrical		
single	Single Not Single		

Extending the Feature Set

Our first approach was to increase the number of features and thereby adding more information about the time series data. We used three different sets of features: The first set (size: 22) contains only those that were suggested in (Beckel et al, 2012). In the second set (size: 64) we added more consumption features with a distinction between consumption on weekdays and at the weekend, such as numbers of a seasonal- and trend-decomposition. In the third set (size: 88) we added features that try to describe the base load and subtract it from the consumption. The classification results are illustrated in Figure 3.

The diagram shows three main aspects:

1. The inclusion of further features can improve the classification results;
2. If the feature set is too big or if the quality of newly added features is not adequate, the classification performance can also decrease;
3. For properties that already exhibit a classification accuracy higher than 60% the extension of the feature set displays no improvement. The extension of the feature set increased average classification accuracy by 3% for the presented properties.

Applying Feature Filtering

The second aspect we evaluated was the impact of feature filtering on the classification quality. Figure 4 shows the accuracy of the classification instances with and without the feature selection methods described in the previous section.

The average classification performance is by 8% higher with any filtering technique than without. In #devices the accuracy could be improved by 12%.

We underline the two most important findings:

First, nearly every classification performs better with a feature filtering approach than without. In the applied FS methods there is no clear favorite, because some algorithms achieve better classification results in some properties, but are worse in others.

Second, in the CombFS method we combine KSBF and CBFS to simultaneously benefit from their strength. This effect holds for the property family and some others, but we were not able to show an overall dominance of one of the presented filtering approaches.

Figure 3. Classification (SVM) results with different feature sets

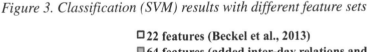

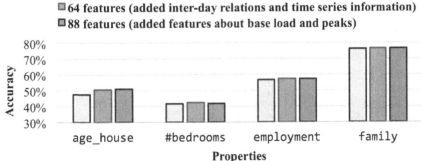

Figure 4. Classification (kNN) with different feature filtering methods

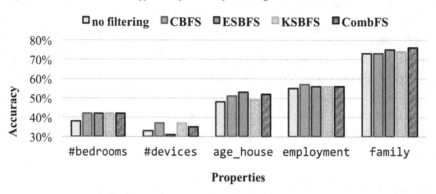

To determine the best feature selection method for every property is a subject for future research.

Refining Property Definition

Finally, we exemplarily tested alternative property definitions and compared them to the results of (Beckel et al, 2013). This achieved an improvement in the classifier's performance in several parts (see Figure 5). The property single and cooking have the same definition in all property sets thus obviously the same performance is achieved in all three definitions. The properties age_house (accuracy = 79%), #devices (accuracy = 53%), and employment (accuracy = 56%) performed better with a different definition of the class labels.

The right choice of the class labels has a large impact on the classification results. This determination of the borders between different classes should be made on the basis of classification results. We only considered two alternative definitions, but there are more possibilities, which is a part of future work.

Comparison with the Reference System

Since our main goal was to improve the classification system presented by Beckel et al. (2013), it seems reasonable to compare the overall improvement of the re-implemented CLASS-system in GNU-R to their results using a Matlab® implementation and wrapper methods for FS.

Figure 5. Classification (kNN) results with different property definitions

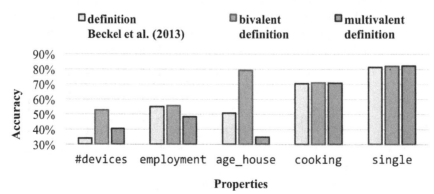

The classification performance of CLASS, a random guess of the right class label of a household (knowing the distribution) and the results of our system in an optimized configuration are presented in Figure 6. We achieved at least the same results as the reference system in most of the properties. With a more precise refining of the properties these results could be further improved, as we can see for age_house: when we define the border of whether a house is old or new as 10 years, the classification accuracy is ~80%, but it is much worse if we use the definition from (Beckel et al, 2013) (30 years).

The three presented approaches (extending the feature set, applying feature filtering methods and refining the properties) improved the classification accuracy of the properties, shown in Figure 6, on average by 3% compared to (Beckel et al, 2013).

6. CONCLUSION

In this chapter we showed three major improvements in household classification system proposed by Beckel et al. (2013).

We extended the feature set from initially 12 to 88 and included thereby more information from the SMD. This increased the classification performance in some features by 7%. Furthermore, we adopted feature filtering and showed that these methods outperform feature selection with wrapper methods in the context of household classification, because of their low computational costs and their classification results which are as good as those who were produced with wrapper approaches. Besides that we have shown that considering the property definition can make a large volume of potential improvements (accuracy was increased by 50% in some properties).

Finally, our contributions to the household classification system presented in (Beckel et al, 2013) increased the classification performance on average by 3% and by 30% against a bias random guess, knowing class size of a property. Our work shows that the results in household classification can be further improved by optimizing the property definitions and applying an optimal feature selection for each property.

Figure 6. Classification (kNN) performance compared with the reference system (Beckel et al, 2013).

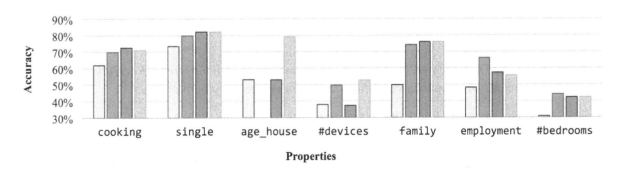

□ bias random guess   ▣ results from Beckel et al. (2013) ▣ results with feature filtering   ▢ results with redefined properties

REFERENCES

Beckel, C., Sadamori, L., & Santini, S. (2012). Towards automatic classification of private households using electricity consumption data. In *Proceedings of the Fourth ACM Workshop on Embedded Sensing Systems for Energy-Efficiency in Buildings* (pp. 169-176). Toronto, Canada: ACM. doi:10.1145/2422531.2422562

Beckel, C., Sadamori, L., & Santini, S. (2013). Automatic socio-economic classification of households using electricity consumption data. In *Proceedings of the fourth international conference on Future energy systems* (pp.75-86). Berkeley, CA: ACM. doi:10.1145/2487166.2487175

Biesiada, J., & Duch, W. (2005). Feature Selection for High-Dimensional Data: A Kolmogorov-Smirnov Correlation-Based Filter. In *Proceedings of the 4th International Conference on Computer Recognition Systems, CORES'05* (pp. 95-103). Springer. doi:10.1007/3-540-32390-2_9

Chicco, G., Napoli, R., Postolache, P., Scutariu, M., & Toader, C. (2003). Customer characterization options for improving the tariff offer. *IEEE Transactions on Power Systems*, *18*(1), 381–387. doi:10.1109/TPWRS.2002.807085

De Silva, D., Xinghuo, Y., Alahakoon, D., & Holmes, G. (2011). A Data Mining Framework for Electricity Consumption Analysis From Meter Data. *IEEE Transactions on Industrial Informatics*, *7*(3), 399–407. doi:10.1109/TII.2011.2158844

Degen, K., Efferson, C., Frei, F., Goette, L., & Lalive, R. (2013). Smart Metering, Beratung oder Sozialer Vergleich: Was beeinflusst den Elektrizitätsverbrauch? Zürich.

Figueiredo, V., Rodrigues, F., Vale, Z., & Gouveia, J. B. (2005). An electric energy consumer characterization framework based on data mining techniques. *IEEE Transactions on Power Systems*, *20*(2), 596–602. doi:10.1109/TPWRS.2005.846234

Guyon, I., & Elisseeff, A. (2003). An introduction to variable and feature selection. *Journal of Machine Learning Research*, *3*, 1157–1182.

Hall, M. A. (1999). *Correlation-based feature selection for machine learning.* (Dissertation). University of Waikato.

Han, J., Kamber, M., & Pei, J. (2011). *Data mining: Concepts and techniques* (3rd ed.). Amsterdam: Elsevier.

Hart, G. W. (1992). Nonintrusive appliance load monitoring. *Proceedings of the IEEE*, *80*(12), 1870–1891. doi:10.1109/5.192069

Irish Social Science Data Archive. (2014). *Data from the Commission for Energy Regulation.* Retrieved Mar. 4 2014 from http://www.ucd.ie/issda/data/commissionforenergyregulationcer/

Meyer, D., Dimitriadou, E., Hornik, K., Weingessel, A., & Leisch, F. (2014). *e1071: Misc Functions of the Department of Statistics.* TU Wien.

Ramsey, F. L., & Schafer, D. W. (2002). *The statistical sleuth: A course in methods of data analysis* (2nd ed.). Pacific Grove, CA: Duxbury.

Räsänen, T., Ruuskanen, J., & Kolehmainen, M. (2008). Reducing energy consumption by using self-organizing maps to create more personalized electricity use information. *Applied Energy*, *85*(9), 830–840. doi:10.1016/j.apenergy.2007.10.012

Richardson, J. T. E. (2011). Eta squared and partial eta squared as measures of effect size in educational research. *Educational Research Review*, *6*(2), 135–147. doi:10.1016/j.edurev.2010.12.001

Saeys, Y., Inza, I., & Larranaga, P. (2007). A review of feature selection techniques in bioinformatics. *Bioinformatics (Oxford, England)*, *23*(19), 2507–2517. doi:10.1093/bioinformatics/btm344 PMID:17720704

Sánchez, I. B., Espinós, I. D., Sarrion, L. M., López, A. Q., & Burgos, I. N. (2009). Clients segmentation according to their domestic energy consumption by the use of self-organizing maps. In *Proceedings of 6th International Conference on the European Energy Market*, (pp. 1–6). Academic Press. doi:10.1109/EEM.2009.5207172

Verdu, S. V., Garcia, M. O., Senabre, C., Marin, A. G., & Franco, F. J. G. (2006). Classification, Filtering, and Identification of Electrical Customer Load Patterns Through the Use of Self-Organizing Maps. *IEEE Transactions on Power Systems*, *21*(4), 1672–1682. doi:10.1109/TPWRS.2006.881133

Zeifman, M., & Roth, K. (2011). Nonintrusive appliance load monitoring: Review and outlook. *IEEE Transactions on Consumer Electronics*, *57*(1), 76–84. doi:10.1109/TCE.2011.5735484

KEY TERMS AND DEFINITIONS

Energy Utility: A company that produces electrical energy or purchases it from electricity producers, feeds it into the public grid, and thus delivers it to the customers.

Feature Extraction: A technique that reduces the amount of input data by distilling its representative descriptive attributes.

Feature Selection: A dimensionality reduction technique that filters all extracted data features and keeps only classification-relevant ones.

Household Classification: A method of predicting household characteristics.

Smart Meter Data: Household related energy consumption time series continuously accumulated at short time intervals (typically 15 to 30 minutes).

Supervised Machine Learning: A set of prediction algorithms that use labeled data to learn from it with the goal to categorize new unlabeled data instances.

Chapter 20
Application of Data Mining Techniques on Library Circulation Data for Library Material Acquisition and Budget Allocation

Md. Hossain
North South University, Bangladesh

Rashedur M. Rahman
North South University, Bangladesh

ABSTRACT

This chapter offers a model for automated library material utilization that is based on knowledge discovery using association rules. Processing the circulation data of the library to extract the statistics and association utilization of the materials for departments is a great achievement that makes the analysis easier for calculating material utilization. Moreover, processing the circulation data of the library, two important dimensions, namely concentration and connection (Kao, Chang, & Lin, 2003), could be explored among departments and library members. This can make the analysis easier by calculating weights in those two important dimensions to make the decision about budget allocation. This chapter analyses the circulation data of North South University Library and suggests that efficient management and budget allocation can be achieved by using the above-mentioned metrics.

1. INTRODUCTION

Data Mining is a fabulous technique to acquire knowledge from any archive of scatterd data. It can easily help us taking any decision based on the collected knowledge. Allocation of budget for a library is important to manage and maintain it properly. Besides, good allocation ensures the maximum and optimum usability of the library materials for the sake of the members of the library. In this occasion

DOI: 10.4018/978-1-4666-7272-7.ch020

data mining can play a vital role to allocate a perfect or nearly perfect budget for a library based on the circulation data. There are a number of research studies reported in the literature that used data mining techniques in the last few years. A large amount of time usually the librarians spend to acquire resources for numbers of library users. However, prior to this panic task, library authority must determine how to list up all the materials that will meet the needs of most of the users. Many studies involved in the literature have observed the increased use of the data mining techniques like association rule in the past few years. In (Hamaker, 1995) it was indicated that usage information showed something different from the collectors' recommendations. More importantly, information such as ''what were the materials most utilized by the students of a particular department'' would be highly useful for acquiring materials (Kao, Chang, & Lin, 2003). In (Budd & Adams, 1989), it was emphasized that circulation statistics could be one of the most significantly references for library managerial decisions. This paper introduces some easier techniques of statistical analysis and goal programming to extract the knowledge which can give us the power to take the decision about the allocation of budget.

In this research we analyze North South University (NSU) Library database for possible allocation of academic library acquisition budget via circulation database mining. We derived weights of acquisition budget allocation by composing the descriptive knowledge via utilization concentration and the suitability via utilization connection (Kao, Chang, & Lin, 2003) for departments concerned. The value of concentration and connection is calculated from the number of records, the distribution of material categories used, and the relation between categories and subjects. We obtained the degree of concentration for a department by measuring information entropy using ID3 algorithm introduced by Quinlan (1986). Finally, we obtain budget allocation table for each department using corresponding weights. We also derived material utilization by composing statistics utilization and association utilization from the knowledge collected from the circulation database. We obtained the degree of support for categories of a department by measuring the association in transactions using association rule mining algorithm and the confidence from the records found in circulation database. We obtained budget allocation table for each department corresponding to material utilization.

The rest of the chapter is organized as follows: Section 2 highlights some related papers that describe similar kind of researches. Section 3 shows the diagram of the database model, Section 4 describes the model in detail. Section 5 presents our research findings and finally Section 6 draws the conclusion.

2. RELATED WORKS

Many research works have been involved into budget allocation for library materials acquisition. Most of them are in common style and with a common objective, some have slightly different in objectives. We report findings from some of the researches related to our work below.

Kao, Chang, & Lin (2003) worked with the circulation database of Kun Shan University of Technology where they used ID3 (Quinlan, 1986) algorithm of Data Mining. Wu, Lee, & Kao (2004) used circulation statistics mechanism and an association rule was applied to discover knowledge. There are several models approached by several researchers like ABAMDM (Kao, Chang, & Lin, 2003), $KDBM_{LMA}$ (Wu, Lee, & Kao, 2004) to help derive the utilization of library material categories. Although many approaches and research reports have been extensively used to help library material acquisitions, the knowledge contained in circulation databases has rarely been used to investigate in-depth how the acquired materials are being used. Wu & Lee (2005) presented a decision support model for library material acquisition and budget allocation using the knowledge derived from circulation databases.

A good research work was done by Rahman & Yousop (2011) focused on three important goals:

1. A balance between continuing commitment and new initiatives,
2. A balance between resources to support undergraduate learning and those to support graduate work and research, and
3. A balance between subject disciplines.

In order to achieve these goals, the specific objectives of the study were to firstly, construct a mathematical model to determine the total amount of the library's budget that should be allocated to each faculty and secondly, construct a mathematical model for faculty's budget allocation in terms of acquisition of books and journals. The model must satisfy the budget allocated for every faculty and at the same time avoid overspending on the purchasing of materials.

Another analytical work by Wu et al. (2003) reports the most beneficial use of the allocated acquisition budget. Similar to their approach we have also explored knowledge in the circulation databases in-depth to relevantly reflect the need of budget allocation. In this research a data mining based model has been introduced based on the feature of ID3 algorithm to use the explanatory knowledge via information theory and statistics to derive appropriateness via utilization gain.

Meo, Psaila, & Ceri (1998) used association rule in their work where they had shown how to extract information from historical data based on the association between elements in transactions.

A very exceptional process has been used in a research by applying formal methods for material acquisitions. In the research work by Ho, Shyu, & Wu (2008), the authors used feature based approach for the acquisition that resembles the practical situations of academic libraries. Here some important features had been considered like the preference, price and its categories. Different techniques, e.g., simulated annealing; genetic algorithm and tabu search have been exploited in this study.

Another research work has been introduced by Knievel, Wicht, & Connaway (2011). In their research, the authors analyzed their work based on three distinct sets of data, the records of borrowing, holding and inter-library loan data at the University of Colorado. Like us they also used Library of Congress classifications for category comparison. They showed a way of the management of collection data from the circulation database of library.

A number of research works (Wise & Perushek, 2000; Wise & Perushek, 1996) used goal programming for the solution of allocating academic library's acquisitions funds. The availability of diverse materials and the varying demands of user needs in a variety of subject disciplines may represent a set of conflicting, incommensurate goals. Lexicographic linear goal programming offers an appropriate allocation methodology for determining an optimal solution with conflicting goals. This research work applies this methodology to 90 funds representing books and periodicals in 45 subject disciplines at the University of Tennessee, Knoxville (UT).

3. DATABASE MODEL

Modified NSU Library Database

We modified original NSU Library Database for our research as seen in Table 1.

Table 1. NSU Library database

Original NSU Library Database	Modified Database for Our Research
books	materials (material_id,call_number,category_code)
client	dept_member (member_id, department_id)
department	department(department_id, department_name)
loanarchive	circulation (material_id, member_id)
there is no table for material_category	*Newly created table for material_category(category_code,description)

There was no table for material_category. We created it with the help of Library of Congress Classification (Library Congress Reference, 2014). Portion of the table is shown in Table 2.

In original NSU books table (we named the books table in our database as materials), there was no category_code attribute. We generated the value for this attribute from call_number. The value of the category_code attribute is the first alphabetic digit part before starting of numeric digits of a call_number which coincides with category_codes described in Library of Congress Classification. For example, if call_number of any material is HD9940.B36Q83 331.4 Q2e 2000, then category_code of this material is HD which means (from Library of Congress Classification) as "Industries, Land use, Labor" that we have stored in material_category table.

Membership table is created by department and material_category tables which contain all departments, categories, and corresponding semantic strengths (we called it matching_level). The semantic strength can be expressed by the degree of the relation between a department and a material category. These values are management definable (Kao, Chang, & Lin, 2003). There are five levels for semantic strength (SS), for example, A, H, M, L, and N, where we consider A as absolutely matching, H as highly matching, M as matching, L as likely matching, N as absolutely not matching. The corresponding importance is: IS (0.4, 0.3, 0.2, 0.1, 0.0).

Membership table with department_id='EECS' and not matching_level='N' is presented in Table 3.

We created level table which describes importance of each level which is shown in Table 4.

Category importance/strength graph for department EECS is shown in Figure 1.

Table 2. Material_category table

Id	Category_Code	Description
1	A	General Works
2	AC	Collections. Series. Collected works
3	AE	Encyclopedias
4	AG	Dictionaries and other general reference works
5	AI	Indexes
6	AM	Museums. Collectors and collecting
7	AN	Newspapers
8	AP	Periodicals
9	AS	Academic and learned societies
10	AY	Yearbooks, Almanacs, Directories

Table 3. Category matching level (membership table)

Id	Department_Id	Category_Code	Matching_Level
13	EECS	BC	H
15	EECS	BF	L
61	EECS	GA	L
64	EECS	GE	L
65	EECS	GF	L
70	EECS	H	L
71	EECS	HA	M
72	EECS	HB	L
73	EECS	HC	L
74	EECS	HD	L

Table 4. Level with importance (level table)

Level	Importance
A	0.4
H	0.3
M	0.2
L	0.1
N	0.0

Figure 1. Strength of different categories for EECS department

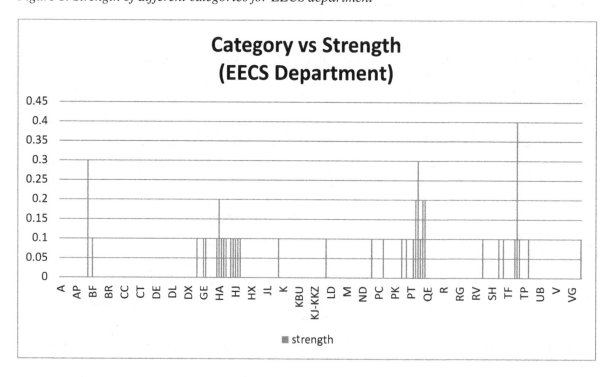

4. MODEL DESCRIPTION

The architecture of our model is illustrated in Figure 2. It contains two stages to achieve the objective of our research. The first stage is to pre-process the circulation data, and the second is to obtain descriptive knowledge, e.g., find out association rules between different categories of library materials; calculate the utilization gain that is used to derive the weights of acquisition budget allocation for departments.

Figure 2. Database model view

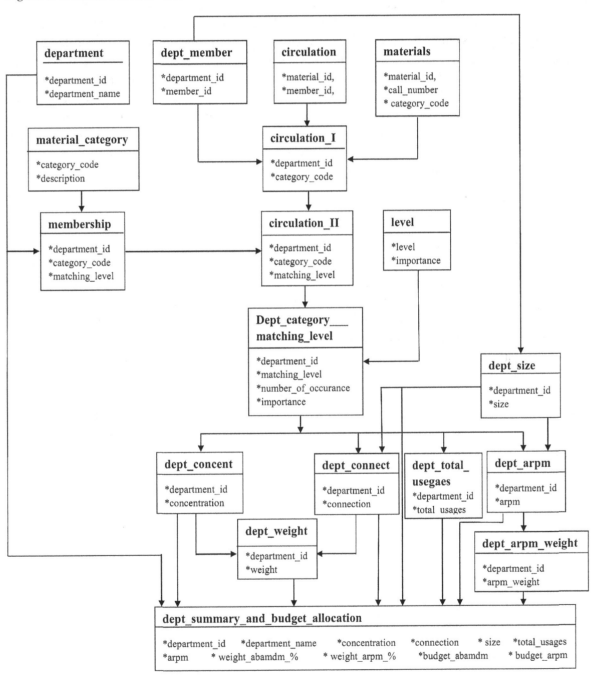

Pre Process of Circulation Data

Circulation table is the heart of Library Database. From this table we generated circulation_I table linking with materials and dept_member tables. In above we already mentioned that we built a new table material_category table with the help of Library of Congress Classification. Membership table is created by department and material_category tables. So membership table has number of rows which is equal to department size X category size. The table has attributes – department_id, category _code, matching_level (semantic strength). The semantic strength can be expressed as the degree of the relation between a department and a material category. These values are management definable. There are five levels for semantic strength, SS(A, H, M, L, N)—A: absolutely matching, H: highly matching, M: matching, L: likely matching, N: absolutely not matching. The corresponding importance is, IS(0.4, 0.3, 0.2, 0.1, 0.0). We created a level table which describes importance of each level.

Now from circulation_I and membership tables, circulation_II is generated. Here all records of original circulation table contained with attributes department_id, category_code and matching_level which is the semantic strength between a department and a category in membership table. After pre-process of circulation_II and linking the pre-processed table with level table, we got the important table titled dep_category_matching_level table which contains all department_id with total number of matching values and their relative importance. A partial view of the data is shown in Table 5.

Association Rule Mining

Now, all of our data analysis will be done from this circulation_II_particular_dept. From this table we generated transactions_members_particular_dept which contains all the member_ids those participated in circulation_ii_particular_dept table. For association rule analysis, all transactions are based on member_id. For a particular department these are in transactions_members particular_dept table.

Statistics utilization simply computes the sum of numeric value of strength for all different types of categories in circulation_II_particular_dept table. For example, if in ACT department, Category A occurs 7 times, its statistics utilization will be 7*0.4=2.8 (from Table 5). We can calculate statistics utilization from this table by applying sql command. A part of the relation for EECS department is given in Table 6.

On the other hand association utilization helps us to predict how the categories are associated which determine the strength of the usability of the material categories. This is why we cannot just rely on the statistics utilization to determine the quality of the library or to understand the perfect usability rather we have to consider the association utilization also. Before describing association utilization, we will briefly discuss association rules.

Table 5. Departments with total number of matching level (dep_category_matching_level_table)

Department_Id	Matching_Level	Number_of_Occurances	Importance
ACT	A	7	0.4
ACT	L	2	0.1
ACT	N	8	0.0
ADMI	H	2	0.3

Table 6. Statistics utilization

Department_Id	Category_Code	Statistics_U
EECS	B	0.0000
EECS	BC	3.3000
EECS	BF	1.8000
EECS	BJ	0.0000
EECS	BL	0.0000
EECS	BP	0.0000
EECS	CT	0.0000
EECS	D	0.0000
EECS	DA	0.0000
EECS	DC	0.0000

If P and Q are two categories of materials then an association rule can written as: $P \rightarrow Q(\alpha, \beta)$, where α and β are support and confidence respectively (Meo, Psaila, & Ceri,1998). Note that, according to the association theory P is being considered as the condition and Q as the conclusion. So, we can say that P can produce Q implicitly. We can give an example here like: an association rule "Electrical engineering => Mechanical engineering and machinery (0.32, 0.41)" can be stated as "if materials in category of Electrical engineering were borrowed in a transaction then Mechanical engineering and machinery was also borrowed in the same transaction where the support is 0.32 and the confidence is 0.41".

In a transaction, user can borrow more than one material. The ratio of the number of transactions observed to the total number of transactions is the support. On the other hand confidence is the ratio of the number of transactions to the number of antecedents.

Considering the above discussion, we firstly created a temporary table, temp_category_each _ transaction where all category_code for each member_id (considering to a transaction) in circulation_II_particular_dept, is temporarily stored uniquely. All possible association rules for this transaction is extracted from this table and further stored in accumulated_rules_for _support_confidence table. Thus all possible rules for all transactions (contained in transactions_members_particular_dept) is accumulated stored in this table. This storing process is done by running a php script. A snapshot of a part of this table is shown in Table 7.

The Table 7 view is for first few transactions (member_ids).

Secondly, we have to calculate support and confidence for every rule in above table. We have done this by two php programming scripts – one for support calculation - and the other for confidence calculation. The calculated values of support and confidence are then updated in accumulated_rules_for _support_confidence table. A portion of the data is shown in the Table 8.

Now, Association utilization for a material category A can be obtained via the following formula (Wu, Lee, & Kao, 2004):

Table 7. Accumulated_rules_for_support_confidence table

Department_Id	Member_Id	Category_Code_Cond	Category_Code_Cocl	Support	Confidence
EECS	CF02102282	QC	E	0.00	0.00
EECS	CF02102282	TK	E	0.00	0.00
EECS	CF02102282	E	QC	0.00	0.00
EECS	CF02102282	TK	QC	0.00	0.00
EECS	CF02102282	E	TK	0.00	0.00
EECS	CF02102282	QC	TK	0.00	0.00
EECS	CF02201982	T		0.00	0.00
EECS	CF03300003	QA		0.00	0.00
EECS	CF04203754	HF	HD	0.00	0.00
EECS	CF04203754	QA	HD	0.00	0.00

Table 8. Updated accumulated_rules_for_support_confidence_table

Department_Id	Member_Id	Category_Code_Cond	Category_Code_Cocl	Support	Confidence
EECS	CF02102282	QC	E	0.01	0.02
EECS	CF02102282	TK	E	0.01	0.01
EECS	CF02102282	E	QC	0.01	0.17
EECS	CF02102282	TK	QC	0.09	0.12
EECS	CF02102282	E	TK	0.01	0.17
EECS	CF02102282	QC	TK	0.09	0.27
EECS	CF02201982	T		0.00	0.00
EECS	CF03300003	QA		0.00	0.00
EECS	CF04203754	HF	HD	0.02	0.06
EECS	CF04203754	QA	HD	0.01	0.01

$$A(U) \equiv \sum_{i}^{k} n_k * \left[\theta * \text{support} + \omega * \text{cofidence} \right]$$

where, n_k is statistics utilization of k_{th} category that can produce A, θ is the intensity of support, ω is the intensity of confidence.

Running php programming, using above formula and using statistics_utilization and accumulated_rules _for _support_confidence tables, we can calculate association utilization and store them in association_utilization table. In our calculation we considered θ as 0.3 and ω as 0.7. A portion of the data from that relation is shown in Table 9.

Material utilization can be defined as the sum of the association utilization and the statistics utilization. We can get this applying following formula and store them in final_material_utilization table (Wu, Lee, & Kao, 2004).

Table 9. Association utilization

Department_Id	Category_Code	Statistics_U	Association_U
EECS	B	0.0000	25.6294
EECS	BC	3.3000	9.9412
EECS	BF	1.8000	7.5910
EECS	BJ	0.0000	0.0245
EECS	BL	0.0000	0.0000
EECS	BP	0.0000	4.3560
EECS	CT	0.0000	0.0560
EECS	D	0.0000	0.2177
EECS	DA	0.0000	0.0000
EECS	DC	0.0000	0.0000

$$M(U) \equiv n_A + A(U)$$

Here n_A is the total statistics utilization.

The final view of portion of this data is given in Table 10.

Obtaining Descriptive Knowledge and Utilization Gain

The descriptive knowledge is stored in table of dept_concent (department_id,concentration) and utilization gain in dept_connect (department_id,connection). Concentration represents how different categories of materials are used by the department. The less value of it indicates that the corresponding department uses materials in various subjects. The more value of it means that it is pure and categories are well distributed towards the department. The connection represents the utilization suitability of a department.

Table 10. Final material utilization

Department_Id	Category_Code	Statistics_U	Association_U	Material_U	Material_U%
EECS	B	0.0000	25.6294	25.6294	0.3452
EECS	BC	3.3000	9.9412	13.2412	0.1783
EECS	BF	1.8000	7.5910	9.3910	0.1265
EECS	BJ	0.0000	0.0245	0.0245	0.0003
EECS	BL	0.0000	0.0000	0.0000	0.0000
EECS	BP	0.0000	4.3560	4.3560	0.0587
EECS	CT	0.0000	0.0560	0.0560	0.0008
EECS	D	0.0000	0.2177	0.2177	0.0029
EECS	DA	0.0000	0.0000	0.0000	0.0000
EECS	DC	0.0000	0.0000	0.0000	0.0000

For example, the descriptive knowledge "EECS department used a good number of materials and most of them are in its subject" can relevantly explain the utilization of the EECS department.

Now we will obtain the concentration for a department. Applying the ID3 algorithm introduced by Quinlan (1986), the following formula has been introduced in (Kao, Chang, & Lin, 2003). We can found the Information (I) of all departments and Entropy(E) of each department:

$$I\left(n_{C_1}, n_{C_2}, \ldots\ldots, n_{C_n}\right)$$
$$= \left(-\frac{n_{C_1}}{M}\log_2\frac{n_{C_1}}{M}\right) + \ldots + \left(-\frac{n_{C_n}}{M}\log_2\frac{n_{C_m}}{M}\right) \tag{1}$$

n_{C_1} is the number of records that return to class C_i, $i=1,2,\ldots, n$ and M is the total number or records

$$E(D) = \sum_{i=1}^{t}\left[\left(\frac{n_{V_i}}{M}\right) I\left(a_{V_i C_1}, a_{V_i C_2}, \ldots a_{V_i Cm}\right)\right] \tag{2}$$

t is the number of different values that the department D can takes on; n_{V_i} is the total number of records that the department D takes value V_i, $i=1, 2,\ldots,t$; $a_{V_i C_j}$ is the total number or records that the department D takes value V_i and returns to class C_j, $i=1, 2,\ldots,t$ and $j=1,2,3\ldots,m$ and M is the total number of records.

From above parameters and using following formula (Kao, Chang, & Lin, 2003), we can calculate concentration for each department:

$$\text{Concentration (D)} = I\left(n_{C_1}, n_{C_2}, \ldots, n_{C_n}\right) - E(D) \tag{3}$$

We wrote PHP programming (using dept_category _matching _ level table) to find out information I and Entropy.

In dept_concent table these values are stored. The table view of portion of this data is shown in Table 11.

Then applying sql command, final concentration is stored in the Table 12.

Now, to obtain the connection for a department, we created the dept_connect (department_id,connection) table by using dept_category_matching_level table (presented in Table 5) and following formula (Kao, Chang, & Lin, 2003):

$$\text{Connection(D)} = \frac{\sum_{i}^{n} n_{L_i}\omega_{L_i}}{N_D} \tag{4}$$

where, N_{L_i} is the number of records of which the matching_level is L_i and ω_{L_i} is the importance of L_i. N_D is the number of members in a department that could be generated from dept_member table.

Table 11. Information and entry for different department table (dept_concent table)

Department_Id	Information	Entropy	Concentration
ACT	2.0898	0.0029	0.0000
ADMI	2.0898	0.0124	0.0000
ARC	2.0898	0.0033	0.0000
BBA	2.0898	0.9673	0.0000

Table 12. Concentration for different departments (updated dept_concent table)

Department_Id	Information	Entropy	Concentration
ACT	2.0898	0.0029	2.0869
ADMI	2.0898	0.0124	2.0774
ARC	2.0898	0.0033	2.0865
BBA	2.0898	0.9673	1.1225

The table view of portion of this data is given in Table 13.

Weight of each department is calculated by following formula (Kao, Chang, & Lin, 2003):

$$Weight(\mathrm{D}) = \frac{\alpha Concentration(D) + (1-\alpha)Connection(D)}{\sum_{i=1}^{m}\left[\alpha Concentration\left(D_i\right) + \left(1-\alpha\right)Connection\left(D_i\right)\right]} \tag{5}$$

It is an assumption that the importance of concentration α and connection $1-\alpha$ are management definable.

We assume this value as 0.3 in our calculation. In dept_weight table, we stored this value and shown in Table 14.

We also created dept_total_usages (department_id,total_usages) and dept_arpm(department_id, arpm) from dept_ category_matching_level table and then dept_arpm_weight(department_id, arpm_weight).

Table 13. Concentration for different departments (department_id, connection table)

Department_Id	Connection
ACT	0.1875
ADMI	0.0795
ARC	0.0490
BBA	0.1504

Table 14. Weight for different departments (dept_ weight table)

Department_Id	Weight
ACT	0.0560
ADMI	0.0502
ARC	0.0488
BBA	0.0327

Finally we created dept_summary_and_budget_allocation table, attributes of which are department_id, department_name, concentration, connection, size, total_usages, arpm, weight_%, weight_arpm_%, budget and budget_arpm.

The table view of left portion of this data is given in Table 15 and right portion in Table 16.

5. RESULTS AND FINDINGS

Material Utilization

There are two parts of our final material utilization data:

1. Statistics utilization,
2. Association utilization.

Table 15. Concentration and connection for departments (left portion of dept_summary_and_budget_allocation table)

Department_Id	Department_Name	Concentration	Connection	Size	Total_Usages
ACT	Accounts	2.0869	0.1875	16	17
ADMI	Administration	2.0774	0.0795	78	63
ARC	Architecture	2.0865	0.0490	104	17
BBA	Bachelor of Business Administration	1.1225	0.1504	7950	4384
BIOT	Biotechnology	2.0851	0.0607	89	20
ECO	Economics	1.9832	0.1670	721	434
EECS	Electrical Engineering and Computer Science	1.7048	0.1930	2201	1605
ENG	English	2.0323	0.1619	373	283
ENV	Environmental Studies	2.0416	0.1769	234	179
ETE	Electronic and Telecommunication Engineering	1.9373	0.2433	515	564

Table 16. Different budget allocation scheme (right portion of dept_summary_and_budget_allocation table)

Total_Usages	ARPM	Weight_%	Weight_ARPM%	Budget	Budget_ARPM
17	1.0625	5.6000	7.4300	56000.0000	74300.0000
63	0.8077	5.0200	5.6400	50200.0000	56400.0000
17	0.1635	4.8800	1.1400	48800.0000	11400.0000
4384	0.5514	3.2700	3.8500	32699.9980	38500.0000
20	0.2247	4.9400	1.5700	49400.0000	15699.9990
434	0.6019	5.2600	4.2100	52600.0000	42100.0000
1605	0.7292	4.7800	5.1000	47800.0000	51000.0000
283	0.7587	5.3500	5.3000	53500.0000	53000.0000
179	0.7650	5.4500	5.3500	54500.0000	53500.0000
564	1.0951	5.5600	7.6500	55600.0000	76500.0000

Table 17 indicates that the department of EECS had used 59 different categories. Part of the statistics utilization for each single category is shown in this table. For the association utilization, the total number of association rules generated was 1242 (including inverse rules), including all single categories in a transaction. Part of the association rules with their corresponding support and confidence are listed in Table 18. For example HF => HD (support(θ): 0.02, confidence(ω): 0.06). Part of the final material utilization is illustrated in Table 10. For example, the utilization of HF was 314.0806 and that of HD was 23.5616, for which the corresponding ratios to the total utilization were 4.2298% and 0.3173%.

Figure 3 illustrates the statistics utilization, association utilization, and material utilization against the categories. In this current study some particular observations as managerial implications are firstly, the category of "Electrical engineering and Electronics" (TK) has the highest value of material utilization which indicates that the department of EECS made the most use of "Electrical engineering and Electronics" at the same time we see the maximum utilization of association is also of this category but

Table 17. Statistics utilization by the department of 'EECS'

Department_Id	Category_Code	Statistics_U
EECS	B	0.0000
EECS	BC	3.3000
EECS	BF	1.8000
EECS	BJ	0.0000
EECS	BL	0.0000
EECS	BP	0.0000
EECS	CT	0.0000
EECS	D	0.0000
EECS	DA	0.0000
EECS	DC	0.0000

Table 18. Association rules by the department of 'EECS'

Department_Id	Member_Id	Category_Code_Cond	Category_Code_Cocl	Support	Confidence
EECS	CF02102282	QC	E	0.01	0.02
EECS	CF02102282	TK	E	0.01	0.01
EECS	CF02102282	E	QC	0.01	0.17
EECS	CF02102282	TK	QC	0.09	0.12
EECS	CF02102282	E	TK	0.01	0.17
EECS	CF02102282	QC	TK	0.09	0.27
EECS	CF02201982	T		0.00	0.00
EECS	CF03300003	QA		0.00	0.00
EECS	CF04203754	HF	HD	0.02	0.06
EECS	CF04203754	QA	HD	0.01	0.01

Figure 3. Final material utilization against the categories

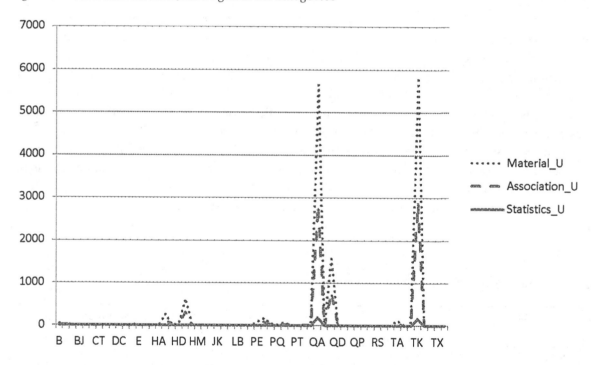

the statistic utilization of this category is not the highest one. From this behaviour we can say that this category was associated to others in most of its transactions. On the other hand if we keep eyes on the category of Mathematics (QA) not having the highest value of association even not that of material utilization, gained the highest value of statistics utilization. This makes sense that the association utilization of a particular department has not been dominated by its statistic utilization while it highly depends on the occurrences associated with other categories in transactions. Table 19 depicts this.

Table 19. Final material utilization (order by material_u)

Department_Id	Category_Code	Statistics_U	Association_U	Material_U	Material_U_%
EECS	TK	171.2000	2713.1975	2884.3975	38.8452
EECS	QA	203.1000	2621.4482	2824.5481	38.0392
EECS	QC	15.0000	770.3930	785.3930	10.5772
EECS	HF	5.8000	308.2806	314.0806	4.2298
EECS	HB	4.3000	127.1036	131.4036	1.7697
EECS	PK	0.0000	87.9510	87.9510	1.1845
EECS	TA	1.6000	66.7864	68.3864	0.9210
EECS	PE	2.0000	41.7944	43.7944	0.5898
EECS	PR	1.6000	36.5954	38.1954	0.5144
EECS	B	0.0000	25.6294	25.6294	0.3452
EECS	PN	0.9000	24.0236	24.9236	0.3357
EECS	HD	1.8000	21.7616	23.5616	0.3173
EECS	HG	1.7000	14.4597	16.1597	0.2176
EECS	Q	2.2000	11.8721	14.0721	0.1895
EECS	BC	3.3000	9.9412	13.2412	0.1783
EECS	DS	0.0000	12.1021	12.1021	0.1630
EECS	PQ	0.0000	11.9161	11.9161	0.1605

Finally, category TK shows the highest material utilization (38.8452%), and thus was allocated the highest budget for this category to reply for its demands. That means the percentage for each category utilized reflects the practical usage information. This indicates on which the department of EECS relies for the next year material acquisitions operation.

Budget Allocation

By utilizing ID3 algorithm by Formula (4) and Formula (5), the results including concentration, connection, weights and Average Record Per Member (ARPM) and allocated acquisition budget for our analysis was shown in Table 20. To determine the budget amount for each depaertment total budget has been considered 1,00,00,000 BDT. Our budget % and ARPM % are percentages of this total budget amount. The results found by ARPM was also included in Table XX. The relationship between concentration and connection was shown in Figure 4 while the number of members, the number of records, and allocated budget is shown in Figure 5.

To fit the graph in this small area, the values of the budget were devided by 100 in Figure 5. From the tables and figures given above, it was found that:

1. Although the department of Electronic and Telecommunication Engineering (ETE) showed the highest ARPM (1.0951 in Table 20), it has obtained the highest connection but not the budget. Good connection and ARPM value here indicates that the members of EECS Department has made a good use of the materials and all of them are related to their areas.

Table 20. The result via our analysis and Arpm (dept_summary_and_budget_allocation table)

Dept_Id	Department_Name	Concentration	Connection	Size	Total_Usage	ARPM	Weight_%	Weight_ARPM_%	Budget	Budget_ARPM
ACT	Accounts	2.0869	0.1875	16	17	1.0625	5.6	7.43	56000	74300
ADMI	Administration	2.0774	0.0795	78	63	0.8077	5.02	5.64	50200	56400
ARC	Architecture	2.0865	0.049	104	17	0.1635	4.88	1.14	48800	11400
BBA	Bachelor of Business Administration	1.1225	0.1504	7950	4384	0.5514	3.27	3.85	32700	38500
BIOT	Biotechnology	2.0851	0.0607	89	20	0.2247	4.94	1.57	49400	15699.999
ECO	Economics	1.9832	0.167	721	434	0.6019	5.26	4.21	52600	42100
EECS	Electrical Engineering & Computer Science	1.7048	0.193	2201	1605	0.7292	4.78	5.1	47800	51000
ENG	English	2.0323	0.1619	373	283	0.7587	5.35	5.3	53500	53000
ENV	Environmental Studies	2.0416	0.1769	234	179	0.765	5.45	5.35	54500	53500
ETE	Electronic & Telecommunication Engineering	1.9373	0.2433	515	564	1.0951	5.56	7.65	55600	76500
GCE	General & Continuing Education	2.0875	0.0229	109	25	0.2294	4.75	1.6	47500	16000.001
IS	Information Services	2.0841	0.18	15	27	1.8	5.56	12.58	55600	125800
LIB	Library	2.0812	0.1033	30	114	3.8	5.15	26.56	51500	265600
LSC	Life Sciences	2.0891	0.0343	175	16	0.0914	4.81	0.64	48100	6400
MBA	Master of Business Administration	2.0455	0.0492	759	226	0.2978	5	2.08	50000	20800
MDS	Master of Development Studies	2.0898	0.0923	26	6	0.2308	5.11	1.61	51100	16100.001
MPH	Masters in Public Health	2.0881	0.0701	147	28	0.1905	5	1.33	50000	13300
PHAR	Pharmacy	2.0683	0.1202	585	208	0.3556	5.21	2.49	52100	24900
REG	Registrar	2.0855	0.0079	114	55	0.4825	4.67	3.37	46700	33700
UKN	Unknown	2.0898	0	28	2	0.0714	4.64	0.5	46400	5000

Figure 4. Department wise concentration-connection graph

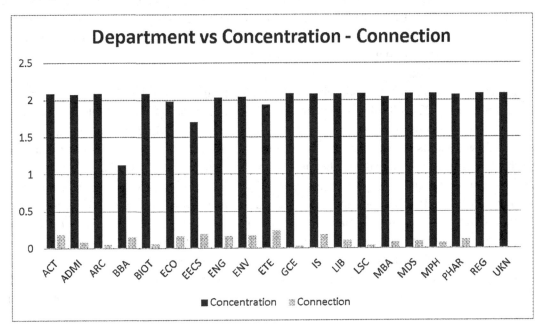

Figure 5. Department vs. member, total_usages and final budget (budget/100)

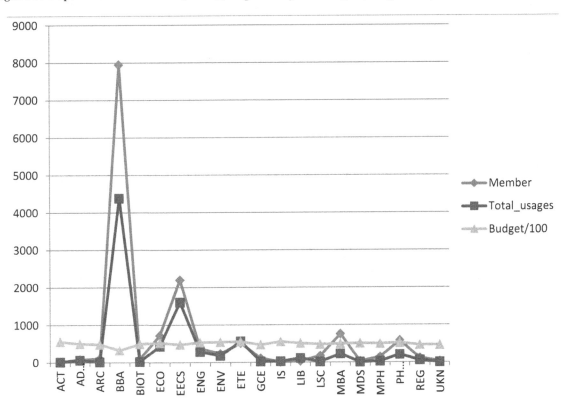

2. In Figure 4, the department of Master of Development Studies (MDS) showed the highest concentration (2.0898 in Table 20). This indicated that the categories used were equally distributed. However, the Figure 4 indicated that it did not get a high value of connection. This indicated that most of the materials used were not in its subject. Figure 5 supported this information and showed that it got the low budget.

3. In Figure 4, the department of Bachelor of Business Administration (BBA) got the lowest value of concentration (1.1225 in Table 20), but the largest number of usage (4,384 in Table 20). Accordingly, it was shown that it used the materials in a variety of categories, which indicated that part of these materials were in its subject, but part were not. Therefore, the total connection it found was not high (in Figure 4), and so was the allocated acquisition budget (in Figure 5).

4. In Figure 4, it was found that the department of ETE got the highest value of connection (0.2433 in Table 20), but the observed concentration was considered to be low (1.9373) in comparison to others (in Figure 4) and the number of members was not high (515 in Table 20). However, it finally got almost highest allocated budget (55600.00 in Table 20). It can be said that the value of importance of concentration took a very significant role in this case.

5. The acquisition budget allocated via ARPM depended totally upon the ARPM. Figure 6 provided the information that the result produced by our analysis was fairly different from that by ARPM.

Figure 6. The allocated acquisition budget via our analysis and ARPM for 20 departments

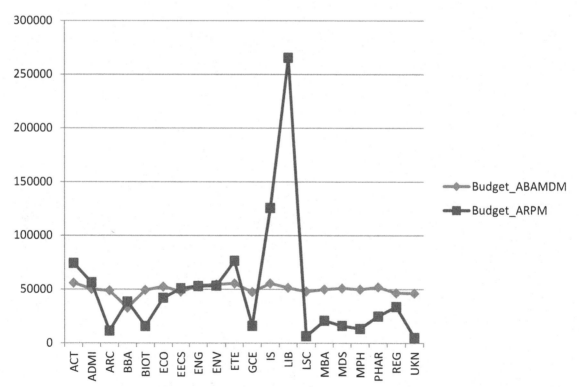

6. CONCLUSION

We derive the statistics utilization and association utilization from circulation databases. Statistics utilization is a part of this study but this was never the aim to determine the amount of transaction for each material category, rather we involved association utilization using association rule to predict the user's need. To achieve this, we collected circulation data for about 8 years and processed the data to get ready for knowledge discovery. We have mined the library circulation data to understand the proportion of budget that should be allocated for the next academic year for different departments. We employed SQL to help pre-process the circulation data if necessary. We also employed the information theory to measure the concentration of categories observed in the circulation data table, and at the same time the utilization connection to derive the weights as a decisional base of acquisition budget allocation with the help of goal programming using a high-level language. In our case we used PHP with MySQL database. The knowledge discovered by our analysis can be used to support making decisions in regard to the acquisition library materials as well budget allocation for North South University or any other university having the similar operation process. This knowledge will help in a great deal to allocate the budget for the library and will save a large amount of time and cost. It also helps to reduce mismanagement of library resources by ensuring appropriate availability of materials for every members of the library.

Finally, a core question remains while budgeting and that is how to capitalize the investment to buy right things. It will really be a ceaseless discovery of unknown information in historical data to support the decisions related to the allocation of budget.

REFERENCES

Budd, J. M., & Adams, K. (1989). Allocation formulas in practice. *Library Acquisitions: Practice and Theory*, *13*(4), 381–390. doi:10.1016/0364-6408(89)90049-5

Hamaker, C. (1995). Time series circulation data for collection development or: You can't intuit that. *Library Acquisition: Practice and Theory*, *19*(2), 191–195. doi:10.1016/0364-6408(95)00019-6

Ho, T. F., Shyu, S. J., & Wu, Y. L. (2008). Material acquisitions in academic libraries. In *Proceedings of Asia-Pacific Services Computing Conference (APSCC)*, (pp. 1465-1470). IEEE.

Kao, C., Chang, H. C., & Lin, C. H. (2003). Decision support for the academic library acquisition budget allocation via circulation database mining. *Information Processing & Management*, *39*(1), 133–147. doi:10.1016/S0306-4573(02)00019-5

Knievel, J. E., Wicht, H., & Connaway, L. S. (2011). Use of circulation statistics and interlibrary loan data in collection management. *College & Research Libraries*, *67*(1), 35–49. doi:10.5860/crl.67.1.35

Library Congress Reference. (2014). Retrieved from http://en.wikipedia.org/wiki/Library_of_Congress_Classification

Meo, R., Psaila, G., & Ceri, S. (1998). An extension to SQL for mining association rules. *Data Mining and Knowledge Discovery*, *2*(2), 195–224. doi:10.1023/A:1009774406717

Quinlan, J. R. (1986). Induction of decision tree. *Machine Learning*, *1*(1), 81–106. doi:10.1007/BF00116251

Rahman, S. A., & Yousop, N. M. (2011). Modeling of budget allocation for university library. *Journal of Statistical Modeling and Analytics*, 2(2), 1–8.

Wise, K., & Perushek, D. E. (1996). Linear goal programming for academic library acquisitions allocations. *Library Acquisitions: Practice & Theory*, 20(3), 311–327. doi:10.1016/0364-6408(96)00065-8

Wise, K., & Perushek, D. E. (2000). Goal Programming as a solution technique. *Library & Information Science Research*, 22(2), 165–183. doi:10.1016/S0740-8188(99)00052-3

Wu, C. H. et al. (2003). Data mining applied to material acquisition budget allocation for libraries: Design and development. *Expert Systems with Applications*, 25(3), 401–411. doi:10.1016/S0957-4174(03)00065-4

Wu, C. H., & Lee, T. Z. (2005). Material acquisitions using discovery informatics approach. In Encyclopaedia of Data Warehousing and Mining, (pp. 705-709). Hershey, PA: IGI Global.

Wu, C. H., Lee, T. Z., & Kao, S. C. (2004). Knowledge discovery applied to material acquisitions for libraries. *Information Processing & Management*, 40(4), 709–725. doi:10.1016/j.ipm.2003.08.010

KEY TERMS AND DEFINITIONS

Budget Allocation: Try to allocate limited budget to satisfy most of the users' needs.

Circulation Data: Loan information about book, CD etc. that are borrowed by users of library.

Data Mining: Method to reveal hidden information from data.

Decision Tree: A tree like structure that is used for classification of different records.

Knowledge Discovery: Explore data to find some useful information.

Material Acquisition: Acquire or make a reservation of materials like books, cd etc to facilitate the need of the users of library.

SQL-Structured Query Language: A special language to retrieve data from a computerized database.

Chapter 21
Some Aspects of Estimators for Variance of Normally Distributed Data

N. Hemachandra
Indian Institute of Technology Bombay, India

Puja Sahu
Indian Institute of Technology Bombay, India

ABSTRACT

Normally distributed data arises in various contexts and often one is interested in estimating its variance. The authors limit themselves in this chapter to the class of estimators that are (positive) multiples of sample variances. Two important qualities of estimators are bias and variance, which respectively capture the estimator's accuracy and precision. Apart from the two classical estimators for variance, they also consider the one that minimizes the Mean Square Error (MSE) and another that minimizes the maximum of the square of the bias and variance, the minmax estimator. This minmax estimator can be identified as a fixed point of a suitable function. For moderate to large sample sizes, the authors argue that all these estimators have the same order of MSE. However, they differ in the contribution of bias to their MSE. The authors also consider their Pareto efficiency in squared bias versus variance space. All the above estimators are non-dominated (i.e., they lie on the Pareto frontier).

1. INTRODUCTION

It is well known that normally distributed data sets are observed in numerous situations. One major reason for this is the following situation. Suppose one has a random error which is the aggregate of a large collection of errors. Then, under mild conditions, by the classical Central Limit Theorem and its variants, as discussed in Billingsley (1995), Chung (2001), Fristedt and Gray (1997), Kallenberg (2002), Wasserman (2005), etc., the standardized sum of the collections of errors (and hence suitable scaling of the centered random error) has approximately the distribution of a zero mean normal random variable.

DOI: 10.4018/978-1-4666-7272-7.ch021

A central theme in statistical inference is that given a sample from a parametric distribution, one is interested in finding a suitable 'best' estimator for a parameter of the distribution. Most of such inference procedures concentrate on the unbiased estimators and finding the 'best' (i.e., the one having the minimum variance) amongst them. These are the classical Uniformly Minimum Variance Unbiased Estimators, (UMVUE) (Casella & Berger, 2002), (DeGroot & Schervish, 2012), etc. However, one can tradeoff the bias of the estimator to achieve lower variance and hence find a better estimator in terms of Mean Squared Error (MSE) as MSE is the sum of squared bias and variance of the estimator, leading to the optimal MSE estimator. Further, one can view both squared bias and variance of an estimator as equally important and hence search for an estimator that minimizes the maximum of these two (undesirable) quantities, the minmax estimator.

In fact, one can view MSE as capturing a quality of an estimator and hence compare various estimators on the basis of their MSEs. Also, one can compare estimators in terms of the percentage of squared bias in MSE. Yet an another way to compare estimators is to view this comparison as a multi-criteria problem involving squared bias and variance and then search for those estimators that are Pareto optimal: the set of estimators such that reducing of one of these quantities leads to increase in the other quantity.

In this chapter, we illustrate the above aspects of estimators and various measures of quality of estimators when the underlying data is normally distributed and the parameter we are interested is the variance of this normal random variable.

Consider a random sample $(X_1, X_2, ..., X_n)$ of size n from a $N(\mu, \sigma^2)$ distribution and consider the two cases for estimation of population variance (σ^2): μ known and μ unknown. For μ known case, the classical unbiased estimator is

$$\hat{\sigma}^2 = \frac{1}{n} \sum_{i=1}^{n} \left(X_i - \mu \right)^2 \tag{1}$$

But one can also consider the following estimators of σ^2:

$$\bar{S}_c^2 = c \sum_{i=1}^{n} \left(X_i - \mu \right)^2, \tag{2}$$

parameterized by coefficients, $c > 0$. $\bar{S}_c^2$ can be viewed as scalings of $\hat{\sigma}^2$.

Similarly for the μ unknown case, we decided to look for estimators for σ^2 of the form

$$S_c^2 = c \sum_{i=1}^{n} \left(X_i - \bar{X} \right)^2, c > 0. \tag{3}$$

It is assumed that the sample size, n, is at least two. Also, we can restrict ourselves to $c > 0$ as estimators of this nature dominate the zero estimator corresponding to $c = 0$, both on MSE as well as minmax criteria. Details on this and related points are in given in the technical report (Hemachandra & Sahu, 2014).

It is known (Casella & Berger, 2002), since χ_n^2 is a random variable of location-scale exponential family, that

$$\frac{\overline{S}_c^2}{c\sigma^2} \sim \chi_n^2,$$

(4)

$$\frac{S_c^2}{c\sigma^2} \sim \chi_{n-1.}^2$$

(5)

2. DIFFERENT RISK CRITERIA AND ESTIMATORS BASED ON THEM

A loss function measures the quality of an estimator. Bias of an estimator can be interpreted as capturing its accuracy while variance can be interpreted as measuring its precision, (Casella & Berger, 2002), (Alpaydin, 2010). One of the most common methods is minimizing the variance over the class of unbiased estimators. This gives us what is called the Uniform Minimum Variance Unbiased Estimator (UMVUE). Another popular loss function is mean squared error (MSE) which is the sum of square of the bias and variance, (Casella & Berger, 2002). So, MSE can be viewed as capturing the tradeoff between the bias and variance of an estimator (Friedman, 1997). Minimizing MSE can be interpreted as minimizing the weighted average of square of bias and variance where weights are equal. Treating each of the squared bias and the variance of an estimator as dissatisfactions associated with that estimator, minimizing the maximum of them can be viewed as attempt towards achieving a certain notion of fairness (towards squared bias and variance); thus, a minmax estimator can be viewed as an estimator with this property. Also, both the optimal MSE estimator and minmax estimator are biased estimators, unlike UMVUE.

2.1 Uniformly Minimum Variance Unbiased Estimator (UMVUE)

The UMVUE is, as the name suggests, the estimator that has the minimum variance among the unbiased estimators for the parameter of interest. Among the two basic measures of the quality of an estimator, the bias is more important factor for UMVUE than the variance. Hence, first the bias is brought down to its minimum possible value, that is zero, and then the 'best' is picked from this class of estimators with the minimum value of bias.

However, the existence of an unbiased estimator cannot always be guaranteed. As pointed out by (Doss & Sethuraman, 1989), when an unbiased estimator does not exist, any attempt to reduce the bias below a given value can result in substantial increment in the variance, thereby providing an even worse estimator on the MSE grounds.

The UMVUE can be obtained analytically by identifying the coefficient, c, as a function of sample size, n, (for a given n) at which squared bias, B_c^2, becomes zero. Note that we could uniquely pin down the coefficient c (and hence the UMVUE) because the set of unbiased estimators for σ^2 is a singleton for both the cases: μ known and μ unknown.

1. **Case:** μ known:

$$B_c = 0$$

$$\Rightarrow E\left(\bar{S}_c^2\right) - \sigma^2 = 0 \lim_{x \to \infty}$$

$$\Rightarrow c\sigma^2 E\left[\frac{\bar{S}_c^2}{c\sigma^2}\right] - \sigma^2 = 0$$

$$\Rightarrow (nc - 1)\sigma^2 = 0 \text{ (using (4))}$$

$$\Rightarrow c = \frac{1}{n} \tag{6}$$

Thus, the UMVUE for σ^2 in the μ known case is $\hat{\sigma}^2 = \frac{1}{n}\sum_{i=1}^{n}\left(X_i - \mu\right)^2$.

2. **Case: μ unknown:**

$$B_c = 0$$

$$\Rightarrow E\left(S_c^2\right) - \sigma^2 = 0$$

$$\Rightarrow c\sigma^2 E\left[\frac{S_c^2}{c\sigma^2}\right] - \sigma^2 = 0$$

$$\Rightarrow [(n - 1)c - \sigma^2] = 0 \text{ (using (5))}$$

$$\Rightarrow c = \frac{1}{n - 1}. \tag{7}$$

The UMVUE for σ^2 in the μ unknown case is $S^2 = \frac{1}{n - 1}\sum_{i=1}^{n}\left(X_i - \bar{X}\right)^2$.

Suppose, for a given sample size, we plot squared bias values on the horizontal axis and variance values on the vertical axis. Then the UMVUE can be determined on the graph as the point where the graph touches the vertical axis, i.e., where the squared bias (and hence the bias) becomes zero. The graphical method for finding the UMVUE for σ^2 for the case of known mean, μ, gives us the estimators shown in Figure 1.

2.2 The Optimal MSE Estimator

The UMVUE gives the best estimator in the class of unbiased estimators. But an optimal MSE estimator tries to minimize the MSE which is the sum of squared bias and variance of the estimator. Thus, the optimal MSE estimator has lower MSE value than the UMVUE since it has significant decrease in the variance as compared to the increment in the bias value.

MSE takes into account both the squared bias and variance and weighs them equally. Hence, it makes sure that the performance of the estimator does not overlook the effects of any one of these components.

Figure 1. UMVUE for normal variance (σ^2) for different sample sizes (n)

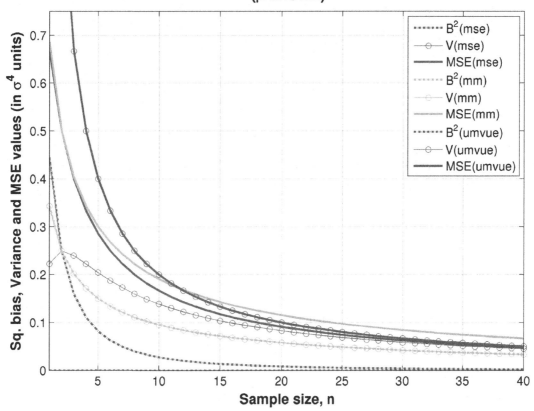

This helps us extend the domain of comparison to the biased estimators as well, unlike the case of UM-VUE, where by definition, we look only for unbiased estimators and choose the optimal amongst them

We use the MSE value as criterion for comparing different estimators in a later section. Hence, as a baseline case, we now derive the optimal MSE estimator here. But before that we define the bias and the variance of an estimator, denoted by B_c and V_c, respectively.

First consider the μ known case. The bias B_c for an estimator $\overline{S}_c^2$ is obtained as:

$$B_c = E\left(\overline{S}_c^2\right) - \sigma^2$$

$$\Rightarrow B_c = c\sigma^2 E\left(\frac{\overline{S}_c^2}{c\sigma^2}\right) - \sigma^2$$

$$\Rightarrow B_c = \left(nc - 1\right)\sigma^2, \tag{8}$$

and the variance of $\bar{S}_c^2$ is given by:

$$V_c = \text{Var}\left(\bar{S}_c^2\right)$$

$$\Rightarrow V_c = c^2\sigma^4\text{Var}\left(\frac{\bar{S}_c^2}{c\sigma^2}\right)$$

$$\Rightarrow V_c = 2nc^2\sigma^4. \tag{9}$$

Similarly for an estimator S_c^2 of σ^2 in the μ unknown case, we obtain the bias and variance values as:

$$B_c = \left[(n-1)c-1\right]\sigma^2 \tag{10}$$

$$V_c = 2(n-1)c^2\sigma^4. \tag{11}$$

Using the property of chi-squared distribution, the MSE of an estimator for the two cases can be calculated as:

1. **Case:** μ known:

$$\left(\text{MSE}(\bar{S}_c^2) = bias\left(\bar{S}_c^2\right)\right)^2 + Var\left(\bar{S}_c^2\right)$$
$$= \left(\left(nc-1\right)\sigma^2\right)^2 + 2nc^2\sigma^4$$

$$= \sigma^4\left[\left(n^2+2n\right)c^2 \overset{*}{-} 2nc + 1\right] \tag{12}$$

The minimum MSE estimator can be found by setting:

$$\frac{\partial}{\partial c}\text{MSE}\left(\bar{S}_c^2\right) = 0$$

$$\Rightarrow d / dc\sigma^4\left[2c\left(n^2+2n\right) - 2n\right] = 0$$

$$\Rightarrow c_{MSE}^* = \frac{1}{n+2}\cdot\left(\because n \geq 1, \sigma^4 \neq 0\right) \tag{13}$$

Thus the minimum MSE estimator for variance of normal distribution when mean is known is:

$$\bar{S}^2_{c*_{MSE}} = \frac{1}{n+2} \sum_{i=1}^{n} \left(X_i - \mu \right)^2 \tag{14}$$

2.   **Case:** μ unknown:

By similar analysis as in previous case,

$$MSE(S_c^2) = [E(S_c^2) - \sigma^2]^2 + Var(S_c^2)$$

$$= \left[\left(n-1 \right) c - 1\sigma^2 \right]^2 + 2 \left(n-1 \right) c^2 \sigma^4$$

$$= \sigma^4 \left[\left(n^2 - 1 \right) c^2 - 2 \left(n-1 \right) c + 1 \right] \tag{15}$$

The minimum MSE estimator in this case is obtained as:

$$\frac{\partial}{\partial c} MSE \left(S_c^2 \right) = 0$$

$$\Rightarrow d \, / \, dc \sigma^4 \left[\left(n^2 - 1 \right) c^2 - 2 \left(n-1 \right) c + 1 \right] = 0$$

$$\Rightarrow c^*_{MSE} = \frac{1}{n+1} \cdot \left(\because n > 1, \sigma^4 \neq 0 \right) \tag{16}$$

Thus the minimum MSE estimator for variance of normal distribution when mean is unknown is

$$S^2_{c*_{MSE}} = \frac{1}{n+1} \sum_{i=1}^{n} \left(X_i - \bar{X} \right)^2 \tag{17}$$

2.2.1 Graphical Illustration

We can identify the optimal MSE estimator for a given sample size, n, graphically by plotting the MSE values (in σ^4 units) versus the coefficient values and picking the coefficient value that has the minimum MSE value on this plot.

We consider the case where the mean, μ, is known and identify the optimal MSE estimator as described above (See Figure 2). The marked points are the coordinates corresponding to coefficient of optimal MSE estimator, c^*_{MSE}, and its MSE value, $MSE \left(\bar{S}^2_{c*_{MSE}} \right)$, which are:

$$c^*_{\text{MSE}} = \frac{1}{n+2} \text{ and } \text{MSE}\left(\bar{S}^2_{c^*_{\text{MSE}}}\right) = \frac{2\sigma^4}{n+2}$$

Hence, as n increases, c^*_{MSE} and $\text{MSE}\left(\bar{S}^2_{c^*_{\text{MSE}}}\right)$ decrease in value, which is also verified from the graph.

Consider the graph of squared bias versus variance values for estimators with coefficients, c in Figure 3 and Figure 4. To spot the optimal MSE estimator on this graph, we draw a line with slope -1 and translate it so at we get a tangent to the curve. At this point of intersection, sits the optimal MSE estimator.

Figure 2. Coefficient of optimal MSE estimator of σ^2 for different sample sizes (n)

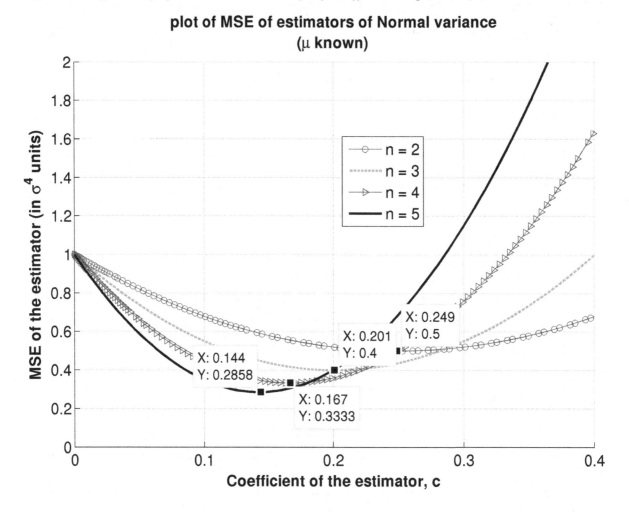

Figure 3. Optimal MSE, classical and minmax estimator of σ^2 with known μ; (a) sample size $n = 2$, (b) sample size $n = 13$

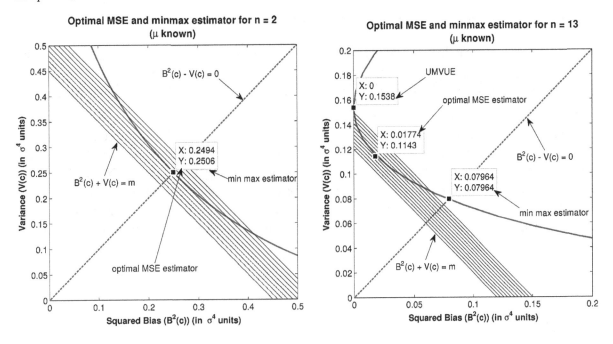

Figure 4. Optimal MSE, classical and minmax estimator of σ^2 with unknown μ; (a) sample size $n = 2$, (b) sample size $n = 12$

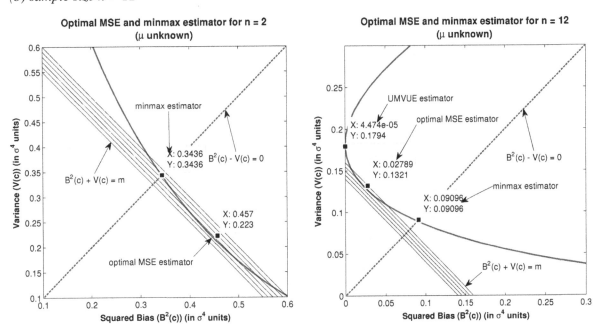

2.3 The Minmax Estimator

Now, instead of using MSE criterion which takes sum of the squared bias and the variance of the estimator, we propose to look at these quantities as vector $\begin{pmatrix} B_c^2 \\ V_c \end{pmatrix}$ and try to find an estimator that compares the two components on the same scale by using minmax criterion: $\min_c \max \left\{ B_c^2, V_c \right\}$. B_c^2 and V_c denote the squared bias and the variance of the estimator.

Squared bias and variance are two different criteria for comparing the estimators; yet it is difficult to weigh one against the other. Even though MSE, as a sum of squared bias and variance of the estimator, gives equal weightage to both of them, the minmax criterion explicitly treats squared bias and variance as equally important and competing risks. Such a minmax estimator minimizes the maximum of squared bias and variance among all the estimators of form given by (2) and (3), as the case may be. minmax estimator helps us look at the worst case risk. We also interpret the minmax estimator as a fixed point for a suitable function.

1. **Case:** μ known:

$$\min_c \max_{B_c^2, V_c} \left(\overline{S}_c^2 \right) = \min_c \max \{ (nc-1)^2 \sigma^4, 2nc^2 \sigma^4 \}$$

where σ^4 is just a positive scaling factor. Now,

$$B_c^2 \geq Vc$$

$$\Leftrightarrow (nc-1)^2 \geq 2nc^2$$

$$\Leftrightarrow (n^2 - 2n)c^2 - 2nc + 1 \geq 0.$$

For a fixed n, the RHS term is a quadratic in c, whose sign can be deduced by looking at its roots. The roots of this quadratic are given as:

$$c = \frac{\sqrt{n} \pm \sqrt{2}}{\sqrt{n}\,(n-2)}$$

Thus, from the definitions of B_c^2 and V_c, one has that

$$B_c^2 \geq V_c \text{ when } 0 \leq c \leq \frac{\sqrt{n} - \sqrt{2}}{\sqrt{n}\,(n-2)} \text{ or } c = \frac{\sqrt{n} + \sqrt{2}}{\sqrt{n}\,(n-2)},$$

and, $B_c^2 < V_c$ when $\dfrac{\sqrt{n} - \sqrt{2}}{\sqrt{n}\,(n-2)} < c < \dfrac{\sqrt{n} + \sqrt{2}}{\sqrt{n}\,(n-2)}$.

The roots $\dfrac{\sqrt{n} - \sqrt{2}}{\sqrt{n}\,(n-2)}$ and $\dfrac{\sqrt{n} + \sqrt{2}}{\sqrt{n}\,(n-2)}$ are the points where $B_c^2 = V_c$. So the minmax estimator is chosen by comparing the variance values at these roots. (We chose variance values over squared bias values for the ease of comparison.)

Say the two roots are c_1 and c_2, then

$$V_{c_1} = 2nc_1^2 = \frac{2(n + 2 - 2\sqrt{2n})}{(n+2)^2}$$

$$V_{c_2} = 2nc_2^2 = \frac{2(n + 2 - 2\sqrt{2n})}{(n-2)^2}$$

Clearly, $V_{c_1} < V_{c_2}$ for $n \geq 1$ except $n = 2$.

Hence, the coefficient of the minmax estimator is

$$c_{mm}^* = \frac{\sqrt{n} - \sqrt{2}}{\sqrt{n}(n-2)} = \frac{1}{\sqrt{n}(\sqrt{n} + \sqrt{2})}, \text{ for } n \neq 2 \tag{18}$$

a. **Special Case:** $n = 2$:

$$B_c^2 \geq V_c$$

$$\Leftrightarrow (2c - 1)^2 \geq 4c^2$$

$$\Leftrightarrow 1 - 4c \geq 0.$$

$$c_{mm}^* = -\frac{1}{4}.$$

This is same as that given by (18) for $n = 2$.

Also, $c_{MSE}^* = \dfrac{1}{n+1} = \dfrac{1}{4}$. Thus, the optimal MSE estimator and the minmax estimator for variance when mean is known are same when sample size is 2.

2. **Case:** μ unknown:

$$\min_{c\ B_c^2 V_c} \max(S_c^2)$$

$$= \sigma^4 \min_c \max\{[(n-1)c-1]^2, 2(n-1)c^2\}$$

since σ^4 is just a positive scaling factor. Now

$$B_c^2 \geq V_c$$

$$\Leftrightarrow [(n-1)c-1]^2 \geq 2(n-1)c^2$$

$$\Leftrightarrow (n^2-4n+3)c^2 - 2(n-1)c + 1 \geq 0$$

The roots of the above quadratic equation are:

$$c = \frac{(\sqrt{n-1}) \pm \sqrt{2}}{\sqrt{(n-1)(n-3)}}.$$

As in the previous case, we compare the variance values at these two roots to choose the coefficient of the minmax estimator. Say the two roots are c_1 and c_2, then

$$V_{c_1} = 2(n-1)c_1^2 = \frac{2(n+1-2\sqrt{2(n-1)})}{(n-3)^2}$$

$$V_{c_2} = 2(n-1)c_2^2 = \frac{2(n+1-2\sqrt{2(n-1)})}{(n-3)^2}.$$

Comparing the numerators we can say that $V_{c_1} < V_{c_2}$ for all $n \geq 2$ except $n=3$. Hence,

$$c_{mm}^* = \frac{(\sqrt{n-1})-\sqrt{2}}{(\sqrt{n-1})(n-3)} = \frac{1}{(\sqrt{n-1})(\sqrt{n-1}+\sqrt{2})}, \text{ for } n \neq 3. \tag{19}$$

a. **Special Case: $n=3$:**

$$B_c^2 \geq V_c$$

$$\Leftrightarrow 1-4c \geq 0$$

$$c_{mm}^* = \frac{1}{4}.$$

Again, this is same as that given by $c_{mm}^* = \dfrac{(\sqrt{n-1}) - \sqrt{2}}{(\sqrt{n-1})(n-3)} = \dfrac{1}{(\sqrt{n-1})(\sqrt{n-1} + \sqrt{2})}$ for $n = 3$.

Also, $c_{MSE}^* = \dfrac{1}{n+1} = \dfrac{1}{4}$.

2.3.1 Minmax Estimator as a Fixed Point

The minmax estimator for a given sample size, n, can be obtained as the fixed point of a function, $f(c)$.

1. For μ known case, the function f is

$$f(c) = \frac{nc - 1}{\sqrt{2n}}$$

One can observe that, for a minmax estimator, squared bias and variance values are equal and obtain f from here.

$$B_c^2 = V_c$$

$$\Leftrightarrow (nc - 1)^2 = 2nc^2$$

$$\Rightarrow c = \frac{nc - 1}{\sqrt{2n}}.$$

2. For μ unknown case, the desired function can be similarly obtained as

$$^\circ\tilde{f}(c^\circ) = \frac{(n-1)c - 1}{\sqrt{2(n-1)}}.$$

2.3.2 Graphical Illustration

The minmax estimator for σ^2 is obtained by looking for the intersection point of the curve with a line whose slope is $+1$ and passes through origin of the graph since this line will have equal values for squared bias and variance.

Figure 3 shows the minmax estimator for a few sample sizes when μ is known. Note that, there may be more than one (ideally, two) intersection points of the curve with the line. We pick the one that is closest to the origin, since it corresponds to the minimum value amongst all the estimators with equal squared bias and variance values. Similarly, we have plotted the mimmax estimator for σ^2 when μ is unknown in the Figure 4.

3. COMPARISON OF THE ESTIMATORS

Since we have more than one estimator for our parameter σ^2, we would like to test their performance on different grounds. For comparison of these estimators, we look at some popular criteria such as Mean Squared Error (MSE). Although MSE is a good enough criterion, it does not take into account the individual contributions of squared bias and variance components. So we devise some other benchmarks for comparison such as ratio of squared bias to the MSE of an estimator, which identifies relative contribution of squared bias towards the MSE, and Pareto efficiency, which treats the comparison as a multi-criteria optimization problem. These have been discussed in the subsequent sections.

3.1 Comparison Based on MSE

The first measure that we use to compare these estimators is the Mean Square Error (MSE) of each estimator.

3.1.1 Case: μ Known

1. Optimal MSE estimator $\overline{S}_{*_{CMSE}}^{-2}$

$$MSE\left(\overline{S}_{*_{CMSE}}^{-2}\right)$$

$$= \sigma^4\left[\left(n^2+2n\right)c_{*MSE}^{*2} - 2n\,c_{*MSE}^* + 1\right]$$

$$= \sigma^4\left[\left(n^2+2n\right)\frac{1}{(n+2)^2} - \frac{2n}{n+2} + 1\right]$$

$$= \frac{2\sigma^4}{n+2}.$$

2. Minmax estimator $\overline{S}_{*_{Cnm}}^{-2}$

$$MSE\left(\overline{S}_{*_{Cmm}}^{-2}\right)$$

$$= \sigma^4\left[\left(n^2+2n\right)\frac{1}{n\left(\frac{\sqrt{n}}{+\sqrt{2}}\right)^2} - \frac{2n}{\sqrt{n}\left(\frac{\sqrt{n}}{+\sqrt{2}}\right)} + 1\right]$$

$$= \sigma^4 \left[(n^2 + 2n) \frac{1}{n \left(\frac{\sqrt{n}}{+\sqrt{2}} \right)^2} - \frac{2n}{\sqrt{n} \left(\frac{\sqrt{n}}{+\sqrt{2}} \right)} + 1 \right]$$

$$= \frac{4\sigma^4}{(\sqrt{n} + \sqrt{2})^2} .$$

3.   Classical unbiased estimator ($\hat{\sigma}^2$)

$$MSE(\hat{\sigma}^2) = \sigma^4 \left[(n^2 + 2n) \frac{1}{n^2} - 2n \frac{1}{n} + 1 \right]$$

$$= \frac{2\sigma^4}{n} .$$

Comparison Results

   a.   Clearly, $\dfrac{1}{n+2} < \dfrac{1}{n} \forall n = 1, 2...$

$\therefore MSE \left(\bar{S}^2_{c_{MSE}} \right) < MSE(\hat{\sigma}^2)$ for $n = 2, 3, ...$

   b.   Consider, $n + 2 \geq 2\sqrt{2n}$ which is true for $n = 2, 3, ...$

$\therefore MSE \left(\bar{S}^2_{c_{MSE}} \right) \leq MSE \left(\bar{S}^2_{c_{mm}} \right)$ for $n = 2, 3, ...$

   c.   Next consider,

$$n - 2 \geq 2\sqrt{2n} \tag{20}$$

which holds true only for $n = 12, 13, ...$
   For $n \in \{2, ..., 11\}$, $n - 2 < 2\sqrt{2n}$. Thus,

$$MSE \left(\bar{S}^{-2}_{c_{mm}} \right) < MSE(\hat{\sigma}^2) \forall n \in \{2, ..., 11\}$$

and $MSE\left(\bar{S}_{\cdot_{c_{mm}}}^{-2}\right) > MSE(\hat{\sigma}^2) \forall n = 12,13,...$

Note that the inequality holds strictly in this case, because there is no integral value of n such that (20) holds with equality.

3.1.2 Case: μ Unknown

1. Optimal MSE estimator $\left(S_{\cdot_{c_{MSE}}}^2\right)$

$$MSE\left(S_{\cdot_{c_{MSE}}}^2\right) = \frac{2\sigma^4}{n+1}.$$

2. Minmax estimator $\left(S_{\cdot_{c_{mm}}}^2\right)$

$$MSE\left(S_{\cdot_{c_{mm}}}^2\right) = \frac{4\sigma^4}{(\sqrt{n-1}+\sqrt{2})^2}$$

3. Classical unbiased estimator (S^2)

$$MSE(\mathrm{S}^2) = Var(\mathrm{S}^2)(\because S^2 \ is \ unbiased)$$
$$= \frac{2\sigma^4}{n+1}$$

4. Classical biased estimator (s^2)

$$MSE(s^2) = \frac{2(n-1)\sigma^4}{n^2}.$$

Comparison Results

  a.   Clearly, $\dfrac{1}{n+1} < \dfrac{1}{n-1} \forall n = 2,3,...$

$\therefore MSE\left(S_{\cdot_{c_{MSE}}}^2\right) < MSE(S^2) for \ n = 2,3,...$

  b. $\dfrac{1}{n^2} < \dfrac{1}{(n-1)^2} \forall n = 2,3,K$

$\therefore MSE\left(s^2\right) < MSE(S^2) for \ n = 2,3,...$

    c. $n - 1 > 0 \; \forall n = 2,3,...$

$$\Rightarrow \frac{(2n-1)}{n^2} > \frac{2}{n+1}$$

$$\Rightarrow MSE(s^2) > MSE\left(S^2_{*_{c_{MSE}}}\right).$$

    Thus, $MSE(S^2) > MSE(s^2) > MSE\left(S^2_{*_{c_{MSE}}}\right)$ for $n = 2,3,....$

    d.   To compare MSE $S^2_{*_{c_{mm}}}$ and MSE $S^2_{*_{c_{MSE}}}$, let us assume

$$MSE\left(S^2_{*_{c_{mm}}}\right) \leq MSE\left(S^2_{*_{c_{MSE}}}\right)$$

$$\Rightarrow \frac{4\sigma^4}{n+1+2\sqrt{2(n-1)}} \leq \frac{2\sigma^4}{n+1}$$

$$\Rightarrow (n-3)^2 \leq 0,$$

which is contradictory for all $n = 2,...$ except for $n = 3$ where equality holds.

$$\therefore MSE\left(S^2_{*_{c_{mm}}}\right) \geq MSE\left(S^2_{*_{c_{MSE}}}\right) \; for \; n = 2,3,...$$

    e.   For comparing MSE $\left(S^2_{*_{c_{mm}}}\right)$ and $MSE(s^2)$, let us assume

$$MSE\left(S^2_{*_{c_{mm}}}\right) \geq MSE(s^2)$$

$$\Rightarrow \frac{4\sigma^4}{n+1+2\sqrt{2(n-1)}} \geq \frac{(2n-1)\sigma^4}{n^2}$$

$$\Rightarrow 2n^2 - 4n\sqrt{2(n-1)} - n + 2\sqrt{2(n-1)} + 1 \geq 0$$

    By explicit computation, the above is true for $n \in \{7,8,...\}$, while for $n \in \{2,...,6\}$,
$\Rightarrow 2n^2 - 4n\sqrt{2(n-1)} - n + 2\sqrt{2(n-1)} + 1 \leq 0$. Thus,

$$MSE\left(S^2_{*_{c_{mm}}}\right) < MSE(s^2) \forall n \in \{2,...,6\}$$

and $MSE\left(S^2_{c_{mm}^*}\right) \geq MSE(s^2) \forall n = 7, 8, \ldots$.

f. Now for comparing $MSE\left(S^2_{c_{mm}^*}\right)$ and $MSE(\text{S}^2)$, we assume

$$MSE\left(S^2_{c_{mm}^*}\right) < MSE(\text{S}^2)$$

$$\Rightarrow \frac{4\sigma^4}{n + 1 + 2\sqrt{2(n-1)}} < \frac{2\sigma^4}{n-1}$$

$$\Rightarrow n - 3 < 2\sqrt{2(n-1)} \tag{21}$$

which holds true only for $n \in \{2, \ldots, 12\}$. The inequality reverses for $n = 13, 14, \ldots$

Thus, $MSE\left(S^2_{c_{mm}^*}\right) < MSE(\text{S}^2) \forall n \in \{2, \ldots, 12\}$, and $MSE\left(S^2_{c_{mm}^*}\right) > MSE(\text{S}^2) \forall n = 13, 14, \ldots$.

Note that the inequality holds strictly in this case, because there is no integral value of n such that (21) holds with equality.

3.2 Ratio of Squared Bias to MSE

While MSE is a good way of simultaneously capturing both accuracy and precision of an estimator, it cannot capture the relative contributions of square of bias and variance. One simple way to capture this is to consider the percentage of square of bias in MSE. So, for an estimator T, we consider a quantity f_c, the ratio of square of the bias of the estimator T to its MSE. Mathematically, in our case, $f_c(\cdot)$ is defined as:

$$f_c\left(S^2_c\right) = \frac{B^2_c}{MSE\left(S^2_c\right)} . \tag{22}$$

In general, $f_c: (0, \infty) \to [0, 1]$. For the above class of estimators that we are considering, we have $f_c: (0, \infty) \to [0, 1)$ (we do not consider $c = 0$, as such an estimator gives inadmissible estimate of zero for the variance σ^2).

3.2.1 Case: μ Known

For a sample of size n, $f_c(.)$ for a general estimator is

$$f_c\left(S^2_c\right) = \frac{(nc - 1)^2}{(nc - 1)^2 + 2nc^2} . \tag{23}$$

The ratios for the estimators of interest are listed as follows:

1. $f_c\left(\overline{S}^{-2}_{*_{c_{mm}}}\right) = 0.5$

2. $f_c\left(\overline{S}^{-2}_{*_{c_{MSE}}}\right) = \left(\dfrac{-2}{n+2}\right)^2 \div \left(\dfrac{2}{n+2}\right) = \left(\dfrac{2}{n+2}\right)$

3. $f_c(\hat{\sigma}^2) = 0$.

3.2.2 Case: μ Unknown

For a sample of size n, $f_c(.)$ for a general estimator is

$$f_c\left(\overline{S}^2_c\right) = \frac{((n-1)c-1)^2}{((n-1)c-1)^2 + 2(n-1)c^2} \,. \tag{24}$$

The ratios for the estimators of interest are listed as follows:

1. $f_c\left(S^2_{*_{c_{mm}}}\right) = 0.5$

2. $f_c\left(S^2_{*_{c_{MSE}}}\right) = \left(\dfrac{-2}{n+1}\right)^2 \div \left(\dfrac{2}{n+1}\right) = \left(\dfrac{2}{n+1}\right)$

3. $f_c(S^2) = \left(\dfrac{-1}{n}\right)^2 \div \dfrac{2n-1}{n^2} = \dfrac{1}{2n-1}$

4. $f_c(S^2) = 0$.

Estimators with f_c close to 0 or 1 have either square of the bias or variance dominating the other. Notice that the ratio f_c is constant for minmax estimator and UMVUE. But for the optimal MSE estimator (and the classical estimator in the μ unknown case), the ratio is a decreasing function of sample size n and is bounded on both sides by the ratios for minmax and UMVUE.

3.3 Pareto Efficiency

We now treat the squared bias-variance aspects of the linear estimators as a multi-criteria problem and plot the Pareto frontier in squared bias and variance space. We first show below that all the estimators that we have considered in the previous sections, are non-dominated points in feasible space, i.e., they are Pareto optimal. Then we identify the Pareto frontier.

3.3.1 Pareto Optimal Estimators

- **Minmax Estimator:** For a given sample size, n, consider the minmax estimator with squared bias, $B^2_{*_{c_{mm}}}$ and variance, $V_{*_{c_{mm}}}$ where $B^2_{*_{c_{mm}}} = V_{*_{c_{mm}}}$. Any estimator with (squared bias, variance) =

$(a, a), a < B^2_{c_{*_{mm}}}$ cannot lie on the curve of squared bias versus variance, by definition and uniqueness of minmax estimator. Therefore, consider an estimator with (B^2_c, V_c). Let $B^2_c < B^2_{c_{*_{mm}}}$, then V_c has to be greater than $V_{c_{*_{mm}}}$, otherwise it contradicts the fact that $\left(B^2_{c_{*_{mm}}}, V_{c_{*_{mm}}}\right)$ is minmax estimator. Similarly, if $V_c < V_{c_{*_{mm}}}$, then B^2_c will have to be more than $B^2_{c_{*_{mm}}}$ to preserve the definition of $\left(B^2_{c_{*_{mm}}}, V_{c_{*_{mm}}}\right)$. Thus, one cannot reduce both squared bias and variance of the minmax estimator, by considering any other estimator in the considered class, parameterized by the coefficient, c. Therefore, minmax estimator is a Pareto point.

- **Optimal MSE Estimator:** When n is fixed, there cannot be an estimator with (B^2_c, V_c) such that $\left(B^2_c + V_c\right) < \left(B^2_{c_{*_{MSE}}} + V_{c_{*_{MSE}}}\right)$ since $\left(B^2_{c_{*_{MSE}}}, V_{c_{*_{MSE}}}\right)$ denotes the optimal MSE estimator. As the optimal MSE estimator is unique, consider an estimator $\left(B^2_c, V_c\right)$ with $\left(B^2_c + V_c\right) > \left(B^2_{c_{*_{MSE}}} + V_{c_{*_{MSE}}}\right)$. Suppose $B^2_c < B^2_{c_{*_{MSE}}}$. This implies that $V_c > V_{c_{*_{MSE}}}$. On the other hand, if for this estimator, $V_c < V_{c_{*_{MSE}}}$, then $B^2_c > B^2_{c_{*_{MSE}}}$ to preserve the optimality of $(B^2_{c_{*_{MSE}}}, V_{c_{*_{MSE}}})$. Hence, the optimal MSE estimator is also a Pareto point.

- **Uniformly Minimum Variance Unbiased Estimator (UMVUE):** UMVUE is characterized by $\left(0, V_{c_{*_{UMVUE}}}\right)$, since by definition its bias has to be zero. Since UMVUE is unique, we cannot have an estimator (B^2_c, V_c) with $B^2_c = 0$ and $V_c < V_{c_{*_{UMVUE}}}$ for a given n. However if we insist on reduced variance, i.e., $V_c < V_{c_{*_{UMVUE}}}$, then B^2_c for this estimator has to be positive, by definition of UMVUE. Thus, UMVUE is another Pareto point on the squared bias versus variance curve for a fixed n.

3.3.2 Pareto Frontier

For a given sample size, n, all the estimators with coefficient c lying on the lower arm of the squared bias versus variance plot are Pareto estimators (refer to Figure 3 and 4). This can be argued as follows:

Consider the μ known case. Let the sample size, n, be fixed. Then the bias and variance of an estimator for σ^2 with coefficient c are,

$$B_c = nc - 1 \tag{25}$$

$$V_c = 2nc^2 \tag{26}$$

From the above two equations, bias and variance of an estimator can be related as:

$$V_c = \frac{2}{n}B^2_c + \frac{4}{n}B_c + \frac{2}{n} \tag{27}$$

Comparing the above equation with the general form of a conic section

$$Ax^2 + Bxy + Cy^2 + Dx + Ey + F = 0,$$

we see that it satisfies the following restriction:

$$B^2 - 4AC = 0.$$

Hence the equation (27) represents a parabola with B_c and V_c as the variables.

Note that, B_c^2 itself is a parabola in variable c, with vertex at $c = \dfrac{1}{n}$. Hence, B_c^2 decreases as c varies over $\left(0, \dfrac{1}{n}\right]$, and increases over $\left(\dfrac{1}{n}, \infty\right)$. On the other hand, V_c, which is also a parabola in c with vertex at $c = 0$, increases monotonically over $(0, \infty)$. Therefore, on the interval $\left(0, \dfrac{1}{n}\right]$, the values of B_c^2 and V_c cannot be increased simultaneously. Thus, this arm of the parabola represents the class of Pareto optimal estimators for σ^2.

Similarly for the μ unknown case, when the sample size n is fixed, the bias and variance of an estimator with coefficient c are:

$$B_c = (n - 1)c - 1$$
$$V_c = 2(n - 1)c^2$$

As in the μ known case, it can be established in the μ unknown case also that B_c^2 and V_c for the estimators trace a parabola. Also, B_c^2 is a parabola in variable c, with vertex at $c = \dfrac{1}{n-1}$ as well as V_c is a parabola in c with vertex at $c = 0$. Thus, B_c^2 decreases monotonically on $c \in \left(0, \dfrac{1}{n-1}\right]$, whereas V_c is ever increasing on this interval. Hence, the estimators with coefficients $c \in \left(0, \dfrac{1}{n-1}\right]$ are Pareto optimal since we cannot simultaneously improve their squared bias and variance.

In fact, it can be seen from Figures 3 and 4 that the optimal MSE estimator, minmax estimator, UMVUE and MLE – all lie on this Pareto frontier, since their coefficients belong to the specified interval that captures the Pareto optimal estimators. The c_{MSE}, S^2 and s^2 estimators are sandwiched between minmax estimator and UMVUE estimators in the variance versus squared bias plot. Another observation is that the c_{MSE}, S^2 (and s^2, when mean of the data is also to be estimated) cluster near the UMVUE estimator in the variance vs. squared-bias plot showing that the variance is a predominant component in the MSE of these estimators. This is also brought out in the f_c measure of these estimators.

4. COMPARISON OF MSE AND f_c VALUES OF DIFFERENT ESTIMATORS AS FUNCTIONS OF n

We have summarized the values of squared bias, variance, MSE and f_c for different estimators under both the cases in Table 1. It can be easily observed that the MSE values of the considered estimators are $O\left(\dfrac{1}{n}\right)$ since the bias can be 0 or $O\left(\dfrac{1}{n^2}\right)$ and the variance is $O\left(\dfrac{1}{n}\right)$.

Considering the μ known case, from the Figure 3, we see that for a fixed sample size, n, optimal MSE estimator has the lowest MSE value in the graphs; while among the remaining two estimators, minmax estimator performs better for small sample sizes ($n \in \{2,...,11\}$), whereas $\hat{\sigma}^2$ performs better for $n \in \{12,13,...\}$ in terms of MSE values. Parallel results can be observed in Figure 4 for the case of unknown μ.

Figure 5 plots the squared bias, variance and MSE values for the considered estimators of σ^2 for a range of sample sizes under both the cases: μ known and μ unknown. Figure 6 compares the ratio of the squared bias to the MSE value of the mentioned estimators for a range of sample sizes under both the cases: μ known and μ unknown.

5. DISCUSSION

In both the cases (μ known and μ unknown), the distribution of the estimators was known (Casella & Berger, 2002) to be chi-squared distribution (with n and $n - 1$ degrees of freedom for μ known and μ unknown cases, respectively) and hence computation of bias, variance and MSE was easy. We proposed an estimator by using minmax criterion over the squared bias and variance of the estimator. We saw that, though the optimal MSE estimator always had the minimum MSE value for a given sample size; the minmax estimator performed better than the classical estimator(s) on the MSE value for small sample sizes. That all these estimators are Pareto optimal shows that the improvement in one of the two competing risks, the variance and squared bias, comes only at the cost of increase of the other risk in these estimators.

Our first conclusion is that as sample size increases, i.e., in the context of 'Big Data', these estimators are nearly same when MSE as a measure of quality of an estimator. When the measure of quality of an estimator is the fraction of squared bias in MSE of an estimator, it is not more than half (for minmax estimator) and zero for UMVUE estimators. Our finding that all these estimators are Pareto optimal in the space of squared bias and variance of estimators complies with the above conclusion by pointing out that for these estimators an attempt to decrease in squared bias (variance) leads to increase in variance (squared bias).

Table 1. MSE values and ratios for different estimators of $\hat{\sigma}^2$ for a sample size n

	μ Known			μ Unknown			
Ratio, f_c	0.5	0.5	0	0.5	$\dfrac{2}{(n+1)}$	$\dfrac{2}{(2n-1)}$	0
MSE in σ^4 units	$\dfrac{4}{(\sqrt{n}+\sqrt{2})^2}$	$\dfrac{2}{\sqrt{n+2}}$	$\dfrac{2}{n}$	$\dfrac{4}{(\sqrt{n-1}+\sqrt{2})^2}$	$\dfrac{2}{\sqrt{n+1}}$	$\dfrac{2n-1}{n^2}$	$\dfrac{2}{n-1}$
$\left(B^2_c, V_c\right)$ in σ^4 units	$\left(\dfrac{2}{(\sqrt{n}-\sqrt{2})^2}, \dfrac{2}{(\sqrt{n}+\sqrt{2})^2}\right)$	$\left(\dfrac{4}{(n+2)^3}, \dfrac{2n}{(n+2)^2}\right)$	$\left(0, \dfrac{2}{n}\right)$	$\left(\dfrac{2}{(\sqrt{n-1}-\sqrt{2})^2}, \dfrac{2}{(\sqrt{n-1}+\sqrt{2})^2}\right)$	$\left(\dfrac{4}{(n+1)^3}, \dfrac{2(n-1)}{(n+1)^2}\right)$	$\left(\dfrac{1}{n^2}, \dfrac{2(n-1)}{n^2}\right)$	$\left(0, \dfrac{2}{(n-1)}\right)$
Definition	$\dfrac{1}{\sqrt{n}(\sqrt{n}+\sqrt{2})}\sum_{i=1}^{n}(X_i-\mu)^2$	$\dfrac{1}{n+2}\sum_{i=1}^{n}(X_i-\mu)^2$	$\dfrac{1}{n}\sum_{i=1}^{n}(X_i-\mu)^2$	$\dfrac{1}{\sqrt{n-1}(\sqrt{n-1}+\sqrt{2})}\sum_{i=1}^{n}(X_i-\bar{X})^2$	$\dfrac{1}{n+1}\sum_{i=1}^{n}(X_i-\bar{X})^2$	$\dfrac{1}{n}\sum_{i=1}^{n}(X_i-\bar{X})^2$	$\dfrac{1}{n-1}\sum_{i=1}^{n}(X_i-\bar{X})^2$
Estimator	Minmax, $\bar{S}^2_{c^*_{mm}}$	Optimal MSE, $\bar{S}^2_{c^*_{MSE}}$	UMVUE/ MLE, $\hat{\sigma}^2$	Minmax, $S^2_{c^*_{mm}}$	Optimal MSE, $S^2_{c^*_{MSE}}$	MLE, s^2	UMVUE, S^2

Figure 5. Comparison of MSE values for the estimators of σ^2; (a) when μ is known, (b) when μ is unknown

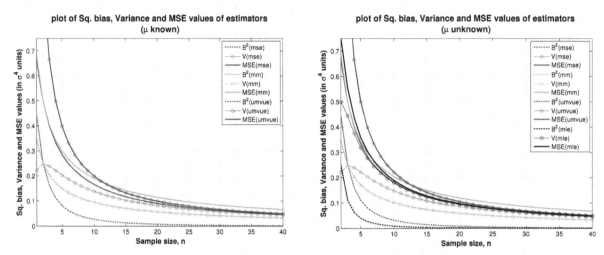

Figure 6. Comparison of ratios f_c for the estimators of σ^2; (a) when μ is known, (b) when μ is unknown

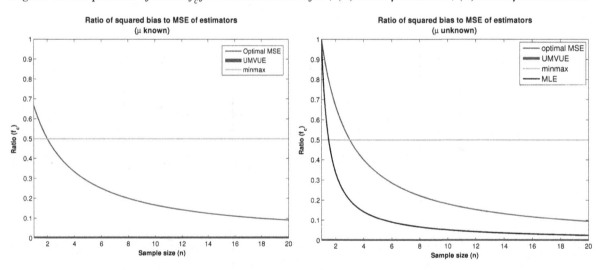

Note that our observations and analysis were restricted to the above class of estimators. As a part of further investigation, one aspect could be to identify a 'better' class of estimators. Another aspect is to consider non-normal data. Similar ideas could be used for estimating the parameters of a linear regression model.

ACKNOWLEDGMENT

We thank Dr. Kartikeya Puranam for inviting us to contribute this chapter to this book. We thank Professor Alladi Subramanyam for bringing the paper by Doss and Sethuraman (1989) to our notice. Puja Sahu was partially supported by a Teaching Assistantship for PhD students offered by MHRD, GoI.

REFERENCES

Alpaydin, E. (2010). *Introduction to machine learning* (2nd ed.). Cambridge, MA: MIT Press.

Billingsley, P. (1995). *Probability and measure* (3rd ed.). New York: John Wiley.

Casella, G., & Berger, R. L. (2002). Statistical inference (2nd ed.). Duxbury: Thomson Learning.

Chung, K. L. (2001). *A course in probability theory* (3rd ed.). New York: Academic Press.

DeGroot, M. H., & Schervish, M. J. (2012). *Probability and statistics* (4th ed.). Addison Wesley Publishing Company Incorporated.

Doss, H., & Sethuraman, J. (1989). The price of bias reduction when there is no unbiased estimate. *Annals of Statistics*, *17*(1), 440–442. doi:10.1214/aos/1176347028

Friedman, J. H. (1997). On bias, variance, 0/1 - loss, and the curse-of-dimensionality. *Data Mining and Knowledge Discovery*, *1*(1), 55–77. doi:10.1023/A:1009778005914

Fristedt, B. E., & Gray, L. F. (1997). *A modern approach to probability theory. Probability and its applications*. Boston: Birkhauser. doi:10.1007/978-1-4899-2837-5

Hemachandra, N., & Sahu, P. (2014). *Some Aspects of Estimators for Variance of Normally Distributed Data* (Technical Report). Mumbai, India: Indian Institute of Technology Bombay, Industrial Engineering and Operations Research. Retrieved from http://www.ieor.iitb.ac.in/files/Variance_Estimators_TechReport.pdf

Kallenberg, O. (2002). *Foundations of modern probability* (2nd ed.). New York: Springer Verlag. doi:10.1007/978-1-4757-4015-8

Wasserman, L. (2005). *All of statistics: A concise course in statistical inference* (2nd ed.). New York: Springer Science.

KEY TERMS AND DEFINITIONS

Bias: The bias of an estimator T of the parameter θ is defined as: $bias\left(T\right) = E_{\theta}\left(T\right) - \theta$.

Minmax Estimator: We define the minmax estimator as the one which minimizes the maximum of the squared bias and the variance values for an estimator with coefficient, c. $c_{mm}^{*} = arg\,\underset{c}{min}\,max\left\{B_{c}^{2}, V_{c}\right\}$.

MSE: Mean Squared Error (MSE) of an estimator T of the parameter θ is defined as: $MSE\left(T\right) = E_{\theta}\left(T - \theta\right)^{2}$, which can be simplified to the following form: $MSE\left(T\right) = bias^{2}\left(T\right) + Var\left(T\right)$.

Pareto Optimality: Pareto optimality or efficiency is achieved over the multi-criteria $\left\{B_{c}^{2}, V_{c}\right\}$ for an estimator, when none of the component can be improved upon without making worse the other component.

Variance: The variance of an estimator T of the parameter θ is defined as:

$$Var\left(T\right) = E_{\theta}\left(T - E_{\theta}\left(T\right)\right)^{2} = E_{\theta}\left(T^{2}\right) - \left(E_{\theta}\left(T\right)\right)^{2}.$$

Chapter 22
An Exploration of Backpropagation Numerical Algorithms in Modeling US Exchange Rates

Salim Lahmiri
ESCA School of Management, Morocco & University of Quebec at Montreal, Canada

ABSTRACT

This chapter applies the Backpropagation Neural Network (BPNN) trained with different numerical algorithms and technical analysis indicators as inputs to forecast daily US/Canada, US/Euro, US/Japan, US/Korea, US/Swiss, and US/UK exchange rate future price. The training algorithms are the Fletcher-Reeves, Polak-Ribiére, Powell-Beale, quasi-Newton (Broyden-Fletcher-Goldfarb-Shanno, BFGS), and the Levenberg-Marquardt (LM). The standard Auto Regressive Moving Average (ARMA) process is adopted as a reference model for comparison. The performance of each BPNN and ARMA process is measured by computing the Mean Absolute Error (MAE), Mean Absolute Deviation (MAD), and Mean of Squared Errors (MSE). The simulation results reveal that the LM algorithm is the best performer and show strong evidence of the superiority of the BPNN over ARMA process. In sum, because of the simplicity and effectiveness of the approach, it could be implemented for real business application problems to predict US currency exchange rate future price.

1. INTRODUCTION

Currency exchange rate forecasting is crucial for financial institutions to estimate currency risk, increase profits, and to monitor strategic financial planning. Additionally, active participants in the foreign exchange market such as traders, investors, and speculators continuously make arbitrage and hedging transactions so as to affect financial institutions wealth and national economies. Consequently, all these participants become dependent on the response in the foreign exchange market. Nowadays, governments, economists and participants in the foreign exchange market are increasingly interested in models that allow accurately predicting currency exchange rate. However, currency markets are generally perceived as nonlinear and no stationary systems which are difficult to predict (Majhi et al, 2012).

DOI: 10.4018/978-1-4666-7272-7.ch022

Statistical models such as the auto regressive moving average (ARMA) (Box et al, 1994) and generalized autoregressive conditional heteroskedasticity (GARCH) (Bollerslev, 1986) models and linear regression methods were largely applied by researchers and scholars in modeling foreign currency exchange rates (Hsieh, 1989; Liu et al, 1994; Brooks, 1996). However, all these linear statistical models require a priori assumptions about the underlying laws governing the data and the model specification. As a result, their applications are restricted to linear specifications of the model. They are also restricted to stationarity and normality distribution of variables and errors. Indeed, these assumptions are not true in real life situations, which lead to poor prediction quality (Hu et al, 1999; Yao & Tan, 2000).

In the last decade, soft computing tools such as multilayer artificial neural networks (ANN) (Rumelhart et al, 1986; Haykin, 2008) were introduced in currency exchange time series forecasting (Hu et al, 1999; Yao & Tan, 2000) since they do not make such assumptions. In addition, they are adaptive and robust to noisy and incomplete data. Furthermore, the ANN employs the traditional empirical risk minimization principle to minimize the error on training data using the backpropagation algorithm. Finally they were proven to be effective and accurate in different time series application problems; including electrical load (Kulkarni, 2013), stock market volatility (Wei, 2013), river flow (Singh & Deo, 2007), car fuel consumption (Wu & Liu, 2012), flood (Feng & Lu, 2010), and rainfall-runoff forecasting (Sedki et al, 2009), in stock market prediction (Lahmiri, 2014; Lahmiri et al, 2014a, 2014b), and also recently in currency exchange rate forecasting (Majhi et al, 2012; Sedki et al, 2009; Majhi et al, 2009; Panda & Narasimhan, 2007; Sermpinis & Laws, 2012; Hussain et al, 2006; Dunis et al, 2011).

For instance, Majhi et al, (2012) used functional link artificial neural network (FLANN) and cascaded functional link artificial neural network (CFLANN) to predict currency exchange rate between US/British Pound, US/Indian Rupees, and US/Japanese Yen. The computer simulation results showed that each neural network outperformed the standard least mean square (LMS) algorithm. In addition, the CFLANN offers superior prediction performance in all cases in comparison with the FLANN. In their study, Majhi et al, (2006) employed Wilcoxon artificial neural network (WANN) and Wilcoxon functional link artificial neural network (WFLANN) to reduce dependency of the network weights to the outliers in the training data. Both networks were found to be robust in the prediction of US/Indian Rupees, US/ British Pound, and US/Japanese. In addition, it was found that WFLANN offers low computational complexity and hence preferable as a robust prediction model for currency exchange rates than WANN. Panda and Narasimhan (2007) found that the neural network has superior in-sample forecast than linear autoregressive and random walk models in the prediction of the weekly Indian rupee/US dollar exchange rate. In addition, the neural network was also found to beat both linear autoregressive and random walk models in out-of-sample forecasting. Anastasakis and Mort (2009) applied both neural networks with active neurons and self-organizing modeling methods for the daily prediction of the US/British Pound and the Deutche/British Pound. They found that both networks are capable to outperform the random walk model and the buy-and-hold strategy. Sermpinis et al, (2012) compared the performance of the Psi sigma neural network (PSI), the gene expression algorithm (GEP), multi-layer perceptron (MLP), recurrent neural network (RNN), genetic programming algorithm (GP), ARMA process, and naïve strategy when applied to the task of modeling and forecasting the EURO/USD exchange rate. They found that the PSI network performs the best. In addition, all models outperformed the ARMA process and naïve strategy. In similar studies, the PSI presented satisfactory results in forecasting the EUR/USD, the EUR/ GBP and the EUR/JPY exchange rates having as benchmarks a HONN model (Hussain et al, 2006). On the other hand, the PSI failed to outperform MLP, RNN and HONN in the prediction of the EUR/USD exchange rate series (Dunis et al, 2011).

From the study of the recent literature on currency exchange rate forecasting, it is concluded that artificial neural networks as nonlinear artificial intelligence technique are well suited for forecasting purpose (Hu et al, 1999; Yao & Tan, 2000; Majhi et al, 2012; Sedki et al, 2009; Majhi et al, 2009; Panda & Narasimhan, 2007; Sermpinis & Laws, 2012; Hussain et al, 2006; Dunis et al, 2011). Although different types of artificial neural networks have been compared in the literature, there is no attention given to the choice of the learning algorithm used to train the neural network for modeling and predicting exchange rate. Indeed, the choice of the training algorithm is crucial for the success of the artificial neural network in predicting currency exchange rate. Therefore, the purpose of our study is to explore the effectiveness of different numerical techniques in the training of the BPNN; including conjugate gradients (Fletcher-Reeves update, Polak-Ribiére update, Powell-Beale restart), quasi-Newton (Broyden-Fletcher-Goldfarb-Shanno, BFGS), and the Levenberg-Marquardt (LM) algorithm (Haykin, 2008; Nocedal & Wright, 2006; Eligius & Boglárka, 2010). The goal is to identify which algorithm allows achieving higher prediction accuracy of the future exchange rate.

The aim of this paper is to predict currency exchange rate by using a set of technical analysis indicators as inputs to artificial neural networks trained with five different numerical algorithms cited previously. The artificial neural network structure used in this study is the backpropagation neutral network (BPNN) since it is the most popular structure. Technical analysis seeks to predict a given asset future price movements based on the analysis of its historical prices (Pring, 1991). Indeed, it assumes that the dynamics of a given asset price are characterized by internal market information, and that its variation will repeat in the future. Therefore, one can explore asset price historical regularities to determine the possible future trends of the asset price. Because of simplicity of technical analysis approach and its effectiveness, it was successfully adopted to predict trends of financial assets (Box et al, 1994; Neely et al, 1997; Sewell & Shawe-Taylor, 2012). In our study, the ARMA process (Box et al, 1994) which is a popular linear statistical model is used as main benchmark for comparison purpose to check the effectiveness of the nonlinear intelligent models namely the BPNN. The genetic algorithms (Goldberg, 1989) will be used to optimize the architecture of the latter. Additionally, real data of six currency exchange rates are considered for modeling and simulation. They are the US/Canada, US/Euro, US/Japan, US/Korea, US/Swiss, and US/UK exchange rate.

The performance of the BPNN and ARMA process is measured by computing the mean absolute error (MAE), mean absolute deviation (MAD), and mean of squared errors (MSE).

This paper is organized as follows. Section 2 describes the BPNN, ARMA process, technical analysis indicators, and statistical metrics used to measure out-of-sample forecasting performance. Section 3 describes the data and provides all simulation results. Finally in Section 4, conclusion and further research directions are presented.

2. METHODS

2.1 Neural Networks

An artificial neural network (Rumelhart et al, 1986; Haykin, 2008) is a nonlinear system with neurons used to process data. A standard architecture has one input layer with x predictive variables, one hidden layer that fulfills the input-output mapping, and an output layer with the predicted variable y. The output y is computed as follows:

$$y_i = f\left(\sum_{j=1}^{m} x_j w_{ij} + \theta_i\right) \tag{1}$$

where w_{ij} is a connecting weight from neural j to neural i, θ denotes the bias, and f($\bullet$) is an activation function employed to control the amplitude of the output. In this study, the well-known sigmoid function is used for activation. It is given by:

$$f(x) = \frac{1 - e^{-2x}}{1 + e^{-2x}} \tag{2}$$

The training of the network is performed by the well-known Backpropagation algorithm (Rumelhart et al, 1986; Haykin, 2008) trained with the steepest descent algorithm given as follows:

$$\Delta w_k = -\alpha_k g_k \tag{3}$$

where, Δw_k is a vector of weights changes, g_k is the current gradient, α_k is the learning rate that determines the length of the weight update. Thus, in the gradient descent learning rule, the update is done in the negative gradient direction. In order to avoid oscillations and to reduce the sensitivity of the network to fast changes of the error surface (Jang et al, 1997), the change in weight is made dependent of the past weight change by adding a momentum term:

$$\Delta w_k = -\alpha_k g_k + p\Delta w_{k-1} \tag{4}$$

where, p is the momentum parameter. Furthermore, the momentum allows escaping from small local minima on the error surface (Ramirez et al, 2003). In our study, the number of neurons in the input layer is set to eight, where each neuron corresponds to a given technical indicator. Technical analysis indicators used in our study will be described lately. Similarly, the number of neurons in the hidden layer is set to eight. Finally, there is one neuron in the output layer corresponding to the currency exchange rate predicted value.

2.2 Training Algorithms

In general, artificial neural networks are trained with gradient descent and gradient descent with momentum algorithms. Some numerical algorithms can be used to faster convergence of the gradient descent. They can be broken into three categories: conjugate gradient algorithms, quasi-Netwon algorithms, and Levenberg-Marquardt algorithm. In particular, this paper compares the prediction performance of the following algorithms: quasi-Newton (Broyden-Fletcher-Goldfarb-Shanno, BFGS), conjugate gradient (Fletcher-Reeves update, Polak-Ribiére update, Powell-Beale restart), and Levenberg-Marquardt algorithm. These numerical algorithms are briefly described in Table 1, and are well presented in Haykin (2008), Nocedal & Wright (2006), and Eligius & Boglárka (2010) for further details.

Table 1. Training algorithms

Algorithm	Search Direction	Description
Fletcher-Reeves (conjugate)	$$p_0 = -g_0$$ $$\Delta w_k = \alpha_k p_k$$ $$p_k = -g_k + \beta_k p_{k-1}$$ $$\beta_k = \frac{g'_k g_k}{g'_{k-1} g_{k-1}}$$	4. Iteration starts by searching in the steepest descent direction. 5. Search line method (Charalambous, 1992) is employed to find the optimal current search direction α. 6. Next (update) search direction β is found such that it is conjugate to previous search directions.
Polak-Ribiere (conjugate)	$$p_0 = -g_0$$ $$\Delta w_k = \alpha_k p_k$$ $$p_k = -g_k + \beta_k p_{k-1}$$ $$\beta_k = \frac{\Delta g'_{k-1} g_k}{g'_{k-1} g_{k-1}}$$	Update is made by computing the product of the previous change in the gradient with the current gradient divided by the square of the previous gradient.
Powell-Beale restarts (conjugate)	$$\left| g'_{k-1} g_k \right| \geq 0.2 \left\| g_k \right\|^2$$	Update of Search direction is reset to the negative of the gradient only when this condition is satisfied.
BFGS (quasi-Newton)	$$\Delta w_k = -H'_k g_k$$	H is the Hessian (second derivatives) matrix.
Levenberg-Marquardt (L-M)	$$\Delta w_k = -H'_k g_k$$ $$H' = J'J$$ $$g = J'e$$	J is the Jacobian matrix (first derivatives) and e is a vector of network errors.

2.3 Genetic Algorithms

The genetic algorithm (Goldberg, 1989) is used to automatically optimize the architectures of TDNN and ATDNN. In a GA, each solution to a problem is called an individual and the solutions are coded as a string of bits or real values. A set of solutions is called a population. Therefore, the GA is a population-based technique because instead of operating on a single potential solution, it uses a population of potential solutions. Thus, the larger the population, the greater the diversity of the members composing the population; but unfortunately, the larger the domain searched by the population.

The GA was chosen for three reasons. First, the architectural design is crucial to the success of a network's information processing capabilities (Yen, 1994). Second, genetic search provides an advantage over expert experience in building neural networks and also over constructive and destructive algorithms (Yen, 1994). Finally, genetic algorithms allow the convergence speed of artificial neural networks to be faster because of the search multiple initial states and the effect of mutation operations (Goldberg, 1989).

The process of a genetic algorithm is iterative and consists of the following steps:

1. Create an initial population of genotypes which are a genetic representation of neural networks, and network architectures are randomly selected.
2. Train and test the neural networks to determine how fit they are by calculating the fitness measure of each trained network *i*. The fitness function is calculated as: $f_i = 1/MSE_i$, where MSE is the mean squared error.
3. Compare the fitness of the networks and keep the best top 10 for future use.
4. Select better networks from each completed population by applying the selection operator.
5. Refill the population back to the defined size.
6. Mate the genotypes by exchanging genes (features) of the networks.
7. Randomly mutate the genotypes according to a given probability.
8. Return back to step 2 and continue this process until stopping criteria (RMSE < ε) is reached.

The initial parameters of the neural networks to be optimized are described in Table 2.

2.4 The ARMA Process

The autoregressive moving average (ARMA) (Box et al, 1994) process has become a popular linear statistical model for stationary time series analysis and forecasting. In the ARMA process, the future value of a variable y is assumed to be a linear function of several past observations and random errors. The ARMA generating process is given by:

$$\varphi(B)y_t = \theta(B)e_k \tag{5}$$

where y_t and e_t are respectively the actual value and random error at time period *t*, *B* is the backshift operator. The error term e_t are assumed to be independently and identically distributed (*iid*) with a mean $E(e_t) = 0$ and a variance $V(e_t) = \sigma^2$. The polynomials $\phi(B)$ and $\theta(B)$ are given by:

Table 2. Genetic algorithm initial parameters

Hidden layers	maximum 2
Neurons by each hidden layer	maximum 8
Activation functions	sigmoid
Size of initial population	30
Selection	0.50%
Refill	cloning
Mating	tail swap
Mutations	random exchange at 0.25%
Number of passes	20 to 50
Learning rate	0.4 to 0.1
Momentum rate	0.3 to 0.1
Hidden layers	maximum 2

$$\varphi\left(B\right) = \left(1 - \varphi_1 B - \dots - \varphi_p B^p\right) \tag{6}$$

$$\theta\left(B\right) = \left(1 - \theta_1 B - \dots - \theta_q B^q\right) \tag{7}$$

where p is the number of autoregressive orders, q is the number of moving average orders, θ is the autoregressive coefficient, and ϕ is the moving average coefficient. In particular, the autoregressive (AR) component is expressed by the coefficients ϕ that represent a linear relationship between the value predicted by the model at time t and the past values of the time series y. Similarly, the moving average (MA) component is expressed by the coefficients θ that represent a linear relationship between the value predicted by the model at time t and the error term e. The autocorrelation function (ACF) and partial autocorrelation function (PACF) are used in conjunction with the Akaike information criterion (AIC) (Box et al, 1994) to determine the order p and q. The AIC is computed as follows:

$$AIC = \log\left(\hat{\sigma}^2\right) + \frac{2\left(p + q\right)}{T} \tag{8}$$

where $\hat{\sigma}$ is the ARMA model estimated variance from errors $e_1, e_2, \dots, e_T$.

2.5 Inputs and Performance Measures

Technical analysis indicators rely on asset historical prices to predict its future trends and cycles. Therefore, they can be used so as to evaluate possible investment opportunities by determining a given asset overbought and oversold conditions. In our study, technical analysis indicators are applied as inputs to BPNN. Indeed, a set of eight widely used indicators by real world traders is composed to form the input block to the BPNN. They are Bollinger bands (middle, upper, lower), moving average convergence/divergence (MACD), nine-period exponential moving average (EMA), relative strength index (RSI), momentum, and acceleration. They are described in Table 2 where C is the current currency exchange rate, t is time script, T is set to 20, n is set to 14, $a = 2/(1+k)$ is a smoothing factor, and Diff $=$ EMA(12)$_t$ $-$ EMA(26)$_t$.

Finally, the performance of the BPNN and ARMA process is measured by computing the mean absolute deviation (MAD), mean absolute error (MAE), and mean of squared errors (MSE) which are defined as follows:

$$MAD = m^{-1}\sum\nolimits_{i=1}^{m}\left|\hat{y}_i - \tilde{y}_i\right| \tag{9}$$

$$MAE = m^{-1}\sum\nolimits_{i=1}^{m}\left|y_i - \hat{y}_i\right| \tag{10}$$

$$MAE = m^{-1}\sum\nolimits_{i=1}^{m}\left(y_i - \hat{y}_i\right)^2 \tag{11}$$

where y is the observed value, $\hat{y}$ is the predicted value, $\tilde{y}$ is the average of the predicted values, and m is the total number of observations in the testing data. The lower are these statistical metrics the better is the accuracy.

3. DATA AND RESULTS

Empirical simulations are carried out in six major US currency exchange markets. They include the US/Canada, US/Euro, US/Japan, US/Korea, US/Swiss, and US/UK exchange rate. The overall sample used for our study span from January 4th 1999 to December 6th 2013, yielding 3756 daily observations. The first 80% of the sample is used for training the BPNN and estimating ARMA process parameters, and the last 20% of the sample is used to conduct out-of-sample simulations. All data was obtained from federal economic database (FRED) of Saint-Louis Federal Reserve Bank. Table 3 to Table 8 list the

Table 3. List of technical indicators

Indicators	Formula
Middle band	$$\frac{\sum_{t=1}^{T} C_t}{T}$$
Upper band	$$Middle\ Band + \left[D \frac{\sum_{t=1}^{T} \left(C_t - Middle\ Band \right)^2}{T} \right]$$
Lower band	$$Middle\ Band - \left[D \frac{\sum_{t=1}^{T} \left(C_t - Middle\ Band \right)^2}{T} \right]$$
Momentum	$$C_t - C_{t-12}$$
Acceleration	$$Momentum\ (t) - Momentum\ (t-12)$$
EMA	$$EMA\left(k\right)_{t-1} + \alpha \left(C_t - EMA\left(k\right)_{t-1} \right)$$
RSI	$$100 - \frac{100}{1 + \left(\sum_{i=0}^{n-1} \frac{Up_{t-i}}{n} \right) \bigg/ \left(\sum_{i=0}^{n-1} \frac{Down_{t-i}}{n} \right)}$$
MACD	$$MACD = MACD\left(n\right)_{t-1} + 2/n + 1 \times \left(Diff_t - MACD\left(n\right)_{t-1} \right)$$

out-of-sample forecasting accuracy obtained by each BPNN training algorithm and the ARMA process for US/Canada, US/Euro, US/Japan, US/Korea, US/Swiss, and US/UK exchange rate respectively.

According to the statistical metrics used to evaluate accuracy, the LM algorithm outperforms all the other numerical algorithms in the prediction of US exchange rates considered in our study. In addition, according to Table 3 to Table 8 simulation results all training algorithms outperform the statistical ARMA process. Indeed, the ARMA process achieved the highest prediction errors in each simulation experiment. Finally, it is worth pointing out that all ANN training algorithms are capable to predict US exchange rates. For instance, Figure 3 to Figure 8 show for each US currency exchange rate the comparison chart between the actual data and the prediction performed by each ANN algorithm. As it can be seen, the values predicted by the neural network followed the trend of all US currency exchange rate series and for all numerical algorithms used to train the ANN.

Summarizing, several observations can be made from the above results. First, the conventional BPNN as nonlinear system is suitable to model and predict US currency exchange rates than a linear statistical model since it is assumptions-free, adaptive and robust to noisy data. Second, all numerical algorithms provide in general accurate forecasts, but the LM algorithm performs the best. Indeed, the LM is a combination of steepest descent and the Gauss-Newton method. Therefore, when the current solution is far from a local minimum, the algorithm behaves like a steepest descent method to converge, and when the current solution is close to a local minimum, it becomes a Gauss-Newton method to exhibit fast

Figure 1. US/Euro predicted and observed series

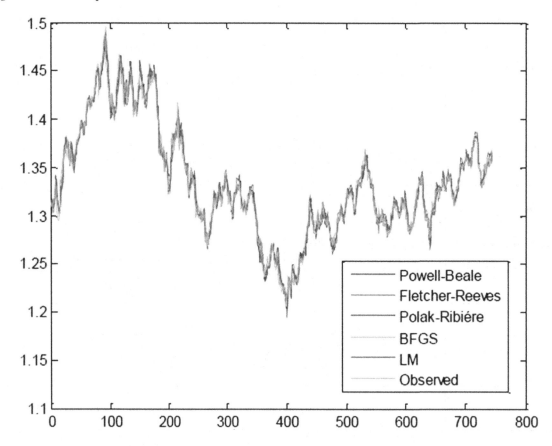

Figure 2. US/Canada predicted and observed series

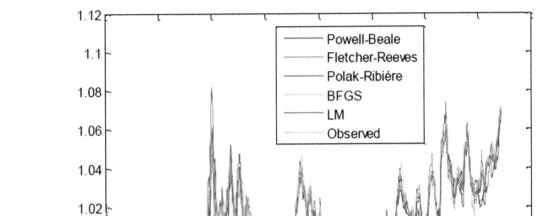

Figure 3. US/UK predicted and observed series

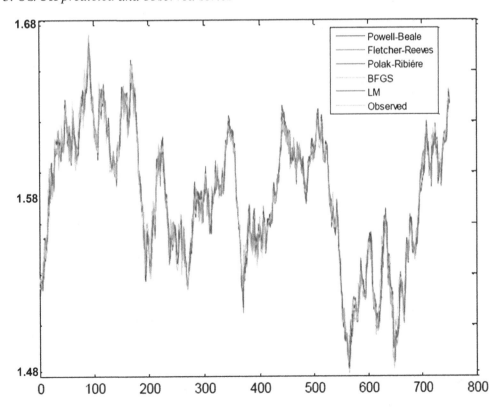

Figure 4. US/Japan predicted and observed series

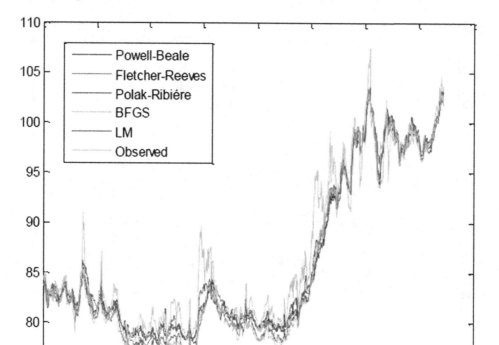

Figure 5. US/Swiss predicted and observed series

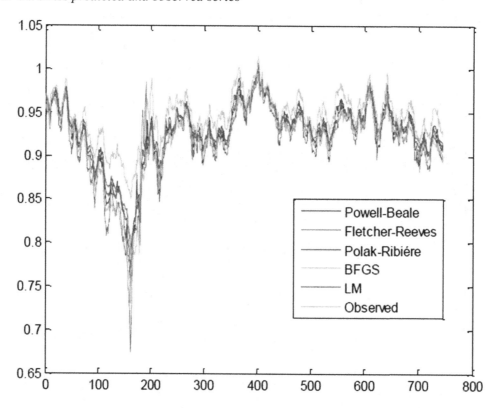

Figure 6. US/Korea predicted and observed series

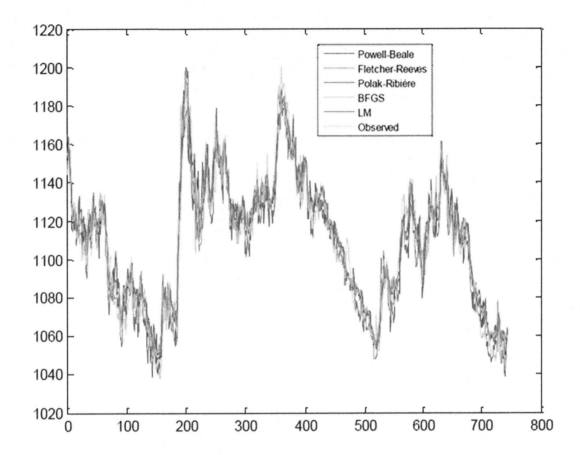

Table 4. US/UK simulation results

	MAD	MAE	MSE
Powell-Beale	0.00425	0.00442	0.00003
Fletcher	0.00566	0.00595	0.00006
Polak-Ribiére	0.00646	0.00662	0.00008
BFGS	0.00626	0.00642	0.00007
LM	**0.00408**	**0.00435**	**0.00003**
ARMA	0.02671	0.07225	0.00626

convergence. As a result, the simple gradient descent and Gauss-Newton iteration are complementary in the advantages they provide. Third, the obtained results suggest that the prediction system based on technical indicators as inputs to BPNN can be practically used by traders and managers in business applications. Overall, the presented approach provides a powerful tool and easy to implement for forecasting US currency exchange rates.

Table 5. US/UK simulation results

	MAD	MAE	MSE
Powell-Beale	0.00788	0.00789	0.00011
Fletcher	0.00861	0.00861	0.00012
Polak-Ribiére	0.00914	0.00913	0.00014
BFGS	0.00731	0.00731	0.00009
LM	**0.00715**	**0.00719**	**0.00009**
ARMA	0.04374	0.04706	0.00393

Table 6. US/Japan simulation results

	MAD	MAE	MSE
Powell-Beale	0.88070	1.05323	1.59570
Fletcher	0.75109	0.94791	1.26765
Polak-Ribiére	0.94276	1.17402	1.94031
BFGS	1.55375	1.99055	6.25410
LM	**0.52515**	**0.54888**	**0.49954**
ARMA	7.58188	14.94661	292.68839

Table 7. US/UK simulation results

	MAD	MAE	MSE
Powell-Beale	5.45500	5.47113	55.56161
Fletcher	5.16905	5.17818	50.27420
Polak-Ribiére	7.32389	8.49899	116.71201
BFGS	7.77740	8.29295	111.90648
LM	**4.62354**	**4.66975**	**42.51976**
ARMA	26.53299	28.86898	1327.97114

Table 8. US/Swiss simulation results

	MAD	MAE	MSE
Powell-Beale	0.00816	0.01112	0.00021
Fletcher	0.00971	0.00971	0.00020
Polak-Ribiére	0.00778	0.01023	0.00019
BFGS	0.01400	0.02789	0.00117
LM	**0.00681**	**0.01011**	**0.00017**
ARMA	0.05184	0.05681	0.00451

Table 9. US/UK simulation results

	MAD	MAE	MSE
Powell-Beale	0.00724	0.00724	0.00008
Fletcher	0.00727	0.00727	0.00008
Polak-Ribiére	0.00701	0.00701	0.00008
BFGS	0.00752	0.00762	0.00009
LM	**0.00681**	**0.00683**	**0.00007**
ARMA	0.03100	0.08683	0.00891

4. CONCLUSION

This paper examines the performance of the conventional backpropagation neural network trained with different numerical algorithms in the prediction of the US/Canada, US/Euro, US/Japan, US/Korea, US/Swiss, and US/UK exchange rate future value. Technical analysis indicators are used to extract hidden historical patterns in exchange rate series and are used as inputs to the BPNN. The architecture of the BPNN is optimized by using genetic algorithms. The forecasting accuracy of the BPNN was compared with that of the popular autoregressive moving average process used as reference model. Based on three forecasting evaluation criteria, it was found that the Levenberg-Marquardt algorithm performs the best among the Fletcher-Reeves, Polak-Ribiére, Powell-Beale, and quasi-Newton numerical algorithm. In addition, it was found that the BPNN largely outperforms the ARMA process for all markets and all training algorithms. This finding provides evidence of the superiority of ANN over the popular statistical model ARMA. From a managerial point of view, we conclude that using technical analysis indicators and BPNN trained with LM algorithm offers a possibility to extract information hidden in exchange rate series to forecast its future value. Indeed, the implementation is easy and the processing and forecasting is fast.

Future research direction could involve advanced optimization of BPNN-LM initial parameters to improve the accuracy and consideration of directions prediction problem along with comparison with advanced neural networks architectures.

ACKNOWLEDGMENT

The author would like to thank the anonymous reviewers and the editor for their insightful comments and suggestions.

REFERENCES

Anastasakis, L., & Mort, N. (2009). Exchange rate forecasting using a combined parametric and non-parametric self-organizing modeling approach. *Expert Systems with Applications, 36*(10), 12001–12011. doi:10.1016/j.eswa.2009.03.057

Bollerslev, T. (1986). Generalized autoregressive conditional heteroskedasticity. *Journal of Econometrics, 31*(3), 307–327. doi:10.1016/0304-4076(86)90063-1

Box, G. E. P., Jenkins, G. M., & Reinsel, G. C. (1994). Time series analysis: Forecasting and control. Englewood Cliffs, NJ: Prentice Hall.

Brooks, C. (1996). Testing for non-linearity in daily sterling exchange rates. *Applied Financial Economics, 6*(4), 307–317. doi:10.1080/096031096334105

Charalambous, C. (1992). Conjugate gradient algorithm for efficient training of artificial neural networks. *IEEE Proceedings, 139*, 301-310.

Dunis, C., Laws, J., & Sermpinis, G. (2011). Higher order and recurrent neural architectures for trading the EUR/USD exchange rate. *Quantitative Finance, 11*(4), 615–629. doi:10.1080/14697680903386348

Eligius, M. T., & Boglárka, G.-T. (2010). *Introduction to Nonlinear and Global Optimization*. Springer.

Feng, L.-H., & Lu, J. (2010). The practical research on flood forecasting based on artificial neural networks. *Expert Systems with Applications, 37*(4), 2974–2977. doi:10.1016/j.eswa.2009.09.037

Goldberg, D. E. (1989). *Genetic Algorithm in Search, Optimization, and Machine Learning*. Addison Wesley.

Haykin, S. (2008). *Neural Networks and Learning Machines*. Prentice Hall.

Hsieh, D. A. (1989). Testing for nonlinear dependence in daily foreign exchange rates. *The Journal of Business, 62*(3), 339–368. doi:10.1086/296466

Hu, M. Y., Zhang, G. P., Jiang, C. X., & Patuwo, B. E. (1999). A cross-validation analysis of neural network out-of-sample performance in exchange rate forecasting. *Decision Sciences, 30*(1), 197–216. doi:10.1111/j.1540-5915.1999.tb01606.x

Hussain, A., Ghazali, R., & Al-Jumeily, D. (2006). Dynamic ridge polynomial neural network for financial time series prediction. In Proceedings of IEEE International Conference on Innovation in Information Technology (IIT06). Dubai, UAE: IEEE.

Jang, J.-S. R., Sun, C.-T., & Mizutani, E. (1997). *Neuro-Fuzzy and Soft Computing: A Computational Approach to Learning and Machine Intelligence*. Prentice-Hall.

Kulkarni, S., Simon, S. P., & Sundareswaran, K. (2013). A spiking neural network (SNN) forecast engine for short-term electrical load forecasting. *Applied Soft Computing, 13*(8), 3628–3635. doi:10.1016/j.asoc.2013.04.007

Lahmiri, S. (2014). Practical machine learning in financial market trend prediction. In *Analytical approaches to strategic decision-making: Interdisciplinary considerations*. Hershey, PA: IGI-Global. doi:10.4018/978-1-4666-5958-2.ch010

Lahmiri, S., Boukadoum, M., & Chartier, S. (2014a). Exploring Information Categories and Artificial Neural Networks Numerical Algorithms in S&P500 Trend Prediction: A Comparative Study. *International Journal of Strategic Decision Sciences*, *5*(1), 76–94. doi:10.4018/IJSDS.2014010105

Lahmiri, S., Boukadoum, M., & Chartier, S. (2014b). (in press). A Supervised Classification System of Financial Data Based on Wavelet Packet and Neural Networks. *International Journal of Strategic Decision Sciences*.

Liu, T.-R., Gerlow, M. E., & Irwin, S. H. (1994). The performance of alternative VAR models in forecasting exchange rates. *International Journal of Forecasting*, *10*(3), 419–433. doi:10.1016/0169-2070(94)90071-X

Majhi, B., Rout, M., Majhi, R., Panda, G., & Fleming, P. J. (2012). New robust forecasting models for exchange rates prediction. *Expert Systems with Applications*, *39*(16), 12658–12670. doi:10.1016/j.eswa.2012.05.017

Majhi, R., Panda, G., & Sahoo, G. (2009). Efficient prediction of exchange rates with low complexity artificial neural network models. *Expert Systems with Applications*, *36*(1), 181–189. doi:10.1016/j.eswa.2007.09.005

Neely, C., Weller, P., & Dittmar, R. (1997). Is technical analysis in the foreign exchange market profitable? A genetic programming approach. *Journal of Financial and Quantitative Analysis*, *32*(4), 405–426. doi:10.2307/2331231

Nocedal, J., & Wright, S. J. (2006). *Numerical Optimization*. Springer.

Panda, C., & Narasimhan, V. (2007). Forecasting exchange rate better with artificial neural network. *Journal of Policy Modeling*, *29*(2), 227–236. doi:10.1016/j.jpolmod.2006.01.005

Pring, M. T. (1991). *Technical Analysis*. New York.

Ramírez, E., Castillo, O., & Soria, J. (2003). Hybrid system for cardiac arrhythmia classification with fuzzy k-nearest neighbors and multi layer perceptrons combined by a fuzzy inference system. In *Proceedings of the International Joint Conference on Neural Networks*. Barcelona, Spain: Academic Press.

Rumelhart, D. E., Hinton, G. E., & Williams, R. J. (1986). Learning representations by back-propagating errors. *Nature*, *323*(6088), 533–536. doi:10.1038/323533a0

Sedki, A., Ouazar, D., & El Mazoudi, E. (2009). Evolving neural network using real coded genetic algorithm for daily rainfall–runoff forecasting. *Expert Systems with Applications*, *36*(3), 4523–4527. doi:10.1016/j.eswa.2008.05.024

Sermpinis, G., Laws, J., Karathanasopoulos, A., & Dunis, C. L. (2012). Dunis, Forecasting and trading the EUR/USD exchange rate with Gene Expression and Psi Sigma Neural Networks. *Expert Systems with Applications*, *39*(10), 8865–8877. doi:10.1016/j.eswa.2012.02.022

Sewell, M., & Shawe-Taylor, J. (2012). Forecasting foreign exchange rates using kernel methods. *Expert Systems with Applications*, *39*(9), 7652–7662. doi:10.1016/j.eswa.2012.01.026

Singh, P., & Deo, M. C. (2007). Suitability of different neural networks in daily flow forecasting. *Applied Soft Computing*, *7*(3), 968–978. doi:10.1016/j.asoc.2006.05.003

Wei, L.-Y. (2013). A GA-weighted ANFIS model based on multiple stock market volatility causality for TAIEX forecasting. *Applied Soft Computing*, *13*(2), 911–920. doi:10.1016/j.asoc.2012.08.048

Wu, J.-D., & Liu, J.-C. (2012). A forecasting system for car fuel consumption using a radial basis function neural network. *Expert Systems with Applications*, *39*(2), 1883–1888. doi:10.1016/j.eswa.2011.07.139

Yao, J., & Tan, C. L. (2000). A case study on using neural networks to perform technical forecasting of forex. *Neurocomputing*, *34*(1-4), 79–98. doi:10.1016/S0925-2312(00)00300-3

Yen, G. (1994). Adaptive time-delay neural control in space structural platforms. In *Proceedings of IEEE World Congress on Computational Intelligence*, (vol. 4, pp. 2622-2627). IEEE. doi:10.1109/ICNN.1994.374635

KEY TERMS AND DEFINITIONS

ARMA Process: A description of stationary stochastic process in terms of an auto-regression and moving average polynomials.

Exchange Rate: The rate at which one currency will be exchanged for another.

Forecasting: A prediction process of unobservable events.

Genetic Algorithms: A heuristic search algorithm that mimics the process of natural selection used for optimization purpose using mutation, selection, and crossover operators.

Gradient Descent: A first-order optimization algorithm used to find a local minimum of a function by taking steps proportional to the negative of the gradient.

Neural Networks: Biologically inspired computing system based on the neural structure of the brain.

Chapter 23
Solving Solid Transportation Problems with Multi-Choice Cost and Stochastic Supply and Demand

Sankar Kumar Roy
Vidyasagar University, India

Deshabrata Roy Mahapatra
Vidyasagar University, India

ABSTRACT

In this chapter, the authors propose a new approach to analyze the Solid Transportation Problem (STP). This new approach considers the multi-choice programming into the cost coefficients of objective function and stochastic programming, which is incorporated in three constraints, namely sources, destinations, and capacities constraints, followed by Cauchy's distribution for solid transportation problem. The multi-choice programming and stochastic programming are combined into a solid transportation problem, and this new problem is called Multi-Choice Stochastic Solid Transportation Problem (MCSSTP). The solution concepts behind the MCSSTP are based on a new transformation technique that will select an appropriate choice from a set of multi-choice, which optimize the objective function. The stochastic constraints of STP converts into deterministic constraints by stochastic programming approach. Finally, the authors construct a non-linear programming problem for MCSSTP, and by solving it, they derive an optimal solution of the specified problem. A realistic example on STP is considered to illustrate the methodology.

INTRODUCTION

The classical transportation problem (TP) can be described as a special case of linear programming problem. Its model is applied to determine an optimal solution of the TP of how many units of commodity to be shipped from each origin to various destinations, satisfying source availability and destination demand and minimizing the total cost of transportation. The amounts of available goods at the supply

DOI: 10.4018/978-1-4666-7272-7.ch023

points and the amounts required at the demand points are the parameters of the TP, and these parameters are not always exactly known and stable. This imprecision may follow from the lack of exact information. The STP is an important extension of the traditional TP. The traditional TP is a well known optimization problem in operations research, in which two kinds of constraints are taken into consideration, i.e., source constraints and destination constraints. But in the real system, we always deal with other constraints besides of source constraints and destination constraints, such as product type constraints or transportation mode constraints. For such cases, the traditional TP turns into STP. The STP is a generalization of the well-known TP in which three items (they are source, destination and conveyance) are taken into account in the constraint set instead of two (source and destination). In many industrial problems, a homogeneous product is delivered from an origin to destination by means of different modes of transport called conveyances, such as trucks, cargo flights, goods trains, ships, etc. In reality, due to changes in market supply and demand, weather conditions, road conditions and other unpredictable factors, the STP is important for both theoretical and practical significance.

Stochastic programming deals with situations where some or all of the parameters of the optimization problem are described by random variables rather than by deterministic quantity. The random variables are defined as sources, destinations and conveyances which are depending on the nature and the type of problem. Decision making problems of stochastic optimization arise when certain coefficients of the optimization model are not fixed or known. In such cases, the quantities are random. In recent years, methods of multi-objective stochastic optimization have become increasingly important in the field of economics, industry, transportation, military purpose and technology. The Cauchy's distribution is a good example of a continuous stable distribution and this distribution is a source of counter examples, having little connection with statistical practice. The Cauchy's distribution is an old and very important problem in the statistical literature. Particularly, in the recent years it has gained more importance. The Cauchy's distribution is empirical as many large data sets exhibit on heavy tails and skewness. The strong empirical evidence for these features combined with the generalized central limit theorem is used for many types of physical and economic systems.

In the recent past normal, log-normal, extreme value distribution and other random variables have been considered in the stochastic programming model. Cauchy's distribution has also two parameters namely location parameter and scale parameter. It has some similarities with normal distribution. Assuming Cauchy's distribution is a suitable one for stochastic programming model, we consider the source, the availability and the conveyance parameters of the transportation problem as Cauchy's distribution. Here, we consider the probability density function of Cauchy's distribution with location parameter α_i and scale parameter β_i as,

$$f\left(x\right) = \frac{\alpha_i}{\pi\left[\beta_i^2 + \left(x - \alpha_i\right)^2\right]},$$

(1.1)

$-\infty < x < \infty$ and $\alpha_i > 0$ and $\beta_i > 0$

An extension of the traditional TP to the STP was stated by Shell (1955). Haley (1962) introduced the solution procedure of STP, which is an extension of the modified distribution method. For finding an optimal solution, the STP requires (m+n+s−2) non-zero values of the decision variables to start with a basic feasible solution. Bit et al. (1993) developed the fuzzy programming model for multi-objective STP. Patel & Tripathy (1989) presented a computationally superior method for a STP with mixed constraints. Jimenez et al. (1998) obtained a solution procedure for uncertain STP. Hitchcock (1941) first considered the problem of minimizing the cost of distribution of products from several factories to a number of customers. He developed a procedure to solve the TP, which has close resemblance with the simplex method for solving TP as the primal simplex transportation method developed by Dantzig (1963) Goicoechea et al. (1982) presented the deterministic equivalents for some stochastic programming involving normal and other distribution. Rao (1984) described the chance constrained and two stage programming methods for solving a stochastic linear programming problem. Mahapatra et al. (2010) have presented the fuzzy programming technique to obtain the compromise solution of multi-objective stochastic transportation problem. They have also discussed the conversion procedure from stochastic constraints into deterministic constraints when the sources and destination parameters involve randomness. Biswal & Acharya (2009) presented the transformation of a multi-choice linear programming problem in which the terms of right hand side in the constraints also satisfy the multi-choices or goals. A method for modeling the multi-choice goal programming problem, using the multiple terms of binary variables with aspiration levels was presented by Chang (2007). He has proposed a revised method for multi-choice goal programming model which does not involve any multiplicative terms of binary variables (2008). Hiller and Lieberman. (1990) and Ravindran et al. (1987) have considered a mathematical model in which an appropriate constraint is to be chosen using binary variables. Roy et al. (2012) and Mahapatra et al. (2013) discussed the multi choice stochastic transportation problem involving extreme value distribution and exponential distribution in which the multi-choice concept involved only in the cost parameters.

In this chapter, we have studied the MCSSTP with three stochastic constraints keeping in view the real life problems. The stochastic constraints are inequality type and the parameters (supply, demand and capacity) are followed by Cauchy's distribution and cost coefficients of objective function which are under multi-choice environment.

MATHEMATICAL MODEL

In the typical STP, we consider the situation having m origins i.e, sources S_i (i=1,2,…,m) and n demands i.e, destinations D_j (j=1,2,…,n). The sources may be production facilities, warehouses, supply points and the destinations are consumption facilities, warehouses or demand points. Let e_k (k=1,2,…,s) denotes the unit of product that can be carried by k different modes of transportation called conveyance, such as land transportation by car or train, airlines and ocean shipping.

The coefficient C_{ijk}^p of the objective function could represent the transportation cost or delivery time or unfulfilled supply and demand, and others, are provided with transporting a unit of product from source i to destination j by means of the k-th conveyance. Most of real world practical problems are modeled with MCSSTP which are measured in different scales and in the same type of conflict.

In this chapter, we have considered the mathematical model for MCSSTP involving Cauchy's distribution in all constraints and cost coefficients of objective function are in multi-choice framework as follows:

- **Model 1**

$$\min: \ Z = \sum_{i=1}^{m}\sum_{j=1}^{n}\sum_{k=1}^{s}\left\{C_{ijk}^{1}, C_{ijk}^{2}, ..., C_{ijk}^{p}\right\}x_{ijk}^{p},$$
$$p = 1, 2, ..., P \tag{2.2}$$

$$subject\,to, \ \Pr\left(\sum_{j=1}^{n}\sum_{k=1}^{s}x_{ijk} \le a_{i}\right) \ge 1 - \gamma_{i},$$
$$i = 1, 2, ..., m \tag{2.3}$$

$$\Pr\left(\sum_{i=1}^{m}\sum_{k=1}^{s}x_{ijk} \ge b_{j}\right) \ge 1 - \delta_{j}, \ j = 1, 2, ..., n \tag{2.4}$$

$$\Pr\left(\sum_{i=1}^{m}\sum_{j=1}^{n}x_{ijk} \ge e_{k}\right) \ge 1 - \eta_{k}, \ k = 1, 2, ..., s \tag{2.5}$$

$$x_{ijk} \ge 0, \ \forall \ i \ , \ \forall j \ and \forall k \tag{2.6}$$

Here z represents the minimum value of the objective function. It is assumed that

$$a_{i} > 0, \ b_{j} > 0 \quad and \ e_{k} > 0 \, and \ \ C_{ijk}^{p} > 0 \ and \sum_{i=1}^{m}a_{i} \ne \sum_{j=1}^{n}b_{j} \ne \sum_{k=1}^{s}e_{k}$$

(for unbalanced solid transportation problem), where specified stochastic levels or predetermined confidence levels are defined as $0 < \gamma_{i} < 1, \ \forall \ i; \ 0 < \delta_{j} < 1, \forall j$, and $0 < \eta_{k} < 1, \forall \ k$.

We assumed that a_{i} (i = 1, 2, ...,m), b_{j} (j = 1, 2, ..., n) and e_{k} (k = 1, 2, ..., s) are specified with Cauchy's distribution and $C_{ijk}^{p} > 0, \ \forall p$ are also defined as multi-choice parameters in each respective decision variable. Now the following cases are to be considered

1. Only a_{i} (i = 1, 2, $\cdots$, m) follows Cauchy's distribution.
2. Only b_{j} (j = 1, 2, $\cdots$, n) follows Cauchy's distribution.
3. Only e_{k} (k = 1, 2, $\cdots$, s) follows Cauchy's distribution.
4. All of a_{i} (i = 1, 2, $\cdots$, m), b_{j} (j = 1, 2, $\cdots$, n) and e_{k} (k = 1, 2, $\cdots$, s) follow Cauchy's distributions.

1.   Only a_i (i = 1, 2, $\cdots$, m) follows Cauchy's Distribution

It is assumed that a_i (i = 1, 2, ..., m) are independent random variables having Cauchy's distribution in which mean and variance do not exist and the i-th variable has two known parameters α_i and β_i (where α_i = location parameter and β_i = scale parameter for sources) which are known to us. The probability density function of Cauchy's distribution for random variable a_i be given by

$$f\left(a_i\right) = \frac{\beta_i}{\pi\left[\beta_i^2 + \left(a_i - \alpha_i\right)^2\right]};$$

(2.7)

$$-\infty < x < \infty \ \ and\, \alpha_i > 0 \ \ and\, \beta_i > 0$$

The stochastic constraints (2.3) having ai (i = 1, 2,...,m) random variables restated as below:

$$\Pr\left(\sum_{j=1}^{n}\sum_{k=1}^{s} x_{ijk} \leq \alpha_i\right) \geq 1 - \gamma_i, \ \ i = 1, 2, ..., m$$

Hence the above stochastic constraints can be reduced to the cumulative density function using the probability density function of Cauchy's distribution as follows:

$$\int_{\sum_{j=1}^{n}\sum_{k=1}^{s} x_{ijk}}^{\infty} f(\alpha_i) d(\alpha_i) \geq 1 - \gamma_i, \ \ i = 1, 2, ..., m$$

(2.8)

$$\int_{\sum_{j=1}^{n}\sum_{k=1}^{s} x_{ijk}}^{\infty} \frac{\beta_i}{\pi\left[\beta_i^2 + (a_i - \alpha_i)^2\right]} d(\alpha_i) \geq 1 - \gamma_i,$$

(2.9)

$$i = 1, 2, ..., m$$

On simplification, we have

$$\left|\sum_{j=1}^{n}\sum_{k=1}^{s} x_{ijk} - \alpha_i\right| \leq \beta_i \tan\left(\pi\gamma_i - \frac{\pi}{2}\right),$$

(2.10)

$$i = 1, 2, ..., m$$

Finally, the stochastic constraints (2.3) can be expressed into equivalent deterministic constraints as follows:

$$\sum_{j=1}^{n}\sum_{k=1}^{s} x_{ijk} \leq \alpha_i + \beta_i \tan\left(\pi\gamma_i - \frac{\pi}{2}\right), i = 1, 2, ..., m$$

(2.11)

2.   Only b_j (j = 1, 2, ..., n) follows Cauchy's Distribution

Assume that bj (j = 1, 2, ..., n) are independent random variables having Cauchy's distribution in which mean and variance do not exist and the j-th random variable has two known parameters α'_j and β'_j (where α'_j = location parameter and β'_j = scale parameter for destinations) which are known to us. The probability density function of Cauchy's distribution for random variable bj be given by

$$f\left(b_j\right) = \frac{\beta'_j}{\pi\left[\beta'^2_j + \left(b_i - \alpha_i\right)^2\right]};$$

$$-\infty < x < \infty \ and \ \alpha'_j > 0 \ and \ \beta'_j > 0$$

(2.12)

The stochastic constraints (2.4) having b_j (j = 1, 2,···, n) random variables restated as follows:

$$\Pr\left(\sum_{i=1}^{m}\sum_{k=1}^{s}x_{ijk} \geq b_j\right) \geq 1 - \delta_j, j = 1, 2, ..., n$$

(2.13)

Hence the above stochastic constraints can be reduced to the cumulative density function using probability density function of Cauchy's distribution as follows:

$$\int_{\sum_{j=1}^{m}\sum_{k=1}^{s}x_{ijk}}^{\infty} f(b_j)d(b_j) \geq 1 - \delta_j; j = 1, 2, ..., n$$

(2.14)

which can be further simplified to

$$\int_{\sum_{j=1}^{m}\sum_{k=1}^{s}x_{ijk}}^{\infty} \frac{\beta'_j}{\pi\left[\beta'^2_j + (b_j - \alpha'_j)^2\right]} d(b_j) \geq 1 - \delta_j,$$

$$j = 1, 2, ..., n$$

(2.14)

On simplification, we have

$$\left(\sum_{i=1}^{m}\sum_{k=1}^{s}x_{ijk} - \alpha'_j\right) \geq \beta'_j \tan\left(\frac{\pi}{2} - \pi\delta_j\right),$$

$$j = 1, 2, ..., n$$

(2.15)

Finally, the stochastic constraints (2.4) can be expressed into equivalent deterministic constraints as follows:

$$\sum_{i=1}^{m}\sum_{k=1}^{s} x_{ijk} \geq \alpha_{j}' + \beta_{j}' \tan\left(\frac{\pi}{2} - \pi\delta_{j}\right), j = 1,2,...,n \tag{2.16}$$

3. Only e_k (k = 1, 2, $\cdots$, s) follows Cauchy's Distribution

Assume that e_k (k = 1, 2, ..., s) are independent random variables having Cauchy's distribution in which mean and variance do not exist and the k-th random variable has two known parameters α_{k}'' and β_{k}'' (where α_{k}'' = location parameter and β_{k}'' = scale parameter for capacities) which are known to us. The probability density function of Cauchy's distribution for random variable e_k be given by

$$f\left(e_{k}\right) = \frac{\beta_{k}''}{\pi\left[\beta_{k}''^{2} + \left(e_{k} - \alpha_{k}''\right)^{2}\right]}; \tag{2.17}$$
$$-\infty < x < \infty \ \ and \ \ \alpha_{j}'' > 0 \ \ and \ \ \beta_{j}'' > 0$$

The stochastic constraints (2.5) having ek, (k = 1, 2, $\cdots$, s) random variables restated as follows:

$$\Pr\left(\sum_{i=1}^{m}\sum_{j=1}^{n} x_{ijk} \geq e_{k}\right) \geq 1 - \eta_{k}, \ \ k = 1,2,...,s$$

Hence the above stochastic constraints can be reduced to cumulative density function using probability density function for Cauchy's distribution as,

$$\int_{\sum_{j=1}^{m}\sum_{k=1}^{n} x_{ijk}}^{\infty} f(e_{k})d(e_{k}) \geq 1 - \eta_{k}; j = 1,2,...,s \tag{2.18}$$

$$\int_{\sum_{j=1}^{m}\sum_{k=1}^{n} x_{ijk}}^{\infty} \frac{\beta_{k}''}{\pi\left[\beta_{k}''^{2} + (e_{k} - \alpha_{k}'')^{2}\right]} d(e_{k}) \leq \eta_{k}; \tag{2.19}$$
$$k = 1,2,...,s$$

On simplification, we have

$$\sum_{i=1}^{m}\sum_{j=1}^{n} x_{ijk} - \alpha_{k}'' \geq \beta_{k}'' \tan\left(\frac{\pi}{2} - \pi\eta_{k}\right), k = 1,2,...,s \tag{2.20}$$

Finally, the stochastic constraints (2.5) can be expressed into deterministic constraints as follows:

$$\sum_{i=1}^{m}\sum_{j=1}^{n} x_{ijk} \geq \alpha_{k}'' + \beta_{k}'' \tan\left(\frac{\pi}{2} - \pi\eta_{k}\right), k = 1,2,...,s \tag{2.21}$$

4. All of a_i (i = 1, 2, ..., m), b_j (j = 1, 2,..., n), and e_k (k = 1, 2, ..., s) follow Cauchy's Distributions

In this case, the equivalent deterministic model of MCSSTP with specified confidence levels γ_i, δ_j and η_k can be represented as:

- **Model 2**

$$\min : Z = \sum_{i=1}^{m}\sum_{j=1}^{n}\sum_{k=1}^{s}\left\{C_{ijk}^1, C_{ijk}^2, ..., C_{ijk}^p\right\} x_{ijk}^p,$$
$$p = 1, 2, ..., P$$

(2.22)

$$\sum_{j=1}^{n}\sum_{k=1}^{s}x_{ijk} \le \alpha_i + \beta_i \tan\left(\pi\gamma_i - \frac{\pi}{2}\right), i = 1, 2, ..., m$$

(2.23)

$$\sum_{j=1}^{n}\sum_{k=1}^{s}x_{ijk} \ge \alpha_j' + \beta_j' \tan\left(\frac{\pi}{2} - \pi\delta_j\right), j = 1, 2, ..., n$$

(2.24)

$$\sum_{i=1}^{m}\sum_{j=1}^{n}x_{ijk} \ge \alpha_k'' + \beta_k'' \tan\left(\frac{\pi}{2} - \pi\eta_k\right), k = 1, 2, ..., s$$

(2.25)

$$x_{ijk} \ge 0, \forall i, \forall j \, and \, \forall k$$

(2.26)

TRANSFORMATION OF AN EQUIVALENT MODEL WITH COST COEFFICIENTS OF OBJECTIVE FUNCTION

The proposed model is specified for twenty choices on the cost coefficients of objective function. For p = 1, the case is trivial. Nineteen cases are expressed in the following form for p = 2, 3, ..., 20.

Step 1: When p = 2:

We rewrite the objective function (2.2) as follows:

$$\min : Z = \sum_{i=1}^{m}\sum_{j=1}^{n}\sum_{k=1}^{s}\left\{C_{ijk}^1, C_{ijk}^2\right\} x_{ijk}, p = 1, 2, ..., P$$

The cost coefficients have two choices namely, $\{C_{ijk}^1, C_{ijk}^2\}$, out of which one is to be selected. Since total number of elements of the set are 2, so only one binary variable is required. Denoting the binary variable Z_{ijk}^1, the above equation is formulated as below:

$$\min : Z = \sum_{i=1}^{m} \sum_{j=1}^{n} \sum_{k=1}^{s} \left\{ C_{ijk}^1 Z_{ijk}^1 + \left(1 - Z_{ijk}^1\right) C_{ijk}^2 \right\} x_{ijk},$$

$$x_{ijk} \geq 0, \ \forall \ i \ , \ \forall j \ and \forall k \ and \ Z_{ijk}^q = 0 \ / \ 1, q = 1$$

Step 2: When p = 3:

We rewrite the objective function (2.2) as follows:

$$\min : Z = \sum_{i=1}^{m} \sum_{j=1}^{n} \sum_{k=1}^{s} \left\{ C_{ijk}^1, C_{ijk}^2, C_{ijk}^3 \right\} x_{ijk},$$

The cost coefficients have three choices namely, $\left\{ C_{ijk}^1, C_{ijk}^2, C_{ijk}^3 \right\}$ out of which one is to be selected. Since $2^1 < 3 < 2^2$, so the total number of elements of the set are 3. Denoting the binary variables as: Z_{ijk}^1, Z_{ijk}^2 and introducing auxiliary constraint in two models are formulated as as follows:

- **Model 2(a)**

$$\min : Z = \sum_{i=1}^{m} \sum_{j=1}^{n} \sum_{k=1}^{s} \left\{ C_{ijk}^1 \left(1 - Z_{ijk}^1\right)\left(1 - Z_{ijk}^2\right) + Z_{ijk}^1 \left(1 - Z_{ijk}^2\right) C_{ijk}^2 + Z_{ijk}^2 \left(1 - Z_{ijk}^1\right) C_{ijk}^3 \right\} x_{ijk}$$

$$Z_{ijk}^1 + Z_{ijk}^2 \leq 1, \ x_{ijk} \geq 0, \ \forall \ i \ , \ \forall j \ and \forall k \ Z_{ijk}^q = 0 \ / \ 1, \ q = 1, 2.$$

- **Model 2(b)**

$$\min : Z = \sum_{i=1}^{m} \sum_{j=1}^{n} \sum_{k=1}^{s} \left\{ C_{ijk}^1 Z_{ijk}^1 Z_{ijk}^2 + Z_{ijk}^1 \left(1 - Z_{ijk}^2\right) C_{ijk}^2 + Z_{ijk}^2 \left(1 - Z_{ijk}^1\right) C_{ijk}^3 \right\} x_{ijk}$$

$$Z_{ijk}^1 + Z_{ijk}^2 \geq 1, \ x_{ijk} \geq 0, \ \forall \ i \ , \ \forall j \ and \forall k \ Z_{ijk}^q = 0 \ / \ 1, \ q = 1, 2.$$

Step 3: When p = 4:

We rewrite the objective function (2.2) as follows:

$$\min : Z = \sum_{i=1}^{m} \sum_{j=1}^{n} \sum_{k=1}^{s} \left\{ C_{ijk}^1, C_{ijk}^2, C_{ijk}^3, C_{ijk}^4 \right\} x_{ijk},$$

The cost coefficients of the objective function have four choices namely, $\left\{ C_{ijk}^{1}, C_{ijk}^{2}, C_{ijk}^{3}, C_{ijk}^{4} \right\}$ out of which one is to be selected. Since the total number of choices are $4 = 2^2$. Denoting the binary variables as: Z_{ijk}^{1}, Z_{ijk}^{2} so we construct the objective function in the following form:

- **Model 3**

$$\min : Z$$

$$= \sum_{i=1}^{m} \sum_{j=1}^{n} \sum_{k=1}^{s} \left\{ Z_{ijk}^{1} Z_{ijk}^{2} C_{ijk}^{1} + Z_{ijk}^{1} \left(1 - Z_{ijk}^{2}\right) C_{ijk}^{2} + Z_{ijk}^{2} \left(1 - Z_{ijk}^{1}\right) C_{ijk}^{3} + \left(1 - Z_{ijk}^{1}\right)\left(1 - Z_{ijk}^{2}\right) C_{ijk}^{4} \right\} x_{ijk}$$

$$x_{ijk} \geq 0, \ \forall \ i \ , \ \forall j \ and \forall k \ \ Z_{ijk}^{q} = 0 \, / \, 1, \ q = 1, 2 \, .$$

Step 4: When p = 5:

We rewrite the objective function (2.2) as follows:

$$\min : Z = \sum_{i=1}^{m} \sum_{j=1}^{n} \sum_{k=1}^{s} \left\{ C_{ijk}^{1}, C_{ijk}^{2}, C_{ijk}^{3}, C_{ijk}^{4}, C_{ijk}^{5} \right\} x_{ijk}$$

The cost coefficients have five choices as $\left\{ C_{ijk}^{1}, C_{ijk}^{2}, C_{ijk}^{3}, C_{ijk}^{4}, C_{ijk}^{5} \right\}$ out of which one is to be selected. Since $2^2 < 5 < 2^3$, so we need three binary variables and they are Z_{ijk}^{1}, Z_{ijk}^{2} , Z_{ijk}^{3}. Then we put restriction to remaining three terms (8 − 5) by introducing auxiliary and additional constraints in three different models which are expressed as given as follows:

- **Model 4(a)**

$$\min : Z = \sum_{i=1}^{m} \sum_{j=1}^{n} \sum_{k=1}^{s} \left\{ \begin{array}{l} Z_{ijk}^{1}\left(1 - Z_{ijk}^{2}\right)\left(1 - Z_{ijk}^{3}\right) C_{ijk}^{1} + Z_{ijk}^{2}\left(1 - Z_{ijk}^{1}\right)\left(1 - Z_{ijk}^{3}\right) C_{ijk}^{2} \\ + Z_{ijk}^{3}\left(1 - Z_{ijk}^{1}\right)\left(1 - Z_{ijk}^{2}\right) C_{ijk}^{3} + Z_{ijk}^{1} Z_{ijk}^{2}\left(1 - Z_{ijk}^{3}\right) C_{ijk}^{4} + Z_{ijk}^{2} Z_{ijk}^{3}\left(1 - Z_{ijk}^{1}\right) C_{ijk}^{4} \end{array} \right\} x_{ijk}$$

$$1 \leq Z_{ijk}^{1} + Z_{ijk}^{2} + Z_{ijk}^{3} \leq 2$$

$$Z_{ijk}^{1} + Z_{ijk}^{3} \leq 1$$

$$x_{ijk} \geq 0, \ \forall \ i \ , \ \forall j \ and \forall k \ Z_{ijk}^{q} = 0 \, / \, 1, \ q = 1, 2, 3 \, .$$

- **Model 4(b)**

$$\min : Z = \sum_{i=1}^{m} \sum_{j=1}^{n} \sum_{k=1}^{s} \left\{ \begin{array}{l} Z_{ijk}^1 (1 - Z_{ijk}^2)(1 - Z_{ijk}^3) \mathrm{C}_{ijk}^1 + Z_{ijk}^2 (1 - Z_{ijk}^1)(1 - Z_{ijk}^3) \mathrm{C}_{ijk}^2 \\ + Z_{ijk}^3 (1 - Z_{ijk}^1)(1 - Z_{ijk}^2) \mathrm{C}_{ijk}^3 + Z_{ijk}^1 Z_{ijk}^2 (1 - Z_{ijk}^3) \mathrm{C}_{ijk}^4 + Z_{ijk}^1 Z_{ijk}^3 (1 - Z_{ijk}^1) \mathrm{C}_{ijk}^4 \end{array} \right\} x_{ijk}$$

$$1 \leq Z_{ijk}^1 + Z_{ijk}^2 + Z_{ijk}^3 \leq 2$$

$$Z_{ijk}^3 + Z_{ijk}^2 \leq 1$$

$$x_{ijk} \geq 0, \forall\, i\,, \forall j \ and \forall k \quad Z_{ijk}^q = 0\,/\,1,\, q = 1, 2, 3\,.$$

- **Model 4(c)**

$$\min : Z = \sum_{i=1}^{m} \sum_{j=1}^{n} \sum_{k=1}^{s} \left\{ \begin{array}{l} Z_{ijk}^1 (1 - Z_{ijk}^2)(1 - Z_{ijk}^3) \mathrm{C}_{ijk}^1 + Z_{ijk}^2 (1 - Z_{ijk}^1)(1 - Z_{ijk}^3) \mathrm{C}_{ijk}^2 \\ + Z_{ijk}^3 (1 - Z_{ijk}^1)(1 - Z_{ijk}^2) \mathrm{C}_{ijk}^3 + (1 - Z_{ijk}^1) Z_{ijk}^2 Z_{ijk}^3 \mathrm{C}_{ijk}^4 + Z_{ijk}^1 (1 - Z_{ijk}^2) Z_{ijk}^3 \mathrm{C}_{ijk}^5 \end{array} \right\} x_{ijk}$$

$$1 \leq Z_{ijk}^1 + Z_{ijk}^2 + Z_{ijk}^3 \leq 2$$

$$Z_{ijk}^1 + Z_{ijk}^2 \leq 1$$

$$x_{ijk} \geq 0, \forall\, i\,, \forall j \ and \forall k \quad Z_{ijk}^q = 0\,/\,1,\, q = 1, 2, 3\,.$$

Step 5: When p = 6:

We rewrite the objective function (2.2) as follows:

$$\min : Z$$
$$= \sum_{i=1}^{m} \sum_{j=1}^{n} \sum_{k=1}^{s} \left\{ C_{ijk}^1, C_{ijk}^2, C_{ijk}^3, C_{ijk}^4, C_{ijk}^5, C_{ijk}^6 \right\} x_{ijk}\,.$$

The cost coefficients have six choices as $\left\{ C_{ijk}^1, C_{ijk}^2, C_{ijk}^3, C_{ijk}^4, C_{ijk}^5, C_{ijk}^6 \right\}$ out of which one is to be selected. Since $2^2 < 6 < 2^3$, so we need three binary variables and they are $Z_{ijk}^1, Z_{ijk}^2, Z_{ijk}^3$. Then we put restriction to remaining two terms $(8 - 6)$ by introducing auxiliary and additional constraints in three different models which are expressed as given:

- **Model 5**

$$
\min : Z = \sum_{i=1}^{m}\sum_{j=1}^{n}\sum_{k=1}^{s}
\begin{bmatrix}
Z_{ijk}^1(1-Z_{ijk}^2)(1-Z_{ijk}^3)\,\mathrm{C}_{ijk}^1 + Z_{ijk}^2(1-Z_{ijk}^1)(1-Z_{ijk}^3)\,\mathrm{C}_{ijk}^2 \\
+(1-Z_{ijk}^1)(1-Z_{ijk}^2)Z_{ijk}^3\,\mathrm{C}_{ijk}^3 + Z_{ijk}^1 Z_{ijk}^2(1-Z_{ijk}^3)\,\mathrm{C}_{ijk}^4 \\
+Z_{ijk}^1\,Z_{ijk}^3(1-Z_{ijk}^2)\,\mathrm{C}_{ijk}^5 + Z_{ijk}^2 Z_{ijk}^3(1-Z_{ijk}^1)C_{ijk}^6
\end{bmatrix} x_{ijk}
$$

$$
1 \le Z_{ijk}^1 + Z_{ijk}^2 + Z_{ijk}^3 \le 2
$$

$$
x_{ijk} \ge 0,\ \forall\, i\ ,\ \forall j\ and \forall k\ Z_{ijk}^q = 0\,/\,1,\ q = 1,2,3\,.
$$

Step 6: When p = 7:

We rewrite the objective function (2.2) as follows:

$$
\min : Z
$$

$$
= \sum_{i=1}^{m}\sum_{j=1}^{n}\sum_{k=1}^{s}\left\{ C_{ijk}^1, C_{ijk}^2, C_{ijk}^3, C_{ijk}^4, C_{ijk}^5, C_{ijk}^6, C_{ijk}^7 \right\} x_{ijk}\,.
$$

The cost coefficients have seven choices as $\left\{ C_{ijk}^1, C_{ijk}^2, C_{ijk}^3, C_{ijk}^4, C_{ijk}^5, C_{ijk}^6, C_{ijk}^7 \right\}$ out of which one is to be selected. Since $2^2 < 7\ < 2^3$, so we need three binary variables and they are $Z_{ijk}^1,\ Z_{ijk}^2, Z_{ijk}^3$. Then we put restriction to remaining two terms $(8-7)$ by introducing auxiliary and additional constraints in three different models which are expressed as given below:

- **Model 6(a)**

$$
\min : Z = \sum_{i=1}^{m}\sum_{j=1}^{n}\sum_{k=1}^{s}
\begin{bmatrix}
(1-Z_{ijk}^1)(1-Z_{ijk}^2)(1-Z_{ijk}^3)\,\mathrm{C}_{ijk}^1 + Z_{ijk}^1(1-Z_{ijk}^2)(1-Z_{ijk}^3)\,\mathrm{C}_{ijk}^2 \\
+(1-Z_{ijk}^3)\,\mathrm{C}_{ijk}^3 + (1-Z_{ijk}^1)(1-Z_{ijk}^2)Z_{ijk}^3\,\mathrm{C}_{ijk}^4 + Z_{ijk}^1 Z_{ijk}^2(1-Z_{ijk}^3)\,\mathrm{C}_{ijk}^5 \\
+Z_{ijk}^1\,Z_{ijk}^3(1-Z_{ijk}^2)C_{ijk}^6 + Z_{ijk}^2 Z_{ijk}^3(1-Z_{ijk}^1)\,\mathrm{C}_{ijk}^7
\end{bmatrix} x_{ijk}
$$

$$
Z_{ijk}^1 + Z_{ijk}^2 + Z_{ijk}^3 \le 2
$$

$$
x_{ijk} \ge 0,\ \forall\, i\ ,\ \forall j\ and \forall k\ Z_{ijk}^q = 0\,/\,1,\ q = 1,2,3\,.
$$

- **Model 6(b)**

$$\min : Z = \sum_{i=1}^{m}\sum_{j=1}^{n}\sum_{k=1}^{s}\left\{\begin{array}{l} Z_{ijk}^{1}(1-Z_{ijk}^{2})(1-Z_{ijk}^{3})\,\mathrm{C}_{ijk}^{1}+Z_{ijk}^{2}(1-Z_{ijk}^{1})(1-Z_{ijk}^{3})\,\mathrm{C}_{ijk}^{2} \\ +(1-Z_{ijk}^{1})(1-Z_{ijk}^{2})Z_{ijk}^{3}\,\mathrm{C}_{ijk}^{3}+Z_{ijk}^{1}Z_{ijk}^{2}(1-Z_{ijk}^{3})\,\mathrm{C}_{ijk}^{4} \\ +Z_{ijk}^{1}Z_{ijk}^{3}(1-Z_{ijk}^{2})\mathrm{C}_{ijk}^{5}+Z_{ijk}^{2}Z_{ijk}^{3}(1-Z_{ijk}^{1})\,\mathrm{C}_{ijk}^{6}+Z_{ijk}^{1}Z_{ijk}^{2}Z_{ijk}^{3}\mathrm{C}_{ijk}^{7} \end{array}\right\}x_{ijk}$$

$$Z_{ijk}^{1}+Z_{ijk}^{2}+Z_{ijk}^{3}\geq 1$$

$$x_{ijk}\geq 0,\ \forall\ i\ ,\ \forall j\ and\forall k\ \ Z_{ijk}^{q}=0\,/\,1,\ q=1,2,3\,.$$

Step 7: When p=8:

We present the objective function (2.2) as follows:

$$\min :\ Z=\sum_{i=1}^{m}\sum_{j=1}^{n}\sum_{k=1}^{s}\left\{\begin{array}{l}C_{ijk}^{1},C_{ijk}^{2},C_{ijk}^{3},C_{ijk}^{4}, \\ C_{ijk}^{5},C_{ijk}^{6},C_{ijk}^{7},C_{ijk}^{8}\end{array}\right\}x_{ijk}\ .$$

The cost coefficients have eight choices as $\left\{C_{ijk}^{1},C_{ijk}^{2},C_{ijk}^{3},C_{ijk}^{4},C_{ijk}^{5},C_{ijk}^{6},C_{ijk}^{7},C_{ijk}^{8}\right\}$ out of which one is to be selected. Since $8=2^{3}$, so we need three binary variables and they are Z_{ijk}^{1}, Z_{ijk}^{2}, Z_{ijk}^{3}. Therefore we have formulated only one model as:

- **Model 7**

$$\min : Z=\sum_{i=1}^{m}\sum_{j=1}^{n}\sum_{k=1}^{s}\left\{\begin{array}{l}(1-Z_{ijk}^{1})(1-Z_{ijk}^{2})\,\mathrm{C}_{ijk}^{8}+Z_{ijk}^{1}(1-Z_{ijk}^{2})(1-Z_{ijk}^{3})\,\mathrm{C}_{ijk}^{7} \\ +(1-Z_{ijk}^{1})Z_{ijk}^{2}(1-Z_{ijk}^{3})\,\mathrm{C}_{ijk}^{6}+(1-Z_{ijk}^{1})(1-Z_{ijk}^{2})Z_{ijk}^{3}\,\mathrm{C}_{ijk}^{5} \\ +Z_{ijk}^{1}Z_{ijk}^{2}(1-Z_{ijk}^{3})C_{ijk}^{4}+Z_{ijk}^{1}Z_{ijk}^{3}(1-Z_{ijk}^{2})\mathrm{C}_{ijk}^{3} \\ +Z_{ijk}^{2}Z_{ijk}^{3}(1-Z_{ijk}^{1})\mathrm{C}_{ijk}^{2}+Z_{ijk}^{1}Z_{ijk}^{2}Z_{ijk}^{3}C_{ijk}^{1} \end{array}\right\}x_{ijk}$$

$$x_{ijk}\geq 0,\ \forall\ i\ ,\ \forall j\ and\forall k\ \ Z_{ijk}^{q}=0\,/\,1,\ q=1,2,3\,.$$

Step 8: When p=9:

We present the objective function (2.2) as follows:

$$\min :Z=\sum_{i=1}^{m}\sum_{j=1}^{n}\sum_{k=1}^{s}\left\{\begin{array}{l}C_{ijk}^{1},C_{ijk}^{2},C_{ijk}^{3},C_{ijk}^{4}, \\ C_{ijk}^{5},C_{ijk}^{6},C_{ijk}^{7},C_{ijk}^{8},C_{ijk}^{9}\end{array}\right\}x_{ijk}\ .$$

The cost coefficients of the objective function have nine choices as $\left\{ C_{ijk}^1, C_{ijk}^2, C_{ijk}^3, C_{ijk}^4, C_{ijk}^5, C_{ijk}^6, C_{ijk}^7, C_{ijk}^8, C_{ijk}^9 \right\}$ out of which one is to be selected. Since $2^3 < 9 < 2^4$, so we need four binary variables and they are $Z_{ijk}^1, Z_{ijk}^2, Z_{ijk}^3, Z_{ijk}^4$. Then we put the restriction to the introducing auxiliary and additional constraints in the mathematical model. Using the four binary variables with additional restrictions we formulate two different models. Again for each model, there are six similar models. To reduce the length of the chapter, we have stated only two models as given below:

- **Model 8(a)**

$$\min : Z$$

$$= \sum_{i=1}^{m} \sum_{j=1}^{n} \sum_{k=1}^{s} \left\{ \begin{array}{l} (1-Z_{ijk}^1)(1-Z_{ijk}^2)(1-Z_{ijk}^3)Z_{ijk}^4\,C_{ijk}^1 + (1-Z_{ijk}^1)(1-Z_{ijk}^2)Z_{ijk}^3(1-Z_{ijk}^4)C_{ijk}^2 \\ +(1-Z_{ijk}^1)Z_{ijk}^2(1-Z_{ijk}^3)(1-Z_{ijk}^4)C_{ijk}^3 + Z_{ijk}^1(1-Z_{ijk}^2)(1-Z_{ijk}^3)(1-Z_{ijk}^4)C_{ijk}^4 \\ +(1-Z_{ijk}^1)(1-Z_{ijk}^2)Z_{ijk}^3\,Z_{ijk}^4\,C_{ijk}^5 + (1-Z_{ijk}^1)(1-Z_{ijk}^3)Z_{ijk}^4\,C_{ijk}^6 \\ +(1-Z_{ijk}^1)Z_{ijk}^2 Z_{ijk}^3(1-Z_{ijk}^4)C_{ijk}^7 + Z_{ijk}^1(1-Z_{ijk}^2)(1-Z_{ijk}^3)C_{ijk}^8 + Z_{ijk}^1(1-Z_{ijk}^2)Z_{ijk}^3(1-Z_{ijk}^4)C_{ijk}^9 \end{array} \right\} x_{ijk}$$

$$1 \le Z_{ijk}^1 + Z_{ijk}^2 + Z_{ijk}^3 + Z_{ijk}^4 \le 2$$

$$Z_{ijk}^1 + Z_{ijk}^2 \le 1$$

$$x_{ijk} \ge 0, \ \forall \ i \ , \ \forall j \ and \forall k \quad Z_{ijk}^q = 0 \,/\, 1, \ q = 1,2,3,4\,.$$

- **Model 8(b)**

$$\min : Z$$

$$= \sum_{i=1}^{m} \sum_{j=1}^{n} \sum_{k=1}^{s} \left\{ \begin{array}{l} (1-Z_{ijk}^1)(1-Z_{ijk}^2)Z_{ijk}^3 Z_{ijk}^4\,C_{ijk}^1 + (1-Z_{ijk}^1)Z_{ijk}^2(1-Z_{ijk}^3)Z_{ijk}^4\,C_{ijk}^2 \\ +(1-Z_{ijk}^1)Z_{ijk}^2 Z_{ijk}^3(1-Z_{ijk}^4)C_{ijk}^3 + Z_{ijk}^1(1-Z_{ijk}^2)(1-Z_{ijk}^3)Z_{ijk}^4\,C_{ijk}^4 \\ +Z_{ijk}^1(1-Z_{ijk}^2)Z_{ijk}^3(1-Z_{ijk}^4)C_{ijk}^5 + Z_{ijk}^1 Z_{ijk}^2(1-Z_{ijk}^3)(1-Z_{ijk}^4)C_{ijk}^6 \\ +(1-Z_{ijk}^1)Z_{ijk}^2 Z_{ijk}^3 Z_{ijk}^4\,C_{ijk}^7 + Z_{ijk}^1(1-Z_{ijk}^2)Z_{ijk}^3 Z_{ijk}^4 C_{ijk}^8 + Z_{ijk}^1 Z_{ijk}^2(1-Z_{ijk}^3)Z_{ijk}^4 C_{ijk}^9 \end{array} \right\} x_{ijk}$$

$$2 \le Z_{ijk}^1 + Z_{ijk}^2 + Z_{ijk}^3 + Z_{ijk}^4 \le 3$$

$$Z_{ijk}^1 + Z_{ijk}^2 + Z_{ijk}^3 \le 2$$

$$x_{ijk} \ge 0, \ \forall \ i \ , \ \forall j \ and \forall k \quad Z_{ijk}^q = 0 \,/\, 1, \ q = 1,2,3,4\,.$$

Step 9: When p = 10:

We rewrite the objective function (2.2) as follows:

$$\min : Z = \sum_{i=1}^{m}\sum_{j=1}^{n}\sum_{k=1}^{s}\left\{C_{ijk}^1, C_{ijk}^2, ..., C_{ijk}^{10}\right\} x_{ijk}.$$

The cost coefficients of the objective function have ten choices as $\left\{C_{ijk}^1, C_{ijk}^2, ..., C_{ijk}^{10}\right\}$ out of which one is to be selected. Since $2^3 < 10 < 2^4$, so we need four binary variables and they are $Z_{ijk}^1, Z_{ijk}^2, Z_{ijk}^3, Z_{ijk}^4$ We express the two sets of binomial coefficients as $\{^4C1, ^4C2\}$ and $\{^4C1, ^4C3\}$ whose individual sum is equal to 10 for the same goal as p = 10. So there does not arise any additional constraint. Two different models are formulated as given below:

- **Model 9(a)**

$$= \sum_{i=1}^{m}\sum_{j=1}^{n}\sum_{k=1}^{s}\left\{\begin{array}{l}(1-Z_{ijk}^1)(1-Z_{ijk}^2)(1-Z_{ijk}^3)Z_{ijk}^4\,C_{ijk}^1 + (1-Z_{ijk}^1)(1-Z_{ijk}^2)Z_{ijk}^3(1-Z_{ijk}^4)C_{ijk}^2 \\ +(1-Z_{ijk}^1)Z_{ijk}^2(1-Z_{ijk}^3)(1-Z_{ijk}^4)C_{ijk}^3 + Z_{ijk}^1(1-Z_{ijk}^2)(1-Z_{ijk}^3)(1-Z_{ijk}^4)C_{ijk}^4 \\ +Z_{ijk}^1(1-Z_{ijk}^2)(1-Z_{ijk}^3)(1-Z_{ijk}^4)C_{ijk}^5 + (1-Z_{ijk}^1)Z_{ijk}^2(1-Z_{ijk}^3)Z_{ijk}^4\,C_{ijk}^6 + (1-Z_{ijk}^1)Z_{ijk}^2 Z_{ijk}^3(1-Z_{ijk}^4)C_{ijk}^7 \\ +Z_{ijk}^1(1-Z_{ijk}^2)(1-Z_{ijk}^3)Z_{ijk}^4 C_{ijk}^8 + Z_{ijk}^1(1-Z_{ijk}^2)Z_{ijk}^3(1-Z_{ijk}^4)C_{ijk}^9 \\ +Z_{ijk}^1 Z_{ijk}^2(1-Z_{ijk}^3)(1-Z_{ijk}^4)C_{ijk}^{10}\end{array}\right\} x_{ijk}$$

$$1 \le Z_{ijk}^1 + Z_{ijk}^2 + Z_{ijk}^3 + Z_{ijk}^4 \le 2$$

$$x_{ijk} \ge 0, \forall\, i\,, \forall j\ and \forall k\ \ Z_{ijk}^q = 0\,/\,1,\ q = 1, 2, 3, 4.$$

- **Model 9(b)**

$$\min : Z = \sum_{i=1}^{m}\sum_{j=1}^{n}\sum_{k=1}^{s}\left\{\begin{array}{l}(1-Z_{ijk}^1)(1-Z_{ijk}^2)Z_{ijk}^3 Z_{ijk}^4\,C_{ijk}^1 + (1-Z_{ijk}^1)Z_{ijk}^2(1-Z_{ijk}^3)Z_{ijk}^4\,C_{ijk}^2 \\ +(1-Z_{ijk}^1)Z_{ijk}^2 Z_{ijk}^3(1-Z_{ijk}^4)C_{ijk}^3 + Z_{ijk}^1(1-Z_{ijk}^2)(1-Z_{ijk}^3)Z_{ijk}^4\,C_{ijk}^4 \\ +Z_{ijk}^1(1-Z_{ijk}^2)Z_{ijk}^3(1-Z_{ijk}^4)C_{ijk}^5 + Z_{ijk}^1 Z_{ijk}^2(1-Z_{ijk}^3)(1-Z_{ijk}^4)C_{ijk}^6 \\ +(1-Z_{ijk}^1)Z_{ijk}^2 Z_{ijk}^3 Z_{ijk}^4 C_{ijk}^7 + Z_{ijk}^1(1-Z_{ijk}^2)Z_{ijk}^3 Z_{ijk}^4 C_{ijk}^8 \\ +Z_{ijk}^1 Z_{ijk}^2(1-Z_{ijk}^3)Z_{ijk}^4 C_{ijk}^9 + Z_{ijk}^1 Z_{ijk}^2 Z_{ijk}^3(1-Z_{ijk}^4)C_{ijk}^{10}\end{array}\right\} x_{ijk}$$

$$2 \le Z_{ijk}^1 + Z_{ijk}^2 + Z_{ijk}^3 + Z_{ijk}^4 \le 3$$

$$x_{ijk} \ge 0, \forall\, i\,, \forall j\ and \forall k\ \ Z_{ijk}^q = 0\,/\,1,\ q = 1, 2, 3, 4.$$

Step 10: When p = 11

We rewrite the objective function (2.2) as follows:

$$\min : Z = \sum_{i=1}^{m}\sum_{j=1}^{n}\sum_{k=1}^{s}\left\{C_{ijk}^{1}, C_{ijk}^{2}, \ldots, C_{ijk}^{11}\right\} x_{ijk}.$$

The cost coefficients of the objective function have eleven choices as $\left\{C_{ijk}^{1}, C_{ijk}^{2}, \ldots, C_{ijk}^{11}\right\}$ out of which one is to be selected. Since $2^{3} < 11 < 2^{4}$, so we need four binary variables and they are $Z_{ijk}^{1}, Z_{ijk}^{2}, Z_{ijk}^{3}, Z_{ijk}^{4}$. We express the two set of binomial coefficients as $\left\{{}^{4}C_{0}, {}^{4}C_{1}, {}^{4}C_{2}\right\}$ and $\left\{{}^{4}C_{1}, {}^{4}C_{2}, {}^{4}C_{3}\right\}$ in respect to two possible models. In each model, the auxiliary constraints depend upon the above specified sets of binomial coefficients and its ranges. The sum of terms of binomial coefficients is just equal to 11, which is the same of the aspiration level as p = 11. So there does not arise any additional constraint. Two different models are formulated as given below:

- **Model 10(a)**

$$\min : Z$$

$$= \sum_{i=1}^{m}\sum_{j=1}^{n}\sum_{k=1}^{s}\left\{\begin{array}{l}(1-Z_{ijk}^{1})(1-Z_{ijk}^{2})(1-Z_{ijk}^{3})(1-Z_{ijk}^{4})\mathrm{C}_{ijk}^{1}+(1-Z_{ijk}^{1})(1-Z_{ijk}^{2})(1-Z_{ijk}^{3})Z_{ijk}^{4}\,\mathrm{C}_{ijk}^{1}\\ +(1-Z_{ijk}^{1})(1-Z_{ijk}^{2})(1-Z_{ijk}^{3})Z_{ijk}^{4}C_{ijk}^{2}+(1-Z_{ijk}^{1})(1-Z_{ijk}^{2})Z_{ijk}^{3}(1-Z_{ijk}^{4})C_{ijk}^{3}\\ +(1-Z_{ijk}^{1})Z_{ijk}^{2}(1-Z_{ijk}^{3})(1-Z_{ijk}^{4})C_{ijk}^{4}+Z_{ijk}^{1}(1-Z_{ijk}^{2})(1-Z_{ijk}^{3})(1-Z_{ijk}^{4})C_{ijk}^{5}\\ +(1-Z_{ijk}^{1})(1-Z_{ijk}^{2})Z_{ijk}^{3}Z_{ijk}^{4}\,\mathrm{C}_{ijk}^{6}+(1-Z_{ijk}^{1})Z_{ijk}^{2}(1-Z_{ijk}^{3})Z_{ijk}^{4}C_{ijk}^{7}\\ +(1-Z_{ijk}^{1})Z_{ijk}^{2}Z_{ijk}^{3}(1-Z_{ijk}^{4})C_{ijk}^{8}+Z_{ijk}^{1}(1-Z_{ijk}^{2})(1-Z_{ijk}^{3})Z_{ijk}^{4}C_{ijk}^{9}\\ +Z_{ijk}^{1}(1-Z_{ijk}^{2})Z_{ijk}^{3}(1-Z_{ijk}^{4})C_{ijk}^{10}+Z_{ijk}^{1}Z_{ijk}^{2}(1-Z_{ijk}^{3})(1-Z_{ijk}^{4})C_{ijk}^{11}\end{array}\right\} x_{ijk}$$

$$Z_{ijk}^{1}+Z_{ijk}^{2}+Z_{ijk}^{3}+Z_{ijk}^{4}\leq 2$$

$$x_{ijk}\geq 0,\ \forall\ i\ ,\ \forall j\ and\ \forall k\ \ Z_{ijk}^{q}=0\,/\,1,\ q=1,2,3,4.$$

- **Model 10(b)**

$$\min : Z = \sum_{i=1}^{m}\sum_{j=1}^{n}\sum_{k=1}^{s}\left\{\begin{array}{l}(1-Z_{ijk}^{1})(1-Z_{ijk}^{2})Z_{ijk}^{3}\,Z_{ijk}^{4}\,\mathrm{C}_{ijk}^{1}+(1-Z_{ijk}^{1})Z_{ijk}^{2}(1-Z_{ijk}^{3})Z_{ijk}^{4}C_{ijk}^{2}\\ +(1-Z_{ijk}^{1})Z_{ijk}^{2}Z_{ijk}^{3}(1-Z_{ijk}^{4})C_{ijk}^{3}+Z_{ijk}^{1}(1-Z_{ijk}^{2})(1-Z_{ijk}^{3})Z_{ijk}^{4}\,\mathrm{C}_{ijk}^{4}\\ +Z_{ijk}^{1}(1-Z_{ijk}^{2})Z_{ijk}^{3}(1-Z_{ijk}^{4})C_{ijk}^{5}+Z_{ijk}^{1}Z_{ijk}^{2}(1-Z_{ijk}^{3})(1-Z_{ijk}^{4})\mathrm{C}_{ijk}^{6}\\ +(1-Z_{ijk}^{1})Z_{ijk}^{2}Z_{ijk}^{3}Z_{ijk}^{4}C_{ijk}^{7}+Z_{ijk}^{1}(1-Z_{ijk}^{2})Z_{ijk}^{3}Z_{ijk}^{4}C_{ijk}^{8}\\ +Z_{ijk}^{1}Z_{ijk}^{2}(1-Z_{ijk}^{3})Z_{ijk}^{4}C_{ijk}^{9}+Z_{ijk}^{1}Z_{ijk}^{2}Z_{ijk}^{3}(1-Z_{ijk}^{4})C_{ijk}^{10}+Z_{ijk}^{1}Z_{ijk}^{2}Z_{ijk}^{3}Z_{ijk}^{4}C_{ijk}^{11}\end{array}\right\} x_{ijk}$$

$$Z_{ijk}^1 + Z_{ijk}^2 + Z_{ijk}^3 + Z_{ijk}^4 \geq 2$$

$$x_{ijk} \geq 0, \forall \ i \ , \ \forall j \ and \ \forall k \ \ Z_{ijk}^q = 0/1, \ q = 1,2,3,4 \ .$$

Step 11: When p = 12:

We rewrite the objective function (2.2) as follows:

$$min : Z = \sum_{i=1}^{m}\sum_{j=1}^{n}\sum_{k=1}^{s} \left\{ C_{ijk}^1, C_{ijk}^2, \ldots, C_{ijk}^{12} \right\} x_{ijk} \ .$$

The cost coefficients of the objective function have twelve choices as $\left\{ C_{ijk}^1, C_{ijk}^2, \ldots, C_{ijk}^{12} \right\}$ out of which one is to be selected. Since $2^3 < 12 < 2^4$, so we need four binary variables and they are $Z_{ijk}^1, \ Z_{ijk}^2, Z_{ijk}^3, \ Z_{ijk}^4$. We consider the set of binomial coefficients as $\left\{ {}^4C_1, {}^4C_2, {}^4C_3 \right\}$ and the sum of terms is 14, which is just greater than the selected aspiration level or goal as p = 12. The auxiliary constraints depend upon the above specified set of binomial coefficient and its ranges, and two (14−12=2) additional constraints are performed. Total six similar models are possible for this aspiration level since p = 12. To reduce the length of the chapter, we have formulated only one model as given below:

- **Model 11**

$min : Z$

$$= \sum_{i=1}^{m}\sum_{j=1}^{n}\sum_{k=1}^{s} \left\{ \begin{array}{l} (1-Z_{ijk}^1)(1-Z_{ijk}^2)(1-Z_{ijk}^3)Z_{ijk}^4 \, \mathrm{C}_{ijk}^1 + (1-Z_{ijk}^1)(1-Z_{ijk}^2)Z_{ijk}^3(1-Z_{ijk}^4)C_{ijk}^2 \\ +(1-Z_{ijk}^1)Z_{ijk}^2(1-Z_{ijk}^3)(1-Z_{ijk}^4)\mathrm{C}_{ijk}^3 + Z_{ijk}^1(1-Z_{ijk}^2)(1-Z_{ijk}^3)(1-Z_{ijk}^4)\mathrm{C}_{ijk}^4 \\ +Z_{ijk}^1 Z_{ijk}^2(1-Z_{ijk}^3)(1-Z_{ijk}^4)\mathrm{C}_{ijk}^5 + Z_{ijk}^1(1-Z_{ijk}^2)Z_{ijk}^3(1-Z_{ijk}^4)\mathrm{C}_{ijk}^6 \\ +(1-Z_{ijk}^2)Z_{ijk}^2(1-Z_{ijk}^3)Z_{ijk}^4 C_{ijk}^7 + (1-Z_{ijk}^1)(1-Z_{ijk}^2)Z_{ijk}^3 Z_{ijk}^4 C_{ijk}^8 \\ +Z_{ijk}^2(1-Z_{ijk}^1)Z_{ijk}^3(1-Z_{ijk}^4)C_{ijk}^9 + Z_{ijk}^1 Z_{ijk}^2(1-Z_{ijk}^1)(1-Z_{ijk}^4)C_{ijk}^{10} \\ +Z_{ijk}^1(1-Z_{ijk}^2)Z_{ijk}^3 Z_{ijk}^4 C_{ijk}^{11} + Z_{ijk}^1(1-Z_{ijk}^3)Z_{ijk}^2 Z_{ijk}^4 C_{ijk}^{12} \end{array} \right\} x_{ijk}$$

$$1 \leq Z_{ijk}^1 + Z_{ijk}^2 + Z_{ijk}^3 + Z_{ijk}^4 \leq 3$$

$$Z_{ijk}^2 + Z_{ijk}^3 + Z_{ijk}^4 \leq 2$$

$$Z_{ijk}^1 + Z_{ijk}^2 + Z_{ijk}^3 \leq 2$$

$$x_{ijk} \geq 0, \forall \ i \ , \ \forall j \ and \ \forall k \ \ Z_{ijk}^q = 0/1, \ q = 1,2,3,4 \ .$$

Step 12: When p = 13:

We rewrite the objective function (2.2) as follows:

$$\min : Z = \sum_{i=1}^{m}\sum_{j=1}^{n}\sum_{k=1}^{s}\left\{C_{ijk}^{1}, C_{ijk}^{2}, ..., C_{ijk}^{13}\right\} x_{ijk} .$$

The cost coefficients of the objective function have thirteen choices as $\left\{C_{ijk}^{1}, C_{ijk}^{2}, ..., C_{ijk}^{13}\right\}$ out of which one is to be selected. Since $2^{3} < 13 < 2^{4}$, so we need four binary variables and they are $Z_{ijk}^{1}, Z_{ijk}^{2}, Z_{ijk}^{3}, Z_{ijk}^{4}$. We consider the set of consecutive terms of binomial coefficients $\left\{^{4}C_{1}, ^{4}C_{2}, ^{4}C_{3}\right\}$ and their sum is exactly equal to 14 which is just greater than the selected aspiration level or goal as $k_{i} =$ 13. Therefore, exactly one auxiliary constraint can be formulated with the help of above binomial coefficients and its ranges. Then we put the restriction to remaining one (i.e, $14 - 13 = 1$) term by introducing additional constraint in the model. Here four similar models are possible for this aspiration level since p = 13. Here, we have formulated only one model:

- **Model 12**

$\min : Z$

$$= \sum_{i=1}^{m}\sum_{j=1}^{n}\sum_{k=1}^{s}\left\{\begin{matrix} Z_{ijk}^{1}(1-Z_{ijk}^{4})(1-Z_{ijk}^{2})(1-Z_{ijk}^{3})C_{ijk}^{1} + Z_{ijk}^{2}(1-Z_{ijk}^{1})(1-Z_{ijk}^{3})(1-Z_{ijk}^{4})C_{ijk}^{2} \\ +(1-Z_{ijk}^{1})Z_{ijk}^{3}(1-Z_{ijk}^{2})(1-Z_{ijk}^{4})C_{ijk}^{3} + (1-Z_{ijk}^{1})(1-Z_{ijk}^{3})(1-Z_{ijk}^{2})Z_{ijk}^{4}C_{ijk}^{4} \\ +Z_{ijk}^{1}Z_{ijk}^{2}(1-Z_{ijk}^{3})(1-Z_{ijk}^{4})C_{ijk}^{5} + Z_{ijk}^{1}Z_{ijk}^{3}(1-Z_{ijk}^{2})(1-Z_{ijk}^{4})Z_{ijk}^{4}C_{ijk}^{6} \\ +Z_{ijk}^{1}Z_{ijk}^{4}(1-Z_{ijk}^{2})(1-Z_{ijk}^{3})C_{ijk}^{7} + Z_{ijk}^{2}Z_{ijk}^{3}(1-Z_{ijk}^{1})(1-Z_{ijk}^{4})C_{ijk}^{8} \\ +(1-Z_{ijk}^{1})(1-Z_{ijk}^{3})Z_{ijk}^{2}Z_{ijk}^{4}C_{ijk}^{9} + Z_{ijk}^{3}Z_{ijk}^{4}(1-Z_{ijk}^{1})(1-Z_{ijk}^{2})C_{ijk}^{10} \\ +Z_{ijk}^{1}(1-Z_{ijk}^{4})Z_{ijk}^{3}Z_{ijk}^{2}C_{ijk}^{11} + Z_{ijk}^{1}(1-Z_{ijk}^{3})Z_{ijk}^{2}Z_{ijk}^{4}C_{ijk}^{12} + Z_{ijk}^{1}Z_{ijk}^{4}Z_{ijk}^{3}(1-Z_{ijk}^{2})C_{ijk}^{13} \end{matrix}\right\} x_{ijk}$$

$$1 \leq Z_{ijk}^{1} + Z_{ijk}^{2} + Z_{ijk}^{3} + Z_{ijk}^{4} \leq 3$$

$$Z_{ijk}^{2} + Z_{ijk}^{3} + Z_{ijk}^{4} \leq 2$$

$$x_{ijk} \geq 0, \forall i, \forall j \text{ and} \forall k \ Z_{ijk}^{q} = 0 / 1, q = 1, 2, 3, 4 .$$

Step 13: When p = 14:

We rewrite the objective function (2.2) as follows:

$$\min : Z = \sum_{i=1}^{m}\sum_{j=1}^{n}\sum_{k=1}^{s}\left\{C_{ijk}^{1}, C_{ijk}^{2}, ..., C_{ijk}^{14}\right\} x_{ijk}.$$

The cost coefficients of the objective function have fourteen choices as $\left\{C_{ijk}^{1}, C_{ijk}^{2}, ..., C_{ijk}^{14}\right\}$ out of which one is to be selected. Since $2^{3} < 14 < 2^{4}$, so we need four binary variables and they are $Z_{ijk}^{1}, Z_{ijk}^{2}, Z_{ijk}^{3}, Z_{ijk}^{4}$. We recall the relation $2^{4} = {}^{4}C_{0} + {}^{4}C_{1} + {}^{4}C_{2} + {}^{4}C_{3} + {}^{4}C_{4}$, and construct a set whose elements are the consecutive binomial coefficients i.e, $\left\{{}^{4}C_{1}, {}^{4}C_{2}, {}^{4}C_{3}\right\}$, and the sum is 14 which is equal to the goal since p = 14. So there does not arise any additional constraint. Hence only one model is formulated:

- **Model 13**

$\min : Z$

$$= \sum_{i=1}^{m}\sum_{j=1}^{n}\sum_{k=1}^{s}\begin{bmatrix} Z_{ijk}^{1}(1-Z_{ijk}^{4})(1-Z_{ijk}^{2})(1-Z_{ijk}^{3})C_{ijk}^{1} + Z_{ijk}^{2}(1-Z_{ijk}^{1})(1-Z_{ijk}^{3})(1-Z_{ijk}^{4})C_{ijk}^{2} \\ +(1-Z_{ijk}^{1})Z_{ijk}^{3}(1-Z_{ijk}^{2})(1-Z_{ijk}^{4})C_{ijk}^{3} + (1-Z_{ijk}^{1})(1-Z_{ijk}^{3})(1-Z_{ijk}^{2})Z_{ijk}^{4}\,C_{ijk}^{4} \\ +Z_{ijk}^{1}Z_{ijk}^{2}(1-Z_{ijk}^{3})(1-Z_{ijk}^{4})C_{ijk}^{5} + Z_{ijk}^{1}Z_{ijk}^{3}(1-Z_{ijk}^{2})(1-Z_{ijk}^{4})Z_{ijk}^{4}\,C_{ijk}^{6} \\ +Z_{ijk}^{1}Z_{ijk}^{4}(1-Z_{ijk}^{2})(1-Z_{ijk}^{3})C_{ijk}^{7} + Z_{ijk}^{2}Z_{ijk}^{3}(1-Z_{ijk}^{1})(1-Z_{ijk}^{4})C_{ijk}^{8} \\ +(1-Z_{ijk}^{1})(1-Z_{ijk}^{3})Z_{ijk}^{2}Z_{ijk}^{4}C_{ijk}^{9} + Z_{ijk}^{3}Z_{ijk}^{4}(1-Z_{ijk}^{1})(1-Z_{ijk}^{2})C_{ijk}^{10} \\ +Z_{ijk}^{1}(1-Z_{ijk}^{4})Z_{ijk}^{3}Z_{ijk}^{2}C_{ijk}^{11} + Z_{ijk}^{1}(1-Z_{ijk}^{3})Z_{ijk}^{2}Z_{ijk}^{4}C_{ijk}^{12} + Z_{ijk}^{1}Z_{ijk}^{4}Z_{ijk}^{3}(1-Z_{ijk}^{2})C_{ijk}^{13} \\ +(1-Z_{ijk}^{1})Z_{ijk}^{2}Z_{ijk}^{3}Z_{ijk}^{4}C_{ijk}^{14} \end{bmatrix} x_{ijk}$$

$$1 \leq Z_{ijk}^{1} + Z_{ijk}^{2} + Z_{ijk}^{3} + Z_{ijk}^{4} \leq 3$$

$x_{ijk} \geq 0, \forall\, i, \forall j\, and \forall k\; Z_{ijk}^{q} = 0/1, q = 1, 2, 3, 4.$

Step 14: When p = 15:

We rewrite the objective function (2.2) as follows:

$$\min : Z = \sum_{i=1}^{m}\sum_{j=1}^{n}\sum_{k=1}^{s}\left\{C_{ijk}^{1}, C_{ijk}^{2}, ..., C_{ijk}^{15}\right\} x_{ijk}.$$

The cost coefficients of the objective function have fifteen choices as $\left\{C_{ijk}^{1}, C_{ijk}^{2}, ..., C_{ijk}^{15}\right\}$ out of which one is to be selected. Since $2^{3} < 15 < 2^{4}$, so we need four binary variables and they are $Z_{ijk}^{1}, Z_{ijk}^{2}, Z_{ijk}^{3}, Z_{ijk}^{4}$. We express 15 as two sets of consecutive terms of binomial coefficients $\left\{{}^{4}C_{0}, {}^{4}C_{1}, {}^{4}C_{2}, {}^{4}C_{3}\right\}$ or $\left\{{}^{4}C_{1}, {}^{4}C_{2}, {}^{4}C_{3}, {}^{4}C_{4}\right\}$ in respect to two different models. The auxiliary constraints are performed with the help of above two sets of binomial coefficients with their restriction as sum of four binary variables does not equal to "0" and product of them is not equal to "1". Therefore two different models are formulated as given in Model 14(a).

- **Model 14(a)**

$\min : Z$

$$
= \sum_{i=1}^{m} \sum_{j=1}^{n} \sum_{k=1}^{s} \left\{ \begin{array}{l} (1-Z_{ijk}^1)(1-Z_{ijk}^2)(1-Z_{ijk}^3)Z_{ijk}^4 \mathrm{C}_{ijk}^1 + Z_{ijk}^1(1-Z_{ijk}^2)Z_{ijk}^3(1-Z_{ijk}^4)C_{ijk}^2 \\ +(1-Z_{ijk}^1)Z_{ijk}^2(1-Z_{ijk}^3)(1-Z_{ijk}^4)\mathrm{C}_{ijk}^3 + (1-Z_{ijk}^1)Z_{ijk}^2(1-Z_{ijk}^3)(1-Z_{ijk}^4)\mathrm{C}_{ijk}^4 \\ +(1-Z_{ijk}^1)(1-Z_{ijk}^2)Z_{ijk}^3 Z_{ijk}^4 \mathrm{C}_{ijk}^5 + (1-Z_{ijk}^1)Z_{ijk}^2(1-Z_{ijk}^3)Z_{ijk}^4 \mathrm{C}_{ijk}^6 \\ +(1-Z_{ijk}^1)Z_{ijk}^2 Z_{ijk}^3(1-Z_{ijk}^4)C_{ijk}^7 + Z_{ijk}^1(1-Z_{ijk}^2)(1-Z_{ijk}^3)Z_{ijk}^4 C_{ijk}^8 \\ +Z_{ijk}^1(1-Z_{ijk}^2)Z_{ijk}^3(1-Z_{ijk}^4)C_{ijk}^9 + Z_{ijk}^1 Z_{ijk}^2(1-Z_{ijk}^3)(1-Z_{ijk}^4)C_{ijk}^{10} \\ +Z_{ijk}^1(1-Z_{ijk}^2)Z_{ijk}^3 Z_{ijk}^4 C_{ijk}^{11} + Z_{ijk}^1(1-Z_{ijk}^3)Z_{ijk}^2 Z_{ijk}^4 C_{ijk}^{12} + Z_{ijk}^1 Z_{ijk}^2 Z_{ijk}^3(1-Z_{ijk}^4)C_{ijk}^{13} \\ +(1-Z_{ijk}^1)Z_{ijk}^2 Z_{ijk}^3 Z_{ijk}^4 C_{ijk}^{14} + (1-Z_{ijk}^1)(1-Z_{ijk}^2)(1-Z_{ijk}^3)(1-Z_{ijk}^4)C_{ijk}^{15} \end{array} \right\} x_{ijk}
$$

$Z_{ijk}^1 + Z_{ijk}^2 + Z_{ijk}^3 + Z_{ijk}^4 \leq 3$

$x_{ijk} \geq 0, \forall\ i\ ,\ \forall j\ and \forall k\ \ Z_{ijk}^q = 0/1,\ q = 1,2,3,4\ .$

- **Model 14(b)**

$\min : Z$

$$
= \sum_{i=1}^{m} \sum_{j=1}^{n} \sum_{k=1}^{s} \left\{ \begin{array}{l} (1-Z_{ijk}^1)(1-Z_{ijk}^2)(1-Z_{ijk}^3)Z_{ijk}^4 \mathrm{C}_{ijk}^1 + Z_{ijk}^1(1-Z_{ijk}^2)Z_{ijk}^3(1-Z_{ijk}^4)C_{ijk}^2 \\ +(1-Z_{ijk}^1)Z_{ijk}^2(1-Z_{ijk}^3)(1-Z_{ijk}^4)\mathrm{C}_{ijk}^3 + (1-Z_{ijk}^1)Z_{ijk}^2(1-Z_{ijk}^3)(1-Z_{ijk}^4)\mathrm{C}_{ijk}^4 \\ +(1-Z_{ijk}^1)(1-Z_{ijk}^2)Z_{ijk}^3 Z_{ijk}^4 \mathrm{C}_{ijk}^5 + (1-Z_{ijk}^1)Z_{ijk}^2(1-Z_{ijk}^3)Z_{ijk}^4 \mathrm{C}_{ijk}^6 \\ +(1-Z_{ijk}^1)Z_{ijk}^2 Z_{ijk}^3(1-Z_{ijk}^4)C_{ijk}^7 + Z_{ijk}^1(1-Z_{ijk}^2)(1-Z_{ijk}^3)Z_{ijk}^4 C_{ijk}^8 \\ +Z_{ijk}^1(1-Z_{ijk}^2)Z_{ijk}^3(1-Z_{ijk}^4)C_{ijk}^9 + Z_{ijk}^1 Z_{ijk}^2(1-Z_{ijk}^3)(1-Z_{ijk}^4)C_{ijk}^{10} \\ +Z_{ijk}^1(1-Z_{ijk}^2)Z_{ijk}^3 Z_{ijk}^4 C_{ijk}^{11} + Z_{ijk}^1(1-Z_{ijk}^3)Z_{ijk}^2 Z_{ijk}^4 C_{ijk}^{12} + Z_{ijk}^1 Z_{ijk}^2 Z_{ijk}^3(1-Z_{ijk}^4)C_{ijk}^{13} \\ +(1-Z_{ijk}^1)Z_{ijk}^2 Z_{ijk}^3 Z_{ijk}^4 C_{ijk}^{14} + Z_{ijk}^1 Z_{ijk}^2 Z_{ijk}^3 Z_{ijk}^4 C_{ijk}^{15} \end{array} \right\} x_{ijk}
$$

$Z_{ijk}^1 + Z_{ijk}^2 + Z_{ijk}^3 + Z_{ijk}^4 \geq 1$

$x_{ijk} \geq 0, \forall\ i\ ,\ \forall j\ and \forall k\ Z_{ijk}^q = 0/1,\ q = 1,2,3,4\ .$

Step 15: When p = 16:

We rewrite the objective function (2.2) as follows:

$$\min : Z = \sum_{i=1}^{m}\sum_{j=1}^{n}\sum_{k=1}^{s}\left\{C_{ijk}^1, C_{ijk}^2, ..., C_{ijk}^{16}\right\} x_{ijk}.$$

The cost coefficients of the objective function have sixteen choices as $\left\{C_{ijk}^1, C_{ijk}^2, ..., C_{ijk}^{16}\right\}$ out of which one is to be selected. Since the choices have satisfied the norms as $2^4 = 16$, so there is no involvement of auxiliary and additional constraints. Hence we need four binary variables and they are $Z_{ijk}^1, Z_{ijk}^2, Z_{ijk}^3, Z_{ijk}^4$. Finally we formulate the above objective function:

- **Model 15**

$\min : Z$

$$= \sum_{i=1}^{m}\sum_{j=1}^{n}\sum_{k=1}^{s}\begin{bmatrix}(1-Z_{ijk}^1)(1-Z_{ijk}^2)(1-Z_{ijk}^3)(1-Z_{ijk}^4)\mathrm{C}_{ijk}^1 + Z_{ijk}^1(1-Z_{ijk}^2)(1-Z_{ijk}^3)(1-Z_{ijk}^4)C_{ijk}^2 \\ +(1-Z_{ijk}^1)Z_{ijk}^2(1-Z_{ijk}^3)(1-Z_{ijk}^4)\mathrm{C}_{ijk}^3 + (1-Z_{ijk}^1)(1-Z_{ijk}^2)Z_{ijk}^3(1-Z_{ijk}^4)\mathrm{C}_{ijk}^4 \\ +(1-Z_{ijk}^1)(1-Z_{ijk}^2)(1-Z_{ijk}^3)Z_{ijk}^4\,\mathrm{C}_{ijk}^5 + Z_{ijk}^1 Z_{ijk}^2(1-Z_{ijk}^3)(1-Z_{ijk}^4)\mathrm{C}_{ijk}^6 \\ +Z_{ijk}^1(1-Z_{ijk}^2)Z_{ijk}^3(1-Z_{ijk}^4)C_{ijk}^7 + (1-Z_{ijk}^1)Z_{ijk}^2 Z_{ijk}^3(1-Z_{ijk}^4)C_{ijk}^9 \\ +Z_{ijk}^1(1-Z_{ijk}^2)(1-Z_{ijk}^3)Z_{ijk}^4 C_{ijk}^8 + (1-Z_{ijk}^1)Z_{ijk}^2(1-Z_{ijk}^3)Z_{ijk}^4 C_{ijk}^{10} \\ +(1-Z_{ijk}^1)(1-Z_{ijk}^2)Z_{ijk}^3 Z_{ijk}^4 C_{ijk}^{11} + Z_{ijk}^1 Z_{ijk}^2 Z_{ijk}^3(1-Z_{ijk}^4)C_{ijk}^{12} \\ +Z_{ijk}^1 Z_{ijk}^2(1-Z_{ijk}^3)Z_{ijk}^4 C_{ijk}^{13} + Z_{ijk}^1(1-Z_{ijk}^2)Z_{ijk}^3 Z_{ijk}^4 C_{ijk}^{14} + (1-Z_{ijk}^1)Z_{ijk}^2 Z_{ijk}^3 Z_{ijk}^4 C_{ijk}^{15} \\ +Z_{ijk}^1 Z_{ijk}^2 Z_{ijk}^3 Z_{ijk}^4 C_{ijk}^{16}\end{bmatrix} x_{ijk}$$

$x_{ijk} \geq 0, \forall\ i\ , \forall j\ and \forall k\ \ Z_{ijk}^q = 0\,/\,1,\ q = 1, 2, 3, 4.$

Step 16: When p = 17:

We rewrite the objective function (2.2) as follows:

$$\min : Z = \sum_{i=1}^{m}\sum_{j=1}^{n}\sum_{k=1}^{s}\left\{C_{ijk}^1, C_{ijk}^2, ..., C_{ijk}^{17}\right\} x_{ijk}.$$

In this case, seventeen $\left\{C_{ijk}^1, C_{ijk}^2, ..., C_{ijk}^{17}\right\}$ are considered as the coefficients of the objective function in the specified multi-choice programming problem, out of which one is to be selected. Since, $2^4 < 17 < 2^5$, so we need five binary variables as: $Z_{ijk}^1, Z_{ijk}^2, Z_{ijk}^3, Z_{ijk}^4, Z_{ijk}^5$. We express the $2^5 = {}^5C_0 + {}^5C_1 + {}^5C_2 + {}^5C_3 + {}^5C_4 + {}^5C_5$, in which the set of consecutive binomial coefficients terms as $\left\{{}^5C_2, {}^5C_3\right\}$, whose sum is $(10\ +\ 10)\ =\ 20$. It is just greater than the number of goals as p = 17. The auxiliary constraints are also depend on the ranges of above said of binomial coefficients. So there are three $(20 - 17\ =\ 3)$ terms of additional constraints are appeared in the possible model which contain altogether 120 similar models. Here only one model is shown, as other models are similar.

- **Model 16**

$$
=\sum_{i=1}^{m}\sum_{j=1}^{n}\sum_{k=1}^{s}
\begin{bmatrix}
(1-Z_{ijk}^1)(1-Z_{ijk}^2)(1-Z_{ijk}^3)Z_{ijk}^4 Z_{ijk}^5\, C_{ijk}^1 + (1-Z_{ijk}^1)(1-Z_{ijk}^2)Z_{ijk}^3(1-Z_{ijk}^4)Z_{ijk}^5 C_{ijk}^2 \\
+(1-Z_{ijk}^1)(1-Z_{ijk}^2)Z_{ijk}^3 Z_{ijk}^4(1-Z_{ijk}^5)C_{ijk}^3 + (1-Z_{ijk}^1)(1-Z_{ijk}^3)(1-Z_{ijk}^4)Z_{ijk}^2 Z_{ijk}^5\, C_{ijk}^4 \\
+Z_{ijk}^2 Z_{ijk}^4(1-Z_{ijk}^1)(1-Z_{ijk}^3)(1-Z_{ijk}^5)C_{ijk}^5 + (1-Z_{ijk}^1)Z_{ijk}^2 Z_{ijk}^3(1-Z_{ijk}^4)(1-Z_{ijk}^5)C_{ijk}^6 \\
+Z_{ijk}^1(1-Z_{ijk}^2)(1-Z_{ijk}^3)(1-Z_{ijk}^4)Z_{ijk}^5 C_{ijk}^7 + Z_{ijk}^1(1-Z_{ijk}^2)(1-Z_{ijk}^3)Z_{ijk}^4(1-Z_{ijk}^5)C_{ijk}^8 \\
+Z_{ijk}^1(1-Z_{ijk}^2)Z_{ijk}^3(1-Z_{ijk}^4)(1-Z_{ijk}^5)C_{ijk}^9 + Z_{ijk}^1 Z_{ijk}^2(1-Z_{ijk}^3)(1-Z_{ijk}^4)(1-Z_{ijk}^5)C_{ijk}^{10} \\
(1-Z_{ijk}^1)(1-Z_{ijk}^2)Z_{ijk}^3 Z_{ijk}^4 Z_{ijk}^5 C_{ijk}^{11} + (1-Z_{ijk}^1)Z_{ijk}^2 Z_{ijk}^3(1-Z_{ijk}^4)Z_{ijk}^5 C_{ijk}^{12} + (1-Z_{ijk}^1)Z_{ijk}^2 Z_{ijk}^3(1-Z_{ijk}^4)Z_{ijk}^5 C_{ijk}^{13} \\
+(1-Z_{ijk}^1)Z_{ijk}^2 Z_{ijk}^3 Z_{ijk}^4(1-Z_{ijk}^5)C_{ijk}^{14} + Z_{ijk}^1(1-Z_{ijk}^2)(1-Z_{ijk}^3)Z_{ijk}^4 Z_{ijk}^5 C_{ijk}^{15} \\
+Z_{ijk}^1(1-Z_{ijk}^2)Z_{ijk}^3(1-Z_{ijk}^4)Z_{ijk}^5 C_{ijk}^{16} + Z_{ijk}^1(1-Z_{ijk}^2)Z_{ijk}^3(1-Z_{ijk}^5)Z_{ijk}^4 C_{ijk}^{17}
\end{bmatrix} x_{ijk}
$$

$$
2 \le Z_{ijk}^1 + Z_{ijk}^2 + Z_{ijk}^3 + Z_{ijk}^4 + Z_{ijk}^5 \le 3
$$

$$
Z_{ijk}^1 + Z_{ijk}^2 + Z_{ijk}^5 \le 2
$$

$$
Z_{ijk}^1 + Z_{ijk}^2 + Z_{ijk}^4 \le 2
$$

$$
Z_{ijk}^1 + Z_{ijk}^2 + Z_{ijk}^3 \le 2
$$

$$
x_{ijk} \ge 0,\ \forall\, i\,,\ \forall j\ and\, \forall k\ \ Z_{ijk}^q = 0\,/\,1,\ q = 1,2,3,4,5.
$$

Step 17: When p = 18:

We rewrite the objective function (2.2) as follows:

$$
\min : Z = \sum_{i=1}^{m}\sum_{j=1}^{n}\sum_{k=1}^{s}\left\{ C_{ijk}^1, C_{ijk}^2, \ldots, C_{ijk}^{18} \right\} x_{ijk}.
$$

The cost coefficients of the objective function have eighteen choices $\left\{ C_{ijk}^1, C_{ijk}^2, \ldots, C_{ijk}^{18} \right\}$ out of which one is to be selected. Since, $2^4 < 18 < 2^5$, so we need five binary variables as: $Z_{ijk}^1,\ Z_{ijk}^2,\ Z_{ijk}^3,\ Z_{ijk}^4,\ Z_{ijk}^5$. We express 18 is just less than as $\left\{ {}^5C_2, {}^5C_3 \right\}$ [whose sum is equal to 20] in which binomial coefficients of its ranges are established for obtaining the auxiliary constraints. Then two $(20 - 18 = 2)$ additional constraints are appear in the possible models. In this case, there are forty five similar models are possible. Here only one model is shown:

- **Model 17**

$\min : Z$

$$
= \sum_{i=1}^{m}\sum_{j=1}^{n}\sum_{k=1}^{s}
\begin{bmatrix}
(1-Z_{ijk}^{1})(1-Z_{ijk}^{2})(1-Z_{ijk}^{3})Z_{ijk}^{4}Z_{ijk}^{5}\,\mathrm{C}_{ijk}^{1}+(1-Z_{ijk}^{1})(1-Z_{ijk}^{2})Z_{ijk}^{3}(1-Z_{ijk}^{4})Z_{ijk}^{5}C_{ijk}^{2} \\
+(1-Z_{ijk}^{1})(1-Z_{ijk}^{2})Z_{ijk}^{3}Z_{ijk}^{4}(1-Z_{ijk}^{5})\mathrm{C}_{ijk}^{3}+(1-Z_{ijk}^{1})(1-Z_{ijk}^{3})(1-Z_{ijk}^{4})Z_{ijk}^{2}Z_{ijk}^{5}\,\mathrm{C}_{ijk}^{4} \\
+Z_{ijk}^{2}Z_{ijk}^{4}(1-Z_{ijk}^{1})(1-Z_{ijk}^{3})(1-Z_{ijk}^{5})\mathrm{C}_{ijk}^{5}+(1-Z_{ijk}^{1})Z_{ijk}^{2}Z_{ijk}^{3}(1-Z_{ijk}^{4})(1-Z_{ijk}^{5})\mathrm{C}_{ijk}^{6} \\
+Z_{ijk}^{1}(1-Z_{ijk}^{2})(1-Z_{ijk}^{3})(1-Z_{ijk}^{4})Z_{ijk}^{5}C_{ijk}^{7}+Z_{ijk}^{1}(1-Z_{ijk}^{2})(1-Z_{ijk}^{3})Z_{ijk}^{4}(1-Z_{ijk}^{5})C_{ijk}^{8} \\
+Z_{ijk}^{1}(1-Z_{ijk}^{2})Z_{ijk}^{3}(1-Z_{ijk}^{4})(1-Z_{ijk}^{5})C_{ijk}^{9}+Z_{ijk}^{1}Z_{ijk}^{2}(1-Z_{ijk}^{3})(1-Z_{ijk}^{4})(1-Z_{ijk}^{5})C_{ijk}^{10} \\
(1-Z_{ijk}^{1})(1-Z_{ijk}^{2})Z_{ijk}^{3}Z_{ijk}^{4}Z_{ijk}^{5}C_{ijk}^{11}+(1-Z_{ijk}^{1})Z_{ijk}^{2}Z_{ijk}^{4}(1-Z_{ijk}^{3})Z_{ijk}^{5}C_{ijk}^{12} \\
+(1-Z_{ijk}^{1})Z_{ijk}^{2}Z_{ijk}^{3}Z_{ijk}^{5}(1-Z_{ijk}^{4})C_{ijk}^{13}+Z_{ijk}^{2}(1-Z_{ijk}^{1})(1-Z_{ijk}^{5})Z_{ijk}^{4}Z_{ijk}^{3}C_{ijk}^{14} \\
+Z_{ijk}^{1}(1-Z_{ijk}^{2})Z_{ijk}^{4}(1-Z_{ijk}^{3})Z_{ijk}^{5}C_{ijk}^{15}+Z_{ijk}^{1}(1-Z_{ijk}^{2})Z_{ijk}^{3}(1-Z_{ijk}^{5})Z_{ijk}^{4}C_{ijk}^{16} \\
+(1-Z_{ijk}^{2})Z_{ijk}^{1}Z_{ijk}^{3}(1-Z_{ijk}^{5})Z_{ijk}^{4}C_{ijk}^{17}+Z_{ijk}^{1}(1-Z_{ijk}^{3})Z_{ijk}^{2}(1-Z_{ijk}^{4})Z_{ijk}^{5}C_{ijk}^{18}
\end{bmatrix}x_{ijk}
$$

$$2 \leq Z_{ijk}^{1}+Z_{ijk}^{2}+Z_{ijk}^{3}+Z_{ijk}^{4}+Z_{ijk}^{5} \leq 3$$

$$Z_{ijk}^{1}+Z_{ijk}^{2}+Z_{ijk}^{4} \leq 2$$

$$Z_{ijk}^{1}+Z_{ijk}^{2}+Z_{ijk}^{3} \leq 2$$

$$x_{ijk} \geq 0, \ \forall \ i \ , \ \forall j \ and \forall k \ \ Z_{ijk}^{q}=0\,/\,1, \ q=1,2,3,4,5.$$

Step 18: When p = 19:

We rewrite the objective function (2.2) as follows:

$$\min : Z = \sum_{i=1}^{m}\sum_{j=1}^{n}\sum_{k=1}^{s}\left\{C_{ijk}^{1}, C_{ijk}^{2}, \ldots, C_{ijk}^{19}\right\}x_{ijk}.$$

The cost coefficients of the objective function have nineteen choices $\left\{C_{ijk}^{1}, C_{ijk}^{2}, \ldots, C_{ijk}^{19}\right\}$ out of which one is to be selected. Since, $2^{4} < 19 < 2^{5}$, so we need five binary variables as: $Z_{ijk}^{1}, Z_{ijk}^{2}, Z_{ijk}^{3}, Z_{ijk}^{4}, Z_{ijk}^{5}$. We express 18 is just less than as $\left\{{}^{5}C_{2}, {}^{5}C_{3}\right\}$ [whose sum is equal to 20] in which binomial coefficients of its ranges are established for obtaining the auxiliary constraints. Then two $(20-19=1)$ additional constraints are appear in the possible models. In this case, there are forty five similar models are possible. Here only one model is shown:

- **Model 18**

$\min : Z$

$$
= \sum_{i=1}^{m}\sum_{j=1}^{n}\sum_{k=1}^{s}
\begin{Bmatrix}
(1-Z_{ijk}^1)(1-Z_{ijk}^2)(1-Z_{ijk}^3)Z_{ijk}^4 Z_{ijk}^5\, \mathrm{C}_{ijk}^1 + (1-Z_{ijk}^1)(1-Z_{ijk}^2)Z_{ijk}^3(1-Z_{ijk}^4)Z_{ijk}^5 C_{ijk}^2 \\
+(1-Z_{ijk}^1)(1-Z_{ijk}^2)Z_{ijk}^3 Z_{ijk}^4(1-Z_{ijk}^5)\mathrm{C}_{ijk}^3 + (1-Z_{ijk}^1)(1-Z_{ijk}^3)(1-Z_{ijk}^4)Z_{ijk}^2 Z_{ijk}^5\, \mathrm{C}_{ijk}^4 \\
+Z_{ijk}^2 Z_{ijk}^4(1-Z_{ijk}^1)(1-Z_{ijk}^3)(1-Z_{ijk}^5)\mathrm{C}_{ijk}^5 + (1-Z_{ijk}^1)Z_{ijk}^2 Z_{ijk}^3(1-Z_{ijk}^4)(1-Z_{ijk}^5)\mathrm{C}_{ijk}^6 \\
+Z_{ijk}^1(1-Z_{ijk}^2)(1-Z_{ijk}^3)(1-Z_{ijk}^4)Z_{ijk}^5 C_{ijk}^7 + Z_{ijk}^1(1-Z_{ijk}^2)(1-Z_{ijk}^3)Z_{ijk}^4(1-Z_{ijk}^5)C_{ijk}^8 \\
+Z_{ijk}^1(1-Z_{ijk}^2)Z_{ijk}^3(1-Z_{ijk}^4)(1-Z_{ijk}^5)C_{ijk}^9 + Z_{ijk}^1 Z_{ijk}^2(1-Z_{ijk}^3)(1-Z_{ijk}^4)(1-Z_{ijk}^5)C_{ijk}^{10} \\
(1-Z_{ijk}^1)(1-Z_{ijk}^2)Z_{ijk}^3 Z_{ijk}^4 Z_{ijk}^5 C_{ijk}^{11} + (1-Z_{ijk}^1)(1-Z_{ijk}^3)Z_{ijk}^2\, Z_{ijk}^4\, Z_{ijk}^5 C_{ijk}^{12} \\
+(1-Z_{ijk}^1)Z_{ijk}^2 Z_{ijk}^3(1-Z_{ijk}^4)Z_{ijk}^5 C_{ijk}^{13} + (1-Z_{ijk}^1)Z_{ijk}^2 Z_{ijk}^3 Z_{ijk}^4(1-Z_{ijk}^5)C_{ijk}^{14} \\
+Z_{ijk}^1(1-Z_{ijk}^2)(1-Z_{ijk}^3)Z_{ijk}^4 Z_{ijk}^5 C_{ijk}^{15} + Z_{ijk}^1(1-Z_{ijk}^2)Z_{ijk}^3(1-Z_{ijk}^4)Z_{ijk}^5 C_{ijk}^{16} \\
+Z_{ijk}^1(1-Z_{ijk}^2)Z_{ijk}^3 Z_{ijk}^4(1-Z_{ijk}^5)C_{ijk}^{17} + Z_{ijk}^1 Z_{ijk}^2(1-Z_{ijk}^3)(1-Z_{ijk}^4)Z_{ijk}^5 C_{ijk}^{18} \\
+Z_{ijk}^1 Z_{ijk}^2(1-Z_{ijk}^3)Z_{ijk}^4(1-Z_{ijk}^5)C_{ijk}^{19}
\end{Bmatrix} x_{ijk}
$$

$$2 \le Z_{ijk}^1 + Z_{ijk}^2 + Z_{ijk}^3 + Z_{ijk}^4 + Z_{ijk}^5 \le 3$$

$$Z_{ijk}^1 + Z_{ijk}^2 + Z_{ijk}^3 \le 2$$

$$x_{ijk} \ge 0,\ \forall\, i\, ,\ \forall j\ and\, \forall\, k\ \ Z_{ijk}^q = 0\,/\,1,\ q = 1,2,3,4,5\,.$$

Step 19: When p = 20:

We rewrite the objective function (2.2) as follows:

$$\min : Z = \sum_{i=1}^{m}\sum_{j=1}^{n}\sum_{k=1}^{s}\Big\{C_{ijk}^1, C_{ijk}^2, ..., C_{ijk}^{20}\Big\} x_{ijk}\,.$$

We state here twenty choices as $\Big\{C_{ijk}^1, C_{ijk}^2, ..., C_{ijk}^{20}\Big\}$ out of which one is to be selected. Since, $2^4 < 20 < 2^5$, so we need five binary variables as: $Z_{ijk}^1,\ Z_{ijk}^2,\ Z_{ijk}^3,\ Z_{ijk}^4,\ Z_{ijk}^5$. We express the consecutive binomial coefficients as $\Big\{{}^5C_2, {}^5C_3\Big\}$ whose sum is 20 which is exactly equal to the number of goal as p = 20. So there does not arise any additional constraint in such model which is given:

- **Model 19**

$\min : Z$

$$= \sum_{i=1}^{m}\sum_{j=1}^{n}\sum_{k=1}^{s}\begin{bmatrix}(1-Z_{ijk}^1)(1-Z_{ijk}^2)(1-Z_{ijk}^3)Z_{ijk}^4 Z_{ijk}^5 \, \mathrm{C}_{ijk}^1 + (1-Z_{ijk}^1)(1-Z_{ijk}^2)Z_{ijk}^3(1-Z_{ijk}^4)Z_{ijk}^5 C_{ijk}^2 \\ +(1-Z_{ijk}^1)(1-Z_{ijk}^2)Z_{ijk}^3 Z_{ijk}^4(1-Z_{ijk}^5)\,\mathrm{C}_{ijk}^3 + (1-Z_{ijk}^1)(1-Z_{ijk}^3)(1-Z_{ijk}^4)Z_{ijk}^2 Z_{ijk}^5 \, \mathrm{C}_{ijk}^4 \\ +Z_{ijk}^2 Z_{ijk}^4(1-Z_{ijk}^1)(1-Z_{ijk}^3)(1-Z_{ijk}^5)\,\mathrm{C}_{ijk}^5 + (1-Z_{ijk}^1)Z_{ijk}^2 Z_{ijk}^3(1-Z_{ijk}^4)(1-Z_{ijk}^5)\,\mathrm{C}_{ijk}^6 \\ +Z_{ijk}^1(1-Z_{ijk}^2)(1-Z_{ijk}^3)(1-Z_{ijk}^4)Z_{ijk}^5 C_{ijk}^7 + Z_{ijk}^1(1-Z_{ijk}^2)(1-Z_{ijk}^3)Z_{ijk}^4(1-Z_{ijk}^5)C_{ijk}^8 \\ +Z_{ijk}^1(1-Z_{ijk}^2)Z_{ijk}^3(1-Z_{ijk}^4)(1-Z_{ijk}^5)C_{ijk}^9 + Z_{ijk}^1 Z_{ijk}^2(1-Z_{ijk}^3)(1-Z_{ijk}^4)(1-Z_{ijk}^5)C_{ijk}^{10} \\ (1-Z_{ijk}^1)(1-Z_{ijk}^2)Z_{ijk}^3 Z_{ijk}^4 Z_{ijk}^5 C_{ijk}^{11} + (1-Z_{ijk}^1)(1-Z_{ijk}^3)Z_{ijk}^2 Z_{ijk}^4 Z_{ijk}^5 C_{ijk}^{12} \\ +(1-Z_{ijk}^1)Z_{ijk}^2 Z_{ijk}^3(1-Z_{ijk}^4)Z_{ijk}^5 C_{ijk}^{13} + (1-Z_{ijk}^1)Z_{ijk}^2 Z_{ijk}^3 Z_{ijk}^4(1-Z_{ijk}^5)C_{ijk}^{14} \\ +Z_{ijk}^1(1-Z_{ijk}^2)(1-Z_{ijk}^3)Z_{ijk}^4 Z_{ijk}^5 C_{ijk}^{15} + Z_{ijk}^1(1-Z_{ijk}^2)Z_{ijk}^3(1-Z_{ijk}^4)Z_{ijk}^5 C_{ijk}^{16} \\ +Z_{ijk}^1(1-Z_{ijk}^2)Z_{ijk}^3(1-Z_{ijk}^5)Z_{ijk}^4 C_{ijk}^{17} + Z_{ijk}^1(1-Z_{ijk}^3)Z_{ijk}^2(1-Z_{ijk}^4)Z_{ijk}^5 C_{ijk}^{18} \\ +Z_{ijk}^1(1-Z_{ijk}^3)Z_{ijk}^2(1-Z_{ijk}^5)Z_{ijk}^3 C_{ijk}^{19} + Z_{ijk}^1(1-Z_{ijk}^4)Z_{ijk}^2(1-Z_{ijk}^5)Z_{ijk}^3 C_{ijk}^{20}\end{bmatrix}x_{ijk}$$

$$2 \le Z_{ijk}^1 + Z_{ijk}^2 + Z_{ijk}^3 + Z_{ijk}^4 + Z_{ijk}^5 \le 3$$

$$x_{ijk} \ge 0, \ \forall \ i \ , \ \forall j \ and \forall k \ \ Z_{ijk}^q = 0/1, \ q = 1,2,3,4,5.$$

NUMERICAL EXAMPLE

A reputed betel leaves (Pan) supplier company transports a variety of Betel leaves from three source points namely Ramnagar of Purba Midnapore, Mecheda of Purba Midnapore and Jahalda of Paschim Midnapore in West Bengal, India by truck or goods train to the four destination centers at Delhi, Patna, Ranchi and Mumbai, India through the eighteen routes. The transportation cost is related with fluctuation in road condition, distance of destination point from source point, consumption of fuel etc. The main purpose is to minimize the transportation cost and maximize the profit against the market price at different markets. The transportation cost of carrying one unit (100 Kg) of Betel leaves from sources to destinations each treated as of multi-choice parameters.

Without using the multi-choice programming methodology, the problem cannot be solved easily. Due to increasing the fuel price rate and road collection tax, the price rates of transportation costs in each route are appended below:

x_{111} route either 10 or 11 or 12 required admissible costs per hundred Rupees.

x_{112} route either 15 or16 required admissible costs per hundred Rupees.

x_{121} route either 18 or 19 or 20 or 21 required admissible costs per hundred Rupees.

x_{122} route either 13 or 14 or 15 required admissible costs per hundred Rupees.

x_{131} route either 12 or 13 required admissible costs per hundred Rupees.

x_{132} route either 10 or 14 required admissible costs per hundred Rupees.

x_{211} route either 9 or 10 or 11 required admissible costs per hundred Rupees.

x_{212} route either 14 or 15 required admissible costs per hundred Rupees.

x_{221} route either 22 or 24 required admissible costs per hundred Rupees.

x_{222} route either 24 or 25 required admissible costs per hundred Rupees.

x_{231} route either 20 or 21 or 22 required admissible costs per hundred Rupees.

x_{232} route either 15 or 20 required admissible costs per hundred Rupees.

x_{311} route either 16 or 17 or 18 required admissible costs per hundred Rupees.

x_{312} route either 19 or 20 required admissible costs per hundred Rupees.

x_{321} route either 17 or 18 required admissible costs per hundred Rupees.

x_{322} route either 12 or 14 or 16 required admissible costs per hundred Rupees.

x_{331} route either 18 or 19 required admissible costs per hundred Rupees.

x_{332} route either 14 or 16 required admissible costs per hundred Rupees.

We formulate a MCSSTP where the objective function and the constraints are as follows:

$$\min : Z = \sum_{i=1}^{3} \sum_{j=1}^{3} \sum_{k=1}^{3} \left\{ C_{ijk}^1, C_{ijk}^2, \ldots, C_{ijk}^p \right\} x_{ijk}, \, , \, p=1,2,3,4$$

subject to $\Pr\left(\sum_{j=1}^{3} \sum_{k=1}^{2} x_{ijk} \leq a_i \right) \geq 1 - \gamma_i$, i=1,2,3

$$\Pr\left(\sum_{i=1}^{3} \sum_{k=1}^{2} x_{ijk} \geq b_j \right) \geq 1 - \delta_j , \text{j=1,2,3}$$

$$\Pr\left(\sum_{i=1}^{3} \sum_{j=1}^{3} x_{ijk} \geq e_k \right) \geq 1 - \eta_k , \text{k=1,2}$$

$x_{ijk} \geq 0, \, \forall i, \forall j$ and $\forall k$.

Due to conflicting situation of market, assume that the parameters supplies (sources) a_i, demands (destinations) b_j and conveyances (capacities) e_k of our specified problem followed by Cauchy's distribution with scale and shape parameters are given in the following three tables: Taking two known parameters of Cauchy's distribution with specified probability level of supplies i.e, a_i for i = 1, 2, 3 are represented in Table 1.

Taking two known parameters of Cauchy's distribution with specified probability level of Demands . i.e, b_j for j = 1, 2, 3 are represented in Table 2.

Taking two known parameters of Cauchy's distribution with specified probability level of conveyances i.e, e_k for k = 1, 2 are represented in Table 3.

Using the data from Tables 1, 2, and 3, the following multi-choice deterministic solid transportation problem is constructed.

Table 1. The values of location and scale parameters with SPL for supply

Location Parameter	Scale Parameter	Specified Probability Level (SPL)
$\alpha_1 = 900$	$\beta_1 = 6.3$	$\gamma_1 = 0.09$
$\alpha_2 = 1000$	$\beta_2 = 6.9$	$\gamma_2 = 0.08$
$\alpha_3 = 1100$	$\beta_3 = 7.5$	$\gamma_1 = 0.07$

Table 2. The values of location and scale parameters with SPL for demand

Location Parameter	Scale Parameter	Specified Probability Level (SPL)
$\alpha_1' = 600$	$\beta_1' = 4.5$	$\delta_1 = 0.06$
$\alpha_2' = 700$	$\beta_2' = 5.0$	$\delta_2 = 0.05$
$\alpha_3' = 800$	$\beta_3' = 5.7$	$\delta_3 = 0.04$

Table 3. The values of location and scale parameters with SPL for conveyance

Location Parameter	Scale Parameter	Specified Probability Level (SPL)
$\alpha_1'' = 300$	$\beta_1'' = 2.0$	$\eta_1 = 0.03$
$\alpha_2'' = 400$	$\beta_2'' = 2.7$	$\eta_2 = 0.02$

$$\min : Z = \{10,\ 11,\ 12\}x_{111} + \{15,\ 16\}x_{112} + \{18,\ 19,\ 20,\ 21\}x_{121} + \{13,\ 14,\ 15\}x_{122}$$
$$+ \{12,\ 13\}x_{131} + \{10,\ 14\}x_{132} + \{9,\ 10,\ 11\}x_{211} + \{14,\ 15\}x_{212} + \{22,\ 24\}x_{221}$$
$$+ \{24,\ 25\}x_{222} + \{20,\ 21,\ 22\}x_{231} + \{15,\ 20\}x_{232} + \{16,\ 17,\ 18\}x_{311} + \{19,\ 20\}x_{312}$$
$$+ \{17,\ 18\}x_{321} + \{12,\ 14,\ 16\}x_{322} + \{18,\ 19\}x_{331} + \{14,\ 16\}x_{332}$$

subject to

$$\sum_{j=1}^{3} \sum_{k=1}^{2} x_{1jk} \leq 899.8582291 \qquad\qquad (4.33)$$

$$\sum_{j=1}^{3} \sum_{k=1}^{2} x_{2jk} \leq 999.8409399 \qquad\qquad (4.34)$$

$$\sum_{j=1}^{3}\sum_{k=1}^{2} x_{3jk} \leq 1099.822992 \tag{4.35}$$

$$\sum_{i=1}^{3}\sum_{k=1}^{2} x_{i1k} \geq 600.1086746 \tag{4.36}$$

$$\sum_{i=1}^{3}\sum_{k=1}^{2} x_{i2k} \geq 700.1234938 \tag{4.37}$$

$$\sum_{i=1}^{3}\sum_{k=1}^{2} x_{i3k} \geq 800.1439115 \tag{4.38}$$

$$\sum_{i=1}^{3}\sum_{j=1}^{3} x_{ij1} \geq 300.051593 \tag{4.39}$$

$$\sum_{i=1}^{3}\sum_{j=1}^{3} x_{ij2} \geq 400.0711325 \tag{4.40}$$

$x_{ijk} \geq 0, \forall i, \forall j$ and $\forall k$

Now using a new transformation technique, we obtain the following a multi-choice deterministic solid transportation problem:

$$\begin{aligned}
\min : Z = {} & t_{111}x_{111} + t_{112}x_{112} + t_{121}x_{121} + t_{122}x_{122} \\
& + t_{131}x_{131} + t_{132}x_{132} + t_{211}x_{211} + t_{212}x_{212} + t_{221}x_{221} \\
& + t_{222}x_{222} + t_{231}x_{231} + t_{232}x_{232} + t_{311}x_{311} + t_{312}x_{312} \\
& + t_{321}x_{321} + t_{322}x_{322} + t_{331}x_{331} + t_{332}x_{332}
\end{aligned}$$

subject to (4.32) to (4.40)

$$t_{111} = 10Z_{111}^1 Z_{111}^2 + 11Z_{111}^1 (1 - Z_{111}^2) + 12(1 - Z_{111}^1)Z_{111}^2$$

$$t_{112} = 15Z_{112}^1 + 16(1 - Z_{112}^1)$$

$$t_{121} = 18Z_{221}^1 Z_{221}^2 + 19Z_{221}^1 (1 - Z_{221}^2) + 20(1 - Z_{221}^1)Z_{221}^2 + 21(1 - Z_{221}^1)(1 - Z_{221}^2)$$

$$t_{122} = 13Z_{212}^1 Z_{212}^2 + 14(1 - Z_{212}^1) + 15(1 - Z_{212}^1)Z_{212}^1$$

$$t_{131} = 12Z_{311}^1 + 13(1 - Z_{311}^1)$$

$$t_{132} = 10Z_{123}^1 + 14(1 - Z_{123}^1)$$

$$t_{211} = 9Z_{121}^1 + 10z_{121}^1(1 - Z_{121}^2) + 11(1 - Z_{121}^1)Z_{121}^2$$

$$t_{212} = 14Z_{122}^1 + 15(1 - Z_{122}^1)$$

$$t_{221} = 22Z_{221}^1 + 24(1 - Z_{221}^1)$$

$$t_{222} = 24Z_{222}^1 + 25(1 - Z_{222}^1)$$

$$t_{231} = 20Z_{321}^1 + 21z_{321}^1(1 - Z_{321}^2) + 22(1 - Z_{321}^1)Z_{321}^2$$

$$t_{232} = 15Z_{322}^1 + 20(1 - Z_{322}^1)$$

$$t_{311} = 16Z_{311}^1 Z_{311}^2 + 17Z_{311}^1(1 - Z_{311}^2) + 18(1 - Z_{311}^1)Z_{311}^2$$

$$t_{312} = 19Z_{312}^1 + 20(1 - Z_{312}^1)$$

$$t_{321} = 17Z_{321}^1 + 18(1 - Z_{321}^1)$$

$$t_{322} = 12Z_{322}^1 Z_{322}^2 + 14Z_{322}^1(1 - Z_{322}^2) + 16(1 - Z_{322}^1)Z_{322}^2$$

$$t_{331} = 18Z_{331}^1 + 19(1 - Z_{331}^1)$$

$$t_{332} = 14Z_{332}^1 + 16(1 - Z_{332}^1)$$

$$1 \le Z_{111}^1 + Z_{111}^2 \le 2$$

$$1 \le Z_{122}^1 + Z_{122}^2 \le 2$$

$$1 \leq Z_{211}^1 + Z_{211}^2 \leq 2$$

$$1 \leq Z_{231}^1 + Z_{231}^2 \leq 2$$

$$1 \leq Z_{311}^1 + Z_{311}^2 \leq 2$$

$$1 \leq Z_{322}^1 + Z_{322}^2 \leq 2$$

$$x_{ijk} \geq 0, \forall i, \forall j \text{ and } \forall k \ Z_{ijk}^q = 0/1; q=1,2.$$

RESULT AND DISCUSSION

The above problem is solved by Lingo10 package and to obtain the optimal solution and the optimal value of the objective function. They are as: $x_{132} = 800.1439$, $x_{211} = 700.1235$, and rest of the decision variables are zero, and the minimum cost of the objective function is 15002.67. The optimal value for multi-choice cost coefficient of x_{ijk} to the objective function are 11, 15, 21, 15, 12, 10, 10, 14, 22, 24, 22, 15, 18, 19, 17, 16, 18, 14 per hundred rupees respectively.

Introduction of binary variables is an important concept in multi-choice programming for selection of one choice from the set of multi-choice. To formulate the proposed model in this chapter we have required the additional/auxiliary constraints which contains the binary variables. The number of binary variables for each choice or goal depend on the relation $\dfrac{\ln(p)}{\ln(2)}$ where p is the number of choice or goal.

When p = 2, or 4, or 8 or 16 there is no auxiliary constraint to construct of our proposed model. When p = 3, or 7, or 11, or 15 only one auxiliary constraint is required which contain the binary variable for construction of our model. When p = 5, or 6, or 9, or 10, or 13, 14, or 19, or 20 then there is needed for two or three auxiliary constraints respectively. Again when p = 12, or 18 then there are four auxiliary constraints respectively. Specially, when p = 17, there are lot of models each of which contain five binary variables and five auxiliary constraints. To reduce the length of the chapter, here we have considered only one model instead of different models in this case. Any model can be considered for optimal solution. Depending on the number of choices or goals, we get different models of our proposed problem and solving all these of choices or goals, we get different models of our proposed problem and solving all these models, we have obtained the same optimal solution. Hence it is necessary to solve only one model.

CONCLUSION AND FUTURE RESEARCH DIRECTIONS

The main aim of this chapter is to present the solution procedure for multi-choice stochastic solid unbalanced transportation problem with consideration of Cauchy's distribution. Initially, we have transformed all the stochastic constraints into equivalent deterministic constraints by stochastic programming approach. Then we have introduced a transformation technique which selects only one choice from a set of multi-choice for each coefficient of objective function and provides an optimal solution of our model.

The transportation phenomena, as a manifestation of the complex human social, economic, and political interactions, are filled with uncertainties. To handle the first uncertainty we have assumed that the cost coefficients of the objective function are of multi-choice rather than of single choice; and the second uncertainty involves supply, demand and capacity which are all followed by Cauchy's distribution. Finally, we have concluded that the formulated model is highly applicable for real-life solid transportation problem and solving this model, the decision maker has provided more information for taking the right decision. A further study is also needed for MCSSTP under multi-objective environment.

ACKNOWLEDGMENT

The authors would like to thank the anonymous reviewers and the editor for their insightful comments and suggestions.

REFERENCES

Biswal, M. P., & Acharya, S. (2009). Transformation of a Multi-choice Linear Programming Problem. *Applied Mathematics and Computation, 210*(1), 182–188. doi:10.1016/j.amc.2008.12.080

Bit, A. K., Biswal, M. P., & Alam, S. S. (1993). Fuzzy Programming Approach to Multi-objective Solid Transportation Problem. *Fuzzy Sets and Systems, 57*(2), 183–194. doi:10.1016/0165-0114(93)90158-E

Chang, C.-T. (2007). Multi-choice Goal Programming, *OMEGA. International Journal of Management Sciences, 35*, 389–396.

Chang, C.-T. (2008). Revised Multi-choice Goal Programming. *Applied Mathematical Modelling, 32*(12), 2587–2595. doi:10.1016/j.apm.2007.09.008

Dantzig, G. B. (1963). *Linear Programming and Extensions*. Princeton, NJ: Princeton University Press.

Goicoechea, A., Hansen, D. R., & Duckstein, L. (1982). *Multi-objective Decision Analysis with Engineering and Business Application*. New York: John Wiley and Sons.

Haley, K. B. (1962). The Solid Transportation Problem. *Operations Research, 11*(4), 448–463. doi:10.1287/opre.10.4.448

Hiller, F., & Lieberman, G. (1990). *Introduction to Operations Research*. New York: Mc Graw-Hill.

Hitchcock, F. L. (1941). The Distribution of a Product from Several Sources to Numerous Localities. *Journal of Mathematics and Physics, 20*, 224–230.

Jimenez, F., & Verdegay, J. L. (1998). Uncertain Solid Transportation Problems. *Fuzzy Sets and Systems, 100*(1-3), 45–57. doi:10.1016/S0165-0114(97)00164-4

Mahapatra, D. R., Roy, S. K., & Biswal, M. P. (2010). Stochastic Based on Multi-objective Transportation Problems Involving Normal Randomness. *Advanced Modeling and Optimization, 12*(2), 205–223.

Mahapatra, D. R., Roy, S. K., & Biswal, M. P. (2011). Computation of Multi-objective Probabilistic Transportation Problems Involving Normal Distribution with Joint Constraints. *The Journal of Fuzzy Mathematics*, *19*(4), 865–876.

Mahapatra, D. R., Roy, S. K., & Biswal, M. P. (2013). Multi-choice stochastic transportation problem involving extreme value distribution. *Applied Mathematical Modelling*, *37*(4), 2230–2240. doi:10.1016/j.apm.2012.04.024

Patel, G., & Tripathy, J. (1989). The Solid Transportation Problem and its Variants. *International Journal of Management and Systems*, *5*, 17–36.

Rabindran, A., Philips Don, T., & Solberg James, J. (1987). *Operations Research: Principles and Practice* (2nd ed.). New York: John Wiley and Sons.

Rao, S. S. (1984). *Optimization Theory and Applications* (2nd ed.). New Delhi: Wiley Eastern Limited.

Roy, S. K., Mahapatra, D. R., & Biswal, M. P. (2012). Multi-choice stochastic transportation problem with exponential distribution. *Journal of Uncertain Systems*, *6*(3), 200–213.

Shell, E. (1955). Distribution of a Product by Several Properties, Directorate of Management Analysis. In *Proceedings of the Second Symposium in Linear Programming*, (vol. 2, pp. 615-642). DCS/Comptroller H.Q.U.S.A.F.

KEY TERMS AND DEFINITIONS

Binary Variable: Variable which takes only two values.

Cauchy's Distribution: It is the distribution of a random variable that is the ratio of two independent standard normal variables.

Mixed-Integer Programming: Mixed integer linear programming (MILP) involves problems in which only some of the variables are constrained to be integers, while other variables are allowed to be non-integers.

Multi-Choice Programming: The Multi-choice programming (MCP) is a mathematical programming technique in which the decision maker collects multiple information exists for all parameters.

Solid Transportation Problem: The STP is an important extension of the traditional TP with constraints besides of source constraints and destination constraints, such as product type constraints or transportation mode constraints.

Stochastic Programming: Stochastic programming is a framework for modeling optimization problems that involve uncertainty.

Transformation Technique: Selects only one choice from a set of multi-choice for each coefficient of objective function and provides an optimal solution to the model.

Transportation Problem: It is a model that is applied to determine how many units of commodity to be shipped from each origin to various destinations, satisfying source availability and destination demand and minimizing the total cost of transportation.

Chapter 24
Default Probability Prediction of Credit Applicants Using a New Fuzzy KNN Method with Optimal Weights

Abbas Keramati
University of Tehran, Iran

Niloofar Yousefi
University of Central Florida, USA

Amin Omidvar
Amirkabir University of Technology, Iran

ABSTRACT

Credit scoring has become a very important issue due to the recent growth of the credit industry. As the first objective, this chapter provides an academic database of literature between and proposes a classification scheme to classify the articles. The second objective of this chapter is to suggest the employing of the Optimally Weighted Fuzzy K-Nearest Neighbor (OWFKNN) algorithm for credit scoring. To show the performance of this method, two real world datasets from UCI database are used. In classification task, the empirical results demonstrate that the OWFKNN outperforms the conventional KNN and fuzzy KNN methods and also other methods. In the predictive accuracy of probability of default, the OWFKNN also show the best performance among the other methods. The results in this chapter suggest that the OWFKNN approach is mostly effective in estimating default probabilities and is a promising method to the fields of classification.

1. INTRODUCTION

The increased demand for consumer credit has led to an intense competition in credit industry. Therefore, credit managers have to develop and apply machine learning methods to handle analyzing credit data in order to save time and reduce errors. Credit scoring can be defined as a technique that helps lenders decide whether to grant credit to the applicants with respect to the applicants' characteristics such as age,

DOI: 10.4018/978-1-4666-7272-7.ch024

income and marital status (M. C. Chen & Huang, 2003). In recent years, several quantitative methods have been proposed for credit risk evaluation. Among all existent approaches, data mining methods have found more popularity than the others because of their ability in discovering practical knowledge from the database and transforming them into useful information. The first researches on credit scoring were done by (Fisher, 1936) and (Durand, 1941) who applied linear and quadratic discriminant analysis respectively to categorize credit applications as "good" or "bad" ones.

Credit scoring models are known as statistical models which have been widely used to predict the default risk of individuals or companies. These are multivariate models which use the main economic and financial indicators of a company or the individuals' characteristics such as age, income and marital status as input and assign them a weight which reflects their relative importance in predicting the default. The result is an index of creditworthiness that is expressed as a numerical score measuring the borrower's probability of default (PD). Default probability is the likelihood that a borrower will be unable to repay a loan and fall into default.

The initial credit scoring models were devised in the 1930s by authors such as (Fisher, 1936) and (Durand, 1941) and have been developed by the studies of (Beaver, 1967), (Altman, 1968) and others from 1960. Many credit scoring methods have been proposed so far, but many of them only focus on classifying customers instead of scoring them. From the viewpoint of risk management, assigning a score to each borrower will be more meaningful than classifying him as a "good" or "bad" applicant. The most important issue in credit scoring is to assign a specific PD to each customer according to his characteristics and financial/economic indicators. In this article we will present a method which is capable of classifying and scoring applicants simultaneously.

In this study, we present a new method which is capable of estimating a default probability for each borrower in addition to classifying him. It will be shown that the PDs generated from this method are very close to their real values. The other advantage of the proposed model is that it does not need any a priori information about the structure of the data. The conventional methods for estimating PD such as discriminant analysis (DA) or logistic regression (LR) are based on fairly unrealistic assumptions (the normality of the data for DA and the existence of a logistic relationship between input variables and PD for LR).

In the next section, we review the most widely used data mining methods and the articles associated with each data mining method applied for credit scoring task from 2000 to 2010. Section 3 describes our methodology for doing this research in detail. Empirical results generated by Optimally Weighted Fuzzy K-Nearest Neighbor (OWFKNN) method on two real world data sets are shown in section 4. Section 5 contains some concluding remarks.

2. LITERATURE SURVEY

This paper presents a comprehensive review of literature related to application of data mining techniques in credit scoring published in academic journals between 2000 and 2010.

For doing this research, we searched online journal databases which some of them are referenced here. These databases include Science Direct; Scopus, Emerald, Springer, IEEE Explore, Jstore, John Wiley, Academic Search Premier. The searched Journals include Expert Systems with Applications, European Journal of Operational Research, Computers & Operations Research, Computer Engineering and Applications, Journal of Empirical Finance, Journal of Banking & Finance, Journal of Business Economics and Management, Mathematics and Economics, IEEE international conference papers.

Credit Scoring, Credit Risk, Credit Rating, Data Mining, Classification, Neural Network, Bayesian Classifier, Discriminant Analysis, Logistic Regression, Decision Tree, K-Nearest Neighbor, Support Vector Machine, Fuzzy Rule-Based System, Survival Analysis and Hybrid Model were the most useful keywords to find articles.

This survey has been done in two stages: in the first stage we selected the articles related to credit scoring by reviewing abstracts and titles. In this stage, two hundred articles were identified and reviewed for their direct relevance to applying data mining techniques in credit scoring. These articles were identified based on the descriptors "credit scoring" and "data mining". Then we extracted the most widely used data mining methods in credit scoring context from the articles and some books. In this stage, we realized ten data mining methods as the most employed techniques for credit scoring. In the next stage, the articles associated with each of the ten data mining methods-applied in credit scoring- were collected from 2000 to 2010. Ninety six articles were subsequently selected, reviewed and classified in this stage.

2.1. Data Mining Techniques Employed for Credit Scoring

Nowadays each individual or organization – business, family or institution – produces and collects a huge volume of data about itself and its environment. According to (Giudici, 2003) "Data mining is the process of selection, exploration, and modeling of large quantities of data to discover regularities or relations that are at first unknown with the aim of obtaining clear and useful results for the owner of the database." Data mining is a useful tool for taking strategic decision, and it plays an important role in market segmentation, customer services, fraud detection, credit and behavior scoring and benchmarking (Giudici, 2001), (Lyn C, 2000).

2.1.1. Neural Network (NN)

Artificial neural networks (ANNs) are non-linear statistical data modeling tools based on the function of the human brain. They are powerful tools for unknown data relationship modeling. ANNs are able to recognize non-linear, non-additive relationship in data and handle both continues and categorical predictors and outcomes. They also can manage multiple outcomes in a single model. These models have some weaknesses as follows: they provide few insights about data; the results are difficult to interpret; the solution may be sensitive to starting point due to multiple locally optimal solutions.

2.1.2. Bayesian Classifier (BC)

A Bayes classifier is a simple probabilistic classifier based on applying Bayes' theorem (from Bayesian statistics) with strong (naive) independent assumptions, and it is particularly suited when the dimensionality of the inputs is high. A naive Bayes classifier assumes that the existence (or nonexistence) of a specific feature of a class is unrelated to the existence (or nonexistence) of any other feature. The major disadvantage of this model is that the predictive accuracy is highly correlated with this assumption. An advantage of this method is that it requires a small amount of training data to estimate the parameters (means and variances of the variables) required for classification.

2.1.3. Discriminant Analysis (DA)

Discriminant analysis which was studied by Fisher as early as 1936 is an alternative for logistic regression which assumes the explanatory variables follow a multivariate normal distribution, and they have a common variance-covariance matrix. This method can separate and classify individuals into multiple groups. The objective of this method is to minimize the distance within each group and to maximize the distance between different groups using discriminant function. The main drawback of this model is that it relies on unrealistic assumptions.

2.1.4. Logistic Regression (LR)

Logistic regression is a form of the linear regression. This model can predict a discrete outcome from a set of variables that may be continuous, discrete, dichotomous, or a combination of any of these. Generally, the dependent or response variable is dichotomous. One advantage of this method is that it does not assume the linearity of relationship between the dependent and independent variables; another advantage of this method is that it does not require normally distributed variables. Logistic regression can accept a large number of independent variables. While this may seem like an advantage, there are many situations when it is not, because the parameter estimation procedure of logistic regression relies heavily on having an adequate number of samples for each combination of independent variables. On the other hand, small sample sizes can lead to widely inaccurate estimates of parameters.

2.1.5. Decision Tree (DT)

A classification tree is a predictive technique with a tree structure, where the branches represent different possible values of input variables, and the leaves refer to the final classification (i.e., output). The advantages of this method are: it is a white box model and so it is simple to understand and explain no processing of data is required, it handles both continues and categorical variables. The limitation of this model is that it cannot be generalized as a designed structure for other contexts.

2.1.6. Survival Analysis (SA)

This method is a new credit scoring model. The conventional methods can distinguish good borrowers from bad ones at the time of loan application, but this model can compute the profitability of the customers over the customers' lifetime, and it can perform profit scoring (Bart. Baesens, Gestel, Stepanova, Poel, & Vanthienen, 2005). SA can predict the time the event will occur instead of predicting the probability of the occurrence of an event. In the other words, it can provide time-varying credit information. The main weakness of this model is that it needs to give unambiguous definition of "death" (e.g., customer's default).

2.1.7. Fuzzy Rule-Based System (FRS)

It helps creditors in designing rules that accurately derive the credit score with explanation, while most of credits scoring models focus on estimating a score without explaining how the results were obtained. The advantage of this model is that the fuzzy rules are capable of handling both quantitative and qualitative factors, so if there are a large set of inputs, scoring results will be less sensitive to small measurement errors. It also provides more specific results with explanation, but this model is more difficult to formulate due to its informal interpretation of data.

2.1.8. Support Vector Machine (SVM)

Support vector machine is a classifier technique, first proposed by (Vapnik, 1995). This method involves three elements. A score formula which is a linear combination of features selected for the classification problem, an objective function which considers both training and test samples to optimize the classification of new data, and an optimizing algorithm for determining the optimal parameters for the objective function of training sample. The advantage of SVM is that, in the nonparametric case, it requires no data structure assumptions such as normal distribution and continuity. SVM can perform a nonlinear mapping from an original input space into a high dimensional feature space and is capable of handling both continuous and categorical predictions. The weaknesses of this method is that it is difficult to interpret unless the features are interpretable and standard formulations do not contain specification of business constraints (Ravi, 2008).

2.1.9. Hybrid Models (HM)

These models are credit scoring models which are developed by integrating two or more existing models. The advantage of these models is that the creditor can benefit form the advantages of two or more models and they can also remove the weakness of a model by combining them with the other models, but these methods are difficult to formulate and implement in comparison with simple methods (Ravi, 2008).

2.1.10. K-Nearest Neighbor (KNN)

K-nearest neighbor is a nonparametric classifier based on learning by similarity. A training data set is collected for which a distance function is introduced between the explanatory variable of observations. For each new observation this method explores the pattern space for the K nearest neighbors that are closest to the new observation in terms of distance between the explanatory variables. The new observation is assigned to the class to which its most KNNs belong. The main advantage of KNN is its simple implementation. Also just distance metric and k parameters must be tuned. As new instances with known classes are presented, the classifier can be updated online at very little cost, moreover, KNN is robust with regard to the search space. KNN has some disadvantages that some of them are mentioned here. First, testing of each instance is expensive as we need to compute its distance to all known instances. Sensitiveness to noisy or irrelevant attributes is another drawback; also the K parameters must be determined before implementation.

2.2. Comparative Studies (CS)

There were some studies among the articles which make a comparative analysis of some different data mining methods with the motivation to understand their classification performance. As these articles might help researchers to select an appropriate method for credit scoring, we have considered them in our literature survey.

Galindo & Tamayo (2000) prepared a study that investigated several classification techniques in terms of their advantages and limitations in credit risk assessment. They considered probit, neural network, decision tree and KNN models and some combination of these methods for this purpose. The KNN method rendered the best result among the mentioned methods. Doumpos, Kosmidou, Baourakis, & Zopounidis, (2002) employed Multi-group Hierarchical DIScrimination (M.H.DIS) method for classifying purpose, and they measured the efficiency of this model against some traditional methods such as discriminant analysis, logit analysis, and probit analysis. They concluded that the proffered model had more classification ability in comparison with benchmark methods. Xiao, Zhao, & Fei, (2006) assessed the ability of some classification methods in handling credit scoring task. These methods include linear discriminant analysis (DA), logistic regression (LA), neural networks (NN), k-nearest neighbor (k-NN), support vector machines (SVM), classification and regression tree (CART) and multivariate adaptive regression splines (MARS). Based on this study, SVM, MARS, logistic regression and neural network yield a very good classification, though LDA and CART are very user-friendly tools in building a credit scoring model. (Huysmans, Baesens, Vanthienen, & Gestel, 2006) probed the suitability of self organization maps (SOMs) for credit scoring. They also noted the advantages of the application of SOM integrated with some supervised classifier instead of using a SOM method per se. (Islam, Wu, Ahmadi, & Sid-Ahmed, 2007) employed a naive Bayes classifier and a K-Nearest neighbor classifier on a credit card dataset. They evaluated the effectiveness of these two classifiers in terms of the correct classification and misclassification. The empirical results show that the accuracy of k-nearest neighbor method is strictly dependent on the selection of k values. (Atish P & Huimin, 2008) compared the profitability of seven data mining classification techniques: naive Bayes, logistic regression, neural network, decision table, decision tree, k-nearest neighbor, and support vector machine with and without unifying domain knowledge. For this purpose, misclassification cost and area under the curve (AUC) were used to analyze the results. Based on their findings, incorporating domain knowledge improves the effectiveness of some data mining methods. (Falangis, 2008) used a Mathematical Programming (MP) Discriminant analysis method, and they compared its performance with Logistic Regression, Discriminant Analysis, KNN classifier and Support Vector machine technique. Based on their results, Discriminant functions generated by MSD (minimize the sum of the deviations) model can acquire equal or better classification performance in comparison with the logistic regression model. They also showed their proposed method outperforms Discriminant Analysis and KNN classifier. Ince & Aktan, (2009) evaluated the ability of discriminant analysis, logistic regression, neural network and classification and regression tree in prediction and classification task. According to this study CART and neural network outperform the other methods in terms of predictive accuracy and type II errors. L. Zhou & Lai, (2009) compared the predictive and classification accuracy of some traditional statistical methods with some artificial intelligence methods, such as Neural Network, Linear Regression, Discriminant Analysis, Decision Tree, Support Vector Machine, etc., using fourteen datasets. Based on their results, it should be applied different methods for problems with different degrees of imbalance. Feng Chia. Li, (2009) explored the classification accuracy of K-Nearest Neighbor, Support Vector Machine and Neural Network, without features selection. The results indicate that integrating these methods with effective feature selection approaches leads to more accurate classifications. (Twala, 2010) investigated the capability of five classifier and pairs of classifier ensembles in handling credit risk prediction. The results show that combining individual classifiers can improve the accuracy of predictive models. Paleologo, Elisseeff, & Antonini, (2010) designed an ensemble credit scoring model that is able to manage missing information, unbalanced data and non ii-d data points.

Several single and hybrid data mining methods are applied for credit scoring problem (Zurada & Lonial, 2005), (Chye Koh, Chin Tan, & Peng Goh, 2006), (Kirkos, Spathis, & Manolopoulos., 2007), (Atish P & Huimin, 2008), (Yeh & Lien, 2009). The most widely used methods in credit scoring problem are derived from classification technique. Classification can involve any context in which some decision or forecast is made on the basis of available information. It can be defined as a method which classifies the members of a given set of instances into some groups in terms of their characteristics. Classification task is highly suited to data mining methods and techniques. The summarized results of literature review are shown in Table 1.

As you can see, most of these studies aim at classifying customers into binary classes. In other words, these methods consider the same PD for each group of customers whereas, it is an unrealistic assumption. Limited information produced by these models can not meet the needs of risk management and at least we must know the PD of an obligator. Different customers have different characteristics and their default probabilities must be different. Based on the individual default probabilities we can assess portfolio risk of commercial banks and rationalize the distribution of limited resources. Therefore with estimating individual defaults probabilities for each applicant we will have a broader view of our system. In this paper we suggest applying OWFKNN method to calculate the default probabilities. This method is built based on KNN models which are popular because of their simplicity and good performance (Duda, Hart, & Stork, 2000).

3. METHODOLOGY

While logistic regression is commonly applied model for calculating default probabilities, but it is not the first method to be used for this purpose. One of the earliest methods in this context was discriminant analysis, but both of these methods have some limitation which decreases their applicability. As mentioned before, the discriminant analysis model assumes that the independent variable follow a multivariate normal distribution; however, empirical analysis illustrate that this hypothesis is an unrealistic assumption. In fact, as many financial/ economic indicators are structurally limited between 0 and 100%, a distribution taking unlimited value, such as normal distribution, in intuitively incorrect. In the logistic regression model, a logistic curve should be fitted to the database to model the probability of occurrence of a class. This model should be fitted correctly, neither over fitting nor under fitting should occur. Moreover, this model can not handle the correlation between explanatory variables and, it may result singular matrix and get wrong models if the explanatory variables correlate heavily. Since there is high correlation between financial indices, it is essential to implement some preprocessing to the data before logistic modeling. This is the reason that we prefer to apply a KNN-based model to calculate PDs which has the ability of handling these problems.

Table 1. Results summary of the literature survey

Approach (Count)	References	Probability of Default	Classification of Applicant	Rating Applicants	Time to Default Estimation
Neural Network (8)	(West, 2000),		✓		
	(Malhotra & Malhotra, 2003),		✓		
	(Nan Chen. Hsieh, 2004),		✓		
	(Angelini, Tollo, & Roli, 2008),		✓		
	(Yu, Wang, & Lai, 2008),		✓		
	(H. Abdou, Pointon, & El-Masry, 2008),		✓		
	(Tsai, Lin, Cheng, & Lin, 2009),		✓		
	(Khashman, 2010)		✓		
Bayesian Classifier (6)	(B. Baesens, Egmont-Petersen, Castelo, & Vanthienen, 2002),		✓		
	(X. S. Li & Guo, 2006),		✓		
	(McNeil & Wendin, 2007),			✓	
	(Kadam & Lenk, 2008),			✓	
	(Stefanescu, Tunaru, & Turnbull, 2009),			✓	
	(Antonakis & Sfakianakis, 2009)		✓		
Discriminant Analysis (5)	(Altman, 1968),		✓		
	(Eisenbeis, 1977),		✓		
	(Taffler & Abassi, 1984),		✓		
	(Kumar & Bhattacharya, 2006),			✓	
	(H. A. Abdou, 2009)		✓		
Logistic Regression (8)	(Steenackers & Goovaerts, 1989),	✓			
	(Laitinen, 1999),			✓	
	(Alfo, Caiazza, & Trovato, 2005),		✓		
	(Tang & Chi, 2005),		✓		
	(Ma & Tang, 2007),	✓			
	(Sohn & Kim, 2007),	✓			
	(J. h. Luo & Lei, 2008),	✓			
	(Liang & Xin, 2009)		✓		

continued on following page

Table 1. Continued

Approach (Count)	References	Probability of Default	Classification of Applicant	Rating Applicants	Time to Default Estimation
Decision Tree (6)	(Mues, Baesens, Files, & Vanthienen, 2004)		✓		
	(Lee, Chiu, Chou, & Lu, 2006),		✓		
	(Zhao, 2007),		✓		
	(Lopez, 2007),			✓	
	(Bastos, 2008),		✓		
	(H. Li, Sun, & Wu, 2010)		✓		
Survival Analysis (11)					
	(Thomas, Ho, & Scherer, 2001),				✓
	(Stepanova & Thomas, 2002),		✓		
	(Bart. Baesens, Gestel, Stepanova, Poel, & Vanthienen, 2005),				✓
	(Noh, Roh, & Han, 2005),		✓		
	(Sohn & Shin, 2006),		✓		
	(Carling, Jacobson, Linde, & Roszbach, 2007),				✓
	(Beran & Djaidja, 2007),				✓
	(Andreeva, Ansell, & Crook, 2007),				✓
	(Bellotti & Crook, 2009a),		✓		
	(Cao, Vilar, & Devia, 2009),				✓
	(Sarlija, Bensic, & Susac, 2009)				✓
Fuzzy Rule-based System (9)					
	(Baetge & Heitmann, 2000)		✓		
	, (Tung, Quek, Cheng, & EWS, 2004),		✓		
	(Tang & Chi, 2005),		✓		
	(Laha, 2007),		✓		
	(Hoffmann, Baesens, Mues, Gestel, & Vanthienen, 2007),		✓		
	(Jiao, Syau, & Lee, 2007),			✓	
	(Lahsasna, Ainon, & Wah, 2008),		✓		
	(Liu, Lai, & Guu, 2009),		✓		
	(Xinhui & Zhong, 2009)		✓		

continued on following page

Table 1. Continued

Approach (Count)	References	Probability of Default	Classification of Applicant	Rating Applicants	Time to Default Estimation
Support Vector Machine (16)					
	(Z. Huang, Chen, Hsu, Chen, & Wu, 2004),			✓	
	(Gestel, Bart Baesens, et al., 2006),			✓	
	(W. H. Chen & Shih, 2006),	·		✓	
	(Gestel, Baesens, et al., 2006),		✓		
	(Yang, 2007),		✓		
	(Martens, Baesens, Gestel, & Vanthienen, 2007),		✓		
	(C. L. Huang, Chen, & Wang, 2007),		✓		
	(Xu, Zhou, & Wang, 2009),		✓		
	(L. Zhou, Lai, & Yu, 2009),		✓		
	(W. Chen, Ma, & Ma, 2009),		✓		
	(S. T. Luo, Cheng, & Hsieh, 2009),		✓		
	(Bellotti & Crook, 2009b),		✓		
	(HÄRDLE, Lee, Schafer, & Yeh, 2009),		✓		
	(L. Zhou, Lai, & Yu, 2010),		✓		
	(Yu, Yue, Wang, & Lai, 2010),		✓		
	(Kim & Sohn, 2010)		✓		
Hybrid Models (12)					
	(Lee, Chiu, Lu, & Chen, 2002),		✓		
	(Malhotra & Malhotra, 2002),		✓		
	(Wang, Wang, & Lai, 2005),		✓		
	(Lee & Chen, 2005),		✓		
	(Nan Chen. Hsieh, 2005),		✓		
	(J. J. Huang, Tzeng, & Ong, 2006),		✓		
	(J. Zhou & Bai, 2008),		✓		
	(Zhang, Hifi, Chen, & Ye, 2008),		✓		
	(Yu, Wang, Wen, Lai, & He, 2008),		✓		
	(Feng Chia. Li, 2009; Lin, 2009),		✓		
	(F. L. Chen & Li, 2010),		✓		
	(Nan Chen. Hsieh & Hung, 2010)		✓		
K-Nearest Neighbor (3)					
	(Paredes & Vidal, 2000),		✓		
	(Hand & Vinciotti, 2003),		✓		
	(Marinakis, Marinaki, Doumpos, & Matsatsinis, 2008)		✓		

continued on following page

Table 1. Continued

Approach (Count)	References	Probability of Default	Classification of Applicant	Rating Applicants	Time to Default Estimation
Comparative Studies (12)					
	(Galindo & Tamayo, 2000)		✓		
	, (Doumpos, Kosmidou, Baourakis, & Zopounidis, 2002),		✓		
	(Xiao, Zhao, & Fei, 2006),		✓		
	(Huysmans, Baesens, Vanthienen, & Gestel, 2006)		✓		
	(Islam, Wu, Ahmadi, & Sid-Ahmed, 2007),		✓		
	(Atish P & Huimin, 2008),		✓		
	(Falangis, 2008),		✓		
	(Ince & Aktan, 2009),		✓		
	(L. Zhou & Lai, 2009),		✓		
	(Feng Chia. Li, 2009),		✓		
	(Twala, 2010),		✓		
	(Paleologo, Elisseeff, & Antonini, 2010)		✓		
Total (96)	96	4	75	10	7

In this section, we explain our methodology for conducting this research. The KNN algorithm is the basis of our method because of its simplicity and its being nonparametric, but one drawback of KNN algorithm is that considering the same importance for all neighbors can reduce the accuracy of the method. To overcome this shortage, the fuzzy KNN model is proposed which assigns a weight to each neighbor according to its distance from the test sample.

In this study, we present a new fuzzy KNN method which applies statistical measures to assign the weights to the neighbors. It will be shown that the new method outperforms the conventional KNN and fuzzy KNN in terms of classification accuracy. The most important ability of this method is its power in default probability prediction. To apply this method, we should first calculate optimal kriging weights for each neighbor using the method described in the next section. For taking into account the overlapping between two classes, the fuzzy membership grade is employed for each labeled sample instead of those crisp values. The method used for this purpose is also briefly explained in section 3.1. Then the fuzzy grade of each test sample in each class can be obtained from a linear combination of the fuzzy membership of k weighted nearest neighbors. The test sample is assigned to the class with maximum fuzzy grade. To predict the default probability of each applicant we can use his fuzzy grade in "bad" class as his default probability. To illustrate the accuracy of the OFWKNN in default probability prediction we apply a new method named Sorting Smoothing Method which is proposed by (Yeh & Lien, 2009). In the next two sections we describe the optimally weighted fuzzy KNN and Sorting Smoothing Method in detail. The research architecture for the proposed method has been shown in Figure 1 and all the details will be explained next.

Figure 1. Research architectures for the proposed OWFKNN method

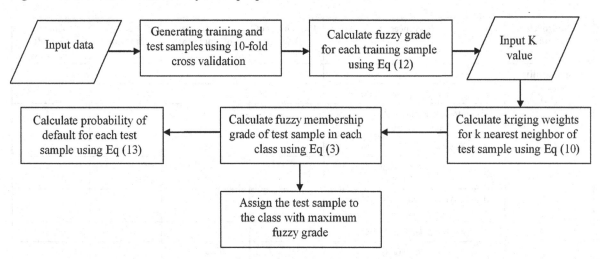

3.1. Optimally Weighted Fuzzy KNN Algorithm (OWFKNN)

Among the mentioned methods k-nearest neighbor (KNN) is a non-parametric method which has been widely used for solving many practical problems. KNN is the most popular classifier because its error rate asymptotically approaches the optimal Bayes error rate (Cover & Hart, 1967) despite its simplicity. But it is shown that considering equal importance for all neighbors can reduce the accuracy of the KNN particularly when there is a strong degree of overlap between the sample vectors (Pham, 2005). To overcome this problem fuzzy KNN algorithm is suggested by (Keller, Gray, & Givens, 1985b) which assigns a fuzzy membership for an unknown sample $\mathbf{x}_u$ to class label y, denoted as μ_{yu} :

$$\mu_{yu} = \frac{\sum_{i=1}^{k} c_i \mu_{yi}}{\sum_{i=1}^{k} c_i} \tag{1}$$

μ_{yu} is a linear combination of the fuzzy membership of k nearest neighbors, μ_{yi} is the fuzzy membership assigned to labeled sample $\mathbf{x}_i$, and c_i is the inverse distance between $\mathbf{x}_i$ and the unknown sample $\mathbf{x}_u$:

$$c_i = \| x_u - x_i \|^{-2/(q-1)} \tag{2}$$

$\| \mathbf{x}_u - \mathbf{x}_i \|$ is the distance between the test sample $\mathbf{x}_u$ and training sample $\mathbf{x}_i$. Different distance measures can be applied, such as Euclidean and Mahalanobis distance measures. In this study, the Euclidean metric which is the most common metric, is used to select nearest neighbors. It can be seen that the conventional fuzzy KNN algorithm assigns a fuzzy membership based on some arbitrary distance measure not based on any optimal criteria, but the proposed model by (Pham, 2005) is based on a statistical measure. (Pham, 2005) propose an optimally weighted fuzzy KNN (OWFKNN) algorithm which is based on a geostatistical technique named kriging. Kriging is the best linear unbiased estimator (Isaaks & Srivastava, 1989) because it tries to estimate a set of optimal weight for labeled sample by minimization the error variance subject to unbiasedness.

Using OWFKNN, we can rewrite Equation (1) as follows:

$$\mu_{yu} = \sum_{i=1}^{k} w_i \mu_{yi} \tag{3}$$

where μ_{yu} and μ_{yi} have the same definition as in Equation 1, and w_i stands for the weights of the neighbors which can be obtained from different approaches. Kriging computes these weights by minimizing the average error of estimation.

The estimation of the unknown sample $\mathbf{x}_u$ can be defined as the weighted linear combination of the neighbors:

$$\hat{\mathbf{x}}_u = \sum_{i=1}^{k} w_i \mathbf{x}_i \tag{4}$$

where $\hat{\mathbf{x}}_u$ is the estimate value of $\mathbf{x}_u$, $\mathbf{x}_i \{i = 1, \dots, k\}$ are the neighbors and $w_i \{i = 1, \dots, k\}$ are optimal kriging weights for available samples obtained by solving the following system of equation:

$$\mathbf{Cw} = \mathbf{D} \tag{5}$$

where

$$\mathbf{C} = \begin{bmatrix} c_{11} & \cdots & c_{1k} & 1 \\ \vdots & \cdots & \vdots & \vdots \\ c_{k1} & \cdots & c_{kk} & 1 \\ 1 & \cdots & 1 & 0 \end{bmatrix} \tag{6}$$

$$\mathbf{w} = \begin{bmatrix} w_1 \dots w_k \, \beta \end{bmatrix}^T \tag{7}$$

and

$$\mathbf{D} = \begin{bmatrix} c_{1u} \dots c_{ku} \, 1 \end{bmatrix}^T \tag{8}$$

where c_{ij} is the covariance of x_i, x_j, $w_1, \dots, w_k$ are optimal kriging weights and β is a Lagrange multiplier. The optimal kriging weights can be obtained by solving:

$$\mathbf{w} = \mathbf{C}^{-1}\mathbf{D} \tag{9}$$

where $\mathbf{C}^{-1}$ is the inverse of the covariance matrix $\mathbf{C}$. The normalization is not needed, because $\sum_{i=1}^{k} w_i = 1$.

Some of the kriging weights can be negative, one way to correct negative weights proposed by (Journel & Rao, 1996) is to determine the largest negative weight and to add an equivalent constant to all weights which are then normalized:

$$w_i^* = \frac{w_i - \alpha}{\sum_{i=1}^{k}(w_i - \alpha)}, \qquad \forall i = 1, \ldots, k \tag{10}$$

where w_i^* is the corrected weight of w_i and

$$\alpha = -\min_i w_i \tag{11}$$

After finding the optimal kriging weights (w_i^*), we can replace them in Equation (1) to obtain the fuzzy membership of a test pattern.

To determine the fuzzy membership grades (μ_{yi}) for sample data, we use the method proposed by (Keller, Gray, & Givens, 1985a). The K nearest neighbors to each sample (x), are selected and the fuzzy membership of x in each class is assigned using the following equations:

$$\mu_y(x_i) = \begin{cases} 0.51 + \left(\dfrac{n_j}{K}\right) * 0.49 & if\, j = y \\ \left(\dfrac{n_j}{K}\right) * 0.49 & if\, j \neq y \end{cases} \tag{12}$$

The value n_j refers to the number of the neighbors which belongs to the jth class. This technique fuzzifies the memberships of the labeled samples which are located in the region where classes have overlap. Moreover, the samples which are well away from this area (Overlapping Area) are assigned with complete membership in the known class.

3.2. Prediction Probability of Default Using OWFKNN

Many credit scoring models, based on data mining methods, can only classify customers into "good" or "bad" classes, while from the perspective of risk management, predicting the probability of default for each applicant, who applies for a credit, will be more meaningful than classifying him into binary classes. For this reason we propose OWFKNN model which has the ability of estimating the probability of default. The advantage of the OWFKNN method is that it can estimate the probability of default (PD) based on statistical criteria. Many of the applied methods for credit scoring only focus on classifying customers, and there are few models which can predict one real PD for each applicant in addition to classifying him. In OWFKNN the fuzzy membership grade in "bad" class can be interpreted as the probability of default when we use crisp membership function for each sample instead of fuzzy membership function (namely in Equation (3) $\mu_{yi} = 0\ or\ 1$).

$$PD = \sum_{i=1}^{k} w_i \mu_{bi} \tag{13}$$

where μ_{bi} is the fuzzy membership of the sample, labeled as "bad" class, and w_i stands kriging weights.

$\mu_{bi} = 1$, if default occurred,

$\mu_{bi} = 0$, if default did not occur.

When we use crisp membership value for the labeled sample (instead of fuzzy membership), we can obtain more accurate results for PD. It can be for this reason that using fuzzy membership grade in Equation (3) changes the cut-off point value in classification task and makes it more meaningful by considering overlapping between classes. The more overlap between the two classes the more difference in PDs obtained from the approaches. This can be associated with the characteristics of the data and the cut-off point value which can separate "good" applicants from "bad" ones. It is noticeable that the sum of fuzzy grades over all classes for an unknown sample is not equal to one when we apply fuzzy memberships for labeled samples. Whereas this total sum would be exactly equal to one in case of using crisp values for labeled samples. It seems that the latter can generate more interpretable PD values. The obtained PD from OWFKNN can be meaningful because it is estimated based on statistical measure (kriging measures). In this study we use the "Sorting Smoothing Method" proposed by (Yeh & Lien, 2009) to explore the predictive accuracy of OWFKNN in prediction of probability of default.

3.3. The Sorting Smoothing Method (SSM)

To estimate the real probability of default using Sorting Smoothing Method (SSM) proposed by (Yeh & Lien, 2009), the validation data from the minimum to the maximum can be ordered according to the predictive probability. Then the real probability of default is obtained as shown in Box 1.where

- P_i is the estimated real probability of default in the ith order of validation data;
    Y_i is the binary variable which represents the real default risk in the ith order of validation, if default happened $Y_i = 1$, and if default did not happen $Y_i = 0$;
- n is the number of data for smoothing; in this study the n=50 is selected.

Box 1.

$$P_i = \frac{Y_{i-n} + Y_{i-n+1} + \dots + Y_{i-1} + Y_i + Y_{i+1} + \dots + Y_{i+n-1} + Y_{i+n}}{2n + 1} \tag{14}$$

After finding the PD, we can apply the two following steps to explore the predictive accuracy of the method in terms of default probability prediction.

1. Scatter plot diagram: the horizontal axis stands for the predictive probability of default, and the vertical axis reveals the obtained actual default probability.
2. Linear regression: the linear regression line *(Y=A+BX)* is fitted to the scatter plot, then the coefficient of determination (R^2) is calculated. If R^2 is close to one, intercept (*A*) is close to zero and regression coefficient (*B*) is close to one, it can be concluded that the predictive probability of default obtained from the method represents the actual default probability (Yeh & Lien, 2009).

4. EMPIRICAL ANALYSIS

4.1. Real Credit Data Set

Two real world data sets from the UCI Repository of Machine Learning Databases are selected (see Table 2). The Australian consumer credit data set consists of 307 "good" creditors and 383 "bad" ones. There are 6 numerical and 8 categorical attributes and 1 class attribute (accepted or rejected) for each sample. To protect confidentiality of the data, all attribute names and values have been changed to meaningless symbols. This dataset is interesting because there is a good mixture of attributes – continuous, nominal with small value numbers, and nominal with larger value numbers. The second data set is the German credit scoring data set which is more unbalanced. 700 applicants are creditworthy and 300 cases are not. Additionally each applicant is described by 24 input variables: the credit history, account balances, loan purpose, loan amount, employment status, personal information, age, housing and job, and 1 class attribute (accepted or rejected).

4.2. Experimental Results of Classification Using OWFKNN

Three approaches were applied in this study: original k-nearest neighbor, conventional fuzzy KNN (FKNN) and optimally weighted fuzzy KNN (OWFKNN). Table 3 and Table 4 summarize the results obtained from three approaches for the two data sets using 10-fold cross-validation. For the Australian data set, the accuracy of KNN is 85.36%, FKNN is 84.2%, and OWFKNN is 85.7%. For the German data set, the accuracy of KNN is 73.4%, FKNN is 74.4%, and OWFKNN is 74.9%. In this study we change values of K from 1 to 20. The accuracy rate of three approaches in different K values for Australian and German data sets are shown in Figure 2 and Figure 3 respectively. The highest accuracy rate for Australian data occurs when K value is equal to 13 in OWFKNN model, and for German data when k value is equal to 7 in OWFKNN model.

Table 2. Datasets from the UCI repository

Datasets	Total Instances	Nominal Features	Numeric Features	Total Features	Number of Classes
Australian	690	6	8	14	2
German	1000	0	24	24	2

Table 3. Results summary with 10-fold cross validation for Australian credit data set

Approaches	Avg.(%)	Std.(%)
KNN	85.36(K=18)	3.708
FKNN	84.2(K=19)	4.55
OWFKNN	86.5(K=13)	4.76

Table 4. Results summary with 10-fold cross validation for German credit data set

Approaches	Avg.(%)	Std.(%)
KNN	73.4(K=16)	4.32
FKNN	74.4(K=17)	5.23
OWFKNN	74.9(K=7)	3.51

Figure 2. The movements of average accuracy over different K values for Australian data set

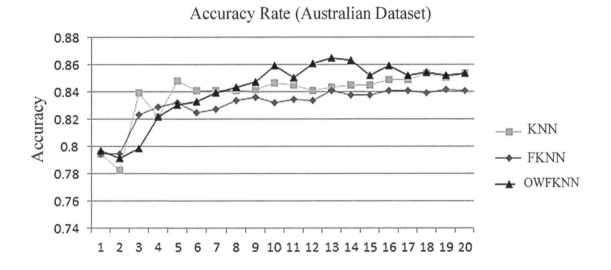

4.3. Comparison with Other Methods in Terms of Classification Accuracy

For the comparison purpose, several common methods which have been recently used in credit scoring context are selected and their results are used as a benchmark to those generated by OWFKNN method. Sensitivity and specificity are statistical measures of the performance of a binary classification test. Let N_1 represent the number of correctly classified instances as good; N_2 represent the number of bad instances incorrectly classified as good; N_3 represent the number of good instances incorrectly classified as bad by the classifier; N_4 represent the number of correctly classified instances as "bad". Performance measures of the classifier are defined as:

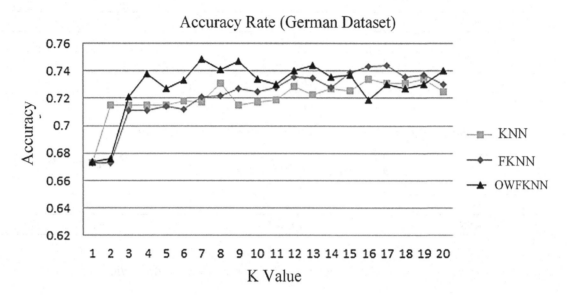

$$sensitivity = \frac{N_1}{N_1 + N_3} \tag{15}$$

Sensitivity shows the fraction of instances which are correctly classified by OWFKNN as good among all good instances.

$$specificity = \frac{N_4}{N_2 + N_4} \tag{16}$$

Specificity shows the fraction of instances which are correctly classified by OWFKNN as bad among all bad instances.

$$hit\,rate\left(accuracy\,percentage\right) = \frac{N_1 + N_4}{N_1 + N_2 + N_3 + N_4} \tag{17}$$

Accuracy shows the fraction of instances that are classified correctly among all instances.

In this section we compare the results of three KNN based models with those generated by Neural network, logistic regression, discriminant analysis, classification and regression tree (CART) and support vector machine referred in (Xiao, et al., 2006).

It is concluded from Table 5 that logistic regression has the highest overall accuracy of 87.2% for Australian data set, and RBF neural network with accuracy of 87.1% yields very similar results to logistic regression. The OWFKKN has classificatory accuracy of 86.5% which has no significant difference with superior models. While Lin-Svm, Pol-Svm, Rbf-Svm and Sig-Svm have overall accuracy of 85.5% to 85.8%.

Table 5. Comparison of different credit scoring models in terms of classification performance (Australian Data)

Approaches	Sensitivity (%)	Specificity (%)	Overall Accuracy (%)
RBF	86.8	87.2	87.1
Neural network BPN	84.6	86.7	85.8
FAR	74.4	76.2	75.4
Logistic regression	85.9	89.0	87.2
Linear discriminant	81.0	92.2	85.9
CART	79.9	92.5	85.5
Lin-Svm	79.9	92.5	85.5
SVM Pol-Svm	83.8	88.6	85.5
Rbf-Svm	80.5	93.0	85.8
Sig-Svm	80.5	92.0	85.6
KNN	78.3	90.8	85.4
KNN-based FKNN	79.28	88.05	84.2
OWFKNN	83.03	89.25	86.5

For the German data set (see Table 6) the highest classificatory accuracy (hit rate) of 77.2% is achieved from Sig-Svm model, while the other three SVM based models have overall accuracy of 77.1%, 77% and 76.5% respectively. The logistic regression with hit rate of 76.3% has the highest accuracy after SVM based models, and OWFKNN with accuracy of 74.9% is better than the rest methods. The least accurate method is FAR neural network for both Australian and German data sets. The results reveal that the proposed method is an acceptable alternative to distinguish "bad" and "good" customers from each other.

Table 6. Comparison of different credit scoring models in terms of classification performance (German Data)

Approaches	Sensitivity (%)	Specificity (%)	Overall Accuracy (%)
RBF	86.5	48.0	74.6
Neural network BPN	86.4	42.5	73.3
FAR	60.0	51.2	57.3
Logistic regression	88.1	48.7	76.3
Linear discriminant	72.3	73.3	72.6
CART	71.2	69.4	70.5
Lin-Svm	88.9	49.1	77.0
SVM Pol-Svm	88.5	48.6	76.5
Rbf-Svm	88.7	49.7	77.1
Sig-Svm	89.0	50.0	77.2
KNN	95.32	22.62	73.4
KNN-based FKNN	94.16	29.0	74.4
OWFKNN	88.42	43.33	74.9

4.4. Predicting the Default Probabilities Using OWFKNN and Comparison with Some Data Mining Methods

The scatter plot, regression line and R^2 obtained from OWFKNN for Australian and German datasets are shown in Figure 4 and Figure 11 respectively. Finally, for the purpose of comparison, the default probabilities of Australian and German applicants are predicted by the six major data mining methods; Multilayer perceptron, RBF network, C4.5 (decision tree), Logistic regression, Linear Discriminant analysis and Naïve Bayes classifier. The regression results for both data sets are summarized in Table 7 and Table 8.

In this study the n=50 was chosen and SSM was employed to estimate the real default probabilities. The scatter plot diagram, the regression line and R^2, produced from the seven data mining methods for Australian data set are shown in Figures 4 to 10 and their results are summarized in Table 7. From the result of R^2, regression coefficient (B) and intercept (A), the predictive default probability produced from OWFKNN has the highest explanatory ability for real default probability.

The scatter plot diagrams of the seven data mining techniques for the German data set are shown below (Figures 11 to 17). From Table 8, the OWFKNN show the best performance based on R^2 (0.9389, close to 1), regression intercept (0.03905, close to 0) and regression coefficient (0.9349, close to 1).

Figure 4. Scatter plot diagram of OWFKNN for Australian dataset

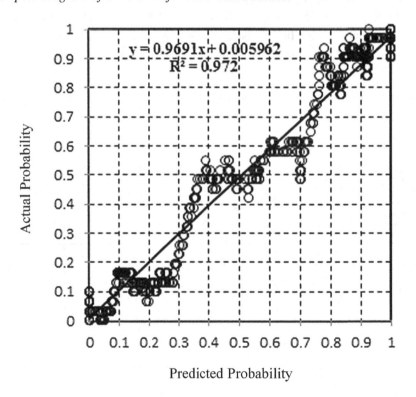

Table 7. Summary of linear regression between real probability and predictive probability of default for Australian dataset

Approach	Regression Coefficient	Regression Intercept	Regression R^2
OWFKNN	0.9691	0.005962	0.972
Multilayer Perceptron	0.725	0.109	0.916
RBF network	0.925	0.006	0.882
C4.5	0.7777	0.078	0.8932
Logistic Regression	0.9201	0.0069	0.955
Naïve Bayes Classifier	0.6785	0.1794	0.7618
Linear Discriminant analysis	0.8071	0.047	0.9388

Table 8. Summary of linear regression between real probability and predictive probability of default for German dataset

Approach	Regression Coefficient	Regression Intercept	Regression R^2
OWFKNN	0.9349	0.03905	0.9389
Multilayer Perceptron	0.3214	0.209	0.7745
RBF	0.8485	0.0427	0.9125
C4.5	0.3955	0.1624	0.5158
Logistic Regression	0.818	0.0413	0.8018
Naïve Bayes Classifier	0.5232	0.1099	0.7373
Linear Discriminant Analysis	0.7878	0.0449	0.8727

5. CONCLUSION

Application of data mining techniques in credit scoring is an emerging trend in the industry. It has attracted the attention of practitioners and academics. The first objective of this paper is to give a research summary on the application of data mining in the credit scoring domain and techniques which are most often used. In this study, ninety six articles were identified related to application of data mining techniques in credit scoring, and published between 2000 and 2010. According to the results of this survey, 78.2% (75 articles) of the articles are related to classification of applicants into binary classes and just 3% (4 articles) were related to predicting probability of default.

As the second objective, this study explored the capability of the optimally weighted fuzzy KNN method in predicting the probability of default. From the perspective of risk management, predicting the probability of default for each applicant will be more meaningful than classifying him into binary classes. Whereas most academic journal papers, considered in this study, only had concentrated on clas-

Figure 5. Scatter plot diagram of multilayer perceptron for Australian dataset

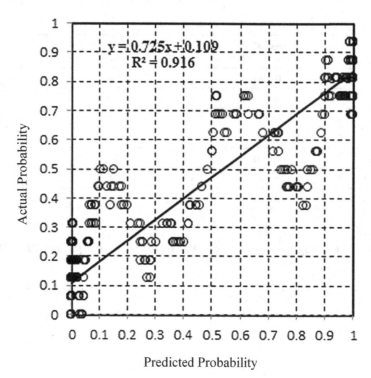

Figure 6. Scatter plot diagram of RBF for Australian dataset

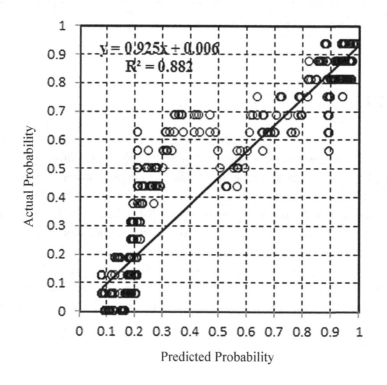

Figure 7. Scatter plot diagram of C4.5 for Australian dataset

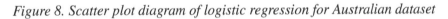

Figure 8. Scatter plot diagram of logistic regression for Australian dataset

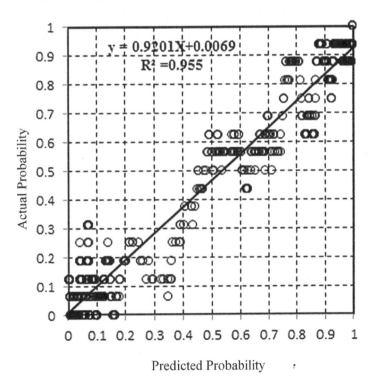

Figure 9. Scatter plot diagram of naive Bayes classifier for Australian dataset

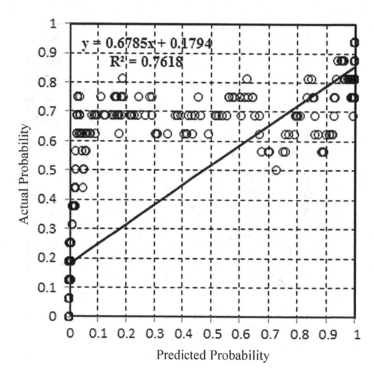

Figure 10. Scatter plot diagram of linear discriminant analysis for Australian dataset

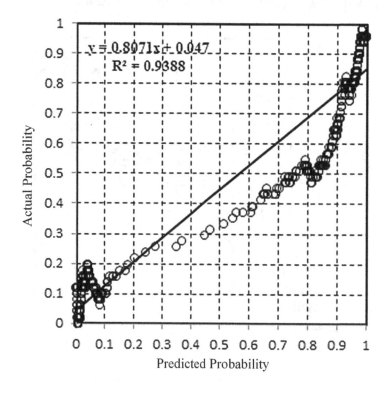

Figure 11. Scatter plot diagram of OWFKNN for German dataset

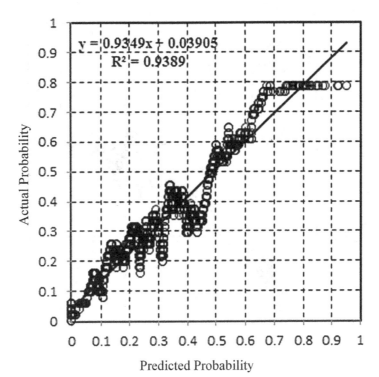

Figure 12. Scatter plot diagram of multilayer perceptron for German dataset

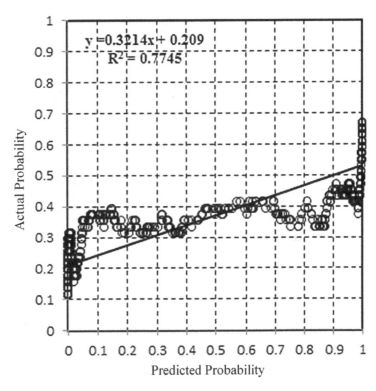

Figure 13. Scatter plot diagram of RBF for German dataset

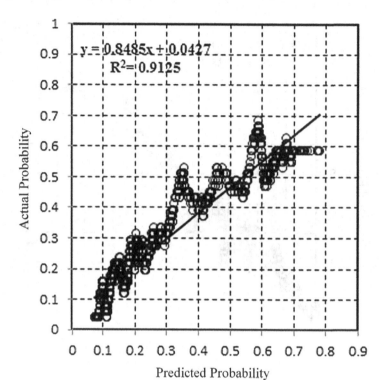

Figure 14. Scatter plot diagram of C4.5 for German dataset

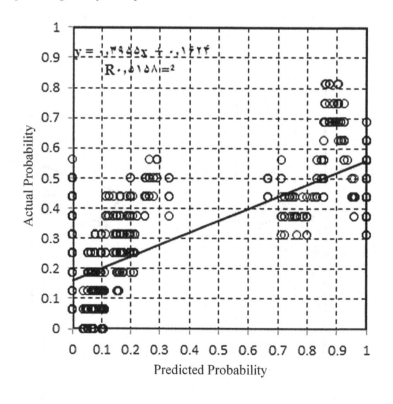

Figure 15. Scatter plot diagram of logistic regression for German dataset

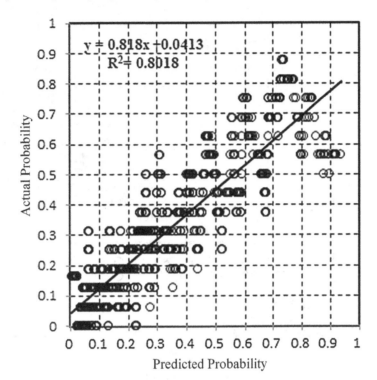

Figure 16. Scatter plot diagram of naive Bayes classifier for German dataset

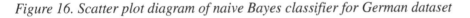
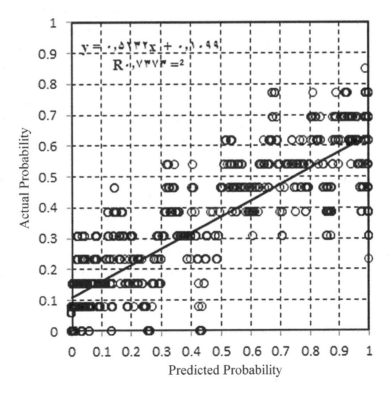

Figure 17. Scatter plot diagram of linear discriminant analysis for German dataset

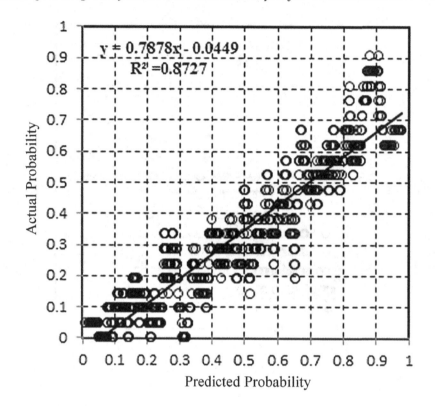

sifying customers, the key idea of this study is to predict a specific default probability for each applicant in addition to classify him as a "good" or "bad" payer. For this reason, we examined the performance of classification and predictive accuracy of OWFKNN method and compared the results with some major data mining techniques.

In the classification task, the results of OWFKNN were used as a benchmark to those produced by the neural network, logistic regression, discriminant analysis, classification and regression tree and four SVM-based models. From the experimental results, we concluded that there is a little difference between the error rates of OWFKNN with the best models. It can be seen that the OWFKNN is very similar to the best models in terms of classification performance. The results of performing this method on two datasets show that the proposed model outperforms the conventional KNN and fuzzy KNN.

In the prediction task, we used a new method called Sorting Smoothing Method proposed by (Yeh & Lien 2009) to prove the accuracy of the estimated default probabilities. Then we compared the PDs predicted by OWFKNN with those estimated by Multilayer perceptron, RBF network, C4.5 (decision tree), Logistic regression, Discriminant analysis and Naïve Bayes classifier. In the predictive accuracy of probability of default, OWFKNN also show the best performance in both data sets based on R^2, regression intercept and regression coefficient.

REFERENCES

Abdou, H., Pointon, J., & El-Masry, A. (2008). Neural nets versus conventional techniques in credit scoring in Egyptian banking. *Expert Systems with Applications*, *35*(3), 1275–1292. doi:10.1016/j. eswa.2007.08.030

Abdou, H. A. (2009). An evaluation of alternative scoring models in private banking. *The Journal of Risk Finance*, *10*(1), 38–53. doi:10.1108/15265940910924481

Alfo, M., Caiazza, S., & Trovato, G. (2005). Extending a Logistic Approach to Risk Modeling through Semiparametric Mixing. *Journal of Financial Services Research*, *28*(1), 163–176. doi:10.1007/s10693-005-4360-8

Altman, E. I. (1968). Financial Ratios, Discriminant Analysis and the Prediction of Corporate Bankruptcy. *The Journal of Finance*, *23*(4), 589–609. doi:10.1111/j.1540-6261.1968.tb00843.x

Andreeva, G., Ansell, J., & Crook, J. (2007). Modelling profitability using survival combination scores. *European Journal of Operational Research*, *183*(3), 1537–1549. doi:10.1016/j.ejor.2006.10.064

Angelini, E., Tollo, G., & Roli, A. (2008). A neural network approach for credit risk evaluation. *The Quarterly Review of Economics and Finance*, *48*(4), 733–755. doi:10.1016/j.qref.2007.04.001

Antonakis, A. C., & Sfakianakis, M. E. (2009). Assessing naive Bayes as a method for screening credit applicants. *Journal of Applied Statistics*, *36*(5), 537–545. doi:10.1080/02664760802554263

Atish, P. S., & Huimin, Z. (2008). Incorporating domain knowledge into data mining classifiers: An application in indirect lending. *Decision Support Systems*, *46*(1), 287–299. doi:10.1016/j.dss.2008.06.013

Baesens, B., Egmont-Petersen, M., Castelo, R., & Vanthienen, J. (2002). *Learning Bayesian network classifiers for credit scoring using Markov Chain Monte Carlo search*. Paper presented at the International Congress on Pattern Recognition. Academic Press. doi:10.1109/ICPR.2002.1047792

Baesens, B., Gestel, T. V., Stepanova, M., Poel, D. V., & Vanthienen, J. (2005). Neural Network Survival Analysis for Personal Loan Data. *The Journal of the Operational Research Society*, *56*(9), 1089–1098. doi:10.1057/palgrave.jors.2601990

Baetge, J., & Heitmann, C. (2000). creating a fuzzy rule-based indicator for the review of credit standing. *Schmalenbach Business Review*, *52*(3), 318–343.

Bastos, J. A. (2008). Credit scoring with boosted decision trees. *MPRA Paper*, *27*(1), 262–273.

Beaver, W. (1967). Financial ratios as predictors of failures. *Empirical Research in Accounting: Selected*, *38*(1), 63-93.

Bellotti, T., & Crook, J. (2009a). Credit scoring with Macroeconomic Variables using Survival Analysis. *The Journal of the Operational Research Society*, *60*(3), 1699–1707. doi:10.1057/jors.2008.130

Bellotti, T., & Crook, J. (2009b). Support vector machines for credit scoring and discovery of significant features. *Expert Systems with Applications*, *36*(2), 3302–3308. doi:10.1016/j.eswa.2008.01.005

Beran, J., & Djaidja, A. Y. K. (2007). Credit risk modeling based on survival analysis with immunes. *Statistical Methodology*, *4*(3), 251–276. doi:10.1016/j.stamet.2006.09.001

Cao, R., Vilar, J. M., & Devia, A. (2009). Modelling consumer credit risk via survival analysis. *Statistics & Operations Research Transactions*, *33*(1), 3–30.

Carling, K., Jacobson, T., Linde, J., & Roszbach, K. (2007). Corporate credit risk modeling and the macroeconomy. *Journal of Banking & Finance*, *31*(3), 845–868. doi:10.1016/j.jbankfin.2006.06.012

Chen, F. L., & Li, F. C. (2010). Combination of feature selection approaches with SVM in credit scoring. *Expert Systems with Applications*, *37*(7), 4902–4909. doi:10.1016/j.eswa.2009.12.025

Chen, M. C., & Huang, S. H. (2003). Credit scoring and rejected instances reassigning through evolutionary computation techniques. *Expert Systems with Applications*, *24*(4), 433–441. doi:10.1016/S0957-4174(02)00191-4

Chen, W., Ma, C., & Ma, L. (2009). Mining the customer credit using hybrid support vector machine technique. *Expert Systems with Applications*, *36*(4), 7611–7616. doi:10.1016/j.eswa.2008.09.054

Chen, W. H., & Shih, J. Y. (2006). A study of Taiwan's issuer credit rating systems using support vector machines. *Expert Systems with Applications*, *30*(3), 427–435. doi:10.1016/j.eswa.2005.10.003

Chye Koh, H., Chin Tan, W., & Peng Goh, C. (2006). A Two-step Method to Construct Credit Scoring Models with Data Mining Techniques. *Journal of Business and Information*, *1*, 96–118.

Cover, T. M., & Hart, P. E. (1967). Nearest neighbor pattern classification. *IEEE Transactions on Information Theory*, *13*(1), 21–27. doi:10.1109/TIT.1967.1053964

Doumpos, M., Kosmidou, K., Baourakis, G., & Zopounidis, C. (2002). Credit risk assessment using a multicriteria hierarchical discrimination approach: A comparative analysis. *European Journal of Operational Research*, *138*(2), 392–412. doi:10.1016/S0377-2217(01)00254-5

Duda, R. O., Hart, P. E., & Stork, D. G. (Eds.). (2000). Pattern Classification. New York: Information Science Reference.

Durand, D. (1941). *Risk elements in consumer instalments financing*. New York: National Bureau of Economic Research.

Eisenbeis, R. A. (1977). Pitfalls in the application of discriminant analysis in business, finance, and economics. *The Journal of Finance*, *32*(3), 875–900. doi:10.1111/j.1540-6261.1977.tb01995.x

Falangis, K. (2008). The use of MSD model in credit scoring. *Operations Research*, *7*(3), 481–504. doi:10.1007/BF03024859

Fisher, R. (1936). The use of multiple measurements in taxonomic problems. *Annals of Eugenics*, *7*(2), 179–188. doi:10.1111/j.1469-1809.1936.tb02137.x

Galindo, J., & Tamayo, P. (2000). Credit Risk Assessment Using Statistical and Machine Learning: Basic Methodology and Risk Modeling Applications. *Basic Methodology and Risk Modeling Applications*, *15*(1-2), 107–143.

Gestel, T. V. (2006). A process model to develop an internal rating system: Sovereign credit ratings. *Decision Support Systems, 42*(2), 1131–1151. doi:10.1016/j.dss.2005.10.001

Gestel, T. V., Baesens, B., Suykens, J. A. K., Poel, D. V., Baestaens, D. E., & Wil, M. (2006). Bayesian kernel based classification for financial distress detection. *European Journal of Operational Research, 172*(3), 979–1003. doi:10.1016/j.ejor.2004.11.009

Giudici, P. (2001). Bayesian data mining, with application to benchmarking and credit scoring. *Applied Stochastic Models in Business and Society, 17*(1), 69–81. doi:10.1002/asmb.425

Giudici, P. (2003). *Applied Data Mining: Statistical Methods for Business and Industry*. New York: John Wiley & Sons.

Hand, D. J., & Vinciotti, V. (2003). Choosing k for two-class nearest neighbor classifiers with unbalanced classes. *Pattern Recognition Letters, 24*(9-10), 1555–1562. doi:10.1016/S0167-8655(02)00394-X

Härdle, W., Lee, Y. J., Schafer, D., & Yeh, Y. R. (2009). Variable Selection and Oversampling in the Use of Smooth Support Vector Machines for Predicting the Default Risk of Companies. *Journal of Forecasting, 28*(2), 512–534.

Hoffmann, F., Baesens, B., Mues, C., Gestel, T. V., & Vanthienen, J. (2007). Inferring descriptive and approximate fuzzy rules for credit scoring using evolutionary algorithms. *European Journal of Operational Research, 177*(1), 540–555. doi:10.1016/j.ejor.2005.09.044

Hsieh, N. C. (2004). An integrated data mining and behavioral scoring model for analyzing bank customers. *Expert Systems with Applications, 27*(4), 623–633. doi:10.1016/j.eswa.2004.06.007

Hsieh, N. C. (2005). Hybrid mining approach in the design of credit scoring models. *Expert Systems with Applications, 28*(4), 655–665. doi:10.1016/j.eswa.2004.12.022

Hsieh, N. C., & Hung, L. P. (2010). A data driven ensemble classifier for credit scoring analysis. *Expert Systems with Applications, 37*(1), 534–545. doi:10.1016/j.eswa.2009.05.059

Huang, C. L., Chen, M. C., & Wang, C. J. (2007). Credit scoring with a data mining approach based on support vector machines. *Expert Systems with Applications, 33*(4), 847–856. doi:10.1016/j.eswa.2006.07.007

Huang, J. J., Tzeng, G. H., & Ong, C. S. (2006). Two-stage genetic programming (2SGP) for the credit scoring model. *Applied Mathematics and Computation, 174*(2), 1039–1053. doi:10.1016/j.amc.2005.05.027

Huang, Z., Chen, H., Hsu, C. J., Chen, W. H., & Wu, S. (2004). Credit rating analysis with support vector machines and neural networks: A market comparative study. *Decision Support Systems, 37*(4), 543–558. doi:10.1016/S0167-9236(03)00086-1

Huysmans, J., Baesens, B., Vanthienen, J., & Gestel, T. (2006). Failure prediction with self organizing maps. *Expert Systems with Applications, 30*(3), 479–487. doi:10.1016/j.eswa.2005.10.005

Ince, H., & Aktan, B. (2009). A Comparison of Data mining Techniques for Credit Scoring in Banking: A managerial Perspective. *Journal of Business Economics and Management, 10*(3), 233–240. doi:10.3846/1611-1699.2009.10.233-240

Isaaks, E. H., & Srivastava, R. M. (1989). *An Introduction to Applied Geostatistics*. New York: Oxford University Press.

Islam, M. J., Wu, Q. M. J., Ahmadi, M., & Sid-Ahmed, M. A. (2007). *Investigating the Performance of Naive- Bayes Classifiers and K- Nearest Neighbor Classifiers*. Paper presented at the International Conference on Convergence Information Technology. New York, NY. doi:10.1109/ICCIT.2007.148

Jiao, Y., Syau, Y. R., & Lee, E. S. (2007). Modelling credit rating by fuzzy adaptive network. *Mathematical and Computer Modelling*, *45*(5-6), 717–731. doi:10.1016/j.mcm.2005.11.016

Journel, A. G., & Rao, S. E. (1996). Deriving conditional distribution from ordinary kriging. Stanford Center for Reservoir Forcasting, Stanford University Report.

Kadam, A., & Lenk, P. (2008). Bayesian inference for issuer heterogeneity in credit ratings migration. *Journal of Banking & Finance*, *32*(10), 2267–2274. doi:10.1016/j.jbankfin.2007.12.043

Keller, J. M., Gray, M. R., & Givens, J. A. (1985). A fuzzy K-nearest neighbor algorithm. *IEEE Transactions on Systems, Man, and Cybernetics*, *15*(4), 580–585. doi:10.1109/TSMC.1985.6313426

Khashman, A. (2010). Neural networks for credit risk evaluation: Investigation of different neural models and learning schemes. *Expert Systems with Applications*, *37*(9), 6233–6239. doi:10.1016/j.eswa.2010.02.101

Kim, H. S., & Sohn, S. Y. (2010). Support vector machines for default prediction of SMEs based on technology credit. *European Journal of Operational Research*, *201*(3), 838–846. doi:10.1016/j.ejor.2009.03.036

Kirkos, E., Spathis, C., & Manolopoulos, Y. (2007). Data Mining techniques for the detection of fraudulent financial statements. *Expert Systems with Applications*, *32*(4), 995–1003. doi:10.1016/j.eswa.2006.02.016

Kumar, K., & Bhattacharya, S. (2006). Artificial neural network vs linear discriminant analysis in credit ratings forecast: A comparative study of prediction performances. *Review of Accounting and Finance*, *5*(3), 216–227. doi:10.1108/14757700610686426

Laha, A. (2007). Building contextual classifiers by integrating fuzzy rule based classification technique and k-nn method for credit scoring. *Advanced Engineering Informatics*, *21*(3), 281–291. doi:10.1016/j.aei.2006.12.004

Lahsasna, A., Ainon, R. N., & Wah, T. Y. (2008). *Credit Risk Evaluation Decision Modeling Through Optimized Fuzzy Classifier*. Paper presented at the International Symposium on Information Technology, ITSim. New York, NY. doi:10.1109/ITSIM.2008.4631606

Laitinen, E. K. (1999). Predicting a corporate credit analyst's risk estimate by logistic and linear models. *International Review of Financial Analysis*, *8*(2), 97–121. doi:10.1016/S1057-5219(99)00012-5

Lee, T. S., & Chen, I. F. (2005). A two-stage hybrid credit scoring model using artificial neural networks and multivariate adaptive regression splines. *Expert Systems with Applications*, *28*(4), 743–752. doi:10.1016/j.eswa.2004.12.031

Lee, T. S., Chiu, C. C., Chou, Y. C., & Lu, C. J. (2006). Mining the customer credit using classification and regression tree and multivariate adaptive regression splines. *Computational Statistics & Data Analysis*, *50*(4), 1113–1130. doi:10.1016/j.csda.2004.11.006

Lee, T. S., Chiu, C. C., Lu, C. J., & Chen, I. F. (2002). Credit scoring using the hybrid neural discriminant technique. *Expert Systems with Applications*, *23*(3), 245–254. doi:10.1016/S0957-4174(02)00044-1

Li, F. C. (2009). *Comparison of the Primitive Classifiers without Features Selection in Credit Scoring*. Paper presented at the International Conference on Management and Service Science. New York, NY. doi:10.1109/ICMSS.2009.5302730

Li, F. C. (2009). *The Hybrid Credit Scoring Model based on KNN Classifier*. Paper presented at the Sixth International Conference on Fuzzy Systems and Knowledge Discovery. New York, NY.

Li, H., Sun, J., & Wu, J. (2010). Predicting business failure using classification and regression tree: An empirical comparison with popular classical statistical methods and top classification mining methods. *Expert Systems with Applications*, *37*(8), 5895–5904. doi:10.1016/j.eswa.2010.02.016

Li, X. S., & Guo, Y. H. (2006). Personal credit scoring models on naive Bayesian classifier. *Computer Engineering and Applications*, *42*(1), 197–201.

Liang, Y., & Xin, H. (2009). *Application of Discretization in the Use of Logistic Financial Rating*. Paper presented at the International Conference on Business Intelligence and Financial Engineering. New York, NY. doi:10.1109/BIFE.2009.90

Lin, S. L. (2009). A new two-stage hybrid approach of credit risk in banking industry. *Expert Systems with Applications*, *36*(4), 8333–8341. doi:10.1016/j.eswa.2008.10.015

Liu, K., Lai, K. K., & Guu, S. M. (2009). *Dynamic Credit Scoring on Consumer Behavior using Fuzzy Markov Model*. Paper presented at the Fourth International Multi-Conference on Computing in the Global Information Technology. New York, NY. doi:10.1109/ICCGI.2009.42

Lopez, R. F. (2007). Modeling of insurers' rating determinants. An application of machine learning techniques and statistical models. *European Journal of Operational Research*, *183*(2), 1488–1512. doi:10.1016/j.ejor.2006.09.103

Luo, J. h., & Lei, H. y. (2008). *Empirical study of corporation credit default probability based on Logit model*. Paper presented at the Wireless Communications, Networking and Mobile Computing. New York, NY. doi:10.1109/WiCom.2008.2276

Luo, S. T., Cheng, B. W., & Hsieh, C. H. (2009). Prediction model building with clustering-launched classification and support vector machines in credit scoring. *Expert Systems with Applications*, *36*(4), 7562–7566. doi:10.1016/j.eswa.2008.09.028

Lyn, C. T. (2000). A survey of credit and behavioural scoring: Forecasting financial risk of lending to consumers. *International Journal of Forecasting*, *16*(2), 149–172. doi:10.1016/S0169-2070(00)00034-0

Ma, R. w., & Tang, C. y. (2007). Building up Default Predicting Model based on Logistic Model and Misclassification Loss. *Systems Engineering - Theory & Practice, 27*(8).

Malhotra, R., & Malhotra, D. K. (2002). differentiating between good credits and bad credits using neuro-fuzzy systems. *European Journal of Operational Research*, *136*(1), 190–211. doi:10.1016/S0377-2217(01)00052-2

Malhotra, R., & Malhotra, D. K. (2003). Evaluating consumer loans using neural networks. *Omega*, *31*(2), 83–96. doi:10.1016/S0305-0483(03)00016-1

Marinakis, Y., Marinaki, M., Doumpos, M., Matsatsinis, N., & Zopounidis, C. (2008). Constantin Zopounidis, Optimization of nearest neighbor classifiers via metaheuristic algorithms for credit risk assessment. *Journal of Global Optimization*, *42*(2), 279–293. doi:10.1007/s10898-007-9242-1

Martens, D., Baesens, B., Gestel, T. V., & Vanthienen, J. (2007). Comprehensible credit scoring models using rule extraction from support vector machines. *European Journal of Operational Research*, *183*(3), 1466–1476. doi:10.1016/j.ejor.2006.04.051

McNeil, A. J., & Wendin, J. P. (2007). Bayesian inference for generalized linear mixed models of portfolio credit risk. *Journal of Empirical Finance*, *14*(2), 131–149. doi:10.1016/j.jempfin.2006.05.002

Mues, C., Baesens, B., Files, C. M., & Vanthienen, J. (2004). Decision diagrams in machine learning: An empirical study on real-life credit-risk data. *Expert Systems with Applications*, *27*(2), 257–264. doi:10.1016/j.eswa.2004.02.001

Noh, H. J., Roh, T. H., & Han, I. (2005). Prognostic personal credit risk model considering censored information. *Expert Systems with Applications*, *28*(4), 753–762. doi:10.1016/j.eswa.2004.12.032

Paleologo, G., Elisseeff, A., & Antonini, G. (2010). Subagging for credit scoring models. *Journal of Operational Research*, *201*(2), 490–499. doi:10.1016/j.ejor.2009.03.008

Paredes, R., & Vidal, E. (2000). A class-dependent weighted dissimilarity measure for nearest neighbor classification problems. *Pattern Recognition Letters*, *21*(12), 1027–1036. doi:10.1016/S0167-8655(00)00064-7

Pham, T. D. (2005). An Optimally Weighted Fuzzy k-NN Algorithm. *Lecture Notes in Computer Science*, *3686*(PART I), 239–247. doi:10.1007/11551188_26

Ravi, V. (2008). *Advances in banking technology and management: impacts of ICT and CRM*. New York: Information Science Reference.

Sarlija, N., Bensic, M., & Susac, M. Z. (2009). Comparison procedure of predicting the time to default in behavioural scoring. *Expert Systems with Applications*, *36*(5), 8778–8788. doi:10.1016/j.eswa.2008.11.042

Sohn, S. Y., & Kim, H. S. (2007). Random effects logistic regression model for default prediction of technology credit guarantee fund. *European Journal of Operational Research*, *183*(1), 427–478. doi:10.1016/j.ejor.2006.10.006

Sohn, S. Y., & Shin, H. W. (2006). Reject inference in credit operations based on survival analysis. *Expert Systems with Applications*, *31*(1), 26–29. doi:10.1016/j.eswa.2005.09.001

Steenackers, A., & Goovaerts, M. J. (1989). A credit scoring model for personal loans. *Insurance, Mathematics & Economics*, *8*(1), 31–34. doi:10.1016/0167-6687(89)90044-9

Stefanescu, C., Tunaru, R., & Turnbull, S. (2009). The credit rating process and estimation of transition probabilities: A Bayesian approach. *Journal of Empirical Finance*, *16*(2), 216–234. doi:10.1016/j.jempfin.2008.10.006

Stepanova, M., & Thomas, L. C. (2002). survival Analysis Methods for Personal Loan Data. *Operations Research, 50*(2), 277–289. doi:10.1287/opre.50.2.277.426

Taffler, R. J., & Abassi, B. (1984). A Model for Predicting Debt Servicing Problems in Developing Countries. *Journal of the Royal Statistical Society. Series A (General), 147*(4), 541–568. doi:10.2307/2981843

Tang, T. C., & Chi, L. C. (2005). Predicting multilateral trade credit risks: Comparisons of Logit and Fuzzy Logic models using ROC curve analysis. *Expert Systems with Applications, 28*(3), 547–556. doi:10.1016/j.eswa.2004.12.016

Thomas, L. C., Ho, J., & Scherer, W. T. (2001). Time will tell: Behavioural scoring and the dynamics of consumer credit assessment. *IMA Journal of Management Mathematics, 12*(1), 89–103. doi:10.1093/imaman/12.1.89

Tsai, M. C., Lin, S. P., Cheng, C. C., & Lin, Y. P. (2009). The consumer loan default predicting model – An application of DEA–DA and neural network. *Expert Systems with Applications, 36*(9), 11682–11690. doi:10.1016/j.eswa.2009.03.009

Tung, W. L., Quek, C., Cheng, P., & Ews, G. (2004). A novel neural-fuzzy based early warning system for predicting bank failures. *Neural Networks 17*(4), 567–587.

Twala, B. (2010). Multiple classifier application to credit risk assessment. *Expert Systems with Applications, 37*(4), 3326–3336. doi:10.1016/j.eswa.2009.10.018

Vapnik, V. (1995). The Nature of Statistical Learning Theory. New York: Springer.

Wang, Y., Wang, S., & Lai, K. K. (2005). *A New Fuzzy Support Vector Machine to Evaluate Credit Risk*. Paper presented at the IEEE Transactions on Fuzzy Systems. New York, NY.

West, D. (2000). Neural network credit scoring models. *Computers & Operations Research, 27*(11-12), 1131–1152. doi:10.1016/S0305-0548(99)00149-5

Xiao, W., Zhao, Q., & Fei, Q. (2006). a comparative study of data mining methods in consumer loans credit scoring management. *Journal of Systems Science and Systems Engineering, 15*(4), 419-435.

Xinhui, C., & Zhong, Q. (2009). *Consumer Credit Scoring Based on Multi-criteria Fuzzy Logic*. Paper presented at the International Conference on Business Intelligence and Financial Engineering. New York, NY. doi:10.1109/BIFE.2009.177

Xu, X., Zhou, C., & Wang, Z. (2009). Credit scoring algorithm based on link analysis ranking with support vector machine. *Expert Systems with Applications, 36*(2), 2625–2632. doi:10.1016/j.eswa.2008.01.024

Yang, Y. (2007). Adaptive credit scoring with kernel learning methods. *European Journal of Operational Research, 183*(3), 1521–1536. doi:10.1016/j.ejor.2006.10.066

Yeh, I. C., & Lien, C. (2009). The comparisons of data mining techniques for the predictive accuracy of probability of default of credit card clients. *Expert Systems with Applications, 36*(2), 2473–2480. doi:10.1016/j.eswa.2007.12.020

Yu, L., Wang, S., & Lai, K. K. (2008). Credit risk assessment with a multistage neural network ensemble learning approach. *Expert Systems with Applications, 34*(2), 1434–1444. doi:10.1016/j.eswa.2007.01.009

Yu, L., Wang, S., Wen, F., Lai, K. K., & He, S. (2008). Designing A Hybrid Intelligent Mining System for Credit Risk Evaluation. *Journal of Systems Science and Complexity*, *21*(4), 527–539. doi:10.1007/s11424-008-9133-7

Yu, L., Yue, W., Wang, S., & Lai, K. K. (2010). Support vector machine based multiagent ensemble learning for credit risk evaluation. *Expert Systems with Applications*, *37*(2), 1351–1360. doi:10.1016/j.eswa.2009.06.083

Zhang, D., Hifi, M., Chen, Q., & Ye, W. (2008). *A Hybrid Credit Scoring Model Based on Genetic Programming and Support Vector Machines*. Paper presented at the Fourth International Conference on Natural Computation. New York, NY. doi:10.1109/ICNC.2008.205

Zhao, H. (2007). A multi-objective genetic programming approach to developing Pareto optimal decision trees. *Decision Support Systems*, *43*(3), 809–826. doi:10.1016/j.dss.2006.12.011

Zhou, J., & Bai, T. (2008). *Credit Risk Assessment using Rough Set Theory and GA-based SVM*. Paper presented at the 3rd International Conference on Grid and Pervasive Computing – Workshops. New York, NY. doi:10.1109/GPC.WORKSHOPS.2008.56

Zhou, L., & Lai, K. K. (2009). Benchmarking binary classification models on data sets with different degrees of imbalance. *Frontiers of Computer Science in China*, *3*(2), 205–216. doi:10.1007/s11704-009-0027-1

Zhou, L., Lai, K. K., & Yu, L. (2009). Credit scoring using support vector machines with direct search for parameters selection. *Soft Computing*, *13*(2), 149–155. doi:10.1007/s00500-008-0305-0

Zhou, L., Lai, K. K., & Yu, L. (2010). Least squares support vector machines ensemble models for credit scoring. *Expert Systems with Applications*, *37*(1), 127–133. doi:10.1016/j.eswa.2009.05.024

Zurada, J., & Lonial, S. (2005). *Comparison of the performance of several data mining methods for bad debt recovery in the healthcare industry*. *The Journal of Applied Business Research*, *21*(2), 37–53.

KEY TERMS AND DEFINITIONS

Classification: Grouping of different objects into mutually exclusive classes.

Credit Risk: Possibility of loss from a borrower's default.

Credit Scoring: Use of analytical techniques including statistical or data mining techniques in consumer loaning for credit approval, and monitoring.

Data Analysis: Evaluating data with analytical and logical perceptive to survey each element of the data.

Data Mining: Extracting useful knowledge from a huge data using analytical techniques such as artificial intelligence techniques, neural networks, and advanced statistical tools.

Probability of Default: Degree of inevitability that a firm will go into failure to pay or a promised customer will not perform affording to the agreement.

Risk Management: Identifying, investigating, valuating, controlling, avoiding, minimizing, or eliminating offensive risks.

APPENDIX

List of Acronyms Used in This Chapter

ANN: Artificial Neural Network.
AUC: Area Under the Curve.
BC: Bayesian Classifier.
CART: Classification And Regression Tree.
DA: Discriminant Analysis.
DT: Decision Tree.
FKNN: Fuzzy K-Nearest Neighbor.
FRS: Fuzzy Rule-based System.
HM: Hybrid Models.
KNN: K-Nearest Neighbor.
LDA: Linear Discriminant Analysis.
LR: Logistic Regression.
MARS: Multivariate Adaptive Regression Splines.
MP: Mathematical Programming.
MSD: Minimize the Sum of the Deviations.
NN: Neural Network.
OWFKNN: Optimally Weighted Fuzzy K-Nearest Neighbor.
PD: Probability of Default.
SA: Survival Analysis.
SOM: Self Organization Maps.
SSM: Sorting Smoothing Method.
SVM: Support Vector Machine.
UCI: University of California, Irvine.

Compilation of References

Abate, J., & Whitt, W. (1987). Transient behavior of M/M/1 queue: Starting at origin. *Queueing Systems, 2*(1), 41–65. doi:10.1007/BF01182933

Abdellaoui, M., Bleichrodt, H., & Paraschiv, C. (2007). Loss aversion under prospect theory: A parameter-free measurement. *Management Science, 53*(10), 1659–1674. doi:10.1287/mnsc.1070.0711

Abdou, H. A. (2009). An evaluation of alternative scoring models in private banking. *The Journal of Risk Finance, 10*(1), 38–53. doi:10.1108/15265940910924481

Abdou, H., Pointon, J., & El-Masry, A. (2008). Neural nets versus conventional techniques in credit scoring in Egyptian banking. *Expert Systems with Applications, 35*(3), 1275–1292. doi:10.1016/j.eswa.2007.08.030

Abdul Muhmin, A. (2005). Instrumental and interpersonal determinants of relationship satisfaction and commitment in industrial markets. *Journal of Business Research, 58*(5), 619–628. doi:10.1016/j.jbusres.2003.08.004

Abdul Wahab, A. (1979). *Decision-Making in Saudi Arabia*. Riyadh: Institute of Public Administration.

Aci, M., Inam, C., & Avci, M. (2010). A hybrid classification method of k nearest neighbors, Bayesian methods and genetic algorithm. *Expert Systems with Applications, 37*(7), 5061–5067. doi:10.1016/j.eswa.2009.12.004

Ackoff, R. (1989). From data to wisdom. *Journal of Applied Systems Analysis, 16*, 3–9.

Acs, Z. J., & Yeung, B. (1999). *Small and Medium-Sized Enterprises in the Global Economy*. University of Michigan Press.

Adhikari, D. R. (2010). Human resource development (HRD) for performance management The case of Nepalese organizations. *International Journal of Productivity and Performance Management, 59*(4), 306–324. doi:10.1108/17410401011038883

Adler, N. J. (2002). International Dimensions of Organizational Behaviour (4ed). Cincinnati, Ohio: South-Western.

Agustin-Blas, L., Salcedo-Sanz, S., Jimenez-Fernandez, S., Carro-Calvo, L., Del-Ser, J., & Portilla-Figueras, J. (2012). A new grouping genetic algorithm for clustering problems. *Expert Systems with Applications, 39*(10), 9695–9703. doi:10.1016/j.eswa.2012.02.149

Aha, D. W., Kibler, D., & Albert, M. K. (1991). Instance-based learning algorithms. *Machine Learning, 6*(1), 37–66. doi:10.1007/BF00153759

Ahmad, K. (2006). *Management from the Islamic Perspective*. Kuala Lumpur: International Islamic University Malaysia.

Ahmad, S., & Schroeder, R. G. (2003). The impact of human resource management practices on operational performance: Recognizing country and industry differences. *Journal of Operations Management, 21*(1), 19–43. doi:10.1016/S0272-6963(02)00056-6

Ahn, S., & Cho, S. B. (2010). Stock Prediction Using News Text Mining and Time Series Analysis. *KIISE 2010 Conference, 37*, 364-369.

Ahn, H. (2001). Applying the balance scorecard concept: An experience report. *Long Range Planning, 34*(4), 441–461. doi:10.1016/S0024-6301(01)00057-7

Aiken, K. D., & Boush, D. M. (2006). Trustmarks, objective-source ratings, and implied investments in advertising: Investigating online trust and the context-specific nature of internet signals. *Journal of the Academy of Marketing Science, 34*(3), 308–323. doi:10.1177/0092070304271004

Akdeniz, B., Calantone, R. J., & Voorhees, C. M. (2013). Effectiveness of Marketing Cues on Consumer Perceptions of Quality: The Moderating Roles of Brand Reputation and Third-Party Information. *Psychology and Marketing, 30*(1), 76–89. doi:10.1002/mar.20590

Al Faleh, M. (1987). Cultural Influences on Arab Management Development: A Case Study of Jordan. *Journal of Management Development, 6*(3), 19–34. doi:10.1108/eb051643

Al Rasheed, A. (2001). Features of Traditional Arab Management and Organization in Jordan Business Environment. *Journal of Transnational Management Development, 6*(1-2), 27–53. doi:10.1300/J130v06n01_02

Alavi, M., & Leidner, D. E. (2001). Review: Knowledge management and knowledge management system: conceptual foundations and research issue. *MIS Quarterly Journal, 25*(1), 107–136. doi:10.2307/3250961

Albaum, G., & Herche, J. (1999). Management style comparisons among five European nations. *Journal of Global Marketing, 12*(4), 5–27. doi:10.1300/J042v12n04_02

Albaum, G., Herche, J., Yu, J., Evangelista, F., Murphy, B., & Poon, P. (2008). Differences in Marketing Managers' Decision Making Styles Within the Asia-Pacific Region. *Journal of Global Marketing, 21*(1), 63–78. doi:10.1300/J042v21n01_06

Albescu, F., Pugna, I., & Paraschiv, D. (2008). Business Intelligence & Knowledge management – Technological support for strategic management in the knowledge based economy. *Revisit Information Economics, 4*(48), 5–12.

Al-Buraey, M. A. (1990). *Management and Administration in Islam*. Saudi Arabia: Al-Dharan.

Alegre, J., Lapiedra, R., & Chiva, R. (2006). A measurement scale for product innovation performance. *European Journal of Innovation Management, 5*(4), 333–346. doi:10.1108/14601060610707812

Alfo, M., Caiazza, S., & Trovato, G. (2005). Extending a Logistic Approach to Risk Modeling through Semiparametric Mixing. *Journal of Financial Services Research, 28*(1), 163–176. doi:10.1007/s10693-005-4360-8

Al-Hegelan, H., & Palmer, M. (1985). Bureaucracy and development in Saudi Arabia. *The Middle East Journal, 39*(Winter), 48–59.

Ali, J. A. (1989). Decision Style and Work Satisfaction of Arab Gulf Executives: A Cross-National Study. *International Studies of Management & Organization, 19*, 22–37.

Ali, J. A. (1990). Management theory in a transitional society: The Arab's experience. *International Studies of Management & Organization, 20*, 7–35.

Ali, J. A. (1993). Decision Making Style, Individualism and Attitudes Toward Risk of Arab Executives. *International Studies of Management & Organization*, (Fall): 23, 53–74.

Ali, J. A. (1995). Cultural discontinuity and Arab management thought. *International Studies of Management & Organization, 25*, 7–30.

Ali, J. A. (1995b). Preface: Management in a sheiko-capitalist system. *International Studies of Management & Organization, 25*, 3–6.

Ali, J. A. (1998). The typology of the Arab individual: Implications for management and business organizations. *The International Journal of Sociology and Social Policy, 18*(11/12), 1–19. doi:10.1108/01443339810788551

Ali, J. A. (2005). *Islamic Perspectives on Management and Organization*. Cheltenham, UK: Edward Elgar Publishing.

Ali, J. A. (2010). Islamic challenges to HR in modern organizations. *Personnel Review, 39*(6), 692–711. doi:10.1108/00483481011075567

Ali, J. A., & Sabri, H. (2001). Organizational culture and job satisfaction in Jordan. *Journal of Transnational Management Development, 6*(1-2), 105–118. doi:10.1300/J130v06n01_06

Ali, J. A., & Schaupp, L. D. (1992). Value Systems as Predictors of Managerial Decision Styles of Arab Executives. *International Journal of Manpower, 13*(3), 19–26. doi:10.1108/01437729210010274

Al-Malik, S. (1989). *Strategic Decision Makers: A Study of Business and Government Executives in Saudi Arabia.* (Unpublished doctoral dissertation). Georgia State University.

Alpaydin, E. (2010). *Introduction to machine learning* (2nd ed.). Cambridge, MA: MIT Press.

Altman, E. I. (1968). Financial Ratios, Discriminant Analysis and the Prediction of Corporate Bankruptcy. *The Journal of Finance, 23*(4), 589–609. doi:10.1111/j.1540-6261.1968.tb00843.x

Alwis, R., & Hartmann, E. (2008). The use of tacit knowledge within innovative companies: Knowledge management in innovation enterprise. *Journal of Knowledge Management, 12*(1), 133–147. doi:10.1108/13673270810852449

Amason, A. C. (1996). Distinguishing the effects of functional and dysfunctional conflict on strategic decision making: Resolving a paradox for top management teams. *Academy of Management Journal, 39*(1), 123–148. doi:10.2307/256633

Amerland, D. (2014). Social Media Analytics: From Return on Investment to Return on Involvement. *Social Media Today.* Retrieved July 8th 2014 from: http://www.socialmediatoday.com/david-amerland/2510061/social-media-analytics-return-investment-return-involvement-video

Anastasakis, L., & Mort, N. (2009). Exchange rate forecasting using a combined parametric and nonparametric self-organizing modeling approach. *Expert Systems with Applications, 36*(10), 12001–12011. doi:10.1016/j.eswa.2009.03.057

Ancona, D. G., Okhuysen, G. A., & Perlow, L. A. (2001). Taking time to integrate temporal research. *Academy of Management Review, 26,* 512–529.

Andersen, B., Henriksen, B., & Aarseth, W. (2006). Holistic performance management: An integrated framework. *International Journal of Productivity and Performance Management, 55*(1), 67–78. doi:10.1108/17410400610635507

Anderson, J. C., & Gerbing, D. W. (1988). Structural equation modeling in practice: A review and recommended two-step approach. *Psychological Bulletin, 103*(3), 411–423. doi:10.1037/0033-2909.103.3.411

Anderson, S. W., & Lanen, W. N. (1999). Economic transition, strategy, and the evolution of management accounting practices: The case of India. *Accounting, Organizations and Society, 24*(5-6), 379–412. doi:10.1016/S0361-3682(97)00060-3

Andreeva, G., Ansell, J., & Crook, J. (2007). Modelling profitability using survival combination scores. *European Journal of Operational Research, 183*(3), 1537–1549. doi:10.1016/j.ejor.2006.10.064

Andreou, A. N., Green, A., & Stankosky, M. (2007). A framework of intangible valuation areas and antecedents. *Journal of Intellectual Capital, 8*(1), 52–75. doi:10.1108/14691930710715060

Angelini, E., Tollo, G., & Roli, A. (2008). A neural network approach for credit risk evaluation. *The Quarterly Review of Economics and Finance, 48*(4), 733–755. doi:10.1016/j.qref.2007.04.001

Anonymous. (2013). YouTube for non profits 101. *GuideStar.* Retrieved July 6th 2014 from: http://www.guidestar.org/ViewCmsFile.aspx?ContentID=4631

Anonymous. (2014a). Give Local America. *Give Local America.* Retrieved July 8th 2014 from: http://www.givelocalamerica.org/#page-1

Anonymous. (2014b). Google for Nonprofits. *Google.* Retrieved July 6th 2014 from: http://www.google.com/nonprofits/join/

Anonymous. (2014c). Join the campaign to end extreme poverty. *One.* Retrieved July 6th 2014 from: http://www.one.org/us/about/

Anonymous. (n.d.a). The Greatest 24 Hours to Crank Up the Giving. *Amplify Austin.* Retrieved July 6th 2014 from: https://amplifyatx.ilivehereigivehere.org/content/whatsAmplify

Anonymous. (n.d.b). *Twitter for Business.* Retrieved July 6th 2014 from: https://business.twitter.com/products/promoted-tweets

Antonakis, A. C., & Sfakianakis, M. E. (2009). Assessing naive Bayes as a method for screening credit applicants. *Journal of Applied Statistics, 36*(5), 537–545. doi:10.1080/02664760802554263

Arbuckle, J. L. (2003). *AMOS 5.0 update to the AMOS user's guide*. Chicago: SPSS.

Archer, N., Bajaj, H., & Zhang, H. (2008). Supply management for home healthcare services. *Information Systems and Operational Research*, *46*(2), 137–145. doi:10.3138/infor.46.2.137

Arendt, S., & Brettel, M. (2010). Understanding the influence of corporate social responsibility on corporate identity: Image, and Firm Performance. *Management Decision*, *48*(10), 1469–1492. doi:10.1108/00251741011090289

Argenti, P. A. (1996). Corporate communication as a discipline–Toward a Definition. *Management Communication Quarterly*, *10*(1), 73–97. doi:10.1177/0893318996010001005

Argenti, P. A. (2007). *Corporate communication*. New York: McGraw-Hill.

Armstrong, M., & Baron, A. (1998). *Performance management handbook*. London, UK: IPM.

Arnold, V., & Sutton, S. G. (2007). The Impact of Enterprise Systems on Business and Audit Practice and the Implications for University Accounting Education. *International Journal of Enterprise Information Systems*, *3*(4), 1–21. doi:10.4018/jeis.2007100101

Arsham, H. (1987). A stochastic model of optimal advertising pulsing policy. *Computers & Operations Research*, *14*(3), 231–239. doi:10.1016/0305-0548(87)90026-8

Arsham, H. (1996). Stochastic optimization of discrete event systems simulation. *Microelectronics and Reliability*, *36*(10), 1357–1368. doi:10.1016/0026-2714(96)00044-3

Arsham, H. (1998a). Techniques for Monte Carlo optimizing. *Monte Carlo Methods and Applications*, *4*(3), 181–230. doi:10.1515/mcma.1998.4.3.181

Arsham, H. (1998b). Algorithms for sensitivity information in discrete-event systems simulation. *Simulation Practice and Theory*, *6*(1), 1–22. doi:10.1016/S0928-4869(97)00011-6

Arsham, H. (2008). *Gradient-based optimization techniques for discrete event systems simulation. In B. W. Wah (Ed.), Wiley Encyclopedia of Computer Science and Engineering* (Vol. 2, pp. 1–17). New York: Wiley.

Arsham, H., Feuerverger, A., McLeish, D., Kreimer, J., & Rubinstein, R. (1989). Sensitivity analysis and the 'what-if' problem in simulation analysis. *Mathematical and Computer Modelling*, *12*(2), 193–219. doi:10.1016/0895-7177(89)90434-2

Asia-Pacific Economic Cooperation. (2013). *SMEs in the APEC Region*. Retrieved from http://www.apec.org/Groups/SOM-Steering-Committee-on-Economic-and-Technical-Cooperation/Working-Groups/~/media/20ABF15DB43E498CA1F233DFF30CF88D.ashx

Atish, P. S., & Huimin, Z. (2008). Incorporating domain knowledge into data mining classifiers: An application in indirect lending. *Decision Support Systems*, *46*(1), 287–299. doi:10.1016/j.dss.2008.06.013

Attafar, A., Sadidi, M., Attafar, H., & Shahin, A. (2013). The Role of Customer Knowledge (CKM) in Proving Organization Customer Relationship. *Middle-East Journal of Science Research*, *13*(6), 829–835.

Austin, J., & Currie, B. (2003). Changing organisations for a knowledge economy: The theory and practice of change management. *Journal of Facilities Management*, *3*(2), 229–243. doi:10.1108/14725960410808221

Avlonitis, G. J., Kouremenos, A., & Tzokas, N. (1994). Assessing the innovativeness of organizations and its antecedents: Project innovstrat. *European Journal of Marketing*, *28*(11), 5–28. doi:10.1108/03090569410075812

Baali, F., & Wardi, A. (1981). *Ibn Khaldun and Islamic Thought Style*. Boston, MA: Haland G K.

Baer, J. (n.d.). 11 Shocking New Social Media Statistics in America. *Convince and Convert*. Retrieved July 6th 2014 from: http://www.convinceandconvert.com/social-mediaresearch/11-shocking-new-social-media-statistics-in-america/

Baesens, B., Egmont-Petersen, M., Castelo, R., & Vanthienen, J. (2002). *Learning Bayesian network classifiers for credit scoring using Markov Chain Monte Carlo search*. Paper presented at the International Congress on Pattern Recognition. Academic Press. doi:10.1109/ICPR.2002.1047792

Baesens, B., Gestel, T. V., Stepanova, M., Poel, D. V., & Vanthienen, J. (2005). Neural Network Survival Analysis for Personal Loan Data. *The Journal of the Operational Research Society*, *56*(9), 1089–1098. doi:10.1057/palgrave.jors.2601990

Baetge, J., & Heitmann, C. (2000). creating a fuzzy rule-based indicator for the review of credit standing. *Schmalenbach Business Review*, *52*(3), 318–343.

Baker, M., & AbouIsmail, F. (1993). Organizational buying behavior in the Gulf. *International Marketing Review*, *10*(6), 42–60. doi:10.1108/02651339310051614

Ballou, D. P., & Tayi, G. K. (1999). Enhancing data quality in data warehouse environments. *Communications of the ACM*, *42*(1), 73–78. doi:10.1145/291469.291471

Banek, M., Vrdoljak, B., Tjoa, A. M., & Skocir, Z. (2008). Automated Integration of Heterogeneous Data Warehouse Schemas. *International Journal of Data Warehousing and Mining*, *4*(4), 1–21. doi:10.4018/jdwm.2008100101

Banerjee, J., & Kane, W. (1996). Informing the accountant. *Management Accounting*, *74*(9), 30–32.

Barakat, H. (1983). *Contemporary Arab Society: An Exploratory Sociological Study*. Beirut, Lebanon: Arab Unity Studies Center. (In Arabic)

Barakat, H. (1993). *The Arab World: Society, Culture and the State*. Berkeley, CA: University of California Press.

Barlow, R., & Proschan, F. (1998). *Statistical Theory of Reliability and Life Testing Probability Models*. New York: Holt Rinehart & Winston.

Barney, J. B. (1991). Firm resources and sustained competitive advantage. *Journal of Management*, *17*(1), 99–120. doi:10.1177/014920639101700108

Barrett, D. J. (2002). Change communication: Using strategic employee communication to facilitate major change. *Corporate Communications*, *7*(4), 219–231. doi:10.1108/13563280210449804

Bartlett, C., & Ghoshal, S. (2013). Building competitive advantage through people. *Sloan Management Review*, *43*(2).

Barton, D., & Court, D. (2012). Making Advanced Analytics Work For You. *Harvard Business Review*, *90*(10), 79–83. PMID:23074867

Baruch, Y., & Holtom, B. C. (2008). Survey response rate levels and trends in organizational research. *Human Relations*, *61*(8), 1139–1160. doi:10.1177/0018726708094863

Baruch, Y., & Ramalho, N. (2006). Communalities and distinctions in the measurement of organizational performance and effectiveness across for-profit and nonprofit sectors. *Nonprofit and Voluntary Sector Quarterly*, *35*(1), 39–65. doi:10.1177/0899764005282468

Bastos, J. A. (2008). Credit scoring with boosted decision trees. *MPRA Paper*, *27*(1), 262–273.

Basu, P., & Nair, S. K. (2012). Supply chain finance enabled early pay: Unlocking trapped value in B2B logistics. *International Journal of Logistics Systems and Management*, *12*(3), 334–353. doi:10.1504/IJLSM.2012.047605

Bauer, J., Tanner, S. J., & Neely, A. (2004). Benchmarking performance measurement: A consortium benchmarking study. In A. Neely, M. Kennerly, & A. Waters (Eds.), *Performance measurement and management: Public and private* (pp. 1021–1028). Cranfield, UK: Centre for Business Performance.

Baum, J. R., & Wally, S. (2003). Strategic decision speed and firm performance. *Strategic Management Journal*, *24*(11), 1107–1129. doi:10.1002/smj.343

Baxter, L. F., & Hirschhauser, C. (2004). Reification and representation in the implementation of quality improvement programmes. *International Journal of Operations & Production Management*, *24*(2), 207–224. doi:10.1108/01443570410514894

Beales, H., Mazis, M. B., Salop, S. C., & Staelin, R. (1981). Consumer search and public policy. *The Journal of Consumer Research*, *8*(1), 11–22. doi:10.1086/208836

Beaver, W. (1967). Financial ratios as predictors of failures. *Empirical Research in Accounting: Selected*, *38*(1), 63-93.

Beckel, C., Sadamori, L., & Santini, S. (2012). Towards automatic classification of private households using electricity consumption data. In *Proceedings of the Fourth ACM Workshop on Embedded Sensing Systems for Energy-Efficiency in Buildings* (pp. 169-176). Toronto, Canada: ACM. doi:10.1145/2422531.2422562

Beckel, C., Sadamori, L., & Santini, S. (2013). Automatic socio-economic classification of households using electricity consumption data. In *Proceedings of the fourth international conference on Future energy systems* (pp.75-86). Berkeley, CA: ACM. doi:10.1145/2487166.2487175

Beekun, R. E. (2006). *Strategic Planning and Implementation for Islamic Organizations*. Herndon, VA: The International Institute of Islamic Thought.

Bellotti, T., & Crook, J. (2009a). Credit scoring with Macroeconomic Variables using Survival Analysis. *The Journal of the Operational Research Society*, *60*(3), 1699–1707. doi:10.1057/jors.2008.130

Bellotti, T., & Crook, J. (2009b). Support vector machines for credit scoring and discovery of significant features. *Expert Systems with Applications*, *36*(2), 3302–3308. doi:10.1016/j.eswa.2008.01.005

Benamati, J. H., Ozdemir, Z. D., & Smith, H. J. (2010). Aligning Undergraduate IS Curricula with Industry Needs. *Communications of the ACM*, *53*(3), 152–156. doi:10.1145/1666420.1666458

Beneventano, D., Bergamaschi, S., Guerra, F., & Vincini, M. (2001). The Momis approach to Information Integration. In *Proceedings of the International Conference on Enterprise Information Systems (ICEIS 2001)*. ICEIS.

Benevenuto, F., Rodrigues, T., Almeida, V., Almeida, J., Zhang, C., & Ross, K. (2008, April). Identifying video spammers in online social networks. In *Proceedings of the 4th International Workshop on Adversarial Information Retrieval on the Web* (pp. 45-52). ACM. doi:10.1145/1451983.1451996

Benveniste, A., Metivier, M., & Priouret, P. (1990). *Adaptive Algorithms and Stochastic Approximations*. New York: Springer-Verlag. doi:10.1007/978-3-642-75894-2

Beran, J., & Djaidja, A. Y. K. (2007). Credit risk modeling based on survival analysis with immunes. *Statistical Methodology*, *4*(3), 251–276. doi:10.1016/j.stamet.2006.09.001

Bergamaschi, S., Castano, S., De Capitani De Vimercati, S., Montanari, S., & Vincini, M. (1998). An Intelligent Approach to Information Integration. In *Proceedings of The 1st Conference on Formal Ontology in Information Systems (FOIS '98)*. FOIS.

Bergamaschi, S., Guerra, F., Orsini, M., Sartori, C., & Vincini, M. (2011). A semantic approach to ETL technologies. *Journal of Data and Knowledge Engineering*, *70*(8), 717–731. doi:10.1016/j.datak.2011.03.003

Bergamaschi, S., Olaru, M. O., Sorrentino, S., & Vincini, M. (2012). Dimension matching in Peer-to-Peer Data Warehousing. In *Proceedings of the International Conference on Decision Support Systems (DSS 2012)*. DSS.

Bergamaschi, S., Sartori, C., Guerra, F., & Orsini, M. (2007). Extracting Relevant Attribute Values for Improved Search. *IEEE Internet Computing*, *11*(5), 26–35. doi:10.1109/MIC.2007.105

Bernhardt, D. (1993). *Perfectly legal competitive intelligence—How to get it, use it and profit from it*. London: Pitman Publishing.

Berrach, L., & Cliville, V. (2007). Towards an aggregation performance measurement system model in a supply chain context. *Computers in Industry*, *58*(7), 709–719. doi:10.1016/j.compind.2007.05.012

Berry, A. J., Coad, A. F., Harris, E. P., Otley, D. T., & Stringer, C. (2009). Emerging themes in management control: A review of recent literature. *The British Accounting Review*, *41*(1), 2–20. doi:10.1016/j.bar.2008.09.001

Beyer, M. A., & Laney, D. (2012). *The importance of 'big data': A definition*. Gartner Report, June version, ID G00235055.

Bhuian, S. (1998). An empirical examination of market orientation in Saudi Arabian manufacturing companies. *Journal of Business Research*, *43*(1), 13–25. doi:10.1016/S0148-2963(97)00130-6

Biesiada, J., & Duch, W. (2005). Feature Selection for High-Dimensional Data: A Kolmogorov-Smirnov Correlation-Based Filter. In *Proceedings of the 4th International Conference on Computer Recognition Systems, CORES'05* (pp. 95-103). Springer. doi:10.1007/3-540-32390-2_9

Billingsley, P. (1995). *Probability and measure* (3rd ed.). New York: John Wiley.

Biswal, M. P., & Acharya, S. (2009). Transformation of a Multi-choice Linear Programming Problem. *Applied Mathematics and Computation*, *210*(1), 182–188. doi:10.1016/j.amc.2008.12.080

Biswas, P., & Sarker, B. R. (2008). Optimal batch quantity models for a lean production system with in-cycle rework and scrap. *International Journal of Production Research*, *46*(23), 6585–6610. doi:10.1080/00207540802230330

Bit, A. K., Biswal, M. P., & Alam, S. S. (1993). Fuzzy Programming Approach to Multi-objective Solid Transportation Problem. *Fuzzy Sets and Systems*, *57*(2), 183–194. doi:10.1016/0165-0114(93)90158-E

Bititci, U. S., Carrie, A. S., & McDevitt, L. (1997). Integrated performance measurement systems: A development guide. *International Journal of Operations & Production Management*, *17*(5), 522–534. doi:10.1108/01443579710167230

Bjerke, B., & Abdulrahim, A. (1993). Culture's consequences: Management in Saudi Arabia. *Leadership and Organization Development Journal*, *14*(2), 30–35. doi:10.1108/01437739310032700

Blili, S., & Raymond, L. (1993). Information Technology: Threats and Opportunities for Small and Medium-Sized Enterprises. *International Journal of Information Management*, *13*(6), 439–448. doi:10.1016/0268-4012(93)90060-H

Boderndort, F., & Kasier, C. (2010). Mining Customer Opinions on the Internet A Case Study in the Automotive Industry. In *Proceedings of Third International Conference on Knowledge Discovery and Data Mining*, (pp. 24-27). Phuket, Thailand: Academic Press.

Boisot, M. (1995). Is your firm a creative destroyer? Competitive learning and knowledge flows in the technological strategies of firms. *Research Policy*, *24*(4), 489–506. doi:10.1016/S0048-7333(94)00779-9

Bollen, J., Mao, H., & Zeng, X. (2011). Twitter mood predicts the stock market. *Journal of Computational Science*, *2*(1), 1–8. doi:10.1016/j.jocs.2010.12.007

Bollen, K. A. (1989). *Structural Equations with Latent Variables*. New York, NY: Wiley. doi:10.1002/9781118619179

Bollen, K. A., & Long, J. S. (1993). *Testing structural equation modeling*. Newbury Park, CA: Sage.

Bollerslev, T. (1986). Generalized autoregressive conditional heteroskedasticity. *Journal of Econometrics*, *31*(3), 307–327. doi:10.1016/0304-4076(86)90063-1

Bolwijn, P. T., & Kumpe, T. (1990). Manufacturing in the 1990s—productivity, flexibility, and innovation. *Long Range Planning*, *23*(4), 44–57. doi:10.1016/0024-6301(90)90151-S

Bontis, N. (1999). Managing organizational knowledge by diagnosing intellectual capital: Framing and advancing the state of the field. *International Journal of Technology Management*, *18*(5-8), 433–462. doi:10.1504/IJTM.1999.002780

Bose, R. (2009). Advanced analytics: Opportunities and challenges. *Industrial Management & Data Systems*, *109*(2), 155–172. doi:10.1108/02635570910930073

Bose, R., & Sugumaran, V. (2003). Application of knowledge management technology in customer relationship management. *Knowledge and Process Management*, *10*(1), 3–17. doi:10.1002/kpm.163

Bourne, M., Neely, A. J., & Platts, K. (2003). Implementing performance measurement systems: A literature review. *The International Journal of Business Performance Management*, *5*(1), 1–24. doi:10.1504/IJBPM.2003.002097

Boussif, D. (2010). Decision-Making Styles of Arab Executives: Insights from Tunisia. *Communications of the IBIMA*, *2010* (2010), article ID 66660955. Retrieved February 12, 2013, http://www.ibimapublishing.com/journals/CIBIMA/cibima.html

Box, G. E. P., Jenkins, G. M., & Reinsel, G. C. (1994). Time series analysis: Forecasting and control. Englewood Cliffs, NJ: Prentice Hall.

Branderburger, A., & Nalebuff, B. (1996). *Co-Opetition*. New York: Doubleday.

Branine, M. (2002). Algeria's employment policies and practice: An overview. *International Journal of Employment Studies*, *10*, 133–152.

Branine, M., & Pollard, D. (2010). Human resource management with Islamic management principles: A dialectic for a reverse diffusion in management. *Personnel Review*, *39*(6), 712–727. doi:10.1108/00483481011075576

Breiman, L. (1996). Bagging predictors. *Machine Learning*, *24*(2), 123–140. doi:10.1007/BF00058655

Brito, T. B., & Botter, R. C. (2012). Feasibility analysis of a global logistics hub in Panama. *International Journal of Logistics Systems and Management*, *12*(3), 247–266. doi:10.1504/IJLSM.2012.047601

Broadbent, J., & Laughlin, R. (2009). Performance management systems: A conceptual model. *Management Accounting Research*, *20*(4), 283–295. doi:10.1016/j.mar.2009.07.004

Brooks, C. (1996). Testing for non-linearity in daily sterling exchange rates. *Applied Financial Economics*, *6*(4), 307–317. doi:10.1080/096031096334105

Brooks, M. (1996). *Zbližanje in ujemanje*. Kranj: Ganeš.

Brother International Corporation. (2013, March 19). *Brother small business survey2013*. Retrieved from http://www.brother-usa.com/PressReleases/brother%20 2013%20smb%20survey%20press%20release%20%20 final.pdf

Brouthers, K. D., Brouthers, L. E., & Werner, S. (2000). Influences on strategic decision-making in the Dutch financial services industry. *Journal of Management*, *26*(5), 863–883. doi:10.1177/014920630002600506

Brown, B., Chui, M., & Manyika, J. (2011). Are you ready for the era of 'big data'. *The McKinsey Quarterly*, *4*, 24–35.

Browning, T. R., & Heath, R. D. (2009). Reconceptualizing the effects of lean on production costs with evidence from the F-22 program. *Journal of Operations Management*, *27*(1), 23–35. doi:10.1016/j.jom.2008.03.009

Brown, J. S., & Duguid, P. (1991). Organizational learning and communities-of-practice: Toward a unified view of working, learning, and innovation. *Organization Science*, *2*(1), 40–57. doi:10.1287/orsc.2.1.40

Brown, R., & Ozgur, C. (1997). Priority Class Scheduling: Production Scheduling for Multi-objective Environments. *Production Planning and Control*, *8*(2), 762–770. doi:10.1080/095372897234650

Bruttel, O. (2005). Are employment zones successful? Evidence from the first four years. *Local Economy*, *20*(4), 389–403. doi:10.1080/00207230500286533

Brynjolfsson, E., & McAfee, A. (2012). Big Data's Management Revolution. In The promise and challenge of big data. Harvard Business Review Insight Center Report.

Buckheit, C. (n.d.). 5 Savvy Nonprofits Using Eye-Catching Online Pledges to Advocate, Educate and Grow Email Lists. *Carol Buckheit RSS*. Retrieved July 8th 2014 from: http://www.carolbuckheit.org/2012/02/29/5-savvy-nonprofits-using-eye-catching-onlinepledges-to-advocate-educate-and-grow-email-lists/

Buckingham, I. (2008). Communicating in a recession: Employee must engage with the brand during tough times. *Strategic Communication Management*, *12*(3), 7.

Budd, J. M., & Adams, K. (1989). Allocation formulas in practice. *Library Acquisitions: Practice and Theory*, *13*(4), 381–390. doi:10.1016/0364-6408(89)90049-5

Budhwar, P., & Mellahi, K. (2006). Human resource management in the Middle East: emerging HRM models and future challenges for research and policy. In Managing Human Resources in the Middle East (pp. 291-301). London: Routledge.

Budhwar, P., & Mellahi, K. (2006). Introduction: Managing human resources in the Middle East. In P. Budhwar & K. Mellahi (Eds.), *Managing Human Resources in the Middle* (pp. 1–19). London: Routledge.

Bueren, A., Schierholz, R., Kolbe, L., & Brenner, W. (2004), Customer knowledge management - improving performance of customer relationship management with knowledge management. In *Proceedings of the 37th Hawaii International Conference on System Sciences*. IEEE. doi:10.1109/HICSS.2004.1265416

Bughin, J., Chui, M., & Manyika, J. (2010). Clouds, big data, and smart assets: Ten tech-enabled business trends to watch. *The McKinsey Quarterly*, *56*(1), 75–86.

Bulcsu, S. (2011). The process of liberalising the rail freight transport markets in the EU: The case of Hungary. *International Journal of Logistics Systems and Management*, *9*(1), 89–107. doi:10.1504/IJLSM.2011.040061

Busco, C., Quattrone, P., & Riccaboni, A. (2007). Management accounting issues in interpreting its nature and change. *Management Accounting Research*, *18*(2), 125–149. doi:10.1016/j.mar.2007.04.003

Busi, M. M., & Bititci, U. S. (2006). Collaborative performance management: Present gaps and future research. *International Journal of Productivity and Performance Management*, *55*(1), 7–25. doi:10.1108/17410400610635471

Bussey, J. (2011, September 16). Seeking safety in clouds. *The Wall Street Journal*, p. B8.

Byun, B., Lee, C., Webb, S., Irani, D., & Pu, C. (2009, July). An anti-spam filter combination framework for text-and-image emails through incremental learning. In *Proceedings of the the Sixth Conference on Email and Anti–Spam (CEAS 2009)*. CEAS.

CACI PC Simscript II.5. (1987). Introduction and User's Manual. San Diego, CA: CACI.

Calvanese, D., Castano, S., Guerra, F., Lembo, D., Melchiori, M., & Terracina, G. et al. (2001). Towards a Comprehensive Methodological Framework for Integration. In *Proceedings of the 8th International Workshop on Knowledge Representation meets Databases (KRDB 2001)*. KRDB.

Camarinha-Matos, L. M., Afsarmanesh, H., & Ollus, M. (2005). Ecolead: A holistic approach to creation and management of dynamic virtual organizations. In L. M. Camarinha-Matos, H. Afsarmanesh, & A. Ortiz (Eds.), *Collaborative networks and their breeding environments* (pp. 3–16). New York, NY: Springer-Verlag. doi:10.1007/0-387-29360-4_1

Campbell, A. J. (2006). The role of organizational knowledge management strategies in the quest for business intelligence. In *Proceedings of IEE International Conference on Engineering Management,* (pp. 231-236). IEE.

Campbell, A. J. (2003). Creating customer knowledge competence: Managing customer relationship management programs strategically. *Industrial Marketing Management*, *32*(5), 375–383. doi:10.1016/S0019-8501(03)00011-7

Cao, R., Vilar, J. M., & Devia, A. (2009). Modelling consumer credit risk via survival analysis. *Statistics & Operations Research Transactions*, *33*(1), 3–30.

Capon, N., Farley, J. U., & Hulbert, J. M. (1987). *Corporate Strategic Planning*. New York, NY: Columbia University Press.

Carlberg, C. (2013). *Predictive Analytics: Microsoft Excel*. Pearson Education, Inc.

Carling, K., Jacobson, T., Linde, J., & Roszbach, K. (2007). Corporate credit risk modeling and the macroeconomy. *Journal of Banking & Finance*, *31*(3), 845–868. doi:10.1016/j.jbankfin.2006.06.012

Carpinetti, L. C. R., & Melo, A. M. D. (2002). What to benchmark? A systematic approach and cases. *Benchmarking: An International Journal*, *9*(3), 244–255. doi:10.1108/14635770210429009

Carr, C. (1997). Strategic investment decisions and short-termism: Germany versus Britain. In V. Papadakis & P. Barwise (Eds.), *Strategic Decisions* (pp. 107–125). Boston, MA: Kluwer Academic Publishers. doi:10.1007/978-1-4615-6195-8_8

Carrillo, P. M., Kamara, J. M., & Anumba, C. J. (2000), Integration of knowledge management within construction business processes. In *Proceeding of the UK National Conference on Objects and Integration for Architecture, Engineering and Construction*, (pp. 95-105). Academic Press.

Carvalho, H., Cruz-Machado, V., & Tavares, J. G. (2012). A mapping framework for assessing supply chain resilience. *International Journal of Logistics Systems and Management*, *12*(3), 354–373. doi:10.1504/IJLSM.2012.047606

Casadesus, M., & de Castro, R. (2005). How improving quality improves supply chain management: Empirical study. *The TQM Magazine*, *17*(4), 345–357. doi:10.1108/09544780510603189

Cascio, W. F. (2006). *Managing human resources: Productivity, quality of life, profits*. Burr Ridge, IL: McGraw-Hill/Irwin.

Casella, G., & Berger, R. L. (2002). Statistical inference (2nd ed.). Duxbury: Thomson Learning.

Cassandras, C. (1993). *Discrete Event Systems: Modeling and Performance Analysis*. Irwin.

Cavaleri, S. A. (2008). Are learning organizations pragmatic? *The Learning Organization*, *15*(6), 474–481. doi:10.1108/09696470810907383

Cenicola, M. (2013, April 29). Three steps to incorporate big data into your small business. *Forbes*. Retrieved from http://www.forbes.com/sites/theyec/2013/04/29/3-steps-to-incorporate-big-data-into-yoursmall-business/

Chamber, C., Kouvelis, P., & Wang, H. (2006). Supply chain management research and production and operations management: Review, trends, and opportunities. *Production and Operations Management*, *15*(3), 449–469.

Chambers, D., Little, M., Lugo, E., Melendez, F., & Vasquez, V. (2014). *Instagram*. Final Deliverable for Spring 2014 Semester BMGT 4381 (section 1) Course. Presented May 8th, 2014 (Unpublished).

Chan, F. T. S., & Kumar, V. (2009). Performance optimization of a legality inspired supply chain model: A CFGTSA algorithm based approach. *International Journal of Production Research*, *47*(3), 777–791. doi:10.1080/00207540600844068

Chang, C.-T. (2007). Multi-choice Goal Programming, OMEGA. *International Journal of Management Sciences*, *35*, 389–396.

Chang, C.-T. (2008). Revised Multi-choice Goal Programming. *Applied Mathematical Modelling*, *32*(12), 2587–2595. doi:10.1016/j.apm.2007.09.008

Charalambous, C. (1992). Conjugate gradient algorithm for efficient training of artificial neural networks. *IEEE Proceedings*, *139*, 301-310.

Cheney, G., & Ashcraft, K. L. (2007). Considering "The Professional" in Communication Studies: Implications for Theory and Research Within and Beyond the Boundaries of Organizational Communication. *Communication Theory*, *17*(2), 146–175. doi:10.1111/j.1468-2885.2007.00290.x

Chen, F. L., & Li, F. C. (2010). Combination of feature selection approaches with SVM in credit scoring. *Expert Systems with Applications*, *37*(7), 4902–4909. doi:10.1016/j.eswa.2009.12.025

Cheng, L., & Peng, P. (2011), Integration knowledge management and Business. In *Proceedings of 2011 Fourth International Conference on Business Intelligence and Financial Engineering (BIFE)*, (pp. 307-310). BIFE. doi:10.1109/BIFE.2011.172

Chen, H., Chiang, R. H., & Storey, V. C. (2012). Business Intelligence and Analytics: From Big Data to Big Impact. *Management Information Systems Quarterly*, *36*(4), 1165–1188.

Chen, H., & Schmeiser, B. (2001). Stochastic root finding via retrospective approximation. *IIE Transactions*, *33*(3), 259–275. doi:10.1080/07408170108936827

Chen, H., & Zimbra, D. (2010). AI and Opinion mining. *IEEE Intelligent Systems*, *25*(3), 74–80. doi:10.1109/MIS.2010.75

Chenhall, R. (2005). Integrative strategic performance measurement systems, strategic alignment of manufacturing, learning and strategic outcomes: An exploratory study. *Accounting, Organizations and Society*, *30*(5), 395–422. doi:10.1016/j.aos.2004.08.001

Chen, I. J., & Popovich, K. (2003). Understanding customer relationship management (CRM), people, process and technology. *Business Process Management Journal*, *9*(5), 672–688. doi:10.1108/14637150310496758

Chen, J., & Tsou, H. (2007). Information technology adoption for service innovation practices and competitive advantage: The case of financial firms. *Information Research*, *12*, 1368–1613.

Chen, M. C., & Huang, S. H. (2003). Credit scoring and rejected instances reassigning through evolutionary computation techniques. *Expert Systems with Applications*, *24*(4), 433–441. doi:10.1016/S0957-4174(02)00191-4

Chen, M., Chang, S., & Hwang, Y. (2005). An empirical investigation of the relationship between intellectual capital and firms' market value and financial performance. *Journal of Intellectual Capital*, *6*(2), 159–176. doi:10.1108/14691930510592771

Chen, R. S., Sun, C. M., Helms, M. M., & Jih, W. J. (2009). Factors Influencing Information System Flexibility: An Interpretive Flexibility Perspective. *International Journal of Enterprise Information Systems*, *5*(1), 32–43. doi:10.4018/jeis.2009010103

Chen, W. H., & Shih, J. Y. (2006). A study of Taiwan's issuer credit rating systems using support vector machines. *Expert Systems with Applications*, *30*(3), 427–435. doi:10.1016/j.eswa.2005.10.003

Chen, W., Ma, C., & Ma, L. (2009). Mining the customer credit using hybrid support vector machine technique. *Expert Systems with Applications*, *36*(4), 7611–7616. doi:10.1016/j.eswa.2008.09.054

Chen, Y., Liu, Y., & Zhang, J. (2012). When do third-party product reviews affect firm value and what can firms do? The case of media critics and professional movie reviews. *Journal of Marketing*, *76*(2), 116–134. doi:10.1509/jm.09.0034

Chen, Y., & Xie, J. (2005). Third-party product review and firm marketing strategy. *Marketing Science*, *24*(2), 218–240. doi:10.1287/mksc.1040.0089

Chevalier, J. F., & Gramme, P. (2008). RANK for spam detection ECML-Discovery Challenge. In *Proceedings of ECML PKDD Discovery Challenge*. PKDD.

Chicco, G., Napoli, R., Postolache, P., Scutariu, M., & Toader, C. (2003). Customer characterization options for improving the tariff offer. *IEEE Transactions on Power Systems*, *18*(1), 381–387. doi:10.1109/TP-WRS.2002.807085

Chiesa, V., Frattini, F., Lazzarotti, V., & Manzini, R. (2009). Performance measurement of research and development activities. *European Journal of Innovation Management*, *12*(1), 25–61. doi:10.1108/14601060910928166

Child, J., & Tsai, T. (2005). The dynamic between firms' environmental strategies and institutional constraints in emerging economies: Evidence from China and Taiwan. *Journal of Management Studies*, *42*(1), 95–125. doi:10.1111/j.1467-6486.2005.00490.x

Chituc, C. M., & Azevedo, A. L. (2005). Multi-perspective challenges on collaborative networks business environment. In L. M. Camarinha-Matos, H. Afsarmanesh, & A. Ortiz (Eds.), *Collaborative networks and their breeding environments* (pp. 25–32). New York, NY: Springer-Verlag. doi:10.1007/0-387-29360-4_3

Choi, B., & Lee, H. (2003). An empirical investigation of KM styles and their effect on corporate performance. *Information & Management*, *40*(5), 403–417. doi:10.1016/S0378-7206(02)00060-5

Chung, K. L. (2001). *A course in probability theory* (3rd ed.). New York: Academic Press.

Chye Koh, H., Chin Tan, W., & Peng Goh, C. (2006). A Two-step Method to Construct Credit Scoring Models with Data Mining Techniques. *Journal of Business and Information*, *1*, 96–118.

Clark, D. (1984). Necessary & sufficient conditions for the Robbins-Monro method. *Stochastic Processes and Their Applications*, *17*(2), 359–367. doi:10.1016/0304-4149(84)90011-5

Clymer, J. (1995). System design & evaluation using discrete event simulation with AI. *European Journal of Operational Research*, *84*(1), 213–225. doi:10.1016/0377-2217(94)00327-9

Cohen, W. M., & Levinthal, D. A. (1990). Absorptive capacity: A new perspective on learning and innovation. *Administrative Science Quarterly*, *35*(1), 128–152. doi:10.2307/2393553

Cohn, D. A., Ghahramani, Z., & Jordan, M. I. (1996). Active learning with statistical models. *arXiv preprint cs/9603104*.

Cosier, R., Schwenk, C. R., & Dalton, D. (1992). Managerial decision making in Japan, the U.S., and Hong Kong. *The International Journal of Conflict Management*, *3*(2), 151–160. doi:10.1108/eb022710

Cover, T. M., & Hart, P. E. (1967). Nearest neighbor pattern classification. *IEEE Transactions on Information Theory*, *13*(1), 21–27. doi:10.1109/TIT.1967.1053964

Cray, D., Mallory, G. R., Butler, R. J., Hickson, D. J., & Wilson, D. C. (1988). Sporadic, fluid and constricted processes: Three types of strategic decision making in organizations. *Journal of Management Studies*, *25*(1), 13–39. doi:10.1111/j.1467-6486.1988.tb00020.x

Croft, L., & Cochrane, N. (2005). Communicating change effectively. *Management Services*, *49*(1), 18.

Croteus, A. M., & Peter, L. (2003). Critical success factors of CRM technological initiatives. *Canadian Journal of Administrative Sciences*, *20*(1), 21–34. doi:10.1111/j.1936-4490.2003.tb00303.x

Curry, E., Freitas, A., & O'Riain, S. (2010). The role of community-driven data curation for enterprises. In D. Wood (Ed.), *Linking enterprise data* (pp. 25–47). Boston, MA: Springer. doi:10.1007/978-1-4419-7665-9_2

D'Aveni, R. (1994). *Hypercompetition*. New York, NY: Free Press.

da Cruz, J. M. M. (2009, December 4). *Méthodologie d'évaluation des filtres anti-spam. Journées Réseaux*.

Dadfar, H. (1993). In search of Arab management, Direction and identity. In *Proceedings of the Arab Management Conference*. Bradford Management Centre, University of Bradford

Daft, R. L. (2000). *Organization theory and design*. Cincinnati, OH: South-Western College.

Dağ, İ. (1991). Rotter'in iç-dış kontrol odağı ölçeğinin üniversite öğrencileri için güvenirliği ve eçerliği. *Psikoloji Dergisi, 7*, 10–16.

Dantzig, G. B. (1963). *Linear Programming and Extensions*. Princeton, NJ: Princeton University Press.

Davenport, T. (2013). *The Rise of Data Discovery*. Retrieved from http://www.asterdata.com/resources/assets/The_Rise_of_Data_Discovery.pdf

Davenport, T., Harris, J., & Kohli, A. (2001, Winter). How do they know their customer so well?. *MIT Sloan Management, Review*, 1-13.

Davenport, T., Harris, J., & Morison, R. (2010). Analytics at Work: Smarter Decisions, Better Results. Boston, MA: Harvard Business School Publishing Corporation. Retrieved from http://www.sas.com/resources/asset/IIA_NewWorldofBusinessAnalytics_March2010.pdf

Davenport, T. (2010). *The New World of "Business Analytics*. International Institute for Analytics.

Davenport, T. (2012). *Enterprise Analytics: Optimize Performance. Process, and Decisions Through Big Data*. FT Press.

Davenport, T. (2014). *Big Data at Work: Dispelling the Myths, Uncovering the Opportunities*. Harvard Business Review Press.

Davenport, T. H. (2006). Competing on Analytics. *Harvard Business Review, 84*(1), 98–107. PMID:16447373

Davenport, T. H., Harris, J., & Shapiro, J. (2010). Competing on Talent Analytics. *Harvard Business Review, 88*(10), 52–58. PMID:20929194

Davenport, T. H., & Patil, D. (2012). Data Scientist: The Sexiest Job of the 21st Century. *Harvard Business Review, 90*(10), 70–76. PMID:23074866

Dawes, P. L., & Massey, G. R. (2005). Antecedents of conflict in marketing's cross-functional relationship with sales. *European Journal of Marketing, 39*(11/12), 1327–1344. doi:10.1108/03090560510623280

Dayal, U., Castellanos, M., Simitsis, A., & Wilkinson, K. (2009). Data integration flows for business intelligence. In *Proceedings of the 12th International Conference on Extending Database Technology: Advances in Database Technology* (pp. 1-11). New York: ACM. doi:10.1145/1516360.1516362

Day, G. S. (1994). The capabilities of market-driven organizations. *Journal of Marketing, 58*(4), 37–54. doi:10.2307/1251915

De Silva, D., Xinghuo, Y., Alahakoon, D., & Holmes, G. (2011). A Data Mining Framework for Electricity Consumption Analysis From Meter Data. *IEEE Transactions on Industrial Informatics, 7*(3), 399–407. doi:10.1109/TII.2011.2158844

de Waal, A. A. (2003). Behavioural factors important for the successful implementation and use of performance management systems. *Management Decision, 41*(8), 688–697. doi:10.1108/00251740310496206

de Waal, A. A., & Coevert, V. (2007). The effect of performance management on the organizational results of a bank. *International Journal of Productivity and Performance Management, 56*(5-6), 397–416. doi:10.1108/17410400710757114

de Waal, A. A., & Counet, H. (2009). Lessons learned from performance management systems implementations. *International Journal of Productivity and Performance Management, 58*(4), 367–390. doi:10.1108/17410400910951026

de Weck, O., & Jones, M. (2006). Isoperformance: Analysis and design of complex systems with desired outcomes. *Systems Engineering, 9*(1), 45–61. doi:10.1002/sys.20043

Dean, J. W., & Sharfman, M. P. (1993). Procedural rationality in the strategic decision-making process. *Journal of Management Studies, 30*(4), 587–610. doi:10.1111/j.1467-6486.1993.tb00317.x

Dean, J. W., & Sharfman, M. P. (1996). Does decision process matter? A study of strategic decision making effectiveness. *Academy of Management Journal, 39*(2), 368–396. doi:10.2307/256784

Dean, J. W., Sharfman, M. P., & Ford, C. A. (1993). The relationship of procedural rationality and political behaviour in strategic decision-making. *Decision Sciences, 24*(6), 1069–1083. doi:10.1111/j.1540-5915.1993.tb00504.x

Dedoussis, E. (2004). A Cross- Cultural Comparison of Organizational Culture: Evidence from Universities in the Arab World and Japan. *Cross Cultural Management, 11*(1), 15–34. doi:10.1108/13527600410797729

Deerwester, S. C., Dumais, S. T., Landauer, T. K., Furnas, G. W., & Harshman, R. A. (1990). Indexing by latent semantic analysis. *JASIS, 41*(6), 391–407. doi:10.1002/(SICI)1097-4571(199009)41:6<391::AID-ASI1>3.0.CO;2-9

Degen, K., Efferson, C., Frei, F., Goette, L., & Lalive, R. (2013). Smart Metering, Beratung oder Sozialer Vergleich: Was beeinflusst den Elektrizitätsverbrauch? Zürich.

DeGroot, M. H., & Schervish, M. J. (2012). *Probability and statistics* (4th ed.). Addison Wesley Publishing Company Incorporated.

Deresky, H. (1994). *International Management: Managing Across Borders and Cultures*. New York, NY: Harper Collins College Publ.

Deshpande, R., Farley, J. U., & Webster, F. E. Jr. (1993). Corporate culture customer orientation and innovativeness in Japanese firms: A quadrat analysis. *Journal of Marketing, 57*(1), 23–27. doi:10.2307/1252055

Dietterichl, T. G. (2002). Ensemble learning. In The handbook of brain theory and neural networks, (pp. 405-408). Academic Press.

Dietterich, T. G. (2000). An experimental comparison of three methods for constructing ensembles of decision trees: Bagging, boosting, and randomization. *Machine Learning, 40*(2), 139–157. doi:10.1023/A:1007607513941

Dijkman, R., Dumas, M., Van Dongen, B., Käärik, R., & Mendling, J. (2011). Similarity of business process models: Metrics and evaluation. *Information Systems, 36*(2), 498–516. doi:10.1016/j.is.2010.09.006

Dippon, J., & Renz, J. (1997). Weighted means in stochastic approximation of minima. *SIAM Journal on Control and Optimization, 35*(5), 1811–1827. doi:10.1137/S0363012995283789

Dodds, W. B., Monroe, K. B., & Grewal, D. (1991). Effects of price, brand, and store information on buyers' product evaluations. *JMR, Journal of Marketing Research, 28*(3), 307–319. doi:10.2307/3172866

Dolphin, R. R. (2005). Internal Communications: Today's Strategic Imperative. *Journal of Marketing Communications, 11*(3), 171–190. doi:10.1080/1352726042000315414

Dorfman, P. W., & Howell, J. P. (1988). Dimensions of national culture and effective leadership patterns: Hofstede revisited. In R. N. Farmer & E. G. McGoun (Eds.), *Advances in International Comparative Management (pp. 127-50)*. New York, NY: JAI.

Doss, H., & Sethuraman, J. (1989). The price of bias reduction when there is no unbiased estimate. *Annals of Statistics, 17*(1), 440–442. doi:10.1214/aos/1176347028

Doumpos, M., Kosmidou, K., Baourakis, G., & Zopounidis, C. (2002). Credit risk assessment using a multicriteria hierarchical discrimination approach: A comparative analysis. *European Journal of Operational Research, 138*(2), 392–412. doi:10.1016/S0377-2217(01)00254-5

Drobo Incorporated. (2012). *SMB IT 2012 Survey Results*. Retrieved from http://www.drobo.com/downloads/docs/SR-0137-00_SMB-virt-survey-q3-q4-2012.pdf

Drucker, P. F. (1991). The new productivity challenge. *Harvard Business Review, 69*(6), 69–76. PMID:10114929

Duda, R. O., Hart, P. E., & Stork, D. G. (Eds.). (2000). Pattern Classification. New York: Information Science Reference.

Dundon, E. (2005). Innovation triangle. *Leadership Excellence, 22*, 16.

Dunis, C., Laws, J., & Sermpinis, G. (2011). Higher order and recurrent neural architectures for trading the EUR/USD exchange rate. *Quantitative Finance, 11*(4), 615–629. doi:10.1080/14697680903386348

Durand, D. (1941). *Risk elements in consumer instalments financing*. New York: National Bureau of Economic Research.

Dwairy, M., Achoui, M., Abouserie, R., Farah, A., Sakhleh, A., Fayad, M., & Khan, H. (2006). Parenting Styles in Arab Societies: A First Cross-regional Research Study. *Journal of Cross-Cultural Psychology, 37*(3), 230–247. doi:10.1177/0022022106286922

Dyson, C. K. (2013, January 9). Can the cloud help small businesses? *Wall Street Journal.* Retrieved from http://online.wsj.com/article/SB10001424127887323706704578230641145851624.html

Džeroski, S., & Ženko, B. (2004). Is combining classifiers with stacking better than selecting the best one? *Machine Learning, 54*(3), 255–273. doi:10.1023/B:MACH.0000015881.36452.6e

Dziczkowski, G., & Wegrzyn-Wolska, K. (2008, December). An autonomous system designed for automatic detection and rating of film reviews. In *Proceedings of the 2008 IEEE/WIC/ACM International Conference on Web Intelligence and Intelligent Agent Technology*(vol. 1, pp. 847-850). IEEE Computer Society. doi:10.1109/WIIAT.2008.262

Earley, P. C. (2006). Leading cultural research in the future: A matter of paradigms and taste. *Journal of International Business Studies, 37*(6), 922–931. doi:10.1057/palgrave.jibs.8400236

Eckerson, W. (2013). *Analytical Modeling is Both Science and Art.* Retrieved from http://searchbusinessanalytics.techtarget.com/opinion/Analytical-modeling-is-both-science-and-art

Eckerson, W. W. (2007a). *2007 TDWI BI benchmark report.* Retrieved December 24, 2013, from http://tdwi.org/~/media/86FE9B6DA255431C84E20570BBFFF3EB.pdf

Eckerson, W. W. (2007b). *Beyond the basics: Accelerating BI maturity.* Retrieved March 8, 2013, from http://download.101com.com/pub/tdwi/Files/SAP_monograph_0407.pdf

Eddy, N. (2012, May 30). *Small-business security spending to top $5.6B in2015.* Retrieved from http://www.eweek.com/c/a/Security/Small-Business-Security-Spending-to-Top-56-Billion-in-2015-IDC875794/?kc=rss

Edvinsson, L., & Malone, M. (1997). *Intellectual capital.* New York: Harper Business.

Eisenbeis, R. A. (1977). Pitfalls in the application of discriminant analysis in business, finance, and economics. *The Journal of Finance, 32*(3), 875–900. doi:10.1111/j.1540-6261.1977.tb01995.x

Eisend, M. (2004). Is it still worth to be credible? A meta-analysis of temporal patterns of source credibility effects in marketing. *Advances in Consumer Research. Association for Consumer Research (U. S.), 31*(1), 352–357.

Eisenhardt, K. M. (1989). Making fast strategic decisions in high-velocity environments. *Academy of Management Journal, 32*(3), 543–576. doi:10.2307/256434

Eisenhardt, K. M. (1997). Strategic decisions and all that jazz. *Business Strategy Review, 8*(3), 1–3. doi:10.1111/1467-8616.00031

Eisenhardt, K. M., & Bourgeois, L. J. I. (1988). Politics of strategic decision making in high-velocity environments: Toward a midrange theory. *Academy of Management Journal, 31*(4), 737–770. doi:10.2307/256337

Elbana, S. (2012). Slack, Planning and Organizational Performance: Evidence from the Arab Middle East. *European Management Review, 9*(2), 99–115. doi:10.1111/j.1740-4762.2012.01028.x

Elbana, S., & Child, J. (2007). Influences on Strategic Decision effectiveness: Development and test of an integrative model. *Strategic Management Journal, 28*(4), 431–453. doi:10.1002/smj.597

Elbanna, S. (2006). Strategic decision making: Process perspectives. *International Journal of Management Reviews, 8*(1), 1–20. doi:10.1111/j.1468-2370.2006.00118.x

Elbanna, S. (2008). Planning and participation as determinants of strategic planning effectiveness: Evidence from the Arabic context. *Management Decision, 46*(5), 779–796. doi:10.1108/00251740810873761

Elbanna, S., Ali, A. J., & Dayan, M. (2011). Conflict in strategic decision making: Do the setting and environment matter? *The International Journal of Conflict Management, 22*(3), 278–299. doi:10.1108/10444061111152973

Elbashir, M. Z., Collier, P. A., & Davern, M. J. (2008). Measuring the effects of business intelligence systems: The relationship between business process and organizational performance. *International Journal of Accounting Information Systems*, *9*(3), 135–153. doi:10.1016/j.accinf.2008.03.001

Eligius, M. T., & Boglárka, G.-T. (2010). *Introduction to Nonlinear and Global Optimization*. Springer.

Erdem, T., Zhao, Y., & Valenzuela, A. (2004). Performance of store brands: A cross-country analysis of consumer store-brand preferences, perceptions, and risk. *JMR, Journal of Marketing Research*, *41*(1), 86–100. doi:10.1509/jmkr.41.1.86.25087

Erickson, G. S., & Rothberg, H. N. (2012). *Intelligence in action: Strategically managing knowledge assets*. London: Palgrave Macmillan. doi:10.1057/9781137035325

European Commission. (2003). *The New SME Definition*. Retrieved from http://ec.europa.eu/enterprise/policies/sme/files/sme_definition/sme_user_guide_en.pdf

Evans, J. R., & Lindner, C. H. (2012). Business Analytics: The Next Frontier for Decision Sciences. *Decision Line*, *43*(2), 4–6.

Evans, S., Roth, N., & Sturm, F. (2004). Performance measurement and added value of networks. In L. M. Camarinha-Matos & H. Afsarmanesh (Eds.), *Collaborative networked organizations: A research agenda for emerging business models* (pp. 147–152). New York, NY: Springer-Verlag. doi:10.1007/1-4020-7833-1_18

Ewusi-Mensah, K. (1997). Critical issues in abandoned information systems development projects. *Communications of the ACM*, *40*(9), 74–80. doi:10.1145/260750.260775

Eyler, A. A., Mayer, J., Rafii, R., Housemann, R., & Brownson, R. C. (1999). Key informant surveys as a tool to implement and evaluate physical activity interventions in the community. *Health Education Research*, *14*(2), 289–298. doi:10.1093/her/14.2.289 PMID:10387507

Falangis, K. (2008). The use of MSD model in credit scoring. *Operations Research*, *7*(3), 481–504. doi:10.1007/BF03024859

Farley, C. (2005). HR's role in talent management and driving business results. *Employment Relations Today*, *32*(1), 55–61. doi:10.1002/ert.20053

Feinberg, F. M., Kahn, B. E., & McAlister, L. (1992). Market share response when consumers seek variety. *JMR, Journal of Marketing Research*, *29*(2), 227–237. doi:10.2307/3172572

Feng, L.-H., & Lu, J. (2010). The practical research on flood forecasting based on artificial neural networks. *Expert Systems with Applications*, *37*(4), 2974–2977. doi:10.1016/j.eswa.2009.09.037

Ferguson, R. B. (2012). Location Analytics: Bringing Geography Back. *MIT Sloan Management Review*, *54*(2), 1–5.

Ferreira, A., & Otley, D. (2009). The design and use of performance management systems: An extended framework for analysis. *Management Accounting Research*, *20*(4), 263–282. doi:10.1016/j.mar.2009.07.003

Ferreira, P. S., Shamsuzzoha, A. H. M., Toscano, C., & Cunha, P. (2012). Framework for performance measurement and management in a collaborative business environment. *International Journal of Productivity and Performance Management*, *61*(6), 672–690. doi:10.1108/17410401211249210

Ferreira, R. P., Silva, J. N., Strauhs, F. R., & Soares, A. L. (2011). Performance management in collaborative networks: A methodological proposal. *Journal of Universal Computer Science*, *17*(10), 1412–1429.

Field, A. (2009). *Discovering Statistics Using SPSS* (3rd ed.). London: Sage Publications, Inc.

Figueiredo, V., Rodrigues, F., Vale, Z., & Gouveia, J. B. (2005). An electric energy consumer characterization framework based on data mining techniques. *IEEE Transactions on Power Systems*, *20*(2), 596–602. doi:10.1109/TPWRS.2005.846234

Firer, S., & Williams, M. (2003). Intellectual capital and traditional measures of corporate performance. *Journal of Intellectual Capital*, *4*(3), 348–360. doi:10.1108/14691930310487806

Fisher, M. (2001). Innovation, knowledge creation and systems of innovation. *The Annals of Regional Science*, *35*(2), 199–216. doi:10.1007/s001680000034

Fisher, R. (1936). The use of multiple measurements in taxonomic problems. *Annals of Eugenics*, *7*(2), 179–188. doi:10.1111/j.1469-1809.1936.tb02137.x

Fjose, S., Grunfeld, L.A., & Green, C. (2010). *SMEs and Growth in Sub-Saharan Africa*. MENON-publication. Number 14/2010.

Fleishe, C. (2014). *Pittsburgh unemployment rate drops to 5.5 percent in May*. Retrieved July 2, 2014 from http://triblive.com/business/headlines/6373154-74/jobs-rate-reported#ixzz36KiyyJTa

Fleisher, C. S., & Bensoussan, B. (2002). *Strategic and competitive analysis: Methods and techniques for analysing business competition*. Upper Saddle River, NJ: Prentice Hall.

Folsom, W. (n.d.). Little Giants, Big Money: Lessons in Social Media Fundraising From a Liberal Arts College. *Nonprofit Hub*. Retrieved July 8th 2014 from: http://www.nonprofithub.org/featured/little-giants-big-money-lessons-social-media-fundraising-liberal-arts-college/

Fonseca, D. (2014). *Peer-to-peer fundraising*. Retrieved July 6th 2014 from: http://info.firstgiving.com/blog/?Tag=peer-to-peer%20fundraising

Forbes, D. P. (2000). *The strategic implications of managerial cognition and firm decision processes: evidence from a new venture context*. (Unpublished PhD thesis). New York University, New York, NY.

Ford, G. T., Smith, D. B., & Swasy, J. L. (1990). Consumer skepticism of advertising claims: Testing hypotheses from economics of information. *The Journal of Consumer Research*, 16(4), 433–441. doi:10.1086/209228

Forstenlechner, I., & Mellahi, K. (2011). Gaining legitimacy through hiring local workforce at a premium: The case of MNEs in the United Arab Emirates. *Journal of World Business*, 46(4), 455–461. doi:10.1016/j.jwb.2010.10.006

Fortuin, F. T. J. M., & Omta, S. W. F. (2009). Innovation drivers and barriers in food processing. *British Food Journal*, 111(8), 839–851. doi:10.1108/00070700910980955

Franceschini, F., Galetto, M., Maisano, D., & Mastrogiacomo, L. (2010). Clustering of European countries based on ISO 9000 certification diffusion. *International Journal of Quality & Reliability Management*, 27(5), 558–575. doi:10.1108/02656711011043535

Franke, G. R., Huhmann, B. A., & Mothersbaugh, D. L. (2004). Information content and consumer readership of print ads: A comparison of search and experience products. *Journal of the Academy of Marketing Science*, 32(1), 20–31. doi:10.1177/0092070303257856

Fredrickson, J. W. (1984). The comprehensiveness of strategic decision processes: Extension, observations, future directions. *Academy of Management Journal*, 27(3), 445–466. doi:10.2307/256039

Fredrickson, J. W., & Laquinto, A. L. (1989). Inertia and creeping rationality in strategic decisions. *Academy of Management Journal*, 32(3), 516–542. doi:10.2307/256433

Fredrickson, J. W., & Terence, R. M. (1984). Strategic Decision Processes: Comprehensiveness and Performance in an Industry with an Unstable Environment. *Academy of Management Journal*, 27(2), 399–423. doi:10.2307/255932

Freitas, A. A. (2002). *Data mining and knowledge discovery with evolutionary algorithms*. Springer. doi:10.1007/978-3-662-04923-5

Freudenberg, B., Tran-Nam, B., Karlinsky, S., & Gupta, R. (2012). A comparative analysis of tax advisers' perception of small business tax law complexity: United States, Australia and New Zealand. *Australian Tax Forum*, 27(4), 677-718. Retrieved from http://ssrn.com/abstract=2190692

Freund, Y., & Schapire, R. E. (1996, July). *Experiments with a new boosting algorithm* (Vol. 96). ICML.

Frey, D., Palladino, J., Sullivan, J., & Atherton, M. M. (2007). Part count and design of robust systems. *Systems Engineering*, 10(3), 203–221. doi:10.1002/sys.20071

Friedman, J. H. (1997). On bias, variance, 0/1 - loss, and the curse-of dimensionality. *Data Mining and Knowledge Discovery*, 1(1), 55–77. doi:10.1023/A:1009778005914

Friedman, L. (1996). *The Simulation Metamodel*. Norwell, MA: Kluwer Academic Publishers. doi:10.1007/978-1-4613-1299-4

Friman, M., Garling, T., Millett, B., Mattsson, J., & Johnston, R. (2002). An analysis of international business-to-business relationships based on the commitment-trust theory. *Industrial Marketing Management, 31*(5), 403–409. doi:10.1016/S0019-8501(01)00154-7

Fristedt, B. E., & Gray, L. F. (1997). *A modern approach to probability theory. Probability and its applications.* Boston: Birkhauser. doi:10.1007/978-1-4899-2837-5

Fu, T., Lee, K., Sze, D., Chung, F., & Ng, C. (2008). Discovering the Correlation between Stock Time Series and Financial News. In *Proceedings of IEEE/WIC/ACM International Conference on Web Intelligence and Intelligent Agent Technology*, (pp. 880-883). Sydney: IEEE. doi:10.1109/WIIAT.2008.228

Fuld, L. M. (1994). *The new competitor intelligence: The complete resource for finding, analyzing, and using information about your competitors.* New York: John Wiley.

Fu, M. (2002). Optimization for simulation: Theory vs. practice. *INFORMS Journal on Computing, 14*(3), 192–227. doi:10.1287/ijoc.14.3.192.113

Galindo, J., & Tamayo, P. (2000). Credit Risk Assessment Using Statistical and Machine Learning: Basic Methodology and Risk Modeling Applications. *Basic Methodology and Risk Modeling Applications, 15*(1-2), 107–143.

Gallupe, R. B., Dennis, R. A., Cooper, A. W., Vallacich, S. G., Bastianutti, M. L., & Nunamaker, G. F. (1992). Electronic brainstorming and group size. *Academy of Management Journal, 35*(2), 350–369. doi:10.2307/256377

Gannon, M. (1994). *Understanding Global Cultures: Metaphorical Journeys Through 17 Countries.* Thousand Oaks, CA: Sage Publications.

GAO Research. (2012). Retrieved from http://www.gaoresearch.com/POS/pos.php

Gardner, O. (n.d.). Why Do Infographics Make Great Marketing Tools? [Infographic] – Unbounce. *Unbounce Latest Posts RSS.* Retrieved July 6th 2014 from: http://unbounce.com/content-marketing/why-do-infographics-make-great-marketing-tools/

Garengo, P., Biazzo, S., & Bititci, U. S. (2005). Performance measurement systems in SMEs: A review for a research agenda. *International Journal of Management Reviews, 7*(1), 25–47. doi:10.1111/j.1468-2370.2005.00105.x

Gartner Inc. (2013). *Press Release: Gartner Executive Program Survey of More Than 2,000 CIOs Shows Digital Technologies Are Top Priorities in 2013.* Available at http://www.gartner.com/newsroom/id/2304615

Gebert, H., Geib, H., Kolbe, L., & Brenner, W. (2003). Knowledge-enabled customer relationship management: Integrating customer relationship management and knowledge management concepts. *Journal of Knowledge Management, 7*(5), 107–123. doi:10.1108/13673270310505421

Geib, M., Reichold, A., Kolbe, L., & Brenner, W. (2005). Architecture for customer relationship management approaches in Financial service. In *Proceedings of the 38th Annual Hawaii International Conference on System Sciences* (HICSS '05), (pp. 240.1-240.10). IEEE.

George, D., & Mallery, P. (2010). *SPSS for Windows Step by Step: A Simple Guide and Reference 18.0 Update* (11th ed.). Boston, MA: Pearson Education, Inc.

Gestel, T. V. (2006). A process model to develop an internal rating system: Sovereign credit ratings. *Decision Support Systems, 42*(2), 1131–1151. doi:10.1016/j.dss.2005.10.001

Gestel, T. V., Baesens, B., Suykens, J. A. K., Poel, D. V., Baestaens, D. E., & Wil, M. (2006). Bayesian kernel based classification for financial distress detection. *European Journal of Operational Research, 172*(3), 979–1003. doi:10.1016/j.ejor.2004.11.009

Gibson, T., & van der Vaart, H. J. (2008). *Defining SMEs: A Less Imperfect Way of Defining Small and Medium Enterprises in Developing Countries.* The Brookings Institute.

Gilad, B. (2003). *Early warning: Using competitive intelligence to anticipate market shifts, control risk, and create powerful strategies.* New York: ANACOM.

Gilad, B., & Herring, J. (Eds.). (1996). *The art and science of business intelligence.* Greenwich, CT: JAI Press.

Gillam, L., Ahmad, K., Ahmad, S., Casey, M., Cheng, D., Taskaya, T., et al. (2002). Economic News and Stock Market Correlation: A Study of the UK Market. In *Proceedings of Conference on Terminology and Knowledge Engineering*. Retrieved January 12, 2014, from http://www.cs.surrey.ac.uk/BIMA/People/M.Casey/downloads/Publications/2002_gillam_ahmad_ahmad_casey_cheng_taskaya_oliveira_manomaisupat_economic_news_and_stock_market_correlation.pdf

Giudici, P. (2001). Bayesian data mining, with application to benchmarking and credit scoring. *Applied Stochastic Models in Business and Society*, *17*(1), 69–81. doi:10.1002/asmb.425

Giudici, P. (2003). *Applied Data Mining: Statistical Methods for Business and Industry*. New York: John Wiley & Sons.

Glykas, M. M. (2011). Effort based performance measurement in business process management. *Knowledge and Process Management*, *18*(1), 10–33. doi:10.1002/kpm.364

Glynn, P. (1990). Likelihood ratio derivative estimation for stochastic systems. *Communications of the ACM*, *33*(10), 75–84. doi:10.1145/84537.84552

Gnatovich, R. (2006). *Business Intelligence Versus Business Analytics—What's the Difference?* Available at http://www.cio.com/article/18095/Business_Intelligence_Versus_Business_Analytics_What_s_the_Difference

Gobeli, D. H., & Brown, W. B. (1994). Technological innovation strategies. *Engineering Management Journal*, *6*, 17–24.

Goering, P. A. (1985). Effects of product trial on consumer expectations, demand, and prices. *The Journal of Consumer Research*, *12*(1), 74–82. doi:10.1086/209036

Goicoechea, A., Hansen, D. R., & Duckstein, L. (1982). *Multi-objective Decision Analysis with Engineering and Business Application*. New York: John Wiley and Sons.

Goldberg, E. (2012). How Nonprofits Used Social Media To Increase Giving In 2012 (INFOGRAPHIC). *The Huffington Post*. Retrieved July 7th 2014 from: http://www.huffingtonpost.com/2012/12/18/nonprofits-social-media-2012_n_2325319.html

Goldberg, D. E. (1989). *Genetic Algorithm in Search, Optimization, and Machine Learning*. Addison Wesley.

Golfarelli, M., Maio, D., & Rizzi, S. (1998). The Dimensional Fact Model: A Conceptual Model for Data Warehouses. *International Journal of Cooperative Information Systems*, *7*(2-3).

Golfarelli, M., Mandreoli, F., Penzo, W., Rizzi, S., & Turricchia, E. (2012). OLAP Query Reformulation in Peer-to-Peer Data Warehousing. *Information Systems*, *37*(5), 393–411. doi:10.1016/j.is.2011.06.003

Golfarelli, M., & Rizzi, S. (2009). *Data Warehouse Design: Modern Principles and Methodologies*. McGraw Hill.

Gow, G. (2014). Why Are Predictive Marketing Analytics A Problem? *Crimson Marketing*. Retrieved July 6th 2014 from: http://crimsonmarketing.com/predictive-marketing-analytics-problem/

Grant, R. M. (1998). Contemporary Strategy Analysis: Concepts, Techniques, Applications (3rd Ed.). Oxford, UK: Blackwell Publishing.

Grant, R. M. (1996). Toward a knowledge-based theory of the firm. *Strategic Management Journal*, *17*(Winter), 109–122. doi:10.1002/smj.4250171110

Greene, R. H. (1993). *Nov način komunikacije: Praktični nasveti za boljše poslovno in družinsko sporazumevanje*. Ljubljana: Alpha Center.

Gregg, G. S. (2005). *The Middle East: A Cultural Psychology*. Oxford, UK: Oxford University Press.

Grimshaw, J., & Barry, M. (2008). How mature is your internal communication: Empowering the function to demonstrate its strategic value to the organization. *Strategic Communication Management*, *12*(3), 28–29.

Gross, D. (2009). *Fundamentals of Queueing Theory*. New York: John Wiley and Sons.

Grunig, J. E., & Hunt, T. (1984). *Managing Public Relations*. New York: Harcourt Brace Jovanovich College Publishers.

Guangming, Z. (2007). CRM-based customer knowledge management. In *Proceeding of International Conference on Enterprise and Management Innovation*, (pp. 417-421). Academic Press.

Guarda, T., Santos, M., Pinto, F., Augusto, M., & Silva, C. (2013). Business intelligence as a competitive advantage for SMEs. *International Journal of Trade, Economics and Finance, 4*(4), 187–190.

Gürhan-Canli, Z., & Batra, R. (2004). When corporate image affects product evaluations: The moderating role of perceived risk. *JMR, Journal of Marketing Research, 41*(2), 197–205. doi:10.1509/jmkr.41.2.197.28667

Guyon, I., & Elisseeff, A. (2003). An introduction to variable and feature selection. *Journal of Machine Learning Research, 3*, 1157–1182.

Gyöngyi, Z., Garcia-Molina, H., & Pedersen, J. (2004, August). Combating web spam with trustrank. In *Proceedings of the Thirtieth International Conference on Very Large Data Bases* (vol. 30, pp. 576-587). VLDB Endowment.

Habul, A., Piav-Velic, A., & Kremic, E. (2012). *Customer Relationship Management and Business. In Advances in Customer Relationship Management* (pp. 1–30). InTech.

Haddad, R. (2003). Taking the Veil: Reem Haddad on Why Lebanese Women Are Covering Up. *New Internationalist, 360*, 3–12.

Hafeez, K., Keoy, K. H. A., Zairi, M., Hanneman, R., & Koh, S. C. L. (2010). E-supply chain operational and behavioral perspectives: An empirical study of Malaysian SMEs. *International Journal of Production Research, 48*(2), 526–546. doi:10.1080/00207540903175079

Hair, F., Anderson, R., Tatham, R., & Black, W. (1995). *Multivariate Data Analysis with Readings* (4th ed.). London, UK: Prentice-Hall.

Hair, J. F., & Anderson, R. E. (2010). *Multivariate data analysis*. Upper Saddle River, NJ: Prentice Hall.

Hair, J. F. Jr. (2007). Knowledge creation in marketing: The role of predictive analytics. *European Business Review, 19*(4), 303–315. doi:10.1108/09555340710760134

Haley, K. B. (1962). The Solid Transportation Problem. *Operations Research, 11*(4), 448–463. doi:10.1287/opre.10.4.448

Halikias, J., & Panayotopoulou, L. (2003). Chief executive personality and export involvement. *Management Decision, 41*(4), 340–349. doi:10.1108/00251740310468072

Hall, M. A. (1999). *Correlation-based feature selection for machine learning*. (Dissertation). University of Waikato.

Hamaker, C. (1995). Time series circulation data for collection development or: You can't intuit that. *Library Acquisition: Practice and Theory, 19*(2), 191–195. doi:10.1016/0364-6408(95)00019-6

Hamidi, M., Farahmand, K., Sajjadi, S. R., & Nygard, K. E. (2012). A hybrid GRASP-tabu search metaheuristic for a four-layer location-routing problem. *International Journal of Logistics Systems and Management, 12*(3), 267–287. doi:10.1504/IJLSM.2012.047602

Hammoud, J. (2011). Consultative Authority Decision Making: On the Development and Characterization of Arab Corporate Culture. *International Journal of Business and Social Science, 2*, 141–148.

Hamou, R. M., Amine, A., & Rahmani, M. (2012). Visualisation and clustering by 3D cellular automata: Application to unstructured data. *International Journal of Data Mining and Emerging Technologies, 2*(1), 15-25.

Hamou, R. M., Lehireche, A., Lokbani, A. C., & Rahmani, M. (2010, October). Text clustering by 2D cellular automata based on the n-grams. In *Proceedings of Cryptography and Network Security, Data Mining and Knowledge Discovery, E-Commerce & Its Applications and Embedded Systems (CDEE),* (pp. 271-277). IEEE.

Hamou, R. M., Amine, A., & Boudia, A. (2013). A New Meta-Heuristic Based on Social Bees for Detection and Filtering of Spam. *International Journal of Applied Metaheuristic Computing, 4*(3), 15–33. doi:10.4018/ijamc.2013070102

Hamou, R. M., Amine, A., & Lokbani, A. C. (2012). The Social Spiders in the Clustering of Texts: Towards an Aspect of Visual Classification. *International Journal of Artificial Life Research, 3*(3), 1–14. doi:10.4018/jalr.2012070101

Hamou, R. M., Amine, A., & Lokbani, A. C. (2013). Study of Sensitive Parameters of PSO: Application to Clustering of Texts. *International Journal of Applied Evolutionary Computation, 4*(2), 41–55. doi:10.4018/jaec.2013040104

Hamou, R. M., Amine, A., Rahmouni, A., Lokbani, A. C., & Simonet, M. (2013). Modeling of Inclusion by Genetic Algorithms: Application to the Beta-Cyclodextrin and Triphenylphosphine. *International Journal of Chemoinformatics and Chemical Engineering*, *3*(1), 19–36. doi:10.4018/ijcce.2013010103

Hamou, R. M., Lehireche, A., Lokbani, A. C., & Rahmani, M. (2010). Representation of textual documents by the approach wordnet and n-grams for the unsupervised classification (clustering) with 2D cellular automata: A comparative study. *Computer and Information Science*, *3*(3), 240–255.

Hana, H., Kanga, J., & Songb, M. (2009). Two-stage process analysis using the process-based performance measurement framework and business process simulation. *Expert Systems with Applications*, *36*(3), 7080–7086. doi:10.1016/j.eswa.2008.08.035

Hanandeh, R., Aiajlouni, M. I. & Nawafleh, S. A. (2012). The impact of knowledge management system on business intelligence optimization. In *Proceeding of Business Intelligence and Knowledge Economy*, (pp. 1119-1125). Academic Press.

Hand, D. J., & Vinciotti, V. (2003). Choosing k for two-class nearest neighbor classifiers with unbalanced classes. *Pattern Recognition Letters*, *24*(9-10), 1555–1562. doi:10.1016/S0167-8655(02)00394-X

Handen, L. (2000). *Customer relationship management: A strategic imperative in the world of e-business*. New York: Join Wiley & Sons.

Handley, H. A., Zaidi, Z. R., & Levis, A. H. (1999). *The use of simulation models in model driven experimentation*. George Mason University.

Han, J., Kamber, M., & Pei, J. (2011). *Data mining: Concepts and techniques* (3rd ed.). Amsterdam: Elsevier.

Harastani, H., & Al-Turki, M. (1985). *Patients Queuing in Out-Patient Clinics in Riyadh's Public Hospitals*. Riyadh, Saudi Arabia: Institute of Public Administration. (In Arabic)

Härdle, W., Lee, Y. J., Schafer, D., & Yeh, Y. R. (2009). Variable Selection and Oversampling in the Use of Smooth Support Vector Machines for Predicting the Default Risk of Companies. *Journal of Forecasting*, *28*(2), 512–534.

Harnish, V. (2012). *The Greatest Business Decisions of All Time*. New York: Time Home Entertainment.

Harris, P., & Moran, R. (1987). *Managing cultural differences* (2nd ed.). Houston, TX: Gulf Publishing Co.

Hart, G. W. (1992). Nonintrusive appliance load monitoring. *Proceedings of the IEEE*, *80*(12), 1870–1891. doi:10.1109/5.192069

Hart, P. M. (1994). Teacher quality of work life: Integrating work experiences, psychological distress and morale. *Journal of Occupational and Organizational Psychology*, *67*(2), 109–132. doi:10.1111/j.2044-8325.1994.tb00555.x

Hashemi, N., & Hajiheydari, N. (2011), Customer knowledge management framework in E-commerce. In *Proceedings of 2011 International Conference on E-business, Management and Economics*. IACSIT Press.

Haskin, H. N., & Krehbiel, T. C. (2011). Business statistics at the top 50 US business programmes. *Teaching Statistics*, 92–98.

Haykin, S. (2008). *Neural Networks and Learning Machines*. Prentice Hall.

Head, T. C., & Sorenson, P. F. (1993). Cultural values and organizational development: A seven-country study. *Leadership and Organization Development Journal*, *14*(2), 3–7. doi:10.1108/01437739310032656

Hedayat, A., Sloane, N., & Stufken, J. (1999). *Orthogonal Arrays: Theory and Applications*. New York, NY: Springer. doi:10.1007/978-1-4612-1478-6

Heffernan, M. M., & Flood, P. C. (2000). An exploration of the relationship between managerial competencies organizational, characteristic and performance in an Irish organization. *Journal of European Industrial Training*, *24*(2), 128–136. doi:10.1108/03090590010321098

Heizer, J., & Render, B. (2011). *Operations Management* (10th ed.). Upper Saddle River, NJ: Prentice Hall.

Hemachandra, N., & Sahu, P. (2014). *Some Aspects of Estimators for Variance of Normally Distributed Data* (Technical Report). Mumbai, India: Indian Institute of Technology Bombay, Industrial Engineering and Operations Research. Retrieved from http://www.ieor.iitb.ac.in/files/Variance_Estimators_TechReport.pdf

Henderson, J., & McAdam, R. (2003). Adopting a learning-based approach to improve internal communications: A large utility experience. *International Journal of Quality & Reliability Management, 20*(6/7), 774–794. doi:10.1108/02656710310491212

Heymann, P., Koutrika, G., & Garcia-Molina, H. (2007). Fighting spam on social web sites: A survey of approaches and future challenges. *IEEE Internet Computing, 11*(6), 36–45. doi:10.1109/MIC.2007.125

Hibbard, C. (2010). How One Man Used Social Media to Raise $91,000 for Charity. *Social Media Examiner RSS*. Retrieved July 7th 2014 from: http://www.socialmediaexaminer.com/howone-man-used-social-media-to-raise-91000-for-charity/

Hickson, D. J., & Pugh, D. S. (1995). *Management worldwide*. London, UK: Penguin Books.

Hickson, D. J., & Pugh, D. S. (2001). *Management worldwide: Distinctive styles Amid globalization* (2nd ed.). London, UK: Penguin Books.

Hill, C., Loch, K., Straub, D. W., & El-Sheshai, K. (1998). A Qualitative Assessment of Arab Culture and Information Technology Transfer. *Journal of Global Information Management, 6*(3), 29–38. doi:10.4018/jgim.1998070103

Hiller, F., & Lieberman, G. (1990). *Introduction to Operations Research*. New York: Mc Graw-Hill.

Hitchcock, F. L. (1941). The Distribution of a Product from Several Sources to Numerous Localities. *Journal of Mathematics and Physics, 20*, 224–230.

Hoffmann, F., Baesens, B., Mues, C., Gestel, T. V., & Vanthienen, J. (2007). Inferring descriptive and approximate fuzzy rules for credit scoring using evolutionary algorithms. *European Journal of Operational Research, 177*(1), 540–555. doi:10.1016/j.ejor.2005.09.044

Hofstede, G. (2008). Dimensionalizing Cultures: The Hofstede Model in Context. *Online Readings in Psychology and Culture*. Retrieved February 10/2013 from Http://www.ac.wwu.edu/~culture/hofstede.htm

Hofstede, G. (2001). *Culture's Consequences: Comparing Values, Behaviors, Institutions and Organizations Across Nations* (2nd ed.). Thousand Oaks, CA: Sage Publications.

Hofstede, G. (2007). Asian management in the 21st century. *Asia Pacific Journal of Management, 24*(4), 411–420. doi:10.1007/s10490-007-9049-0

Hofstede, G. (2010). The Hofstede model: Applications to global branding and advertising strategy and research. *International Journal of Advertising, 29*(1), 85–110. doi:10.2501/S026504870920104X

Hofstede, G., & Hofstede, G. J. (2004). *Cultures and Organizations: Software for the Mind. Intercultural Cooperation and Its Importance for Survival* (2nd ed.). New York, NY: McGraw-Hill.

Holloway, J., Lewis, J., & Mallory, G. (1995). *Performance measurement and evaluation*. London, UK: Sage.

Holmberg, S. (2000). A system perspective on supply chain measurement. *International Journal of Physical Distribution & Logistics, 30*(10), 847–868. doi:10.1108/09600030010351246

Holte, R. C. (1993). Very simple classification rules perform well on most commonly used datasets. *Machine Learning, 11*(1), 63–90. doi:10.1023/A:1022631118932

Holtz, S. (2004). *Corporate conversations: a guide to crafting effective and appropriate internal communications*. New York: AMACOM.

Hope, J., & Player, S. (2012). *Beyond Performance Management: Why, When, and How to Use 40 Tools and Best Practices for Superior Business Performance*. Harvard Business Review Press.

Hoque, Z., & James, W. (2000). Linking balanced scorecard measures to size and market factors: Impact on organizational performance. *Journal of Management Accounting Research, 12*(1), 1–18. doi:10.2308/jmar.2000.12.1.1

Hoskisson, R. E., Hitt, M. A., Johnson, R. A., & Grossman, W. (2002). Conflicting voices: The effects of institutional ownership heterogeneity and internal governance on corporate innovation strategies. *Academy of Management Journal, 45*(4), 697–716. doi:10.2307/3069305

Ho, T. F., Shyu, S. J., & Wu, Y. L. (2008). Material acquisitions in academic libraries. In *Proceedings of Asia-Pacific Services Computing Conference (APSCC)*, (pp. 1465-1470). IEEE.

Hotho, A., Jäschke, R., Schmitz, C., & Stumme, G. (2006). *Information retrieval in folksonomies: Search and ranking*. Springer Berlin Heidelberg.

Hough, J. R., & White, M. A. (2003). Environmental dynamism and strategic decision-making rationality: An examination at the decision level. *Strategic Management Journal*, 24(5), 481–489. doi:10.1002/smj.303

House, R. J., Hanges, P. J., Javidan, M., Dorfman, P. W., & Gupta, V. (2004). *Leadership, Culture, and Organizations: The GLOBE Study of 62 Societies*. Thousand Oaks, CA: Sage.

Hoving, R. (2007). Information technology leadership challenges - past, present, and future. *Information Systems Management*, 24(2), 147–153. doi:10.1080/10580530701221049

Howell, J. M., & Higgins, C. A. (1990). Champions of technological innovation. *Administrative Science Quarterly*, 35(2), 317–341. doi:10.2307/2393393

Hox, J. (2002). *Multilevel analysis: Techniques and applications*. Mahwah, NJ: Lawrence Erlbaum Associates.

Hsieh, D. A. (1989). Testing for nonlinear dependence in daily foreign exchange rates. *The Journal of Business*, 62(3), 339–368. doi:10.1086/296466

Hsieh, N. C. (2004). An integrated data mining and behavioral scoring model for analyzing bank customers. *Expert Systems with Applications*, 27(4), 623–633. doi:10.1016/j.eswa.2004.06.007

Hsieh, N. C. (2005). Hybrid mining approach in the design of credit scoring models. *Expert Systems with Applications*, 28(4), 655–665. doi:10.1016/j.eswa.2004.12.022

Hsieh, N. C., & Hung, L. P. (2010). A data driven ensemble classifier for credit scoring analysis. *Expert Systems with Applications*, 37(1), 534–545. doi:10.1016/j.eswa.2009.05.059

Huang, C. L., Chen, M. C., & Wang, C. J. (2007). Credit scoring with a data mining approach based on support vector machines. *Expert Systems with Applications*, 33(4), 847–856. doi:10.1016/j.eswa.2006.07.007

Huang, J. J., Tzeng, G. H., & Ong, C. S. (2006). Two-stage genetic programming (2SGP) for the credit scoring model. *Applied Mathematics and Computation*, 174(2), 1039–1053. doi:10.1016/j.amc.2005.05.027

Huang, Z., Chen, H., Hsu, C. J., Chen, W. H., & Wu, S. (2004). Credit rating analysis with support vector machines and neural networks: A market comparative study. *Decision Support Systems*, 37(4), 543–558. doi:10.1016/S0167-9236(03)00086-1

Huber, G. P. (1990). A theory of the effects of an advanced information technologies on organization designs intelligence and decision making. *Academy of Management Review*, 15, 47–71.

Hu, M. Y., Zhang, G. P., Jiang, C. X., & Patuwo, B. E. (1999). A cross-validation analysis of neural network out-of-sample performance in exchange rate forecasting. *Decision Sciences*, 30(1), 197–216. doi:10.1111/j.1540-5915.1999.tb01606.x

Hussain, A., Ghazali, R., & Al-Jumeily, D. (2006). Dynamic ridge polynomial neural network for financial time series prediction. In Proceedings of IEEE International Conference on Innovation in Information Technology (IIT06). Dubai, UAE: IEEE.

Hutton, R., & Klein, G. (1999). Expert decision making. *Systems Engineering*, 2(1), 32–45. doi:10.1002/(SICI)1520-6858(1999)2:1<32::AID-SYS3>3.0.CO;2-P

Huynh, T. (2011). Orthogonal array experiment in systems engineering and architecting. *Systems Engineering*, 14(2), 208–222. doi:10.1002/sys.20172

Huysmans, J., Baesens, B., Vanthienen, J., & Gestel, T. (2006). Failure prediction with self organizing maps. *Expert Systems with Applications*, 30(3), 479–487. doi:10.1016/j.eswa.2005.10.005

IBM. (2012). *Bringing Big Data to the Enterprise*. Retrieved from http://www-01.ibm.com/software/data/bigdata/

IDC. (2012, March). *U.S. small and medium-sized business 2012–2016 forecast: Sizing the SMB markets for PCs and peripherals, systems and storage, networking equipment, packaged software, and IT services.* IDC.

Ince, H., & Aktan, B. (2009). A Comparison of Data mining Techniques for Credit Scoring in Banking: A managerial Perspective. *Journal of Business Economics and Management, 10*(3), 233–240. doi:10.3846/1611-1699.2009.10.233-240

INFORMS Analytics. (n.d.). Retrieved from https://www.informs.org/Sites/Getting-Started-With-Analytics/What-Analytics-Is

Inmon, H. (1992). *Building the Data Warehouse.* New York: John Wiley & Sons, Inc.

Iqbal, A. (2011). Creativity and innovation in Saudi Arabia: An overview. *Innovation: Management. Policy & Practice, 13*(3), 391–406. doi:10.5172/impp.2011.13.3.376

Ireland, R., & Bruce, R. (2000). CPFR: Only the beginning of collaboration. *Supply Chain Management Review, 4*(4), 80–89.

Irish Social Science Data Archive. (2014). *Data from the Commission for Energy Regulation.* Retrieved Mar. 4 2014 from http://www.ucd.ie/issda/data/commission-forenergyregulationcer/

Isaaks, E. H., & Srivastava, R. M. (1989). *An Introduction to Applied Geostatistics.* New York: Oxford University Press.

Islam, M. J., Wu, Q. M. J., Ahmadi, M., & Sid-Ahmed, M. A. (2007). *Investigating the Performance of Naive-Bayes Classifiers and K-Nearest Neighbor Classifiers.* Paper presented at the International Conference on Convergence Information Technology. New York, NY. doi:10.1109/ICCIT.2007.148

Ittner, C. D., & Larcker, D. F. (2003). Coming up short on nonfinancial performance measures. *Harvard Business Review, 81*(11), 88–98. PMID:14619154

Ittner, C. D., Larcker, D. F., & Randall, T. (2003). Performance implications of strategic performance measurement in financial service firms. *Accounting, Organizations and Society, 28*(7-8), 715–741. doi:10.1016/S0361-3682(03)00033-3

Jacoby, J., & Szybillo, G. J. (1995). Consumer research in FTC versus Kraft (1991): A case of heads we win, tails you lose? *Journal of Public Policy & Marketing,* 1–14.

Jacoby, J., Szybillo, G. J., & Busato-Schach, J. (1977). Information acquisition behavior in brand choice situations. *The Journal of Consumer Research, 3*(4), 209–216. doi:10.1086/208669

Jang, J.-S. R., Sun, C.-T., & Mizutani, E. (1997). *Neuro-Fuzzy and Soft Computing: A Computational Approach to Learning and Machine Intelligence.* Prentice-Hall.

Jarrar, Y. F., & Zairi, M. (2001). Future trends in benchmarking for competitive advantage: A global survey. *Total Quality Management, 12*(7-8), 906–912. doi:10.1080/09544120100000014

Jarvis, C. B. (1998). An exploratory investigation of consumers' evaluations of external information sources in prepurchase search. *Advances in Consumer Research. Association for Consumer Research (U. S.), 25*(1), 446–452.

Jasinsky, D., Bravo, E., Olsen, A., Solano, J., & Rodriguez, K. (2014). *You Tube.* Final Deliverable for Spring 2014 Semester BMGT 4381 (section 1) Course. Presented May 8th, 2014 (Unpublished).

Jayashree, S., & Shojace, S. (2011). A critical analysis customer relationship management from strategic perspective. In *Proceedings of 2010 International Conference on E-business Management and Economics.* IACSIT Press.

Jiang, P., Jones, D. B., & Javie, S. (2008). How third-party certification programs relate to consumer trust in online transactions: An exploratory study. *Psychology and Marketing, 25*(9), 839–858. doi:10.1002/mar.20243

Jiao, Y., Syau, Y. R., & Lee, E. S. (2007). Modelling credit rating by fuzzy adaptive network. *Mathematical and Computer Modelling, 45*(5-6), 717–731. doi:10.1016/j.mcm.2005.11.016

Jimenez, F., & Verdegay, J. L. (1998). Uncertain Solid Transportation Problems. *Fuzzy Sets and Systems, 100*(1-3), 45–57. doi:10.1016/S0165-0114(97)00164-4

John, G. H., & Langley, P. (1995, August). Estimating continuous distributions in Bayesian classifiers. In *Proceedings of the Eleventh Conference on Uncertainty in Artificial Intelligence* (pp. 338-345). Morgan Kaufmann Publishers Inc.

Johnson, J. (2012). *Big Data + Big Analytics = Big Opportunity*. Financial Executive International.

Jones, L. W. (1993). *High Speed, Management: Time-Based Strategies for Managers and Organizations*. San Francisco, CA: Jossey-Bass.

Jones, R. E., Jacobs, L. W., & Spijker, W. V. (1992). Strategic decision processes in international firms. *Management International Review, 32*, 219–237.

Joreskog, K. G., & Sorbom, D. (2004). *LISREL 8.7 for Windows, (computer software)*. Lincolnwood, IL: Scientific Software International INC.

Jo, S., & Shim, S. W. (2005). Paradigm shift of employee communication: The effect of management communication on trusting relationships. *Public Relations Review, 31*(5), 277–280. doi:10.1016/j.pubrev.2005.02.012

Joshi, P. L. (2001). The international diffusion of new management accounting practices: The case of India. *Journal of International Accounting, Auditing & Taxation, 10*(1), 85–109. doi:10.1016/S1061-9518(01)00037-4

Jourdan, Z., Rainer, R. K., & Marshall, T. E. (2008). Business intelligence: An analysis of the literature. *Information Systems Management, 25*(2), 121–131. doi:10.1080/10580530801941512

Journel, A. G., & Rao, S. E. (1996). Deriving conditional distribution from ordinary kriging. Stanford Center for Reservoir Forcasting, Stanford University Report.

Judge, W. Q., & Miller, A. (1991). Antecedents and outcomes of decision speed in different environmental contexts. *Academy of Management Journal, 34*(2), 449–463. doi:10.2307/256451 PMID:10111313

Jugdev, K., & Müller, R. (2005). A retrospective look at our evolving understanding of project success. *Project Management Journal, 36*(4), 19–31.

Justinek, G., & Sedej, T. (2011). Knowledge sharing as a part of internal communication within internationalized companies. In *Knowledge as business opportunity: Proceedings of the Management, Knowledge and Learning International Conference 2011*. Celje: International School for Social and Business Studies.

Kabasakal, H., Dastmalchian, A., Karacay, G., & Bayraktar, S. (2012). Leadership and culture in the MENA region: An analysis of the GLOBE project. *Journal of World Business, 47*(4), 519–529. doi:10.1016/j.jwb.2012.01.005

Kadam, A., & Lenk, P. (2008). Bayesian inference for issuer heterogeneity in credit ratings migration. *Journal of Banking & Finance, 32*(10), 2267–2274. doi:10.1016/j.jbankfin.2007.12.043

Kahneman, D., & Tversky, A. (1979). Prospect theory: An analysis of decision under risk. *Econometrica, 47*(2), 263–291. doi:10.2307/1914185

Kalaian, S. A. (2008). Multilevel Modeling Methods for E-Collaboration Data. In N. Kock (Ed.), *Encyclopedia of E-Collaboration* (pp. 450–456). Hershey, PA: IGI Global.

Kalaian, S. A., & Kasim, R. M. (2006). Hierarchical Linear Modeling. In L. Salkind (Ed.), *Encyclopedia of Measurement and Statistics* (pp. 433–436). Thousand Oaks, CA: SAGE.

Kalakota, R. (2011). *Gartner says – BI and Analytics a $12.2 Bln market*. Available at http://practicalanalytics.wordpress.com/2011/04/24/gartner-says-bi-and-analytics-a-10-5-bln-market/

Kalla, H. (2005). Integrated internal communications: A multidisciplinary perspective. *Corporate communication. International Journal (Toronto, Ont.), 10*(4), 302–314.

Kalleberg, A. L., & Rognes, J. (2000). Employment Relations in Norway: Some Dimensions and Correlates. *Journal of Organizational Behavior, 21*(3), 315–335. doi:10.1002/(SICI)1099-1379(200005)21:3<315::AID-JOB23>3.0.CO;2-1

Kallenberg, O. (2002). *Foundations of modern probability* (2nd ed.). New York: Springer Verlag. doi:10.1007/978-1-4757-4015-8

Kanich, C., Kreibich, C., Levchenko, K., Enright, B., Voelker, G. M., Paxson, V., & Savage, S. (2008, October). Spamalytics: An empirical analysis of spam marketing conversion. In *Proceedings of the 15th ACM Conference on Computer and Communications Security* (pp. 3-14). ACM. doi:10.1145/1455770.1455774

Kao, C., Chang, H. C., & Lin, C. H. (2003). Decision support for the academic library acquisition budget allocation via circulation database mining. *Information Processing & Management*, *39*(1), 133–147. doi:10.1016/S0306-4573(02)00019-5

Kapin, A. (2012). *Infographic a peek inside donation trends and why we support charities*. Retrieved July 7th 2014 from: http://www.frogloop.com/care2blog/2012/3/23/infographic-2012-nonprofit-benchmarks.html

Kaplan, R. S., & Norton, D. P. (1992). The balanced scorecard: Measures that drive performance. *Harvard Business Review*, *70*(1), 71–79. PMID:10119714

Kaplan, R. S., & Norton, D. P. (1996). *The balanced scorecard: Translating strategy into action*. Boston, MA: Harvard Business School Press.

Kaplan, R. S., & Norton, D. P. (1996). Using the balanced scorecard as a strategic management system. *Harvard Business Review*, *74*(1), 75–85.

Kaplan, R. S., & Norton, D. P. (2004). *Strategy maps: Converting intangible assets into tangible outcomes*. Boston, MA: Harvard Business School Press.

Kaplan, R. S., & Norton, D. P. (2008). Mastering the management system. *Harvard Business Review*, *86*(1), 63–77. PMID:18271319

Kaplan, S. N., & Minton, B. A. (1994). Outside activity in Japanese companies: Determinants and managerial implications. *Journal of Financial Economics*, *36*(2), 225–258. doi:10.1016/0304-405X(94)90025-6

Karl, W. (1997). Knowledge management: An Introduction and Perspective. *Journal of Knowledge Management*, *1*(1), 6–14. doi:10.1108/13673279710800682

Kass, L. (2013, May 07). *Survey results reveal top five reasons small businesses are turning to cloud file management*. Retrieved from http://www.sugarsync.com/blog/2013/05/07/survey-results-reveal-top-fivereasons-small-business-are-turning-to-cloud-file-management/

Katos, A. V. (2010). The influence of information and communication technologies on enabling trade: A cross-country investigation. *Journal of Information Technology Impact*, *10*, 15–24.

Kavoossi, M. (2000). *The Globalization of Business and the Middle East: Opportunities and Constraints*. Westport, CT: Quorum Books.

Keller, J. M., Gray, M. R., & Givens, J. A. (1985). A fuzzy K-nearest neighbor algorithm. *IEEE Transactions on Systems, Man, and Cybernetics*, *15*(4), 580–585. doi:10.1109/TSMC.1985.6313426

Kelloway, E. K. (1998). *Using LISREL for structural equation modelling: a researcher's guide*. Newbury Park, CA: SAGE Publications.

Kelman, H. C., & Hovland, C. I. (1953). Reinstatement" of the communicator in delayed measurement of opinion change. *Journal of Abnormal and Social Psychology*, *48*(3), 327–335. doi:10.1037/h0061861 PMID:13061165

Kennerley, M., & Neely, A. (2003). Measuring performance in a changing business environment. *International Journal of Operations & Production Management*, *23*(2), 213–229. doi:10.1108/01443570310458465

Kenny, G. (2005). *Strategic planning and performance management: Develop and measure a winning strategy*. London, UK: Butterworth-Heinemann/Elsevier.

Kepner-Tregoe, G. (2001). Hurry up and decide. *Business Week*, *3732*, 16.

Ketikidis, P. H., Hayes, O. P., Lazuras, L., Gunasekaran, A., & Koh, S. C. L. (2013). Environmental practices and performance and their relationships among Kosovo construction companies: A framework for analysis in transition economies. *International Journal of Services and Operations Management*, *15*(1), 115–130. doi:10.1504/IJSOM.2013.050565

Khalifa, A. S. (2001). *Towards and Islamic Foundation of Strategic Business Management*. Kuala Lumpur, Malaysia: International Islamic University Malaysia.

Khalil, O. E. M., & Mady, T. (2005). IT Adoption and Industry Type: Some Evidence from Kuwaiti Manufacturing Companies. *International Journal of Enterprise Information Systems*, *1*(4), 39–55. doi:10.4018/jeis.2005100103

Khaliq, A. (2009). Leadership and work motivation from the cross cultural perspective. *International Journal of Commerce and Management*, *19*(1), 72–84. doi:10.1108/10569210910939681

Khashman, A. (2010). Neural networks for credit risk evaluation: Investigation of different neural models and learning schemes. *Expert Systems with Applications, 37*(9), 6233–6239. doi:10.1016/j.eswa.2010.02.101

Khatri, N., & Alvin, H. N. (2000). The role of intuition in strategic decision making. *Human Relations, 53*(1), 57–86. doi:10.1177/0018726700531004

Kiefer, J., & Wolfowitz, J. (1952). Stochastic estimation of the maximum of a regression function. *Annals of Mathematical Statistics, 23*(3), 462–466. doi:10.1214/aoms/1177729392

Kimbal, R., & Ross, M. (2002). *The Data Warehouse Toolkit: The Complete Guide to Dimensional Modeling.* New York: John Wiley & Sons, Inc.

Kim, H. D., Lee, I., & Lee, C. K. (2013). Building Web 2.0 enterprises: A study of small and medium enterprises in the United States. *International Small Business Journal, 31*(2), 156–174. doi:10.1177/0266242611409785

Kim, H. S., & Sohn, S. Y. (2010). Support vector machines for default prediction of SMEs based on technology credit. *European Journal of Operational Research, 201*(3), 838–846. doi:10.1016/j.ejor.2009.03.036

Kim, K. J., & Han, I. (2000). Genetic algorithms approach to feature discretization in artificial neural networks for the prediction of stock price index. *Expert Systems with Applications, 19*(2), 125–132. doi:10.1016/S0957-4174(00)00027-0

Kim, Y., Kim, N., & Jeong, S. R. (2012). Stock-index Invest Model Using News Big Data Opinion Mining. *Journal of Intelligent Information Systems, 18*(2), 143–156.

Kim, Y., Song, K., & Lee, J. (1993). Determinants of technological innovation in the small firms of Korea. *R & D Management, 23*(3), 215–226. doi:10.1111/j.1467-9310.1993.tb00824.x

Kini, R. B., & Basaviah, S. (2013). Critical Success Factors in the Implementation of Enterprise Resource Planning Systems in Small and Midsize Businesses: Microsoft Navision Implementation. *International Journal of Enterprise Information Systems, 9*(1), 97–117. doi:10.4018/jeis.2013010106

Kirkos, E., Spathis, C., & Manolopoulos, Y. (2007). Data Mining techniques for the detection of fraudulent financial statements. *Expert Systems with Applications, 32*(4), 995–1003. doi:10.1016/j.eswa.2006.02.016

Kitchen, J. P. (1997). *Public relationship: Principles and Practice.* London: International Thomson Business Press.

Kitchen, J. P., & Daly, F. (2002). Internal communication during the change management. *Corporate communications. International Journal (Toronto, Ont.), 7*(1), 46–53.

Klatt, T., Schlafke, M., & Moller, K. (2011). Integrating business analytics into strategic planning for better performance. *The Journal of Business Strategy, 32*(6), 30–39. doi:10.1108/02756661111180113

Kleijnen, J., & Rubinstein, R. (1996). Optimization and sensitivity analysis of computer simulation models by score function method. *European Journal of Operational Research, 88*(3), 413–427. doi:10.1016/0377-2217(95)00107-7

Kleinberg, J. M. (1999). Authoritative sources in a hyperlinked environment. *Journal of the ACM, 46*(5), 604–632. doi:10.1145/324133.324140

Klein, L. R., & Ford, G. T. (2003). Consumer search for information in the digital age: An empirical study of prepurchase search for automobiles. *Journal of Interactive Marketing, 17*(3), 29–49. doi:10.1002/dir.10058

Kloot, L., & Martin, J. (2000). Strategic performance management: A balanced approach to performance management issues in local government. *Management Accounting Research, 11*(2), 231–251. doi:10.1006/mare.2000.0130

Knievel, J. E., Wicht, H., & Connaway, L. S. (2011). Use of circulation statistics and interlibrary loan data in collection management. *College & Research Libraries, 67*(1), 35–49. doi:10.5860/crl.67.1.35

Knuth, D. (2011). *The Art of Computer Programming.* New York: Addison-Wesley Professional.

Kodama, M. (2005). Customer value creation through knowledge creation with customers: Case studies of IT and multimedia business in Japan. *International Journal of Innovation and Learning, 2*(4), 357–385. doi:10.1504/IJIL.2005.006661

Kogut, B., & Zander, U. (1992). Knowledge of the firm, combinative capabilities, and the replication of technology. *Organization Science*, *3*(3), 383–397. doi:10.1287/orsc.3.3.383

Kopalle, P. K., & Lehmann, D. R. (1995). The effects of advertised and observed quality on expectations about new product quality. *JMR, Journal of Marketing Research*, *32*(3), 280–290. doi:10.2307/3151981

Kopalle, P. K., & Lehmann, D. R. (2006). Setting quality expectations when entering a market: What should the promise be? *Marketing Science*, *25*(1), 8–24. doi:10.1287/mksc.1050.0122

Kovacic, A. (2007). Benchmarking the Slovenian competitiveness by system of indicators. *Benchmarking: An International Journal*, *14*(5), 553–574. doi:10.1108/14635770710819254

Kozan, M. K. (1993). Cultural and industrialization level influences on leadership attitudes for Turkish managers. *International Studies of Management & Organization*, *23*, 7–17.

Kraft, K. (1990). Are product- and process-innovations independent of each other? *Applied Economics*, *22*(8), 1029–1038. doi:10.1080/00036849000000132

Kreps, G. L. (1990). *Organizational Communication: Theory and Practice* (2nd ed.). New York: Longman.

Kuhns, M., & Johnson, K. (2013). *Applied Predictive Modeling*. New York: Springer. doi:10.1007/978-1-4614-6849-3

Kulkarni, S., Simon, S. P., & Sundareswaran, K. (2013). A spiking neural network (SNN) forecast engine for short-term electrical load forecasting. *Applied Soft Computing*, *13*(8), 3628–3635. doi:10.1016/j.asoc.2013.04.007

Kumar, K., & Bhattacharya, S. (2006). Artificial neural network vs linear discriminant analysis in credit ratings forecast: A comparative study of prediction performances. *Review of Accounting and Finance*, *5*(3), 216–227. doi:10.1108/14757700610686426

Kumar, P., Shankar, R., & Yadav, S. S. (2011). Global supplier selection and order allocation using FQFD and MOLP. *International Journal of Logistics Systems and Management*, *9*(1), 43–68. doi:10.1504/IJLSM.2011.040059

Kurzweil, R. (2005). *The singularity is near*. New York: Viking.

Kuznetsky, D. (2010). *What is big data?*. Academic Press.

La Forme, L., Genoulaz, F. A. G., & Campagne, J. P. (2007). A framework to analyze collaborative performance. *Computers in Industry*, *58*(7), 687–697. doi:10.1016/j.compind.2007.05.007

Lab, Y. N. (2013). YouTube playbook guide. *YouTube*. Retrieved July 6th 2014 from: http://static.googleusercontent.com/media/www.youtube.com/en/us/yt/advertise/medias/pdfs/playbook-for-good.pdf

Laha, A. (2007). Building contextual classifiers by integrating fuzzy rule based classification technique and k-nn method for credit scoring. *Advanced Engineering Informatics*, *21*(3), 281–291. doi:10.1016/j.aei.2006.12.004

Lahmiri, S. (2014). Practical machine learning in financial market trend prediction. In *Analytical approaches to strategic decision-making: Interdisciplinary considerations*. Hershey, PA: IGI-Global. doi:10.4018/978-1-4666-5958-2.ch010

Lahmiri, S., Boukadoum, M., & Chartier, S. (2014a). Exploring Information Categories and Artificial Neural Networks Numerical Algorithms in S&P500 Trend Prediction: A Comparative Study. *International Journal of Strategic Decision Sciences*, *5*(1), 76–94. doi:10.4018/IJSDS.2014010105

Lahmiri, S., Boukadoum, M., & Chartier, S. (2014b). (in press). A Supervised Classification System of Financial Data Based on Wavelet Packet and Neural Networks. *International Journal of Strategic Decision Sciences*.

Lahsasna, A., Ainon, R. N., & Wah, T. Y. (2008). *Credit Risk Evaluation Decision Modeling Through Optimized Fuzzy Classifier*. Paper presented at the International Symposium on Information Technology, ITSim. New York, NY. doi:10.1109/ITSIM.2008.4631606

Laitinen, E. K. (1999). Predicting a corporate credit analyst's risk estimate by logistic and linear models. *International Review of Financial Analysis*, *8*(2), 97–121. doi:10.1016/S1057-5219(99)00012-5

Lammers, J. C., & Barbour, J. B. (2006). An Institutional Theory of Organizational Communication. *Communication Theory, 16*(3), 356–377. doi:10.1111/j.1468-2885.2006.00274.x

Laney, D. (2001). *3D data management: Controlling data volume, velocity and variety.* Retrieved November 1, 2013 from http://blogs.gartner.com/doug-laney/files/2012/01/ad949-3D-Data-Management-Controlling-Data-Volume-Velocity-and-Variety.pdf

Langley, A. (1999). Strategies for theorizing from process data. *Academy of Management Review, 24*(4), 691–710.

Lau, C. M., & Woodman, R. W. (1995). Understanding organizational change: A schematic perspective. *Academy of Management Journal, 38*(2), 537–554. doi:10.2307/256692

Laurent, A. (1983). The Cultural Diversity of Western Conceptions of Management. *International Studies of Management & Organization, 13*, 75–96.

Lawson, R., Stratton, W., & Hatch, T. (2003). The benefits of a scorecard system. *CMA Management, 77*(4), 24–26.

Le Dain, M. A., Calvi, R., & Cheriti, S. (2011). Measuring supplier performance in collaborative design: Proposition of a framework. *R & D Management, 41*(1), 61–79. doi:10.1111/j.1467-9310.2010.00630.x

L'Ecuyer, P. (1995). Note: On the interchange of derivative and expectation for likelihood derivative estimation. *Management Science, 41*(4), 738–748. doi:10.1287/mnsc.41.4.738

Lee, J. (2014). Facebook Posts See More Engagement After Hours, Weekends [Study]. *ClickZ.* Retrieved July 7th 2014 from: http://www.clickz.com/clickz/news/2349587/facebook-posts-see-more-engagement-after-hours-weekends-study

Lee, T. S., & Chen, I. F. (2005). A two-stage hybrid credit scoring model using artificial neural networks and multivariate adaptive regression splines. *Expert Systems with Applications, 28*(4), 743–752. doi:10.1016/j.eswa.2004.12.031

Lee, T. S., Chiu, C. C., Chou, Y. C., & Lu, C. J. (2006). Mining the customer credit using classification and regression tree and multivariate adaptive regression splines. *Computational Statistics & Data Analysis, 50*(4), 1113–1130. doi:10.1016/j.csda.2004.11.006

Lee, T. S., Chiu, C. C., Lu, C. J., & Chen, I. F. (2002). Credit scoring using the hybrid neural discriminant technique. *Expert Systems with Applications, 23*(3), 245–254. doi:10.1016/S0957-4174(02)00044-1

Lengel, R., & Daft, R. L. (1988). The selection of communication media as an executive skill. *The Academy of Management Executive, 11*(3), 225–232. doi:10.5465/AME.1988.4277259

Lenzerini, M. (2002). Data Integration: A Theoretical Perspective. In *Proceedings of the Symposium on Principles of Database Systems (PODS 2002)*. PODS.

Lev, B., & Radhakrishnan, S. (2003). The measurement of firm-specific organizational capital. *NBER Working Paper #9581.*

Levy, M., Loebbecke, C., & Powel, P. (2001). SMEs, CO-Opetition and Knowledge Sharing: The IS Role. In *Proceedings of the 9th European Conference on Information Systems*. Academic Press.

Levy, M., & Powell, P. (2004). *Strategies for growth in SMEs: The role of information and information systems.* Oxford, UK: Butterworth-Heinemann.

Lewin, A. Y., & Stephens, C. U. (1994). CEO attributes as determinants of organization design: An integrated model. *Organization Studies, 15*(2), 183–212. doi:10.1177/017084069401500202

Lewis, L. K. (1999). Disseminating information and soliciting input during planned organizational change: Implementers' targets, sources and channels for communicating. *Management Communication Quarterly, 13*(1), 43–75. doi:10.1177/0893318999131002

Li, F. C. (2009). *Comparison of the Primitive Classifiers without Features Selection in Credit Scoring.* Paper presented at the International Conference on Management and Service Science. New York, NY. doi:10.1109/ICMSS.2009.5302730

Li, F. C. (2009). *The Hybrid Credit Scoring Model based on KNN Classifier*. Paper presented at the Sixth International Conference on Fuzzy Systems and Knowledge Discovery. New York, NY.

Liang, Y., & Xin, H. (2009). *Application of Discretization in the Use of Logistic Financial Rating*. Paper presented at the International Conference on Business Intelligence and Financial Engineering. New York, NY. doi:10.1109/BIFE.2009.90

Liautaud, R., & Hammond, M. (2002). *E-business intelligence: Turning information into knowledge into profit*. New York: McGraw-Hill.

Library Congress Reference. (2014). Retrieved from http://en.wikipedia.org/wiki/Library_of_Congress_Classification

Liebowitz, J. (2005). Linking social network analysis with the analytical hierarchy process for knowledge mapping in organizations. *Journal of Knowledge Management, 9*(1), 76–86. doi:10.1108/13673270510582974

Liebowitz, J. (Ed.). (2013). *Big data and business analytics*. Boca Raton, FL: CRC Press/Taylor & Francis. doi:10.1201/b14700

Li, H., Sun, J., & Wu, J. (2010). Predicting business failure using classification and regression tree: An empirical comparison with popular classical statistical methods and top classification mining methods. *Expert Systems with Applications, 37*(8), 5895–5904. doi:10.1016/j.eswa.2010.02.016

Lima, R. H. P., Guerrini, F. M., & Carpinetti, L. C. R. (2011). Performance measurement in collaborative networks: A proposal of performance indicators for the manufacturing industry. *International Journal of Business Excellence, 4*(1), 61–79. doi:10.1504/IJBEX.2011.037249

Linke, A., & Zerfass, A. (2011). Internal communication and innovation culture: Developing a change framework. *Journal of Communication Management, 15*(4), 332–348. doi:10.1108/13632541111183361

Lin, S. L. (2009). A new two-stage hybrid approach of credit risk in banking industry. *Expert Systems with Applications, 36*(4), 8333–8341. doi:10.1016/j.eswa.2008.10.015

Li, S., Ragu-Nathan, B., Ragu-Nathan, T., & Subba Rao, S. (2006). The impact of supply chain management practices on competitive advantage and organizational performance. *Omega, 34*(2), 107–124. doi:10.1016/j.omega.2004.08.002

Li, T., & Calantone, R. J. (1998). The impact of market knowledge competence on new product advantage: Conceptualization and empirical examination. *Journal of Marketing, 62*(4), 13–29. doi:10.2307/1252284

Liu, K., Lai, K. K., & Guu, S. M. (2009). *Dynamic Credit Scoring on Consumer Behavior using Fuzzy Markov Model*. Paper presented at the Fourth International Multi-Conference on Computing in the Global Information Technology. New York, NY. doi:10.1109/ICCGI.2009.42

Liu, T.-R., Gerlow, M. E., & Irwin, S. H. (1994). The performance of alternative VAR models in forecasting exchange rates. *International Journal of Forecasting, 10*(3), 419–433. doi:10.1016/0169-2070(94)90071-X

Li, X. S., & Guo, Y. H. (2006). Personal credit scoring models on naive Bayesian classifier. *Computer Engineering and Applications, 42*(1), 197–201.

Li, Y. H., Huang, J. W., & Tsai, M. T. (2009). Entrepreneurial orientation and firm performance: The role of knowledge creation process. *Industrial Marketing Management, 38*(4), 440–449. doi:10.1016/j.indmarman.2008.02.004

Longe, O. B. (2011). On the use of Imagebased Spam Mails as Carriers for Covert Data Transmission. Computer & Information Systems Journal, 15(1).

Lopez, V., Martinez, C., Rowell, E., Rodriguez, A., Speakmon, A., & Torres, A. (2014). *Twitter*. Final Deliverable for Spring 2014 Semester BMGT 4381 (section 1) Course. Presented May 8th, 2014 (Unpublished).

Lopez, R. F. (2007). Modeling of insurers' rating determinants. An application of machine learning techniques and statistical models. *European Journal of Operational Research, 183*(2), 1488–1512. doi:10.1016/j.ejor.2006.09.103

Luna-Arocas, R., & Camps, J. (2008). A model of high performance work practices and turnover intentions. *Personnel Review, 37*(1), 26–46. doi:10.1108/00483480810839950

Luo, J. h., & Lei, H. y. (2008). *Empirical study of corporation credit default probability based on Logit model.* Paper presented at the Wireless Communications, Networking and Mobile Computing. New York, NY. doi:10.1109/WiCom.2008.2276

Luo, S. T., Cheng, B. W., & Hsieh, C. H. (2009). Prediction model building with clustering-launched classification and support vector machines in credit scoring. *Expert Systems with Applications*, *36*(4), 7562–7566. doi:10.1016/j.eswa.2008.09.028

Luss, R., & Nyce, S. A. (2004). *Connecting Organizational Communication to Financial Performance: The Methodology Behind the 2003/2004 Communication ROI Study.* Retrieved April 30, 2007, from http://www.watsonwyatt.com/research/reports.asp

Lustig, I., Dietrich, B., Johnson, C., & Dziekan, C. (2010). *The Analytics Journey. Retrieved from analyticsmagazine.com*

Lydon, S. (2006). *Common Sense in a Changing world: Ipsos MORI Employee Relationship Management.* Retrieved may 15, 2011, from http://www.ipsos-mori.com/_assets/erm/common-sense-in-a-changing-world.pdf

Lyn, C. T. (2000). A survey of credit and behavioural scoring: Forecasting financial risk of lending to consumers. *International Journal of Forecasting*, *16*(2), 149–172. doi:10.1016/S0169-2070(00)00034-0

Lynn, S. (2013, June 4). Small business cloud myths: Busted! *PC Magazine*. Retrieved from http://www.pcmag.com/article2/0,2817,2419823,00.asp

Ma, R. w., & Tang, C. y. (2007). Building up Default Predicting Model based on Logistic Model and Misclassification Loss. *Systems Engineering - Theory & Practice, 27*(8).

MacMillan, D. (2009). *Netflix, AT&T are Real Winners of Netflix Prize.* Available at http://www.businessweek.com/the_thread/techbeat/archives/2009/09/netflix_att_are.html

Madden, S. (2012). From Databases to Big Data. *IEEE Internet Computing*, *16*(3), 4–6. doi:10.1109/MIC.2012.50

Madhavan, J., Bernstein, P. A., & Rahm, E. (2001). Generic Schema Matching With Cupid. In *Proceedings of the International Conference on Very Large Data Bases (VLDB 2001).* VLDB.

Mahapatra, D. R., Roy, S. K., & Biswal, M. P. (2010). Stochastic Based on Multi-objective Transportation Problems Involving Normal Randomness. *Advanced Modeling and Optimization*, *12*(2), 205–223.

Mahapatra, D. R., Roy, S. K., & Biswal, M. P. (2011). Computation of Multi-objective Probabilistic Transportation Problems Involving Normal Distribution with Joint Constraints. *The Journal of Fuzzy Mathematics*, *19*(4), 865–876.

Mahapatra, D. R., Roy, S. K., & Biswal, M. P. (2013). Multi-choice stochastic transportation problem involving extreme value distribution. *Applied Mathematical Modelling*, *37*(4), 2230–2240. doi:10.1016/j.apm.2012.04.024

Maire, J., Bronet, V., & Pillet, M. (2005). A typology of best practice for a benchmarking process. *Benchmarking: An International Journal*, *12*(1), 45–60. doi:10.1108/14635770510582907

Maisel, L. S., & Cokins, G. (2014). *Predictive Business Analytics: Forward Looking Capabilities to Improve Business Performance.* Hoboken, NJ: John Wiley & Sons, Inc.

Majhi, B., Rout, M., Majhi, R., Panda, G., & Fleming, P. J. (2012). New robust forecasting models for exchange rates prediction. *Expert Systems with Applications*, *39*(16), 12658–12670. doi:10.1016/j.eswa.2012.05.017

Majhi, R., Panda, G., & Sahoo, G. (2009). Efficient prediction of exchange rates with low complexity artificial neural network models. *Expert Systems with Applications*, *36*(1), 181–189. doi:10.1016/j.eswa.2007.09.005

Malhotra, R., & Malhotra, D. K. (2002). differentiating between good credits and bad credits using neuro-fuzzy systems. *European Journal of Operational Research*, *136*(1), 190–211. doi:10.1016/S0377-2217(01)00052-2

Malhotra, R., & Malhotra, D. K. (2003). Evaluating consumer loans using neural networks. *Omega*, *31*(2), 83–96. doi:10.1016/S0305-0483(03)00016-1

Malshe, A., Al-Khatib, J., Al-Habib, M., & Ezzi, S. (2012). Exploration of sales-marketing interface nuances in Saudi Arabia. *Journal of Business Research, 65*(8), 1119–1125. doi:10.1016/j.jbusres.2011.08.006

Manning, N. P. D. (2009). Knowledge management. *Development Journal, 5*(2), 31–34.

Manovich, L. (2011). Trending: The Promises and the Challenges of Big Social Data. In M. K. Gold (Ed.), *Debates in the Digital Humanities*. Minneapolis, MN: The University of Minnesota Press.

Manyika, J., Chui, M., Brown, B., Bughin, J., Dobbs, R., Roxburgh, C., & Byers, A. H. (2011). *Big data: The next frontier for innovation, competition, and productivity.* Available at http://www.mckinsey.com/insights/business_technology/big_data_the_next_frontier_for_innovation

Manyika, J., Chui, M., Brown, B., Bughin, J., Dobbs, R., Roxburgh, C., & Hung Byers, A. (2011). *Big data: The next frontier for innovation, competition and productivity.* McKinsey Global Institute.

Marchant, A. (2010). Obstacles to the flow of requirements verification. *Systems Engineering, 13*(1), 1–13.

Marinakis, Y., Marinaki, M., Doumpos, M., Matsatsinis, N., & Zopounidis, C. (2008). Constantin Zopounidis, Optimization of nearest neighbor classifiers via metaheuristic algorithms for credit risk assessment. *Journal of Global Optimization, 42*(2), 279–293. doi:10.1007/s10898-007-9242-1

Mark, S. (1997). Delaying decisions stifles: Industrial management decision-making progress. *Management Decision, 45*, 1622–1635.

Marr, B., & Schiuma, G. (2001). Measuring and managing intellectual capital and knowledge assets in new economy organisations. In M. Bourne (Ed.), Handbook of performance measurement. London: Gee.

Marshall, J. J., & Vredenburg, H. (1992). An empirical study of factors influencing innovation implementation in industrial sales organizations. *Journal of the Academy of Marketing Science, 20*(3), 205–215. doi:10.1007/BF02723407

Martens, D., Baesens, B., Gestel, T. V., & Vanthienen, J. (2007). Comprehensible credit scoring models using rule extraction from support vector machines. *European Journal of Operational Research, 183*(3), 1466–1476. doi:10.1016/j.ejor.2006.04.051

Martinsons, G. M., & Robert, D. M. (2007). Strategic decision making and support systems: Comparing American, Japanese and Chinese management. *Decision Support Systems, 43*(1), 284–300. doi:10.1016/j.dss.2006.10.005

Massey, A., Montoya-Weiss, M. M., & Holcom, K. (2001). Re-engineering the customer relationship: Leveraging knowledge assets at IBM. *Decision Support Systems, 32*(2), 155–170. doi:10.1016/S0167-9236(01)00108-7

Mateen, A., & More, D. (2013). Applying TOC thinking process tools in managing challenges of supply chain finance: A case study. *International Journal of Services and Operations Management, 15*(4), 389–410. doi:10.1504/IJSOM.2013.054882

Mathirajan, M., Manoj, K., & Ramachandran, V. (2011). A design of distribution network and development of efficient distribution policy. *International Journal of Logistics Systems and Supply Management, 9*(1), 108–137. doi:10.1504/IJLSM.2011.040062

Matson, E., Patiath, P., & Shavers, T. (2003). Stimulating knowledge sharing: Strengthening your organizations' internal knowledge market. *Organizational Dynamics, 32*(3), 275–285. doi:10.1016/S0090-2616(03)00030-5

McAfee, A., & Brynijolfsson, E. (2012). Big Data: The Management Revolution. *Harvard Business Review, 90*(10), 61–68. PMID:23074865

McCroskey, J. C., & Teven, J. J. (1999). Goodwill: A reexamination of the construct and its measurement. *Communication Monographs, 66*(1), 90–103. doi:10.1080/03637759909376464

McDougall, M. (2012). Prioritizing internal communications. *Canadian HR Reporter, 25*(14), 22.

McEvily, S., & Chakravarthy, B. (2002). The persistence of knowledge-based advantage: An empirical test for product performance and technological knowledge. *Strategic Management Journal, 23*(4), 285–305. doi:10.1002/smj.223

McGonagle, J., & Vella, C. (2002). *Bottom line competitive intelligence*. Westport, CT: Quorum Books.

McKenna, B. (2013). What does a petabyte look like? *Computer Weekly*. Retrieved from http://www.computerweekly.com/feature/What-does-a-petabyte-look-like

McKinsey & Company. (2009). *Hal Varian on how the Web challenges managers*. Available at http://www.mckinsey.com/insights/innovation/hal_varian_on_how_the_web_challenges_managers

McNeil, A. J., & Wendin, J. P. (2007). Bayesian inference for generalized linear mixed models of portfolio credit risk. *Journal of Empirical Finance*, *14*(2), 131–149. doi:10.1016/j.jempfin.2006.05.002

Meek, G., and Ozgur, C. (1989, August). Prevailing Locknut Torque Variations. *Journal of Fastener Technology International*, 58-60.

Meek, G., & Ozgur, C. (1991). Torque Variation Analysis. *Indagationes Mathematicae*, *41*(1), 1–16.

Melewar, T. C., Turnbull, S., & Balabanis, G. (2000). International advertising strategies of multinational enterprises in the Middle East. *International Journal of Advertising*, *19*, 529–547.

Mellahi, K. (2003). National culture and management practices: The case of GCCs. In M. Tayeb (Ed.), *International management: Theory and practices*. London, UK: Prentice-Hall.

Mellahi, K. (2006). Human resource management in Saudi Arabia. In P. Budhwar & K. Mellahi (Eds.), *Managing Human Resources in the Middle East*. London, UK: Routledge.

Mellahi, K., & Al-Hinai, S. (2000). Local workers in Gulf co-operation countries: Assets or liabilities? *Middle Eastern Studies*, *36*(3), 177–190. doi:10.1080/00263200008701323

Mellahi, K., & Budhwar, P. (2010). Introduction: Islam and human resource management. *Personnel Review*, *39*(6), 685–691. doi:10.1108/00483481011075558

Mellers, B. A., Schwartz, A., Ho, K., & Ritov, I. (1997). Decision affect theory: Emotional reactions to the outcomes of risky options. *Psychological Science*, *8*(6), 423–429. doi:10.1111/j.1467-9280.1997.tb00455.x

Meo, R., Psaila, G., & Ceri, S. (1998). An extension to SQL for mining association rules. *Data Mining and Knowledge Discovery*, *2*(2), 195–224. doi:10.1023/A:1009774406717

Merrell, P. (2012). Effective Change Management: The Simple Truth. *Management Services*, *56*(2), 20–23.

Mertler, C. A., & Vannatta, R. A. (2005). *Advanced and Multivariate Statistical Methods* (3rd ed.). Glendale, CA: Pyrczak Publishing.

Metcalfe, B. D. (2007). Gender and human resource management in the Middle East. *International Journal of Human Resource Management*, *18*(1), 54–74. doi:10.1080/09585190601068292

Meyer, D., Dimitriadou, E., Hornik, K., Weingessel, A., & Leisch, F. (2014). *e1071: Misc Functions of the Department of Statistics*. TU Wien.

Meyer, A. D., & Goes, J. B. (1988). Organizational assimilation of innovations: A multilevel contextual analysis. *Academy of Management Journal*, *31*(4), 897–923. doi:10.2307/256344

Michalski, M., & Yurov, K.M. & Montes, Botella, J. L. (2014). Trust and IT innovation in asymmetric environments of the supply chain management process. *Journal of Computer Information Systems*, *54*(3), 10–24.

Micheli, P., & Manzoni, J. F. (2010). Strategic performance measurement: Benefits, limitations and paradoxes. *Long Range Planning*, *43*(4), 465–476. doi:10.1016/j.lrp.2009.12.004

Miguel, P. L., & Brito, L. A. L. (2011). Supply chain management measurement and its influence on operational performance. *Journal of Operations and Supply Chain Management*, *4*(2), 56–69.

Miller, C. C., Burke, M. L., & Glich, H. M. (1998). Cognitive Diversity among Upper-Echelon Executives: Implications for strategic decision processes. *Strategic Management Journal*, *19*(1), 39–58. doi:10.1002/(SICI)1097-0266(199801)19:1<39::AID-SMJ932>3.0.CO;2-A

Miller, D., & Droge, C. (1986). Psychological and traditional determinants of structure. *Administrative Science Quarterly*, *31*(4), 539–560. doi:10.2307/2392963

Miller, D., & Friesen, P. H. (1982). Innovation in conservative and entrepreneurial firms: Two models of strategic momentum. *Strategic Management Journal, 3*(1), 1–25. doi:10.1002/smj.4250030102

Minkov, M. L., & Hofstede, G. (2011). The evolution of Hofstede's doctrine. *Cross Cultural Management: An International Journal, 18*(1), 10–20. doi:10.1108/13527601111104269

Mintzberg, H. (1985). The organization as a political arena. *Journal of Management Studies, 22*(2), 133–154. doi:10.1111/j.1467-6486.1985.tb00069.x

Mintzberg, H. (1998). *Strategy Safari: a Guided Tour Through the Wilds of Strategic Management*. London, UK: Prentice-Hall.

Mitchell, M. L., & Mulherin, J. H. (1994). The Impact of Public Information on the Stock Market. *The Journal of Finance, 49*(3), 923–950. doi:10.1111/j.1540-6261.1994.tb00083.x

Mitchell, V. W., & McGoldrick, P. J. (1996). Consumer's risk-reduction strategies: A review and synthesis. *International Review of Retail, Distribution and Consumer Research, 6*(1), 1–33. doi:10.1080/09593969600000001

Mittermayer, M. A., & Knolmayer, G. F. (2006). NewsCATS: A News Categorization and Trading System. In *Proceedings of 6ᵗʰ International Conference in Data Mining*, (pp. 1002-1007). Hong Kong: Academic Press.

Mohamed, M. S., O'Sullivan, K. J., & Ribiere, V. (2008). A Paradigm Shift in the Arab Region Knowledge Evolution. *Journal of Knowledge Management, 12*(5), 107–220. doi:10.1108/13673270810902975

Moore, D. S. (2001). Undergraduate Programs and the Future of Academic Statistics. *The American Statistician, 55*(1), 1–6. doi:10.1198/000313001300339860

More, D., & Babu, A. S. (2012). Benchmarking supply chain flexibility using data envelopment analysis. *International Journal of Logistics Systems and Management, 12*(3), 288–317. doi:10.1504/IJLSM.2012.047603

Morrice, D., & Bardhan, I. (1995). A weighted least squares approach to computer simulation factor screening. *Operations Research, 43*(5), 792–806. doi:10.1287/opre.43.5.792

Moss, F. (2011). *The sorcerers and their apprentices: How the digital magicians of the MIT media lab are creating the innovative technologies that will transform our lives*. New York: The Crown Publishing Group.

Motiwalla, L., & Aiken, M. (1993). An organizational communications perspective on knowledge-based mail systems. *Information & Management, 25*(5), 265–272. doi:10.1016/0378-7206(93)90075-5

Mouritsen, J. (2004). Measuring and intervening: How do we theorize intellectual capital management? *Journal of Intellectual Capital, 5*(2), 257–267. doi:10.1108/14691930410533687

Moutot, J. M., & Bascoul, G. (2008). Effects of sales force automation use on sale force activities and customer relationship management processes. *Journal of Personal Selling and Sales, 28*(2), 167–184. doi:10.2753/PSS0885-3134280205

Mowbray, M. (2009). *The fog over the grimpen mire: Cloud computing and the law*. HP Laboratories: HPL-2009-99. Retrieved from http://www.hpl.hp.com/techreports/2009/HPL-2009-99.pdf

Mozy, Inc. (2009). *How much is a petabyte?* Retrieved from http://mozy.com/blog/misc/how-much-is-apetabyte/

Mues, C., Baesens, B., Files, C. M., & Vanthienen, J. (2004). Decision diagrams in machine learning: An empirical study on real-life credit-risk data. *Expert Systems with Applications, 27*(2), 257–264. doi:10.1016/j.eswa.2004.02.001

Mumel, D. (2008). *Komuniciranje v poslovnem okolju*. Maribor: De Vesta.

Muna, F. (1980). *The Arab Executive*. New York, NY: St. Martin's Press.

Murfitt, S. (2001). *Using Business Intelligence*. Retrieved 14 August 2013, from http://www.digitrends/net/scripts

Murray-Smith, D. (2013). The application of parameter sensitivity analysis methods to inverse simulation models. *Mathematical and Computer Modelling of Dynamical Systems, 19*(1), 67–90. doi:10.1080/13873954.2012.696271

Nahapiet, J., & Ghoshal, S. (1998). Social capital, intellectual capital, and the organizational advantage. *Academy of Management Review, 23*(2), 242–266.

National Small Business Association. (2010). *Small business technology survey*. Washington, DC: Author.

Neely, A. D., Adams, C., & Kennerley, M. (2002). *The performance prism: The scorecard for measuring and managing stakeholder relationship*. London, UK: Financial Times Prentice Hall.

Neely, A. (2011). *Business Performance Measurement: Theory and Practice*. London: Cambridge University Press.

Neely, A. D., Gregory, M. J., & Platts, K. W. (1995). Performance measurement system design: A literature review and research agenda. *International Journal of Operations & Production Management*, *15*(4), 80–116. doi:10.1108/01443579510083622

Neely, C., Weller, P., & Dittmar, R. (1997). Is technical analysis in the foreign exchange market profitable? A genetic programming approach. *Journal of Financial and Quantitative Analysis*, *32*(4), 405–426. doi:10.2307/2331231

Neill, S., & Rose, G. M. (2006). The effect of strategic complexity on marketing strategy and organizational performance. *Journal of Business Research*, *59*(1), 1–10. doi:10.1016/j.jbusres.2004.12.001

Nelson, P. (1970). Information and consumer behavior. *Journal of Political Economy*, *78*(2), 311–329. doi:10.1086/259630

Nelson, R. R., & Winter, S. G. (1982). *An evolutionary theory of economic change*. Cambridge, MA: Harvard University Press.

Nevitt, C. (2013, March 18). What is a petabyte? *Financial Times*. Retrieved from http://www.ft.com/cms/s/2/bc7350a6-8fe7-11e2-ae9e-00144feabdc0.html#axzz2WD55Twcz

Nichols, W. (2013). Advertising Analytics 2.0. *Harvard Business Review*, *91*(3), 60–68. PMID:23593768

Nisar, T. (2006). *Organising electronic-based channels of internal communications*. Southampton, UK: University of Southampton, Information and Management.

Nocedal, J., & Wright, S. J. (2006). *Numerical Optimization*. Springer.

Noh, H. J., Roh, T. H., & Han, I. (2005). Prognostic personal credit risk model considering censored information. *Expert Systems with Applications*, *28*(4), 753–762. doi:10.1016/j.eswa.2004.12.032

Nonaka, I., & Takeuchi, H. (1995). *The knowledge-creating company: How japanese companies create the dynamics of innovation*. New York: Oxford University Press.

Nonthaleerak, P., & Hendry, L. (2008). Exploring the six sigma phenomenon using multiple case study evidence. *International Journal of Operations & Production Management*, *28*(2), 279–303. doi:10.1108/01443570810856198

Nucleus Research. (2011). *Analytics Pays Back $10.66 for every dollar spend*. Available at http://nucleusresearch.com/research/search/

Nunnally, J. (1978). *Psychometric theory*. New York, NY: McGraw-Hill.

Nutt, P. C. (1984). Types of organizational decision processes. *Administrative Science Quarterly*, *29*(3), 414–450. doi:10.2307/2393033 PMID:10268867

Nutt, P. C. (1998). Evaluating alternatives to make strategic choices. *Omega*, *26*(3), 333–354. doi:10.1016/S0305-0483(97)00068-6

O'Brien, J. A., & Marakas, G. M. (2007). *Introduction to information Systems*. New York: McGraw-Hill.

O'Connor J., & Seymour, J. (1996). *Spretnosti sporazumevanja in vplivanja*. Žalec: Sledi.

O'Grady, W., Rouse, P., & Gunn, C. (2010). Synthesizing management control frameworks. *Measuring Business Excellence*, *14*(1), 96–108. doi:10.1108/13683041011027481

O'Neil, J. (2008). Measuring the Impact of Employee Communication on Employee Comprehension and Action: A Case Study of a Major International Firm. *The Public Relations Journal*, *2*(2), 1–17.

Obermiller, C., & Spangenberg, E. R. (1998). Development of a scale to measure consumer skepticism toward advertising. *Journal of Consumer Psychology*, *7*(2), 159–186. doi:10.1207/s15327663jcp0702_03

Olbrich, S., Poppelbuß, J., & Niehaves, B. (2012). Critical contextual success factors for business intelligence: A Delphi study on their relevance, variability, and controllability. In *Proceedings of the 45th Hawaii International Conference on System Science* (pp. 4148-4157). Washington, DC: IEEE Computer Society. doi:10.1109/HICSS.2012.187

Oliver, J. E., Jose, P. E., & Brough, P. (2006). Confirmatory Factor Analysis of the Work Locus of Control Scale. *Educational and Psychological Measurement, 66*(5), 835–851. doi:10.1177/0013164405285544

Olson, E. M., & Slater, S. F. (2002). The balanced scorecard, competitive strategy, and performance. *Business Horizons, 45*(3), 11–16. doi:10.1016/S0007-6813(02)00198-2

Olszak, C. M., & Ziemba, E. (2003, June). Business intelligence as a key to management of an enterprise. *Proceeding of Information Science,* 855-863.

Olszak, C. M., & Ziemba, E. (2007). Approach to building and implementing business intelligence systems. *Interdisciplinary Journal of Information, Knowledge and Management, 2,* 135–148.

Omar, A. (1984). *The Role of Training in Saudi Arabian Public Agencies.* Riyadh, Saudi Arabia: Institute of Public Administration.

Opitz, D., & Maclin, R. (1999). Popular ensemble methods: An empirical study. *Journal of Artificial Intelligence Research, 11,* 169–198.

Orsini, B. (2000). Improving internal communications. *Internal Auditor, 57*(6), 28–33.

Osmundson, J. (2000). A systems engineering methodology for information systems. *Systems Engineering, 3*(2), 68–76. doi:10.1002/1520-6858(2000)3:2<68::AID-SYS2>3.0.CO;2-A

Otley, D. T. (1999). Performance management: A framework for management control systems research. *Management Accounting Research, 10*(4), 363–382. doi:10.1006/mare.1999.0115

Ouchi, W. G. (1980). Markets, bureaucracies, and clans. *Administrative Science Quarterly, 25*(1), 129–141. doi:10.2307/2392231

Oxford Economics. (2013). *SMES: Equipped to compete.* Retrieved from http://cdn.news-sap.com/wp-content/blogs.dir/1/files/SAP-SME-analysis-presentation.pdf

Ozgur, C. (1998). Capacity Constrained Resource Scheduling: A Decision Utility Approach. *International Journal of Operations and Quantitative Management, 4*(3), 1–21.

Ozgur, C., & Bai, L. (2010, March/June). Hierarchical Composition Heuristic for Asymmetric Sequence Dependent Single Machine Scheduling Problems. *Operations Management Research, 3*(1), 98–106. doi:10.1007/s12063-010-0031-5

Ozgur, C., & Brown, J. R. (1995). A Two-Stage Traveling Salesman Procedure for the Single Machine Sequence Dependent Scheduling Problem. *OMEGA, International Journal of Management Science, 23*(2), 205–219. doi:10.1016/0305-0483(94)00057-H

Pagell, M., & Gobeli, D. (2009). How plant managers' experiences and attitudes toward sustainability relate to operational performance. *Production and Operations Management, 18*(3), 278–299. doi:10.1111/j.1937-5956.2009.01050.x

Paik, W., Kyoung, M. H., Min, K. S., Oh, H. R., Lim, C., & Shin, M. S. (2007). Multi-stage News Classification System for Predicting Stock Price Changes. *Journal of the Korea Society for Information Management, 24*(2), 123–141. doi:10.3743/KOSIM.2007.24.2.123

Paksoy, T., & Cavlak, E. B. (2011). Development and optimisation of a new linear programming model for production/distribution network of an edible vegetable oils manufacturer. *International Journal of Logistics Systems and Management, 9*(1), 1–21. doi:10.1504/IJLSM.2011.040057

Paleologo, G., Elisseeff, A., & Antonini, G. (2010). Subagging for credit scoring models. *Journal of Operational Research, 201*(2), 490–499. doi:10.1016/j.ejor.2009.03.008

Pal, M. (2007). Ensemble learning with decision tree for remote sensing classification. *World Academy of Science. Engineering and Technology, 36,* 258–260.

Panda, C., & Narasimhan, V. (2007). Forecasting exchange rate better with artificial neural network. *Journal of Policy Modeling, 29*(2), 227–236. doi:10.1016/j.jpolmod.2006.01.005

Pang, B., & Lee, L. (2008). Opinion Mining and Sentiment Analysis. *Foundations and Trends in Information Retrieval*, *2*(1-2), 1–35. doi:10.1561/1500000011

Papadakis, V. M. (1998). Strategic investment decision processes and organizational performance: An empirical examination. *British Journal of Management*, *9*(2), 115–132. doi:10.1111/1467-8551.00078

Papadakis, V. M., Lioukas, S., & Chambers, D. (1998). Strategic decision-making processes: The role of management and context. *Strategic Management Journal*, *19*(2), 115–147. doi:10.1002/(SICI)1097-0266(199802)19:2<115::AID-SMJ941>3.0.CO;2-5

Paquette, S. (2006). *Customer knowledge management. In Encyclopedia of knowledge management*. Idea Group Inc.

Paredes, R., & Vidal, E. (2000). A class-dependent weighted dissimilarity measure for nearest neighbor classification problems. *Pattern Recognition Letters*, *21*(12), 1027–1036. doi:10.1016/S0167-8655(00)00064-7

Park, B.-N., & Min, H. (2013). Global supply chain barriers of foreign subsidiaries: The case of Korean expatriate manufacturers in China. *International Journal of Services and Operations Management*, *15*(1), 67–78. doi:10.1504/IJSOM.2013.050562

Parnell, A. J., & Hatem, T. (1999). Cultural Antecedents of Behavioural Differences between American and Egyptian managers. *Journal of Management Studies*, *36*(3), 399–418. doi:10.1111/1467-6486.00142

Patel, G., & Tripathy, J. (1989). The Solid Transportation Problem and its Variants. *International Journal of Management and Systems*, *5*, 17–36.

Paulk, M. C., Curtis, B., Chrissis, M. B., & Weber, C. V. (1993). Capability maturity model. *IEEE Software*, *10*(4), 18–27. doi:10.1109/52.219617

Payne, A., & Frow, P. (2005). A strategic framework for customer relationship management. *Journal of Marketing Management*, *69*(4), 167–176. doi:10.1509/jmkg.2005.69.4.167

Payne, A., & Frow, P. (2006). Customer relationship management: From strategy to implementation. *Journal of Marketing Management*, *22*(1-2), 135–168. doi:10.1362/026725706776022272

Perko, L., & Bobek, S. (2007). An agent model in BI knowledge intensive environment. In *Proceedings of International Conference on Information Technology Interfaces*. Academic Press. doi:10.1109/ITI.2007.4283821

Peterson, J. E. (2006). Qatar and the World: Branding for a Micro-State. *The Middle East Journal*, *60*, 732–748.

Petrini, M., & Pozzebon, M. (2009). Managing sustainability with the support of business intelligence: Integrating socio-environmental indicators and organisational context. *The Journal of Strategic Information Systems*, *18*(4), 178–191. doi:10.1016/j.jsis.2009.06.001

Pettersson, A. I., & Segerstedt, A. (2011). Performance measurements in supply chains within Swedish industry. *International Journal of Logistics Systems and Management*, *9*(1), 69–88. doi:10.1504/IJLSM.2011.040060

Pettigrew, A. M. (1987). Strategy formulation as a political process. *International Studies of Management & Organization*, *7*, 78–87.

Pham, T. D. (2005). An Optimally Weighted Fuzzy k-NN Algorithm. *Lecture Notes in Computer Science*, *3686*(PART I), 239–247. doi:10.1007/11551188_26

Phan, P. H. (2000). *Taking Back the Boardroom*. Singapore: McGraw-Hill.

Piller, C. (1999). Everyone is a critic in cyberspace. *Los Angeles Times, 3*(12), A1.

Pintér, J. (2010). *Global Optimization in Action: Continuous and Lipschitz Optimization: Algorithms. Implementations and Applications*. New York: Springer.

Plakoyiannaki, E., & Saren, M. (2006). Time and the customer relationship management process: Conceptual and methodological insights. *Journal of Business and Industrial Marketing*, *2*(4), 218–230. doi:10.1108/08858620610672588

Polanyi, M. (1967). *The tacit dimension*. New York: Doubleday.

Poon, P., & Wagner, C. (2001). Critical success factors revisited: Success and failure cases of information systems for senior executives. *Decision Support Systems*, *30*(4), 393–418. doi:10.1016/S0167-9236(00)00069-5

Popova, V., & Sharpanskykh, A. (2010). Modeling organizational performance indicators. *Information Systems, 35*(4), 505–527. doi:10.1016/j.is.2009.12.001

Porter, M. E. (2008). Why America needs an economic strategy. *Business Week, 4107*, 39-42. Retrieved September 15, 2014 from http://reddog.rmu.edu:2060/pqdweb?did=1589842131&sid=1&Fmt=2&clientId=2138&RQT=309&VName=PQD

Porter, M. E. (1996). What is strategy? *Harvard Business Review, 74*(6), 61–78. PMID:10158474

Porter, M. E., & Kramer, M. R. (2006). Strategy and society: The link between competitive advantage and corporate social responsibility. *Harvard Business Review, 84*(12), 78–92. PMID:17183795

Poter, M. E., & Milar, V. E. (1985). How Information Gives you Competitive advantage. *Harvard Business Review, 4*, 149–160.

Power, D. J. (2002). *Decision support systems: Concepts and resources for managers*. Westport, CT: Greenwood Publishing Group.

Prajogo, I. D., & Amrik, S. S. (2006). The integration of TQM and technology/R&D management in determining quality and innovation performance. *Omega, 34*(3), 296–312. doi:10.1016/j.omega.2004.11.004

Prastacos, G., Soderquist, K., Spanos, Y., & Wassenhove, L. V. (2002). An integrated framework for managing change in the new competitive landscape. *European Management Journal, 20*(1), 55–71. doi:10.1016/S0263-2373(01)00114-1

Pratap Jain, S., Buchanan, B., & Maheswaran, D. (2000). Comparative versus noncomparative advertising: The moderating impact of prepurchase attribute verifiability. *Journal of Consumer Psychology, 9*(4), 201–211. doi:10.1207/S15327663JCP0904_2

Prescott, J. E., & Miller, S. H. (2001). *Proven strategies in competitive intelligence: Lessons from the trenches*. New York: John Wiley and Sons.

Pring, M. T. (1991). *Technical Analysis*. New York.

Provost, F., & Fawcett, T. (2013). *Data Science for Business*. Sebastopol, CA: O'Reilly Media, Inc.

Pulic, A. (2004). Intellectual capital—does it create or destroy value? *Measuring Business Excellence, 8*(1), 62–68. doi:10.1108/13683040410524757

Quinlan, J. R. (1986). Induction of decision tree. *Machine Learning, 1*(1), 81–106. doi:10.1007/BF00116251

Quinlan, J. R. (1993). *C4. 5: Programs for machine learning* (Vol. 1). Morgan Kaufmann.

Rababah, K. Mohd, H. & Ibrahim, H. (2011). Customer Relationship Management (CRM) process from Theory to Practice: The pre-implementation Plan of CRM System. *International Journal of e-Education, e-Business, e-Management, e-Learning, 1*(1), 22-27.

Raber, D., Wortmann, F., & Winter, R. (2013). Situational business intelligence maturity models: An exploratory analysis. In *Proceedings of the 46th Hawaii International Conference on System Sciences* (pp. 4219-4228). Wailea, HI: IEEE Computer Society. doi:10.1109/HICSS.2013.483

Rabindran, A., Philips Don, T., & Solberg James, J. (1987). *Operations Research: Principles and Practice* (2nd ed.). New York: John Wiley and Sons.

Raft, A., & Lord, M. (2002). Acquiring new technologies and capabilities: A grounded model of acquisition implementation. *Organization Science, 13*(4), 420–441. doi:10.1287/orsc.13.4.420.2952

Ragins, E. J., & Greco, A. J. (2003). Customer Relationship Management and E-Business: More than a Software Solution. *Review of Business, 24*(1), 25–30.

Rahman, S. A., & Yousop, N. M. (2011). Modeling of budget allocation for university library. *Journal of Statistical Modeling and Analytics, 2*(2), 1–8.

Rajagopalan, N., Rasheed, M. A., & Datta, D. (1993). Diversification and performance: Critical review and future directions. *Journal of Management, 19*, 349–384. doi:10.1177/014920639301900207

Rajapakshe, T., Dawande, M., & Sriskandarajah, C. (2013). On the trade-off between remanufacturing and recycling. *International Journal of Services and Operations Management, 15*(1), 1–53. doi:10.1504/IJSOM.2013.050560

Rajeev, V. (2013). Impact of service co-creation on performance of firms: The mediating role of market oriented strategies. *International Journal of Services and Operations Management*, *15*(4), 449–466. doi:10.1504/IJSOM.2013.054885

Ramamurthy, K., Sen, A., & Sinha, A. P. (2008). An empirical investigation of the key determinants of data warehouse adoption. *Decision Support Systems*, *44*(4), 817–841. doi:10.1016/j.dss.2007.10.006

Ramírez, E., Castillo, O., & Soria, J. (2003). Hybrid system for cardiac arrhythmia classification with fuzzy k-nearest neighbors and multi layer perceptrons combined by a fuzzy inference system. In *Proceedings of the International Joint Conference on Neural Networks*. Barcelona, Spain: Academic Press.

Ramsey, F. L., & Schafer, D. W. (2002). *The statistical sleuth: A course in methods of data analysis* (2nd ed.). Pacific Grove, CA: Duxbury.

Ranadive, A. (2013). Promoted Tweets drive offline sales for CPG brands. *Twitter Blogs*. Retrieved July 6th 2014 from: https://blog.twitter.com/2013/promoted-tweetsdrive-offline-sales-for-cpg-brands

Rao, S. S. (1984). *Optimization Theory and Applications* (2nd ed.). New Delhi: Wiley Eastern Limited.

Raouch, D., & Santi, P. (2001). Competitive intelligence adds value: Five intelligence attitudes. *European Management Journal*, *19*(5), 552–559. doi:10.1016/S0263-2373(01)00069-X

Räsänen, T., Ruuskanen, J., & Kolehmainen, M. (2008). Reducing energy consumption by using self-organizing maps to create more personalized electricity use information. *Applied Energy*, *85*(9), 830–840. doi:10.1016/j.apenergy.2007.10.012

Rasmussen, N., Goldy, P. S., & Solli, P. Q. (2002). *Financial business intelligence, trends, technology, software selection, and implementation*. John Wiley & Sons.

Raudenbush, S. W., & Bryk, A. S. (2002). *Hierarchical Linear Models: Applications and Data Analysis Methods* (2nd ed.). Thousand Oaks, CA: Sage Publications, Inc.

Raudenbush, S. W., Bryk, A. S., Cheong, Y., & Congdon, R. T. (2004). *HLM 6: Hierarchical Linear and Nonlinear Modeling*. Chicago: Scientific Software International.

Ravi, V. (2008). *Advances in banking technology and management: impacts of ICT and CRM*. New York: Information Science Reference.

Razzouk, N., & Al-Khatib, J. (1993). The nature of television advertising in Saudi Arabia: Content analysis and marketing implications. *Journal of International Consumer Marketing*, *6*(2), 65–90. doi:10.1300/J046v06n02_06

Reinartz, W., Krafft, M., & Hoyer, W. D. (2004). The customer relationship management process: Its measurement and impact on performance. *JMR, Journal of Marketing Research*, *41*(3), 293–305. doi:10.1509/jmkr.41.3.293.35991

Rettab, B., Ben Brik, A., & Mellahi, K. (2009). Study of management perceptions of the impact of corporate social responsibility on organisational performance in emerging economies: The case of Dubai. *Journal of Business Ethics*, *89*(3), 371–390. doi:10.1007/s10551-008-0005-9

Review, H. B. (2011). *Making Smart Decisions*. Harvard Business Review Press.

Ricardo, R., & Wade, D. (2001). *Corporate performance management: How to build a better organization through measurement driven strategies alignment*. Oxford, UK: Butterworth-Heinemann.

Rice, G. (1999). Islamic ethics and the implications for business. *Journal of Business Ethics*, *18*(4), 345–358. doi:10.1023/A:1005711414306

Richard, P. J., Devinney, T. M., Yip, G. S., & Johnson, G. (2009). Measuring organizational performance: Towards methodological best practice. *Journal of Management*, *35*(3), 718–804. doi:10.1177/0149206308330560

Richardson, J. T. E. (2011). Eta squared and partial eta squared as measures of effect size in educational research. *Educational Research Review*, *6*(2), 135–147. doi:10.1016/j.edurev.2010.12.001

Richardson, P., & Denton, K. (1996). Communicating change. *Human Resource Management*, *35*(2), 203–216. doi:10.1002/(SICI)1099-050X(199622)35:2<203::AID-HRM4>3.0.CO;2-1

Riddle, L., Ralston, D. A., Mellahi, K., Butt, A. N., & Dalgic, T. (2007). *Middle East managerial values: Evidence from five countries*. Philadelphia, PA: Academy of Management Meeting.

Riel van, C. (2005). Principles of Corporate Communication. Harlow, MA: Prentice-Hall.

Robbins, H., & Monro, S. (1951). A stochastic approximation method. *Annals of Mathematical Statistics, 22*(3), 400–407. doi:10.1214/aoms/1177729586

Robertazzi, Th. (2000). *Computer Networks & Systems: Queueing Theory and Performance Evaluation.* New York, NY: Springer. doi:10.1007/978-1-4612-1164-8

Robertson, J. C., Al–Khatib, A. J., Al–Habib, D. M., & Lanoue, D. (2001). Beliefs about Work in the Middle East and the Convergence Versus Divergence of Values. *Journal of World Business, 36*(3), 223–244. doi:10.1016/S1090-9516(01)00053-0

Rohlfer, S. (2004). Benchmarking concepts in the UK and Germany: A shared understanding among key players? *Benchmarking: An International Journal, 11*(5), 521–539. doi:10.1108/14635770410557735

Rossier, J., Dahourou, D., & Mccrae, R. R. (2005). Structural and Mean-Level Analyses of the Five-Factor Model and Locus of Control: Further Evidence From Africa. *Journal of Cross-Cultural Psychology, 36*(2), 227–246. doi:10.1177/0022022104272903

Ross, Ph. (1996). *Taguchi Techniques for Quality Engineering.* New York: McGraw Hill.

Ross, R., & Lam, G. (2011). *Building Business Solutions: Business Analysis with Business Rules.* New York: Business Rule Solutions Inc.

Rothberg, H. N., & Erickson, G. S. (2005). *From knowledge to intelligence: Creating competitive advantage in the next economy.* Woburn, MA: Elsevier Butterworth-Heinemann.

Rotter, J. B. (1954). *Social Learning and Clinical Psychology.* New York, NY: Prentice-Hall. doi:10.1037/10788-000

Rotter, J. B. (1966). Generalized expectancies for internal versus external control of reinforcement. *Psychological Monographs, 80*(1), 1–28. doi:10.1037/h0092976 PMID:5340840

Rowe, K., & Schlacter, J. (1978). Integrating social responsibility into the corporate structure. *Public Relations Quarterly, 23*(3), 7–12.

Rowley, J. (2002). Reflections on customer knowledge management in e-business. *Qualitative market Research:An Internal Journal, 4*, 268–280.

Rowley, J. (2004). Relationship Marketing and Knowledge Management: Partnering Paradigms? *Industrial Management & Data Systems, 104*(2), 149–157. doi:10.1108/02635570410522125

Rowley, J., Baregheh, A., & Samhrook, S. (2011). Towards an innovation-type mapping tool. *Management Decision, 49*(1), 73–86. doi:10.1108/00251741111094446

Roy, S. K., Mahapatra, D. R., & Biswal, M. P. (2012). Multi-choice stochastic transportation problem with exponential distribution. *Journal of Uncertain Systems, 6*(3), 200–213.

Rubinstein, R., & Shapiro. (1998). A. *Discrete Event Systems: Sensitivity Analysis and Stochastic Optimization by the Score Function Method.* Wiley.

Rumelhart, D. E., Hinton, G. E., & Williams, R. J. (1986). Learning representations by back-propagating errors. *Nature, 323*(6088), 533–536. doi:10.1038/323533a0

Rumelt, R. P. (1987). *The competitive challenge.* Cambridge, MA: Ballinger.

Ruppert, D. A. (1985). Newton-Raphson version of the multivariate Robbins-Monro procedure. *Annals of Statistics, 13*(2), 236–245. doi:10.1214/aos/1176346589

Russell, S., Haddad, M., Bruni, M., & Granger, M. (2010). Organic evolution and the capability maturity of business intelligence. In *Proceedings of the 16th Americas Conference on Information Systems* (pp. 4271-4280). Lima, Peru: AMCIS.

Sabri, H. (2004). Socio-cultural values and organizational culture. In K. Becker (Ed.), *Islam and Business.* New Brunswick, NJ: Haworth Press.

Sabri, H. (2007). Jordanian managers' leadership styles in comparison with the International Air Transport Association (IATA) and prospects for knowledge management in Jordan. *International Journal of Commerce and Management, 17*(1/2), 56–72. doi:10.1108/10569210710774758

Sacu, C., & Spruit, M. (2010). BIDM: The business intelligence development model. In *Proceedings of the 12th International Conference on Enterprise Information Systems* (pp. 288-293). Lisboa, Portugal: SciTePress.

Saeys, Y., Inza, I., & Larranaga, P. (2007). A review of feature selection techniques in bioinformatics. *Bioinformatics (Oxford, England), 23*(19), 2507–2517. doi:10.1093/bioinformatics/btm344 PMID:17720704

Sahami, M., Dumais, S., Heckerman, D., & Horvitz, E. (1998, July). A Bayesian approach to filtering junk e-mail. In *Learning for text categorization:Papers from the 1998 workshop* (Vol. *62*, pp. 98-105). Academic Press.

Sahoo, C. K., & Jena, S. (2012). Organizational performance management system: Exploring the manufacturing sectors. *Industrial and Commercial Training, 44*(5), 296–302. doi:10.1108/00197851211245059

Salim, I. M., & Sulaiman, M. (2011). Impact of organizational innovation on firm performance: Evidence from Malaysian-hased ICT companies. *Business and Management Review, 1*, 10–16.

Salton, G., & Buckley, C. (1988). Term-weighting approaches in automatic text retrieval. *Information Processing & Management, 24*(5), 513–523. doi:10.1016/0306-4573(88)90021-0

Sánchez, I. B., Espinós, I. D., Sarrion, L. M., López, A. Q., & Burgos, I. N. (2009). Clients segmentation according to their domestic energy consumption by the use of self-organizing maps. In *Proceedings of6th International Conference on the European Energy Market*, (pp. 1–6). Academic Press. doi:10.1109/EEM.2009.5207172

Sande, T. (2009). Taking charge of change with confidence. *Strategic Communication Management, 13*(1), 28–31.

Sankar, C. S. (2010). Factors that improve ERP implementation strategies in an organization. *International Journal of Enterprise Information Systems, 6*(2), 15–34. doi:10.4018/jeis.2010040102

Saporta, G. (2011). *Probabilités, analyse des données et statistique*. Editions Technip.

Sarlija, N., Bensic, M., & Susac, M. Z. (2009). Comparison procedure of predicting the time to default in behavioural scoring. *Expert Systems with Applications, 36*(5), 8778–8788. doi:10.1016/j.eswa.2008.11.042

SAS Business Intelligence Solutions. (2012). *Data Visualization Techniques: From Basics to Big Data with SAS® Visual Analytics*. Retrieved from http://www.sas.com/offices/NA/canada/downloads/IT-World2013/Data-Visualization-Techniques.pdf

Sawyerr, O. O., Ebrahimi, B. P., & Luk, V. W. M. (2003). Environment, executive information search activities, and firm performance: A comparative study of Hong Kong and Nigerian decision-makers. *International Journal of Cross Cultural Management, 3*(1), 67–92. doi:10.1177/1470595803003001851

Schlafke, M., Silvi, R., & Moller, K. (2013). A framework for business analytics in performance management. *International Journal of Productivity and Performance Management, 62*(1), 110–122. doi:10.1108/17410401311285327

Schneider, S. C., & Barsoux, J. L. (2003). Managing across cultures. (2ed.) Harlow, England: Prentice Hall.

Schneider, S. C. (1989). Strategy formulation: The impact of national cultural. *Organization Studies, 10*(2), 149–168. doi:10.1177/017084068901000202

Schneider, S. C., & Meyer, D. A. (1991). Interpreting and responding to strategic issues: The impact of national culture. *Strategic Management Journal, 12*(4), 307–320. doi:10.1002/smj.4250120406

Schroeck, M., Shockley, R., Smart, J., Romero-Morales, D., & Tufano, P. (2012). *Analytics: The real world use of big data*. Somers, NY: IBM Corporation.

Schulz, M., & Jobe, L. A. (2001). Codification and tacitness as knowledge management strategies: An empirical exploration. *The Journal of High Technology Management Research, 12*(1), 139–165. doi:10.1016/S1047-8310(00)00043-2

Schumaker, R. P., & Chen, H. (2009). Textual Analysis of Stock Market Prediction Using Breaking Financial News: The AZFinText System. *ACM Transactions on Information Systems, 27*(2), 12. doi:10.1145/1462198.1462204

Schumpeter, J. A. (1934). *The theory of economic development*. Cambridge, MA: Harvard University Press.

Schwartz, S. H. (1999). A theory of cultural values and some implications for work. *Applied Psychology, 48*(1), 23–47. doi:10.1111/j.1464-0597.1999.tb00047.x

Scriabina, N. (2011). Organize how you innovate. *Quality Progress*, *44*, 16–22.

Sedki, A., Ouazar, D., & El Mazoudi, E. (2009). Evolving neural network using real coded genetic algorithm for daily rainfall–runoff forecasting. *Expert Systems with Applications*, *36*(3), 4523–4527. doi:10.1016/j.eswa.2008.05.024

Sehgal, V., & Song, C. (2009). SOPS: Stock Prediction using Web Sentiment. In *Proceedings of Seventh IEEE International Conference on Data Mining – Workshop*, (pp. 21-26). IEEE.

Sen, A., Sinha, A. P., & Ramamurthy, K. (2006). Data warehousing process maturity: An exploratory study of factors influencing user perceptions. *IEEE Transactions on Engineering Management*, *53*(3), 440–455. doi:10.1109/TEM.2006.877460

Sermpinis, G., Laws, J., Karathanasopoulos, A., & Dunis, C. L. (2012). Dunis, Forecasting and trading the EUR/USD exchange rate with Gene Expression and Psi Sigma Neural Networks. *Expert Systems with Applications*, *39*(10), 8865–8877. doi:10.1016/j.eswa.2012.02.022

Sewell, M., & Shawe-Taylor, J. (2012). Forecasting foreign exchange rates using kernel methods. *Expert Systems with Applications*, *39*(9), 7652–7662. doi:10.1016/j.eswa.2012.01.026

Sexton, R. S., Sriram, R. S., & Etheridge, H. (2003). Improving decision effectiveness of artificial neural networks: A modified genetic algorithm approach. *Decision Sciences*, *34*(3), 421–442. doi:10.1111/j.1540-5414.2003.02309.x

Shacklett, M. (2010). Supply chain software: The big spend. *World Trade, 100*, 16-18, 20, 22.

Shane, S., Venkataraman, S., & MacMillan, I. (1995). Cultural differences in innovation championing strategies. *Journal of Management*, *21*(5), 931–952. doi:10.1177/014920639502100507

Shanks, G., Bekmamedova, N., Adam, F., & Daly, M. (2012). Embedding business intelligence systems within organisations. In A. Respicio & F. Burstein (Eds.), *Fusing Decision Support Systems into the Fabric of the Context* (pp. 113–124). Amsterdam, The Netherlands: IOS Press.

Shariat, M., & Hightower, R. Jr. (2007). Conceptualizing business intelligence architecture. *Marketing Management Journal*, *17*(2), 40–46.

Sharma, R. S., & Djiaw, V. (2011). Realising the strategic impact of business intelligence tools. *VINE: The Journal of Information and Knowledge Management Systems*, *41*(2), 113–131. doi:10.1108/03055721111134772

Shehzad, R., & Khan, M. N. A. (2013). Integrating knowledge management with business intelligence process for enhance organizational learning. *International Journal of Software Engineering and its Applications*, *7*(2), 83-92.

Shell, E. (1955). Distribution of a Product by Several Properties, Directorate of Management Analysis. In *Proceedings of the Second Symposium in Linear Programming*, (vol. 2, pp. 615-642). DCS/Comptroller H.Q.U.S.A.F.

Sheth, A., & Larson, J. (1990). Federated database systems for managing distributed, heterogeneous, and autonomous databases. *ACM Computing Surveys*, *22*(3), 183–236. doi:10.1145/96602.96604

Shim, J. P., Warkentin, M., Courtney, J. F., Power, D. J., Sharda, R., & Carlsson, C. (2002). Past, present, and future of decision support technology. *Decision Support Systems*, *33*(2), 111–126. doi:10.1016/S0167-9236(01)00139-7

Shollo, A., & Kautz, K. (2010). Towards an understanding of business intelligence. In *Proceedings of the 21st Australasian Conference on Information Systems* (pp. 1-10). Brisbane, Australia: ACIS.

Shrivastava, P., & Grant, J. H. (1985). Empirically derived models of strategic decision-making process. *Strategic Management Journal*, *6*(2), 97–113. doi:10.1002/smj.4250060202

Siegel, E. (2014). *Predictive Analysis: The Power to Predict Who will Click, Buy, Lie, or Die*. Indianapolis, IN: John Wiley & Sons, Inc.

Sikora, R., & Piramuthu, S. (2005). Efficient genetic algorithm based data mining using feature selection with Hausdorff distance. *Information Technology Management*, *6*(4), 315–331. doi:10.1007/s10799-005-3898-3

Silk, S. (1998). Automating the balanced scorecard. *Management Accounting*, *79*(11), 38–44.

Simons, R. (1995). *Levers of control, how managers use innovative control systems to drive strategic renewal.* Boston, MA: Harvard Business Review Press.

Singh, P., & Deo, M. C. (2007). Suitability of different neural networks in daily flow forecasting. *Applied Soft Computing, 7*(3), 968–978. doi:10.1016/j.asoc.2006.05.003

SINTEF. (1992). *TOPP: A productivity program for manufacturing industry.* Trondheim, Norway: NTNF/NTH.

SMEAfrica. (2014). Retrieved from http://smeafrica.net

Smidts, A., Pruyn, A. T. H., & Van Riel, C. B. M. (2001). The impact of employee communication and perceived external prestige on organizational identification. *Academy of Management Journal, 44*(5), 1051–1062. doi:10.2307/3069448

Smith, A. A., Smith, A. D., & Baker, D. J. (2011). Inventory management shrinkage and employee anti-theft approaches. *International Journal of Electronic Finance, 5*(3), 209–234. doi:10.1504/IJEF.2011.041337

Smith, A. D. (2011). Corporate social responsibility implementation: Comparison of large not-for-profit and for-profit companies. *International Journal of Accounting and Information Management, 19*(3), 231–246. doi:10.1108/18347641111169241

Smith, A. D. (2012). Gender perceptions of management's green supply chain development among the professional workforce. *International Journal of Procurement Management, 5*(1), 55–86. doi:10.1504/IJPM.2012.044154

Smith, A. D., & Synowka, D. P. (2014). Lean operations and SCM practices in manufacturing firms: Multi-firm case studies in HRM and visual-based metrics. *International Journal of Procurement Management, 7*(2), 183–200. doi:10.1504/IJPM.2014.059554

Smith, B. P., Achoui, M., & Harb, C. (2007). Unity and Diversity in Arab Managerial Styles. *International Journal of Cross Cultural Management, 7*(3), 275–289. doi:10.1177/1470595807083374

Smythe, J. (1996). The changing role of internal communication in tomorrow's company. *Managing Service Quality, 6*(2), 41–44. doi:10.1108/09604529610109756

Snell, P. (2007). Focus on supply chain to retain edge. *Supply Management, 12*(8), 8.

Snijders, C., Matzat, U., & Reips, U.-D. (2012). Big data: Big gaps of knowledge in the field of internet science. *International Journal of Internet Science, 1*, 1–5. Retrieved from http://www.ijis.net/ijis7_1/ijis7_1_editorial.pdf

Sohn, S. Y., & Kim, H. S. (2007). Random effects logistic regression model for default prediction of technology credit guarantee fund. *European Journal of Operational Research, 183*(1), 427–478. doi:10.1016/j.ejor.2006.10.006

Sohn, S. Y., & Shin, H. W. (2006). Reject inference in credit operations based on survival analysis. *Expert Systems with Applications, 31*(1), 26–29. doi:10.1016/j.eswa.2005.09.001

Sousa, G. W. L., Carpinetti, L. C. R., Groesbeck, R. L., & Van Aken, E. (2005). Conceptual design of performance measurement and management systems using a structured engineering approach. *International Journal of Productivity and Performance Management, 54*(5-6), 385–399. doi:10.1108/17410400510604548

Spall, J. (2000). Adaptive stochastic approximation by the simultaneous perturbation method. *IEEE Transactions on Automatic Control, 45*(10), 1839–1853. doi:10.1109/TAC.2000.880982

Spall, J. (2003). *Introduction to Stochastic Search and Optimization: Estimation, Simulation, and Control.* New York, NY: Wiley. doi:10.1002/0471722138

Spiceworks. (2013). *Annual Report on Small and Midsize Business Technology Plans and Purchase Intent.* Retrieved from http://itreports.spiceworks.com/reports/spiceworks_voice_of_it_state_of_smb_2013_1h.pdf

Spoull, L., & Kiesler, S. (1986). Reducing social context cues: Electronic mail in organizational communication. *Management Science, 32*(11), 1492–1512. doi:10.1287/mnsc.32.11.1492

Steenackers, A., & Goovaerts, M. J. (1989). A credit scoring model for personal loans. *Insurance, Mathematics & Economics, 8*(1), 31–34. doi:10.1016/0167-6687(89)90044-9

Stefanescu, C., Tunaru, R., & Turnbull, S. (2009). The credit rating process and estimation of transition probabilities: A Bayesian approach. *Journal of Empirical Finance, 16*(2), 216–234. doi:10.1016/j.jempfin.2008.10.006

Stein, K. (2014). 7 facts your CEO needs to know about the work you do on social media. *Dog-eared Social.* Retrieved July 8th 2014 from: http://www.kierastein.com/7-facts-your-ceo-needs-to-know-about-the-work-you-do-on-social-media/#sthash.lJew1cYc.dpuf

Stein, A. (2006). Employee communications and community: An exploratory study. *Journal of Public Relations Research*, *18*(3), 249–264. doi:10.1207/s1532754xjprr1803_3

Stepanova, M., & Thomas, L. C. (2002). survival Analysis Methods for Personal Loan Data. *Operations Research*, *50*(2), 277–289. doi:10.1287/opre.50.2.277.426

Stevenson, H., & Gumpert, D. (1985). The heart of entrepreneurship. *Harvard Business Review*, *63*, 85–94.

Stewart, T. A. (1997). *Intellectual capital: The new wealth of nations.* New York: Doubleday.

Subramanian, A., & Nilakanta, S. (1996). Organizational innovativeness: Exploring the relationship between organizational determinants of innovation, types of innovations, and measures of organizational performance. *Omega*, *24*(6), 631–647. doi:10.1016/S0305-0483(96)00031-X

Su, C. T., Chen, Y. H., & Sha, D. A. (2006). Linking innovative product development with customer knowledge: A data-mining approach. *Technovation*, *26*(7), 784–795. doi:10.1016/j.technovation.2005.05.005

Sugarsynch. (2013). Retrieved from http://www.sugarsync.com/blog/2013/05/07/survey-results-reveal-topfive-reasons-small-business-are-turning-to-cloud-file-management/

Sunasses, N., & Sewry, D. A. (2002). A theoretical framework for knowledge management implementation. In *Proceeding of 2002 Annual Research Conference of the South African Institute of Computer Scientists and Information Technologies on Enablement through Technology (SAICSIT).* Port Elizabeth, South Africa: SAICSIT.

Supply Chain Sustainability: A Practical Guide for Continuous Improvement. (2010). *United Nations Global Compact Report.* Retrieved September 15, 2014 from http://www.bsr.org/reports/BSR_UNGC_SupplyChain-Report.pdf

Sveiby, K.-E. (2010). *Methods for measuring intangible assets.* Retrieved from http://www.sveiby.com/articles/IntangibleMethods.htm

Tabachnick, B. G., & Fidell, L. S. (1996). *Using Multivariate Statistics* (3rd ed.). New York: Harper Collins.

Taffler, R. J., & Abassi, B. (1984). A Model for Predicting Debt Servicing Problems in Developing Countries. *Journal of the Royal Statistical Society. Series A (General)*, *147*(4), 541–568. doi:10.2307/2981843

Taiwan Ministry of Economic Affairs. (2006). *White Paper on Small and Medium Enterprises in Taiwan.* Retrieved from http://www.moeasmea.gov.tw/eng/2006whitepaper/2006white.asp)

Tallon, P. P. (2008). Inside the adaptive enterprise: An information technology capabilities perspective on business process agility. *Information Technology Management*, *9*(1), 21–36. doi:10.1007/s10799-007-0024-8

Tang, T. C., & Chi, L. C. (2005). Predicting multilateral trade credit risks: Comparisons of Logit and Fuzzy Logic models using ROC curve analysis. *Expert Systems with Applications*, *28*(3), 547–556. doi:10.1016/j.eswa.2004.12.016

Tan, H. P., Plowman, D., & Hancock, P. (1997). Intellectual capital and the financial returns of companies. *Journal of Intellectual Capital*, *9*(1), 76–95.

Tapia, R. S., Daneva, M., & van Eck, P. (2007). Validating adequacy and suitability of business-IT alignment criteria in an inter-enterprise maturity model. In *Proceedings of the 11th IEEE International Enterprise Distributed Object Computing Conference* (pp. 202-213). Washington, DC: IEEE Computer Society. doi:10.1109/EDOC.2007.19

Taras, V., Rowney, J., & Steel, P. (2009). Half a century of measuring culture: Review of approaches, challenges, and limitations based on the analysis of 121 instruments for quantifying culture. *Journal of International Management*, *15*(4), 357–373. doi:10.1016/j.intman.2008.08.005

Taticchi, P. (2010). *Business Performance Measurement and Management: New Contexts, Themes and Challenges.* New York: Springer. doi:10.1007/978-3-642-04800-5

Taticchi, P., Tonelli, F., & Cagnazzo, L. (2010). Performance measurement and management: A literature review and a research agenda. *Measuring Business Excellence*, *14*(1), 4–18. doi:10.1108/13683041011027418

TDWI. (2008). *TDWI BI benchmark report: Organizational and performance metrics for BI teams.* Retrieved December 19, 2013, from http://mfhammond.com/yahoo_site_admin/assets/docs/TDWI-BIBenchmarkReport.242122912.pdf

Teece, D. J. (1998). Capturing value from knowledge assets: The new economy, markets for know-how, and intangible assets. *California Management Review*, *40*(3), 55–79. doi:10.2307/41165943

Teece, D., Pisano, G., & Shuen, A. (1997). Dynamic capabilities and strategic management. *Strategic Management Journal*, *18*(7), 509–533. doi:10.1002/(SICI)1097-0266(199708)18:7<509::AID-SMJ882>3.0.CO;2-Z

Teixeira, P., Brandão, P. L., & Rocha, A. (2012). Promoting Success in the Introduction of Health Information Systems. *International Journal of Enterprise Information Systems*, *8*(1), 17–27. doi:10.4018/jeis.2012010102

Theaker, A. (2004). *Priročnik za odnose z javnostmi.* Ljubljana: GV Založba.

Theriou, G. N., & Chatzoglou, P. D. (2008). Enhancing performance through best HRM practices, organizational learning and knowledge management - A conceptual framework. *European Business Review*, *20*(3), 185–207. doi:10.1108/09555340810871400

Thomas, J. C., Kellogg, W. A., & Erickson, T. (2001). The knowledge management puzzle: Human and social factors in knowledge management. *IBM Systems Journal*, *40*(4), 863–884. doi:10.1147/sj.404.0863

Thomas, L. C., Ho, J., & Scherer, W. T. (2001). Time will tell: Behavioural scoring and the dynamics of consumer credit assessment. *IMA Journal of Management Mathematics*, *12*(1), 89–103. doi:10.1093/imaman/12.1.89

Tidd, J., Bessant, J., & Pavitt, K. (1997). *Managing innovation: integrating technological, market, and organizational change.* Chichester, UK: Wiley.

Tobin, J., & Brainard, W. (1977). Asset markets and the cost of capital. In R. Nelson & B. Balassa (Eds.), *Economic progress, private values, and public policy: Essays in honor of William Fellner.* Amsterdam: North Holland.

Topbas, G. (2013, 08 April). Empowering Qatar's SMEs using cloud technology. *The Edge: Qatar's Business Magazine.* Retrieved from http://www.theedge.me/empowering-qatars-entrepreneurs-and-smes-using-cloud-technology/

Torben, J. A. (2001). Information technology, strategic decision approaches and organizational performance in different industrial settings. *The Journal of Strategic Information Systems*, *10*(2), 101–119. doi:10.1016/S0963-8687(01)00043-9

Torlone, R. (2008). Two Approaches to The Integration of Heterogeneous Data Warehouses. *Distributed and Parallel Databases*, *23*(1), 69–97. doi:10.1007/s10619-007-7022-z

Totka, M. (2013, May 21). How a small business can use big data. *Small Business Operations.* Retrieved from http://smallbiztrends.com/2013/05/small-business-can-use-big-data.html

Tressler, S. (2013). *Ten of San Antonio's Top Tweeters.* Retrieved July 6th 2014 from: http://www.mysanantonio.com/news/local/article/Ten-of-San-Antonio-s-top-tweeters-4755978.php

Triandis, H. C., & Suh, E. M. (2002). Cultural influences on personality. *Annual Review of Psychology*, *53*(1), 133–160. doi:10.1146/annurev.psych.53.100901.135200 PMID:11752482

Trkman, P. (2010). The critical success factors of business process management. *International Journal of Information Management*, *30*(2), 125–134. doi:10.1016/j.ijinfomgt.2009.07.003

Trompenaars, F., & Hampden-Turner, C. (1997). *Riding the Waves of Culture: Understanding Cultural Diversity in Business* (2nd ed.). London, UK: McGraw-Hill.

Truong, D. (2005). Methodologies for Evaluating Investment in Electronic Data Interchange. *International Journal of Enterprise Information Systems*, *1*(3), 56–68. doi:10.4018/jeis.2005070104

Tsai, M. C., Lin, S. P., Cheng, C. C., & Lin, Y. P. (2009). The consumer loan default predicting model – An application of DEA–DA and neural network. *Expert Systems with Applications*, *36*(9), 11682–11690. doi:10.1016/j.eswa.2009.03.009

Tucker, B., Thorne, H., & Gurd, B. (2009). Management control systems and strategy: What's been happening. *Journal of Accounting Literature*, *28*(1), 123–163.

Tufte, E. R. (2010). *Visual Explanations*. Cheshire, CT: Graphics Press LLC.

Tuma, E. H. (1988). Institutionalized Obstacles to Development: The Case of Egypt. *World Development*, *16*(10), 1185–1198. doi:10.1016/0305-750X(88)90085-X

Tung, W. L., Quek, C., Cheng, P., & Ews, G. (2004). A novel neural-fuzzy based early warning system for predicting bank failures. *Neural Networks 17*(4), 567–587.

Turner, P. (2003). *Organisational communication: The role of HR professional*. London: CIPD.

Tushman, M., & Nadler, D. (1986). Organizing for innovation. *California Management Review*, *28*(3), 74–92. doi:10.2307/41165203

Twala, B. (2010). Multiple classifier application to credit risk assessment. *Expert Systems with Applications*, *37*(4), 3326–3336. doi:10.1016/j.eswa.2009.10.018

Twenge, M. J., Zhang, L., & Im, C. (2004). It's Beyond My Control: A Cross-Temporal Meta-Analysis of Increasing Externality in Locus of Control,1960-2002. *Personality and Social Psychology Review*, *8*(3), 308–319. doi:10.1207/s15327957pspr0803_5 PMID:15454351

UCI Machine Learning Repository. (n.d.). *Center for Machine Learning and Intelligent Systems*. Retrieved from http://archive.ics.uci.edu/ml/

Ulrich, E., & Eppinger, S. (2011). Product Design and Development. McGraw-Hill/Irwin.

Umarji, V. (2013, May 27). Gujarat SMEs increase IT spending by 20%. *Business Standard*. Retrieved from http://www.business-standard.com/article/sme/gujarat-smes-increase-it-spending-by-20-113052700986_1.html

United States International Trade Commission. (2010). *Small and Medium-Sized Enterprises: Overview of Participation in U.S. Exports*. Retrieved from http://www.usitc.gov/publications/332/pub4125.pdf

United States Small Business Administration. (2012). Washington, DC: Author.

van Weele, A., & van Raaij, E. (2014). The future of purchasing and supply management research: About relevance and rigor. *Journal of Supply Chain Management*, *50*(1), 56–72. doi:10.1111/jscm.12042

Vance, A. (2010, April 22). Start-up goes after big data with hadoop helper. *New York Times Blog*. Retrieved from http://bits.blogs.nytimes.com/2010/04/22/start-up-goes-after-big-data-with-hadoophelper/?dbk

Vance, A. (2011a, September 12). The data knows. *Bloomberg Businessweek*, 70-74.

Vance, A. (2011b, March 7). The power of the cloud. *Bloomberg Businessweek*, 52-59.

Vandenbosch, B. (1999). An empirical analysis of the association between the use of executive support systems and perceived organizational competitiveness. *Accounting, Organizations and Society*, *24*(1), 77–92. doi:10.1016/S0361-3682(97)00064-0

Vapnik, V. (1995). The Nature of Statistical Learning Theory. New York: Springer.

Vassiliadis, P. (2009). A Survey of Extract–Transform–Load Technology. *International Journal of Data Warehousing and Mining*, *5*(3), 1–27. doi:10.4018/jdwm.2009070101

Venkatadri, M., Hanumat, G. S., & Manjunath, G. (2010). A novel business intelligence system framework. *Universal Journal of Computer Science and Engineering Technology*, *1*(2), 112–116.

Verdu, S. V., Garcia, M. O., Senabre, C., Marin, A. G., & Franco, F. J. G. (2006). Classification, Filtering, and Identification of Electrical Customer Load Patterns Through the Use of Self-Organizing Maps. *IEEE Transactions on Power Systems*, *21*(4), 1672–1682. doi:10.1109/TPWRS.2006.881133

Vigoda-Gadot, E., Shoham, A., Ruvio, A., & Schwabsky, N. (2005). *Innovation in the Public Sector*. Oslo, Norway: The University of Haifa & NIFU STEP.

Vigoda-Gadot, E., & Cohen, A. (2004). *Citizenship and Management in Public Administration: Integrating Behavioral Theory and Managerial Thinking*. Cheltenham, UK: Edward Elgar.

Vitt, E., Luckevich, M., & Misner, S. (2010). *Business intelligence: Making better decisions faster*. Redmond, WA: Microsoft Press.

Vogel, E. F. (1979). *Japan as Number One. Lessons for America*. Cambridge, MA: Harvard University Press. doi:10.4159/harvard.9780674366299

Vrgovic, P., Glassman, B., Walton, A., & Vidicki, P. (2012). Open innovation for SMEs in developing countries - an intermediated communication network model for collaboration beyond obstacles. *Innovation: Management. Policy & Practice, 14*(3), 290–303. doi:10.5172/impp.2012.14.3.290

Wailgum, T. (2010). *Biggest barriers to business analytics adoption: People*. Retrieved November 12, 2013, from http://www.cio.com.au/article/367783/biggest_barriers_business_analytics_adoption_people/

Walker, D. M., Walker, T., & Schmitz, J. (2003). *Doing Business Internationally: The Guide to cross-Cultural Success* (2nd ed.). New York, NY: McGraw-Hill.

Wally, S., & Baum, J. R. (1994). Personal and structural determinants of the pace of strategic decision-making. *Academy of Management Journal, 37*(4), 932–956. doi:10.2307/256605

Wang, Y., Wang, S., & Lai, K. K. (2005). *A New Fuzzy Support Vector Machine to Evaluate Credit Risk*. Paper presented at the IEEE Transactions on Fuzzy Systems. New York, NY.

Wang, R., & Dagli, C. (2011). Executable system architecting using systems modeling language in conjunction with colored Petri nets in a model-driven systems development process. *Systems Engineering, 14*(4), 383–409. doi:10.1002/sys.20184

Wang, S., & Yi, X. (2012). Organizational justice and work withdrawal in Chinese companies: The moderating effects of allocentrism and idiocentrism. *International Journal of Cross Cultural Management, 12*(2), 211–228. doi:10.1177/1470595812439871

Wan, W. P., & Hoskisson, R. E. (2003). Home country environments, corporate diversification strategies, and firm performance. *Academy of Management Journal, 45*(1), 27–45. doi:10.2307/30040674

Wasserman, L. (2005). *All of statistics: A concise course in statistical inference* (2nd ed.). New York: Springer Science.

Watson, H. J. (2013). The Business Case for Analytics. *BizEd, 12*(3), 49–54.

Watson, H. J., & Wixom, B. H. (2007). Enterprise agility and mature BI capabilities. *Business Intelligence Journal, 12*(3), 4–6.

Weidong, Z., Weihui, D., & Kunlomg, K. (2010). The relationship of business intelligence and knowledge. In *Proceedings of the 2nd IEE International Conference on Informational Management and Engineering (ICIE)*, (pp. 26-29). IEE.

Wei, L.-Y. (2013). A GA-weighted ANFIS model based on multiple stock market volatility causality for TAIEX forecasting. *Applied Soft Computing, 13*(2), 911–920. doi:10.1016/j.asoc.2012.08.048

Weir, D. (1998). The fourth paradigm. In A. Al Shamali & J. Denton (Eds.), *Management in the Middle East*. Kuwait: Gulf Management Centre.

Weir, D. (2000). Management in the Arab Middle East. In M. Tayeb (Ed.), *International Business: Theories, Policies and Practices*. London, UK: Prentice Hall.

Weir, D. (2000). Management in the Arab World: A Fourth Paradigm? In A. Al-Shamali & J. Denton (Eds.), *Arab Business: The Globalisation Imperative*. Kuwait: Arab Research Center.

Weir, D., & Hutchings, K. (2005). Cultural embeddedness and contextual constraints: Knowledge sharing in Chinese and Arab cultures. *Knowledge and Process Management, 12*(2), 89–98. doi:10.1002/kpm.222

Weka-3: Data Mining with Open Source Machine Learning Software in Java. (n.d.). Retrieved from http://www.cs.waikato.ac.nz/ml/weka/

Wenrich, K. I., & Ahmad, N. (2009). Lessons Learned During a Decade of ERP Experience: A Case Study. *International Journal of Enterprise Information Systems*, *5*(1), 55–75. doi:10.4018/jeis.2009010105

Wernerfelt, B. (1984). The resource-based view of the firm. *Strategic Management Journal*, *5*(2), 171–180. doi:10.1002/smj.4250050207

West, D. (2000). Neural network credit scoring models. *Computers & Operations Research*, *27*(11-12), 1131–1152. doi:10.1016/S0305-0548(99)00149-5

West, M., & Anderson, N. (1996). Innovation in top management teams. *The Journal of Applied Psychology*, *81*(6), 680–693. doi:10.1037/0021-9010.81.6.680

White, K. Jr. (1998). Systems design engineering. *Systems Engineering*, *1*(4), 285–302. doi:10.1002/(SICI)1520-6858(1998)1:4<285::AID-SYS4>3.0.CO;2-E

White, M. A., & Bruton, G. D. (2011). *The Management of Technology and Innovation*. Mason, OH: South-Western.

Whiteoak, J. W., Crawford, N. G., & Mapstone, R. H. (2006). Impact of gender and generational differences in work values and attitudes in an Arab culture. *Thunderbird International Business Review*, *48*(1), 77–91. doi:10.1002/tie.20086

Whitley, R. (2000). *Divergent Capitalisms. The Social Structuring and Change of Business Systems*. Oxford, UK: Oxford University Press.

Whitt, W. (1989). Planning queueing simulation. *Management Science*, *35*(11), 1341–1366. doi:10.1287/mnsc.35.11.1341

Wilder, C. R., & Ozgur, C. O. (forthcoming). Business Analytics Curriculum for Undergraduate Majors. *INFORMS Transactions on Education*.

Williams, S., & Williams, N. (2007). *The profit impact of business intelligence*. San Fracisco, CA: Morgan Kaufmann.

Wilson, H., Daniel, E., & McDonald, M. (2002). Factors for success in customer relationship management (CRM) systems. *Journal of Marketing Management*, *18*(1-2), 193-219.

Winer, E. (2001). A framework for customer relationship management. *California Management Review*, *43*(4), 6–14. doi:10.2307/41166102

Wise, K., & Perushek, D. E. (1996). Linear goal programming for academic library acquisitions allocations. *Library Acquisitions: Practice & Theory*, *20*(3), 311–327. doi:10.1016/0364-6408(96)00065-8

Wise, K., & Perushek, D. E. (2000). Goal Programming as a solution technique. *Library & Information Science Research*, *22*(2), 165–183. doi:10.1016/S0740-8188(99)00052-3

Wixom, B. (2011). *Survey Finds Disconnect Between BI Education, Industry Needs*. Available at http://www.itbusinessedge.com/cm/community/features/interviews/blog/survey-finds-disconnect-between-bi-education-industry-needs/?cs=47562

Wixom, B. H., Ariyachandra, T., & Mooney, J. (2013). *BI Congress Communications*. Available at http://www2.commerce.virginia.edu/bic3/communications.asp

Wixom, B., Ariyachandra, T., Goul, M., Gray, P., Kulkarni, U., & Phillips-Wren, G. (2011). The Current State of Business Intelligence in Academia. *Communications of the Association for Information Systems*, *29*, 299–312.

Wixom, B., Watson, H., & Werner, T. (2011). Developing an enterprise business intelligence capability: The Norfolk Southern journey. *MIS Quarterly Executive*, *10*(2), 61–71.

Wojtecki, J. G., & Peters R. G. (2000). Communicating organizational change: information technology meets the carbon-based employee unit. *The 2000 Annual*, *2*, 1-16.

Wolf, J. (2014). The relationship between sustainable supply chain management, stakeholder pressure and corporate sustainability performance. *Journal of Business Ethics*, *119*(3), 317–328. doi:10.1007/s10551-012-1603-0

World Bank. (2012). Retrieved from http://data.worldbank.org/indicator/FB.POS.TOTL.P5

Wright, M., Filatotchev, I., Hoskisson, R. E., & Peng, M. W. (2005). Strategy Research in Emerging Economies: Challenging the Conventional Wisdom. *Journal of Management Studies*, 42(1), 1–33. doi:10.1111/j.1467-6486.2005.00487.x

Wright, S., Picton, D., & Callow, J. (2002). Competitive intelligence in UK firms, A typology. *Marketing Intelligence & Planning*, 20(6), 349–360. doi:10.1108/02634500210445400

Wu, C. H., & Lee, T. Z. (2005). Material acquisitions using discovery informatics approach. In Encyclopaedia of Data Warehousing and Mining, (pp. 705-709). Hershey, PA: IGI Global.

Wu, C. H. et al. (2003). Data mining applied to material acquisition budget allocation for libraries: Design and development. *Expert Systems with Applications*, 25(3), 401–411. doi:10.1016/S0957-4174(03)00065-4

Wu, C. H., Lee, T. Z., & Kao, S. C. (2004). Knowledge discovery applied to material acquisitions for libraries. *Information Processing & Management*, 40(4), 709–725. doi:10.1016/j.ipm.2003.08.010

Wu, J.-D., & Liu, J.-C. (2012). A forecasting system for car fuel consumption using a radial basis function neural network. *Expert Systems with Applications*, 39(2), 1883–1888. doi:10.1016/j.eswa.2011.07.139

Wu, W.-Y., Lin, C.-T., & Kung, J.-Y. (2013). Supplier Selection in Supply Chain Management by Using Fuzzy Multiple-Attribute Decision-Making Method. *Journal of Intelligent & Fuzzy Systems*, 24(1), 175–183.

Xavier, M. J., Srinivasan, A., & Thamizhvanan, A. (2011). Use of analytics in Indian enterprises: An exploratory study. *Journal of Indian Business Research*, 3(3), 168–179. doi:10.1108/17554191111157038

Xiao, W., Zhao, Q., & Fei, Q. (2006). a comparative study of data mining methods in consumer loans credit scoring management. *Journal of Systems Science and Systems Engineering*, 15(4), 419-435.

Xinhui, C., & Zhong, Q. (2009). *Consumer Credit Scoring Based on Multi-criteria Fuzzy Logic*. Paper presented at the International Conference on Business Intelligence and Financial Engineering. New York, NY. doi:10.1109/BIFE.2009.177

Xu, X., Zhou, C., & Wang, Z. (2009). Credit scoring algorithm based on link analysis ranking with support vector machine. *Expert Systems with Applications*, 36(2), 2625–2632. doi:10.1016/j.eswa.2008.01.024

Yakowitz, S., L'Ecuyer, P., & Vazquez-Abad, F. (2000). Global stochastic optimization with low-dispersion point sets. *Operations Research*, 48(6), 939–950. doi:10.1287/opre.48.6.939.12393

Yamin, S., Mavondo, F., Gunasekaran, A., & Sarros, J. A. (1997). Study of competitive strategy, organizational innovation and organizational performance among Australian manufacturing companies. *International Journal of Production Economics*, 52(1-2), 161–172. doi:10.1016/S0925-5273(96)00104-1

Yang, J., Liu, H., Gao, S., & Li, Y. (2012). Technological innovation of firms in China: Past, present, and future. *Asia Pacific Journal of Management*, 29(3), 819–840. doi:10.1007/s10490-010-9243-3

Yang, Y. (2007). Adaptive credit scoring with kernel learning methods. *European Journal of Operational Research*, 183(3), 1521–1536. doi:10.1016/j.ejor.2006.10.066

Yao, J., & Tan, C. L. (2000). A case study on using neural networks to perform technical forecasting of forex. *Neurocomputing*, 34(1-4), 79–98. doi:10.1016/S0925-2312(00)00300-3

Yeh, I. C., & Lien, C. (2009). The comparisons of data mining techniques for the predictive accuracy of probability of default of credit card clients. *Expert Systems with Applications*, 36(2), 2473–2480. doi:10.1016/j.eswa.2007.12.020

Yen, G. (1994). Adaptive time-delay neural control in space structural platforms. In *Proceedings of IEEE World Congress on Computational Intelligence*, (vol. 4, pp. 2622-2627). IEEE. doi:10.1109/ICNN.1994.374635

Yerazunis, W. S. (2004, January). The spam-filtering accuracy plateau at 99.9% accuracy and how to get past it. In *Proceedings of the 2004 MIT Spam Conference*. MIT.

Yin, Y., Qin, S., & Holland, R. (2011). Development of a design performance measurement matrix for improving collaborative design during a design process. *International Journal of Productivity and Performance Management*, 60(2), 152–184. doi:10.1108/17410401111101485

You, H. (2010). A knowledge Management Approach for real-time business intelligence. In *Proceedings of the 2nd IEE International Workshop on Intelligent Systems and Application (ISA)*. IEE.

Young, M., & Post, J. E. (1993). Managing to communicate, communicating to manage: How leading companies communicate with employees. *Organizational Dynamics*, 22(1), 31–43. doi:10.1016/0090-2616(93)90080-K

Yu, L., Wang, S., & Lai, K. K. (2008). Credit risk assessment with a multistage neural network ensemble learning approach. *Expert Systems with Applications*, 34(2), 1434–1444. doi:10.1016/j.eswa.2007.01.009

Yu, L., Wang, S., Wen, F., Lai, K. K., & He, S. (2008). Designing A Hybrid Intelligent Mining System for Credit Risk Evaluation. *Journal of Systems Science and Complexity*, 21(4), 527–539. doi:10.1007/s11424-008-9133-7

Yu, L., Yue, W., Wang, S., & Lai, K. K. (2010). Support vector machine based multiagent ensemble learning for credit risk evaluation. *Expert Systems with Applications*, 37(2), 1351–1360. doi:10.1016/j.eswa.2009.06.083

Yune, H., Kim, H., & Chang, J. Y. (2010). An Efficient Search Method of Product Review using Opinion Mining Techniques. *Journal of KIISE: Computing Practices and Letters*, 16(2), 222–226.

Yusuff, R. M. (2004). Manufacturing best practices of the electric and electronics firms in Malaysia. *Benchmarking: An International Journal*, 11(4), 361–369. doi:10.1108/14635770410546764

Yu, Y., Kim, Y., Kim, N., & Jeong, S. R. (2013). Predicting the Direction of the Stock Index by Using a Domain-Specific Sentiment Dictionary. *Journal of Intelligent Information Systems*, 19(1), 92–110.

Zacharia, Z. G., Nix, N. W., & Lusch, R. F. (2009). An analysis of supply chain collaborations and their effect on performance outcomes. *Journal of Business Logistics*, 30(2), 101–123. doi:10.1002/j.2158-1592.2009.tb00114.x

Zack, M. H. (1999). Managing codified knowledge. *Sloan Management Review*, 40(4), 45–58.

Zahra, S. (2011). Doing research in the (new) Middle East: Sailing with the wind. *The Academy of Management Perspectives*, 25(4), 6–21. doi:10.5465/amp.2011.0128

Zalud, B. (2013, February). Nine Shades of Analytics, Anything but Grey. *Security*, 50(2), 36–50.

Zander, U., & Kogut, B. (1995). Knowledge and the speed of transfer and imitation of organizational capabilities: An empirical test. *Organization Science*, 6(1), 76–92. doi:10.1287/orsc.6.1.76

Zanjani, M. S., Rouzbehani, R., & Dabbagh, H. (2008). proposes a conceptual model of customer knowledge Management: A study of CKM tools in British Dotcoms. *International Journal of Humanities and Social Science*, 3(5), 363–367.

Zehir, C., & Ozsahin, M. (2008). A field research on the relationship between strategic decision-making speed and innovation performance in the case of Turkish large-scale firms. *Management Decision*, 46(5), 709–724. doi:10.1108/00251740810873473

Zeifman, M., & Roth, K. (2011). Nonintrusive appliance load monitoring: Review and outlook. *IEEE Transactions on Consumer Electronics*, 57(1), 76–84. doi:10.1109/TCE.2011.5735484

Zeleny, M. (1987). Management support systems: Towards integrated knowledge management. *Human Systems Management*, 7(1), 59–70.

Zeng, L., Li, L., Duan, L., Lu, K., Shi, Z., & Wang, M. et al. (2012). Distributed data mining: A survey. *Information Technology Management*, 13(4), 403–409. doi:10.1007/s10799-012-0124-y

Zhang, D., Hifi, M., Chen, Q., & Ye, W. (2008). *A Hybrid Credit Scoring Model Based on Genetic Programming and Support Vector Machines*. Paper presented at the Fourth International Conference on Natural Computation. New York, NY. doi:10.1109/ICNC.2008.205

Zhang, H., & Ma, D. (2005). A Systems Engineering approach to Occupant Protection System design and optimization through modeling and simulation. *Systems Engineering*, 8(1), 51–61. doi:10.1002/sys.20020

Zhao, D. (2013). Frontiers of big data business analytics: Patterns and cases in online marketing. In J. Liebowitz (Ed.), *Big data and business analytics* (pp. 43–68). Boca Raton, FL: CRC Press/Taylor & Francis. doi:10.1201/b14700-4

Zhao, H. (2007). A multi-objective genetic programming approach to developing Pareto optimal decision trees. *Decision Support Systems*, *43*(3), 809–826. doi:10.1016/j.dss.2006.12.011

Zhou, J., & Bai, T. (2008). *Credit Risk Assessment using Rough Set Theory and GA-based SVM*. Paper presented at the 3rd International Conference on Grid and Pervasive Computing – Workshops. New York, NY. doi:10.1109/GPC.WORKSHOPS.2008.56

Zhou, L., & Lai, K. K. (2009). Benchmarking binary classification models on data sets with different degrees of imbalance. *Frontiers of Computer Science in China*, *3*(2), 205–216. doi:10.1007/s11704-009-0027-1

Zhou, L., Lai, K. K., & Yu, L. (2009). Credit scoring using support vector machines with direct search for parameters selection. *Soft Computing*, *13*(2), 149–155. doi:10.1007/s00500-008-0305-0

Zhou, L., Lai, K. K., & Yu, L. (2010). Least squares support vector machines ensemble models for credit scoring. *Expert Systems with Applications*, *37*(1), 127–133. doi:10.1016/j.eswa.2009.05.024

Zhuang, L., Jing, F., & Zhu, X. (2006). Movie Review Mining and Summarization. In *Proceedings of 15th ACM International Conference on Information and Knowledge Management*, (pp. 43-50). New York, NY: ACM.

Zhuang, L., Williamson, D., & Carter, M. (1999). Innovate or liquidate—are all organisations convinced? A two-phased study into the innovation process. *Management Decision*, *37*(1), 57–71. doi:10.1108/00251749910252030

Zineldin, M. (2002). Globalisation, strategic co-operation and economic integration among Islamic/Arab countries. *Management Research News*, *25*(4), 35–61. doi:10.1108/01409170210783188

Zuboff, S. (1988). *In the Age of the Small Machine*. New York, NY: Basic Books.

Zurada, J., & Lonial, S. (2005). *Comparison of the performance of several data mining methods for bad debt recovery in the healthcare industry. The Journal of Applied Business Research*, *21*(2), 37–53.

About the Contributors

Madjid Tavana is a Professor and Distinguished Chair of Business Systems and Analytics at La Salle University, where he served as Chairman of the Management Department and Director of the Center for Technology and Management. He is a Distinguished Research Fellow at Kennedy Space Center, Johnson Space Center, Naval Research Laboratory at Stennis Space Center, and Air Force Research Laboratory. He was recently honored with the prestigious Space Act Award by NASA. He holds a MBA, PMIS, and PhD in Management Information Systems and received his Post-Doctoral Diploma in Strategic Information Systems from the Wharton School at the University of Pennsylvania. He is the Editor-in-Chief of *Decision Analytics, International Journal of Applied Decision Sciences, International Journal of Management and Decision Making, International Journal of Strategic Decision Sciences,* and *International Journal of Enterprise Information Systems.* He has published several books and over 150 research papers in academic journals such as *Information Sciences, Decision Sciences, Information Systems, Interfaces, Annals of Operations Research, Advances in Space Research, Omega, Information and Management, Knowledge-Based Systems, International Journal of Production Research, Expert Systems with Applications, European Journal of Operational Research, Journal of the Operational Research Society, Computers and Operations Research, Energy Economics, Applied Soft Computing,* and *Energy Policy.*

Kartikeya Puranam is an Assistant Professor of Business Systems and Analytics at La Salle University. He received his PhD in Supply Chain Management from Rutgers Business School. He received his Master's and bachelor's degrees in Mechanical Engineering from the Indian Institute of Technology in Bombay. His research interests include bidding strategies in auctions, learning in sequential auctions, inventory management, marketing and operations interface, Markov chains and Markov decision processes, and supply chain management. He has published in *Operations Research Letters* and *European Journal of Operational Research.*

* * *

Galanou Ekaterini is an Assistant Professor in management. She obtained her PhD from the University of Nottingham (Business School), UK. Her teaching interests are Management Science, Organization Change and Design, International Business, Business Strategy, Business Leadership, Business Cycles, and Forecasting. Her research interests are Leadership, Strategical Thinking, Management Models, Change Management. She has published in journals such as *International Journal of Training and Development, International Journal of Business and Management, Archives of Economic History, Management Research Review, Advances in Applied Economics and Finance.*

Ola Al-Laymoun is a PhD candidate at the College of Business, University of Texas at Arlington. She received her MS in Information Systems from University of Texas at Arlington in 2010. Her research interests are in Data Mining, Information Systems, and Gamification.

Abdelmalek Amine received an Engineering degree in Computer Science from the Computer Science Department of Djillali Liabes University of Sidi-Belabbes, Algeria, and PhD from the same university. He has several publications in the field of text mining. His research interests include data mining, text mining, ontology, classification, clustering, neural networks, genetic programming, biomimetic optimization method. Dr. Amine is an associate professor and the head of Mathematics and Computer Science Department of UTMS University of Saida, Algeria. He also collaborates with the "knowledge base and database" team of the TIMC laboratory at the Joseph Fourier University of Grenoble.

Hossein Arsham is the Harry Wright Distinguished Research Professor at the University of Baltimore. All of Dr. Arsham's higher-education degrees are concentrated on modeling. He has earned his BSc in Physics from Aryam-Meher Technical University, Tehran, Iran; his MSc in Management Science from Cranefield University, UK; and DSc General Operations Research from The George Washington University, Washington, DC. Dr. Arsham's teaching, research, and consulting activities are multidisciplinary and interdisciplinary. His research concentration includes new advances in discrete event system simulation. He has recently received The Regent's Faculty Award for Excellence in Research from The University System of Maryland. Currently, he is teaching graduate courses at The Johns Hopkins University, Baltimore, MD.

Dennis Crossen has more than 30 years of teaching and professional experience in numerous areas of business, engineering, and applicable analytics. In his professional business career, he has managed teams in the commercial and government sectors including responsibilities as technical architect for the United Nations information network, U.S. Department of State, NASA Kennedy Space Center, the Pentagon, and other culturally diverse global organizations. Professor Crossen has been a member of several international and local standards boards, including assignments on the ACT/IAC IPv6 working group in Washington, D.C., where he co-authored a white paper for determining how large organizations would manage the implementation of Internet Protocol version 6 (IPv6). He has consulted and lectured within the continental U.S., Alaska, Cuba, Europe, Japan, the Russian Federation, and South America.

M. Deniz Dalman currently works as branding and marketing consultant based in Istanbul, Turkey. He earned his PhD in Marketing from the State University of New York at Binghamton. His research interests include branding, word-of-mouth, cross-cultural marketing, and marketing of higher education, and his publications have appeared in *Innovative Marketing Journal, International Journal of Marketing Studies, Advances in Consumer Research, Academy of Marketing Science*, and *AMA Summer Educators' Proceedings*.

G. Scott Erickson is Professor of Marketing in the School of Business at Ithaca College, Ithaca, NY, where he has also served as Department Chair and Interim Associate Dean. He holds a PhD from Lehigh University, Masters degrees from Thunderbird and SMU, and a BA from Haverford College. He served as Fulbright Research Chair at The Monieson Centre for the Study of Knowledge-Based Enterprises at Queen's Business School, Kingston, ON, in 2010/2011. He has published widely on intellectual capital, knowledge management, and competitive intelligence and is the Associate Editor for America of the *Journal of Intelligence Studies in Business.*

Reda Mohamed Hamou received an Engineering degree in Computer Science from the Computer Science Department of Djillali Liabes University of Sidi-Belabbes, Algeria, and PhD (Artificial intelligence) from the same university. He has several publications in the fields of BioInspired and Metaheuristics. His research interests include data mining, text mining, classification, clustering, computational intelligence, neural networks, evolutionary computation, and biomimetic optimization methods. He is a head of research team in GecoDe laboratory. Dr. Hamou is an associate professor in technology faculty in UTMS University of Saida, Algeria. Dr. Reda Mohamed Hamou has published in journals such as *International Journal of Applied Evolutionary Computation (IJAEC), International Journal of Applied Metaheuristic Computing (IJAMC), International Journal of Artificial Life Research (IJALR), International Journal of Chemoinformatics & Chimical Engineering (IJCCE),* and *International Journal of Data Mining & Emerging Technologies,* among others.

N. Hemachandra is a Professor in Industrial Engineering and Operations Research, IIT Bombay. His current academic interests include various operations research methodologies like queueing models, Markov decision models, game theory, stochastic approximations, etc., and their applications for decision making in logistics, supply chains, communication networks, power systems.

Konstantin Hopf is a research associate of the Energy Efficient Systems group at the University of Bamberg in Germany. He holds BSc and MSc in Business Information Systems from the University of Bamberg. His research interests are machine learning, statistics, and smart metering.

Md. Hossain was born in Dhaka, Bangladesh, in 1967. He received BSc degree in Electrical and Electronics Engineering from Bangladesh University of Engineering and Technology (BUET), Dhaka, Bangladesh, in 1992. He is currently pursuing his MSc degree in Computer Science and Engineering from North South University, Dhaka, Bangladesh. He has been working as Deputy General Manager – IT in Tradesworth Group, Bangladesh, since 2001. He also worked as a senior computer programmer and software developer in Electronics and Computers Ltd., Bangladesh, from 1997 to 2000. From 1995 to 1997, he worked as a software developer in Aurora System Ltd., Bangladesh. He has published two scientific papers in the field of data mining and fuzzy logic. His current research interest is in database, data mining, and software engineering, especially development of efficient library management software by incorporating knowledge engineering techniques.

Michelle Jeong is a Doctoral student at the Annenberg School for Communication at the University of Pennsylvania. She holds a BA and MA in Communication, both from the University of Pennsylvania. Her primary areas of interest are in health communication and the role of interpersonal communication in the context of mass media, and she is currently exploring the possibilities of applying opinion mining methodology to such areas. Her research has appeared in journals such as *American Journal of Preventive Medicine* and *Journal of Nutrition Education and Behavior.*

Seung Ryul Jeong is a Professor in the Graduate School of Business IT at Kookmin University, Korea. He holds a BA in Economics from Sogang University, Korea, an MS in MIS from University of Wisconsin, and a PhD in MIS from the University of South Carolina, USA. Dr. Jeong has published extensively in the information systems field, with over 60 publications in refereed journals like *Journal of MIS, Communications of the ACM, Information and Management, Journal of Systems and Software,* among others. Dr. Jeong's areas of interest are Opinion Mining, Process Management, Software Engineering, and Information Resource Management.

Sema Kalaian is a Professor of Statistics and Research Methods in the College of Technology at Eastern Michigan University. She received her Masters and Ph. D. in Quantitative Research Methods from Michigan State University. Professor Kalaian was a recipient of the (1) "Best Paper" award from the American Educational Research Association (AERA), and (2) "Distinguished Paper Award" from the Society for the Advancement of Information Systems (SAIS). Over the years, Dr. Kalaian taught introductory and advanced statistical courses such as Research Methods, Research Design, Multivariate Statistics, Regression Analysis, Survey Research, Multilevel Modeling, Structural Equation Modeling, Meta-Analysis, and Program Evaluation. Professor Kalaian's research interests focus on the development of new statistical methods and its applications. Much of her methodological developments and applications have focused on the (a) development of the multivariate meta-analytic techniques for combining evidence from multiple primary studies, (b) applications of the meta-analysis methods to various projects in different fields of study, and (c) developments of statistical methods for analyzing Delphi survey data.

Kijpokin Kasemsap received his BEng degree in Mechanical Engineering from King Mongkut's University of Technology Thonburi, his MBA degree from Ramkhamhaeng University, and his DBA degree in Human Resource Management from Suan Sunandha Rajabhat University. He is a Special Lecturer at Faculty of Management Sciences, Suan Sunandha Rajabhat University based in Bangkok, Thailand. He is a Member of International Association of Engineers (IAENG), International Association of Engineers and Scientists (IAEST), International Economics Development and Research Center (IEDRC), International Association of Computer Science and Information Technology (IACSIT), International Foundation for Research and Development (IFRD), and International Innovative Scientific and Research Organization (IISRO). He also serves on the International Advisory Committee (IAC) for International Association of Academicians and Researchers (INAAR). He has numerous original research articles in top international journals, conference proceedings, and book chapters on business management, human resource management, and knowledge management published internationally.

Rafa Kasim is a professor of statistics and research design in the College of Education at Indiana Tech University. He also works in the private sector as a statistician and research consultant. Previously, he was a senior statistician at the Evaluation, Management & Training Associates Inc. (EMT). He received his Masters and Ph. D. in Quantitative Research Methods from Michigan State University. His research focused on the application of multilevel analysis to study the effects of educational and social contexts on educational outcomes and human development in large-scale longitudinal data sets. Some of Dr. Kasim work has also addressed the issues of selection and attrition bias in multi-site large studies. He has collaborated on numerous studies in fields such as adult literacy, education, and substance abuse treatments. Some of his work appears in a book chapter in *Application of Multilevel Models, Journal of Educational and Behavioral Statistics, Harvard Educational Review*, and *Advances in Health Sciences Education*.

Marios I. Katsioloudes is a Professor in Management. He obtained his PhD in Management from the University of Pennsylvania, USA. His teaching interests are Strategic Management, International Business, Entrepreneurship, Change Management, and Innovation and Leadership. His research interests are strategic management in the for-profit and nonprofit sectors and the participation of employees in the process, strategic planning process in the SMEs, challenges, issues, motivations of entrepreneurs in a number of countries, and field research and write-up of case studies in the above areas. He has published in journals such as *Economics Management and Financial Markets, Int. J. Entrepreneurial Venturing International Journal for Business Innovation and Research, International Journal of Foresight and Innovation Policy, Journal of Business Strategy, Management Research Review*.

Dennis Kennedy is an Associate Professor of Business Systems and Analytics at La Salle University. He has a BS from the Pennsylvania State University and an MBA and PhD from Temple University. His research interests include multi-criteria decision making, expert systems, group decision support systems, distributed consensus building, the conceptual framework of accounting, earnings recognition, and valuation in financial reporting. He has published research in the *International Journal of Business Analytics, Energy Policy, International Journal of Applied Decision Sciences, International Journal of Information Technology and Decision Making, Business Journal, Benchmarking: An International Journal, Information and Management, Journal of Behavioral Decision Making, Omega, Accounting Enquiries, Journal of Management Systems, Journal of Accounting, Auditing and Finance*, and *Interface*.

Abbas Keramati is an Associate Professor of Industrial and Systems Engineering at the University of Tehran. He received his BS, MS, and PhD from Sharif University of Technology, University of Tehran and Tarbiat Modarres University in Iran, respectively. He received the 2007–2008 Teaching Award at the College of Engineering, University of Tehran. He has published several papers in international journals such as *International Journal of Production Research, Industrial Marketing Management*, and *Applied Soft Computing*. He is interested on topics in IT/IS investment evaluation, CRM, multivariate analysis, and intelligent systems and modeling.

Yoosin Kim is a visiting researcher at the College of Business at the University of Texas – Arlington. He received a PhD in Management Information Systems from Kookmin University, Korea. He had worked at Accenture as a Data Scientist, SK C&C as an Application Analyst, and ICT consulting companies as an IS expert for over 10 years in financial, medical, and e-commerce fields. His current research interests include stock prediction, consumer behavior analysis, customer complaint assessment, social media monitoring, and market sensing based on social big data analysis. His research has appeared in journals such as *Journal of Intelligent Information System, Journal of Internet Computing and Services*, and *International Journal of Advances in Soft Computing and Applications*.

Salim Lahmiri is with ESCA School of Management in Casablanca, Morocco. He holds a PhD degree in Cognitive Informatics from UQÀM and a Master's of Engineering (MEng) from École de Technologie Supérieure, Montreal, Canada. His research interests are in pattern recognition, intelligent decision systems, and times series analysis and forecasting.

Ming-Chang Lee is Assistant Professor at National Kaohsiung University of Applied Sciences. His qualifications include a Master's degree in Applied Mathematics from National Tsing Hua University and a PhD degree in Industrial Management from National Cheng Kung University. His research interests include knowledge management, parallel computing, and data analysis. His publications include articles in the *Journal of Computer & Mathematics with Applications, International Journal of Operation Research, Computers & Engineering, American Journal of Applied Science and Computers, Industrial Engineering, International Journal innovation and Learning, Int. J. Services and Standards, Lecture Notes in computer SCIENCE (LNCS), International Journal of Computer Science and Network Security, Journal of Convergence Information Technology, International Journal of Advancements in Computing Technology, International Journal of Artificial Intelligence & Application (IJAIA), International Journal of Software Engineering and its Application (IJSEIA)*, and *International Journal of Management and Enterprise Development (IJMED)*.

Deshabrata Roy Mahapatra is a Doctoral student at the Department of Applied Mathematics with Oceanology and Computer Programming of Vidyasagar University, West Bengal, India. He holds a MSc and BSc in Applied Mathematics from Kalyani University in India. His research interests are in Transportation Problem, Multi Choice Programming, and Fuzzy Set Theory. Deshabrata Roy Mahapatra has published in journals such as *The Journal of Fuzzy Mathematics, Journal of Uncertain Systems, International Journal of Mathematics and Scientific Computing Advanced Modelling and Optimization, Bulletin of Calcutta Mathematical Society, Applied Mathematical Modelling, Journal of Physical Sciences*.

Junhong Min is an assistant professor of Marketing at Michigan Technological University. He earned his PhD in Marketing from the State University of New York at Binghamton and Master's of Marketing Research degree from the Southern Illinois University at Edwardsville, USA. Prior to joining his university, he used to work for Nielsen, NY, and Matritz Marketing Research, MO, USA. His publications have appeared in *Journal of Behavioral Decision Making, Innovative Marketing Journal, Advances in Consumer Research, European Advances in Consumer Research, Decision Science Institute, Society for Marketing Advances*, and *Academy of Marketing Science*.

Damijan Mumel obtained his Doctorate in Psychology at University of Ljubljana, Slovenia. He works as a Professor of Marketing at the University of Maribor, Faculty of Economics and Business. He is a Head of Marketing institute and Vice Dean for Research. His main areas of interest and also lecturing are consumer behaviour, research methodology, qualitative research, and communication. He presents his work at international scientific conferences and publishes original scientific papers in domestic and foreign scientific journals. He is a member of the Slovenian Marketing Association, the Slovenian Psychologists' Association, as well as European Marketing Academy (EMAC). Recently, he focuses more on the management of the Faculty of Economics and Business.

Marius Octavian Olaru received his Bachelor's and Master's Degree in Information Engineering, both cum laude, and his PhD in Information and Communication Technology from the Department of Engineering "Enzo Ferrari," University of Modena and Reggio Emilia, Italy. His research interests are mainly focused on data integration, semantics, data warehousing, business intelligence, and business strategies. His research results have been published in national and international conferences.

Patrick C. Olson is a Professor at National University. He earned his PhD in the Management of Information Systems at Claremont Graduate School. He also holds a Master of Science in Systems Management from the University of Southern California and Bachelor of Arts in Communications from University of Montana. He worked in industry at Hughes Aircraft and held administrative and faculty positions in higher education since 1988. He was on the team that deployed the first commercial Cisco Voice Over IP enterprise system. Dr. Olson has served as an Examiner for the State of California Malcolm Baldridge Quality Awards.

Amin Omidvar received his BS in Information Technology from Amirkabir University of Technology (2009-Iran), and his MS in E-Commerce from Amirkabir University (2012-Iran). He is currently a data engineer and researcher of data mining leaders company, Tehran, Iran. He taught undergraduate and graduate courses in Information Technology with emphasis on data mining and data engineering at Amirkabir University. Amin Omidvar is involved in researches in Business Intelligence (BI), Data Mining, Text Mining, Knowledge Management (KM), Social Network Analysis (SNA), Reputation and Trust in Social Networks, Anti Money Laundering (AML), Fraud Detection, and Applying Data Mining in E-Learning Environments. He has published 16 papers at national and international conferences and journals.

In Lih Ong is currently a Master's degree student of Computer Science at Universiti Tunku Abdul Rahman. She has also obtained her Bachelor's degree in Computer Science from Universiti Tunku Abdul Rahman. Her research interests lie in the areas of business intelligence and management information systems. She has worked as a research assistant in Faculty of Engineering and Science, Universiti Tunku Abdul Rahman, for the past two years. She is involved in conducting background research on maturity models for business intelligence as well as conducting data collection and analysis in Malaysian organizations. She has published her research work in a variety of journals and conference proceedings.

Ceyhun Ozgur is a professor of information and decision sciences in the College of Business at Valparaiso University. He earned a BS in Industrial Management, a MS in Management from the University of Akron, and a PhD in Business (Operation Management/Operations Research) from Kent State University. He published a textbook by McGraw-Hill titled *Introduction to Management Science with Spreadsheets* with William J. Stevenson. Among others, Dr. Ozgur has published in *Operations Management Research, Decision Sciences Journal of Innovative Education, Quality Management, Production Planning & Control, INTERFACES,* and *OMEGA.*

Rashedur M. Rahman is working as an Associate Professor in Electrical and Computer Engineering Department in North South University, Dhaka, Bangladesh. He received his PhD in Computer Science from University of Calgary, Canada, and Master's from University of Manitoba, Canada, in 2007 and 2003, respectively. He has published more than 60 research articles in peer-reviewed journals and conference proceedings, mainly in the area of parallel, distributed, grid, and cloud computing, knowledge and data engineering. His current research interest is in data mining particularly on financial, medical and educational data, data replication on grid, cloud load characterization, optimization of cloud resource placements, and computational finance. He has been serving in the editorial board of a number of journals in the knowledge and data engineering field. He also served as reviewer of couple of journals published by Elsevier, Springer, and Wiley. He also serves as an organizing committee member of different international conferences organized by IEEE and ACM in home and abroad.

Helen Rothberg is Professor of Strategy in the School of Management at Marist College, Poughkeepsie, NY. She holds a PhD and MPhil from City University Graduate Center, and an MBA from Baruch College, CUNY. She is on the faculty of the Fuld-Gilad-Herring Academy of Competitive Intelligence and is principal of HNR Associates. She has published extensively on topics including competitive intelligence and knowledge management. Helen's latest book, with Scott Erickson, is *Intelligence in Action: Strategically Managing Knowledge Assets,* published by Palgrave Macmillan in 2012.

Sankar Kumar Roy is an Associate Professor of Mathematics and Head of the Department of Applied Mathematics with Oceanology and Computer Programming of Vidyasagar University, West Bengal, India. He received his PhD in Operations Research at Department of Mathematics, Indian Institute of Technology, Kharagpur, India, in 2003. His research interests are Operations Research (Transportation Problem, Game Theory), Lattice in Discrete Mathematics, Rough Set Theory, Fuzzy Set Theory, Stochastic Programming, and Multi-Choice Programming. He has credit of several research papers published in various journals such as *Applied Mathematical Modelling, Journal of Uncertainty Analysis and Applications, The Journal of Fuzzy Mathematics, Journal of Uncertain Systems, International Journal of Mathematics and Scientific Computing, Ricerca Operativa, International Journal of Operational Research, CiiT International Journal of Fuzzy Systems, Advanced Modelling and Optimization, Bulletin of Calcutta Mathematical Society, Journal of Physical Sciences, Journal of Information and Computing Sciences, Opsearch, International Journal of Uncertainty, Fuzziness and Knowledge Based Systems.*

Puja Sahu is a research scholar in Industrial Engineering and Operations Research, IIT Bombay, working with Prof. N. Hemachandra. Her thesis is based on "Adaptive Learning with Support Vector Machines." Her research interests lie in the topics like Support Vector Machines, Machine Learning, and Statistical Learning Theory.

Donna M. Schaeffer has taught at universities in the United States, Germany, and Korea. She earned her PhD in the Management of Information Systems at Claremont Graduate School. Dr. Schaeffer participates on the Internet Advisory Caucus for the U.S. Congress and the Business Advisory Forum of the United Nations. She has published over 50 articles and book chapters. She is active in the Churchill Club, Computer History Museum, Consortium of Computing Sciences in Colleges, Decision Sciences Institute, John Dewy Society, Institute of Electrical and Electronics Engineers, Women's High Tech Forum, Women in International Security, and World Affairs Council.

Tanja Sedej holds MSc in Business and Economic Science and is a Doctoral candidate at the Faculty of Business and Economics, University of Maribor, Slovenia. She is a founder and director of Research and Research, LLC, and has more than 10 years of practical experience from the field of marketing and communication. She is also author and co-author of several scientific and expert papers from the field of marketing, corporate communication, entrepreneurship, and international economy.

Shaya Sheikh obtained his Ph.D. from Case Western Reserve University in 2013. He has worked as Scheduling and Optimization Scientist in Lancaster Laboratories and as adjunct faculty instructor in Virginia Commonwealth University. He is now a visiting assistant professor at the University of Baltimore. He has published about 20 papers in technical journals and conference proceedings. In his work, multiple criteria decision making and sequencing theories are developed and applied to solve a variety of business problems.

Pei Hwa Siew is an Assistant Professor in the Department of Multimedia Design & Animation, Faculty of Creative Industries at the Universiti Tunku Abdul Rahman. She obtained her PhD in Information Science, Master's degree in Information Technology, and Bachelor's degree in Psychology from National University of Malaysia. Her areas of research and teaching interest have expanded into the field of information systems, e-commerce, multimedia design and development, and research methodology in IS. Throughout her career, she has conducted many academic and applied researches and published numerous articles and book chapters. Her current research topics are on multimedia learning, business intelligence, and information technology acceptance and appropriation. She has delivered many courses in the areas of multimedia learning, multimedia design and development, e-commerce, etc. for more than 10 years. She has also been actively involved in many conferences and has been an active reviewer for several journals and many conferences.

Riyaz Sikora is an Associate Professor of Information Systems at College of Business, University of Texas at Arlington. He received his PhD from the University of Illinois at Urbana-Champaign. His current research interests are in the area of learning in multi-agent information systems, machine learning, data mining, and business applications of evolutionary computation. He is a senior editor for *Journal of Information Systems and e-Business Management*, serves on the editorial boards of the *Journal of Database Management* and *International Journal of Intelligent Information Technologies*, and is a founding co-chair of the Association of Information Systems SIG on Agent-based Information Systems.

Alan D. Smith is presently University Professor of Operations Management in the Department of Management and Marketing at Robert Morris University, located in Pittsburgh, PA. Previously, he was Chair of the Department of Quantitative and Natural Sciences and Coordinator of Engineering Programs at the same institution, as well as Associate Professor of Business Administration and Director of Coal Mining Administration at Eastern Kentucky University. He holds concurrent PhDs in Engineering Systems/Education from The University of Akron and in Business Administration (OM and MIS) from Kent State University. He is the author of numerous articles and book chapters.

Mariya Sodenkamp is a director of Data and Decision Analytics Lab at the University of Bamberg in Germany and a senior researcher at Bits to Energy Lab, a joint research initiative of ETH Zürich, University of Bamberg, and University of St. Gallen. She holds a PhD in Business Information Systems from the University of Paderborn, as well as a MSc in Computer Science and a BSc in Economics. Her research interests are decision support systems, data analytics, energy-efficient systems, multi-criteria analysis, and uncertainty modeling. Dr. Sodenkamp has several publications in referred scholar journals and book chapters.

Thorsten Staake is full professor of MIS, specializing in Energy Efficient Systems, at the University of Bamberg, Germany. He is also director of the Bits to Energy Lab, a joint research initiative of ETH Zurich, the University of St. Gallen, and the University of Bamberg. His work is dedicated to bringing together information technology with insights from behavioral science to build products that motivate and help consumers to conserve energy. Prior to his appointment at Bamberg, Thorsten worked as chair of Information Management at ETH Zurich, in the Auto-ID Labs at the Massachusetts Institute of Technology, Infineon Technologies, and Clariant. He holds a PhD in business administration from the University of St. Gallen and a diploma in Electrical Engineering from TU Darmstadt. Thorsten is also cofounder of two clean-tech startups, Amphiro AG and BEN Energy AG.

Kathryn Szabat is an Associate Professor in the Business Systems and Analytics Department at La Salle. She received her PhD in Statistics, with cognate field in Operations Research, from the Wharton School of University of Pennsylvania. Dr. Szabat's instructional responsibilities include teaching of business statistics and management science to undergraduate and MBA students. Her current interests include promoting the inclusion of business analytics in business school curriculums and the development of analytical capabilities of business students. Dr. Szabat's research has been published in *International Journal of Applied Decision Sciences, Accounting Education, Journal of Applied Business and Economics, Journal of Healthcare Management,* and *Journal of Management Studies.* Scholarly chapters have appeared in *Managing Adaptability, Intervention, and People in Enterprise Information Systems; Managing Trade, Economies, and International Business; Encyclopedia of Statistics in Behavioral Science;* and *Statistical Methods in Longitudinal Research.* She is currently a co-author of two statistics textbooks: *Statistics for Managers Using Microsoft Excel* and *Basic Business Statistics.*

David Vequist is the Founder and Director of the Social Predictive Analytics Institute (SPA^n). Dr. Vequist has years of experience in consulting with corporations on technology implementations (including data warehousing, ERP, and CRM systems), developing integrated technology solutions and as an executive in the healthcare and nonprofit sectors. He is also a Professor of Management in the H-E-B School of Business & Administration at the University of the Incarnate Word (UIW) in San Antonio, Texas, USA. He is an accomplished speaker, author, researcher, and futurist on the topic of social media analytics, training, development, leadership, medical tourism, and technology management.

Maurizio Vincini received his Master's degree in Computer Engineer and his PhD in Electronic and Computer Engineer from University of Modena, Italy. He is currently associate professor of Computer Engineering at the Engineer Department of the University of Modena e Reggio Emilia, Italy. Maurizio Vincini teaches Fundamentals of Computer Science, Database Technologies, and Information Systems at the Faculty of Information Engineering of the University of Modena and Reggio Emilia. His research activity has been mainly devoted to information management and knowledge representation, with a particular reference to information integration of heterogeneous sources by means of ontologies and representation languages based on Semantic Web. He has published papers in international journals and international and national conferences in the area of Web information integration and virtual enterprises information systems, defining semantic representation models for ontologies. He participated to national and European Community-Funded research projects.

Coleen Wilder is an assistant professor of information and decision sciences in the College of Business at Valparaiso University. She earned a BS in Mathematics Education from Indiana University and an MBA with concentrations in Finance and Operations Management from the University of Chicago. Her PhD is in Management Science from the Illinois Institute of Technology. Dr. Wilder has 18 years of experience in the steel industry and 5 years in the real estate industry.

Niloofar Yousefi is a second-year PhD student in Dept. of Industrial Engineering. She is working in Machine Learning Lab at the Dept. of Electrical and Computer Science. She is currently doing her research in Support Vector Machine and Kernel-based method. She received a Bachelor of Science in Applied Math and a Master's of Science in Operation Research.

Index